W9-AHM-426

Puerto Rico

Brendan Sainsbury
Nate Cavalieri

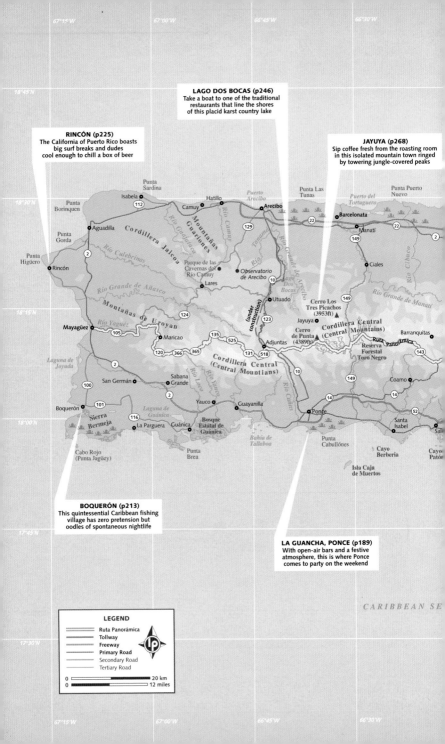

RINCÓN (p225)
The California of Puerto Rico boasts big surf breaks and dudes cool enough to chill a box of beer

LAGO DOS BOCAS (p246)
Take a boat to one of the traditional restaurants that line the shores of this placid karst country lake

JAYUYA (p268)
Sip coffee fresh from the roasting room in this isolated mountain town ringed by towering jungle-covered peaks

BOQUERÓN (p213)
This quintessential Caribbean fishing village has zero pretension but oodles of spontaneous nightlife

LA GUANCHA, PONCE (p189)
With open-air bars and a festive atmosphere, this is where Ponce comes to party on the weekend

CARIBBEAN SE

LEGEND

	Ruta Panorámica
	Tollway
	Freeway
	Primary Road
	Secondary Road
	Tertiary Road

0 — 20 km
0 — 12 miles

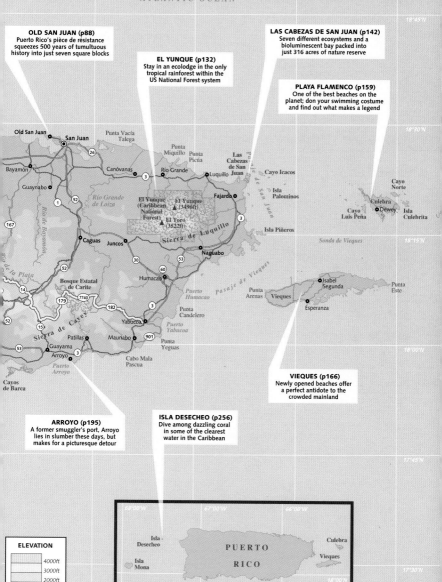

OLD SAN JUAN (p88)
Puerto Rico's pièce de résistance squeezes 500 years of tumultuous history into just seven square blocks

EL YUNQUE (p132)
Stay in an ecolodge in the only tropical rainforest within the US National Forest system

LAS CABEZAS DE SAN JUAN (p142)
Seven different ecosystems and a bioluminescent bay packed into just 316 acres of nature reserve

PLAYA FLAMENCO (p159)
One of the best beaches on the planet; don your swimming costume and find out what makes a legend

VIEQUES (p166)
Newly opened beaches offer a perfect antidote to the crowded mainland

ARROYO (p195)
A former smuggler's port, Arroyo lies in slumber these days, but makes for a picturesque detour

ISLA DESECHEO (p256)
Dive among dazzling coral in some of the clearest water in the Caribbean

ATLANTIC OCEAN

Old San Juan
San Juan
Punta Vacía Talega
26
Punta Miquillo
Punta Picúa
Bayamón
Canóvanas
3
Río Grande
Luquillo
Las Cabezas de San Juan
Fajardo
Cayo Icacos
Cayo Norte
Guaynabo
52
1
Río Grande de Loíza
El Yunque (Caribbean National Forest)
El Yunque (3496ft)
Isla Palominos
Cayo Luis Peña
Culebra
Dewey
Isla Culebrita
167
El Toro (3522ft)
Sierra de Luquillo
3
Isla Piñeros
Río de Bayamón
Caguas
Juncos
30
53
Naguabo
Sonda de Vieques
Río de la Plata
52
Bosque Estatal de Carite
60
Humacao
Pasaje de Vieques
Isabel Segunda
Punta Este
14
179
7740
182
Puerto Humacao
Punta Arenas
Vieques
52
Punta Candelero
3
Esperanza
15
Sierra de Cayey
Yabucoa
Puerto Yabucoa
53
Guayama
Patillas
Maunabo
901
Arroyo
3
Punta Yeguas
Cayos de Barca
Puerto Arroyo
Cabo Mala Pascua

ELEVATION
4000ft
3000ft
2000ft
1000ft
0

Isla Desecheo
Isla Mona
PUERTO RICO
Culebra
Vieques

0 ——— 100 km
0 ——— 60 miles

On the Road

BRENDAN SAINSBURY

Cycling on the tropical island of Vieques can be hot work – especially when you've got a human cargo fast asleep in the back seat. This is me drinking freshly squeezed lemonade just outside the former Camp Garcia a few miles north of Esperanza. Garcia marked the entrance to the former US military training zone that was given over to the US Fish and Wildlife Refuge in May 2003. Five years ago it wasn't uncommon to experience the loud whoosh of live arms fire going off near this site. Now all you can hear is the twitter of the odd Adelaide warbler – and my son snoring.

NATE CAVALIERI

Certainly not my most flattering shot, but that half-dazed look is one of pure triumph: it was snapped at the peak of the hilly road that enters the Bosque Estatal de Guánica. With no lack of sweat (and probably a few tears) I had scaled it just moments earlier on a bike, surviving the climb to the likely disappointment of watchful vultures who circled overhead. The park's thorn-lined trails and breezy Caribbean vantages offered a two-day adventure of hiking and biking, and sweet respite from the thumping clubs of Ponce.

For full author biographies see p309.

HIDDEN PUERTO RICO

You thought you'd seen it all...but you haven't. There's that extra special wave that only breaks two or three times a year in Rincón; that rugged way-out beach in Vieques that no one can ever remember the name of; and that strange, ritualistic festival in San Juan where pious devotees walk backwards into the sea in the middle of the night. As soon as you start believing Puerto Rico is becoming boring and predictable, it floors you with a phantom right-punch – an island the size of Connecticut with the diversity of a small continent.

Beaches

Some are insanely crowded, others wonderfully tranquil; still more are barely discovered. Puerto Rico's beaches don't just grace the front covers of surfing magazines; they also provide a fascinating insight into the moods, emotions and identity of an island of nearly four million fun-loving Latinos.

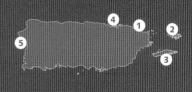

1 Playa Luquillo
The populist's choice. On summer weekends, it seems the whole island descends onto the silky white sands of Playa Luquillo (p138) to lap up the balmy tropical rays. It would be a shame to miss out on the national party.

2 Playa Flamenco
Regularly touted as one of the most coveted scimitars of sand on the planet, glistening Playa Flamenco (p159) is indeed a sight to behold. Head east to idyllic Culebra and find out what all the fuss is about.

3 Secret Beach
Twenty-one mile long Vieques is studded with a golden cache of barely visited 'secret' beaches. This one (p173) is situated somewhere east of Esperanza on the old US military range, but locals are reluctant to divulge its exact location.

4 Ocean Park Beach
Wedged between the towering condos of Condado and the swanky resorts of Isla Verde, Ocean Park (p103) is the savvy solitude-seeker's alternative. Take your iPod and some cool shades and get down to some serious people-watching.

5 Tres Palmas
Ah…the sunsets, the swells, the sights and – more to the point – the surfers. Tres Palmas (p229) is the O'ahu of Puerto Rico, where monster waves erupt like miniature bombs in front of breathtaking Rincón sunsets.

Culture

Think Puerto Rico and you automatically think culture – a small island with a big personality that has enriched the planet with its colorful contributions to music, dance, literature and cuisine. The secret for anthropologists is in the genes, a brightly spiced melting pot of Taíno Indian, colonial Spanish, Afro-Caribbean and modern American.

❶ Architecture

After dark, lovers stroll around Ponce's stately Plaza Las Delicias (p187) and toss pennies into the softly lit Fuente de Leones (Fountain of Lions). The historic nexus of Ponce, the plaza's understated architecture has won it a whole host of local and foreign admirers.

❷ History

The European history of the Americas was first christened on a rocky promontory of land that guards the entrance to San Juan harbor. Miraculously, Old San Juan (p88) is still there, barely blemished by the passing of time, encased in a compact and easily navigable urban quarter full of delicious nooks and crannies that await artful exploration.

❸ Cuisine

Combine the chic appeal of New York's SoHo with the historical authenticity of Cuzco, Peru and you've got SoFo (p116), San Juan's emblematic restaurant district, where *comida criolla* (traditional cuisine) is fused with everything from Sichuan noodles to Mexican cerviche.

❹ Salsa

Some say it was invented in Cuba, others claim it was first ignited by Puerto Ricans living in New York. Whatever your argument, there are few islanders who can't play it, sing it, dance it and feel it well into the small hours – especially in San Juan's Nuyorican Café (p119).

❺ Taíno

Virtually gone but not forgotten, Puerto Rico's indigenous Taíno culture is evident in everything from traditional wood-carving to the stone-decorated ceremonial ball parks that once hosted ancient sporting spectaculars. Visit the Parque Ceremonial Indígena Caguana (p245) near Lares and absorb the mystical memories of millennia past.

Ecoactive

Cars honking, planes landing, casinos jangling and late-night clubs vibrating – in Puerto Rico you sometimes have to think innovatively to get ecoactive. Volunteer for a turtle-watch, stay in a rustic ecolodge, or negotiate the narrow lanes and bumpy trails of the far southwest on a bicycle. There's only one way to find out about Puerto Rico's ecoactive underbelly – and that's to get out.

① Coffee Haciendas

A perfect antidote to skinny decaf lattes and generic worldwide coffee chains, classic Puerto Rican *café* is aromatic, shade-grown, and as earthy as the ground that it was grown on; which – when you're up in the Central Mountains – is probably just a few feet from where you're sitting while drinking it.

② Turtle-watching

The magic of watching a leatherback sea turtle crawl across a deserted starlit beach on the untainted shores of Culebra is hard to beat. Enlist as a volunteer in a turtle-watch (p158) and make all your romantic ecodreams come true.

③ Cycling

As a small island overrun with cars, Puerto Rico desperately needs more cyclists. Become a pioneer and spin your wheels around a handful of attractive new routes that traverse dry forests, skirt spectacular surfing beaches and crisscross abandoned military zones recently given over to wildlife refuges.

④ Hiking

Beyond the short, paved paths of El Yunque, you might have to get your feet dirty navigating the unkempt, sketchily mapped trails of Puerto Rico's territorial parks. On the plus side (if dirty feet aren't your thing), there's a dearth of tourist crowds and you'll feel a palpable sense of DIY adventure.

⑤ Bird-watching

While the island's endemic land mammals are a little thin on the ground (bats aside), Puerto Rico's bird life is healthily abundant. The Holy Grail is an all-too-rare sighting of the critically endangered Puerto Rican parrot.

Water World

Venture beyond the island's exotic shores
and the view becomes increasingly surreal,
whether you're balancing deftly on a
surfboard or blinking disbelievingly from
behind your dive mask as you sink 50ft
beneath the Atlantic breakers. Discovering
this multifarious water world is a spirit-lifting
experience. Hang ten in Rincón,
commandeer a kayak in Boquerón, or dive
deep in La Parguera. The sea is your oyster.

❶ Diving the Wall

The salt-washed southwestern town of La Parguera (p206) is a magnet for divers from across the island who plunge down to explore 'the Wall', a 20-mile-long coral reef which drops to inky depths of 1500ft.

❷ Surfing

Tres Palmas. Spanish Wall. Jobos. Crashboat. To the uninitiated they may sound like rather an odd collection of wartime memorabilia. But, to trusted aficionados, these rugged beaches are the K2s and Kilimanjaros of the local surfing scene. Go to Rincón (p228) and become a dude or dudette for the day.

❸ Bioluminescent Bays

There are only about a dozen in the world and tiny Puerto Rico has three – yes, THREE – of them. Swimming after dark in the glowing translucent purple waters of Bahía Mosquito (p171) on Vieques is one of the best legal psychedelic experiences on the planet.

❹ Kayaking

The bicycle of the waterways, the ecofriendly, zero-carbon-emission kayak doesn't just get you from A to B, it also offers a whole new take on familiar locations. Go for a paddle in Boquerón (p214) and see the coastline from a different angle.

❺ Deep-sea Fishing

The beer is in the cooler, the radio's playing salsa and the fishing line's stretched way out back searching hopefully for blue marlin. No, it's not a scene from an Ernest Hemingway novel; it's what sun-darkened fishing captains in Fajardo (p145) do every day of the year.

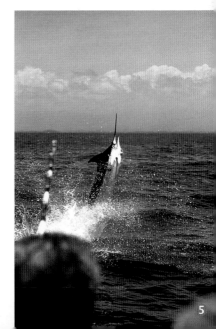

Off the Beaten Track

Escape – as the native Taíno did – to the Central Mountains or the tranquil outlying islands, and Puerto Rico becomes Borinquen, a legendary pre-Columbian archipelago brought to life in the verses of local poets and the oral traditions of the indigenous people. Penetrate fecund forests, wander deserted beaches, or share a cup of gourmet coffee with the congenial locals. Whatever you do, keep the itinerary open.

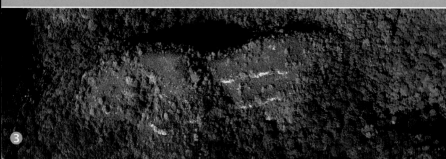

1 Vieques' Beaches

Only 3% of Puerto Rico's five million annual visitors make it as far as Vieques (p171), so the island's plentiful beaches – closed until 2003 due to military exercises – are deliciously unsullied.

2 Isla Mona

With a human population of precisely zero, along with a rich selection of rare flora and fauna, Mona Island (p234) is an ecological outpost well worthy of its 'Galapagos of Puerto Rico' title.

3 Karst Country

Punctuated by bulbous *mogotes* (hillocks) and riddled with hidden sinkholes, Puerto Rico's karst country (p248) provides a natural barrier to the encroaching urbanization of the north coast. Hidden amid the crinkly topography are a plethora of solitary surprises, including luxuriant forests, hushed mountain retreats and placid lakes.

4 Públicos

Stigmatized as being slow, crowded and unreliable, Puerto Rico's public buses are not as antiquated as you might think. They're also one of the best places to meet the locals on their own turf. Hop on a ride in San Juan (p141) and see where the journey takes you.

5 Jíbaros

Straw sombrero pulled roughly over the eyes, well-chewed cigar jammed firmly between the lips, and the winning domino hovering triumphantly over the foldaway games table, the traditional Puerto Rican *jíbaro* is as much rural myth as modern reality. Hang around in Jayuya (p268) and see if he turns up.

Volunteer to help preserve the endangered leatherback sea turtle (p158)

Contents

Regional Map Contents

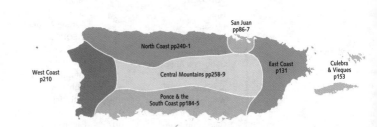

Destination Puerto Rico

Puerto Rico is where the easygoing Caribbean collides with the slick efficiency of modern America over syncopated Latin rhythms and rose-tinted tropical sunsets. The result is a colorful, diverse and culturally unique island that is often as confusing as it is cosmopolitan. Hip funky restaurants nestle next to 15th-century Spanish forts; sprawling concrete shopping malls encroach upon fecund tropical rainforests; and glitzy casinos lie juxtaposed against some of the most stunning beaches, caves and offshore coral reefs in the Caribbean.

History is another inviting draw card. While the United States struggles to emulate the erstwhile glories of 'old world' Europe, Puerto Rico gets out its killer trump card: beguiling Viejo (Old) San Juan, one of the oldest and best preserved colonial cities in the Americas. Cocooned in the crucible of Spain's once illustrious colonial empire, five centuries of checkered history continue to slowly unravel. Neighborly pensioners recline languidly in creaking rocking chairs, *bomba* drums light up the somnolence of a diminutive baroque plaza, and the walls of two great military forts rise like wizened sentinels above the depths of the untamed Atlantic.

Racing headlong into the 21st century, contemporary Puerto Rico can sometimes present a bewildering picture to culture-seeking visitors. Decades of unchecked American-style development have meant that, despite significant economic advances, the modern world has stamped its ugly mark on the idyllically named *Isla del Encanto* (Island of Enchantment). Witness the ever expanding San Juan suburbs, the asphyxiating traffic gridlock, the insipid fast-food outlets, and the plethora of generic international resorts that pepper the northeast coast. But purists can take heart. In Puerto Rico what you see isn't always what you get. Scratch under the surface and the soul of the island will serendipitously reveal itself – though finding it can sometimes present a challenge or two. Hop on a local bus, disappear into the central mountains, or pedal your way around the beautiful island of Vieques; just be sure to tear up any cast-iron itineraries and let the open road lead you where it will.

A commonwealth of the United States of America, Puerto Rico is a semi-autonomous territory whose constitutional status has long been a political oxymoron. The island's cultural manifestations are similarly ridden with contradiction. Puerto Ricans love big American cars, but drive them more like they're in Mexico City; they have served in numerous foreign wars under the banner of stars and stripes, yet share a closer historical identity to communist Cuba; they have exported over half of their ebullient population to the east coast of the United States, but still exhibit a fierce loyalty to their beloved Borinquen, the island they will always call home.

Confused? Don't worry. Even native Puerto Ricans sometimes have difficulty in unraveling the baffling intricacies of their much-debated political system. When asked in a 1998 referendum if they would prefer to 1) adopt US statehood, 2) claim outright independence, or 3) remain as a commonwealth of the US, 50.3% of Puerto Ricans voted for an inconclusive 'none of the above.' Postponed for future discussion – the debate rages on.

FAST FACTS

Population: 3.9 million

Population growth rate: 0.39%

GDP (per capita): $19,600

Life expectancy: 78.5 years

Literacy rate: 94.1%

Unemployment rate: 12%

Cell phones: 3.3 million

Internet users: 915,000

Miles of paved road: 15,220

Getting Started

Puerto Rico offers a plethora of plush, easy-to-negotiate resorts similar in quality to facilities in North America and Europe. Book a package through a New York travel agent, catch a charter to Aeropuerto Internacional de Luis Muñoz Rivera (LMM) in San Juan, and unpack your suitcase in the exclusive Palmas del Mar resort on the east coast, and your trip could be as smooth as a two-week sojourn to South Beach, Florida. But what about the real Puerto Rico that lies invitingly outside those well-guarded hotel gates? A whole island awaits serendipitous exploration, but where do you start?

The key for discerning travelers is less about the intricacies of finding a room or booking an early morning fishing trip, and more about forging a path through the ubiquitous tourist brochure gloss and uncovering the authentic Puerto Rico that lies underneath.

To get a real take on the island's colorful personality, you'll need to be prepared for a lot of spontaneity and a large dose of DIY adventure. Plenty of travel literature would have you believe that Puerto Rico is impossible to traverse without a car and severely lacking in any form of budget accommodations. However, while the public bus system might be a little confusing and the campsites and cabins annoyingly difficult to find, anything is possible as long as you've got the interest and inclination to burrow beneath the surface.

So pack your salsa shoes, arm yourself with a good Spanish phrasebook and hit the road with an open mind and a gung-ho sense of adventure.

WHEN TO GO

The best time to visit Puerto Rico is mid-December through late-April. The upside of visiting at this time is the weather, which is sunny (but not too hot) and free from the threat of hurricanes. The downside is that prices get hiked up and crowds are generally heavier. Skirt the edges of the high season (ie November and May) and you could get lucky with both the weather and cut-price rates.

See Climate Charts (p276) for more information.

The Caribbean hurricane season runs from June to November, with the highest storm risk in September and October. Every year is different, however, and booking your trip around the weather can be a bit of lottery. The island's last big whammy was Hurricane Georges in 1998.

Puerto Rico has plenty of colorful Latin festivals (p278) and you may want to arrange your trip to coincide with one of them. Other travelers, on the other hand, may prefer to dodge the crowds. Either way, be sure to plan ahead. Puerto Rico has a rather old-fashioned approach to national holidays (p280), with businesses shutting down completely and the whole country seemingly grinding to a halt. Easter and Christmas are good times to avoid if you can't bear the inconvenience of closed shops and ghostly town centers. Beware also the months of January and July which both have four official holidays.

COSTS & MONEY

The good news is that Puerto Rico on a budget is possible. The bad news is that you'll need a lot of ingenuity to achieve it. Stay in the big resorts and eat in the better restaurants and prices on the island are comparable to any large US city. But step outside of the standard tourist sector and into a público (shared taxi) or *friquitines* (roadside kiosk), and you could be laughing all the way to the bank.

Transport is the first big issue. Puerto Rico has swallowed the US car culture hook, line and sinker, meaning that there is no decent countrywide rail

DON'T LEAVE HOME WITHOUT...

Puerto Rico's status as a US commonwealth means travelers will find plenty of well-known stores selling familiar medicines, food and clothing – you could just buy what you need on the island to keep luggage to a minimum. But these essentials should come from home:

- A valid international driver's license if you're planning on renting a car (p291).
- A passport, if you're from outside Puerto Rico and the United States.
- Any prescription medicines you need (p295).
- Bug spray to ward off the night-time visitors (p299).
- A Spanish phrasebook to break down cultural barriers and integrate with the locals.
- Sunblock and a water bottle.
- A day-pack and a good pair of walking shoes.
- Energy bars to get you through the more difficult hikes.
- Something dressy for San Juan's late night casinos and clubs.
- A good, super-cool pair of sunglasses.

or bus system. Thus the only viable means of getting around for those without a car is by the hard-to-fathom público system that links the commonwealth's main towns via a fleet of 15-seater minibuses. Using públicos requires reams of patience and plenty of street savvy (see box p141), but if you master the basics you'll quickly end up saving buckets of money – for example, the San Juan–Fajardo run costs $80 in a taxi but only $5 by público. Fortunately for capital dwellers, San Juan has an excellent public transportation system enabling travelers to cross the city (and dodge the notorious traffic jams) for less than a dollar. Don't even think about renting a car here.

Food is cheaper if you stick to the shabbier, traditional places that, more often than not, serve up formidable home-style cooking. A small step up (but not extortionate) are the government-sponsored Mesónes Gastronómicos listed in the free tourist magazine *Qué Pasa*, available from tourist info centers and many hotels. Kiosks are another reliable option and most towns have their ever-ready cluster of mobile street vendors dispatching tasty – though not always healthy – snacks. For a sweet dessert, drop by one of the island's ubiquitous (and cheap) bakeries. A full blown *comida criolla* (traditional cuisine) meal in a family restaurant should cost no more than $10. At a Mesón Gastronómico, bank on $10 to $15. If you're really strapped for cash, hit the fast food franchises that haunt almost every town in the country. Breakfast and lunch will rarely set you back more than $5 if you eat like the locals – in small bakeries, tavernas and at the *friquitines*, which sell salty, deep-fried snacks. Restaurant dinners can range from $8 to $30 and up.

Some of the best deals on the island come in a glass during happy hour, when mixed drinks can go as low as $2. Even during normal hours drinks rarely jump above $4 (outside of the pricier places in San Juan, of course).

Accommodations are likely to be your biggest investment in Puerto Rico. The best midrange options are the government-sponsored paradores that lie scattered across the island. Prices range from $75 to $150 per night depending on the season, and facilities, while not luxurious, are invariably quirky and family-friendly. Real budget accommodations are woefully lacking and generally confined to camping, cabins and a few inferior hotels. If you're sticking around for a week or more you may want to look into renting an apartment. With the right number of people and flexibility with your dates you could cut a deal worth about $60 per person per night.

TRAVELING RESPONSIBLY

Since our inception in 1973, Lonely Planet has encouraged our readers to tread lightly, travel responsibly and enjoy the magic independent travel affords. International travel is growing at a jaw-dropping rate, and we still firmly believe in the benefits it can bring – but, as always, we encourage you to consider the impact your visit will have on both the global environment and the local economies, cultures and ecosystems.

Puerto Rico is one of the most densely populated islands in the world and its diverse ecosystems struggle constantly against a rising tide of burgeoning resorts and mass tourism. Fortunately there are now enough environmentally sensitive operators to make a low-impact trip possible, as long as you're prepared to be selective. Stay at small hotels and ecolodges rather than large resorts, use public transport whenever possible (or, better still, cycle), and support the 'green' local businesses listed in this book's GreenDex.

Puerto Rican públicos are a safe and perfectly viable way of traveling between the island's larger towns if you're willing to decipher the sometimes complicated bus system and muck in with the locals. The rewards are free Spanish lessons, higher ecocredentials and a far more vivid cross-cultural experience.

The following are some helpful websites covering sustainable travel options in Puerto Rico.

Golden Heron (www.golden-heron.com) Golden Heron runs ecotours, and their website provides travel planning information.

El Yunque (www.elyunque.com) Information, sleeping and activities listings for the El Yunque rainforest and how to travel responsibly there.

Elenas Vieques (www.elenas-vieques.com) Ecotourism information about Vieques.

AdvenTours (www.adventourspr.com) The website for AdvenTours, which runs tours for the ecosensitive traveler.

TRAVEL LITERATURE

Probably the best and most evocative fictional account of Puerto Rico at an important turning point in its history is *The Rum Diary* by the late Hunter S Thompson. Although written in the early '60s, it wasn't published until the late '90s, and follows the capers of an expatriate journalist caught in a culture of corruption, jealousy and excessive alcohol consumption. See p97 for further discussion of Thompson's San Juan sojourn.

Stories from Puerto Rico by Robert L Muckley and Adela Martinez-Santiago will fill you in on how the natives discovered the Spaniards weren't Gods, and other local legends.

Boricuas: Influential Puerto Rican Writings – An Anthology by Roberto Santiago showcases the very best Puerto Rican writers from modern to colonial times.

Divided Borders: Essays on Puerto Rican Identity by Juan Flores dissects in greater detail the Puerto Rican struggle to define and maintain indigenous identities as the island becomes more homogeneous. Flores also wrote *From Bomba to Hip-Hop,* a wide-ranging series of essays.

The following titles are rather difficult to get hold of, but are well worth a read if you do manage to find a copy. *Puerto Rico Mio: Four Decades of Change* is a sizable picture book by Jack Delano, who has been photographing Puerto Rico since 1941; Stan Steiner's *The Islands: The Worlds of the Puerto Ricans* stands out for its vivid evocation of islanders and their anecdotal histories; and *The Other Puerto Rico,* by Kathryn Robinson, depicts the island through the eyes of a keen naturalist.

HOW MUCH?

Airport taxi to Old San Juan $20

Average price for day of diving $65

Rental car cost per day $45

One night in a midrange San Juan hotel $125

Round-trip ferry to Vieques $4.50

TOP 10   PUERTO RICO

FESTIVALS

Puerto Rico celebrates all of the US national holidays in addition to nine of its own. Each town also has a patron saint festival that can last up to 10 days. Mostly Catholic in nature, these festivals often incorporate African and indigenous elements left over from the days when Taíno and Yoruba slaves wove their native rituals into colonial culture.

1 Festival San Sebastián, January 20, San Juan (p108)

2 Coffee Harvest Festival, February, Maricao (p279)

3 Carnaval, February, Ponce (p190)

4 José de Diego Day, April 16, nationwide (p279)

5 Fiesta Nacional de la Danza, May, Ponce (p190)

6 Fiesta de San Juan Bautista Day, June 24, San Juan (p108)

7 Festival de Flores, June, Aibonito (p279)

8 Fiesta de Santiago, July, Loíza Aldea (p279)

9 Culinary Festival, early November, San Juan (p108)

10 Festival Casals, dates vary, San Juan (p108)

IT ISN'T EASY BEING GREEN

Palm trees and jungle-covered mountains aside, Puerto Rico isn't the world's most ostensibly 'green' country. But with a bit of advanced planning and a dip into this book's brand-new GreenDex there's nothing to stop you treading lightly around one of the Caribbean's most heavily populated islands.

1 Staying at the Casa Cubuy Ecolodge (p136)

2 Hiking in the Bosque Estatal de Guanica (p203)

3 Tackling the Tradewinds Trail in El Yunque (p137)

4 Catching a público (p141)

5 Bird-watching on the Corozo Salt Flats (p211)

6 Strolling the streets of Old San Juan (p88)

7 Surfing on Playa Jobos (p251)

8 Drinking local coffee in the Hacienda San Pedro (p269)

9 Using an electric boat in the bioluminescent Laguna Grande (p142)

10 Kayaking in La Paguera (p205)

TOP READS

The following offer great insight into Puerto Rican culture and history.

1 *When I Was Puerto Rican* by Esmeralda Santiago (p46)

2 *Sataniada* by Alejandro Tapia y Rivera (p45)

3 *The Rum Diary* by Hunter S Thompson (p97)

4 *La llamarada* by Dr Enrique Laguerre (p46)

5 *Song of the Simple Truth: The Complete Poems of Julia De Burgos* (p45)

6 *Spiks* by Pedro Juan Soto (p46)

7 *Puerto Rican Obituary* by Pedro Pietri (p46)

8 *The Benevolent Masters* by Enrique A Laguerre (p46)

9 *El Gíbaro* by Manuel Alonso (p45)

10 *The History of Puerto Rico: From the Spanish Discovery to the American Occupation* by RA Van Middeldyk (p32)

INTERNET RESOURCES

Escape to Puerto Rico (http://escape.topuertorico.com) A detailed overview of island life, plus links to other informative sources.

LonelyPlanet.com (www.lonelyplanet.com) There's no better place to start your web explorations.

Puerto Rico Tourism Company (www.gotopuertorico.com) Run by the island's tourism company, this site contains loads of useful information and 'travel planner' features to help you sketch out itineraries.

Puerto Rico Wow (www.puertoricowow.com) This for-profit site has good information in between the ads for cars, restaurants and other island products.

Welcome to Puerto Rico (http://welcome.topuertorico.org/index.shtml) A travel guide plus information on the people of Puerto Rico and some great criollo recipes.

World Factbook (www.cia.gov/cia/publications/factbook) All the latest information from the CIA about safe travel in Puerto Rico and some background material too.

Itineraries
CLASSIC ROUTES

PUERTO RICO IN A FLASH
One Week / San Juan to San Juan

Since time is limited, fly to **San Juan** (p83) and make it your home base. With only seven days to spend in Puerto Rico, get right on the beach: **Isla Verde** (p103), **Condado** (p103) or **Ocean Park** (p103). Spend the next day weaving your way through **Old San Juan** (p88), being sure to stop by **El Morro** (p88), **Fuerte San Cristóbal** (p89) and **Calle Fortaleza** (p116). If you're up for some nightlife, stay right there.

The next few days require a rental car. With an early start, you can be the first in line to go inside the caves at **Parque de las Cavernas del Río Camuy** (p245). You'll have plenty of time in the afternoon for a drive up the winding mountain road to the **Observatorio de Arecibo** (p245) and the world's largest radio telescope.

Don't linger too long, though, because you want to get through the mountains to **Parque Ceremonial Indígena Caguana** (p245). Continue on to **Hacienda Gripiñas** (p269) for a restful night on this restored plantation. The next day, follow part of the **Ruta Panorámica** to **Yabucoa**, and then up to famed **Playa Luquillo** (p138), settling into the famed white, sandy crescent to care for your tan; sleep at a nearby **ecoresort** (p137).

For a dramatically different next day, explore the cool, green interior of **El Yunque** (p132) and spend the night in **Fajardo** (p146). Sign up for a kayak ride through **Laguna Grande** (p142), the bioluminescent bay. Then it's back to San Juan via **Loíza Aldea** (p126), where you can pick up a *vejigante* mask and get in a little snorkeling or surfing off the wild and lovely beaches. Test your luck at the gaming tables that night at any of the **Isla Verde** and **Condado** hot spots (p121) in San Juan.

This trip covers about 45 miles, hits all the major highlights and still fits in plenty of beach time.

lonelyplanet.com

THE BEST OF THE ISLAND   Two Weeks / San Juan to North Coast

Spend five days in **San Juan** (p83) and surrounding areas, making sure to see **Old San Juan** (p88), the terrific **beaches** (p247), and the **Observatorio de Arecibo** (p245), a worthwhile day trip a couple of hours' drive to the west. Rent a car and drive east to **El Yunque** (p132) for a day of hiking. That night you can take the bioluminescent bay tour in **Fajardo** (p142) or wait until the next day when you go to **Vieques** (p166) on the ferry.

If you arrive early enough, you can zip right over to **Esperanza** (p170) – just make sure to rent a scooter or car in advance. Once there, hit the beautiful **beaches** (p171). Spend that night and the next day in Esperanza, then return to **Isabel Segunda** (p169); check out **Fortín Conde de Mirasol** (p170) and assess the nightlife at **Al's Mar Azul** (p179). Don't stay out until too late, though, because at 6am the next morning you'll be on a ferry to **Culebra** (p154). More fabulous beaches await, and great snorkeling, diving and glass-bottomed boat trips, too.

Now that you're nice and relaxed it's time to return to Fajardo, but only long enough to pick up your car and hit the road for **Ponce** (p183). Spend a few days exploring the colonial city's sights, such as **La Guancha Paseo Tablado** (p189), **Museo Castillo Serailles** (p189) and the **Centro Ceremonial Indígena de Tibes** (p194).

Definitely allow one day (preferably with an early morning start so you can be done by mid-afternoon when the sun's at its hottest) for **Bosque Estatal de Guánica** (p201). After hiking, drive scenic Rte 333 along the south coast and stop to swim wherever you wish.

The next morning, the San Juan–Ponce Autopista will get you back to the north coast in less than two hours.

This trip gives you plenty of time to explore the major island attractions, as well as the Spanish Virgin Islands. Including ferry rides, the whole jaunt covers about 100 miles.

ROADS LESS TRAVELED

RUTA PANORÁMICA
Three Days / San Juan to Observatorio de Arecibo

Head south from **San Juan** (p83) to **Bosque Estatal de Carite** (p258) on Hwy 184 for a morning of beautiful hiking and swimming in cold-water pools (in nonholiday weeks Carite is almost empty). On your way out in early afternoon grab lunch from one of the *lechoneras* (suckling pig restaurants) that line the highway near **Guavate** (p261). Head to **Aibonito** (p261) next and check out the views from **Cañón de San Cristóbal** (p262) and **Mirador La Piedra Degetau** (p262). Take a stroll around Aibonito's little plaza if you need to stretch your legs before bedding down at the **El Coquí Posada Familiar** (p263).

The next day begins in **Barranquitas** (p264) and the numerous museums dedicated to la Familia Muñoz, the closest thing Puerto Rico had to a political dynasty. Track west along the island's windiest road toward the **Reserva Forestal Toro Negro** (p265) where you can rouse a park ranger (if you're lucky) and set off on a couple of short hikes.

Divert off the Ruta Panorámica briefly on Rte 144 to the mountain town of **Jayuya** (p268) where you can visit the surreal **Museo del Cemí** (p269) and stock up on coffee at the **Hacienda San Pedro** (p269). Spend the night in the tranquil confines of **Hacienda Casa Taína** (p269), a refreshingly unique mountain escape.

Day three can begin with a drive/hike to the top of **Cerro de Punta** (p266), Puerto Rico's highest peak followed by the long decent into **Adjuntas** (p270) where you can visit the environmental protectionists at the **Casa Pueblo** (p270).

Continue via the fecund **Bosque Estatal de Guilarte** (p270) to romantic **Maricao** (p271). From this point you can easily jump off to **Bosque Estatal de Guánica** (p201), or the **Parque de las Cavernas del Río Camuy** (p245). If you've come this far, seriously consider a side trip to the **Observatorio de Arecibo** (p245) before heading back toward the capital.

Ideally this route takes three days, but it's easy to do smaller chunks if you prefer. The entire east–west trip, which includes some mountainous roads, covers 165 miles.

TAILORED TRIPS

FOR NATURE LOVERS

Start with what many believe to be the crown jewel of Puerto Rico's nature reserves, **El Yunque** (p132). Soak up the cool jungle interiors of this unique tropical ecosystem before heading for **Las Cabezas de San Juan Reserva Natural 'El Faro'** (p142), near Fajardo. From there you can ferry to Culebra and the **National Wildlife Refuge** (p156), which includes the coastline as well as more than 20 offshore cays. **Vieques National Wildlife Refuge** (p169) is also a fabulous place to cycle, hike, snorkel and swim on newly opened beaches and pristine land – you can visit one or both, as you wish.

Back on the mainland, head for **Bosque Estatal de Carite** (p258) at the mouth of the Ruta Panorámica. That road leads to the **Reserva Forestal Toro Negro** (p265), a remarkable forest with lush, flowery vegetation very unlike what you'll find at nearby **Bosque Estatal de Guánica** (p201), which is short on greenery but long on bird-watching and stunning ocean views. For the truly adventurous, a trip to **Isla Mona** (p234) is imperative – you'll really feel like an out-of-place guest in this animal kingdom.

Bosque Estatal de Guajataca (p249) is next, followed by **Lago dos Bocas** (p246), **Bosque Estatal de Río Abajo** (p246) and **Bosque Estatal de Cambalache** (p243).

FOR CYCLISTS

Test your brakes in central San Juan before heading east through the traffic-calmed streets of Condado to the bike paths of **Piñones** (p125). Here among gorgeously undone beaches you can cycle to your heart's content with nary a car or truck to bother you.

Hop on a ferry next for the island of **Culebra** (p154) and strike out for the golden crescent of **Playa Flamenco** (p159) and some seriously steep and rutted roads. The switch to **Vieques** (p166) is welcome and seamless – it's one of the best places in Puerto Rico to make a spontaneous bike trip with a local guide.

Back on the mainland, avoid the car chaos of Yabucoa on the southeast coast and veer off on the panoramic **Hwy 901** (p149) that traces the coast until **Maunabo**. Following the south coast beyond Ponce you'll encounter the dry forest of **Guánica** (p201), where a network of trails provide plenty of options.

The **Cabo Rojo** (p211) area is, arguably, the island's best cycling haven. From **La Parguera** (p205) head west toward the famous Las Salinas salt flats and Los Morrillos lighthouse. Spin north after lunch for a seafood dinner in **Boquerón** (p213).

Another little heralded cyclist's paradise is hidden in the roads around Isabela. Spin out of the Ramey Base near Aguadilla before hooking up with spectacular **Hwy 466** (p251) and a full-on surfing show at Playa Jobos.

On the way back to San Juan a couple of protected areas offer plentiful off-road adventures. Try the eight miles of single track in the **Bosque Estatal de Cambalache** (p243) or make a sedate circumnavigation of **Laguna Tortuguero** (p243).

History

Puerto Rico occupies a crux position in the history of the American continent. Colonized by Spanish explorer Juan Ponce de León in 1508, the island contains the oldest European-founded settlement under US jurisdiction. Long before Sir Walter Raleigh and the Pilgrim Fathers had tested the waters of the tempestuous Atlantic, the first granite ramparts of El Morro fort in Old San Juan had been chiseled deftly into place. Nearly 500 years later, they're still there.

As countless historical writers have noted, Puerto Rico is flavored with contrast and contradiction, a blending of cultures and nations that is highly eclectic and not easy to pigeonhole. While technically a US commonwealth, some natives still feel that the island should be a full-blown American state, others an independent nation, and still more, a compromise solution that is neither of the above. Then there is the exotic cultural breakdown: the caustic blending of ancient Taíno with brutally exploited Africans into a historical melting pot that contained Spanish, French, Cuban, Dominican and even Lebanese elements. What you're left with is the essence of modern Puerto Rico, a proud Caribbean nation with a distinctly Latin temperament that also happens to be good friends with the USA.

Read a quick but refreshingly succinct overview of Puerto Rican history in five easy-to-decipher chapters on www .solboricua.com.

TAÍNO CULTURE

The Taíno were an Arawakan Indian group who inhabited Puerto Rico and the other Greater Antilles (Cuba, Hispaniola and Jamaica) at the time of Columbus' arrival in 1493. Arawaks had first started settling on the island around AD 700, following a gradual migration north from the Orinoco River delta in present-day Venezuela, and by the year 1000 a distinctive Taíno culture had begun to emerge based on agriculture, fishing, hunting and the production of cassava bread. Taíno believed in a complex religious cosmology and lived in small, round wooden huts called *bohíos* where they smoked *cohibas* (cigars) and slept in *hamacas* (hammocks). They called their newly adopted island Borinquen (Land of the Noble Lord) and practiced basic crafts such as pottery, basket weaving and wood carving. The native society was relatively democratic and organized around a system of *caciques* (chiefs). Below the *caciques* was a rank of medicine men, subchiefs and, below them, the workers. At the time of Ponce de León's arrival in 1508, the chief of all chiefs was a *cacique* called Agüeybana who presided over Borinquen's largest settlement sited on the Guayanilla River near present-day Guánica.

For leisure, the Taíno built several ceremonial ball parks where they played a soccer-like game with a rubber ball between opposing teams of 10 to 30 players. Winning was supposed to ensure good health and a favorable

The Taínos: The Rise and Decline of the People Who Greeted Columbus, by Irving Rouse, offers a whole book's worth of information on a topic that usually only gets a couple of paragraphs.

Juan Ponce de Leon and the Spanish Discovery of Puerto Rico and Florida, by Robert H Fuson, sheds some light on the man who founded modern Puerto Rico.

TIMELINE

2000 BC	430–250 BC	1000
Punto Ferro Man, a native from the Ortoiroid culture that had migrated north from the Orinoco basin in present-day Venezuela, lives on the island of Vieques.	The Ortoiroids are gradually displaced by the Saladoids, a horticultural people skilled in the art of pottery. Saladoids spoke an Awarak Indian language and laid the early building blocks for a singular Caribbean culture.	The Taíno – who arrived in a second migratory wave from the Orinoco River basin – emerge as the island's dominant culture; they name the island Boriken, meaning 'the Great Land of the Valiant and Noble Lord'.

JUAN PONCE DE LEÓN

Soldier, sailor, governor, dreamer and politician, the life story of Juan Ponce de León reads like a *Who's Who* of late-15th- and early-16th-century maritime exploration. Aside from founding the Spanish colony of Puerto Rico in 1508, this daring, yet often short-sighted, Spanish adventurer partook in Columbus' second trans-Atlantic voyage, charted large tracts of the Bahamas, discovered the existence of the Gulf Stream, and was the first recorded European to set foot in what is now known as Florida.

Born in Valladolid, Spain, in 1460, de León served his military apprenticeship fighting against the Moors during the Christian reconquest of Granada in 1492. The following year he arrived in the New World on Columbus' second expedition and settled on the island of Hispaniola where he was proclaimed deputy governor of the province of Higüey after ruthlessly suppressing a native revolt. Following Columbus' death in 1506, the Spanish crown asked de León to lead the colonization of Borinquen, an island first explored by Columbus in 1493. De León landed on the south coast in 1508 with five ships and 200 people and established the first settlement in Caparra, a few miles inland from present-day San Juan.

Despite initially currying favor with the native Taíno Indians, the Spaniard's relationship with his new neighbors quickly deteriorated. After being made governor of Puerto Rico in 1509, de León ruthlessly exploited the Taíno in his avaricious search for gold, and his position and reputation gradually suffered as a result. Finally in 1512, after much legal wrangling, the explorer was removed from his governor's post in favor of Columbus' son, Diego, before being given title to explore the lands north of Cuba.

De León set sail with three ships in 1513, and tracked north in search of the legendary healing waters of the fountain of youth. According to the natives of Borinquen, the waters were hidden in a place known as Bimini (in the Bahamas), but de León, after circumnavigating the archipelago, elected to divert northwest and, in the process, inadvertently 'discovered' Florida.

After several forays along Florida's coast (which de León thought was an island), the explorer returned to Puerto Rico via Cuba and Guadalupe in 1515 and stayed there for the next six years. In 1521 de León organized another trip to Florida with two ships and 200 people. This time they landed on the west coast of Florida near the Caloosahatchee River but were quickly beaten back by Calusa Indians. Wounded in the thigh by a poisoned arrow, de León was shipped back to Havana where he died in July 1521. His remains were returned to Puerto Rico where they are interred in the Catedral de San Juan (p94).

harvest. At Tibes near Ponce in the south, and at Caguana near Utuadu in the north, archaeologists have discovered and preserved these impressive courts that were marked by rows of massive stone blocks. Here, native rituals were practiced – tribal events that brought the communities together and kept the collective spiritual and social memory alive. Drums made from hollow trunks, as well as maracas and *güiros*, provided the percussive accompaniment – instruments that still fill the sounds of Puerto Rican traditional and popular music today.

1493	1508	1509
On November 19, during his second voyage to the New World, Christopher Columbus lands in Puerto Rico somewhere on the west coast. He christens the island *San Juan Bautista* in honor of St John the Baptist.	Juan Ponce de León leads Spanish colonists to Puerto Rico in search of gold. He establishes the island's first colony – Caparra – in the north on swampy land close to San Juan harbor.	Ponce de León is named the first governor of San Juan Bautista (Puerto Rico) after the Spanish authorities refuse to grant Columbus' son, Diego, rights to the lands discovered by his (recently deceased) father.

Approximately 100 years before the arrival of the Spanish, Taíno culture was challenged by the Caribs, a fierce and warlike tribe from South America who raided Taíno villages in search of slaves and fodder for their cannibalistic rites. The simmering tensions that developed between the Taíno and Caribs were still very much in evidence when Ponce de León took possession of the island in 1508 and was probably misinterpreted by the Spanish as Taíno aggression. In reality the Taíno were a friendly, sedentary people who put up little initial resistance to the new colonizers and ultimately paid a huge price.

Testimonies vary as to how many Taíno inhabited Borinquen at the time of the Spanish invasion, though most anthropologists place the number between 20,000 and 50,000. In 1515 – after nearly a decade of maltreatment, a failed rebellion, disease and virtual slavery – only about 4000 remained. Thirty years later, a Spanish bishop put the number at 60. Some historians have claimed that a small group of Taíno escaped the 16th-century genocide and hid in Puerto Rico's central mountains where they survived until the early 19th century, but the claims have no proof and are impossible to substantiate.

While Taíno blood may have all but disappeared in modern Puerto Rico, the native traditions live on. Puerto Rican Spanish is dotted with traditional native words such as yucca (a root vegetable), iguana, *manatí* (manatee – a sea mammal), maracas and *Ceiba* (Puerto Rico's national tree); and some terms have even found their way into modern English: think *huracan* for hurricane and *hamaca* for hammock. Musically, the Taíno contributed the maracas and the *güiro* to modern percussion, while gastronomically their heavy use of root vegetables has found its way into traditional *comida criolla* (Puerto Rican cuisine).

THE INVADERS

In the golden age of piracy, Puerto Rico was revered by booty-seeking buccaneers like no other Spanish port. Everyone from daring British dandy Francis Drake to common cutthroats such as Blackbeard tried their luck against San Juan's formidable defenses. Few were successful.

One of the colony's earliest invaders, Francis Drake first arrived in Puerto Rico in 1595 in pursuit of a stricken Spanish galleon – holding two million gold ducats – that had taken shelter in San Juan harbor. While the plucky Brit may have singed the king of Spain's beard in Cádiz a decade earlier, the Spaniards quickly got their own back in Puerto Rico when they fired a cannonball into Drake's cabin, killing two of his men, and – allegedly – shooting the great explorer's stool from underneath him. Drake, who had initiated his attack by burning a dozen Spanish frigates in the harbor, was forced to make a hasty retreat and left the island empty-handed. He died the following year of dysentery in Panama.

On a stinging revenge mission, San Juan was attacked by the British navy again three years later under the command of the third earl of Cumberland.

Get the lowdown on San Juan's historic forts on the US National Park Service official website at www.nps.gov/saju.

Alexander O'Reilly was an Irish-born Spanish Field Marshal who became known as the 'Father of the Puerto Rican Militia' for his military training methods and crucial work to strengthen San Juan's beleaguered forts in the 1760s.

The first black person to arrive in Puerto Rico was Juan Garrido, a conquistador allied to Juan Ponce de León. He first set foot on the island in 1509.

1511	**1513**	**1521**
Subjected to brutal exploitation by the Spanish, the Taíno stage their first unsuccessful revolt against their new overlords. Ponce de León is subsequently replaced as governor in favor of Diego Columbus.	Following the decimation of the local Indian population through disease and outright slaughter, the first West African slaves arrive on the island to work in the new economy.	The city of San Juan is founded in its present site and the island changes its name from San Juan Bautista to Puerto Rico.

Learning from Drake's mistakes, Cumberland's 1700-strong army landed in what is now Condado and advanced upon the city from the east, crossing into San Juan via the San Antonio Bridge. After a short battle with Spanish forces, the city surrendered and the British occupied it for the next 10 weeks, before a dysentery epidemic hit and forced an ignominious withdrawal.

In response to frequent British incursions, San Juan's defensive walls were repeatedly strengthened in the early 17th century, a measure that allowed the Spanish to successfully repel an ambitious attack by the Netherlands in 1625. Acting under the command of Captain Boudewijn Hendricksz, the Dutch fired over 4000 cannonballs into the city walls before landing 2000 men at La Puntilla. Although the invaders managed to occupy the city temporarily and even break into the Fortaleza palace, the Spanish continued to hold El Morro fort and, after less than a month, with Puerto Rican reinforcements arriving, Hendricksz beat a hasty retreat, razing the city as he went.

San Juan's second great fort, San Cristóbal, was inaugurated in the 1630s and the city saw no more major attacks for almost two centuries. It wasn't until 1797 that the British, at war again with the Spanish, tried their luck one last time. The armada, which consisted of over 60 ships and 10,000 men, was one of the largest invasion forces ever to take on the Spanish in the American territories, but after two weeks of often vicious fighting, the British commander Sir Ralph Abercromby withdrew in exasperation. Noble in defeat, Abercromby reported that San Juan could have resisted an attack force 10 times greater than the British had used.

AFRICAN CULTURE

As it was throughout the Caribbean, slavery was employed to develop the Puerto Rican economy, primarily in the late 18th and early 19th centuries. The two types of slaves that were brought to the island – ladinos, born and acculturated in Spain, and bozales and Yoruba people, brought from Africa – were first used to mine the limited gold and silver deposits. Once these deposits were depleted, the slaves were used primarily in the sugarcane industry and other areas of agriculture, predominantly in the coastal areas of the island. While the rest of the population experienced normal growth due to reproduction and voluntary migration, the slave population rose much faster throughout the late 18th century, with census figures in 1765 showing the slave population was 5400. By 1830 the slave population had increased to more than 31,000, mainly due to the introduction of new slaves directly from Africa and other parts of the Caribbean. However, despite these increases, by 1795 the majority (more than 60%) of black and mulatto people living in Puerto Rico were free. This trend, unusual for the Caribbean at the time, is often attributed to the island's asylum policy, which granted freedom to fugitive slaves from throughout the region.

1528	1595	1598
The French sack and burn the new west coast settlement of San Germán, ushering in over two and a half centuries of piracy and foreign competition.	British privateer Sir Francis Drake attempts to attack and loot San Juan with 26 ships but is repelled by the city's formidable defenses.	On a revenge mission, George Clifford, earl of Cumberland, lands in Santurce and attacks San Juan by land. He occupies the city for several months before abandoning it due to an outbreak of dysentery.

There is considerable historic debate as to how slaves were actually treated on the large sugarcane estates. Some accounts claim conditions were better in Puerto Rico than in other colonies due to Spain's relatively strict slave code, which provided more protections and benefits than elsewhere. Other studies discount this argument, pointing to evidence of runaway slaves who preferred living as fugitives to living on a plantation. Regardless, by the late 1830s, as it became increasingly apparent that slavery was not going to be justifiable for much longer, plantation owners began enacting measures guaranteeing cheap access to other laborers – *jornaleros*. The landed sugar elite utilized both low-wage *jornaleros* and slaves to generate wealth for themselves and grow the island's economy. In both cases, the exploitation by European whites of African- and island-born blacks and mulattos led to the perpetuation of racial myths that allowed for the continuation of social inequities and racism.

Many slave uprisings occurred on the island, some larger than others. Later this resistance by the black population ran parallel with a political movement for emancipation led by Julio Vizcarrondo, a Puerto Rican abolitionist living in Spain, as well as island-based political leaders such as Segundo Ruiz Belvis, Roman Baldorioty de Castro and Ramón Emeterio Betances. After years of struggle, the Spanish National Assembly abolished slavery on March 22, 1873.

Today the African presence in Puerto Rican culture is striking, described by the late Puerto Rican cultural and social writer Jose Luis González as *el primer piso*, or 'the first floor' of Puerto Rican culture. In its music, art and religious icons, African traditions are powerfully felt. And despite the racial stereotypes and inequalities that continue to exist on the island and within the Puerto Rican diaspora, Puerto Rico will always be considered an Afro-Indigenous-Caribbean experience.

FROM SPANISH COLONY TO AMERICAN COMMONWEALTH

As two Greater Antilles islands ruled by Spain for nearly four centuries, Cuba and Puerto Rico share a remarkably similar history. Both were colonized in the early 1500s, both retain vestiges of their indigenous Taíno culture, both were heavily influenced by the African slave trade (a cultural stimulant that contributed to their unique hybrid music and distinct Afro-Christian religious beliefs) and both remained Spanish colonies a good 80 years after the rest of Latin America had declared independence. The irony, of course, lies in their different paths post 1898 and the fact that today, Puerto Rico remains a staunch US ally, whereas Cuba is 'public enemy number one', a former Soviet satellite state that has been ostracized with the most draconian (and longest) trade embargo in modern history. So what happened?

In 1816 the great South American liberator, Simón Bolívar, stopped briefly in Vieques for an unplanned visit while fleeing defeat in Venezuela. It was the only time he would set foot on Puerto Rican soil.

The father of the Puerto Rican Independence movement, Ramón Emeterio Betances was also a successful surgeon and ophthalmologist who stamped out a critical cholera epidemic that broke out in Mayagüez in 1856.

The total number of American soldiers killed in Puerto Rico during the Spanish-American War of 1898 was four.

1625	1797	1825
The Dutch navy besieges the city of San Juan and burns it to the ground, but they are prevented from taking total control by Spanish forces manning the fortifications in El Morro.	A third and final attempt by the British to take San Juan is led by General Abercromby during the Seven Years War, but the Spanish once again stand firm.	Spanish authorities hire the American schooner *Grampus* to capture 'El Pirata Cofresí', Puerto Rico's nautical Robin Hood, who robbed rich foreign ships to feed the poor of Cabo Rojo; he is executed in El Morro fort.

Two Wings of the Same Dove

While the bulk of Spain's American colonies rose up under the leadership of Simón Bolívar in the 1820s, Puerto Rico and Cuba's conservative Creole landowners, rich on sugar and spice and all things nice, elected to stay put – at least for the time being. But, as economic conditions worsened and slavery came to be seen as an ailing colonial anachronism, the mood started to change.

During the 1860s, links were formed between nationalists and revolutionaries on both islands, united by the same language and a common Spanish foe. The cultural interchange worked both ways. Great thinkers such as Cuban national hero José Martí drew a lot of his early inspiration from Puerto Rican surgeon and nationalist Ramón Emeterio Betances, while Mayagüez-born general Juan Rius Rivera later went on to command the Cuban Liberation Army in the 1895–98 war against the Spanish.

Ironically it was the Puerto Rican nationalists who acted first, proclaiming the abortive Grito de Lares (see opposite) in 1868. Following their lead two weeks later, Cuba's machete-wielding *mambises* (19th-century Cuban independence fighters) unleashed their own independence cry and, with wider grassroots support and better leadership, were able to wage a brutal, though ultimately unsuccessful, 10-year war against the Spanish.

While the rapid defeat in Puerto Rico was a major political setback for the nationalist movement, all was not yet lost. Igniting a second Cuban-Spanish Independence War in 1895, José Martí proclaimed that Cuba and Puerto Rico still stood shoulder to shoulder as 'two wings of the same dove' and, had it not been for the timely intervention of the Americans in 1898 when the Spanish were almost defeated, history could have been very different.

Cuba and Puerto Rico's political divergence began in 1900 when the US Congress passed the Foraker Act (1900), making Puerto Rico the first unincorporated territory of the US. Cuba meanwhile, thanks to the so-called Teller Amendment (passed through Congress before the Spanish-American War had started), gained nominal independence with some strings attached in 1902.

Resistance to the new arrangement in Puerto Rico was spearheaded by the Partido Unión de Puerto Rico (Union Party), which for years had been calling for a resolution to their lack of fundamental democratic rights. The Union Party was led by Luis Muñoz Rivera, one of the most important political figures in the history of Puerto Rico. But unlike his more radical Cuban contemporaries, such as José Martí and – later on – Fidel Castro, Muñoz Rivera was a diplomat who was willing to compromise with the US on key issues. Under pressure from President Woodrow Wilson he ultimately ceded on his demand for outright independence in favor of greater autonomy via an amendment to the Foraker Act.

Former leader of the Puerto Rican Nationalist party, Pedro Albizu Campos was of African, Taíno and Basque descent. He graduated from Harvard University with a law degree in 1921 and was fluent in eight languages.

Ronald Fernandez' *The Disenchanted Island: Puerto Rico and the United States in the 20th Century* explores the complicated relationship between the island and the US.

1850–67	1868	1873
The Puerto Rican liberation movement gathers strength under the inspirational leadership of Ramón Emeterio Betances, a poet, politician, diplomat and eminent surgeon.	Revolutionaries inspired by Betances take the town of Lares and declare a Puerto Rican republic, but the uprising is repelled within hours by Spanish forces sent from nearby San Sebastián.	In the wake of the Grito de Lares, the Spanish authorities institute various political and social reforms in Puerto Rico, including the abolition of slavery.

GRITO DE LARES

As well as boasting the world's largest radio telescope and its youngest ever boxing champion, Puerto Rico also holds the dubious distinction of having created history's shortest-lived republic. The independent republic of Puerto Rico, proclaimed during the abortive Grito de Lares (Cry of Lares) in 1868, lasted slightly less than 24 hours.

Worn down by slavery, high taxes and the asphyxiating grip of Spain's militaristic rulers, independence advocates in the Caribbean colonies of Puerto Rico and Cuba were in the ascendancy throughout the 1850s and '60s. Ironically, it was the Puerto Ricans who acted first. Under the auspices of exiled intellectual and physician Dr Ramón Emeterio Betances, an insurrection was planned in the western town of Lares for September 29, 1868. A ship carrying armed reinforcements from the Dominican Republic was supposed to act as backup but, due to an anonymous betrayal a few weeks beforehand, it was apprehended by the Spanish authorities along with various key rebel leaders. Flailing from the setback, the remaining rebels elected to bring their planned revolt forward six days to September 23, a move that would ultimately cost them dearly.

Meeting at a farm, codenamed Centro Bravo, owned by Venezuelan-born rebel Manuel Rojas on the evening of September 23, over 600 men and women marched defiantly on the small town of Lares near Mayagüez, where they were met with minimal Spanish resistance. Declaring a Puerto Rican republic from the main square, the rebels placed a red, white and blue flag – designed by Betances – on the high altar of the main church and named Francisco Ramírez Medina head of a new provisional government. Fatefully, the glory wasn't to last. Electing next to march on the nearby town of San Sebastián, the poorly armed liberation army walked into a classic Spanish military trap and were quickly seen off by superior firepower. A handful of the militia were killed by Spanish bullets while hundreds more – including Rojas and Medina – were taken prisoner.

While the Grito de Lares was decapitated swiftly and never won widespread grassroots support on the island, the action did lead to some long-term political concessions. In the years that followed, the colonial authorities passed liberal electoral reforms, granted Puerto Rico provincial status and offered Spanish citizenship to all *criollos* (island-born people of European descent). The biggest victory, however, came in 1873 with the abolition of slavery and granting of freedom to over 30,000 previously incarcerated slaves.

In 1917, just months after Muñoz Rivera's death, President Woodrow Wilson signed the Jones Act. It granted US citizenship to all Puerto Ricans and established a bicameral legislature whose decisions could be vetoed by the US president. No Puerto Ricans were involved in the debate over citizenship.

A Question of Status

Questioned by many before the ink had even dried, the Jones Act failed to provide any long-term solutions. On the contrary, the debate over the future of Puerto Rico's relationship with the US continued to intensify and helped define the political careers of two major figures who would emerge in the late 1920s and early '30s on the island: Pedro Albizu Campos, leader

1897	1898	1900
The Carta Autonómica is instituted by Spain, chartering Puerto Rico as an autonomous state under a Spanish governor with representation in the Spanish Cortés (Parliament).	US forces blockade San Juan and land a 16,000-strong force unopposed at Guánica on the south coast, ending the Spanish-American War; Spain cedes Puerto Rico to the USA.	The US Congress passes the Foraker Act, granting a US-run civil government to Puerto Rico; American Charles Allen is installed as the island's first governor and is aided by an 11-man executive council that includes five Puerto Ricans.

of the pro-independence Partido Nacionalista (Nationalist Party); and Luis Muñoz Marín, who established the Partido Popular Democrático (PPD; Popular Democratic Party) in 1938.

As son of the widely respected Muñoz Rivera, Luis Muñoz Marín avoided the radical politics of Albizu, and took a more conciliatory approach to challenging the colonial situation of Puerto Rico. While the US Congress sidestepped the status question, Muñoz Marín's PPD pressed for a plebiscite that would allow Puerto Ricans to choose between statehood and independence as their final options. In the late 1930s and early 1940s, the majority of the PPD favored independence. However, neither President Franklin D Roosevelt nor the Congress seriously considered it as an option, and laws were enacted to criminalize independence activities such as those waged by the Nationalists.

Rather than take to the mountains to fight – as Fidel Castro later would do – Muñoz Marín decided to adopt a strategy that incorporated the status question with other issues affecting the Puerto Rican people, such as the dire economic and social effects of the Great Depression. His crux moment came in 1946 when he rejected independence as an option and threw his political weight behind a new status granted by Congress in 1948, referred to today as Estado Libre Associado, or ELA, the Free Associated State. This approach was meant to give the island more political autonomy, yet maintain and even embrace the very close relationship between the US and Puerto Rico.

In 1952 this status description was approved by a referendum held on the island. The voters also approved a Constitution that for the first time in Puerto Rico's history was written by islanders. Muñoz Marín became the first governor of Puerto Rico to be elected by Puerto Ricans. Nevertheless, despite claims by the new governor and his supporters that the status question was finally resolved with ELA, for all intents and purposes, nothing changed: the Congress still had plenary powers over Puerto Rico. Although islanders were now exempt from paying federal income taxes, they still had no representation in Congress (apart from a nonvoting delegate), could not vote in US national elections, and were still being drafted into the US Armed Forces to fight alongside young Americans in foreign wars.

Over the years a number of referenda and plebiscites have been held, ostensibly to allow the Puerto Rican people to decide the future of the island's status. Two official plebiscites, in 1967 and 1993, resulted in victories for 'commonwealth' status, that is, the ELA. Other votes have been held, with the status options, as well as the approach to self-determination, defined in different ways. All of these popular votes have been shaped by the ruling party at the time of the vote, either the pro-ELA PPD, or the pro-statehood Partido Nuevo Progresista (PNP; New Progressive Party). None of the plebiscites held over the years have been binding for the US Congress.

In 1998, as the island was getting ready to mark the 100th anniversary of US control, another attempt to address the issue came in the form of a bill

Blanca Canales, leader of the abortive Jayuya Uprising in 1950, is popularly considered to have been the first woman to have led an armed revolt against the US government.

It was technically illegal to fly the Puerto Rican flag on the island until the adoption of the commonwealth's new constitution in 1952.

A special cask of high-grade rum was set aside by a brewer in 1942 with orders that it be opened only when Puerto Rico becomes an independent nation. When (or if) that happens, free drinks for everyone!

1917	1937	1948
The Jones Act makes Puerto Rico a territory of the US and unilaterally grants islanders US citizenship and a bill of rights; English becomes the official language.	Student *independentista*s (independence advocates) clash with police on Palm Sunday; 20 people die and over 100 are injured in what becomes known as the 'Masacre de Ponce'.	With US Congressional approval, Puerto Ricans craft their own constitution and elect their first governor, Luis Muñoz Marín, former president of the Senate, who holds the post for 16 years.

SHALL WE KILL THE PRESIDENT?

Deep in the forgotten archives of history lays an event that came to within a gunshot of altering the nature of Puerto Rican–American relations forever.

On November 1, 1950 two Puerto Rican nationalists, Oscar Collazo and Griselio Torresola, attempted to assassinate American President Harry S Truman as he lay taking a nap in his underwear in the Blair House (the presidential residence while the White House was being renovated) in Washington, DC. The act occurred at a particularly volatile moment in Puerto Rican history. The 1940s had seen a rise of political nationalism on the island in the wake of the 1937 Ponce massacre (see p187) the subsequent imprisonment of Nationalist Party leader Pedro Albizu Campos. Released in 1947, Campos quickly began plotting afresh and on October 30, 1950, after a police raid on his San Juan home, he gave a nationalistic call to arms.

First to answer his plea was Blanca Canales, a passionate female independence advocate from the small town of Jayuya in the central mountains. Arming a small group of fellow *independistas* from a cache of hidden weapons, Canales led a fiery uprising in her home town (in what became known as the Jayuya Uprising), burning a post office, cutting telephone lines and declaring a Puerto Rican republic from the town square. But cocooned in the mountains with little outside support, the revolt lasted just three days before it was stamped out by a superior US Air Force that bombed Jayuya and forced the rebels to surrender.

Meanwhile in Washington, DC, news of the Jayuya bombings triggered US-based Puerto Rican nationalists Collazo and Torresola to make the quick but fatal decision to assassinate the US president. The shooting drama was short but incisive. Converging on the Blair House from opposite directions, the two Puerto Ricans opened fire almost simultaneously on security staff guarding the building's entrance. It was Torresola who acted first, firing four shots at White House policeman Leslie Coffelt at close range before wounding another officer as he ran to escape. The assassin then stopped to reload as President Truman rushed to the window to see what all the commotion was about. It was at this point that the mortally wounded Coffelt struggled to his feet and shot Torresola from 30yd, killing him instantly. Stunned by the effort, Coffelt quickly fell to the ground and was rushed to hospital where he died four hours later, his place in history assured as the man who potentially saved the life of an American president.

Collazo, meanwhile, had been incapacitated by a shot in the chest and was promptly arrested. After a much publicized trial he was sentenced to death by electrocution, but his sentence was commuted to life imprisonment by President Truman in 1952. Collazo served 25 years of his sentence before he was released in 1979 after being pardoned by President Carter. Back in Puerto Rico he was received as a homecoming hero in some quarters and as a common terrorist in others. In a grating show of solidarity, Cuban leader Fidel Castro honored him with a hero's medal a few months later. Collazo died aged 80 in 1994.

introduced by Alaskan Republican Don Young. For the first time, Congress acknowledged that the current status was no longer viable. The Young Bill called for a plebiscite on the island where Puerto Ricans would vote on only two status options: either statehood or independence. It did not provide ELA or

1950	1952	1954
A nationalist revolt in the mountain town of Jayuya is quickly suppressed by the US Air Force; in response two nationalists in Washington DC try unsuccessfully to assassinate the US president, Harry Truman.	The Constitution of Puerto Rico is approved by referendum and the island becomes an Estado Libre Associado (a US commonwealth); the Puerto Rican flag is flown – legally – for the first time.	Four Puerto Rican nationalists open fire inside the US House of Representatives in Washington, DC, wounding five US congressmen; they all receive long prison terms.

any other form of 'enhanced commonwealth' as an option, angering members of the PPD. Ultimately, the Young Bill went nowhere. While it was approved in the House by a narrow margin, the Senate never seriously considered it.

CURRENT POLITICS

Puerto Rico's status remains a major point of contention for its political leaders and often overshadows discussions about how to resolve other issues affecting the island, such as economic development, unemployment, education and crime. In the 1990s politics were dominated by pro-statehood Governor Pedro Roselló who, when reelected to a second term in 1996, received more votes than any other governor before him. However, his obsession with the status issue and his almost fanatical desire to convince Washington to make Puerto Rico a state overwhelmed his administration, especially in his second term, when he campaigned tirelessly for the Young Bill and other status-related measures.

In the end, charges of corruption in his administration left him somewhat discredited as he left office in 2001, turning over the reigns of the governor's mansion to the first woman ever elected into the office, Sila Maria Calderón, the standard-bearer of the PPD.

Calderón was committed to bringing back integrity to the governorship, and, not surprisingly, pushed the status issue off the agenda during her four years in office. She took a very vocal position against the US Navy and lobbied regularly to make certain that Washington would stick to its commitment to close down the Vieques bombing range and remove its forces from the island, despite opposition from certain elements within the Pentagon and more hawkish members of the US Congress. However, she did not run for reelection, instead passing the baton to Aníbal Acevedo Vilá, the young former resident commissioner for Puerto Rico (nonvoting delegate to the Congress).

Ironically, Acevedo's primary opponent in the November 2004 election was Pedro Roselló. Once again, the voters were split almost precisely down the middle, with Acevedo narrowly beating the former governor by 3566 votes, a result that was immediately challenged by Roselló. In the latest example of the contradictions in Puerto Rican politics and its relations with federal authorities, the ultimate winner was not officially declared until the first US Circuit Court of Appeals in Boston ruled in late December that a federal court in Puerto Rico did not have jurisdiction in the recount dispute involving the November 2 gubernatorial election. Once again, a non-Puerto Rican entity, in this case a US court, had the final word in determining who was to be governor of the island.

In January 2005 Acevedo was sworn in as the island's eighth democratically elected governor but he soon faced a hostile legislature dominated by the opposing PNP. Blankly refusing to accept Acevedo's budget-balancing proposals, the legislature came up with its own plan which the new governor promptly vetoed. A stalemate ensued, a situation which ultimately led to a

---

A 1991 law which made Spanish the official language in Puerto Rico was revoked just two years later to reinstate both Spanish and English as joint commonwealth languages.

Military Power and Popular Protest: The US Navy in Vieques, Puerto Rico, by Katherine T McCaffrey, provides every detail of the civil disobedience that drove the navy off Vieques.

In 2006 the US Navy estimated that it would take three years and $76 million to remove remaining ordnance and toxins from Vieques.

1967

Puerto Rico holds its first plebiscite on the issue of Puerto Rico becoming a US state, but votes overwhelmingly to remain a commonwealth; the independence parties gain only 1% of the votes

1978

Two independence supporters are gunned down by police posing as revolutionary sympathizers on Cerro Maravilla in the Central Mountains in an incident that exposes deep political fissures and government corruption.

1999

Major protests break out on the island of Vieques against the US Navy, following the killing of islander David Sane Rodríguez during military target practice.

THE GREAT MIGRATION

Long attracted by the lure of the American Dream, the Puerto Ricans rank alongside the Irish in their long-standing tendency to migrate to the United States – in particular to New York City. Indeed, by the late 1990s, the Puerto Rican diaspora in the US was as large as the island's total home-based population, with close to 3.8 million expats living stateside. Puerto Rican émigrés have even fermented their own US-based culture, creating such hybrid musical genres as salsa and reggaeton, and spawning a plethora of foreign-based – but proudly Puerto Rican – superstars such as Ricky Martin, Jennifer Lopez and Mark Anthony.

Although migration to the US has been common since the early 1800s, the largest exodus didn't occur until the mid-20th century, when the granting of US citizenship to all Puerto Ricans, coupled with the lack of economic opportunities on the island, led to tens of thousands of people flocking north. The process snowballed in the late 1940s when a new air link to New York sent another wave of homecoming GIs and dispossessed agricultural workers to the Big Apple where they settled in East Harlem, a quarter that was promptly rechristened 'Spanish Harlem' or – in Latin lingo – El Barrio. In the year 1953 alone an estimated 75,000 Puerto Ricans arrived in New York City and by 1960, over half a million called the Big Apple home.

In the early years, the migrant experience wasn't always a harmonious one, with Puerto Ricans invariably gravitating towards New York's poorest neighborhoods, where they faced economic hardship and discrimination. The situation wasn't aided by a failed assassination attempt on President Truman in 1950 and an abortive shooting on Capitol Hill four years later, both acts perpetuated by Puerto Rican nationalists. Subsequently islanders came to be seen as unpatriotic and were often viewed with distrust and suspicion. As a defensive mechanism many Puerto Ricans banded together in groups and began to re-assert their cultural identity. This led, in part, to the birth of the art-house Nuyorican movement in the 1960s and '70s. Centered at the Nuyorican Poet's Café on New York's Lower East Side, this progressive artistic movement helped to promote salsa music and showcase classic Puerto Rican–inspired movies such as *Carlito's Way*.

With economic conditions improving since the 1980s, many Puerto Ricans have worked their way up the career ladder and moved towards more white-collar jobs. As a result, sizable Puerto Rican enclaves now exist in the affluent suburbs of cities such as Miami and Chicago, and a number of US-born Puerto Ricans have moved back to the old country where they have invested in second homes.

massive budgetary crisis that wracked Puerto Rico in May 2006, when the government was forced to literally 'shut down' after it ran out of funds to pay over 100,000 public sector employees. The crisis lasted two weeks before a grudging compromise was reached, but it made a laughing stock out of the Puerto Rican government and drew intense criticism from business leaders, Puerto Rican celebrities and the general public.

In March 2008 Acevedo was indicted by the US on corruption charges after a two-year grand jury investigation. He has denied any wrongdoing and faces up to 20 years in prison if convicted.

2000	**2003**	**2006**
Puerto Ricans elect ex San Juan mayor Sila Maria Calderón of the Popular Democratic Party as the first woman governor of the commonwealth.	After four years of protests and worldwide publicity, the US Navy pulls out of Vieques after 60 years of occupation; the former military land is promptly designated a US Fish and Wildlife Refuge.	An acute budgetary crisis forces the shutdown of schools and government offices across the island for two weeks as legislative officials try to address a $740-million deficit in public funds.

The Culture

REGIONAL IDENTITY

Think of Puerto Rico as a kaleidoscope with four distinct but intermingling elements: Taíno Indian, Spanish, African and North American. The first group comprises the island's earliest inhabitants (the Taíno), the second arrived with European colonization in the early 16th century, the third is a legacy of over 300 years of slavery, and the last group is a result of Puerto Rico's ongoing relationship as a commonwealth dependency of the United States.

The end product is a dynamic population of rare eclecticism whose diverse personality is often incredibly hard to classify. You won't know you're outside America as you see Puerto Ricans driving into Burger King in ridiculously large American cars; the next moment you're sure you're in Latin America as a local gesticulates passionately; later you wonder if you've somehow taken a wrong turn and landed in Africa, as the people around you gyrate their hips to exotic, rhythmic music in a club.

Modern practicalities have meant that, for three or four generations now, many Puerto Ricans have grown up bouncing back and forth between mainland US cities and their beloved island. Even those who elect to stay put assimilate a great deal by proxy. The full scope of their bilingual and multicultural existence can take a long time for outsiders to comprehend. Lots of Puerto Ricans are perfectly comfortable striding down Manhattan's Fifth Ave during the week for a little shopping, then passing the weekend eating with family at *friquitines* (street vendors) along Playa Luquillo.

From Rincón to Vieques, Puerto Ricans are incredibly friendly and open; they like nothing better than to show off their beloved Boriken (the island's Taíno name). You'll note that, despite their obsession with American cars, Puerto Ricans are much more into experiences than material things. A favorite island pastime is to wade into warm beach waters just before sunset – beer in hand and more in the cooler – to shoot the breeze with whoever else is out enjoying the glorious changing skies. Bank executive, schoolteacher, fisherman – it doesn't matter who you are, as long as you share an appreciation for how good life is in Puerto Rico.

Although Puerto Rico shares many characteristics with other Caribbean nations in its food, ethnicity and general laid-back ambience, Spanish colonial and more recent American influences have lent the island certain distinct traits. Despite its close historical and cultural ties to Cuba and the Dominican Republic, Puerto Rico has easily outpaced its former colonial cousins economically, thanks to over a century of US aid. As a result, the island has become the most modern in the Caribbean with high-rises, heavy traffic and a high percentage of American tourists.

LIFESTYLE

About 60% of the island still lives in what the US defines as poverty, but the remaining 40% is doing quite well – they are the managers of the ever-present pharmaceutical factories, the beneficiaries of the burgeoning tourism business or bankers or business owners in Hato Rey. San Juan is the only city that has much of a middle class – people who do administrative and clerical work in restaurants, hotels, tourism businesses and so on. Many were born in Puerto Rico and raised in the US then returned to the island after college to find work. This return migration is a boon for the island businesses, which need skilled workers, but has made it harder for Puerto Ricans with high-school diplomas to fill those spots.

Informative website Boricua.com bills itself as the website for Puerto Ricans by Puerto Ricans, but anyone with more than a passing interest in the island and its worldwide diaspora will find plenty of hidden nuggets here.

According to the recent World Values Survey, Puerto Ricans are the happiest people on the planet, with a 'happiness rating' of 4.67 out of five. The United States came 15th with a rating of 3.47.

LIVING WITH UNCLE SAM

Puerto Rico's political status inspires a curious mix of guarded ambivalence and grudging acceptance. For many, the idea of living with Uncle Sam has become more a habit than a passion. Suspended constitutionally between full-blown US state and sovereign independent nation, the island's population remains in a curious state of limbo. It seems as if the people can't decide what they want their country to be. Last put to the vote in 1998, the advocates of statehood were pipped at the post by supporters of the existing status quo, ie a commonwealth or unincorporated dependent territory of the United States. The various independence parties, meanwhile, continue to come in a distant third.

Triggered historically by the Grito de Lares in 1868 and reignited briefly in the 1950s, the independence issue has long been a perennial damp squib. Compromise is invariably touted as a more desirable modern option. Cemented in the 1952 Constitution Act, the current relationship between Puerto Rico and the US was largely the work of iconic national governor Luís Muñoz Marín. A prophetic democrat, Muñoz believed that to push for political independence from the Americans was a folly akin to economic suicide. In order to liberate the masses from the crippling poverty of the inter-war years, the island needed to maintain an arm's-length relationship with the US while at the same time retaining its distinct Latin legacy. Steering a fine line between free-thinking commonwealth and obedient colonial lapdog during the '50s and '60s, Muñoz successfully lifted the island out of its economic coma. He also professed to have safeguarded Puerto Rico's cultural identity and political 'freedom' for future generations.

It's a sentiment with which many would concur. While few Puerto Ricans play the out-and-out nationalist card these days, most continue to uphold an unspoken cultural resistance toward their venerable American neighbors in the north. Ubiquitous shopping malls and Burger Kings aside, the proud *boricuas* have consistently resisted swallowing the American Dream hook, line and sinker. Distinctive cultural manifestations pulsate everywhere. From the Spanish language, to the hip-gyrating music, to the way they over-enthusiastically drive their cars – patriotic islanders have always been Puerto Rican first and American a distant second. It's a cultural paradigm that looks set to continue for some time yet.

With an unemployment rate of 12% and average salaries around $15,000, many Puerto Ricans can't afford to pay the real-estate taxes the government has been levying of late, and consequently are losing their traditional homes – old farms that have been handed down for generations. Those who left Puerto Rico in their youth and return to live off an American pension find that their dollars don't stretch quite as far as they used to.

Still, this is the strongest economy in the Caribbean, and you'll see that almost every household owns at least one car. Puerto Rico hasn't quite got to the point of having 'two countries' living on the island, but the economic disparities are growing more apparent. Tons of fast-food outlets and strip malls cater to the working-class families, while trendy eateries doing fancy *comida criolla* (traditional cooking) pull in not just tourists but also a newly created yuppie class of American-educated 30-somethings enjoying their relative prosperity.

ECONOMY

While the wealth of Puerto Rico may pale in comparison to most US states, it actually boasts one of the most dynamic economies in the Caribbean. If you've just come here from Jamaica or the Dominican Republic the differences will be palpable. Rather than trying to judge the island alongside New York or California, outsiders need to view Puerto Rico in a relative context. With huge historical and political differences still existing between the island and the US, the economic strides achieved in the commonwealth since the dark days of the 1930s and '40s have been truly remarkable.

Dreamt up in the 1950s and '60s, Operation Bootstrap succeeded in converting Puerto Rico from a poor agricultural society into a modern industrial powerhouse. Tax incentives first introduced by prophetic island governor Luis Muñoz Marín have led to long-term US investment on the island and a growth in both the pharmaceutical and tourism industries. That said, Puerto Rico's per capita GDP is still marginally lower than the US's poorest state (Mississippi) while its unemployment rate (12%) is a good 7% above the US average.

POPULATION

Puerto Rico – with nearly four million inhabitants – is one of the most densely populated islands in the world. According to US census figures there are about 1000 people per sq mile, a ratio higher than that of many American states. But the figures are misleading: approximately one-third of the population is concentrated in the San Juan–Carolina–Bayamón metropolitan area. Other large cities, such as Caguas, Hatillo, Arecibo and Adjuntas, are attracting new residents every day, with manufacturing and agro-businesses providing jobs. In comparison, the coastal sections along the west and south coast, and much of the lush interior mountain territory, are practically desolate. You can drive for miles and see absolutely nothing but a few slow-moving iguanas and maybe a wild horse or two. Avoid the *tapones* (traffic jams) that blight the major highways and you'll simply have no idea that you are close to any urban sprawl.

Annually, five million visitors to Puerto Rico supply the economy with approximately $1.8 billion a year. More than one third of these tourists are made up of cruise-ship passengers.

SPORTS

If Puerto Rico has an official sport, *béisbol* is probably it. The Caribbean boasts a Puerto Rican Winter League, Dominican Winter League and Panamanian Winter League, and in the off-season Major Leaguers from the US come down to test their mettle against these up-and-comers. Major League teams also hold spring training camps in Puerto Rico and regularly use the island's league as a farm team. Early-season exhibition games are held every spring, and you can see teams like the Montreal Expos work out the winter kinks at bargain prices.

Peleas de gallos (cockfights) have long been a popular pastime in Puerto Rico and the rest of Latin America. The 'sport' of placing specially bred and trained *gallos de pelea* (fighting cocks) in a pit to battle each other for the delight of humans goes back thousands of years to ancient Persia, Greece and Rome.

Cockfighting was outlawed when the US occupation of the island began in 1898. After almost four decades underground, cockfighting was once again legalized on the island in the 1930s.

During the 20-minute fight the cocks try to peck and slash each other to pieces with sharpened natural spurs, or with steel or plastic spurs taped or tied to their feet, causing feathers to fly and blood to splatter. The fight usually ends with one bird mortally wounded or dead. Then the aficionados collect their winnings or plunk down more money – to get even – on the next fight. Betting usually starts at $100 and goes well into the thousands.

Roberto Clemente is probably the most famous Puerto Rican baseball star of all time, with a career batting average of .317. He was posthumously inducted into the Baseball Hall of Fame in 1973 after his death in a plane crash.

MULTICULTURALISM

Like most Caribbean cultures, Puerto Ricans are an ethnic mix of Native American, European and African genes. About 80% of the island classifies itself as white (meaning of Spanish origin, primarily), 8% as black, 10% as mixed or 'other', and 4% as Taíno Indian. Along the coast of Loíza Aldea, where the African heritage is most prominent, distinct features from the Yoruba people abound, while, in the mountains, a handful of people still claim distant Taíno bloodlines.

SMALL COUNTRY, BIG PUNCH

For a country the size of Connecticut, Puerto Rico has spawned enough fighters to fill its own boxing Hall of Fame, a list that includes the youngest world champion in boxing history (at any weight) and one of the sport's greatest-ever knockout specialists.

The standard was set in the 1930s by wily bantamweight Sixto Escobar, who became the first Puerto Rican to capture a world championship belt when he knocked out Mexican Baby Casanova in Montreal in 1936 for the world bantamweight title. In his homeland, Escobar – who hailed from Barceloneta on the north coast – became an overnight hero and it was 30 years before another Puerto Rican was able to emulate his achievements.

The 1970s brought the two Wilfredos – Benitez and Gómez – to the fore. The former, nicknamed 'The Radar,' was a Puerto Rican childhood boxing sensation, raised in New York City, who became the youngest-ever world champion when he defeated Columbian Antonio Cervantes in a World Junior Welterweight championship bout in San Juan in 1976. The victory shocked the boxing world and the prodigious Benitez, who was only 17 at the time, went on to defend his title three times before losing to Sugar Ray Leonard in 1979. Gómez, known affectionately as Bazooka, was a punching phenomenon from San Juan who still retains one of the highest knockout ratios in professional boxing with 42 KOs in 46 fights. Rated at No 13 in *Ring* magazine's list of all-time best punchers, Gómez was the subject of a 2003 documentary shot in New York City entitled *Bazooka: The Battles of Wilfredo Gómez.*

As much a showman as a fighter, Hector 'Macho' Camacho was Puerto Rico's most flamboyant star. Born in Bayamón near San Juan but raised in New York, Camacho aped the style of Muhammad Ali by leaping into the ring dressed as Captain America before a fight. In a career that spanned two decades he fought everyone from Roberto Duran to Julio César Chávez and tested loyalties in his homeland during an all–Puerto Rican world-title fight against fellow countryman Felix Trinidad.

Trinidad, from Cupey Alto, is another modern boxing legend who won world titles at three different weights, including a 1999 victory over Californian 'Golden Boy,' Oscar de la Hoya, after which he received a hero's welcome at Luís Muñoz Marín international airport. He recently passed his mantle over to current superstar Miguel Cotto, part of a famous boxing family dynasty and a product of the famous Bairoa gym in Caguas. As of early 2008, Cotto remains unbeaten with a record of 31 wins, 25 of them by knockout.

Puerto Ricans will tell you that ethnic discrimination doesn't exist on their island, but politically correct Spanish speakers may be aghast at some of the names Puerto Ricans use to refer to each other – words like *trigueño* (wheat-colored) and *jabao* (not quite white). It may sound derogatory (and sometimes it is), but it can also simply be a less-than-thoughtful way of identifying someone by a visible physical characteristic, a habit found in much of Latin America. You'll also hear terms like *la blanquita,* for a lighter-skinned woman, or *el gordo* to describe a robust man.

Identifying which terms are racial slurs, rather than descriptive facts, will be a hard distinction for non-islanders to make, and it's wisest to steer clear of all such vernacular. Compared with much of the Caribbean, Puerto Rico is remarkably integrated and even-keeled about ethnicity.

The island's most important challenge is to correct the historical fact that the poorest islanders – those descended from the slaves and laborers who were kept from owning land until the early 20th century – have been short-changed when it comes to higher education. As in the United States, the issue of racial and economic inequality in Puerto Rico – while still visible – has improved immeasurably in the last 40 years. While urban deprivation and a lack of provision of housing are ongoing issues, the relative economic conditions in modern Puerto Rico are significantly better than in most other countries in the Caribbean.

Escape to Puerto Rico http://escape.topuertorico.com is a good starting point for up-to-date information on hotel prices, car rental and flights to the island.

WOMEN IN PUERTO RICO

Puerto Rican culture is often stigmatized as a 'macho' world where women bear children, cook meals and care for the home. That is superficially true: women generally do all those things and more. Stereotypes paint men as possessive, jealous and prone to wild acts of desperation when in love, and that's also superficially true. Both sexes seem to enjoy the drama that comes along with these intertwined roles – pay close attention to couples twirling on the dance floor to a salsa song or, better yet, a steamy bolero, and you'll see clearly what game they are both happily playing.

None of that has prevented Puerto Rican women from excelling at business, trade and, most importantly, politics. San Juan elected a female mayor decades before a woman won a comparable office in the US, and, in 2000, a woman called Sila Maria Calderón was elected governor of Puerto Rico. She ran on a campaign that promised to end government corruption, and clean house she did.

Abortion is legal in Puerto Rico (although the rest of the Caribbean, outside of Cuba, is completely antichoice) and politicians remain acutely aware of the effects of a high birthrate on family living and quality of life. The facts of life are taught early in the home, but it's worth noting that high-school-aged Puerto Rican girls wait longer to have sex, are better informed about sex, and use condoms more responsibly when they do have sex than their American counterparts – and that's according to the US government's own figures. Puerto Rican culture still has plenty of macho myths that pose a challenge to full empowerment of women, but no more so than any other Western culture.

> Rita Moreno, who was born in Humacao in 1931, is the first and only Puerto Rican actress to have won an Academy Award, a Grammy, a Tony and an Emmy.

MEDIA

Puerto Rico's largest newspaper in terms of circulation is *El Nuevo Día,* a Spanish language periodical founded in the southern city of Ponce in 1909 that currently shifts in the vicinity of 155,000 copies daily. Its largest competitor is *El Vocero,* a tabloid-style newspaper that focuses less on politics and more on sensationalist news, although its tone has become more serious in recent years. The island's primary English-language newspaper is the *San Juan Star* (now also available in Spanish). Founded in 1959, the *Star* won a Pulitzer Prize for its journalistic writing a year after its inception and was famously fictionalized as the *Daily News* in Hunter S Thompson's seminal Puerto Rican novel *The Rum Diary* (p97). While none of the commonwealth's newspapers can be considered radical in their stance on the status issue, it is the Spanish-speaking media that is generally more attuned to the Puerto Rican viewpoint. The *Star* invariably takes a right-of-center stance and employs many 'gringo' writers.

Although Puerto Rican TV is saturated with US shows and channels, home-grown sitcoms and Spanish-language soap operas and chat shows are also perennially popular.

> *El Boricua* is an online monthly bilingual cultural magazine for Puerto Ricans worldwide. It can be found at www.elboricua.com.

RELIGION

Protestantism and Roman Catholicism are the two most widely (or openly) practiced religions on the island – 40% each – but followers of both have been widely influenced by centuries of indigenous and African folkloric traditions. Slaves brought from West Africa between the 16th and 19th centuries carried with them a system of animistic beliefs that they passed on through generations of their descendants.

You can hear it in the cadences of the African drums in traditional music like *bomba* and, more recently, in salsa. You also hear Africa in dance names like rumba and in variations on 'Changó,' the name of the Yoruba god of fire and war, like *machango, changuero, changuería* and *changuear* (all are island words that relate people, things and behavior to Changó).

The little wooden *santos* figurines that have been staple products of Puerto Rican artists for centuries descend to some degree from Santería beliefs in the powers of the saints (although many Puerto Ricans may not be aware of the sources of this worship). Many Puerto Ricans keep a collection of their favorite *santos* enshrined in a place of honor in their homes, similar to shrines West Africa's Yoruba people keep for their *orishas* (spirits) like Yemanjá, the goddess of the sea.

Belief in the magical properties of small carved gods also recalls the island's early inhabitants, the Taíno, who worshipped little stone *cemíes* (figurines) and believed in *jupías,* spirits of the dead who roam the island at night to cause mischief.

Tens of thousands of islanders consult with *curanderos* (healers) when it comes to problems of love, health, employment, finance and revenge. Islanders also spend significant amounts of money in *botánicas*: shops that sell herbs, plants, charms, holy water and books on performing spirit rituals.

Practice your Spanish by reading *El Nuevo Día,* Puerto Rico's biggest selling daily newspaper online at www.elnuevodia.com.

ARTS

Abundant creative energy hangs in the air all over Puerto Rico (maybe it has something to do with the Bermuda Triangle), and its effects can be seen in the island's tremendous output of artistic achievement. Puerto Rico has produced renowned poets, novelists, playwrights, orators, historians, journalists, painters, composers and sculptors. While it's known for world-class art in many mediums, music and dance are especially synonymous with the island.

Literature

The island began inspiring writers in the earliest years of the Spanish colonial period. In 1535, Spanish friar Gonzalo Fernández de Oviedo wrote the *Historia general y natural de las Indias* (General and Natural History of the Indies), in which he painted a lush portrait of the island Ponce de León and his company found.

About 100 years later, two thorough accounts of colonial life on the island came from the pen of the Bishop of Puerto Rico, Fray Damián López de Haro, and that of Diego Torres Vargas.

Puerto Rico was without a printing press until 1807, and Spain's restrictive administrative practices inhibited education and kept literacy rates extremely low on the island during almost 400 years of colonial rule. But an indigenous literature developed nonetheless, particularly in the realms of poetry (which was memorized and declaimed) and drama. The 19th century saw the rise of a number of important writers in these fields. Considered the father of Puerto Rican literature, Alejandro Tapia y Rivera (1826–82) distinguished himself as the author of poems, short stories, essays, novels and plays. His long, allegorical poem, the *Sataniada,* raised islanders' eyebrows with its subtitle, 'A Grandiose Epic Dedicated to the Prince of Darkness.' Tapia y Rivera's play *La cuarterona* (The Quadroon) depicted the struggles of a biracial woman in San Juan.

In 1849, Manuel Alonso wrote *El Gíbaro,* a classic collection of prose and poetry vignettes that delineate the cockfights, dancing, weddings, politics, race relations and belief in *espiritismo* (spiritualism) that characterize the island *jíbaro* – an archetypal witty peasant who lives in the mountains. When the US claimed the island as a territory in 1898, scores of island writers responded with protest literature. Out of that activity emerged Julia de Burgos (1914–53), one of the island's major female poets. Her work came to embody

Welcome to Puerto Rico http://welcome.topuerto rico.org is a website set up by a Puerto Rican currently based in Georgia, USA. It provides an excellent in-depth look at the island's culture, history, geography and ecology.

two intertwining elements of Boricua national identity – an intense, lyrical connection to nature and an equally passionate commitment to politics.

In the 1930s, Puerto Rico's first important novelist, Dr Enrique Laguerre, published *La llamarada* (Blaze of Fire), which takes place on a sugarcane plantation, where a young intellectual wrestles with the destitution of his island in the wake of US corporate exploitation. During this epoch of intellectual foment, the architect of the modern Puerto Rican Commonwealth, Luis Muñoz Marín, was composing poetry and sowing the seeds of his Partido Popular Democrático.

As more islanders migrated to the US in the 1950s, the Puerto Rican 'exiles,' known as Nuyoricans, became grist for fiction writers. One of the most successful authors to take on this subject is Pedro Juan Soto, whose 1956 short-story collection *Spiks* (a racial slur aimed at Nuyoricans) depicts life in the New York barrios with the biting realism that the musical *West Side Story* could only hint at. Luis Piñero, Miguel Algarin and Pedro Pietri started a Latino beatnik movement on Manhattan's Lower East Side, creating the first Nuyorican Café and holding poetry slams long before such things were considered cool. All three became major poets – honored by both English and Spanish readers – although only Algarin is still living today.

More recently, Esmeralda Santiago's 1986 memoir, *Cuando era puertorriqueña* (When I Was Puerto Rican), has become a standard text in many US schools.

Better known by the nickname Diplo, Ramón Rivero was the king of Puerto Rican comedy who kept islanders laughing through times of intense economic hardship in the 1940s and '50s. He also starred in one of Puerto Rico's finest films, *Los peloteros* (The Baseball Players).

Cinema & TV

Movie and TV producers have always known that Puerto Rico's weather, geography, historic architecture and modern infrastructure make it a great place to shoot background scenes. But a homegrown movie industry only started to flourish in the late 1980s, thanks largely to one director: Jacobo Morales. He wrote, directed and starred in *Dios la cría* (God Created Them). He was no stranger to the big screen at that point, having appeared in Woody Allen films in 1971 and 1972, but *Dios la cría* was his first turn behind the camera, shooting in his native land. The movie, which offers a critical look at Puerto Rican society, was lauded by both critics and fans. His next movie, *Lo que le pasó a Santiago* (What Happened to Santiago?) won him an Academy Award nomination in 1990 for best foreign film. *Linda Sara* (Pretty Sara), his follow-up film in 1994, earned him a second Oscar nomination for best foreign film.

Famous Hollywood movies filmed in Puerto Rico include Woody Allen's *Bananas*, Steven Spielberg's *Amistad* and the James Bond movie *Goldeneye*.

Marcos Zurinaga also made a name for himself in the 1980s, first with *La gran fiesta* (The Big Party) in 1986, which focuses on the last days of San Juan's biggest casino, where all the hotshots met, and then *Tango Bar* (1988) and the acclaimed *Disappearance of Garcia Lorca* (1997). The most widely distributed and financially successful Puerto Rican film is probably Luis Molina's 1993 tragic comedy, *La guagua aérea* (The Arial Bus), which explores the reasons behind Puerto Ricans' push to emigrate in the 1960s.

Nowadays, Puerto Ricans are making splashes on the big and small screens – Rita Moreno, one of the first Puerto Rican actresses to star on Broadway and in a major American film, is considered a cultural icon, and Jimmy Smits, a popular TV actor, is also a proud Boricua.

Of course, for sheer glitz and glamour, nobody can compete with power couple Jennifer Lopez and Marc Anthony, both Nuyoricans with close island ties. Oscar winners Raul Julia – who died in 1994 – and smoldering Benicio del Toro are considered two of the best actors to come out of Puerto Rico.

Folk Art

Four forms of folk art have held a prominent place in the island's artistic tradition since the early days of the colony. Some of the island's folk art draws upon the artistic traditions of the Taíno, like their 1ft- to 2ft-high statues of minor gods, called *cemíes*. Crafted from stone, wood or even gold, the idols were prized for the power they were believed to bestow on their owners. Visitors can see collections of the simple, primitive-looking *cemíes* at a number of museums on the island.

Shortly after the arrival of the Spaniards in 1508, the Taíno and their civilization were assimilated. But the islanders' affection for magical statuary did not vanish. Instead, the Taíno and their immediate descendants – who were quickly converted to Christianity – found a new outlet for their plastic arts in the colonial Spaniards' attachment to small religious statues called *santos* (saints). Like the *cemíes, santos* represent religious figures and are enshrined in homes to bring spiritual blessings to their keepers. Importing the *santos* from Spain was both difficult and expensive, so islanders quickly began making their own.

Puerto Rico is also famous for its *mundillo,* a type of lace made only in Spain and on the island. The tradition came to the island with the early nuns, who practiced the art in order to finance schools and orphanages. Over the 17th, 18th and 19th centuries, the nuns perfected the art in their schools and convents, but the intricate process was almost lost in the face of mass-produced textiles during the 20th century. Renewed interest in island folk arts, generated by the Instituto de Cultura Puertorriqueña, has revived the process.

Máscaras (masks), the frightening and beautiful headpieces traditionally worn at island fiestas, have become popular pieces of decorative folk art in recent years. The tradition of masked processions goes back to the days of the Spanish Inquisition and perhaps earlier, when masqueraders known as *vejigantes* brandished balloonlike objects (called *vejigas*) made of dried, inflated cow bladder, and roamed the streets of Spanish towns as 'devils' bent on terrifying sinners into returning to the fold of the church.

Spaniards brought their tradition to Puerto Rico, where it merged with masking traditions of the African slaves. Red-and-yellow papier-mâché masks with a multitude of long horns, bulging eyes and menacing teeth are typical of the headpieces created for festivals in Ponce, Loíza and Hatillo.

The first nondocumentary film shot in Puerto Rico was *Un drama en Puerto Rico* by Rafael Colorado D'Assoy, made in 1912. D'Assoy went on to form the Film Industrial Society of Puerto Rico but his groundbreaking first movie has since been lost.

Architecture

The most dramatic architectural achievements of Old San Juan are the fortresses of El Morro (p88) and San Cristóbal (p89), the stone ramparts surrounding the city and the mammoth seaside entry gate – all built from sandstone gathered from the shore and built in the 16th century. But visitors shouldn't underestimate the rest of the Old City, which exhibits a veritable treasure trove of eclectic architecture from decorative baroque to streamlined art deco.

A visit to Puerto Rico's important southern city of Ponce brings visitors to an equally large cache of historical architecture, particularly Plaza Las Delicias (p187), which holds a 16th-century church and several colonial houses from the 18th century.

Visual Arts

San Juan's Museo de San Juan (p93) is a perfect symbol of Puerto Rico's dedication to the visual arts, which can be traced back to the very early days of Spanish colonization. The first great local artist to emerge was self-taught painter José Campeche (1752–1809), who burst onto the scene. Masterpieces such as *Lady on Horseback* and *Governor Ustauriz* demonstrate Campeche's mastery of the genres of landscape and portraiture, as well as his most frequent subject – the story of Jesus.

Francisco Oller (1833–1917), the next big thing to come out of Puerto Rico, did not gain recognition until the second half of the 19th century. Oller was a very different artist from Campeche; he studied in France under Gustave Courbet and felt the influence of acquaintances such as Paul Cézanne. Like his mentor Courbet, Oller dedicated a large body of his work to the portrayal of scenes from humble, everyday island life. Bayamón, Oller's birthplace, maintains a museum (p129) dedicated to its native son, and many of his works are in San Juan's Museo de Arte (p100). Both Oller and Campeche are honored for starting an art movement that drew inspiration from Puerto Rican nature and life, and helped formulate the idea of a distinct cultural and artistic identity for the island.

When the US gained control of the island, Puerto Rico's artists began to obsess over political declarations of national identity. During this period, the island government funded extensive printmaking, commissioning artists to illustrate pre-existing literary texts. Poems, lines of prose, memorable quotations and political declarations all inspired poster art. Among the best of these practitioners have been Mari Carmen Ramírez and Lorenzo Homar. In Homar's masterworks, such as *Unicornio en la isla* (Unicorn on the Island), a poster becomes a work of art, as it has in the hands of some of his students, including Antonio Martorell and José Rosas.

In the midst of the storm of poster art that covered the island in visual and verbal images during the 1950s and '60s, serious painters such as Julio Rosado de Valle, Francisco Rodón and Myrna Báez – as well as Homar himself – evolved a new aesthetic in Puerto Rican art, one in which the image rebels against the tyranny of political and jingoistic slogans and reigns by itself. Myrna Báez is one of a new generation of female artists, building on Puerto Rico's strong visual traditions to create new and exciting installation art. Her work is exhibited in many San Juan galleries.

Today, one of the island's most famous artists is actually a Nuyorican – Rafael Tufiño, who was born in Brooklyn to Puerto Rican parents. Using vivid colors and big canvases, Turfiño paints scenes of poverty: one of his most well-known works is *La Perla,* named after the picturesque slum that sits right under the nose of El Morro in San Juan. Another celebrated living artist is Tómas Batista, who does 3-D art made from wood. Trained in New York and Spain, Batista settled in Luquillo some years ago and has made numerous pieces of public art for the island. Look for Batista statues in plazas in Río Piedras, Luquillo and Ponce.

The film *Angel,* written and directed by Jacobo Morales, follows the story of a corrupt police captain and the man he wrongly imprisoned. It narrowly missed out on a 2008 Academy Award nomination.

Theater & Dance

Theater is considerably popular in Puerto Rico, particularly in San Juan. The Santurce-based Luis A Ferré Center for the Performing Arts (p121) and the wonderfully gilded Teatro Tapia (p121) act as the main nexus points, staging regular performances from touring companies. Shows include top class ballet, plays, opera and comedy.

You don't have to be in Puerto Rico long to realize that the locals love to dance – and, with their natural rhythm and refreshing lack of North American 'reserve,' they're extremely good at it.

Stylistically speaking, Puerto Rican dance is closely intertwined with the island's distinctive music. Over time, many classifiable musical forms – such as *bomba*, salsa, *plena* and *danza* – have evolved complimentary dances that work off their syncopated rhythms and melodies. Early examples can be seen in formal styles such as *danza*, an elegant ballroom dance that was imported from Cuba in the 1840s and later largely redefined by Puerto Rican composers such as Manuel Tavarez.

Bomba is another colorful import, with influences brought via slaves from Africa. Non-contact but boisterously energetic, *bomba* has spawned a plethora of subgenres such as *sica, yuba* and *holandes,* and is both spontaneous and exciting to watch.

More recognizable to modern dancers is salsa, Puerto Rico's signature dance that has spawned imitators worldwide and can be learnt and enjoyed everywhere from Barcelona to Vancouver. Salsa is a libidinous and red-blooded dance that is relatively easy to learn, although, with its sensuous moves and strong African beat, it was seemingly invented with Puerto Rican bodies in mind. Dancing as close-knit couples and making light work of the four beat quick-quick-slow steps, the loose-limbed locals make it look as simple as walking.

To become involved in Puerto Rican dance head to one of San Juan's numerous bars or nightclubs, where shaking a leg on a Friday night is as common as ordering a mojito. La Rumba (p120) and Nuyorican Café (p119) in Old San Juan are two notable highlights.

The **Le Lo Lai Festival** (☎ 787-721-2400 ext 3901) is an ongoing cultural and entertainment program run by the Puerto Rican Tourist Company. It puts on a traditional music and dance show at a series of revolving venues (often hotels) around the island. You can get more information on when and where they'll be performing by calling the number listed above.

The 1993 movie *Carlito's Way,* starring Al Pacino and Sean Penn, follows the exploits of Carlito Brigante, a Puerto Rican drug dealer in New York who struggles to go straight after his release from prison.

Music

The music of Puerto Rico is a sonic reflection of the destination itself, a sound shaped by a proud and dynamic history of revolution, colonialism, and the cultural cross-currents that waft between the island, New York City, Spain and Africa. Even compared with other destinations in the Caribbean, Puerto Rico is something of an island unto its own.

The sound synonymous with Puerto Rico is certainly salsa, but that which pounds from the open doorways of most of the island's nightspots these days is just as often reggaeton, a blazing blend of hip-hop, Caribbean syncopations and molar-rattling thud of dancehall.

The dominance of reggaeton has almost run the hallmark genre of salsa out of island nightclubs entirely, and travelers to the island who imagine themselves sashaying to the gate of a brassy salsa combo every night should be advised: it probably ain't happenin'. Aside from some packed spots in San Juan, scattered destinations around the island and weekly residences at upscale resorts (which don't exactly ooze authenticity), catching traditional music in Puerto Rico is a surprisingly difficult task, especially considering its role in the birth of the art form. The island's sonic movements beyond salsa – heavily rhythmic styles like *bomba y plena, danza,* merengue and cha-cha-cha – are even more obscure, with performances mostly relegated to museum demonstrations and holiday festivals.

POPULAR MUSIC

For a history lesson on Puerto Rican music in under four minutes, cue up 'Tradicional A Lo Bravo,' a hugely popular single from current Puerto Rican reggaeton hitmaker Tego Calderon. Calderon's rapid-fire lyrical delivery and the pounding syncopated bass line is emblematic of the reggaeton movement, but the song also borrows a little something from the important musical traditions of the island. The brassy horns pay homage to salsa bands from the 1960s. The nylon string guitar nods to the colonial traditions and rural *jíbaro* music. The loping syncopation of the hand drums reference African-rooted Puerto Rican *bomba.* Somewhere, hidden amongst Calderon's macho swagger, you'll even hear the grinding scrape of a *güiro,* a percussion instrument made from a notched, hollowed gourd which was a part of the musical battery of indigenous Taíno tribes.

From the precolonial folk music to the macho rapid-fire of reggaeton, Puerto Rican music has always been an evolving part of, not a departure from, past traditions. Then and now, these traditions often place as much importance on dance-floor expressions as the sound itself.

Bomba y Plena

The bewildering conflux of traditions that collide in Puerto Rican music can be seen in the earliest popular music on the island, *bomba y plena,* two distinct yet often associated types of folk music. With origins in European, African and native Caribbean cultures, this is the basis for many of the sounds still associated with Puerto Rico and, like salsa, a musical form inexorably tied with dance.

The most directly African in origin is the *bomba,* a music developed by West and Central African slaves who worked on sugar plantations. A typical *bomba* ensemble included drums made from rum barrels and goat skin, *palitos* or *cuás* (wooden sticks that are hit together or on other wooden surfaces), maracas and sometimes a *güiro.* In the oldest forms (documented as early as the 1680s), dancers led the band, furiously competing with each other and

José Feliciano, a six-time Grammy award winner, taught himself to play guitar despite being born blind.

Menudo was one of the original boy bands conceived by producer Edgardo Diaz in 1977. It went on to record phenomenal worldwide success with a light brand of teen pop music and celebrated former members such as Ricky Martin.

The Puerto Rican Cuatro Project (www.cuatro-pr .org) is a nonprofit organization that has adopted the island's national instrument as a means of keeping its cultural memories alive. Its website has priceless information on the island's traditional instruments and music.

the percussionists in an increasingly frenzied physical and rhythmic display. The tunes ended when either dancer or drummer became too exhausted to continue. Loíza Aldea, on the northeast coast, claims *bomba* as its invention, and the streets rumble with it throughout the summer, particularly during the festival for St James the Moor Slayer, which begins during the last week of July and lasts for nine days. Partiers don bright *vejigante* masks and take to the streets, celebrating all night.

Plena, which originated in Ponce, is also drum-based but with lighter textures. Introduced by *cocolocos,* slaves who migrated north from islands south of Puerto Rico, *plena* uses an assortment of hand-held percussion instruments. Locals once referred to the form as *el periodico cantado* (the sung newspaper), because the songs typically recounted, and often satirized, current events. *Plena* often uses *panderos,* which resemble Irish and Brazilian frame drums, but according to musicologists, *panderos* were introduced to the island by Spaniards, who had lifted them from their Moorish neighbors. The *plena* beat has strong African roots and is a close cousin to calypso, *soca* and dancehall music from Trinidad and Jamaica.

One of the definitive articles on the origin of the name 'salsa' can be found on www.salsaroots.com.

Bomba y plena developed side-by-side on the coastal lowlands, and inventive musicians eventually realized the call-and-response of *bomba* would work well with *plena*'s satirical lyrical nature, which is why the forms are often played back-to-back by bands. If you catch *bomba y plena* today, a historical performance will be rare; in the 1950s a modernization of the sound paved the way for salsa by adding horns, pan-Caribbean rhythmic elements and the clatter of Cuban percussion.

Salsa

For most gringos, salsa's definition as a catch-all term for the interconnected jumble of Latin and Afro-Caribbean dances and sounds isn't easy to get a handle on, but for those who live in its areas of origin – Puerto Rico, Cuba and New York City – it's as much a lifestyle as a genre, with cultural complexities that go well beyond the 'spicy' jargon that's often bandied about. For the essence of salsa, read between the lines of Yuri Buenaventura's neotraditional anthem, 'Salsa,' where it's called 'the rhythm that gives life.' Better yet, don't read anything – just get out there and dance.

Pondering salsa's definition will quickly lead you to the question of where it comes from, and the debate about its Cuban or Puerto Rican origins is as unanswerable as the chicken and the egg. Debating this topic is likely to raise the blood pressure of any proud *puertorriqueño*, but most will agree that salsa was born in the nightclubs of New York City in the 1960s and has deep roots in both Puerto Rico and Cuba.

Music & Dance in Puerto Rico from the Age of Columbus to Modern Times by Donald and Annie Thompson is a simple timeline of music and dance in Puerto Rico that has great information on the origins of mambo, son, salsa and more.

ORIGINS & VARIATIONS OF SALSA

In addition to the mishmash of African traditions that spread through the islands via the slave trade, Cuba's *son* – a traditional style that was widely reintroduced to global audiences in the '90s though *Buena Vista Social Club* – is a crucial ingredient in salsa. Originating in eastern Cuba, *son* first became popular in the 1850s, mixing guitar-based Spanish *canción*s and Afro-Cuban percussion, a basic formula that still makes the foundation of many salsa songs. Variations of *son* spread through the islands and became internationally popular throughout the early 20th century, with variations including the rumba, mambo and cha-cha-cha.

Another element of salsa is meringue, which takes root in Puerto Rico's neighboring island, the Dominican Republic, where it is the national dance. With its even-paced steps and a signature roll of the hips, it's probably the easiest Latin dance for beginners.

Of all the variations that helped bring salsa into being, none is more important than the mambo – a flamboyant style of music and dance that marries elements of swinging American jazz with *son*. Again, the musical dialogue of the Caribbean islands is evident right down to the style's name; mambo is a Haitian word for a voodoo priestess.

Unlike the blurry origins of other traditions, historians credit its creation to brothers Cachao and Orestes López, who wrote a tune called 'Mambo' in 1938, and Cuban bandleader Pérez Prado, who introduced the complicated dance steps to Havana's La Tropicana nightclub in 1943. What they started in Cuba, Tito Puente (below), Tito Rodríguez, Machito and Xavier Cugat carried to the US, where it was eagerly embraced by Latino and North American audiences.

Music of Puerto Rico (www.musicofpuerto rico.com) gives an excellent rundown on the complex musical genres of the island including audio clips and printed song lyrics.

THE BIRTH & NEAR-DEATH OF SALSA

So, even if we know that most elements of salsa – which literally translates to 'sauce' – were imported to Puerto Rico, how can it remain as one of the country's most prideful exports? Much of that has to do with two artists in New York: Puerto Rican percussionist Tito Puente and Cuban vocalist Celia Cruz. By the time these two became household names in the 1960s, the Latin/Caribbean-influenced style of big band music, which used congas, bass, cowbells (a Puerto Rican addition), bongos, maracas, a horn section, bass and multiple singers, had come to dominate American social dancing.

In 1963, Johnny Pacheco, a visionary producer, created Fania Records, a record label that began to snap up talented Nuyorican musicians like Willie Colón, whose hip-popping music drew rave reviews from critics and brought crowds to the clubs. The only thing the craze lacked was a name. As the story goes, a 1962 record by Joe Cuba made the first mention of 'salsa' music, and the rest was magic. It wasn't long before Charlie Palmieri, another Nuyorican, released 'Salsa Na' Mas.' Scores of Puerto Rican, Cuban and Nuyorican singers became household names in the '60s, and when Carlos Santana's now-ubiquitous rock song 'Oye Como Va' hit the music stores in 1969, it may have marked the crest of the Latin wave.

THE 'BRIDGE' OF TITO PUENTE

Puerto Ricans and Cubans jovially argue over who invented salsa, but the truth is neither island can claim to be the commercial center of salsa success. That honor belongs to the offshore colony known as El Barrio: the Latin Quarter, Spanish Harlem, New York City. In the euphoria following the end of WWII, New York's nightclub scene bloomed as dancers came in droves to the Palladium on 52nd St to bump and grind to the sound of the mambo bands they heard, or dreamed of hearing, in the casinos of Havana, Cuba. At the time, the music carried a basic Latin syncopated beat, punctuated by horn sections that were typical of the great swing bands of Stan Kenton and Count Basie.

Then young Puerto Rican drummer Tito Puente came into the picture. After serving three years in the US Navy and attending New York's Juilliard School of Music, Puente began playing and composing for Cuban bands in New York City. He gained notoriety for spicing up the music with a host of rhythms with roots in Puerto Rican *bomba*. Soon Puente had formed his own band, the Latin Jazz Ensemble, which was playing way beyond the old Cuban templates.

When Fania Records came around, Puente was already a star. Celia Cruz, the late Héctor Lavoe, Eddy Palmieri, Gilberto Santa Rosa, El Gran Combo de Puerto Rico and plenty of other *salseros* have made their mark on the world, but none can claim quite the same place as Tito Puente, who became the face of the salsa boom and bridged cultural divides with his music decades before multiculturalism was even considered a real word. Shortly after the legendary *salsero's* death in 2000, at the age of 77, a stretch of road in Harlem – East 112th Street at Lexington Ave – was renamed Tito Puente Way.

PUERTO RICO PLAYLIST

It's nearly a crime to distil three generations of Puerto Rico's vibrant club music into an iPod playlist, but the following romp includes singles spanning half a century, from classic salsa to contemporary reggaeton.

- Tito Puente: 'Ran Kan Kan,' from 1951's *Babarabatiri*
- Cortijo Y Su Combo: 'El Bombon De Elena,' from 1957's ...*Invites You To Dance*
- Celia Cruz: 'Chango Ta Vani,' from 1958's *La Incomparable*
- Willie Colón: 'Te Conozco,' from 1969's *Cosa Nuestra*
- El Gran Combo De Puerto Rico: 'No Hay Cama Pa' Tanta Gente,' from 1971's *Nuestra Musica*
- Ismael Marinda: 'Se Casa La Rumba,' from 1972's *Abran Paso!*
- Eddie Palmieri: 'Nunca Contigo,' from 1973's *The Sun Of Latin Music*
- Fania All-Stars: 'Ella Fue (She Was The One),' from 1977's *Rhythm Machine*
- Frankie Ruiz: 'Me Dejo,' from 1989's *Mas Grande Que Nunca*
- Marvin Santiago: 'Fuego A La Jicotea,' from 1991's *Fuego A La Jicotea*
- Vico C: 'Calla,' from 1998's *Aquel Que Había Muetro*
- Yuri Buenaventura: 'Salsa,' from 2000's *Yo Soy*
- Tego Calderon: 'Guasa, Guasa,' from 2003's *Abayarde*
- Daddy Yankee: 'Gasolina,' from 2004's *Barrio Fino*
- Ivy Queen: 'Quiero Bailar,' from 2004's *Diva*
- N.O.R.E.: 'Oye Mi Canto,' from 2006's *N.O.R.E. y la Familia...Ya Tú Sabe*
- Tito el ambino: 'El Tra,' from 2007's *It's My Time*
- Don Chezina: 'Songorocosongo,' from 2008's *Tributo Urbano A Hector Lavoe*

Though the craze left a mark on American pop and jazz traditions, the crowds dwindled in subsequent decades as musical tastes shifted radically in the 1970s. While Puerto Rican youth turned to rock-and-roll imports from the US through the '80s, traditionalists celebrated the sappy *salsa romantica* typified by crooners like José Alberto.

SALSA TODAY

It wasn't until the 1990s that a modern Nuyorican – salsa crooner Marc Anthony, aka Mr JLo – brought salsa back from the brink of obscurity, braiding its traditional elements with those of sleek modern pop. Long before his wife even conceived of her breakout Latina-influenced 1999 pop album *On the 6*, Marc's music packed New York's Madison Square Garden several times over with delirious crowds (the DVD of these performances are required viewing in many a Puerto Rican watering hole to this day). Although Lopez and Anthony remain salsa's premiere couple, American audiences have also had fleeting infatuations with Ricky Martin (Mr La Vida Loca) and hunky Spaniard Enrique Iglesias.

Among Tito Puente's many honors are five Grammys, a Presidential Commendation medal (for service in WWII) and having a special session of the Puerto Rican Senate dedicated to him.

Reggaeton

The raucous bastard-child of reggae, salsa and hip-hop is reggaeton, a rough-and-tumble urban sound that took over the unpaved streets of Loíza Aldea, proudly popping its blue collar as the Caribbean's answer to the ethos of American thug life. Recently it's made a wholesale takeover of most dance clubs in the Caribbean and rattles roofs in New York, Chicago and Los Angeles.

PUERTO RICAN MUSIC: ALIVE AND KICKING

Through slush and snow, you've been daydreaming all winter about that idyllic Puerto Rican night on the town, when rum flows like water, the band is hot as a tin roof and the likelihood of dislocating something on the dance floor is high. Catching live traditional music isn't as easy as you might hope, but the following nightspots are the cream of the crop.

- Nuyorican Café (p119) – San Juan's coziest dance floor host live combos playing traditional favorites

- La Rumba (p120) – tight bands and hip patrons groove long into the morning

- Café Hijos de Borinquen (p120) – throaty folk ballads and pounding DJ sets make the soundtrack to this quaint boho dive

- Museo de la Música Puertorriqueña (p188) – Ponce's home of traditional music performances, in a museum setting

- Ponce Hilton (p191) – touristy and a bit tacky, but also the most reliable place for traditional music in the south

---

As the name suggests, it draws heavily on reggae, though the simplest reduction of its sound is a Spanish-language hip-hop driven by the crushing bass of Jamaican raga, a bossy, electro-infused spin on reggae. The earliest forms are traced to Panama, thanks to Jamaican laborers who helped build the Panama Canal, but a more aggressive strain of reggaeton developed in urban areas of Puerto Rico in the 1980s, circulated underground on self-released mix tapes. In the 1990s it incorporated thunderous elements of Jamaican raga and came unto its own. Toss in the thud of a drum-machine and some X-rated lyrics and you have yourself a bona fide musical revolution.

Unlike most traditionally postured Puerto Rican music/dance combos, reggaeton dance floors feature a deliriously oversexed free-for-all, with its most popular move known as *perreo*, or dog dance – which leaves little to the imagination. Reggaeton stars like Tego Calderon, Daddy Yankee, Don Omar and Ivy Queen have played to crowds of thousands in the US and are gradually sneaking on to mainstream urban radio.

Ricky Martin released *Life*, his first English-language album in five years, in 2005. It debuted at number six on the Billboard Top 200 Albums Chart.

FOLK

The earliest folk music on the island started with the percussion and wind instruments of the Taíno, and grew to incorporate elements as disparate as the island's ethnic composition: Spanish guitars, European parlor music and drums and rhythms from West Africa. All are in the DNA of the island's contemporary music, but the long, varied identity of Puerto Rican music incorporates a number of curious indigenous styles and instruments, notably including at least half a dozen guitar-like string instruments that are native to the island, such as the aptly named four-string guitar-like *cuatro*.

Perhaps the most structurally complex of the island's folk music, *danza* is considered Puerto Rico's classical music. *Danza's* exact lineage is unknown, but it's generally considered to be modeled after *contradanza*, a social music and dance from Europe. *Danza* popularity blossomed in 1840 when it incorporated new music and dance steps called *habaneras* (another export of Cuba), which freed the style of movements. Its expressive nature was wildly popular with youth but quite taboo with parents, and so it was banned for a period. Composer Juan Morel Campos is the national hero of the form; he wrote more than 300 expressive *danzas* before he died at 38. The Puerto Rico national anthem, 'La Borinqueña,' is based on a *danza*.

Probably the most appealing colonial-era music found on the island is the *décima* – the vehicle through which the *jíbaros* (rural mountain residents) express joy and sorrow.

A *décima* is based on a 10-line poem and requires multiple instruments – the three-, four- and six-stringed guitars known appropriately enough as the *tres, cuatro* and *seis* and a rhythm section usually comprised of *güiro* and drums. Like other music of the island, a degree of wit and improvisation is expected of the singers. Often a band will have two lead singers who alternate stanzas and try to outdo each other with sizzling rhymes and acrid political statements.

Today, many Puerto Ricans associate *jíbaro* music with Christmas because of *parrandas,* a tradition in which groups of friends stroll from house to house singing joyful *aguinaldos* (Christmas songs set to mountain music) and begging for treats.

CLASSICAL

Puerto Rico's offerings for typical classical fare are limited mostly to the San Juan area, where the Orquesta Sinfónica de Puerto Rico presents standard orchestral rep and hosts visiting luminaries. The symphony shares a space with a distinguished national opera company at Centro de Bellas Artes (p121) whose guests have included renowned Puerto Rican bassist Justino Diaz.

To see the best classical music the island has to offer you can do no better than visit during the Festival Casals (p108), held for two weeks every year.

The festival is named for cellist Pablo Casals, who despite being born in Barcelona, is considered Puerto Rico's most distinguished son (his mother was from Mayagüez). In the years before WWI, he earned a reputation as the pre-eminent cellist of his era. Avidly political, he left Spain in 1936 to protest the Franco regime and eventually settled in Puerto Rico, where he lived out the rest of his days. In 1957 he founded the Festival Casals, which is attended by music fans from around the world, and went on to form the Puerto Rico Symphony Orchestra and the Puerto Rico Conservatory of Music.

By the time he died in 1973 at the age of 97, he considered himself – and was considered by his compatriots – to be Puerto Rico's greatest champion of classical music.

Puerto Rico's national anthem *La Borinqueña* is actually a *danza* that was later subtly altered in order to make it sound more grandiose and anthem-like.

Food & Drink

Thanks to a full-on culinary revolution, Puerto Rico now offers the best selection of food choices in the Caribbean, and restaurants in cities such as San Juan could confidently compete with their stateside counterparts in New York or San Francisco. However, though many of the island's menus popularly describe their food as 'fusion' or 'eclectic,' most owe more than a passing nod to Puerto Rico's real deal – *comida criolla* or *cocina criolla*. The irony, for food lovers, is that *comida criolla* is itself a fusion of numerous international influences, from the indigenous natives to the colonizing Spanish. The mélange can be traced back to the pre-Columbian Taíno who survived on a diet of root vegetables, fish and tropical fruits. With the arrival of the Spanish came an infusion of more European flavors such as olive oil, rice, peppers, beef, pork, and spices like cilantro and cumin. Slavery brought African influences to Puerto Rico including yams, plantains and coffee, and a style of cooking that favored deep-fried food and stews. The US influence in Puerto Rican food is reflected more in the fast food boom than in *comida criolla* per se, though the Americans did introduce corn oil (for cooking), sausages, and various fruits such as papaya, tomatoes and avocados.

Learn about Puerto Rican food, ingredients, recipes and cooking methods on Caribbean Choice (www.caribbeanchoice.com).

A typical *comida criolla* dish today can consist of many different ingredients, though roast pork, rice, beans, deep fried plantains and yucca are all popular staples.

STAPLES & SPECIALTIES
Soups & Stews

Soups and stews are staples in *comida criolla,* and in these brews you can taste a fusion of Taíno, European and African recipes and ingredients. Many soups use unique island vegetables to add texture, taste and vitamins. Some of these vegetables, such as yautia (tanier), *batata* (sweet potato), yucca, chayote (squash), *berzas* (collard greens) and *grelos* (turnip greens) might seem odd to North Americans and Europeans. But you'll learn to love these sprouts and tubers when the greens are simmering in a *caldero* (iron/aluminum kettle) with a peculiar mix of *criollo* spices. *Sancocho* (Caribbean soup) is a blend of many of the vegetables mentioned earlier, along with plantains – peeled and diced – and coarsely chopped tomatoes, green pepper, chili pepper, cilantro leaves, onion and corn kernels. To this mix, the cook adds water, tomato sauce, chopped beef and a few pork ribs for flavoring before cooking it over low heat.

Plantains are in such demand on the island they must be imported from the Dominican Republic.

Perhaps the best-known island concoction to come from a simmering *caldero* is *asopao de pollo.* This is a rich and spicy chicken stew that is fragrant with the ever-present and distinctive seasoning called adobo (garlic, oregano, paprika, peppercorns, salt, olive, lime juice and vinegar crushed into a paste for seasoning meat). Adobo comes from Spain and exists in many Spanish-inspired cuisines, including Filipino, with which it's most often associated.

In addition to adobo, another seasoning that infuses the taste of many criollo dishes is *sofrito.* You can now buy this seasoning on the spice shelves of pueblo supermarkets, but discerning diners say there is nothing like the taste of *sofrito* made from scratch. Certainly the smells that waft from the mix of garlic, onion and pepper browned in olive oil and capped with *achiote* (annato seeds) are enough to make the effort worth it to many cooks.

Meat

Puerto Ricans claim that the modern barbecue descends from the pork roast that the Taíno called *barbicoa*. In this vein, *lechón asado* (roast suckling pig), cooked on a spit over a charcoal fire, is the centerpiece of fiestas and family banquets, particularly at holiday gatherings. Of course, this barbecued pig has been liberally seasoned with adobo, and cooks baste it with *achiote* and the juice from *naranjas* (the island's sour oranges). When cooked to crispness, the meat is served with *ajili-mójili* (a tangy garlic sauce).

For less festive occasions, Puerto Rican dinners will almost always include the staples of *arroz con habichuelas* (rice and beans) and *tostones,* which are fried green plantains, or *panapen* (breadfruit). To these staples, the cook almost always adds a meat dish such as roasted *cabro* (kid goat), *ternera* (veal), *pollo* (chicken) or *carne mechada* (roast beef) – all seasoned with adobo.

The website www.rican recipes.com specializes in recipes from the Enchanted Island, with a comprehensive list that includes everything from brazo gitano to pollo en fricasé.

Seafood

Surprisingly, Puerto Ricans do not eat a lot of fish, but one of the most popular ways to prepare a variety of fish – from *pulpo* (octopus) to *mero* (sea bass) – is *en escabeche*. This technique yields a fried then chilled seafood pickled in vinegar, oil, peppercorns, salt, onions, bay leaves and lime juice. Fried fish generally comes with a topping of *mojo isleño* (a piquant sauce of vinegar, tomato sauce, olive oil, onions, capers, pimentos, olives, bay leaves and garlic). Land crabs – *jueyes* – have long been a staple of islanders who can simply gather the critters off the beaches. An easy way to enjoy the taste is to eat *empanadillas de jueyes,* in which the succulent crab meat has been picked from the shells, highly seasoned and baked into a wrap made of *casabe* paste, a flour made from yucca. Of course, grilled or boiled *langosta* (local tropical lobsters without claws) is a pricey delicacy for both islanders and travelers alike. If you like shellfish, try the *ostiones* (miniature oysters). Fish lovers should also try a bowl of *sopón de pescado* (fish soup), with its scent of onions and garlic and subtle taste of sherry.

Fruits

Puerto Rico grows and exports bananas, papayas, fresh and processed pineapples, as well as a bewildering variety of exotic tropical fruits such as guavas, *tamarindos* (tamarinds), *parchas* (passion fruit) and *guanábanas* (soursops). It's also the third-largest producer of citron – behind Italy and Greece – and you'll see a long swath of fields around Adjuntas dedicated to this fruit.

DRINKS
Nonalcoholic Drinks

Fruit juices, like *guanábana* juice, are locally made and popular with Puerto Ricans (there are carbonated and noncarbonated versions). Other local favorites are carbonated and noncarbonated cans of piña colada (the creamy mix of pineapple juice and coconut cream that can form the basis for a rum drink). *Mavi* is something like root beer, made from the bark of the ironwood tree. As in much of the tropics, beach and street vendors sell chilled green coconuts – *cocos fríos* – to the thirsty.

Featuring renowned island chefs, Puerto Rico: Grand Cuisine of the Caribbean by José Luis Diaz de Villegas is an excellent exploration of the ways in which comida criolla is infusing and being infused with other culinary cultures.

Coffee, grown in Adjuntas and many of the mountain regions, is a staple at all hours and hardly a meal ends without a cup of steaming java.

Alcoholic Drinks

Because Puerto Rico is a major producer of alcoholic beverages – and since the government has not levied outlandish taxes on alcohol – Puerto Rico is clearly one of the cheapest places to drink in the Caribbean, and perhaps the world. The importance of rum to Puerto Rico can hardly be exaggerated.

PUERTO RICO'S TOP CHOICES

- Mamacitas (p164) – the culinary capital of Culebra
- Smilin' Joe's (p233) – surf talk over scrumptious suppers
- Belly Button's (p178) – best (and biggest) breakfasts in Vieques, nay Puerto Rico
- Café Cala'o (p113) – best coffee on the island, hands down
- La Bombonera (p113) – simple food in an authentic Old Town setting
- Restaurant Vinny (p149) – plastic forks and delicious *empanadillas* on scruffy Playa Húcares
- Casa Grande Mountain Retreat (p247) – cordon bleu cuisine produced out of nowhere
- Kasalta's (p117) – mind-bogglingly diverse Ocean Park bakery
- Parrot Club (p115) – SoFo classic; the original and best
- La Casa de los Pasteliollos (p197) – fresh octopus and *pastelillos* to die for

---

Simply put, *ron* (rum) is the national drink. Puerto Rico is the largest producer of rum in the world, and the distilleries bring hundreds of millions of dollars into the island economy. The headquarters for the famous Bacardi Rum Factory is in Cataño (p127), but most Puerto Ricans drink the locally made Don Q, Ronrico, Castillo and Captain Morgan (spiced rum).

There are two island-brewed beers that generally cost no more than $2 in local bars. The India brand has been around for years; Medalla is a popular light pilsner that quite a few islanders drink like water.

CELEBRATIONS

Recipes from La Isla by Robert and Judith Rosado features an extensive listing of recipes, using traditional cooking methods and ingredients (but sometimes with healthier substitutions), and describes the authentic tools and techniques originally used.

Food is an intrinsic part of Puerto Rican culture, so it's no wonder festivals celebrating regional specialties take place practically year-round. The southern region of Salinas, known for seafood, is host to the Salinas Carnival in April. Shrimp lovers should consider visiting the western town of Moca in May for the Festival del Camarón de Río (River Shrimp Festival), where local restaurants and kiosks hold tastings and showcase local recipes. In Lares, located in the mountains, one can sample at least 12 varieties of bananas at the Banana Festival. Those with a sweet tooth should visit the island during the last weekend of August for the Puff Pastry Festival in the western town of Añasco.

In October, the northern town of Corozal hosts the National Plantain Festival. The coastal town of Arecibo, where the sardine is considered a delicacy, holds the annual Cetí (a miniature relative of the sardine) Festival. These are just a few of the culinary celebrations that visitors traveling to Puerto Rico might stumble across at any time of year.

WHERE TO EAT & DRINK

There's room for all price ranges in Puerto Rico. Budget-minded diners can easily eat for under $12, while a midrange meal will set you back between $13 and $29. Top end ($30 plus) can go as high as you want it – but you'll get your money's worth.

Usually eaten between about 7am and 9am, typical Puerto Rican breakfasts are light and simple, except on weekends and holidays, when people have more time to cook egg dishes such as *tortilla española* (Spanish omelette) or French toast. You can get American breakfasts at chains like Denny's…and many Puerto Ricans do. More traditional islanders stop at a *repostelría* (bakery) for a long, sweet cup of *café con leche* (a blend of coffee and steamed milk) and a couple of slices of *pan criollo* (a bit like French bread) with butter or *queso de papa* (a mild island cheese). Folks with more of an appetite may get a sandwich. Those with a sweet tooth favor *la mallorca* (a type of sweet pastry that is covered with powdered sugar).

Lunch is available between 11:30am and 2pm. Puerto Ricans usually go cheap on this event, flocking to fast-food outlets for burgers and the like, or gathering around *friquitines* (street vendors) selling a variety of fried finger foods. To a large degree, islanders avoid leisurely luncheon meals in upscale restaurants, and you will find the noon meal the best time of day to sample good Puerto Rican cooking. The restaurants are not crowded and you can often find fixed-price specials for as little as $6.

Dinners, served between about 6pm and 10pm, are more expensive, and a legion of prosperous islanders have developed a tradition of going out to restaurants – especially on Thursday, Friday and Saturday – as a prelude to a long 'night on the town.' Be prepared to wait for a table if you do not call ahead for reservations at popular spots (some of the better restaurants require reservations). The same is true for the big Sunday afternoon *cena* (lunch) at resort destinations near the beach, in the mountains or at a parador.

Dinner specials may also be available, but they are usually quite a bit more expensive than virtually the same lunch specials.

Travelers who want to take some of the risk out of sampling island cuisine can take advantage of the Mesónes Gastronómicos program, sponsored by the **Puerto Rico Tourism Company** (PRTC; www.gotopuertorico.com). This program has identified a collection of restaurants around the island that feature Puerto Rican cuisine, and has screened those restaurants according to the highest standards of quality. The PRTC publishes a list of these restaurants in its bimonthly magazine, *Qué Pasa*.

> In 2003, Aquaviva (p116) in Old San Juan was listed as one of the top 75 restaurants in the world in a survey by *Condé Nast Traveler*.

VEGETARIANS & VEGANS

There is a growing number of vegetarian restaurants in Puerto Rico, particularly in Old San Juan and San Juan, but even regular restaurants often carry vegetarian dishes nowadays. It's noted in this book when a restaurant specifically does vegetarian/vegan food, but chefs in many restaurants are very often willing to prepare vegetarian dishes upon request.

Vegans should be very careful, as butter or meat renderings often find their way into beans and rice, and many other dishes that can be listed as 'vegetarian' by people who don't fully understand that an absence of actual meat doesn't automatically make a meal vegan.

A MOVEABLE FEAST

Cheap, cheerful and indisputably Puerto Rican, kiosks, or small food stands, offer some of the island's best snacks for prices listed in cents rather than dollars. Running the gamut from smoky holes-in-the-wall to tiny mobile cooking units that materialize seemingly out of nowhere, kiosks offer fast food without the franchise names, meaning the snacks they display are invariably homemade, locally sourced and surprisingly tasty.

The island's most famous cluster of permanent kiosks (over 50 in all) lines the palm-shaded beachfront at Luquillo (p140). Other more moveable feasts operate at weekends in places such as Piñones near San Juan or Boquerón on the west coast, although you can bump into a spontaneous kiosk-gathering in the most unlikely places.

Tasty treats to look out for are *surullitos* (fried cornmeal and cheese sticks), *empanadillas* (meat or fish turnovers), *alcapurrias* (fritters made with mashed plantains and ground meat) and *bacalaitos* (salt-cod fritters seasoned with oregano, garlic and sweet chili peppers). The sellers with the most brightly-colored carts are the *piragüeros*, vendors who sell syrupy *piraguas*, cones of shaved ice covered in sweet fruity sauces such as raspberry, guava, tamarind or coconut.

EATING WITH KIDS

Children are welcome everywhere in Puerto Rico, but it would be a faux pas to bring extremely young children to some of the sleeker restaurants in San Juan. Generally most restaurants are happy to do things like heat up a baby bottle for you, but know that microwaves aren't employed widely outside of San Juan. Baby chairs are often available (this is especially the case in fast-food restaurants) and you will see entire families dining out at a wide range of restaurants; you needn't worry that you'll be the only one with kids.

The traditional recipes are good in *A Taste of Puerto Rico* by Yvonne Ortiz, but more intriguing are the descriptions of some of the more modern dishes appearing on the island, especially the new emphasis on healthy seafood.

HABITS & CUSTOMS

There are very few tricks to dining out easily in Puerto Rico – you can eat with your left or right hand, hold your utensils American or British style, follow basic table manners and get along fine.

Breakfast and lunch tend to be quick, unless you're having a business meal (these can drag on forever). Dinner in restaurants is always a social and festive affair, so solitary diners will stick out a bit. Lunch is much easier to navigate solo. Smoking and belching are best done outside, but otherwise there's little you can do that will upset easygoing Puerto Ricans (aside from criticizing their cooking, that is).

If invited to someone's house, a gift bottle of rum, beer or wine will be well received (more so than flowers). Don't argue when the hosts serve you a gargantuan portion; it's probably more than they would eat in a week, but as their guest, you get special treatment.

EAT YOUR WORDS
Useful Phrases

See the Language chapter (p300) for other useful Spanish words and phrases, and pronunciation guidelines.

If you've got a hankering to try your hand at *aranitas, maduritos* or seafood *asopao*, grab *Puerto Rican Cuisine in America: Nuyorican and Bodega Recipes* by Oswald Rivera. It's a truly mouthwatering book.

Table for…, please.
   Una mesa para…, por favor.   oo·na me·sa pa·ra… por fa·vor

Can I see the menu please?
   ¿Puedo ver el menú, por favor?   pwe·do ver el me·noo por fa·vor

How late are you open?
   ¿El restoran está abierto hasta cuándo?   el re·sto·ran e·sta a·byer·to ha·sta kwan·do

Is this the smoking section?
   ¿Aquí se puede fumar?   a·kee se pwe·de foo·mar

Is there a table with a view available?
   ¿Hay una mesa con vista?   ai oo·na me·sa con vis·ta

I'm a vegetarian.
   Soy vegetariana/o.   soy veg·khe·ta·rya·na/o

What's in this dish?
   ¿Qué ingredientes tiene este plato?   ke een·gre·dyen·tes tye·ne es·te pla·to

What is today's special?
   ¿Cuál es el plato del día?   kwal es el pla·to del dee·a

I'll try what she/he's having.
   Probaré lo que ella/él está comiendo.   pro·ba·ray lo ke e·lya/el es·ta ko·myen·do

Can I have a (beer) please?
   Una (cerveza), por favor.   oo·na (ser·ve·sa) por fa·vor

Thank you, that was delicious.
   Muchas gracias, estaba buenísimo.   moo·chas gra·syas es·ta·ba bwe·nee·see·mo

The check/bill, please.
   La cuenta, por favor.   la kwen·ta por fa·vor

Food Glossary

Following is a handy list of common Puerto Rican menu items.

aguacate	a·gwa·*ka*·te	avocado
ajo	*a*·kho	garlic
alcapurrias	al·ka·*pu*·ree·as	fish, pork or crab fried in a batter of ground plaintains
amarillos en dulce	a·ma·*ree*·lyos en *dul*·se	ripe plaintains fried in sugar, red wine and cinnamon
almejas frescas	al·*me*·khas *fres*·kas	cherrystone clams
al ajillo	al a·*khee*·lyo	with garlic or cooked in garlic
a la parilla	a la pa·*ree*·lya	grilled
al horno	al *or*·no	oven-baked
asado	a·*sa*·do	roasted and seasoned with sofrito
asopao	a·sa·*pa*·o	an island specialty, a delicious thick stew often with seafood
arroz	a·*roz*	rice
bacalaítos	ba·ka·la·*ee*·tos	fried codfish fritters
bien-me-sabe	byen·me·*sa*·be	a coconut sauce over sponge cake
bistec pizzaola	bi·*stek* pit·za·o·la	breaded beef cutlets
caldo de gallina or *sopa de pollo criollo*	*kal*·do de ga·*lyee*·na *so*·pa de *po*·lyo kree·o·lyo	creole chicken soup
camarones	ka·ma·*ro*·nes	shrimp
carrucho	ka·*roo*·cho	conch
cebolla	se·*bo*·lya	onion
chicharrones de pollo	chee·cha·*ro*·nes·de *po*·lyo	chicken crisps
chicharrón	chee·cha·*ron*	crisp pork rind
chillo	*chee*·lyo	snapper
chuletas	choo·*le*·tas	pork chops
churrasco	choo·*ra*·sko	charcoal-broiled Argentinean steak
cocina del kiosko	ko·*see*·na del·*kyo*·sko	food-stand offerings
dulce de leche	*dul*·se de *le*·che	candied milk
empanadilla	em·pa·na·*dee*·lya	plantain or yucca dough stuffed with meat or fish and fried
ensalada mixta	en·sa·*la*·da *mik*·sta	mixed salad
ensalada verde	en·sa·*la*·da *vair*·de	green salad
flan	flan	custard
filete a la criolla	fi·*le*·te a la kree·o·la	creole steak
filete a la parrilla	fi·*le*·te a la pa·*ree*·lya	broiled steak
frito	*free*·to	fried
guineas al vino	gee·*nay*·as al *vee*·no	guinea hen in wine
guisado	gee·*sa*·do	stewed
habichuelas	ha·bee·*chwe*·las	beans
langosta	lan·*gos*·ta	lobster
lechón asado	le·*chon* a·*sa*·do	roast pig
maní	ma·*nee*	peanuts
mariscos	ma·*ris*·kos	shellfish
medallon de filete	me·da·*lyon* de fi·*le*·te	beef medallions
mero	*me*·ro	sea bass
mofongo	mo·*fong*·go	balls of mashed plaintains mixed with pork rind and spices and fried; sometimes stuffed with crab or lobster
parrillada	pa·ree·*lya*·da	spicy grilled steak
natilla	na·*tee*·lya	ice cream
pastelillos de chapin	pa·ste·*lee*·los de cha·*pin*	fried dumplings of trunk fish

The somewhat boringly named *Puerto Rican Cookery* by Carmen Aboy Valldejuli is considered to be the definitive text on *comida criolla* recipes. As if to prove the point, it is now in its 15th printing.

pescado	pe·*ska*·do	fish
pionono	pyo·*no*·no	cone of mashed plantains stuffed with seasoned ground meat, deep-fried in batter
piragua	pee·*ra*·gwa	cup of shaved ice covered with a fruity syrup in the tradition of a US snow cone
pulpo	*pul*·po	octopus
sopa	*so*·pa	soup
tembleque	tem·*ble*·ke	pudding made from coconut
tostones	tos·*to*·nes	twice-fried plantains, sometimes coated with honey
vegetales	ve·khe·*ta*·les	vegetables

Environment

THE LAND

Cartographers group Puerto Rico with the Caribbean's three largest islands – Cuba, Jamaica and Hispaniola – in the so-called Greater Antilles. But at 100 miles long and 35 miles across, Puerto Rico is quite clearly the little sister, stuck off to the east of Hispaniola at about 18° north latitude, 66° west longitude. With its four principal satellite islands – Mona and Desecheo to the west, Culebra and Vieques to the east – and a host of cays hugging its shores, Puerto Rico claims approximately 3500 sq miles of land, making the commonwealth slightly larger than the Mediterranean island of Corsica.

Like almost all the islands ringing the Caribbean Basin, Puerto Rico owes its existence to a series of volcanic events. These eruptions built up layers of lava and igneous rock and created an island with four distinct geographical zones: the central mountains, karst country, the coastal plain and the coastal dry forest. At the heart of the island, running east to west, stands a spine of steep, wooded mountains called the Cordillera Central. The lower slopes of the cordillera give way to foothills, comprising a region on the island's north coast known as 'karst country.' In this part of the island, erosion has worn away the limestone, leaving a karstic terrain of dramatic sinkholes, hillocks and caves.

Forty-five non-navigable rivers and streams rush from the mountains and through the foothills to carve the coastal valleys, particularly on the east and west ends of Puerto Rico, where sugarcane, coconuts and a variety of fruits are cultivated. The island's longest river is the Río Grande de Loíza, which flows north to the coast. Other substantial rivers include the Río Grande de Añasco, the Río Grande de Arecibo and the Río de la Plata.

Little of the island's virgin forest remains, but second- and third-growth forests totaling 140 sq miles now comprise significant woodland reserves, mostly in the center of the island.

The San Fermin earthquake that hit western Puerto Rico in October 1918 measured 7.6 on the Richter scale and triggered a 20ft tsunami. The event caused over $4 million of damage to the cities of Mayagüez and Aguadilla and killed 116 people.

WILDLIFE
Animals

Very few of the land mammals that make their home in Puerto Rico are native to the island; most mammal species – from cows to rats – have been either accidentally or intentionally introduced to the island over the centuries. Among the most distinctive of these is the Paso Fino horse, which is a small-boned, easy-gaited variety. The Paso Finos have been raised in Puerto Rico since the time of the Spanish conquest, when they were introduced to the New World to supply the conquistadores on their expeditions throughout Mexico and the rest of the Americas. They now number 8000 and are unique to Puerto Rico. The horses are most dramatic on the island of Vieques, where they roam in semiwild herds on vast tracts of ex-military land.

Not far from Vieques lies the 39-acre Cayo Santiago, where a small colony of rhesus monkeys, introduced for scientific study in 1938, has burgeoned into a community of more than 700 primates.

Bats are the only native terrestrial mammals in Puerto Rico. Notable marine mammals include humpback whales, which breed in the island's warm waters in the winter. They are best spotted off the coast of Rincón in early December (see p229). Another aquatic resident is the endangered Antillean manatee (the town of Manatí, on the north coast, is named after the mammal) that inhabit shallow coastal areas where they forage on sea

Above and below ground, and under water, *Puerto Rico and Virgin Islands Wildlife Viewing* by David W Nellis gives you all the facts on the flora and fauna of Puerto Rico.

grasses and plants. Manatee numbers have dropped in recent decades due to habitat loss, poaching and entanglement with fishing nets.

Puerto Rico is home to 25 species of amphibian and 61 reptiles. The most famous amphibian is the tiny but highly vocal *coquí* frog (its distinctive nighttime croak has been measured at 10 decibels), which has been adopted as a national symbol.

Iguanas are often kept as semiwild pets and pose unlikely obstacles on numerous Puerto Rican golf courses. The most notable wild species is the Mona ground iguana, which still survives in large numbers on the western island of Mona – often dubbed the 'Galápagos of the Caribbean' because of its unique biological diversity.

Despite rampant coastal development (see p68), a handful of the island's beaches are still nesting sites for hawksbill and leatherback sea turtles. An excellent place to view the nesting process (and help out as a volunteer) is on the isolated northern beaches of the island of Culebra (see p158).

Puerto Rico boasts 11 varieties of snake, none of which is poisonous. The most impressive is the endemic special boa, which can grow to a length of more than 12ft.

Though not native to the island, spectacled caimans have become something of a pest in the areas around Lake Tortuguero on the north coast. Introduced as a macho pet in the 1990s, many of these minicrocs were abandoned by their owners and dumped in the vicinity of Puerto Rico's only freshwater lake where they have played havoc with the fragile ecosystem. Local rangers are currently trying to bring their numbers under control.

The island also has a supply of unusual flying and crawling insects, including a large tropical relative of the firefly called the *cucubano,* and a centipede measuring more than 6in in length with a sting that can kill. Much to the chagrin of generations of foreign visitors there are zillions of blood-hungry mosquitoes.

With more than 250 species spread over 3500 sq miles, Puerto Rico is an excellent place to dust off your binoculars and engage in a bit of tropical bird-watching. The commonwealth's most famous bird is also its rarest: the Puerto Rican parrot. Numbers of the bird were down in the mid teens during the 1970s, but thanks to concerted conservation efforts the population has recovered to a precarious 35 to 40. The parrots still exist in the wild in the El Yunque and Río Abajo forest reserves, although seeing one is akin to winning a lottery ticket.

Another endemic bird is the Puerto Rican tody, a small green, yellow and red creature that frequents the moist mountains of the Cordillera Central and the dense thickets of the south coast where it feeds on insects. If you're lucky you'll also encounter various South American families such as tyrant flycatchers, bananaquits and tanagers.

The coastal dry forest of Guánica features more than 130 bird species, comprising largely songbirds. Some of these are migratory fowl, such as the prairie warbler and the northern parula. Many are nonmigratory species, including the lizard cuckoo and the endangered Puerto Rican nightjar. One of the joys of winter beachcombing is watching the aerial acrobatics of brown pelicans as they hunt for fish.

For more information on birding activities see p82.

Plants

Mangrove swamps and coconut groves dominate the north coast, while El Yunque's rainforest, at the east end of the island, supports mahogany trees and more than 50 varieties of wild orchid. Giant ferns thrive in the

Learn all about the *coquí* frog and other animals that inhabit Puerto Rico in *Natural Puerto Rico* by Alfonso Silva Lee, an exhaustive but entertaining book on island wildlife.

All you need to know about the insects, reptiles, four-legged mammals and greenery that they inhabit is in *The Nature of the Islands: Plants and Animals of the Eastern Caribbean* by Virginia Barlow. Very helpful for campers.

The Puerto Rican parrot is one of the 10 most endangered species in the world, with only an estimated 35 to 40 birds still existing in the wild.

rainforest as well as in the foothills of karst country, while cacti, mesquite forest and bunchgrass reign on the dry southwest tip of the island, which has the look of the African savanna.

Exotic shade trees have long been valued in this sunny climate, and most of the island's municipal plazas spread beneath canopies of magnificent ceibas or kapoks (silk-cotton tree), the *flamboyán* (poinciana), with its flaming red blossoms, and the African tulip tree.

Islanders often adorn their dwellings with a profusion of flowers such as orchids, bougainvillea and poinsettias, and tend lovingly to fruit trees that bear papaya, *uva caleta* (sea grape), *carambola* (star fruit), *panapen* (breadfruit) and *plátano* (plantain). Of course, sugarcane dominates the plantations of the coastal lowlands, while farmers raise coffee on the steep slopes of the Cordillera Central.

TERRITORIAL PARKS & RESERVES

Puerto Rico has more than a dozen well-developed and protected wilderness areas, which offer an array of exploration and a few camping opportunities. Most of these protected areas are considered *reservas forestales* (forest reserves) or *bosques estatales* (state forests), although these identifiers are often treated interchangeably in government-issued literature and maps.

Bosque Estatal de Carite (p258), Bosque Estatal de Guilarte (p270) and Bosque Estatal de Maricao (p271) are all on the slopes of the cordillera and accessible via the Ruta Panorámica.

The Bosque Estatal de Río Abajo (p246) covers 5000 acres in karst country near the Observatorio de Arecibo. Bosque Estatal de Guajataca (p249) is a smaller preserve near the northwest corner of the island, while the immense 10,000-acre Bosque Estatal de Guánica (p201), on the southwest coast, is home to a tropical dry-forest ecosystem and a Unesco biosphere forest.

Another notable coastal preserve is the 316-acre Las Cabezas de San Juan Reserva Natural 'El Faro' (p142), at the northeast corner of Puerto Rico, where El Faro (The Lighthouse) stands guard over the offshore cays. Meanwhile, glimmering to the east lay the Spanish Virgin Islands of Culebra and Vieques, both of which have designated large tracts of land as National Wildlife Refuges under the control of the US Fish & Wildlife Service. With 18,000 acres, Vieques National Wildlife Refuge (p169) is the largest protected natural reserve in Puerto Rico.

Some 300 acres of wilderness make up the Parque de las Cavernas del Río Camuy (p245), near Lares, in karst country; the park marks the entrance to one of the largest known cave systems in the world and is also the site of one of the world's largest underground rivers.

The most isolated of Puerto Rico's nature sanctuaries, Isla Mona (p234) lies about 50 miles east of Mayagüez, across the often-turbulent waters of Pasaje de la Mona.

This tabletop island is sometimes called Puerto Rico's 'Galápagos' or 'Jurassic Park' – because of the island's isolation. It's a tag made all the more eerie by its 200ft limestone cliffs, honeycomb caves and giant iguanas.

Commonwealth or US federal agencies administer most of the natural reserves on the island, and you will find that admission to these areas is generally free.

Private conservation groups own and operate a few of the nature preserves, including Las Cabezas de San Juan Reserva Natural 'El Faro'; visitors to these places should expect to pay an entrance fee (which is usually under $5). The best time to visit nearly all of the parks is from November to March; however, Bosque Estatal de Guánica is an inviting destination year-round.

For birders heading to Puerto Rico or the Caribbean, *A Guide to the Birds of Puerto Rico and the Virgin Islands* by Herbert Raffaele is a must-have. It will help you spy lots of hard-to-find birds in the dense forests of nature reserves.

Check out the website www.elyunque.com. Aside from excellent information on the island's national forest, this site lists many other activities on the island and is regularly updated with topical environmental news.

In April 2007, an executive order signed by US President George W Bush rechristened the Caribbean National Forest as El Yunque National Forest to blend in more with Puerto Rico's cultural inheritance.

TERRITORIAL PARKS & RESERVES

Name	Features	Activities	Page
Bosque Estatal de Carite	easy hikes through pristine forest	hiking, kayaking, camping	p258
Bosque Estatal de Guajataca	pretty artificial lakes in natural settings	hiking	p249
Bosque Estatal de Guánica	arid scenery, beautiful birds	hiking, swimming, biking, birding	p201
Bosque Estatal de Río Abajo	karst country formations, aviary	hiking	p246
Culebra National Wildlife Refuge	wild turtles, sleepy iguanas, rolling hills	hiking, cycling, diving, sailing, swimming	p201
El Yunque (El Yunque National Forest)	lush forests, sun-splashed peaks	hiking, mountain biking	p132
Isla Mona	limestone cliffs, giant iguanas	hiking, caving	p234
Las Cabezas de San Juan Reserva Natural 'El Faro'	coastal views, mangroves	hiking, kayaking	p142
Parque de las Cavernas del Río Camuy	caves, sinkholes, petroglyphs	hiking, caving	p245
Reserva Forestal Toro Negro	misty mountain tops	hiking	p265
Vieques National Wildlife Refuge	wild turtles, sleepy iguanas, rolling hills	hiking, cycling, snorkeling, sailing, swimming	p169

Organizations

The **National Park Service** (NPS; www.nps.gov), part of the US Department of the Interior, oversees San Juan's El Morro (p88) and San Cristóbal (p89) forts which together are classified as the San Juan National Historic Site.

The **Departamento de Recursos Naturales y Ambientales** (DRNA; Department of Natural Resources) administers all of the island's *bosques estatales* and *reservas forestales*, and issues camping permits. Their main office is in San Juan (p87).

The **US Forest Service** (USFS; ☎ campground & reservation info 800-280-2267; www.fs.fed .us) is a part of the Department of Agriculture and manages the use of forests such as El Yunque. National forests are less protected than parks, allowing commercial exploitation in some areas (usually logging or privately owned recreational facilities). Current information about national forests can be obtained from ranger stations (contact information is given in the individual forest sections of this book).

Puerto Rico maintains regional **US Fish & Wildlife Service** (FWS; www.fws.gov) offices that can provide information about viewing local wildlife. Their phone numbers appear in the white pages of the local telephone directory under 'US Government, Interior Department,' or you can call the **Federal Information Center** (☎ 800-688-9889; www.pueblo.gsa.gov).

The National Astronomy & Ionosphere Center runs www.naic.edu, a site about the Observatorio de Arecibo that has information for the general public as well as academic types.

ENVIRONMENTAL ISSUES

Puerto Rico has long suffered from a number of serious environmental problems, including population growth and rapid urbanization, deforestation, erosion of soil, water pollution and mangrove destruction. While Puerto Ricans still have a long way to go toward undoing generations of environmental damage and preserving their natural resources, the past few decades have seen a gradual increase in the level of awareness, resources and action dedicated to conservation efforts.

Without a doubt, population growth and rapid urbanization have long posed the greatest threat to the island's environment. Shortsighted solutions, including locking out blacks and the poor or – later in the 19th century – knocking down the fortress wall marking the eastern edge of Old San Juan, have been among the island's ways of coping with its booming population.

The most recent attempts to isolate elements of the citizenry as a means of reducing population density have included large, low-income federal housing projects called *caserios*. As recently as 15 years ago, sociologists identified the *caserios* as a nightmare vision of the island's future.

They saw Puerto Rico's population density approaching that of Singapore and projected that the expansion of metropolitan San Juan would envelop virtually all land within a 20-mile radius of the old city.

All this has come to pass, but the birthrate on the island has fallen from almost four children per mother to two.

The current birthrate puts the island on track for zero population growth by the end of the decade.

Deforestation & Soil Erosion

During the late 19th and early 20th centuries, massive logging operations denuded much of the island. Consequently, untold acres of rich mountain topsoil have eroded away to clog the mouths of rivers and streams. But in the 1920s and '30s, thoughtful islanders and forward-looking conservationists in the island's US colonial government began to set aside and reforest an extensive network of wilderness reserves, mostly in karst country and the Cordillera Central.

Today these reserves are mature forests, and nearly the entire central part of the island – about one-third of Puerto Rico's landmass – is sheltered by a canopy of trees.

While the creation of wilderness reserves and reforestation have retarded Puerto Rico's erosion problems, much damage has been done by clearing hillside land for housing subdivisions in places such as Guaynabo and

---

BRIGHT LIGHTS, BLACK WATER

There are seven known regions worldwide that are phosphorescent – meaning they glow in the dark thanks to little microorganisms, known as dynoflagellates, in the water – but the ones in Puerto Rico are considered to be the brightest and the best.

There are three places on the island where you can view this psychedelic phenomenon: Bahía Mosquito (p171) in Vieques, Bahía de Fosforescente (p205) at La Parguera, and Laguna Grande (p142) north of Fajardo. The most abundant of the many organisms in Puerto Rico's 'phosphorous' bays is *Pirodinium bahamense*. The term 'Pirodinium' comes from 'pyro,' meaning fire, and 'dirium,' meaning rotate.

When any movement disturbs these creatures, a chemical reaction takes place in their little bodies that makes the flash. Scientists speculate about the purpose of the flash, though many think that the dynoflagellates have developed this ability to give off a sudden green light as a defense mechanism to ward off predators.

You can see these microorganisms flashing like tiny stars in Atlantic waters as far north as New England in the summer, but never in the brilliant concentrations appearing in Puerto Rico. Enclosed mangrove bays, where narrow canals limit the exchange of water with the open sea, are the places that let the dynoflagellates breed and concentrate. In a sense, the bay is a big trap, and vitamins produced along the shore provide food for the corralled microorganisms.

Not surprisingly, bioluminescent bays support precarious ecosystems. To avoid damaging them, only book tours with operators who use kayaks or electric motors. Island Adventures (p174) is on Vieques, which has the best bay of the three.

Yokahú Kayaks (p145) covers the Fajardo bay, which is the second-best option.

Sadly, in La Parguera (p205), home to the third bay, most tour operators use only motorized engines. The bioluminescence has been greatly reduced as a consequence. If you're offered a ride, check that it will be in a boat that's safe for the environment. If not, turn the operator down and make sure to tell them why you are saying no.

CONSTRUCTION VERSUS CONSERVATION

Unchecked development has long been Puerto Rico's biggest environmental threat. On a small island where space is limited and tourists mean money, the territory's sultry Caribbean beauty has often been its undoing. Big developers and hotel companies regularly eye the country's lush coastline and pristine beaches in search of the next high-rise condo tower or 18-hole golf course. But, as economically beneficial as tourism might be, its continued expansion could ultimately lead to a law of diminishing returns. If the famed Isla del Encanto (Enchanted Isle) suffers many more reconfigured coastlines or bulldozed palm groves, it will no longer be worthy of its illustrious nickname.

Many argue that development – particularly in the tourist sector – has already gone too far. Puerto Rico currently has a higher population density than any of the 50 US states, with an average 1000 people per sq mile. It also supports one of the highest concentrations of roads in the world. Outside of the central mountains, it is rare to drive for more than a mile or two without being engulfed by a housing complex, a shopping mall or a fast-food restaurant, and the island's peripheral coast road is often more redolent of a giant parking lot than a well-ordered highway.

One perennial worry for environmentalists is the flouting of property laws, a factor that regularly sees buildings going up on protected land. Side-stepping protection laws, large hotel properties often merely act as a cover for future subdivisions and within a couple of years you'll often find a comparatively new resort shuttered up to make way for a new housing estate.

The good news is that grassroots pressure has already begun to yield results against some of the more politically aligned property developers. In 2007, a proposed condo development known as Costa Serena was indefinitely blocked by community groups in Loiza, near San Juan. If realized, this project would have erected an 880-unit gated community, along with 1350 parking spaces, a casino, tennis courts and a beach club at Piñones on what is currently one of Puerto Rico's most authentic and undeveloped beaches.

Seen by many as a refreshing antidote to the resort strip of Isla Verde, Piñones is home to Puerto Rico's largest mangrove habitat and acts as a natural protective barrier against coastal flooding in the area.

Another weighty tourist project was similarly stalled a couple of months later in Luquillo, when the Puerto Rican government signed a protection order on a 270-acre parcel of land that had been earmarked by two major hotel chains for a luxury resort. According to the Sierra Club's recently inaugurated Puerto Rican Chapter, this project would have severely jeopardized an important nesting beach for leatherback turtles and endangered numerous other species in the so-called northeast ecological corridor.

But, as important as these hard-won victories may be, they are merely small, prickly skirmishes in an ongoing war. With the government pledging increased tourist numbers throughout 2008, the battle against the bulldozers looks set to continue.

Trujillo Alto, both suburbs of San Juan. Consequently, when heavy rains and hurricanes strike, mudslides and hillside streets that turn into rivers threaten life and property.

Water Pollution

Reforestation, the creation of wilderness reserves to preserve mountain watersheds, and generally thoughtful creation of mountain reservoirs have gone a long way toward assuring that the island's freshwater resources remain pollution-free. Nevertheless streams, rivers and estuaries on the coastal plain have long been polluted by agricultural runoff, industry and inadequate sewer and septic systems. And while a number of environmental groups lobby for the cleanup of these cesspools, little has been accomplished. Visitors should not be tempted to swim in rivers, streams or estuaries near the coast (including Bahía de San Juan) – nor should they eat fish or shellfish from these waters – because of the risk of disease and chemical pollutants.

Mangrove Destruction

As with the island's other environmental problems, mangrove destruction was at its worst decades ago when Operation Bootstrap and the rush to develop business and housing lots saw the devastation of vast mangrove swamps, particularly along the island's north shore in the vicinity of Bahía de San Juan. Small bays such as Laguna Condado, now lined with hotels, homes and businesses, were rich mangrove estuaries just 60 years ago.

Environmentalists began fighting to preserve the island's remaining mangrove estuaries in the mid-1970s, and the late 1990s brought a number of significant victories in this arena.

Environmentalists won a court battle in 1998 to preserve as wilderness most of the land at the western end of Laguna de Piñones, long slated for development as resort property. Environmentalists have won a similar battle to protect the mangroves around La Parguera, on the island's southwest shore.

The creation of the huge 2883-acre Reserva Nacional de Investigación Estuarina de Bahía de Jobos (p198) assures the preservation of the island's largest mangrove estuary, although one power plant stands on the fringe and a second may be coming.

In 2005, the well-known American environmental organization Sierra Club (www.sierraclub.org) welcomed a group of members from Puerto Rico as its 64th chapter.

Heavy-Metal Pollution

Nobody knows for sure what cumulative damage has been done to the land and sea life around Vieques during the years of persistent naval bombardment. When the US Army pulled out of Culebra decades ago, it left an underwater legacy of unexploded ordnance that divers and boaters still have to be wary of.

The environmental movement has come a long way since then, and when the US Navy announced its departure from Vieques in 2003, locals immediately began asking who was going to be responsible for the cleanup and who would be paying for any latent health issues that might appear in the future.

Studies done as far back as the 1980s show that the soil of the eastern end of the island is laced with heavy-metal pollution, and quite a few residents of Vieques have been tested and found to have dangerous levels of heavy metals in their bodies. The navy has promised to continue regular testing of residents.

The US government deemed Vieques a Superfund site shortly after the pullout, which made its cleanup a federal responsibility organized and implemented by the Environmental Protection Agency (EPA). Environmental assessors and navy contractors did visual inspections of Red Beach and Blue Beach, and deemed them safe for public use.

The Live Impact Area, which encompassed 900 acres on the tip of the eastern end, was designated a Wilderness Area and closed to public access by an Act of Congress in 2003.

Many other areas of the Vieques National Wildlife Refuge are closed to the public until heavy metals, unexploded ordnance and leftover fuels and chemicals can be taken care of. According to the US Fish & Wildlife Service, the cleanup will take quite a few years but it will include underwater sites as well. Progress may be hampered, though, by recent revelations from the US government that the Superfund itself – which raised money through a small tax on the chemical and oil industry – is now bankrupt.

Recycling

Although Puerto Rico has a government recycling campaign, there are very few receptacles in public places for the recycling of aluminum cans or other materials, and recycling has yet to become an ingrained habit. The Solid Waste Management Authority collects cans, glass, paper and plastic on the second Saturday of every month, as if recycling day is simply another religious feast day to observe and forget.

Conservation Groups

To combat the mounting destruction of the island's environment, citizens in many municipalities have formed local environmental action groups. Contact one of these organizations listed if you see or hear of a problem or – even better – want to collaborate with professionals and volunteers to help save the island:

Caribbean Environmental Information (☎ 787-751-0239)
Conservation Trust of Puerto Rico (☎ 787-722-5834)
Natural History Society of Puerto Rico (☎ 787-726-5488; www.naturalhistorypr.org)
Puerto Rican Association of Water Resources (☎ 787-977-5870)
Puerto Rican Conservation Foundation (☎ 787-763-9875)

Puerto Rico Outdoors

Few people travel to the Caribbean islands to sit around indoors playing tiddlywinks (except perhaps during a hurricane) and Puerto Rico is no exception. With its diverse forests, exotic birdlife, balmy beaches and crinkled karst formations, this is a place to get out and discover the great outdoors, both sensuously and adventurously, whether by foot, kayak, bicycle, surfboard or boat.

The highly rated World's Best 10k Race (WB10k) is considered to be one of the most competitive road running races in the world. In 2003, British Olympian Paula Radcliffe completed the course in a world record time of 30 minutes 21 seconds.

Lapped on four sides by warm ocean, Puerto Rico is famous for its water sports, particularly surfing, though within the diving community it has secured an equally favorable reputation for its clear waters and pristine coral. Several upscale marinas plus the commonwealth's proximity to the US Virgin Islands have also meant that sailing and deep-sea fishing remain popular. On land, a century of American influence has ensured that Puerto Rico is now considered to be the golf capital of the Caribbean with nearly two dozen courses.

WATER ACTIVITIES

SWIMMING

Finding safe swimming in Puerto Rico is easy thanks to an island-wide system of balnearios (public beaches). Scattered liberally around the coastline, balnearios feature lockers, showers and parking at nominal rates. Many of them also employ lifeguards and a flag system that indicates how good conditions are for swimming. On most balnearios you will find a roped-off rectangle of ocean close to the shore, inside which it is safe to swim. These beaches are closed on Monday, Election Day (usually in early November) and Good Friday. Hours are 9am to 5pm in summer, 8am to 5pm in winter. For a complete list, contact the **Departamento de Recreación y Deportes** (Department of Recreation & Sports; ☎ 787-722-5668).

All the balnearios are in lovely settings offering shade and calm waters, though travelers should beware of theft (never leave belongings unattended) and heavy crowds in the summer months. Camping is available in

---

ALTERNATIVE ADVENTURES

- Hit the Reserva Forestal Toro Negro with San Juan–based adventure company Acampa Nature Adventure Tours (p268) and you could find yourself **rappelling** off 60ft cliffs and zip-lining above the tree line.

- **Kitesurfing** is the latest craze on Playa Isla Verde in San Juan. Get kitted out at the locally based Kitesurfpr (p104).

- Rincón is the best place to go for **whale-watching**, where humpbacks appear in the Pasaje de la Mona around December. You can organize a boat trip (p229) or sometimes catch a glimpse from outside the Punta Higüero lighthouse.

- Of the various **yoga retreats** on the island, the most transcendental in both mood and setting has to be the early-morning classes at the Casa Grande Mountain Retreat (p247).

- Test your mettle in one of Puerto Rico's famous **running road races**. Events include the World's Best 10k Race (WB10K), the Rincón Triathlon (p229) and the San Blás de Illescas Marathon in Coamo (p199).

some balnearios, though it is not always 100% safe off-season. Two excellent beaches for safe camping are Playa Seven Seas (p143) in Las Croabas and Playa Flamenco (p163) on the island of Culebra. Puerto Rico's two most idyllic – and hence most popular – balnearios are Luquillo (p138) in the northeast and Boquerón (p213) in the southwest. Other decent options include Escambrón (p103) and Carolina (p103) in San Juan, Sun Bay (p172) in Esperanza, Vieques, and Cerro Gordo (p243), near Dorado.

San Juan boasts some of the best municipal beaches in the Caribbean in an unbroken strip that runs from Condado, through Ocean Park and Isla Verde, all the way to Piñones. The safest swimming can be found at Playa Isla Verde (p103).

Should you wish to escape the beach madness for a little more privacy, almost all of Puerto Rico's resorts and its two dozen or more paradores have swimming pools.

Compact and easily carried, *Snorkeling Guide to Marine Life* by Paul Humann is an excellent guide that lists all the fish, corals, invertebrates and plants found in less than 15ft of water. Great photographs, too.

DIVING & SNORKELING

Most Caribbean islands boast a formidable diving scene and Puerto Rico can compete with the best of them with an exciting selection of walls, drop-offs, reefs and underwater caves. Two specific dive areas on the island can be described as world-class: the massive drop-off near La Parguera in the south, popularly known as the Parguera Wall (p206), and the undisturbed crystal-clear waters that surround the outlying island of Desecheo (p256), 12 miles northwest of Aguadilla. The former constitutes an underwater wall that falls from 60ft to over 1500ft due to a huge drop in the continental shelf below the sea bed. With more than 25 named dive sites, the area is awash with trenches, valleys, coral gardens and colorful fish. Desecheo, meanwhile, has an similar number of dive sites and visibility that reaches over 100ft in places. Real adventurers head out to Isla Mona (p237), where unblemished waters are frequented by turtles and seals.

RESPONSIBLE DIVING & SNORKELING

Please consider the following tips when diving and snorkeling and help preserve the ecology and beauty of reefs:

- Never use anchors on the reef and take care not to ground boats on coral.
- Avoid touching or standing on living marine organisms or dragging equipment across the reef. Polyps can be damaged by even the gentlest contact. If you must hold on to the reef, only touch exposed rock or dead coral.
- Be conscious of your fins. Even without contact, the surge from fin strokes near the reef can damage delicate organisms. Take care not to kick up clouds of sand, which can smother organisms.
- Practice and maintain proper buoyancy control. Major damage can be done by divers descending too fast and colliding with the reef.
- Take great care in underwater caves. Spend as little time within them as possible as your air bubbles may be caught within the roof and thereby leave organisms high and dry. Take turns to inspect the interior of a small cave.
- Resist the temptation to collect or buy corals or shells or to loot marine archaeological sites (mainly shipwrecks).
- Ensure that you take home all your rubbish and any litter you may find as well. Plastics in particular are a serious threat to marine life.
- Do not feed fish.
- Minimize your disturbance of marine animals. *Never* ride on the backs of turtles.

The best snorkeling can be found off the sheltered islands of Vieques (p174) and Culebra (p161) or around the small cays east of Fajardo, such as Palominos (p145) and Icacos (p145). The south coast with its clear Caribbean waters and low river run-off is another exciting option. Try Isla Caja de Muertos (p190) near Ponce or the warm waters around La Parguera (p206). On Culebra and Vieques you can snorkel directly from the beach. The former offers Playa Melones or the wonderfully isolated Carlos Rosario, the latter boasts Green Beach or the handily located municipal beach in the main southern settlement of Esperanza. Generally speaking, the waters off the north and west coasts of Puerto Rico are rough and better suited to surfing. You may, however, get some luck on calm days snorkeling the fringe reefs off Condado (p103) and Playa Isla Verde (p103) in San Juan or at either Playa Shacks or Playa Steps in Rincón.

Dive operators run day trips out of the major ports and resort hotels around the island (see the regional chapters for more details). If you are in the San Juan area, consider a dive trip to the caves and overhangs at Horseshoe Reef, Figure Eight or the Molar. There's decent diving along the chain of islands called 'La Cordillera,' east of Las Cabezas de San Juan (in the Fajardo area), with about 60ft to 70ft visibility. Catch the Drift or the Canyon off Humacao.

Top dive operators include Aquatica Dive & Surf (p254) near Aguadilla for Isla Desecheo trips, West Divers (p206) near the eponymous fishing village for the famous wall, and Sea Ventures Pro Dive Center (p145) in Fajardo for the northeastern cordillera. Centrally based San Juan operators (p104) can take you almost anywhere.

For information on diving safety, see p77.

KAYAKING

Kayaking can be either blissfully relaxing or ruggedly adventurous in Puerto Rico with various freshwater and open-sea options offering brand-new perspectives on strangely familiar sights. One of the highlights is the unique opportunity to dip your paddle in one of the island's three bioluminescent bays (p67), a gentle but wonderfully psychedelic kayak through water that glimmers purple with every touch of the oar. Another restful daytime option is the Laguna de Piñones (p125) in the eponymous barrio just east of Isla Verde with easy boat hire at the nearby Centro Cultural Ecoturístico de Piñones.

One of the island's best ecosensitive kayak companies is **Las Tortugas Adventures** (787-809-0253), based in Canovanas in the east, which runs off-the-beaten-track kayak excursions on Puerto Rico's only navigable waterway, the Río Espiritu Santo near Río Grande. Freshwater kayaking is also possible on some of the island's artificial but ecologically diverse lakes, including Lago Dos Bocas (p246) and Lago Guajataca (p248).

In general, beaches that are good for surfing aren't so good for kayaking and vice versa. The best sea-kayaking options are often in the south and east of the main island or around the two eastern islands of Culebra and Vieques.

SAILING

The semiprotected waters off the east end of Puerto Rico, which include the islands of Culebra and Vieques, provide the setting for racing and cruising aboard sailboats. You can count on the trade winds blowing 12 to 25 knots out of the east almost every day. A number of marinas meet sailors' needs in the Fajardo area. The largest is the Puerto del Rey Marina (p144), with 750 slips and room for vessels up to 200ft long. A number of yachts carry passengers on picnic/snorkeling/sailing day charters out of Puerto del Rey and the four other marinas in the area (see p145). These trips cost about $55 per person for a six-hour sail and offer good value if you want to enjoy a day of the cruisers' life.

For constantly updated information and insider tips on the best diving spots around Puerto Rico, see www.prdiving.com.

Colleen Ryan and Brian Savage's *The Complete Diving Guide: The Caribbean (Volume 2)* has instructions, directions, depths and visibility for just about every dive in the Caribbean.

One of Puerto Rico's biggest sailing events is the Copa Velasco Regatta for ocean racing that takes place at the Palmas del Mar Resort on the East Coast.

SURFING MAP

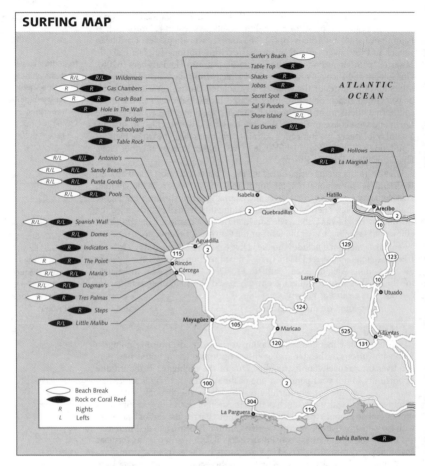

SURFING

Thanks to legendary surf breaks such as Tres Palmas, Crash Boat and Jobos, Puerto Rico has developed its own ingrained surfing culture based around some of the best waves in the Americas. In 1968 the World Surfing Championships were held at Rincón, and the island hasn't looked back since. Surfers from around the world come here for an annual season that runs from October through April and is centered on the northwest coastal regions of Rincón (p228), Aguadilla (p254) and Isabela (p251). Surfing facilities in these enclaves are comprehensive but suitably laid-back, and first-timers should have few problems integrating with the experts.

In 2007, Rincón played host to the ISA World Masters surfing tournament. Local surfer Juan Ashton posted first in the Master's Division.

Should you feel the waves are too big or the dudes too cool out west, then there are a number of lesser-known options for surfers further afield. Along the north coast there are decent breaks around Manatí (p243) and Dorado (p240), while in the far east you can get to grips with the curls and barrels at La Pared (p139) in Luquillo or the newly inaugurated wildlife reserve at La Selva (p139). There's even reasonable surfing to be had in the capital, San Juan (p104). Diehards practice off Playa Escambrón in

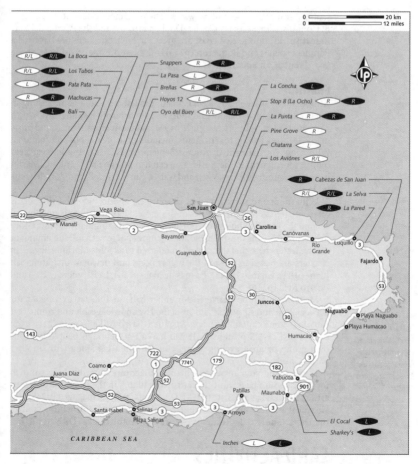

Puerta de Tierra while the best stuff can be found over in Piñones at Los Aviónes.

There are numerous surf shops spread around the island's hot spots. Try WoW Surfing School (p104) in San Juan, the West Coast Surf Shop (p228) in Rincón or Aquatica Dive & Surf (p254) in Aguadilla. Aside from renting equipment, these establishments also offer lessons and can impart information about local conditions and weather. Board rentals start at approximately $25 per day. Lessons go from anywhere between $65 and $95 per session.

WINDSURFING

Puerto Rico played host to the Ray Ban Windsurfing World Cup in 1989 and the sport has been booming here ever since. Hotdoggers head for the surfing beaches at Isla Verde (p104) or – better yet – the rough northwest coast. Some of the favorite sites include Playas Crash Boat and Wilderness (p254) in Aguadilla and Playas Shacks and Jobos (p251) near Isabela.

If you are just getting started, try the Laguna del Condado in San Juan (p104) or Ensenada Honda at Culebra (p161), where there are windsurfing schools, constant wind and no waves. The protected waters off Wyndham El Conquistador Resort & Golden Door Spa (p146) and the Palmas del Mar Resort (p148) on the east coast are great for novices, as are the bays at La Parguera (p206) and Boquerón (p213). All the shoreside resort hotels have board rentals and instruction.

FISHING

Although not as legendary as in Cuba or the Bahamas, big-game fishing in Puerto Rico is still a Blue Riband sport and, for aspiring Hemingways, worth a trip in its own right. Attracting heavyweight competition, the island hosts many deep-sea fishing tournaments, including the prestigious International Billfishing Tournament in August/September, which is the longest-held billfish tournament in the world. You can fish for tuna all year long. Marlin is a spring/summer fish, sailfish and wahoo run in the fall, and dorado show up in the winter.

With the island surrounded by deep water, Puerto Rico's best fishing is often situated within 30 minutes of the shore. Decent fishing is possible all around the island although the north coast, with its abundance of migratory fish, is probably the most reliable and exciting spot to set a line. So abundant are the waters here that they are often referred to as 'Blue Marlin Alley.' Fish charters are based in most of the bigger ports and marinas, including San Juan (p104), Fajardo (p145), Palmas de Mar (p148), La Parguera (p206) and Puerto Real (p216).

Most boats can be chartered for either half- or full-day excursions for between four and six people and are staffed by knowledgeable and competent captains. Some captains, such as San Juan–based Mike Benitez, have even entertained ex-US presidents. If you haven't got enough people for your own group or are traveling alone, you can often tag along with another party. Check ahead.

If you bring your own equipment and acquire a permit, you can fish for large-mouth bass, sunfish, catfish and tilapia in the island's numerous artificial lakes. Lakes Carite (p258), Dos Bocas (p246), Guajataca (p248) and Guayabal, on the south coast, are all popular. For more information, contact the Departamento de Recursos Naturales y Ambientales (DRNA; p87).

The Puerto Rico Trench that surrounds the north coast is the deepest point in the Atlantic – approximately 27,880ft.

LAND ACTIVITIES

HIKING

Hiking in Puerto Rico has plenty of potential. But what you actually get out of it depends largely on your individual expectations and how willing you are to strike out on your own (often without a decent map). It would be wrong to paint a picture of the island as some kind of hiker's nirvana. Although the scenery is invariably lush and the coastline wonderfully idyllic, a lack of well-kept paths and a dearth of accurate printed information have thwarted many a spontaneous hiker. Added to this is the commonwealth's compact size; the whole island is only marginally bigger than Yellowstone National Park in the US and supports a population of nearly 4 million, meaning true backcountry adventures are understandably limited.

The most popular hikes by far are in the emblematic El Yunque National Forest (p133), where a 23-mile network of largely paved trails has opened up the area to mass tourism. Hikes here are usually short and easily accessible, and there are plenty of ecominded tour operators happy

LET'S BE CAREFUL OUT THERE

Safety Guidelines for Diving

Before embarking on a scuba-diving, skin-diving or snorkeling trip, carefully consider the following points to ensure a safe and enjoyable experience:

- Possess a current diving certification card from a recognized scuba-diving instructional agency (if scuba diving).
- Be sure you are healthy and feel comfortable diving.
- Obtain reliable information about physical and environmental conditions at the dive site (eg from a reputable local dive operation).
- Be aware of local laws, regulations and etiquette about marine life and the environment.
- Dive only at sites within your realm of experience; if available, engage the services of a competent, professionally trained dive instructor or dive master.
- Be aware that underwater conditions vary significantly from one region, or even one site, to another. Seasonal changes can significantly alter any site and dive conditions. These differences influence the way divers dress for a dive and what diving techniques they use.
- Ask about the environmental characteristics that can affect your diving and how trained local divers deal with these considerations.

Safety Guidelines for Hiking

Before embarking on a hiking trip, consider the following points to ensure a safe and enjoyable experience:

- Pay any fees and obtain any permits required by local authorities.
- Be sure you are healthy and feel comfortable walking for a sustained period.
- Obtain reliable information about physical and environmental conditions along your intended route (eg from park authorities).
- Be aware of local laws, regulations and etiquette about wildlife and the environment.
- Walk only in regions, and on trails, within your realm of experience.
- Be aware that weather conditions and terrain vary significantly from one region, or even from one trail, to another. Seasonal changes can significantly alter any trail. These differences influence the way walkers dress and the equipment they carry.
- Ask before you set out about the environmental characteristics that can affect your walk and how experienced local walkers deal with these considerations.

to guide you through the main sights. The forest also contains Puerto Rico's only true backcountry adventure, the seven-hour trek to the top of El Toro (3522ft) and back.

Two other forest reserves with relatively well-marked paths and available maps are the dry forest in Bosque Estatal de Guánica (p201) and Bosque Estatal de Guajataca (p249), south of Isabela. The latter's 27-mile network of rough trails, including a side trip to the spooky Cueva del Viento, is one of the commonwealth's most extensive.

For more dramatic and isolated hikes you have to head toward the center of the island and the Reserva Forestal Toro Negro (p265) on Puerto Rico's misty rooftop. Be prepared to get your shoes dirty here as clouds often shroud the peaks and the trails are invariably damp and muddy. Typical of the numerous forest reserves scattered along the Ruta Panorámica – others include Maricao, Carite and Guilarte – Toro Negro is rarely staffed off-season and you'll be lucky to spot more than a handful of fellow hikers enjoying the views.

TRAIL DILEMMAS

With its lush mountains, numerous protected parks and highly developed infrastructure, Puerto Rico ought to be a country perfectly suited to hiking. Yet in reality, decent well-signposted trails are few and far between, and many of the commonwealth's carefully protected forest reserves are rarely utilized.

This paucity of backcountry information can be something of a shock to aspiring wilderness hikers fresh from bushwhacking their way through the Sierra Nevada or dragging their crampons across the European Alps. But, contrary to what the gushing tourist brochures would have you believe, Puerto Rico is no Yosemite. Nor are the Puerto Ricans – with some obvious exceptions – a nation of hikers. Instead, most islanders would rather drive their cars to the top of the nearest mountain than get their shoes dirty hiking up on a trail. Indeed, Punta de Cerro, the commonwealth's highest peak, has a paved road to within a mile of its summit while the poorly maintained hiking path that originates in Jayuya is barely used – except by the odd adventurous visitor.

The key, for confused hikers, is to manage your expectations and do some homework before setting out. In Puerto Rico finding the trailhead can often be more difficult than completing the trail itself.

Outside of El Yunque National Forest (p132), the island's two dozen or so forest reserves are invariably poorly staffed and lacking in any accurate trail maps. But, plan ahead and a little-used Eden is yours for the taking. Persistence is important. Try the Departamento de Recursos Naturales y Ambientales (DRNA; p87) in San Juan, ask around at the various adventure tour agencies and – best of all – question the more outdoor-minded locals. You'll be surprised by what you can find.

Several companies in San Juan can organize group trips to Toro Negro that incorporate hiking with various other activities. Acampa Nature Adventure Tours (p268) do a day trip that mixes hiking with zip-lining and climbing with a harness up a waterfall.

To make an organized trek in the company of serious Puerto Rican hikers, take a weekend hike through the Cañón de San Cristóbal (p262) near Barranquitas, where steep cliffs and spectacular waterfalls contribute to some of the island's most serendipitous scenery.

Some of the commonwealth's best DIY hiking exists on the eastern islands of Culebra (p161) and Vieques (p169).

The former has some excellent bushy scrambles to several isolated beaches while the latter has recently turned over extensive tracts of former military land to a wildlife refuge where barely touched trails are still being forged and discovered.

Getting to the island of Mona is an adventure in itself, and one that requires plenty of planning and organization. But once there you'll feel like you're hiking in another world. For more details on organized Mona trips, see p237.

Fondo de Mejoramiento (☎ 787-759-8366) runs day hikes covering the entire length of the island from east to west along the Cordillera Central (Central Mountains). The idea is to cover the whole Ruta Panorámica in different weekend segments over a period of three months (February to April). The 'Ruta' was actually designed by Luis Muñoz Marín in the 1950s primarily as a hiking route.

During specialized Fondo walks – all of which are confined to the paved road – a police escort is provided to ward off the famously zippy Puerto Rican traffic.

For information on hiking safety, see p77.

CYCLING & MOUNTAIN BIKING

On an island infested with cars, cycling is still in its infancy. But as the traffic gridlock proliferates, it can only be a matter of time before both locals and visitors rediscover the time-saving and health-extolling benefits of two-wheeled transportation.

The key to problem-free cycling adventures is to stay off the main roads. Toll roads such as Expressways 22, 52 and 53 are a definite no-no, as are the two main highways that constitute the island's peripheral ring road, Hwys 2 and 3. The Ruta Panorámica is another potential obstacle course that all but the most experienced cyclists would do well to avoid. While the steep twists and turns might look inviting to visiting Lance Armstrong wannabes, the endless blind corners and speeding Puerto Rican drivers with little or no cycling awareness add too much risk to an already dangerous route.

What you're left with are secondary roads, off-road trails and various designated cycling routes.

The best area for cycle touring is along the secondary roads on the southwest coast of the island, through the gently rolling hills of the coastal plain around Guánica, Cabo Rojo and Sabana Grande. There are enough roads and tracks here to schedule a two- or three-day trip, including roughshod trails around the Cabo Rojo lighthouse and in the Cabo Rojo Wildlife Refuge. This is the site of the International Cycling Competition held each May, and every Sunday morning local cycling club Las Piratas de Boquerón forms a colorful peloton when they hit the road for popular group rides. Reliable bike rental can be procured at the Wheel Shop (p212) in Cabo Rojo (El Pueblo).

Other excellent areas for cycling that have nearby rental facilities include the Isabela coast (p251), the island of Culebra (p161) and the specially designated bike trail in Piñones (p125) that bisects mangroves, beaches and coastal forest over a collection of paths and raised boardwalks. The jewel in the crown, however, has to be pristine Vieques, undoubtedly the best place in Puerto Rico to organize a creative cycling tour; see p175.

If you've got your own bike and transportation you can try out shorter trails in Bosque Estatal de Guánica (p201), Laguna Tortuguero (p243) and Bosque Estatal de Cambalache (p243). The Hacienda Carabali (p139) also rents bikes to tackle its narrow trails on the edge of the El Yunque rainforest.

For more general information, contact the **Puerto Rican Cycling Federation** (☎ 787-721-7185) or Hot Dog Cycling (p105) in Isla Verde. These bodies know the touring and trail-riding scenes on the island and they can point you to an expanding network of safe bike routes.

For a varied ride around some of Puerto Rico's safest and most cycle-friendly terrain see p28.

GOLF

Many travelers come to Puerto Rico and never get past the golf links. There's plenty to keep them busy, with 23 expansive courses (eight of them championship) caressed by warm ocean breezes and framed by stunning ocean vistas. Everyone from President Dwight Eisenhower to Laurence Rockefeller have converged here to swing their nine irons in what golfing fanatics have come to call the 'Scotland of the Caribbean.'

Dorado, on the north coast, is the operations center for aficionados (see p240). It has five courses in as many miles, including the top links on the island, the so-called 'East Course' designed by Robert Trent Jones at the now fallow Hyatt Dorado Beach Resort. This 18-hole golfing extravaganza features breathtaking sea views and some of the most challenging drives in the Caribbean, including the legendary 4th hole deemed by Jack Nicklaus to be one of the 10 toughest in the world.

Puerto Rico's main island (population 3.9 million) is roughly the same size as Yellowstone National Park in the US, which has a human population of approximately 300.

For articles, reviews and good general information about golf on the island, type 'Puerto Rico' into the search engine of www.worldgolf.com.

RESPONSIBLE HIKING

To help preserve the ecology and beauty of Puerto Rico, consider the following tips when hiking.

Rubbish

- Carry out *all* your rubbish. Don't overlook easily forgotten items, such as tin foil, orange peel, cigarette butts and plastic wrappers. Empty packaging should be stored in a dedicated rubbish bag. Make an effort to carry out rubbish left by others.

- Never bury your rubbish: digging disturbs soil and ground cover and encourages erosion. Buried rubbish will likely be dug up by animals, who may be injured or poisoned by it. It may also take years to decompose.

- Minimize waste by taking minimal packaging and no more food than you will need. Take reusable containers or stuff sacks.

- Sanitary napkins, tampons, condoms and toilet paper should be carried out despite the inconvenience. They burn and decompose poorly.

Human Waste Disposal

- Contamination of water sources by human faeces can lead to the transmission of all sorts of nasties. Where there is a toilet, please use it. Where there is none, bury your waste. Dig a small hole that's 6in deep and at least 320ft from any watercourse. Cover the waste with soil and a rock. In snow, dig down to the soil.

- Ensure that these guidelines are applied to a portable toilet tent if one is being used by a large hiking party. Encourage all party members, including porters, to use the site.

Washing

- Don't use detergents or toothpaste in or near watercourses, even if they are biodegradable.

- For personal washing, use biodegradable soap and a water container (or even a lightweight, portable basin) at least 160ft away from the watercourse. Disperse the waste water widely to allow the soil to filter it fully.

- Wash cooking utensils 160ft from watercourses using a scourer, sand or snow instead of detergent.

Erosion

- Hillsides and mountain slopes, especially at high altitudes, are prone to erosion. Stick to existing trails and avoid short cuts.

Gary Player designed the 18-hole course at the exclusive Palmas del Mar Resort (p148), on the east end of the island, where holes 11 to 15 have been called the 'toughest five successive holes in the Caribbean.' Also on the east end of the island, the precipitous Arthur Hill–designed course at El Conquistador Resort & Golden Door Spa (p146) logs over 200ft in elevation changes and sits perched atop a 300ft cliff overlooking the Atlantic.

Nearby, the two courses at the Río Mar Beach Resort & Country Club (p140), designed by Greg Norman and Tom and George Fazio, sport bunkers and water features plus the occasional iguana.

Golf courses thin out as you head south and west, though there are a couple of secluded links for serious addicts. The Club Deportivo de Oeste (p214) at Cabo Rojo (El Pueblo) is a Jack Bender–designed course that opened as a nine-hole in 1965, but was expanded to an 18-hole in 2003. More charming is the Punta Borinquen course (p254) near the former Ramey base close

- If a well-used trail passes through a mud patch, walk through the mud so as not to increase the size of the patch.
- Avoid removing the plant life that keeps topsoils in place.

Fires & Low-Impact Cooking

- Don't depend on open fires for cooking. The cutting of wood for fires in popular hiking areas can cause rapid deforestation. Cook on a lightweight kerosene, alcohol or Shellite (white gas) stove and avoid those powered by disposable butane gas canisters.
- If you patronize local accommodations, select those places that do not use wood fires to heat water or cook food.
- Fires may be acceptable below the tree line in areas that get very few visitors. If you light a fire, use an existing fireplace. Don't surround fires with rocks. Use only dead, fallen wood. Remember the adage 'the bigger the fool, the bigger the fire.' Use minimal wood, just what you need for cooking. In huts, leave wood for the next person.
- Ensure that you fully extinguish a fire after use. Spread the embers and flood them with water.

Wildlife Conservation

- Do not engage in or encourage hunting. It is illegal in all parks and reserves. On an island where the only indigenous land mammals are bats you're better off leaving your hunting ambitions at home.
- Don't buy items made from endangered species.
- Don't attempt to exterminate animals in huts. In wild places, they are likely to be protected native animals.
- Discourage the presence of wildlife by not leaving food scraps behind you. Place gear out of reach and tie packs to rafters or trees.
- Do not feed the wildlife as this can lead to animals becoming dependent on hand-outs, to unbalanced populations and to diseases.

Camping & Walking on Private Property

- Always seek permission to camp from landowners.
- Public access to private property without permission is acceptable where public land is otherwise inaccessible, so long as safety and conservation regulations are observed.

to Aguadilla, which was once a favorite stomping ground of US president Dwight Eisenhower.

HORSEBACK RIDING

In days of yore, horses were the primary means of transportation in mountainous Puerto Rico and every self-respecting *jíbaro* had a decent mount on which to travel from village to village. But, with the advent of the motorcar and the transformation of *jíbaros* into upwardly mobile city dwellers, the opportunities for off-road equestrian adventures became a little more limited. If you're still adamant to recapture that centuries-old tradition of saddle and stirrups, a handful of horseback-riding outfits spread around the island can replicate some memorable journeys.

Palmas del Mar Resort (p148) in Humacao has the island's largest equestrian facility, Rancho Buena Vista, which serves the public with more than

40 horses. Here you will find instruction, trail rides and schooled hunters for jumping. Riders should also check out Tropical Trail Rides (p251) in Isabela and Hacienda Carabaldi (p139) in Mameyes, near Luquillo, at the east end of the island. There are also wilder, more off-the-beaten-track options in Vieques (p174). Horses at these stables will cost you around $30 an hour.

The Paso Fino horse has a smooth gait and sturdy endurance. It was originally bred by Spanish landowners in Puerto Rico and Columbia to work on the plantations.

BIRD-WATCHING

Though land mammals may be rare in Puerto Rico, the exotic birdlife is refreshingly abundant with the island supporting 266 species, 11 of them endemic and 10 of them endangered, including the rarely seen Puerto Rican parrot. The most obvious place for budding ornithologists to brandish their binoculars is El Yunque National Forest, a tree-carpeted swathe of verdant tropical foliage that is both easily accessible and situated close to the capital. The El Portal Visitor's Center (p132) on Hwy 191 can divulge some good basic information on the local birdlife, though for a more detailed insight you can rummage through the bookstores of San Juan for more specialist bird literature.

The island's richest species diversity can be spied in the Cabo Rojo area, particularly around Las Salinas salt flats, where migratory birds from as far away as Canada populate a unique and highly varied ecosystem. Call in at the Centro Interpretativos Las Salinas de Cabo Rojo (p212) to speak to informed local experts.

San Juan

Take note New York! Modern America started here. Well, almost. Established in 1521, San Juan is the second-oldest European-founded settlement in the Americas (after Santo Domingo) and the oldest under US jurisdiction. Shoehorned onto a tiny islet that guards the entrance to San Juan harbor, the atmospheric 'Old City' juxtaposes historical authenticity with pulsating modern energy in a seven-square-block grid of streets that was inaugurated almost a century before the *Mayflower* laid anchor in present day Massachusetts. Surreal sounds and exotic sights resonate everywhere. A stabbing salsa stanza in sonorous Calle San Sebastián, timid cats scurrying under winking lanterns in shady Plaza San José, and the omnipresent roar of Atlantic breakers battling mercilessly with the sturdy 500-year-old fortifications of El Morro.

Beyond its timeworn 15ft-thick walls, San Juan is far more than a dizzying collection of well-polished colonial artifacts. To get the full take on Puerto Rico's capricious capital, visitors must first run the gamut of its distinct but ever-evolving neighborhoods. There's seen-it-all Condado where Cuba's 24-hour gambling party got washed up in the early 1960s; tranquil Ocean Park with its gated villas and strategically located B&Bs; gritty Santurce relaunched with art galleries after a two-decade-long depression; and swanky Isla Verde awash with luxurious resort hotels and kitschy casinos.

Choked by bumper-to-bumper traffic and inundated with nearly five million tourists annually, parts of San Juan can leave you wondering if you took a wrong turn at Miami airport in Florida. But the confusion rarely lingers. Cultural borrowing has long been this city's pragmatic hallmark. For every gleaming office block, you'll also stumble upon a colorful Spanish fiesta, an African religious ritual, a delicate native woodcarving and architecture that could easily have been ripped out of Seville, Cartagena, Buenos Aires, or even Paris.

HIGHLIGHTS

- Savoring a night of colonial luxury in the exquisite **Gran Hotel El Convento** (p109)
- Rekindling the spirit of salsa at the culture defining **Nuyorican Café** (p119)
- Enjoying the prized tranquility of **Ocean Park Beach** (p103)
- Getting a feel for the national sporting passion during a hotly contested game of baseball at the **Hiram Bithorn Stadium** (p122)
- Exploring bike paths, beaches, ramshackle restaurants and precarious coastal ecology in down-to-earth **Piñones** (p124)

- POPULATION: 1.6 MILLION

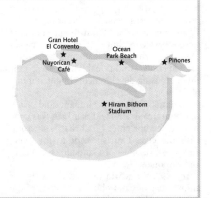

HISTORY

It's hard to believe that San Juan was once a deserted spit of land dominated only by dramatic headlands and strong trade winds, but such was the picture when the Spaniards first arrived with their colonization plans in the early 1500s.

Unable to stave off constant Indian attacks or mosquito-borne malaria in the lower lands, they retreated to the rocky outcrop in 1521 and christened it Puerto Rico ('Rich Port'). (A Spanish cartographer accidentally transposed San Juan Bautista – what Spaniards called the island – with 'Puerto Rico' on some maps a few years later, and the name change stuck permanently.)

The gigantic fortress of El Morro, with its 140ft-high ramparts, quickly rose above the ocean cliffs.

The Catholic Church arrived en masse to build a church, a convent and a cathedral. For the next three centuries, San Juan was the primary military and legislative outpost of the Spanish empire in the Caribbean and Central America. But economically it stagnated, unable to prosper from the smuggling that was pervasive elsewhere on the island.

That all changed after the Spanish-American War of 1898. The US annexed the island as a 'territory' and designated San Juan as the primary port. Agricultural goods such as sugar, tobacco and coffee flowed into the city. *Jíbaros* (country people) flocked to the shipping terminals for work and old villages like Río Piedras were swallowed up.

The unchecked growth surge was a nightmare for city planners, who struggled to provide services, roads and housing. By the 1980s, franchises of US fast-food restaurants were everywhere, but there were few places to get a gourmet meal featuring the island's *comida criolla* (traditional Puerto Rican cuisine). Housing developments blighted much of the area.

Unemployment was rampant, and crime was high. Ironically, Old San Juan was considered the epicenter of all that was wrong with the city. Tourists kept to the overdeveloped beaches of Condado, Isla Verde and Miramar.

In 1992, the world marked the 500-year anniversary of Columbus' 'discovery' of the Americas. That celebration gave city leaders the impetus needed to focus on the historic restoration of Old San Juan. The energy and finesse that characterized that effort waned slightly as the decade ended. However, the new century has brought several successful urban regeneration projects such as the superefficient Tren Urbano (metro) that opened in 2005, a space-age convention center situated in the neighborhood of Miramar and a clutch of redeveloped hotels in revitalized Condado.

CLIMATE

San Juan is blessed with strong trade winds that keep mosquitoes at bay and somewhat lessen the sun's vigor.

In the summer months (June to September), the city gets increasingly hot and humid, averaging in the high 80s. Rains come from late September through early November. San Juan isn't hit as hard as the El Yunque area to the east, but gets a good amount of overflow.

December through May the weather is at its best – highs in the mid-80s, lows in the high 70s (sometimes those trade winds will have you reaching for a sweater at night) with little humidity.

ORIENTATION

Starting at the westernmost tip of the city and working east toward the Aeropuerto Internacional de Luis Muñoz Marín (LMM; Map pp86–7), you've got Old San Juan, the tourist center and most visually appealing part of town.

Following the coast, Condado is next, flashy and full of big buildings and hotels along Av Ashford.

Miramar and Santurce, to the west and southeast of Condado, respectively, and set back from the beach, are filled with a mix of middle- and working-class families.

Ocean Park is a private community (with gates) lying along the water between Condado and Isla Verde; its big street is Av McLeary. The final stop in the city is Isla Verde (although, technically speaking, it is in Carolina, a suburb of San Juan). Av Isla Verde is a long stretch of hotels and casinos along a narrow but pretty white beach. Its drawback is the proximity of the airport – large jets thunder overhead every 20 minutes or so for most of the day.

Hato Rey is the name of the business district of high-rise banks and offices that flanks Av Ponce de León, south of Santurce. Further south, beyond Hato Rey, is Río Piedras, home to the largest campus of the Universidad de Puerto Rico (UPR).

Maps

Travelers will find tourist maps of Old San Juan, Condado and Isla Verde readily available through the tourist information offices run by the Puerto Rico Tourism Company (p88). The standard complimentary map can also be found online at www.travelmaps.com.

If you are driving or want a more complete view of the city, Rand McNally publishes foldout maps of San Juan/Puerto Rico that include a detailed overview of the metro area.

This map is widely available from most bookstores and drugstores in the city's tourist zones for about $5. See p281 for maps covering other island destinations.

Once you have a map, study it with someone who has good local knowledge

regarding traffic jams, damaged roads and crime (p88).

INFORMATION
Bookstores

Bell, Book & Candle (Map pp98-9; ☎ 787-728-5000; 102 Av José de Diego, Condado) Pulls in the vacation crowd and offers a wide range of English titles.

Bookworm (Map pp98-9; ☎ 787-722-3344; 1129 Av Ashford, Condado) Gay literature in Spanish and English as well as mainstream picks. Very helpful and friendly staff.

Librería Thekes (Map pp86-7; ☎ 787-765-1539; Plaza Las Américas, 525 Av FD Roosevelt, Hato Rey) Novels, travel books, bios, thrillers and magazines in both English and Spanish.

Emergency

You may find that the telephone directory and tourist publications list nonfunctioning local numbers for emergency services. In *any* kind of emergency, call ☎ 911.

SAN JUAN NEIGHBORHOODS

Metro San Juan, in common with many great cities, is an amalgamation of its neighborhoods, with each area exhibiting its own vicissitudes, atmosphere and charms. Here's a quick rundown of what to expect.

- **Viejo San Juan** The soul of the city and a gastronome's delight, Old San Juan's seven-square-block Unesco World Heritage site is packed with priceless historical relics and equally pricey restaurants.

- **Puerta de Tierra** This thin slither of land that links Old San Juan with the rest of the city is a strange amalgam of tatty housing projects, salubrious parks and one of the best municipal beaches on the island.

- **El Condado** San Juan's original resort strip has recently transformed itself from a tacky tourist zone into a revitalized urban neighborhood replete with designer shops and salubrious parks.

- **Ocean Park** An attractive beachside residential community punctuated by classy B&Bs and a quiet, gay-friendly stretch of beach.

- **Miramar** A leafy residential quarter of eclectic middle-class houses and plush lakeside condos that showcases San Juan's new state-of-the-art convention center.

- **Santurce** The once vital city center suffered from dilapidation in the '80s and '90s, but a fine arts center, myriad nightclubs, and a couple of well-appointed galleries have placed it back in the urban reckoning.

- **Hato Rey** San Juan's mini Wall Street is a dense cluster of glass tower blocks and is home to the island's most prestigious ballpark and the Caribbean's largest shopping mall.

- **Río Piedras** The low-rise academic quarter is, not surprisingly, replete with cheap shops, a thriving market and an exotic botanical garden.

- **Isla Verde** The city's premier hotel strip plays host to a mishmash of craning condo towers and swanky resorts that are big on luxury but short on authenticity.

SAN JUAN

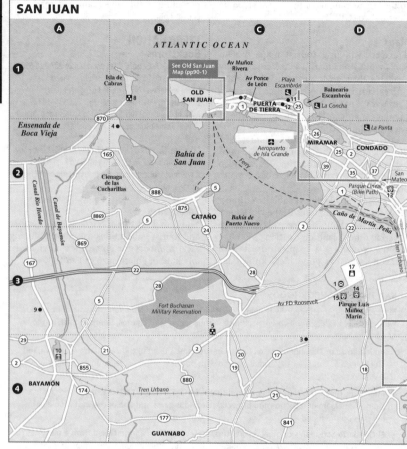

Fire (☎ 787-722-1120, 343-2330)
Hurricane warnings (☎ 787-253-4586)
Isla Verde police (☎ 787-449-9320)
Medical emergencies (☎ 787-754-2550)
Rape crisis hotline (☎ 877-641-2004, 800-981-5721, 787-765-2285)
Río Piedras police (☎ 787-765-6439)
Tourist zone police (☎ 911, 787-726-7020; ⊗ 24hr)
English spoken.

Internet Access

Cybernet Café Condado (Map pp98-9; ☎ 787-724-4033; 1128 Av Ashford; ⊗ 9am-11pm; per hr $5-6); Isla Verde (Map p101; ☎ 787-791-3138; 5980 Av Isla Verde; ⊗ 9am-10:30pm; per hr $5-6)
Diner's Internet (Map pp90-1; ☎ 787-724-6276; 311 Tetuán, Old San Juan)

Internet@active (Map pp90-1; ☎ 787-289-0345; JA Corretjer; per 15min $4)

Laundry

La Lavandería (Map pp90-1; ☎ 787-717-8585; 201 Sol near Cruz, Old San Juan) This is arguably the laundromat that has the best views in town. Service washes are available.
Laundry Condado Cleaners (Map pp98-9; ☎ 787-721-9254; 63 Calle Condado) Promises a fast turnaround, and delivers too.

Medical Services

Ashford Memorial Community Hospital (Map pp98-9; ☎ 787-721-2160; 1451 Av Ashford) This is probably the best-equipped and most convenient hospital for travelers to visit.

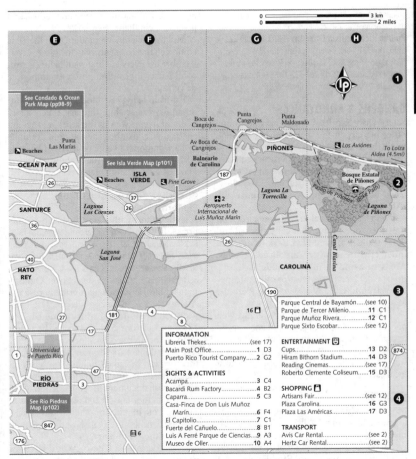

| 0 | 3 km |
| 0 | 2 miles |

INFORMATION
Librería Thekes....................(see 17)
Main Post Office.........................**1** D3
Puerto Rico Tourist Company.....**2** G2

SIGHTS & ACTIVITIES
Acampa..**3** C4
Bacardi Rum Factory....................**4** B2
Caparra...**5** C3
Casa-Finca de Don Luis Muñoz
Marín.......................................**6** F4
El Capitolio...................................**7** C1
Fuerte del Cañuelo.......................**8** B1
Luis A Ferré Parque de Ciencias...**9** A3
Museo de Oller...........................**10** A4

Parque Central de Bayamón.....(see 10)
Parque de Tercer Milenio...........**11** C1
Parque Muñoz Rivera................**12** C1
Parque Sixto Escobar.............(see 12)

ENTERTAINMENT
Cups..**13** D2
Hiram Bithorn Stadium...............**14** D3
Reading Cinemas....................(see 17)
Roberto Clemente Coliseum......**15** D3

SHOPPING
Artisans Fair...........................(see 12)
Plaza Carolina............................**16** G3
Plaza Las Américas.....................**17** D3

TRANSPORT
Avis Car Rental.......................(see 2)
Hertz Car Rental....................(see 2)

Walgreens Old San Juan (Map pp90-1; ☎ 787-722-6690; cnr Cruz & San Francisco); Condado (Map pp98-9; ☎ 787-725-1510; 1130 Av Ashford; ⏰ 24hr) US drugstore chains including Walgreens are all over the city.

Money
Banco Popular LMM airport (☎ 787-791-0326; Terminal C); Old San Juan (Map pp90-1; ☎ 787-725-2635; cnr Tetuán & San Justo) Near the cruise ship piers and Paseo de la Princesa; Condado (Map pp98-9; Av Ashford); Isla Verde (Map p101; Av Isla Verde) Charges only 1% commission to cash traveler's checks.

Post
Greater San Juan has about 20 post offices.
Main Post Office (Map pp86-7; ☎ 787-767-2890; 585 Av FD Roosevelt, Hato Rey; ⏰ 7:30am-4:30pm Mon-Fri, 8:30am-noon Sat) General delivery mail comes here.

Old San Juan Post Office (Map pp90-1; ☎ 787-723-1281; 100 Paseo de Colón; ⏰ 8am-4pm Mon-Fri, 8am-noon Sat) The one likely to be most convenient for travelers.

Tourist Information
Puerto Rico Tourism Company (PRTC) distributes information in English and Spanish at two venues in San Juan, the LMM airport and La Casita in Old San Juan.

At the airport, stop at the information counter between Terminals B and C or visit the PRTC's desk on the lower (arrivals) areas of Terminals B and C.

Departamento de Recursos Naturales y Ambientales (DRNA; Department of Natural Resources; Map p102; ☎ 787-999-2200; www.drna.gobierno.pr in Spanish; Rte 8838 Km 6.3, Sector El Cinco, Río Piedras) For information on camping, including reservations and permits, contact this department or visit its office.

Puerto Rico Tourism Company (PRTC; ☎ 800-223-6530, 787-721-2400; www.prtourism.com) LMM airport (Map pp86-7; ☎ 787-791-1014; ⏱ 9am-5:30pm); Old San Juan (Map pp90-1; ☎ 787-722-1709; La Casita, Calle Comercio & Plaza de la Darsena near Pier 1)

DANGERS & ANNOYANCES

Safety-wise, San Juan is comparable to any other big city in the mainland US. Though you'll hear stories of robberies, drugs and carjackings, the worst most visitors will face is tripping up over an uneven paving stone on the way back from the local bar. Take all the usual precautions and you'll minimize any risk of trouble.

Don't leave your belongings unguarded on the beach, don't leave your car unlocked and don't wander around after dark in deserted inner-city areas or on unpoliced beaches. Areas to avoid at night include La Perla, Puerta de Tierra, parts of Santurce (especially around Calle Loíza) and the Plaza del Mercado in Río Piedras.

Old San Juan is relatively safe and well policed. However, visitors are not encouraged to enter the picturesque yet poverty-stricken enclave of La Perla (p96) just outside the north wall at any time of day or night without a local escort.

SIGHTS

Most of San Juan's major attractions, including museums and art galleries, are in Old San Juan.

There are a few sights worth visiting in Condado, Santurce and Río Piedras, but schedule serious time for the old town. Be aware that most museums are closed on Mondays.

Old San Juan

Old San Juan is a colorful kaleidoscope of life, music, legend and history and would stand out like a flashing beacon in any country, let alone one as small as Puerto Rico.

Somnolent secrets and beautiful surprises await everywhere. From the blue-toned cobblestoned streets of Calle San Sebastián, to the cutting-edge gastronomic artistry of SoFo, you could spend weeks, even months, here and still only get the smallest taste.

Add to this the quarter's sensuous yet subtle mood swings: tranquil at dawn, languid during the midday heat, romantic at dusk and positively ebullient after dark.

Mixing ancient with modern, San Juan has embraced the 21st century in the same way as it embraced every era that went before – with confidence, innovation and a dynamic joie de vivre.

Far from being just another drop off point on a busy cruise ship itinerary, this is a city that still lives: listen to the creaking rocking chairs on Calle de Sol, the clatter of dominos in La Bombonera Café, or the spontaneous African drumming ritual echoing around Plaza de Armas. Pure magic.

COLONIAL FORTS & BUILDINGS
El Morro

A six-level fort with a gray, castellated lighthouse, **El Morro** (Fuerte San Felipe del Morro; San Felipe Fort; Map pp90-1; ☎ 787-729-6960; www.nps.gov/saju/morro .html; adult/child $3/free; ⏱ 9am-5pm Jun-Nov, 9am-6pm Dec-May, free tours at 10am & 2pm in Spanish, 11am & 3pm in English) juts aggressively over Old San Juan's bold headlands, glowering across the Atlantic at would-be conquerors. The 140ft walls (some up to 15ft thick) date back to 1539, and El Morro is said to be the oldest Spanish fort in the New World.

The National Park Service (NPS) maintains this fort and the small military museum on the premises. Displays and videos in Spanish and English document the construction of the fort, which took almost 200 years, as well as El Morro's role in rebuffing the various attacks on the island by the British and the Dutch, and later the US military.

It was declared a Unesco World Heritage site in 1983. The lighthouse on the 6th floor is the island's oldest light station still in use today (although the tower itself dates from 1906).

If you do not join one of the free guided tours, at least try to make the climb up the ramparts to the sentries' walks along the **Sta Barbara Bastion** and **Austria Half-Bastion** for the views of the sea, the bay, Old San Juan, modern San Juan, El Yunque and the island's mountainous spine.

On weekends, the fields leading up to the fort are alive with picnickers, lovers and kite flyers. The scene becomes a kind of impromptu festival with food vendors' carts on the perimeter.

You also gain entry to both El Morro and Fuerte San Cristóbal for $5.

SAN JUAN IN...

Two Days
Find a midrange hotel or apartment in Old San Juan. Explore the historical sights of the colonial quarter and dine along **Calle Fortaleza** (p116) before heading to **La Rumba** (p120) or **Nuyorican Café** (p119) after dark for mojitos and salsa music. Wander over to **Condado** (p98) on day two for some solitary sunbathing or beachside water sports.

Four Days
Add a gallery crawl around **Old San Juan** (opposite) and throw in a visit to the Bayamón **Bacardí Rum Factory** (p127). Find an ecotour company to run you out to **El Yunque** (p132) for a day. Finally, scour the nightclubs of the big hotels in **Condado** (p110) and **Isla Verde** (p111), or dine in one of the beautiful restaurants at **Gran Hotel El Convento** (p109).

One Week
Head into the 'burbs for Santurce's two new **art museums** (p100) or head further south to the **Museo de Oller** (p129) in Río Piedras. Rent a bike and cycle out to **Piñones** (p124). Hit the beach kiosks for lunch and take in the Friday night *bomba* performances in **Café Búho** (p126). Round it up by hiring some beach toys on Playa Isla Verde or booking a surf lesson on **Playa Escambrón** (p104).

Fuerte San Cristóbal

San Juan's second major fort is **Fuerte San Cristóbal** (San Cristóbal Fort; Map pp90-1; ☎ 787-729-6777; www.nps .gov/saju/sancristobal.html; adult/child $3/free; ☑ 9am-5pm Jun-Nov, 9am-6pm Dec-May), one of the largest military installations the Spanish built in the Americas. In its prime, San Cristóbal covered 27 acres with a maze of six interconnected forts protecting a central core with 150ft walls, moats, booby-trapped bridges and tunnels.

The fort was constructed to defend Old San Juan against land attacks from the east via Puerta de Tierra. The imaginative design came from the famous Irish mercenary Alejandro O'Reilly and his compatriot Thomas O'Daly (hired by Spain). Construction began in 1634 in response to an attack by the Dutch a decade previously, though the main period of enlargement occurred between 1765 and 1783. Seven acres were lopped off the fort in 1897 to ease congestion in the Old Town, and the following year the Spanish marked Puerto Rico's entry into the Spanish-American War by firing at the battleship USS *Yale* from its cannon battery. The fort became a National Historic site in 1949 and a Unesco World Heritage site in 1983. Facilities include a fascinating museum, a store, military archives, a reproduction of a soldier's barracks and prime city views. There are also regular historical reenactments. You can gain entry to both Fuerti San Cristóbal and El Morro for $5.

La Fortaleza

A steep climb along Recinto Oeste takes you to the top of the city wall and the guarded iron gates of **La Fortaleza** (The Fortress; Map pp90-1; ☎ 787-721-7000 ext 2211 or 2358; admission free; ☑ 9am-3:30pm Mon-Fri). Also known as El Palacio de Santa Catalina, this imposing building is the oldest executive mansion in continuous use in the western hemisphere, dating from 1533. Once the original fortress for the young colony, La Fortaleza eventually yielded its military pre-eminence to the city's newer and larger forts, and was remodeled and expanded to domicile island governors for more than three centuries. You can join a guided tour that includes the mansion's Moorish gardens, the dungeon and the chapel. Free guided tours generally run on weekdays except holidays; tours in English leave on the hour, in Spanish on the half-hour. Call in advance to make sure the grounds are not closed for a government function.

El Arsenal

On the point of land called La Puntilla is a low, gray fortress with a Romanesque proscenium entrance. This is **El Arsenal** (The Arsenal; Map pp90-1; ☎ 787-724-1877, 787-724-5949; admission free; ☑ 8:30am-4pm Mon-Fri), a former Spanish naval station that was the last place to house Spanish military forces after the US victory in the Spanish-American War. Today, the arsenal is home to the fine- and decorative-arts divisions of

OLD SAN JUAN

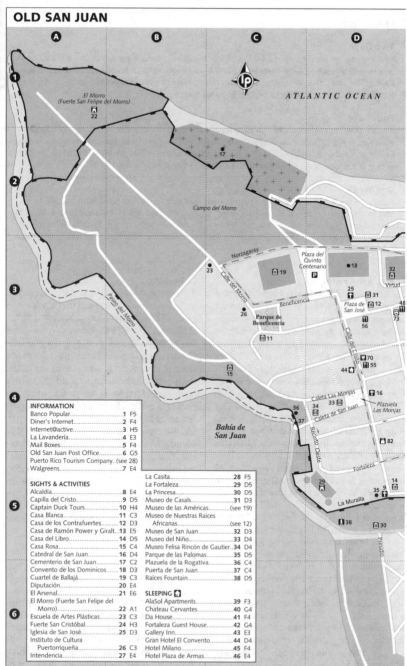

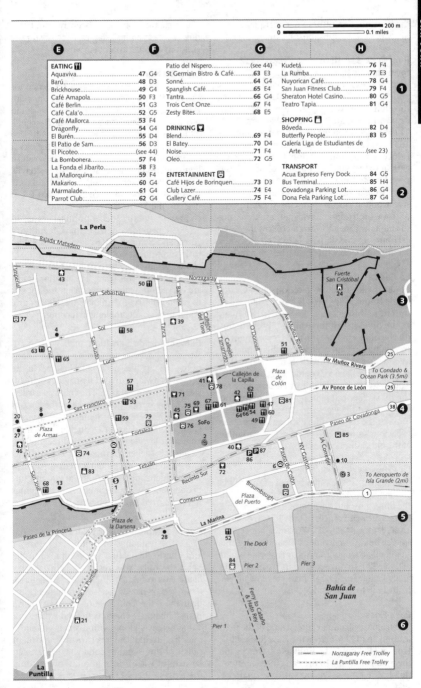

EATING 🍴
Aquaviva......................**47** G4
Barú............................**48** D3
Brickhouse..................**49** G4
Café Amapola..............**50** F3
Café Berlín..................**51** G3
Café Cala'o..................**52** G5
Café Mallorca..............**53** F4
Dragonfly....................**54** G4
El Burén.......................**55** D4
El Patio de Sam............**56** D3
El Picoteo..................(see 44)
La Bombonera.............**57** F4
La Fonda el Jíbarito......**58** F3
La Mallorquina.............**59** G4
Makarios.....................**60** G4
Marmalade..................**61** G4
Parrot Club..................**62** G4

Patio del Níspero........(see 44)
St Germain Bistro & Café...**63** E3
Sonné..........................**64** G4
Spanglish Café.............**65** E4
Tantra..........................**66** G4
Trois Cent Onze............**67** F4
Zesty Bites...................**68** E5

DRINKING 🍷
Blend............................**69** F4
El Batey........................**70** D4
Noise............................**71** F4
Oleo.............................**72** G5

ENTERTAINMENT 🎭
Café Hijos de Borinquen...**73** D3
Club Lazer....................**74** E4
Gallery Café..................**75** F4

Kudetá.........................**76** F4
La Rumba......................**77** E3
Nuyorican Café.............**78** G4
San Juan Fitness Club....**79** F4
Sheraton Hotel Casino....**80** G5
Teatro Tapia..................**81** F4

SHOPPING 🛍
Bóveda........................**82** D4
Butterfly People............**83** E5
Galería Liga de Estudiantes de
  Arte.........................(see 23)

TRANSPORT
Acua Expreso Ferry Dock...**84** G5
Bus Terminal.................**85** H4
Covadonga Parking Lot....**86** D4
Dona Fela Parking Lot.....**87** G4

the Instituto de Cultura Puertorriqueña, and hosts periodic exhibitions in three galleries.

Puerta de San Juan

Spanish ships once anchored in the cove just off these ramparts to unload colonists and supplies, all of which entered the city through a tall red portal known as Puerta de San Juan (San Juan Gate; Map pp90–1). This tunnel through the wall dates from the 1630s. It marks the end of the Paseo de la Princesa, and stands as one of three remaining gates into the old city (the others lead into the cemetery and the enclave of La Perla). Once there were a total of five gates, and the massive wooden doors were closed each night to thwart intruders. Turn right after passing through the gate and you can follow the **Paseo del Morro** northwest, paralleling the city walls for approximately three-quarters of a mile.

La Casita

Looking like a yellow gatehouse, La Casita (Little House; Map pp90–1) greets visitors near the cruise ship docks in 'lower' Old San Juan, in the outskirts of the walled city that rises on the hill to the north. The Department of Agriculture & Commerce built this miniature neoclassical structure with its red-tiled roof in 1937 to serve the needs of the burgeoning port. Today, La Casita is the information center for the PRTC (see p88). Stop here for maps and to check out the weekend craft market. Also look for the food vendors selling icy *piraguas* (delicious snow cones) or taste the local coffee at the old-fashioned hexagonal stand.

La Princesa

Poised against the outside wall of the city is La Princesa (Map pp90–1). Once a harsh jail, the long, gray and white stone structure now houses the main offices of the PRTC (p88) and an **art gallery** (☎ 787-721-2400; admission free; ⏰ 9am-4pm Mon-Fri) with welcome air-conditioning and frequently changing shows by first-rate island artists. The bronze statue in front depicts Doña Felisa Gautier, San Juan's revered mayor from 1946 to 1968 (see opposite).

Casa Rosa

The tropical villa in the foreground of the field leading up to El Morro is the Casa Rosa (Pink House; Map pp90–1). Built as a barracks for the Spanish militia in the early 19th century, this house long served as officers' quarters.

The structure has since been restored and now serves as a plush day-care facility for the children of government employees.

Casa Blanca

First constructed in 1521 as a residence for Puerto Rico's pioneering governor, Juan Ponce de León (who died before he could move in), the **Casa Blanca** (White House; Map pp90–1; ☎ 787-724-4102; adult/child $2/1; ⏰ 9am-noon & 1-4:30pm Tue-Sun, guided tours Tue-Fri by appointment) is the oldest continuously occupied house in the western hemisphere. For the first 250 years after its construction it served as the ancestral home for the de León family. In 1779 it was taken over by the Spanish military, then with the change of Puerto Rico's political status in 1898, it provided a base for US military commanders until 1966. Today it is a historic monument containing a museum, secluded grounds, a chain of fountains and an Alhambra-style courtyard. The interior rooms are decked out with artifacts from the 16th to the 20th century. An animated guide can give you a theatrical complementary tour.

Cementerio de San Juan

Sitting just outside the northern fortifications of the old city, the neoclassical chapel in the cemetery (Map pp90–1) provides a focal point among the graves. The colony's earliest citizens are buried here, as well as the famous Puerto Rican freedom fighter Pedro Albizu-Campos. This Harvard-educated chemical engineer, lawyer and politician led the agricultural workers' strikes in 1934 and was at the forefront of the movement for Puerto Rican independence until his arrest and imprisonment in 1936. A number of muggings have occurred here, so be careful.

Casa de Ramón Power y Giralt

Once the residence of a political reformer and Puerto Rico's first representative to the Spanish court, this restored 18th-century **house** (Map pp90–1; ☎ 787-722-5882; 155 Tetuán; admission free; ⏰ 9am-5pm Tue-Sat) is now the headquarters of the Conservation Trust of Puerto Rico. The house contains limited exhibits of Taíno artifacts along with a small gift shop, and highlights the precarious nature of much of the island's ecology. The staff can be helpful with information about visiting the trust's other island properties.

TOP HISTORICAL HITS

- Fuerte San Cristóbal (p89)
- Casa Blanca (p92)
- Catedral de San Juan (p94)
- Caparra (p129)
- Casa-Finca de Don Luis Muñoz Marín (p102)

Museo de Nuestras Raices Africanas

Housed in the 18th-century **Casa de los Contra-fuertes** (House of Buttresses) on the Plaza de San José, the compact **museum** (Museum of Our African Roots; Map pp90-1; admission $2; 8:30am-4:30pm Tue-Sat) displays masks, sculptures, musical instruments, documents and prints that highlight Puerto Rico's connections to West Africa. One exhibit recreates living conditions in a slave ship.

MUSEUMS
Instituto de Cultura Puertorriqueña

Once a home for the poor, this buff building with green trim, near the intersection with Calle Norzagaray, houses the executive offices of this **institute** (Institute of Puerto Rican Culture; Map pp90-1; 787-724-0700; www.icp.gobierno.pr; Calle del Morro; admission free; 9:30am-5pm Tue-Sun). The agency has been shepherding the flowering of the arts and cultural pride on the island since the 1950s. Its plazas, sheltered from the tourist traffic in the streets outside, are pleasantly tranquil.

Cuartel de Ballajá & Museo de las Américas

Built in 1854 as a military barracks, the **cuartel** (Map pp90-1; off Norzagaray) is a three-story edifice with large gates on two ends, ample balconies, a series of arches and a protected central courtyard that served as a plaza and covers a reservoir. It was the last and largest building constructed by the Spaniards in the New World. Facilities included officer quarters, warehouses, kitchens, dining rooms, prison cells and stables. Now its 2nd floor holds the **Museo de las Américas** (Museum of the Americas; 787-724-5052; admission free; 10am-4pm Tue-Fri, 11am-5pm Sat & Sun, guided tours 10:30am, 11:30am, 12:30pm & 2pm Tue-Fri) which gives an overview of cultural development in the New World. It features changing exhibitions and Caribbean and European American art, most notably an impressive *santos* (religious statuettes) collection. Hours for both the barracks and the museum are the same.

Museo de San Juan

Located in a Spanish colonial building at the corner of Calle MacArthur, the **Museo de San Juan** (Map pp90-1; 787-724-1875; 150 Norzagaray; admission free, donations accepted; 9am-4pm Tue-Fri, 10am-4pm Sat & Sun) is the definitive take on the city's 500-year history. The well laid-out exhibition showcases pictorial and photographic testimonies from the Caparra ruins to the modern-day shopping malls. There's also a half-hour TV documentary about the history of San Juan (in both Spanish and English).

Museo del Niño

The pink and green building that sits on the edge of a small, shady park houses this **museum** (Children's Museum; Map pp90-1; 787-722-3791; 150 Calle del Cristo; adult/child $7/5; 9am-5pm Tue-Fri, 11:30-5:30pm Sat & Sun). Kids love these hands-on exhibits – particular favorites include the short-wave radio display that lets them talk with children in other countries, the miniature town touting the benefits of recycling and a tour through the human heart.

Museo Felisa Rincón de Gautier

This **museum** (Map pp90-1; 787-723-1897; 51 Caleta de San Juan; admission free; 9am-4pm Mon-Fri) is an attractive neoclassical town house that was once the long-time home of San Juan's beloved mayor, Doña Felisa. She presided over the growth of her city with personal style and political acumen for more than 20 years during the Operation Bootstrap days of the 1940s, '50s and '60s. This historic home is a monument to the life of an accomplished public servant.

Casa del Libro

Tucked away on a very pretty street is the **Casa del Libro** (House of Books; Map pp90-1; 787-723-0354; 255 Calle del Cristo; admission free; 11am-4:30pm Tue-Sat, closed holidays), yet another of the old city's tiny museums. This restored 18th-century town house contains more than 5000 manuscripts and texts that date back 2000 years. The collection includes one of the most respected assemblages of *incunabula* (texts produced prior to 1501) in the Americas, including documents signed by King Ferdinand II and his wife Isabela.

SAN JUAN

Escuela de Artes Plásticas

The monumental gray-and-white building with a red-roofed rotunda across from El Morro is actually the **Escuela de Artes Plásticas** (Academy of Fine Arts; Map pp90-1; Norzagaray). Built as an insane asylum during the 19th century, this grand building looks more like a seat of government with its symmetrical wings, columns, Romanesque arches, porticos, courtyards and fountains.

Today it is the source of more than a few jokes by contemporary art students about the mad dreams that continue to take shape within its walls. See for yourself when student shows go on display at the end of each academic term, or take a look at the sculpture court on the right-hand side of the building, where students can be seen chipping new images from granite. The courtyard on the left-hand side has a kiosk.

Museo de Casals

On Plaza de San José is the **Museo de Casals** (Casals Museum; Map pp90-1; ☎ 787-723-9185; adult/child $1/0.50; ⏱ 9:30am-5:30pm Tue-Sat). A native of Spain's proud but repressed province of Catalonia, world-famous cellist Pablo Casals moved to his mother's homeland of Puerto Rico in 1956 to protest the dictatorial regime of Francisco Franco in Spain. He quickly established the respected Festival Casals for classical music, which became a principal force in the subsequent flowering of the arts on the island (p54).

If you loved the man, you'll surely love the museum.

CHURCHES
Catedral de San Juan

Although noticeably smaller and more austere than other Spanish churches, the **Catedral de San Juan** (Map pp90-1; ☎ 787-722-0861; 153 Calle del Cristo; admission free; ⏱ 8am-4pm) nonetheless retains a simple earthy elegance. Founded originally in the 1520s, the first church on this site was destroyed in a hurricane in 1529.

A replacement was constructed in 1540 and, over a period of centuries, it slowly evolved into the Gothic/neoclassical-inspired monument seen today.

Most people come to see the marble tomb of Ponce de León and the body of religious martyr St Pio displayed under glass. However, you can get quite a show here on Saturday afternoons when the limos roll up and bridal parties requisition the front steps. The main entrance to the cathedral faces a beautiful shaded park replete with antique benches and gnarly trees.

Capilla del Cristo

Over the centuries, tens of thousands of penitents have come to pray for miracles at the **Capilla del Cristo** (Christ's Chapel; Map pp90-1; ⏱ 10am-4pm Tue), the tiny outdoor sanctuary adjacent to Parque de las Palomas (Dove Park). One legend claims that the chapel was built to prevent people from falling over the city wall and into the sea. Another claims that citizens constructed the chapel to commemorate a miracle.

As the story goes, a rider participating in a race during the city's San Juan Bautista festivities miraculously survived after his galloping horse carried him down Calle del Cristo, off the top of the wall and into the sea.

Over the years, believers of the fable have left hundreds of little silver ornaments representing parts of the body – called *milagros* (miracles) – on the altar before the statues of the saints as tokens of thanks for being cured of some infirmity.

You can see the chapel any time, but the iron fence across the front is only open during the listed hours.

Iglesia de San José

What it lacks in grandiosity it makes up for in age; the **Iglesia de San José** (Map pp90-1; ☎ 787-725-7501; admission free; ⏱ 8:30am-4pm Mon-Sat, mass noon Sun) in the Plaza de San José is the second-oldest church in the Americas, after the cathedral in Santo Domingo in the Dominican Republic. Established in 1523 by Dominicans, this church with its vaulted Gothic ceilings still bears the coat of arms of Juan Ponce de León (whose family worshipped here), a striking carving of the Crucifixion and ornate processional floats. For 350 years, the remains of Ponce de León rested in a crypt here before being moved to the city's cathedral, down the hill. Another relic missing from the chapel is a Flemish carving of the Virgin of Bethlehem, which came to the island during the first few years of the colony and disappeared in the early 1970s.

It's also the final resting place of José Campeche (p47), one of Puerto Rico's most revered artists.

Convento de los Dominicos

Next to the Iglesia de San José is the **Convento de los Dominicos** (Map pp90-1; ☎ 787-721-6866; ⏰ 9am-5pm Wed-Sun), a Dominican convent which dates from the 16th century. After centuries of use as a convent, the building became a barracks for Spanish troops and was later used as a headquarters for US occupational forces after the Spanish-American War of 1898. It has been restored to its colonial grandeur and houses the arts/crafts/music/book store of the Instituto de Cultura Puertorriqueña, as well as a small chapel museum. Cultural events are sometimes held in the patio, and art exhibitions in the galleries.

PARKS & PLAZAS
Plaza de Armas

Follow Calle San Francisco into the heart of the old city and it opens on to the Plaza de Armas (Army Plaza; Map pp90-1). This is the city's nominal 'central' square, laid out in the 16th century with the classic look of plazas from Madrid and Mexico.

In its time, the plaza has served as a military parade ground (hence its name), a vegetable market and a social center. Shade trees, banks of seats, and a couple of old-fashioned coffee booths still make the plaza the destination of choice for couples taking their evening stroll. The beat of a *bomba* drum has also been known to light up an otherwise humdrum evening.

One of the highlights of the plaza is the **Alcaldía** (City Hall; Map pp90-1; ☎ 787-724-7171; ⏰ 9am-5pm Mon-Fri), which dates from 1789 and has twin turrets resembling those of its counterpart in Madrid. This building houses the office of the mayor of San Juan and is also the site of periodic exhibitions.

At the western end of the plaza, the **Intendencia** (Administration Building; Map pp90-1) and the **Diputación** (Provincial Delegation Building; Map pp90-1) are two other functioning government buildings adding to the charms of the plaza. Both represent 19th-century neoclassical architecture, and come complete with cloisters.

Plazuela de la Rogativa

This tiny gem of a park, the Plazuela de la Rogativa (Small Plaza of the Religious Procession; Map pp90-1), has lovely vistas overlooking the bay and is home to a whimsical bronze sculpture of the bishop of San Juan and three women bearing torches. According to legend, the candles held by the women who walked through this plaza one night in 1797 tricked British lieutenant Abercromby – who was getting ready to lay siege to San Juan with his 8000 troops and flotilla of more than 50 vessels – into believing that reinforcements were flooding the city from the rest of the island. Fearful of being outnumbered, Abercromby and his fleet withdrew.

Paseo de la Princesa

Emanating a distinctly European flavor, the Paseo de la Princesa (Walkway of the Princess; Map pp90-1) is a 19th-century esplanade situated just outside the city walls. Lined with antique street lamps, shade trees, statues, benches, fruit vendors' carts and street entertainers, this romantic walkway culminates at the magnificent **Raíces Fountain**, a stunning statue/water feature that depicts the island's eclectic Taíno, African and Spanish heritage.

The Paseo is an ideal place to indulge in that most refined of Latin pastimes, the evening stroll – an activity best enjoyed at sunset when the breeze blows stiffly off the bay, the fountain shimmers under haunting colored lights and assorted vendors tempt passersby with their sugary *piraguas*.

Plaza de Colón

Tracing its roots back more than a century to the 400-year anniversary of the first Columbus expedition, the Plaza de Colón (Columbus Plaza; Map pp90-1) lies across the street from the lower part of Fuerte San Cristóbal. The city wall on this end of Old San Juan was torn down in 1897, and the plaza, with its statue of the 'Discoverer' atop a pillar, stands on the site of one of the city's original gated entries, Puerta Santiago. Today, the plaza acts as a gateway to much of the traffic entering the city from Av Muñoz Rivera. Buses and taxis congregate on the plaza's south side.

Plaza del Quinto Centenario

It's surprising to find such a modern square shoehorned in among all the architectural antiques, but this small plaza (Map pp90-1) was built in 1992 to honor the 500-year anniversary of Christopher Columbus's first voyage to the Americas. Constructed for a rumored cost of $10 million and decorated with a craning totem pole – **El Tótem Telúrico** – of ambiguous significance, the plaza offers great views over El Morro and the ocean and, from a distance, blends in subtly with the surrounding buildings.

Parque de las Palomas

On the lower end of Calle del Cristo, Parque de las Palomas (Pigeon Park; Map pp90–1) is a cobblestone courtyard shaded with trees at the top of the city wall. *Paloma* means 'dove' or 'pigeon' in Spanish and it's the latter variety you'll encounter here, in their hundreds. Some brave souls come here for the view it affords of Bahía de San Juan. Others just turn up to feed the pigeons. (You can buy birdseed from a vendor by the gate.) Devout Christians have long believed that if you feed the birds and one 'anoints' you with its pearly droppings, you have been blessed by God. Agnostics prefer to look upon it as just plain old bad luck.

Plaza de San José

Adjacent to the uppermost terrace of the Plaza del Quinto Centenario, where it meets Calle San Sebastián, is the Plaza de San José. This relatively small cobblestone plaza is dominated by a statue of Juan Ponce de León, cast from an English cannon captured in the raid of 1797. The plaza is probably the highest point in this city and serves as a threshold to four cultural sites on its perimeter. The neighborhood around the plaza, on San Sebastián and the intersecting Calle del Cristo, is the original home of the restaurant, bar and café scene that began in Old San Juan more than a decade ago. There are still plenty of places to grab a bite to eat in a shady building or outside in the plaza. See p113 for a description of your options, or just follow your nose. The smells of *sofrito* (an island seasoning), grilled chicken, garlic, fresh dorado and lime permeate the air.

La Perla

Wedged tightly between the roaring Atlantic surf and San Juan's thick perimeter walls, the compact neighborhood of La Perla (Map p90-1) marks a rather odd juxtaposition. In truth, this ramshackle hodge-podge of pastel-colored houses and steep, narrow access roads is one of Puerto Rico's most notorious slums – though, as slums go, it's remarkably picturesque (at least, from a distance).

The standard advice given out by San Juan tour companies is for tourists to steer well clear of La Perla, a potentially dangerous *barrio* whose international infamy was cemented in a 1966 nonfiction book called *La Vida* by American anthropologist Oscar Lewis. Lewis detailed the tragic cycle of poverty and prostitution lived out by people growing up in La Perla and won a National Book Award for his efforts, though his views weren't particularly welcomed by the quarter's long-suffering residents.

Generally speaking, the cautionary advice on La Perla is pertinent. This is a gritty, high-crime neighborhood with a seemingly incurable drug problem and it would be unwise for a foreigner to wander around. But it's not all hopelessness.

Hidden among the decrepitude lies a community center, a senior citizen's home, some abstract murals, and a handful of talented local artists. Then there's the shabby magnificence of the houses themselves – the turbulent blues, the glinting greens and the foamy browns – that seem pulled right from the ocean.

During the mid-2000s, the Puerto Rican government made regular (unsuccessful) bids to buy out La Perla's residents and redevelop the area. Recent reports suggest Donald Trump has plans to turn it into a casino/resort.

Puerta de Tierra

Less than 2 miles in length and only one-quarter of a mile broad, this district occupies the lowland, filling the rest of the area that was colonial San Juan. Puerta de Tierra (Map pp86–7) takes its name from its position as the 'gateway of land' leading up to the walls of Old San Juan, which was the favored route of land attack by waves of English and Dutch invaders. For centuries, Puerta de Tierra was a slum much like La Perla, although far less picturesque. It was a place where free blacks and multiracial people lived, excluded from the protection of the walled city where the Spaniards and *criollos* (islanders of European decent) postured like European gentry and maneuvered for political favor.

Today, the district is a major driveway for cars entering Old San Juan. There's a housing project here on the south side, but the north coast is the most dramatic oceanside vista in the metropolitan area. Overlooking the wild spectacle of Balneario Escambrón you'll find the Romanesque Capitolio, the Fuerte San Gerónimo and the sun-dappled Parque

FEAR & LOATHING IN SAN JUAN

Long before *Fear and Loathing in Las Vegas* and the sharp, stylized prose that gave birth to 'Gonzo' journalism, US writer Hunter S Thompson earned a meager living as a scribe for a fledgling Puerto Rican English language weekly called *El Sportivo*, based in San Juan.

Thompson first arrived in the Puerto Rican capital in 1960 on the cusp of an unprecedented tourist boom. With the Americans recently ushered out of Cuba by a belligerent Fidel Castro, the rum party had moved defiantly east as corrupt businessmen and nascent tour companies attempted to recreate the tawdry nightlife and glitzy casinos that had once run rampant in Havana.

Attracted raucously into the melee, Thompson lapped up the louche bars with hungry relish. To finance his Caribbean sojourn he vied for a job with the *San Juan Star,* a newspaper then edited by subsequent Pulitzer Prize winner William Kennedy (author of the novel *Ironweed*) but, after being passed over in favor of more reliable fodder, he set his sights dangerously lower. For the literary world, it was a fortuitous demotion. Money was tight but rum mysteriously abundant in 1960s San Juan and, while many of Thompson's experiences quickly evaporated in back-to-back drinking binges, the essence of the era was later to emerge rather dramatically in his seminal book, *The Rum Diary*. Published in 1998 (nearly 40 years after it was written), the novel is a thinly veiled account of Thompson's alcohol-fuelled journalistic exploits as seen through the eyes of Paul Kemp, a struggling freelance writer caught in a Caribbean boomtown that was battling against an incoming tide of rich American tourists. Kemp, rather like Thompson, was a young chancer, eager to make his mark in a city that was getting its first insight into the decadence and depravity of the American Dream. Transfixed and reviled in equal measure, he regularly plied the streets of Old San Juan drinking rum for breakfast and gate-crashing free press parties for lunch.

However, built on precarious foundations, Thompson's Puerto Rican honeymoon didn't last. The writer left San Juan nine months after he arrived and made tracks for America's west coast. His characteristically manic *Rum Diary* scribblings, released 40 years later, offer a rare glimpse of an island at an important turning point in its history and a snapshot of a journalistic genius in the making. Hailed today as a modern classic, the book has been made into a Hollywood movie starring Johnny Depp, due for release in 2009.

Muñoz Rivera. The road is a popular jogging route in the day time but is best negotiated by taxi at night.

FUERTE SAN GERÓNIMO

This half-forgotten fort (Map pp98–9) is situated at the east end of Puerta de Tierra and was completed in 1788 to guard the entrance to the Condado Lagoon. It was barely up and running in 1797 when the British came marching through on their way to San Juan and a short-lived occupation. Restored in 1983, San Gerónimo today is hemmed in by tall modern hotels, but is still worth a closer look. Entered via the walkway behind the Caribe Hilton, the interior of the fort is rarely open, though the exterior walls and ramparts are usually accessible and offer rather fetching views of Condado across the inlet.

EL CAPITOLIO

Sandwiched between Av Muñoz Rivera and Av Ponce de León, just east of Fuerte San Cristóbal, is **El Capitolio** (The Capitol; Map pp86-7;

☎ 787-721-6040; admission free; ☼ 9am-4pm Mon-Fri, tours by appointment only) of the commonwealth. Resembling a smaller, Romanesque version of the US Capitol, the building commands an authoritative position in Puerta de Tierra overlooking the wave-lashed coast. The much-revered constitution of the commonwealth, which moved the island a step closer to its citizens' dreams of freedom from colonialism in 1951, is on display inside the 80ft rotunda. Regular sessions of the legislature meet inside, while rallies for and against statehood occur outside every time the government calls for an island-wide plebiscite on the issue.

PARQUES MUÑOZ RIVERA & SIXTO ESCOBAR

Spanning half the width of Puerta de Tierra between the Atlantic and Av Ponce de León, this green space, known as Parque Muñoz Rivera (Map pp86–7), dates back over 50 years and injects some much needed breathing space into the surrounding urbanity. It has shade trees, trails, a kid's playground, and a

'Peace Pavilion,' which sometimes hosts community events. An artisans' fair is held here and at the adjacent **Parque Sixto Escobar** (Map pp86–7; ☎ 787-277-9200) on most weekends.

Parque Sixto Escobar – named for the famed Puerto Rican boxer – was the site of the eighth Pan American Games, held in 1979, and is now home to an Olympic athletics track and the gusty Balneario Escambrón. The park also hosts the annual Heineken Jazz Festival.

Condado

On the cusp of a ritzy rehabilitation, beachfront Condado (Map pp98–9) is swinging once again to the sound of jangling money – and equally clangorous slot machines. In the 1960s, this is where Puerto Rico's explosive tourist boom was first ignited, spearheaded by exiled Cuban businessmen and rum-drunk Americans in search of the next big thing. But, as fashions ebbed and flowed, Condado's moment as the next Miami Beach never quite arrived. Instead, the more refined action edged gradually east to Isla Verde and abandoned Condado became a lonely hearts club for an unsavory crowd of prostitutes, pimps, drug dealers and high rollers crying into their piña coladas.

It was in the '90s that things first started to turn around and by the mid-2000s they had almost come full circle. As mainstream tourism headed east, Condado plugged the gaps, attracting assorted celebrities, gay socialites

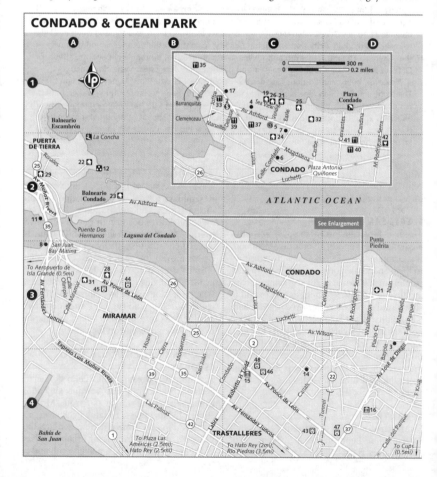

CONDADO & OCEAN PARK

and those in search of the odd hotel bargain. Today, dotted in among the new high-rises and condo towers, you'll still find a few old eclectic 1920s villas, along with a handful of pretty parks that serve as spacious windows to the sea. With its traffic-calmed streets and clustered hotels, Condado also retains the kind of relaxed nighttime street scene that Isla Verde lacks.

Ocean Park

At the east end of Condado lies Ocean Park (Map pp98–9), with its associated neighborhood of **Punta Las Marías**, a largely residential collection of private homes and beach retreats that include a handful of plush seaside guesthouses. The more tranquil beach here is an open secret among the 'in' crowd and is great for windsurfing.

Miramar

Tucked behind Condado Lagoon is the upscale neighborhood of Miramar (Map pp98–9), named for its lovely sea views, all but blotted out these days by the trim new condo towers of Condado. Distinguished by its mature tree-lined streets and handful of unusual Prairie School architectural creations (think Frank Lloyd Wright meets Arts & Craft), the area isn't as homogenous as it once was, though the yachts berthed at the **Club Náutico** still gleam like polished diamonds and the spanking new Convention Center drops a few jaws with its outlandish

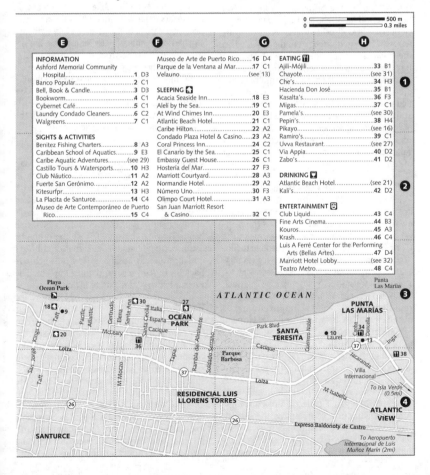

INFORMATION		
Ashford Memorial Community Hospital	**1**	D3
Banco Popular	**2**	C1
Bell, Book & Candle	**3**	D3
Bookworm	**4**	C1
Cybernet Café	**5**	C1
Laundry Condado Cleaners	**6**	C2
Walgreens	**7**	C1

SIGHTS & ACTIVITIES		
Benitez Fishing Charters	**8**	A3
Caribbean School of Aquatics	**9**	E3
Caribe Aquatic Adventures	(see 29)	
Castillo Tours & Watersports	**10**	H3
Club Náutico	**11**	A2
Fuerte San Gerónimo	**12**	A2
Kitesurfpr	**13**	H3
La Placita de Santurce	**14**	C4
Museo de Arte Contemporáneo de Puerto Rico	**15**	C4

Museo de Arte de Puerto Rico	**16**	D4
Parque de la Ventana al Mar	**17**	C1
Velauno	(see 13)	

SLEEPING		
Acacia Seaside Inn	**18**	E3
Aleli by the Sea	**19**	C1
At Wind Chimes Inn	**20**	E3
Atlantic Beach Hotel	**21**	C1
Caribe Hilton	**22**	A2
Condado Plaza Hotel & Casino	**23**	A2
Coral Princess Inn	**24**	C2
El Canario by the Sea	**25**	C1
Embassy Guest House	**26**	C1
Hostería del Mar	**27**	F3
Marriott Courtyard	**28**	A3
Normandie Hotel	**29**	A2
Número Uno	**30**	F3
Olimpo Court Hotel	**31**	A3
San Juan Marriott Resort & Casino	**32**	C1

EATING		
Ajili-Mójili	**33**	B1
Chayote	(see 31)	
Che's	**34**	H3
Hacienda Don José	**35**	B1
Kasalta's	**36**	F3
Migas	**37**	C1
Pamela's	(see 30)	
Pepin's	**38**	H4
Pikayo	(see 16)	
Ramiro's	**39**	C1
Uvva Restaurant	(see 27)	
Via Appia	**40**	D2
Zabo's	**41**	D2

DRINKING		
Atlantic Beach Hotel	(see 21)	
Kali's	**42**	D2

ENTERTAINMENT		
Club Liquid	**43**	C4
Fine Arts Cinema	**44**	B3
Kouros	**45**	A3
Krash	**46**	C4
Luis A Ferré Center for the Performing Arts (Bellas Artes)	**47**	D4
Marriott Hotel Lobby	(see 32)	
Teatro Metro	**48**	C4

modernist design. Unless you're accommodated here in a hotel or you're paying a special visit to the Fine Arts cinema, the most you'll probably see of Miramar is from one of its notorious traffic bottlenecks.

Santurce

Santurce is one of San Juan's most important barrios that actually incorporates Condado and Miramar, but is usually used to describe the area south of Expressway 26 and north of Hato Rey. Buried in the heart of the modern city, its fortunes have fluctuated markedly since its founding by a Basque Country Count in the 1870s.

The '40s and '50s were a boom time, when color and life seeped from its energetic streets, spurred on by the buoyancy of Operation Bootstrap. Back then, Santurce was a financial center and a residential quarter of some repute. The nosedive began in the 1970s when the business district headed south to Hato Rey and Santurce suffered a similar fate to many US cities as the upwardly mobile middle-classes left to colonize the new suburbs. Left to fester, abandoned with high crime rates and unsightly graffiti, Santurce has worked hard to turn the corner. Its recent 21st-century renaissance has been spearheaded by new art galleries, a performing arts center and a host of trendy clubs.

MUSEO DE ARTE DE PUERTO RICO

While the Old Town's historic attractions are universally famous, fewer people are aware that San Juan boasts one of the largest and most celebrated art museums in the Caribbean. The **Museo de Arte de Puerto Rico** (MAPR; Map pp86-7; ☎ 787-977-6277, for tours ext 2230 or 2261; www.mapr.org; 299 Av José de Diego, Santurce; adult/child & senior $6/3; ☺ 10am-5pm Tue-Sat, 10am-8pm Wed, 11am-6pm Sun) opened in 2000 and rapidly inserted itself as a important nexus in the capital's vibrant cultural life. Housed in a splendid neoclassical building that was once the city's Municipal Hospital, MAPR is located in the city's revived Santurce district and boasts 18 exhibition halls spread over an area of 130,000 sq ft.

But there's far more to this cultural 'tour de force' than just a collection of paintings. Adding distinction to diversity, the facility also boasts a 5-acre sculpture garden, a conservation laboratory, a computer-learning center, a 400-seat theater, a museum

shop and the very highly regarded Pikayo restaurant (p118).

The artistic collection traces paintings, sculptures, posters and carvings from the 17th to the 21st century, chronicling such renowned Puerto Rican artists as José Campeche, Francisco Oller, Nick Quijano and Rafael Ferrer.

Do not miss the opportunity to take a walk through the gardens, where winding paths invite visitors to stroll past 14 sculptures and more than 100,000 plants in a scene reminiscent of Monet's water lilies.

MUSEO DE ARTE CONTEMPORÁNEO DE PUERTO RICO

Another recent recipient of the makeover brush, the **Museo de Arte Contemporáneo de Puerto Rico** (Map pp86-7; ☎ 787-977-4030; www.museocontemporaneopr.org; cnr Av Ponce de León & Roberto H Todd; admission free; ☺ 10am-4pm Tue-Sat, noon-4pm Sun) sits just down the road from the Museo de Arte in a similarly eye-catching classical Georgian building – the former Rafael M Labra school – dating from 1918. The museum displays art from the mid-20th century onwards and showcases artists from Puerto Rico, the Caribbean and Latin America.

Isla Verde

Culturally speaking, modern Isla Verde (Map p101), is about as Puerto Rican as skiing in Aspen. Then again, most people don't arrive here to sample home-cooked *mofongo* (mashed plantains) or run off in search of the island's elusive *jíbaros*. Rather, they come for a lavish helping of what the tourist brochures promote: a Cancún-style strip of international hotels and dimly lit casinos that offer an all-inclusive package of sun, sea, sand and escapism. The Puerto Rican part is purely incidental.

Hato Rey

As you head south from Santurce, the urban inquietude of the former business district is replaced by the sleekness of its modern successor. The first signs of the brave new world can be seen at Sagardo Corazon station, a space-age temple to the metro train that is the first stop on San Juan's spanking new Tren Urbano. Welcome to Hato Rey (Map pp86-7), the Caribbean's wannabe Wall Street, a gleaming cluster of glass-sheeted office towers and international banks that reflect not only the crimson afternoon sun but also the lucid

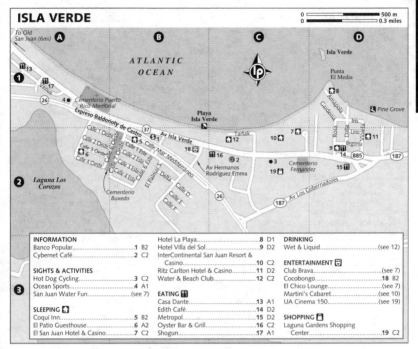

ISLA VERDE

INFORMATION
Banco Popular.....................................**1** B2
Cybernet Café....................................**2** C2

SIGHTS & ACTIVITIES
Hot Dog Cycling................................**3** C2
Ocean Sports.....................................**4** A1
San Juan Water Fun.....................(see 7)

SLEEPING
Coquí Inn..**5** B2
El Patio Guesthouse........................**6** A2
El San Juan Hotel & Casino............**7** C2

Hotel La Playa..................................**8** D1
Hotel Villa del Sol...........................**9** D2
InterContinental San Juan Resort &
  Casino..**10** C2
Ritz Carlton Hotel & Casino...........**11** D2
Water & Beach Club.......................**12** C2

EATING
Casa Dante..**13** A1
Edith Café...**14** D2
Metropol..**15** D2
Oyster Bar & Grill.............................**16** C2
Shogun...**17** A1

DRINKING
Wet & Liquid...............................(see 12)

ENTERTAINMENT
Club Brava.....................................(see 7)
Cocobongo......................................**18** B2
El Chico Lounge............................(see 7)
Martini's Cabaret.........................(see 10)
UA Cinema 150.............................(see 19)

SHOPPING
Laguna Gardens Shopping
  Center..**19** C2

dreams of Puerto Rico's economic miracle. Aside from the ubiquitous financial institutions, Hato Rey's primary attractions revolve around shoppers and sports. Just west of the 'Miracle Mile' business district lies the massive Plaza Las Américas (see p122), the largest mall in the Caribbean, along with two major sports arenas – the Hiram Bithorn Stadium and the Roberto Clemente Coliseum.

Río Piedras

Keep pushing south and the flatness of Hato Rey soon gives way to the leafy uplands of Río Piedras (Map p102). Founded in 1714 and existing as a separate town until 1951, Río Piedras is the home of the renowned University of Puerto Rico and harbors a thriving academic community. You'll find cheap cafés and amply stocked bookshops here as well as a cut-price shopping street (José de Diego), and the island's largest farmers market. The university building itself is set in lush, palm-filled grounds and is distinguished by its signature minaretlike clock tower. This is a great place to hang out, shoot the breeze and start taking up those good Puerto Rican vibrations.

MERCADO DE RÍO PIEDRAS

If you like the smell of fish and oranges, the bustle of people, and trading jests in Spanish as you bargain for a bunch of bananas, this **market** (Paseo de Diego; Map p102; 9am-6pm) is for you. As much a scene as a place to shop, the market continues the colonial tradition of an indoor market that spills into the streets.

The four long blocks of shops and inexpensive restaurants lining Paseo de Diego and facing the market have been closed to auto traffic, turning the whole area into an outdoor mall. You can shop or just watch as the local citizens negotiate for everything from *chuletas* (pork chops) and *camisas* (shirts) to cassettes featuring Puerto Rican pop-music wonders like Menudo. Shoppers will find the market and stores along Paseo de Diego open from early morning to late evening, Monday to Saturday.

JARDÍN BOTÁNICO

This 75-acre tract of greenery is the site of the **Estación Experimental Agrícola de Puerto Rico** (Experimental Agricultural Station of Puerto Rico; Map p102; 787-763-4408, 787-767-1710; admission free;

6am-6pm, closed holidays, tours available), but is open to the public. Hiking trails lead to a lotus lagoon, an orchid garden with more than 30,000 flowers, and a plantation of more than 120 species of palm. The air smells of heliconia blossoms, as well as of nutmeg and cinnamon trees.

One of the reasons the garden is so serene is that it's difficult to find. The entrance is nearly hidden on the south side of the intersection of Hwy 1 and Hwy 847, a walk of about a mile from the center of the UPR campus. Call ahead to book a tour; it can be difficult to get the phone answered.

MUSEO DE ANTROPOLOGÍA, HISTORIA Y ARTE

This small but quite engaging **museum** (Map p102; ☎ 787-764-0000 ext 2452; admission free; ⏲ 9am-4:30pm Mon-Fri, 9am-3pm Sat & Sun) of anthropology, history and art is worth a stop to see examples of the trove of Taíno Indian artifacts unearthed by university scholars in recent digs. In addition, this museum features revolving art shows and offers scholarly perspectives on island history. Finally, visiting the

museum gives travelers a legitimate reason to be snooping around the university campus and opens opportunities for connecting with the students and faculty. The opening hours vary, so call ahead. It lies just inside the entrance to the UPR campus, next to the Biblioteca Lazaro.

CASA-FINCA DE DON LUIS MUÑOZ MARÍN

This house and farm were once home to the godfather of the Partido Popular Democrático (PPD) and the man who shepherded Puerto Rico into commonwealth status – as well as a 20th-century industrialized market economy in the 1950s and '60s. Today, it is a **museum** (Map p102; ☎ 787-755-7979; Hwy 181 Km 1.3; admission $3; ⏲ 10am-2pm Wed-Sun) honoring the memory of this legendary Puerto Rican figure, and it also serves as a venue for concerts and experimental theater. Call for events, and visit if you want to find out more about the pretty astounding political career of Luis Muñoz Marín. Also take a minute to check out the great vegetation and expansive grounds. Look for the house on the east side of Río Piedras.

Beaches

San Juan has some of the best municipal beaches this side of Rio de Janeiro. Starting half a mile or so east of the Old Town, you can go from rustic to swanky and back to rustic all in the space of 7.5 miles.

PUERTA DE TIERRA

Balneario Escambrón (Map pp98–9). Imagine it – a sheltered arc of raked sand, decent surf breaks, plenty of local action and the sight of a 17th-century Spanish fort shimmering in the distance.

But, hang on a minute. Are you really still only a stone's throw from Old San Juan and the busy tourist strip of Condado? Balneario Escambrón is almost too good to be true, which is probably why a lot of people miss it. Perched on the north end of the slither of land that *is* Puerta de Tierra and abutting majestic Parque del Tercer Milenio, this palm-fringed yet rugged beach just might be one of the best municipal options offered anywhere. Adding convenience to enchantment, there are lifeguards, restrooms, and snack bars on hand along with a large parking lot.

CONDADO

Hemmed in by hotel towers and punctuated by rocky outcrops, Condado's narrow beaches are busier than Ocean Park's but less exclusive than Isla Verde's. Expect splashes of lurid graffiti, boisterous games of volleyball and plenty of crashing Atlantic surf.

The area's official public beach is **Balneario Condado** (Map pp98–9), a small arc of sand, adjacent to the Dos Hermanos bridge, that faces west toward the Fuerte San Gerónimo across the inlet. A line of rocks breaks the water here, meaning that the sea is calm and bathing relatively safe. Lifeguards police the area on weekdays and snack bars are open daily, but bathrooms are few and far between. You can rent beach chairs.

Condado's Atlantic-facing beaches are very popular, especially among families who congregate around the big hotels, and with gay men, who seem to like the stretch of sand in front of Calle Condado. Urban redevelopment is ongoing and a number of salubrious parks – most notably **Parque de la Ventana al Mar** (Window to the Sea; Map pp98–9) – have opened up recently, enhancing both beach views and access.

OCEAN PARK

Ocean Park's (Map pp98–9) lesser fame is its hidden blessing. Fronted by leafy residential streets and embellished by the odd luxury B&B, this wide sweep of fine, diamond dust sand is protected by offshore reefs and caressed by cooling seasonal trade winds. Although largely the preserve of trendy lovers of tranquility, anyone can enjoy the very different ambience here. Just pick a road through the neighborhood's low-rise gated community and follow it toward the water.

PLAYA ISLA VERDE

Resort pluggers will tell you that Playa Isla Verde (Map p101) is the Copacabana of Puerto Rico with its legions of tanned bodies and dexterous beach bums flexing their triceps around the volleyball net. Other more savvy travelers prefer to dodge the extended families and colonizing spring-break hedonists that stake space here and head west to Ocean Park. Whatever your subjective view, this broad mile-long wedge of sand that lies between Punta Las Marías and Piñones is an undeniable beauty. The downside – if there is one – is access. Cutting in front of the towering condos and plush hotels of Av Isla Verde, the beach is completely obscured from the road and, as a result, lacks the inclusive atmosphere of more open municipal beaches.

BALNEARIO DE CAROLINA

Wedged in between the high rise hotel strip of Isla Verde and rustic delights of Piñones, the **Balneario de Carolina** (Map pp86–7; Rte 187; ☒ 8am-6pm) is a fine, clean beach that lacks natural shelter and is positioned a little incongruously right in front of LMM international airport. Equipped with plenty of lifeguards, bathrooms, showers, barbecue pits and rather weird red sculptures, the beach can be pleasantly peaceful in the week if you can ignore the noise from 747s taking off. Parking costs $3.

ACTIVITIES
Hiking

A favorite store for climbers and hikers in Puerto Rico, **Aventuras Tierra Adentro** (Map p102; ☎ 787-766-0470; www.aventuraspr.com; 268a Av Jesús T Piñero, Río Piedras; day trip $150; ☒ 10am-6pm Tue-Sat, tours available upon demand) is also a tour operator specializing in rock climbing and rappelling trips to the Río Camuy caves (p245). Guides also take people on trips through Río Tanama and Angeles Cave, and there's a very good trip for children to Yuyu Cave in the karst region. Novices are welcome – all expeditions begin with a short lesson.

Diving & Snorkeling

While Puerto Rico is well known for its first-class diving, San Juan is not the best place for it: strong winds often churn up the water. Condado has an easy dive that takes you through a pass between the inner and outer reefs into coral caverns, overhangs, grottoes and tunnels.

Eco-Action Tours (☎ 787-791-7509; www.ecoaction tours.com; tours $40-130) can do just about any tour imaginable, from rappelling to nature walks. It operates out of a van and comes to you. Check out its website or phone them. The guides are knowledgeable and very accommodating.

Caribe Aquatic Adventures (Map pp98-9; ☎ 787-281-8858; 499 Av Muñoz Rivera; snorkel/dive $50/135) operates out of the Normandie Hotel in Puerta de Tierra, but you needn't be a guest to use the services. This outfit does dives near San Juan, but also further afield around the islands off the coast of Fajardo (Icacos for snorkeling and Palomino and Palominito for diving). Lunch and transportation from San Juan are included in trips to Fajardo. The company's shore dives from the beach behind the hotel are regarded as some of the best in the Caribbean. Cruise passengers love utilizing this place.

Ocean Sports (Map p101; ☎ 787-268-2329; www.osdiv ers.com; 77 Av Isla Verde) has a dive store in Isla Verde. It can also organize shore dives, deep dives, night dives, wall dives and cavern dives. It has a full service facility that provides Nitrox, Trimix and rebreathers.

Castillo Tours & Watersports (right) offers snorkeling excursions that include equipment, instruction, lunch and transportation.

Kayaking

Ecoquest (☎ 787-6167543; www.ecoquestpr.com) offers a great three-hour trip to Piñones and its adjacent lagoon. The excursion includes information on local flora and fauna, a one-hour kayak on the lagoon and some traditional food from one of the famous local fish restaurants. Prices start at $69 per person.

Copladet Nature & Adventure Tours (☎ 787-765-8595; www.copladet.com in Spanish) also offers lots of good tours, including kayaking on the Laguna de Piñones (p125).

Fishing

Captain José Castillo of **Castillo Tours & Watersports** (Map pp98-9; ☎ 787-791-6195; www.castil lotours.com; 2413 Laurel, Punta Las Marías; trips $65-450) offers deep-sea fishing for blue marlin, wahoo, tuna and mahimahi, as well as snorkeling and sailing excursions.

Benitez Fishing Charters (Map pp98-9; ☎ 787-723-2292; San Juan Bay Marina, Miramar) is captained by the celebrated Mike Benitez, who has carried the likes of former US President Jimmy Carter. If you want to trade White House gossip while fishing for dolphin, tuna, wahoo and white and blue marlin, book a space on his deluxe 45' boat for some serious deep-sea fishing. Prices start at $185 per person for a four-hour excursion.

Surfing, Sailing & Water Sports

San Juan is hardly Rincón in the surfing stakes, but no matter. You'll find the best waves and biggest *surferos* scene east of Isla Verde out towards Piñones and beyond, when the morning and evening breezes glass off a 4ft swell. Popular breaks include Pine Grove, Los Avióñes and La Concha along Hwy 187.

WoW Surfing School (☎ 787-955-6059; www.gosur fpr.com) – WoW stands for Walk on Water – runs full surfing lessons from Playa Escambrón in Puerta de Tierra or Pine Grove on Playa Isla Verde. Lessons include boards, stretching, safety drills, dry land practice and the real thing. Board rentals ($30 to $40 per day) are also available.

Velauno (Map p101; ☎ 787-982-0543; www.velauno .com; 2430 Loíza, Punta Las Marías; longboards/windsurfers per day $35/75) is a great place to start learning how to surf, windsurf or kitesurf. On weekends it rents equipment right from the beach, and there is a discount for rentals longer than a day. Classes in all three disciplines offered.

You can learn how to kitesurf, windsurf or just plain surf at **Kitesurfpr** (Map pp98-9; ☎ 787-221-0635; 2434 Loíza, Punta Las Marías).

San Juan Waterfun (Map p101; ☎ 787-643-4510; El San Juan Hotel & Casino, 6063 Av Isla Verde, Isla Verde Beach, Isla Verde) can rent you pretty much anything that floats: banana boats, wave runners, kayaks ($20 per hour), small catamarans (with captain; $70 per hour), jet skis, water skis and knee boards. Or get airborne with some parasailing ($65 per person). It's situated on Playa Isla Verde in front of the El San Juan Hotel.

Castillo Tours & Watersports (opposite) puts together catamaran sailing trips as well as snorkeling and fishing excursions. To rent a small sailboat or powerboat, contact the **Caribbean School of Aquatics** (Map pp98-9; ☎ 787-728-6606; 1 Taft, Suite 10f, Condado).

Cycling

Forget the notorious traffic jams; cycling in San Juan can actually be good fun, as long as you know where to go. In fact, it is perfectly feasible to work your way along the safe coastline from Old San Juan out as far as Carolina and the bike paths of Piñones.

In Isla Verde, **Hot Dog Cycling** (Map p101; ☎ 787-791-0776; www.hotdogcycling.com; 5916 Av Isla Verde; ⊗ 10am-5pm), situated in the small Plazoleta shopping center, rents excellent 21-speed mountain bikes from $25 per day. These guys are handily situated near the start of the designated Isla Verde–Piñones bike route. Also ask about their bike tours.

WALKING TOUR

Start with an early morning pick-me-up in **Café Cala'o** (**1**; p113) next to Pier 2, before heading west to **La Casita** (**2**; p92), a historic neoclassical gatehouse that acts as the modern HQ for the Puerto Rican Tourist Company. After picking up some informative literature on the sights and sounds that lie ahead, stroll west along the **Paseo de la Princesa** (**3**; p95), a 19th-century esplanade that tracks alongside the formidable old city walls to the brink of the Bahía de San Juan. As you feel the refreshing Atlantic breeze hit you face-on, you'll spy an imposing bronze sculpture and fountain called **Raíces** (**4**; p95) that depicts Taíno, European and African figurines rising amid a shower of cascading water.

Behind the fountain, follow the Paseo de la Princesa as it cuts northwest along the waterfront with excellent views over San Juan Bay toward the Bacardí Rum factory. You'll see turreted guard towers called *garitas* carved into the thick city walls here, distinctive conical structures that have become symbolic of Puerto Rico and its rich colonial history. In the 17th and 18th centuries, Spanish ships once anchored in the cove just off these ramparts to unload colonists and supplies, all of which entered the city through a tall red portal known as **Puerta de San Juan** (**5**; p92) dating from the 1630s.

Pass through the gate and turn right on Recinto Oeste. This short cobblestone street leads to the guarded iron gates of **La Fortaleza** (**6**; p89), a one-time fort that today is more redolent of a well-preserved classical palace. After stopping for a guided tour, head back northwest, stopping for a moment to gaze out over the water from the diminutive **Plazuela de la Rogativa** (**7**; p95).

Follow the leafy Caleta de San Juan up the slope to the beautiful Plazuela Las Monjas (Nun's square) where stray cats sunbathe and romantic couples linger. On the north side is **Gran Hotel El Convento** (**8**; p109), Puerto Rico's grandest hotel, well worth a casual inspection. To the east lies the **Catedral de San Juan** (**9**; p94), a relatively austere religious building whose importance is enhanced by its age (dating from 1540) and the fact that the remains of Juan Ponce de León rest inside.

Cut along Luna for a block before heading right down San José. Take a left onto San Francisco, which will bring you to the **Plaza de Armas** (**10**; p95), a small but important square and the hub of the Old City. If the effects of your first coffee have worn off you can procure excellent top-ups here from one of the traditional booths that decorate the plaza. Drop south one block and continue east along Fortaleza and you'll soon fall upon the urban inquietude of **SoFo** (**11**; p116), Old San Juan's funky restaurant and nightlife quarter that has successfully injected vitality and hipness into the aged colonial core. Fortaleza ends in the **Plaza de Colón** (**12**; p95), named for the great Genoese explorer and site of the former land entrance to the walled city from Puerta de Tierra. Cut north up Av Muñoz Rivera here and you'll come to **Fuerte San Cristóbal** (**13**; p89), the old city's other major fortification, which harbors an interesting museum and theatrical military re-enactments.

Walking west along Norzagaray, you can look down at the faded pastel houses of La Perla, San Juan's poorest and most notorious neighborhood, that affronts the fierce and tempestuous Atlantic. Hidden in a former market building to your left is the **Museo de San Juan** (**14**; p93), which will fill the historical gaps in the story of one of America's oldest colonial settlements. A block or two west the **Plaza del Quinto Centenario** (**15; p95**), built in 1992 to commemorate the 500th anniversary of Christopher Columbus' 'discovery' of the New World, blends in seamlessly with the older neighboring Cuartel de Ballajá. The latter building houses the **Museo de las Américas** (**16**; p93), a museum of changing exhibits on Caribbean and European art. Across the grass expanses of Campo del Morro the **El Morro** (**17**; p88) beckons like a brooding sentinel. If you bought a joint ticket from Fuerte San Cristóbal, you'll get in here at a reduced rate.

On your return bypass down Calle del Morro to the **Casa Blanca** (**18**; p92), the ancestral

home for 250 years of the descendants of Juan Ponce de León and the oldest permanent residence in the Americas.

A stone's throw to the east lies the **Plaza de San José** (**19**; p96), with its statue of Juan Ponce de León, cast from an English cannon captured in the raid of 1797. More antiquity overlooks the plaza from the north in the shape of the **Iglesia de San José** (**20**; p94), the second-oldest church in the Americas.

You can cut back to the Puerta de San Juan via a network of steep narrow backstreets punctuated with stone staircases. Exiting the city via the old gate, turn right and follow the mile-long **Paseo del Morro** (**21;** p92) which hugs the city walls to the far tip of El Morro fort. This stroll is most evocative at the end of the

---

WALK FACTS

Distance 3 miles
Duration Three to four hours

WALKING TOUR

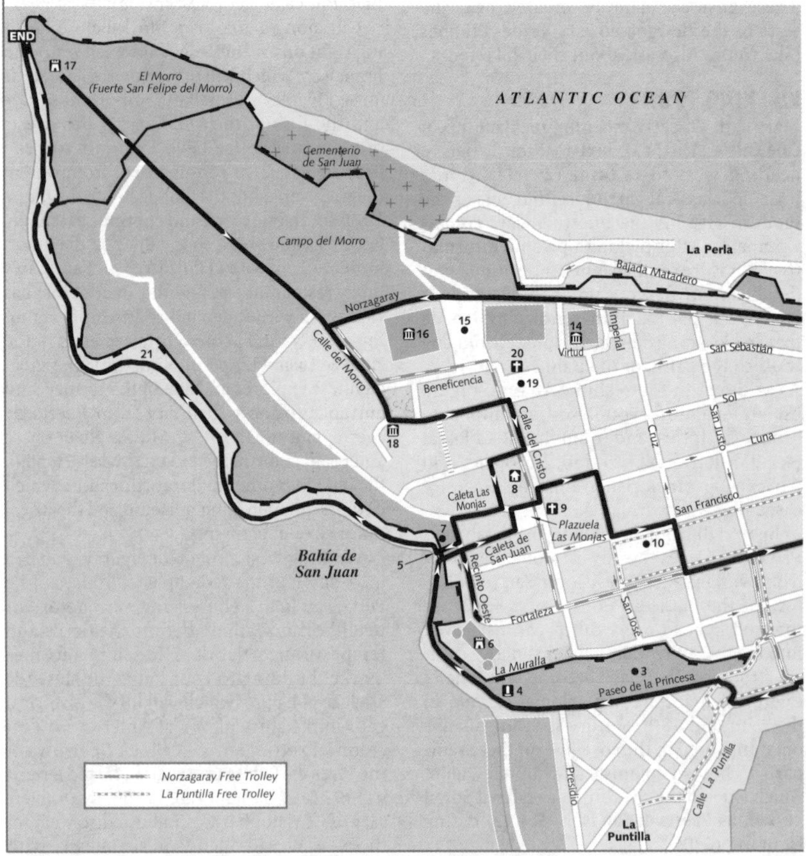

day as the sun sets over the bay and the dark grey shapes of Cataño are transformed into twinkling lights.

SAN JUAN FOR CHILDREN

Puerto Ricans love children – it doesn't matter who they belong to – and they love family, so traveling with youngsters is rarely a hassle, because the Puerto Ricans are doing it too. There are some hotels that won't take children under a certain age, but they are few. Several museums and hotels offer cheaper rates or discounts for children – don't be afraid to ask. If renting a car, make sure that the rental agency has a child seat for you, and if taking a taxi any long distance, bring one with you. Children should carry some form of ID in case

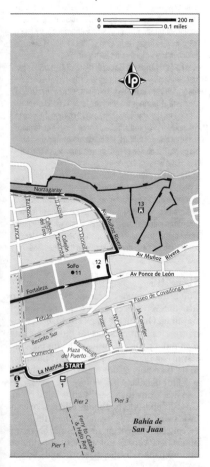

there's an emergency. You'll rarely encounter any icy or disdainful looks when dining out with your child, but some of the trendier places in Old San Juan, Condado and Isla Verde would be the exception to that rule.

In and around San Juan there are several attractions that children really enjoy. The Museo del Niño (p93) is always a big hit, as is the Luis A Ferré Parque de Ciencias (p129) in Bayamón. Isla Verde is the most child-friendly beach, with safe swimming and plenty of beach toys, or you can always head further east to Luquillo (p138). For some outdoor exercise hit the bike trails of Piñones, or go kayaking on the nearby lagoon (p125).

Captain Duck (p108) does a fun water/land tour in an amphibious bus. Alternatively you can hop on one of Old San Juan's two handy trolleys. For an educational but entertaining delve into Puerto Rican history check out the two splendid forts, El Morro (p88) and San Cristóbal (p89).

Baby sitters are not easily found in San Juan or elsewhere in Puerto Rico. There are no organizations that offer this service, but all the larger hotels have vetted baby sitters on speed dial – usually staff who are happy to make some extra money on the side.

QUIRKY SAN JUAN

Maybe it's San Juan's heterogeneous people that make it quirky, or the silent competition between its neighborhoods that simmers unabashedly beneath the surface. Whatever the reason, here in the crucible of Puerto Rican culture you can expect to encounter oddly delicious food fusions, exotic religious iconography and uncensored alfresco belly dancers all in the same evening.

Top of the quirky stakes has to be the decidedly odd Fiesta de San Juan Batista (p108), a June festival where devotees walk backwards into the ocean in the middle of the night – apparently for good luck. First prize for the city's quirkiest hotel goes to the Harry Potter-esque Gallery Inn (p109) and its quirkiest shop, the entomologist's favorite, Butterfly People (p122). In the restaurant scene, SoFo has plenty of quirky contenders, though the zany Parrot Club (p115) and bordello-like (not literally) Dragonfly (p115) are hard to match. If you harbor a *Dirty Dancing* fantasy, hit El Chico Lounge (p120) for some real bump-n-grind.

TOURS

Debbie Molina-Ramos is a well-respected guide for **Legends of Puerto Rico** (☎ 787-605-9060; www.legendsofpr.com), whose wildly popular 'Night Tales in Old San Juan' tour books up pretty fast. She also does 'Legends of San Juan' (from $30 to $35 per person) and many others, including a coffee plantation tour, an eating and drinking tour, and tours to El Yunque. Bus trips are available, as are special discounts for families with children (and child-friendly tours, too), as well as wheelchair-accessible tours (advance booking required). Aside from English and Spanish, tours can be arranged in German, French and Italian.

Captain Duck Tours (Map pp90-1; ☎ 787-447-0077; www.captainduck.com; JA Corretjer) operates amphibious bus tours lasting 90 minutes: 45 minutes on land and 45 minutes floating around San Juan harbor, without once having to leave your seat. The tour skirts Old San Juan and Puerta de Tierra and enters the water in Parque Central west of Hato Rey before motoring around the harbor. Tours usually run twice daily at 11am and 1pm except Tuesday. Tickets cost adult/child/senior $24/17/21.

FESTIVALS & EVENTS

Aside from Noches de Galerias and Festival San Sebastián, which become more adult-oriented during the evening, all of the following festivals retain a congenial atmosphere that is favorable to families. Unless otherwise noted, information on the following events can be obtained by contacting the PRTC (p88).

Festival Casals Renowned soloists and orchestras come here from all over the world to join the Puerto Rican Symphony Orchestra in giving night after night of virtuoso concerts, primarily at the Luis A Ferré Center for the Performing Arts. Tickets run at around $40, but there are big discounts for students, children and seniors. Dates vary. Check out www.festcasalspr.gobierno.pr for details.

Noches de Galerías (Gallery Nights) Galleries stay open late on the first Tuesday of the month (February to May, September to December) to showcase special exhibitions and present up-and-coming talent. Enthusiastic art lovers have also turned this into something of a pub crawl, especially along San Sebastián, Plaza de Armas, Calle del Cristo and Plaza San Sebastián. Look for nearby museums like El Arsenal and Museo de las Américas to hold special exhibits for this event.

Festival San Sebastián For a full week in mid-January, the old city's famous party street, San Sabastián, hums with semireligious processions, music, food stalls and larger-than-ever crowds. During the day, it's folk art and crafts; at night, it's drunken revelry.

Jazz Festival (Late May to early June) Puerto Rico's largest jazz fest, courtesy of Heineken and held from late May to early June, attracts the best Latin jazz artists from all over the Caribbean. The late, great Tito Puente sometimes played here, and Eddie Palmieri still does.

Fiesta de San Juan Bautista Celebration of the patron saint of San Juan and a summer solstice party, Latin style. Staged during the week preceding June 24, the heart of the action – including religious processions, wandering minstrels, fireworks, food stalls, drunken sailors and beauty queens (straight and otherwise) – is in Old San Juan, but the rest of the city gets into the act as well and parties down on the last day of the fiesta at Playa Isla Verde.

Fiesta de Película Screens about 100 new films over one week in October, all of which relate to the Caribbean in some way. Given the number of Puerto Ricans/Nuyoricans making good on the big screen – J Lo, Benicio del Toro, Jimmy Smits (and Raul Julia, who was given a state funeral when he died of cancer in 1994) – this event has been pulling in bigger luminaries each year.

Fiesta Artisanos de Bacardí (Bacardí Artisans Fair; first two Sundays of December) With the feel of a big county fair back in the USA (complete with carnival rides), the fiesta also brings together the largest collection of artisans on the island. As many as 125 crafters show up to compete, display and sell their wares. This is a good place to see an array of folk art, including *santos*, and shop for bargains. The *bomba y plena* singers add a touch of tradition to the whole affair.

Culinary Festival (November) SoFo's alfresco culinary festival is a moveable feast that in recent years has tended to happen during the first week of November. For three nights a two-block wedge of Fortaleza is closed to traffic and commandeered by local restaurateurs who set up their tables in the street and rustle up their best dishes. Live bands drop by, belly dancers entertain the diners and the food is sizzlingly good.

SLEEPING

You'll find ample accommodations in San Juan for every price range except one – budget traveling. Outside of a few affordable guesthouses, it's slim pickings for those watching their money. On the upside, rates for places to stay in San Juan vary significantly (sometimes more than 30%) from season to season. See p273 for details.

Aside from that, San Juan is wide open. Upscale, midscale, boutique or B&B: take your pick. Condado and Ocean Park have the highest concentration of guesthouses and big resort hotels. Isla Verde's got a few ritzy boutique options flanked by mega-resorts, and Old San

Juan's got a handful of historical havens, including the exquisite El Convento, surely the most evocative hotel on the island.

Old San Juan

BUDGET

Fortaleza Guest House (Map pp90-1; ☎ 787-721-7112; 361 Fortaleza; r without bathroom per week from $65) Budget accommodations in Old San Juan are not for the fussy. For this price you get a tiny room with air-con and not a lot else – except for perhaps a few multilegged creatures skittering by (ants, not roaches). Phone ahead as this place books up fast.

MIDRANGE

Da House (Map pp90-1; ☎ 787-977-1180; 312 San Francisco; r $80; ✗ ☐) Make no mistake; Da House is da place to be. Old San Juan's newest and funkiest hotel is also one of its best bargains, with 27 boutique-style rooms kitted out with chic furnishings and decorated with eye-catching contemporary art. Rather uniquely each room is dedicated to a different local artist whose work is displayed within, complete with tantalizing price tags to ponder over. For the musically inclined one of San Juan's best salsa bars, the Nuyorican, is situated downstairs; for the less enamored (or sleep-deprived), the reception staff will ruefully give out ear plugs.

Hotel Plaza de Armas (Map pp90-1; ☎ 787-722-9191; www.ihphoteles.com; 202 San José; r $90-175; ✗) Location, location, location – but not a lot else. The Plaza de Armas is a rather characterless hotel situated in San Juan's most character-loaded quarter. Run by the Howard Johnson chain, the lobby has some funky modern touches, but upstairs the rooms are worn, the furnishings exhausted, and the lack of windows enough to strike terror into the heart of any visiting claustrophobic.

Hotel Milano (Map pp90-1; ☎ 787-729-9050; www.hotelmilanopr.com; 307 Fortaleza; r incl breakfast $95-185; ✗ ☐) Sandwiched into the happening hub of Fortaleza St, the Milano is a safe, reliable, if slightly austere option. Rooms are clean but unexciting, there's wi-fi in the lobby and up on the roof there's an open-to-the-elements restaurant with peek-a-boo views of the harbor. It's a handy and comfortable midrange option within easy staggering distance of some of San Juan's best bars and restaurants.

AlaSol Apartments (Map pp90-1; ☎ 787-724-4456; 318 Sol; apt per night/wk $100/500; P ✗) These handy one bedroom apartments (three-night

minimum) have to be one of the best bargains in Old San Juan. Located on neighborly Sol with all of the restaurant and museum action a hop, skip and jump away, the traditional but comfortable rooms have a double bed, futon, kitchen, bathroom, living room, phone, TV and – almost unheard of in Old San Juan – a parking space out front. Priceless!

TOP END

Chateau Cervantes (Map pp90-1; ☎ 787-724-7722; 329 Recinto Sur; r/ste $225/975; P ✗ ☐) Twelve rooms on six floors, an intimate decor and a stunning level of all-round opulence, the Cervantes is about as luxurious as Puerto Rico gets. Designed as a boutique hotel of the highest class by local guru, Nono Maldonado, the hotel is hard to find and barely advertises itself from the street – probably because it doesn't need to. Once inside, 'chateau' is definitely the right word in this Parisian-influenced city beauty with its eye-catching art (original, of course) and up-to-the-minute electronic gadgets deftly splashed around rooms that retain a tangible old town feel. Despite its city-center location, privacy is a premium here and the service is refreshingly discreet.

Gallery Inn (Map pp90-1; ☎ 787-722-1808; www.thegalleryinn.com; 204-206 Norzagaray; r incl breakfast $225-325; P ✗ ☐) Get ready to double-take here. This quirky artist-owned hotel will make you feel as if you've wandered inadvertently onto the set of a Harry Potter movie. Showcasing masks, caged birds, trickling water, antiques, paintings and well-thumbed books, the Gallery Inn's cavernous 18th-century compound is the property of local artists Jan D'Sopo and Manuco Gandía (who'll meet guests for a daily 5pm cheese and wine tour). Perched romantically above the Atlantic waves and boasting 23 eclectic and whimsical rooms, it will be like nowhere else you have ever visited. Three hundred years of art, antiques and history stuffed into one building – staggering.

our pick Gran Hotel El Convento (Map pp90-1; ☎ 787-723-9020; www.elconvento.com; 100 Calle del Cristo; r $235-420; P ✗ ☐ ☐) Historic monument, tapas restaurant, meeting place, coffee bar, and evocative colonial building…without a doubt El Convento is Puerto Rico's most complete atmospheric and multifaceted hotel. Built in 1651 as the New World's first Carmelite convent, this sturdy baroque beacon oozes with priceless old world relics and subtle 'Siglo de Oro' charm. Check out the Goya-esque tapestries in the hallway or the late afternoon tranquility of the enclosed inner courtyard, or wander up onto the roof deck for a plunge in the tiny pool and Jacuzzi that frame sweeping city views over the Cathedral and Old San Juan. El Convento's 58 rooms and six suites are gorgeously decorated with Andalusian tiles, mahogany and thick rugs, plus the service from the bar to the front desk is impeccable. Oh – and there's no casino!

Condado & Ocean Park

BUDGET

Alelí by the Sea (Map pp98-9; ☎ 787-725-5313; 1125 Sea View; r $65-100; **P** **✄**) Condado on the cheap – it's still possible; though judging by the number of cranes and bulldozers that surround this diminutive hotel, it might not be for too much longer. If the Marriot's normally your thing you'll undoubtedly hate this modest nine-room guesthouse positioned right on the beach. If you've just returned from a backpacking trip around Southeast Asia, the delightful surfside terrace and simple but clean rooms will seem like luxury.

Embassy Guest House (Map pp98-9; ☎ 800-468-0615; 1126 Sea View; r $65-125; **P** **✄** **✄**) A favorite budget spot among gay travelers – although others like it too – the Embassy is a motel-standard crash pad that has so far resisted the glitzy Condado makeover. The rooms show their age a bit, but since the oceanfront location is sublime, it's hardly worth fussing about.

MIDRANGE

At Wind Chimes Inn (Map pp98-9; ☎ 800-946-3244; www.atwindchimesinn.com; 53 Taft; r $80-155; **P** **✄** **✄** **✄**) Linked to the nearby Acacia Inn, At Wind Chimes is modeled along the same lines: a Spanish-style villa that mixes intimacy with low-key luxuries. It's a pleasant antidote to the resort feel of Condado's other luxury piles. Prices drop in the off-season, making this even more of a bargain.

Hostería del Mar (Map pp98-9; ☎ 787-727-3302; hostelria@caribe.net; 1 Tapia; r $89-199; **P** **✄** **✄**) If the nearby Número Uno can live up to its priceless premier tag, then the Hostería del Mar has to be a close *número dos*. Sharing an equally desirable beachside location and greeting guests with an artsy water feature and eye-catching antiques, this whitewashed Ocean Park guesthouse is quiet, intimate and definitively Caribbean. There's no pool,

but there is an excellent restaurant (p122) in an enclosed gazebo overlooking the beach. Rooms are furnished with a simple rattan-inspired elegance.

Atlantic Beach Hotel (Map pp98-9; ☎ 787-721-6900; www.atlanticbeachhotel.net; 1 Vendig; r $90-170; **✄**) This place is regularly held up as the nexus of the Caribbean's gay community, though in recent years many visitors have derided it for its dingy rooms and lackluster service – it all depends on your expectations. Wedged up against the beach at the end of one of Condado's tattier streets, the Atlantic certainly has a great ocean side location and, with a buzzing bar scene, rooftop Jacuzzi and famous Sunday drag shows, it's a good place to hang out and meet other gay travelers. The sticking point for many is the rooms, which, though clean, are long past their prime – which was sometime in the early 1980s.

El Canario by the Sea (Map pp98-9; ☎ 787-533-2649; www.canariohotels.com; 4 Calle Condado; r $105-150; **✄**) There are actually three different Canario inns around Condado – agents here at the By the Sea site can assist you in reserving at any one of the properties. Each of the small hotels has 25 to 40 units with cable TV, phone and continental breakfast. You get a quiet, clean, well-lit place.

Acacia Seaside Inn (Map pp98-9; ☎ 787-728-0668; 8 Taft; r $105-185; **✄** **✄**) How's this for a makeover! The former Arcade Inn – now more exotically renamed the Acacia – was, until a couple of years ago, a grandiose Spanish colonial–style mansion with a seemingly terminal illness. The recent recipient of a full-on TV-design-show–style renovation, this mini-hotel has transformed itself into a chic smorgasbord of sophistication and style. We're talking funky wall art, a salubrious fern-filled restaurant, and an impossibly luxurious Jacuzzi complete with granite surround and Buddha statue imported from China. *Tranquilo,* man.

Coral Princess Inn (Map pp98-9; ☎ 787-977-7700; 1159 Magdalena; r 125-195; **✄** **✄** **✄**) Now we're talking. An independent inn that can compete in the quality stakes with the bigger and plusher opposition. The Coral Princess is a small 25-room boutique hotel that punches way above its weight. Sitting in Condado's midrange bracket, it offers all the luxuries of the fancy resorts – flat-screen TVs, marble floors and original art – but with enough intimacy and Latin flavor to remind you that you're still in Puerto Rico.

Número Uno (Map pp98-9; ☎ 787-726-5010; 1 Santa Ana; r $130-200; P ✗ 🖳 🐂) Pinch yourself – you're still in the middle of San Juan: Ocean Park, to be more precise, the discerning traveler's antidote to Condado and Isla Verde. Hidden behind the walls of a whitewashed 1940s beachfront house, the glowing Número Uno is one of those whispered secrets that gets passed around surreptitiously by word of mouth. Surrounded by palms and topped by a luminous kidney-shaped swimming pool, the property is run by a former New Yorker whose soaring vision has inspired an inn of spiffy rooms, intimate service and one of San Juan's newest culinary legends, Pamela's (p117), an exquisite on-site seafood restaurant. Número Uno? Not far off.

TOP END

Normandie Hotel (Map pp98-9; ☎ 787-729-2929; www .normandiepr.com; 499 Av Muñoz Rivera; r $200-325; P ✗ 🖳 🐂) A classic example of late art deco–style architecture, the Normandie is characterized by its minimalist front facade, which represents the curved bows of a cruise liner guarding the busy entrance to Puerta de Tierra. Once a haven for scandalous 1950s jet-setters who used to cavort nude in the rear pool, the hotel's contemporary incarnation has fewer accessories but more soul than the neighboring Caribe. The centerpiece is a towering, if austere, open-plan lobby where bemused cruise-liner refugees have replaced the lounge lizards of lore.

Caribe Hilton (Map pp98-9; ☎ 787-721-0303; www .hiltoncaribbean.com/sanjuan; Rosales; r $260-450; P ✗ 🖳 🐂) Situated quite literally at the *puerta* (door) of Puerta de Tierra, the Caribe was the first Hilton hotel outside mainland America. Constructed in 1949 after an architectural competition had chosen a utilitarian modern design drawn up by a local firm, the hotel played host to numerous celebrities throughout the 1950s and '60s. Showing its age a bit of late, the Caribe has undergone some long-awaited renovations though reviews remain mixed. There's good beach access and Old San Juan is a not unpleasant 30-minute walk away.

San Juan Marriott Resort & Casino (Map pp98-9; ☎ 787-722 7000; www.marriotthotels.com; 1309 Av Ashford; r $265-525; P ✗ 🖳 🐂) The infamous Hotel Dupont Plaza once stood on this site before an arson attack burnt it to the ground, claiming 97 lives, in 1986. Rising in its place a decade later, Marriot has turned a den of notoriety into a pretty beachfront property, with two pools and 525 units. A lot more personable than other resorts in its class, the Marriott boasts enviably modern rooms, a lavish breakfast buffet and some mean salsa entertainment where even the staff join in.

Condado Plaza Hotel & Casino (Map pp98-9; ☎ 727-721-1000; 999 Av Ashford; r $300-1350; P ✗ 🖳 🐂) Guarding the entrance to Condado like a sparkling concrete sentinel, the Condado Plaza straddles the thin wedge of land that separates the area's eponymous *laguna* from the Atlantic Ocean. Housed in two concrete towers connected by an overhead walkway above Ashford Av, the hotel offers the best of both worlds with stunning views extending in both directions. A swanky lobby redolent of a designer movie set hints at luxury, and guests in the newly renovated oceanfront rooms generally aren't disappointed. Other highlights include a fitness center, spa, live entertainment, a celebrated Italian restaurant and a lovely arc of raked sand that faces the formidable walls of Fuerte San Gerónimo across the inlet.

Isla Verde

BUDGET

El Patio Guesthouse (Map p101; ☎ 787-726-6298; 87 Calle 3; r $69-90; ✗ 🐂) Your average Isla Verde visitor probably wouldn't poke a stick at this place, but in the cheaper price bracket it's not a bad bet – although gamblers will be disappointed to know that there's no casino on-site. A little villa close to the beach and other amenities, it is run by a little old lady who'll bend over backwards to make sure that your rooms are spick and span.

MIDRANGE

Coqui Inn (Map p101; ☎ 787-726-4330; 36 Calle Mar Mediterráneo; r $89-119; P 🐂) Bisected by a major expressway, Isla Verde has its ugly side and you'll get a face full of it here. But location aside, the Coqui Inn – which is an amalgamation of three formerly adjacent hotels: the Mango Inn, the Green Island Inn and Casa Mathiesen – is quite the bargain. Expect clean, modern but simple rooms with kitchenette and plenty of handy extras, such as wi-fi, free coffee/pastries, morning newspapers, cable TV and maid service. Visitors with ear plugs can take comfort in the price and the proximity to the beach – a short walk across a concrete bridge.

GAY & LESBIAN SAN JUAN

Considered to be the most gay-friendly destination in the Caribbean, San Juan has long buried its stereotypical macho image and replaced it with a culture that is remarkable for its tolerance and openness. The beach areas of Condado and Ocean Park are the nexus of the club and cruising scene, but with so many of the capital's hotels and restaurants now run by gay professionals, the finer details of one's sexual preference are usually irrelevant.

One of the oldest gay meeting spots is the Atlantic Beach Hotel (p119) in Condado, though the establishment has been criticized of late – for its declining room standards more than anything – and some travelers have moved on to more mixed spots such as Número Uno (p111) in Ocean Park, the San Juan Marriott Resort & Casino (p111) and the delectable Gran Hotel El Convento (p109) in the heart of the Old City.

For a decent social scene, the beach and bar in front of the Atlantic Beach Hotel is still the best place to meet other gay travelers, though with big new condo developments now enveloping Condado many gay clubs have migrated to grittier Santurce (p120). High energy nightspots to look out for are Krash for men, Cups for women, and Kouros for a good mix of both.

Most dining spots can be considered gay-friendly but perennially popular with the gay community are Parrot Club (p115) in SoFo, Pamela's (p117) inside the Número Uno guesthouse and El Picoteo (p114) in the Gran Hotel El Convento.

Hotel La Playa (Map p101; ☎ 787-791-1115; www.hotellaplaya.com; 6 Amapola; r $95-135) Isla Verde isn't all glitz. At the eastern end of the beach and the bottom end of the quality bracket lies Hotel La Playa which, while living up to its name (it's literally on the beach), probably isn't what your average fun-in-the-sun honeymooner is looking for, but if price is your major determinant and you're not a sucker for cleanliness, give it a whirl. If you're in Isla Verde to get what Isla Verde is famous for, the Ritz Carlton (opposite) is just around the corner.

Hotel Villa del Sol (Map p101; ☎ 787-791-2600; 4 Rosa; r $100-160; P ⚟ ⚓) Up a side street in Isla Verde, the Villa del Sol provides an adequate economical alternative to the larger resorts. Embellished with Spanish colonial architecture and blessed with an attractive pool area, spacious rooms and a popular bar/grill, the hotel gives off a sunny tropical aura without stretching your purse strings.

Water & Beach Club (Map p101; ☎ 787-728-3610; 2 Tartak; r $150-650; P ⚟ ⚏ ⚓) Breaking the resort ubiquity of Isla Verde, the Water & Beach Club is – along with the Horned Dorset (p232) in Rincón – Puerto Rico's most celebrated 'boutique' hotel. With a reception area straight out of *Architectural Digest* and elevators that sport glassed-in waterfalls, this is probably the closest San Juan comes to emulating South Beach, Florida. The minimalist rooms are artfully designed and benefit from spectacular beach views, and you have close proximity to two trendy nightspots (p119). There's also a chicer-than-chic swimming pool on the roof.

TOP END

El San Juan Hotel & Casino (Map p101; ☎ 800-468-2818; www.elsanjuanhotel.com; 6063 Av Isla Verde; r $325-450; P ⚟ ⚏ ⚓) Dimly lit, frigidly air-conditioned and decked out in throwback 1970s furnishings, the lobby of El San Juan is redolent of a Roger Moore–era James Bond movie: you half expect to see the dapper 007 lounging around in his tux at the baccarat table. Instead you get a veritable fashion parade of everyone who is anyone in San Juan prancing in for the legendary nightly entertainment. Renowned for its flashy casino and rollicking nightlife, El San Juan does its best to recreate 'tourist brochure paradise' in among the Isla Verde skyscrapers. If you want decent rooms, unlimited water features, classy restaurants, Starbucks coffee and a heaving nightlife all in one big happy package, this is the place for you.

InterContinental San Juan Resort & Casino (Map p101; ☎ 800-443-2009; www.intercontinental.com; 187 Av Isla Verde; r $399-539; P ⚟ ⚏ ⚓) Probably the least interesting of Isla Verde's craning tourist piles, the Intercontinental is, nonetheless, opulent with all of the usual gadgets and marketing ploys you'd expect in a well-appointed four star. An expensive refurbishment a few years back was designed to put it on a par with El San Juan next door and, although the rooms and facilities are spiffy enough, the latter still wins first prize for character and panache.

Ritz Carlton Hotel & Casino (Map p101; ☎ 800-241-3333; www.ritzcarlton.com; 6961 Av Los Gobernadores; r $400-2500; P ⊠ ⌨ ⊠) Ritz equals posh, you'd better pack the trendy slacks and bring along a platinum credit card before booking a night here. Decked out in expensive marble and embellished with Alhambra-esque lions that line the path to the swimming pool, this is San Juan at its swankiest and a favorite hangout of visiting celebrities. Rooms are plush, service heavy on the 'yes sirs and madams' and the communal areas shimmer like winning entries in an international design competition. Parceled inside this carefully manicured tropical 'paradise' are a resident spa, numerous eating facilities and yes, that obligatory casino, which incidentally is the largest of its kind in the Caribbean.

Miramar & Río Piedras

While these areas have none of the seaside attractions of Old San Juan, Condado/Ocean Park or Isla Verde, the commercial heart of the city does offer a handful of viable accommodations options.

Olimpio Court Hotel (Map pp98-9; ☎ 787-724-0600; 603 Calle Miramar; r $65-135; P ⊠) Cocooned in upscale Miramar, the Olimpio isn't as fancy as its location would suggest; but, no matter. This place is all about price, cleanliness and good down-to-earth service. Santurce as well as Condado are within walking distance and Old San Juan is just a short (50c) bus ride away.

Marriott Courtyard (Map pp98-9; ☎ 787-721-7400; 801 Av Ponce de León; r $140-230; P ⊠ ⌨ ⊠) The former Excelsior Hotel was transformed into a Marriott Courtyard in 2006 and gleams thanks to a stellar renovation. A melting pot for business travelers bound for the nearby convention center and cruise passengers heading for the piers, it's a straightforward, upright sort of place with efficient staff and a renowned on-site restaurant (Augustos). Situated in leafy Miramar its location is a toss-up – central to everywhere, but close to nowhere.

EATING

Few would argue that San Juan offers the best eating in the Caribbean. Indeed, there are probably enough cutting edge restaurants here to justify a trip in its own right. The latest craze is fusion cuisine – expect to see all sorts of creative combinations: Asian–Latino, Puerto Rican–European, Caribbean with a Middle Eastern twist. When in doubt, head to Calle Fortaleza in Old San Juan, the eclectic heart of San Juan's 21st century gastronomic revolution. Most restaurants have vegetarian-friendly dishes, although they may not be billed as 'vegetarian.' Vegans may have a more difficult time as butter and meat renderings are common ingredients. See p58 for further details.

Old San Juan
BUDGET

Café Cala'o (Map pp90-1; ☎ 787-724-4607; Pier 2; muffins $2) It looks just like any other small coffee bar you might roll into in Chicago or Seattle, but in reality Café Cala'o is very different. There are two main reasons for this: the Puerto Rican coffee – which is hand-picked from various small farms in the Central Mountains – is smooth, earthy and not at all bitter, and the people who confect it are trained experts who know as much about coffee as an oenologist knows about wine. The muffins aren't bad either.

Spanglish Café (Map pp90-1; ☎ 787-722-2424; 105 Cruz; dishes $5-10; ☾ lunch & dinner) A homey hole-in-the-wall that does good business with the lunchtime office crowd, Spanglish Café is generally more *Span* than *glish*, so go with a decent phrasebook and get ready to order your $6 set lunch with a few *por favors* and *muchas gracias*. Try the *fricassee de pollo* (chicken fricassee) or the *pernil asado* (roasted pork) and don't forget to leave a *propina* (tip).

La Bombonera (Map pp90-1; ☎ 787-722-0658; 259 San Francisco; mains $5-10; ☾ 8am-4pm) The old-fashioned coffee machine hisses like a steam engine, career waiters in black trousers appear like royal footmen at your table, and a long line of seen-it-all *sanjuaneros* populate the lengthy row of bar stools, catching up on the local breakfast gossip. It shouldn't take you long to work out that La Bombonera is a city institution: it's been around since 1902 and still sells some of the best cakes in town. Come here for breakfast, lunch or an early evening snack attack and soak up the unique Latin ambience over a copy of the *San Juan Star*.

Café Mallorca (Map pp90-1; ☎ 787-724-4607; 400 San Francisco; dishes $5-10; ☾ 7am-7pm) If you spent the previous night in Marmalade or some other *haute couture* restaurant/club/fashion parade, then bring yourself back down to earth with a life-saving coffee and breakfast in this cozy nook on San Francisco. Cheap and simple, the Mallorca is where all-night ravers share pick-me-ups and American journalists sift through their travel notes. Zero pretension, but plenty of warm familiarity.

Zesty Bites (Map pp90-1; ☎ 787-721-5436; 151 Tetuán; sandwiches $5-12; ☺ 7am-5pm; **V**) Could this be the future of Puerto Rican fast food? Let's hope so. Organic salads, artisan yogurts, wraps, granola, oatmeal and the don't-leave-without-tasting-one smoothies are just a few of the healthy but zesty treats on offer here. Positioned in the heart of the historic district, Zesty fills a gap in the market that few others seem to be tackling – ie fresh, delicious food served fast. It's also dog-friendly, kid-friendly, bike-friendly, ecofriendly, computer nerd-friendly, and rather easy on the wallet.

Café Amapola (Map pp90-1; ☎ 787-392-9811; 280 Norzagaray; mains $6-12; ☺ 8am-6pm, closed Thu) Ah the view! Watch crashing surf lash the pastel-colored shantytown of La Perla as you perch on the upstairs terrace at Café Amapola. Welcome to Old San Juan's only oceanfronted eating establishment, an unpretentious café-cum-restaurant that sells memorable homegrown coffee and tasty *criolla*-spiced appetizers. Take a seat barside and the waiters will impart a whole host of insider knowledge about where to go and what to see island-wide.

ourpick **St Germain Bistro & Café** (Map pp90-1; ☎ 787-725-5830; 156 Sol; dishes $7-15; ☺ breakfast, lunch & dinner, closed Mon; **V**) Kudos to the chef for transforming the main course salads – so often the dullest dish on the menu – into something fresh, tasty and filling. Then there's the aromatic Puerto Rican coffee, the delicious *paninis* and the homemade cakes which can only be described as melt-in-your-mouth heavenly. Nestled on the corner of Sol and Cruz, the St Germain is a bright neighborhood place with down-to-earth service, interesting clientele and a distinct European feel. Perfect for breakfast, lunch or a light dinner.

MIDRANGE

La Fonda El Jibarito (Map pp90-1; ☎ 787-725-8375; 280 Sol; dishes $8-22; ☺ 11am-11pm) Welcome to the neighborhood, *hermano*. El Jibarito is the kind of salt-of-the-earth, unpretentious place that you should reserve to sample your first *mofongo* or *arroz con habichuelas* (rice and beans). A favorite of local families, in-the-know tourists and passing *New York Times* journalists, the meals are simple but hearty with good pork and prawns, or plantains smashed, mashed and fried just about any way you want. Pull up a pew and chow with the locals.

El Picoteo (Map pp90-1; ☎ 787-723-9020; 100 Calle del Cristo; tapas $8-24; ☺ lunch & dinner) One of El Convento's culinary highlights is this terrace tapas bar that could rival anything in Andalusia. Perennial favorites include tortilla, meatballs, garlic prawns, garbanzos and various cheeses. If you're after something more substantial there's also pizza and paella washed down with sangria. Suspended above the hotel's central courtyard the ambience at Picoteo is terrific and, during the afternoon, the canned music is punctuated by the familiar clack of dominoes.

Patio de Nispero (Map pp90-1; ☎ 787-723-9020; 100 Calle del Cristo; sandwiches $9.50-12, platters $14-24; ☺ lunch) Every great Spanish-colonial hotel has its shady courtyard and the one at El Convento is the home of the deliciously cool Patio de Nispero, so named for the 350-year-old Nispero tree that resides in its midst. You can enjoy breakfast and lunch here or, even better, escape the hot sun-bleached streets to savor a coffee or an icy mojito during the lazy siesta hour.

Café Berlin (Map pp90-1; ☎ 787-722-5205; 407 San Francisco; dishes $10-25; ☺ 10am-10pm Mon-Fri, 8am-10pm Sat & Sun; **V**) You've probably heard about the Taíno, the Spanish, the French and the Americans, but the German influence in Puerto Rico is less well documented, unless you wind up sampling sweet pastries on the pleasant terrace here. In a setting that's more Viennese than Caribbean, the Café Berlin serves fresh European-style food with a strong vegetarian/vegan bias. Check out the veggie pizza, the tofu done any which way you want and don't leave without ordering a manjito (a mango-flavored mojito). The sweet Teutonic deserts are positively sinful and the German rye bread is so popular that they fly it on demand over to Culebra.

Barú (Map pp90-1; ☎ 787-977-7107; 150 San Sebastián; dishes $13-30; ☺ 6pm-midnight) Very popular with food lovers and martini drinkers, Baru doubles as a nightspot as well as a trendy restaurant. Dishes include 'yuccafongo' (yucca made like a *mofongo*) with shrimp, beef carpaccio with basil essence or the mahimahi topped with crispy onions.

Makarios (Map pp90-1; ☎ 787-723-8653; 361 Tetuán; dishes $15-20; ☺ noon-midnight) Just when you thought you'd already circumnavigated the culinary globe in Fortaleza St, you move a block south and end up in Lebanon, or Turkey, or is it Greece? Makarios is San Juan's rather boisterous, but authentic, take on Middle Eastern cuisine that shimmies to the rhythms of its resident belly dancers on weekend nights. Arrive with your water pipe (plenty do), tuck into falafel, hummus or delicious lamb kabobs, and ponder the alfresco antics of San Juan's musical youth as they prance and pose outside.

El Patio de Sam (Map pp90-1; ☎ 787-723-1149; 102 San Sebastián; dishes $16-28; ☺ 11:30am-midnight) This legendary Old Town staple overlooks San Juan's oldest square and a statue of Ponce de León, who looks on jealously as drinkers down cheap margaritas and tackle juicy burgers with hungry relish. Part of the San Sebastián nightly music fest, there's glimmering neon on the inner patio along with live Brazilian jazz music at weekends.

Tantra (Map pp90-1; ☎ 787-977-8141; 356 Fortaleza; dishes $18-27; ☺ noon-midnight) For purists, eating Masala Dosa in Puerto Rico is probably about as incongruous as chomping on *mofongo* in Madras, but for those willing to drop the cultural blinkers, Tantra's adventurous 'Indo-Latin fusion' cuisine is actually rather authentic. It helps that the chef's from South India. It also helps that the restaurant's Asian-inspired decor, which places exotic lampshades among carved Buddhas, sets your taste buds traveling inexorably east. The pièce de résistance is the belly dancing that kicks off nightly at nine-ish.

El Burén (Map pp90-1; ☎ 787-977-5023; 103 Calle del Cristo; dishes $18-30; ☺ noon-midnight Tue-Sun, 5:30pm-midnight Mon) If you rate intimacy over elbow room, inhale deeply and pull up one of the 24 chairs at this stylish purple and tangerine bistro. As trendy as it is tiny, El Burén offers an eclectic menu with distinct Puerto Rican flourishes, with food delivered to your table like art on a plate. Check out the lamb, prawns or lobster.

Dragonfly (Map pp90-1; ☎ 787-977-3886; 364 Fortaleza; dishes $20-29; ☺ 5:30-11pm Mon-Wed, 5:30-midnight Thu-Sun) Duck nachos – say no more! Safe in its mantle as the hippest of the hip, Dragonfly is SoFo's most stylish culinary innovator; the G-spot of the Latin-Asian fusion movement that brims nightly with a plethora of self-assured, well-dressed and, frankly, beautiful people. Presuming you pass the dress inspection on the door and survive the shock of your initial entrance (the place resembles a dark red bordello – all dim lamp shades and decorative mirrors), try following up with a hard-hitting Dragon Punch cocktail before you dive into a menu awash with the wonderful and the plain weird (yes, those duck nachos).

Trois Cent Onze (Map pp90-1; ☎ 787-725-7959; 311 Fortaleza; dishes $20-30; ☺ noon-3pm & 6:30-11:30pm) After putting all his creative energy into his food, French owner Christophe Gourdain presumably couldn't muster up enough energy to think up an original name for his formidable culinary extravaganza: hence Trois Cent Onze (311), the place's numerical address on Fortaleza St. With its well-established French connection, 311 has the words 'elegant,' 'refined' and 'sophisticated' written all over it, conjuring up classy European cuisine without too many of those Latino-fusion makeovers (alas, no *mofongo* with a camembert twist here). Glide into one of the island's most romantic interiors, awash with billowing white curtains, flickering candles and delightful Moorish-Andalusian tiles and order from a menu replete with scallops, duck and foie gras. Not surprisingly, there's a wine list to rival anything in France.

Parrot Club (Map pp90-1; ☎ 787-725-7370; 363 Fortaleza; dishes $20-32; ☺ noon-3pm & 6-11pm) The menu's in Spanglish, the decor's a lurid mix of orange, blue and yellow, and the waitress could quite conceivably be sporting a pink wig. Welcome to the Parrot Club, where Puerto Rican politicians wind down and enamored gringos live it up. Until the Parrot's opening in 1996, the concept of SoFo didn't even exist. But, with its caustic blend of live jazz and tasty 'nuevo Latino' cuisine, this restaurant quickly set new standards and spawned the ultimate in neighborhood chic – an acronym. Now well into its second decade the menu continues to win kudos with its eclectic crabcakes *caribeños*, pan-seared tuna and vegetarian tortes.

TOP END

Sonné (Map pp90-1; ☎ 787-721-0136; 385 Fortaleza; dishes $20-68; ☺ 5pm-midnight) A Latin-fusion steakhouse with mood lighting and background jazz, Sonné is as much SoHo as SoFo which probably accounts for the extortionate prices, including $68 for a steak. Occupying a prime

LATIN FUSION IN OLD SAN JUAN

While Old San Juan is well known for its historic Spanish forts and atmospheric cobbled plazas, few outsiders arrive expecting to find a clutch of cutting edge gourmet restaurants shoehorned in among the quaint 16th-century facades. But hidden inside one of America's oldest urban quarters, streets that once played host to cutlass-brandishing pirates are now the preserve of knife-wielding chefs. San Juan's culinary nexus is situated in the compact neighborhood of SoFo (an acronym for 'South Fortaleza St'), a trendy but constantly changing strip of funky wine bars and dimly lit restaurants that has sent many a holidaying food critic home happy. Small, cozy and architecturally interesting, these engaging eating establishments are famous for their Latin-fusion cuisine, an eclectic mix of traditional Latin American ingredients such as rice, beans, pork and plantains, blended with more exotic flavors from Asia, Europe and beyond.

A relatively recent phenomenon, SoFo didn't exist until 1996 when the groundbreaking Parrot Club (p115) opened, spearheading a full-on gastronomic revolution. Within a few years, the neighborhood has burgeoned into an internationally renowned restaurant strip that celebrates its own annual culinary festival and has drawn in a plethora of talented chefs from around the globe. OOF Restaurants, owners of the original Parrot Club, have led the way supplementing their initial food foray with two additional eating joints, the Asian-influenced Dragonfly (p115) and the seafood extravaganza, Aquaviva (below). These days you can tour the globe in just two blocks. For South Indian fusion try Tantra (p115), for Puerto Rico with a Lebanese twist visit Makarios (p115), or for up-to-the-minute nouveau cuisine head for Marmalade (below) or Sonné (p115).

As the new nexus for contemporary Caribbean cuisine, SoFo is a font of experimental food fashions. As a result, different restaurants come and go remarkably quickly. Readers should thus treat this book's eating recommendations as a basic list of ingredients on an ever-evolving menu.

position on Fortaleza, it's one of the newest establishments in the ever-evolving San Juan culinary fest. Word on the street suggests it's a stayer.

La Mallorquina (Map pp90-1; ☎ 787-722-3261; 207 San Justo; dishes $22-35) A must for historically-minded food buffs, or food-minded history buffs, La Mallorquina is the grande dame of Old San Juan eateries: it's been around for 150 years, quite a feat in the musical chairs of Fortaleza St and its surrounds. It's worth a gander, if only to have a drink at the immense slab of mahogany that is the bar. Should the smells from the kitchen tempt you to stay, try the house specialty, *asopao*, a rice broth stewed with all type of herbs, seafood or meat.

Marmalade (Map pp90-1; ☎ 787-724-3969; 317 Fortaleza; dishes $25-39; ⊗ 6pm-midnight) With a name liable to dupe over-excited Brits who've been missing out on their early morning toast and marmalade fix, it is somewhat surprising to find that Marmalade doesn't actually serve the stuff at all, except perhaps in a marinade. Promoted as SoFo's latest culinary innovator in a street full of them, this starkly minimalist eating establishment is decked out like the Korova Milk Bar in Stanley Kubrick's *A Clockwork Orange*. Step

inside the trendy interior to sample house specialties such as paella bites or grilled nectarines with Parma ham.

Aquaviva (Map pp90-1; ☎ 787-722-0665; 364 Fortaleza; dishes $30-40; ⊗ 6-11pm Mon-Wed, 6pm-midnight Thu-Sat, 4-10pm Sun) Cerviche's the word at Aquaviva, the third of SoFo's trendy restaurant trio and owned by the same company as Dragonfly and the Parrot Club. Designed with an arty water/sea-life theme – all turquoise blues and brilliant whites – the house specialty is seafood, in particular the cerviches, with plenty of patrons rolling in just to savor an appetizer with a pre-dinner cocktail. Often packed to the rafters, Aquaviva was invented with the word 'hip' in mind. Everything from the open-view kitchen to the catwalk clientele is slavishly stylish. But the real test is the food: fresh oysters, calamari filled with shredded beef, and dorado with lightly grilled bell peppers, seasoned with garlic and served with plantains. It has been voted one of the top 75 restaurants in the world.

Condado & Ocean Park

Don't let the prevalence of second-rate hotel restaurants, tourist traps and fast-food chains deter you – there's good eating to be found along this stretch of beach.

BUDGET

Hacienda Don José (Map pp98-9; ☎ 787-722-5880; 1025 Av Ashford; dishes $3-12; ☽ 7am-11pm) Condado on the cheap – it can still be done. Indeed, the Don José is more redolent of a Mexican beach bar than a plush tourist trap. Waves lash against the rocks within spitting distance of your pancakes and huevos rancheros, and busy waitresses shimmy around the tiled tables and colorful murals. If your swanky hotel's all-you-can-eat breakfast buffet has worn you out, drop by here for a little bit of local hospitality.

Kasalta's (Map pp98-9; ☎ 787-727-7340; 1966 McLeary; dishes $4-10; ☽ 6am-10pm) Wake up with a jolt at Kasalta's, a popular early-morning breakfast haunt and the sort of authentic Puerto Rican bakery and diner that you'll find yourself crossing town to visit. Tucked into Ocean Park's residential enclave, the coffee here is as legendary as the sweets that fill a long glass display case and encapsulate everything from Danish pastries to iced buns. Plentiful seating, myriad newspapers and a buzzing local ambience add even more icing to the cake.

Pepin's (Map pp98-9; ☎ 787-728-6280; 2479 Av Isla Verde; tapas $5-13; ☽ lunch & dinner) Once you've got past the rather draconian dress code here – no sandals, singlets, shorts, earrings, hats, or people under 25 – you can join whoever's left at this surprisingly popular tapas bar in the Punta Las Marías neighborhood, halfway between Isla Verde and Ocean Park. The tapas start at $5 and there's usually a fair smattering of expats.

Via Appia (Map pp98-9; ☎ 787-725-8711; Av Ashford; pizzas $7-14; ☽ 11am-11pm) The good thing about Condado is that it still retains a smattering of family-run jewels among all the Starbucks and 7-Elevens. Via Appia is one such gem, a no-nonsense Italian restaurant where the pizza is classic and the gentlemanly waiters could quite conceivably have walked off the set of *The Godfather*. Munch on garlic bread or feast on meatballs alfresco, as the multilingual mélange of Av Ashford goes strolling by. There's a small store inside where you can stock up on wine or olive oil.

MIDRANGE

Uvva Restaurant (Map pp98-9; ☎ 787-727-3302; 1 Tapia; dishes $12-20; ☽ breakfast, lunch & dinner; **V**) Almost lost among Ocean Park's whitewashed villas lies one of San Juan's most understated culinary treats: an intimate vegetarian-friendly restaurant right on the beach. The menu at this eatery in the Hostería del Mar (p110) changes frequently, but tofu, brown rice and onion dishes with a side salad are always there or thereabouts.

Zabó's (Map pp98-9; ☎ 787-725-9494; 14 Candida; dishes $12-30; ☽ 6-11pm Tue-Sat) Over in condo land, this older colonial-style villa hints at something different. The variations continue inside in an intimate restaurant-cum-bar where trendsetters sup on martinis and gastronomes tuck into creative dishes such as mango and curry rice, and rosemary pork chops with garlic merlot sauce. There's music some nights, everything from Latin jazz to Flamenco.

Migas (Map pp98-9; ☎ 787-721-5991; 1400 Magdalena; dishes $15-35; ☽ 6-11pm Mon-Wed, 6pm-midnight Thu-Sat) A newish boutique restaurant on Magdalena, Migas is high on the list of bar-hopping *sanjuaneros*. Some come for drinks (champagne mainly) and others for the food – miso-glazed salmon, classic French steak frites, spicy duck with orange glaze. Real lounge lizards, meanwhile, arrive just to hang out amid the sleek elegance and fashionable buzz.

Pamela's (Map pp98-9; ☎ 787-726-5010; 1 Santa Ana; dishes $20-30; ☽ noon-10:30pm) Right on the beach and right on the money, Pamela's is encased inside the elegant Numero Uno guesthouse. Diners sup wine and munch on scallops beside a teardrop-shaped swimming pool while the ocean crashes just feet away. The menu specializes in fresh ingredients plucked from the nearby sea – think jalapeño-ginger shrimp and seafood chowder – though there are surprise twists with everything from Asian to Puerto Rican influences. The place is tucked away, but that hasn't prevented it from becoming an open secret. Reserve ahead.

TOP END

Ajili-Mójili (Map pp98-9; ☎ 787-725-9195; 1052 Av Ashford; dishes from $25; ☽ lunch & dinner) The waiters wear hats and the reception displays aromatic cigars from the Dominican Republic, so leave your sandals and singlet in your room and venture out to this classy Condado classic. Housed in one of the neighborhood's few remaining eclectic mansions, the menu is high-end *comida criolla* – such as island-style pork loin with *mofongo* – while the atmosphere is refined and romantic. Expect discreet service and sky-high prices.

Ramiro's (Map pp98-9; ☎ 787-721-9049; 1106 Magdalena; dishes $25-37; ☽ lunch & dinner) In the subjective battle to find San Juan's best all-round restaurant, Ramiro's is often in the running. Situated in the heart of rejuvenated Condado, the flavor here is Spanish with New World infusions. Expect guava sauce with your lamb, avocado with your crabmeat and banana chutney with your halibut. Ambience is elegant and reservations are a good idea.

Isla Verde

Shogun (Map p101; ☎ 787-268-4622; 35 Av Isla Verde; dishes $5-14; ☺ lunch & dinner) Lots of Japanese restaurants line the Isla Verde strip. This is one of the most popular, serving standard fare like tuna, maki and California rolls, or specialty rolls that you can put together yourself or choose from the à la carte menu.

Edith Café (Map p101; ☎ 787-253-1281; Av Isla Verde Km 6.3; dishes $6-15; ☺ 24hr) No frills, no formalities, but good food – and it's open 24 hours, though you'd think it wasn't operating at all looking at the heavily tinted windows. Come here for breakfast after one of those exuberant all-night parties and nip your hangover in the bud with two fried eggs, bacon and ham washed down with a strong cup of coffee.

Che's (Map pp98-9; ☎ 787-726-7202; 35 Caoba; dishes $12-24; ☺ lunch & dinner) Che T-shirts aren't too common in Puerto Rico, where the man who promised to 'create two, three…many Vietnams' in the Americas is regarded with a certain degree of suspicion. That said, you might see the odd red-starred beret in here tucking into *churrasco* and *parrillada* (grilled, marinated steak), or veal chops with a kind of revolutionary zeal. Generally considered to be the best Argentinean food around, Che's is popular with *sanjuaneros* and expats of all political persuasions who allow themselves to be united momentarily by a bloody good steak.

Metropol (Map p101; ☎ 787-791-5585; Av Isla Verde; dishes $12-26; ☺ dinner) You can't miss this place – it's right next to the cockfighting arena. It's a neighborhood favorite well known for the plentiful portions and simple (but not plain) Spanish fare. Wandering tourists are sometimes lured out of their upscale resorts and into its inviting fold.

Casa Dante (Map p101; ☎ 787-726-7310; 39 Av Isla Verde; dishes $14-22; ☺ lunch & dinner) Casa Dante is a family-run restaurant that serves more variations of *mofongo* than one would think humanly feasible. All are delicious, and you can stick to fajitas or enchiladas or a basic steak if that's what you prefer.

Oyster Bar & Grill (Map p101; ☎ 787-726-2161; Condominio La Posada, Av Isla Verde; mains $20-30; ☺ lunch & dinner) Rubbing up against the fancy joints in Isla Verde, the Oyster looks like a rather lackluster alternative. But step inside to taste the spicy crawfish and signature oysters and you could be in for a surprise. Surprise number two comes later on when a dance-happy, salsa-loving crowd hits the floor for a party that doesn't finish until 4am at weekends.

Miramar & Santurce

Chayote (Map pp98-9; ☎ 787-722-9385; 603 Av Miramar; dishes $22-30; ☺ lunch & dinner) Named for a flavorful island vegetable, Chayote is situated in the understated and none too trendy Olimpio Court Hotel (p113). But with its robust *criollo* cooking injected with French, Hindu, African, Spanish and Central American flavors, the restaurant easily trumps the sometimes iffy rooms. International celebrities have been spotted among the traditional wicker and contemporary art furnishings here.

Pikayo (Map pp98-9; ☎ 787-721-6194; 299 Av José de Diego; dishes $25-40; ☺ noon-3pm Tue-Fri & 6-11pm Mon-Sat) Wilo Benet is the island's very own Gordon Ramsey (without the expletives), a celebrity chef par excellence who has uncovered the soul of Caribbean cooking by infusing colonial era Puerto Rican cuisine with various African and Indian elements. Adding atmosphere to authenticity, Pikayo, Benet's showcase restaurant, is situated inside San Juan's stunning Museo de Arte de Puerto Rico (p100) where – with unprecedented transparency – diners can watch the action in the kitchen on closed-circuit TVs. Intrigued? Well, shimmy on over.

Río Piedras

Taquería Azteca (Map p102; ☎ 787-763-0929; 52 Universidad; dishes $7-15) If you're in the area, this unfussy Mexican place near the university does burritos, nachos and empanadas *muy rápido* with all the right ingredients. A great place to meet tomorrow's literati.

DRINKING
Old San Juan

El Batey (Map pp90-1; 101 Calle del Cristo; ☺ 3pm-late) If Hunter S Thompson were still alive and living in Puerto Rico, this is where you'd probably find him. Cool, crusty and unashamedly bohemian, the walls of this cavernous drinking joint are covered in graffiti while the low-key lighting will have you groping in your pockets for spare change to light up the suitably retro jukebox. Across the road from the exquisite El Convento Hotel, El Batey is a place to down shots, shoot pool and ramble soulfully about when Elvis was king and the Bacardí bottles still came from Cuba.

Blend (Map pp90-1; ☎ 787-977-7777; 309 Fortaleza; ☯ 6pm-late) Blend has been described as uber-chic; it's certainly ubernew and – later on in the evening – uberbusy. Cocooned in an old colonial building on Fortaleza St, this fashionable dining and nightlife spot belts out electronic music from its cavernous and moodily lit interior.

Noise (Map pp90-1; ☎ 787-724-3426; 203 Tanca; ☯ 10pm-late) And plenty of it – mainly of the hip-hop variety; salsa-searchers look elsewhere. Brave ladies get in free on Friday nights. There's a metal detector and airport style pat-down at the door. Enough said.

Oleo (Map pp90-1; ☎ 787-977-1083; 305 Recinto Sur; ☯ 6pm-2am) This is Nuevo Old San Juan at its best or worst – depending on your musical persuasion. Forget that image of straw-hatted, guitar strumming *jíbaros*. Olio is all loud dance music, minimalist furnishings, expensively-clad 20-somethings and an atmosphere that's more Vegas than Borinquen. Communication is via shouting or sleek Latino body language.

Condado & Isla Verde

Kali's (Map pp98-9; ☎ 787-721-5104; 1407 Av Ashford; ☯ 6pm-late Tue-Sat) Sophisticated *sanjuaneros* love this moody, Asian-themed restaurant and bar. Sheer curtains flutter against dark maroon walls while trendy patrons sip cocktails and order Indian-influenced appetizers at a big bar adorned with candles.

Atlantic Beach Hotel (Map pp98-9 ☎ 787-721-6900; www.atlanticbeachhotel.net; 1 Vendig; ☯ from noon) Some will tell you that the Caribbean's gay scene begins and ends at this beach-side establishment. Others – while acknowledging its historical importance in the growth of gay nightlife – claim that it slid downhill since its 1980s peak. Whatever your viewpoint, the Atlantic's still crowded, well known and very much part of the scene.

Wet & Liquid (Map p101; ☎ 787-728-3666; Water Club, 2 Calle Tartak) Here they are, the beautiful people, perched on zebra-striped stools or lounging on strategically positioned sofas, martinis in hand. The buffed body-builders, the fashionistas, the 20-something wannabe actresses corseted into tight black dresses. Popularly considered to be two of San Juan's most esteemed watering holes, Wet and Liquid comprise two separate bars situated in Isla Verde's Water & Beach Club (p112). Liquid dominates the ground floor, Wet inhabits the roof. Interconnected by a space-age elevator that is decorated rather surreally with its own water feature, this is where San Juan's well-heeled and the well-endowed come to swap email addresses. The real glitterati arrive some time after midnight.

ENTERTAINMENT

Old San Juan is the G-spot of the city's nightlife, hosting what is popularly considered to be the hottest and hippest entertainment scene in the Caribbean. Walk the aesthetic streets of the historical quarter after dark and you'll encounter all sorts of cross-cultural surprises: an exotic belly dancer in a colorful Asian-fusion restaurant, a spontaneous drumming ritual in Plaza de Armas, live jazz seeping out from underneath the winking louvers along Paseo de la Princesa. For a condensed late-night scene, hit San Sebastián with its dive bars and musical clubs, or Calle Fortaleza with its trendy yet undeniably tasty restaurants.

Isla Verde is an alternative nexus with most of the action confined to a trio of international class hotels. Further west, resurgent Condado plays hosts to one of the Caribbean's biggest gay scenes. Down-at-heel Santurce also has a handful of late-night dance clubs that you'll need a taxi or car to negotiate to and from.

Live Music

OLD SAN JUAN

ourpick **Nuyorican Café** (Map pp90-1; ☎ 787-977-1276; 312 San Francisco; ☯ 7pm-late) Now, this is more like it. If you came to Puerto Rico in search of authentic salsa music, the legend still lives on at the Nuyorican Café. San Juan's hottest nightspot is a congenial hub of live Latino sounds and hip-gyrating locals that easily emulates its famous New York namesake. Stuffed into an alley off Fortaleza, opposite a nameless drinking hole, you get everything from poetry readings to six-piece salsa bands that squish onto the stage here. And you'll meet people too – the Nuyorican is refreshingly devoid of pretensions or dance snobbery. Things usually get interesting around 11pm-ish.

SAN JUAN

Gallery Café (Map pp90-1; ☎ 787-725-8676; 305 Fortaleza; ☽ 7pm-1am) This café in the old city features jazz on Wednesday night, and funk, hip-hop, Latin jazz and techno Thursday to Saturday. Happy-hour specials run till 9pm on Friday. You get a well-dressed local yuppie gang here.

CONDADO & ISLA VERDE

Marriott Hotel Lobby (Map pp98-9; ☎ 787-722-7000; 1309 Av Ashford; ☽ from 6pm) Salsa springs up in the unlikeliest of places, including in the lobby of this international hotel chain. But this is no standard tourist show. Indeed the authenticity and variety of the music here is something to behold – and people dance too (including the staff). Thursday through Saturday is salsa and meringue dancing, Wednesday is Nueva Trova with a Cuban influence, and Sunday through Tuesday is a live salsa sextet.

Martini's Cabaret (Map p101; ☎ 787-791-6100; InterContinental San Juan Resort & Casino, 187 Av Isla Verde; admission around $30; ☽ from 8pm) A luminously lit discotheque and lounge that has booked headliners such as Whitney Houston and Jay Leno in its day – Martini's in Isla Verde's InterContinental is where you go for live music, dancing or the odd celeb surprise. There's more than a hint of Las Vegas in the surroundings – and the drink prices.

Dance Clubs

OLD SAN JUAN

La Rumba (Map pp90-1; ☎ 787-725-4407; 152 San Sebastián; ☽ 11pm-late) This is what you came to Puerto Rico for – a club so packed with people of all ethnicities and ages that it matters not if you are an expert twirler or a rank neophyte who can't even spell syncopation. It won't get busy until after 11pm, when the live bands start warming up, but soon enough the trickle of people through the door will turn into a torrent and you'll be caught up in a warm tropical crush of movement. Expect salsa, samba, reggaeton, rock and, of course, rumba music.

Kudetá (Map pp90-1; ☎ 787-721-3548; 314 Fortaleza; ☽ 10pm-5am) In the snakes and ladders of San Juan nightlife, Kudetá (coup d'état – geddit?) is a precocious newcomer. It is also part of an emerging new trend: a Pan-Asian restaurant that metamorphoses after hours into a hip club with a hidden upstairs lounge where diners can disappear to dance off their Indonesian barbecued baby-back ribs and Cuba Libre–cured salmon roll salad. They've even invented their own furniture – the suede-covered Kudetá Collection.

Club Lázer (Map pp90-1; ☎ 787-721-4479; 251 Cruz; ☽ 11pm-late) It's been around for a while, but it's still a big draw. Cruise-ship escapees, employees on a night off, young, old, gay and straight pack into Club Lazer for a wild night of fun. Probably the most 'alternative' of all San Juan discos. The music ranges from house, electronica, reggaeton (sometimes) to rap and hip-hop.

Café Hijos de Borinquen (Map pp90-1; ☎ 787-723-8126; 51 San José; ☽ 8pm-late Tue-Sun) Gotta wedge your way in on weekend nights. DJs, acoustic guitars, sing-a-long sets and even a bit of patriotic fervor as the clock hand approaches midnight. And that's just the start. The so-named 'Sons of Borinquen' has been known to keep going until 6am.

CONDADO & ISLA VERDE

Club Brava (Map p101; ☎ 787-791-2781; El San Juan Hotel & Casino, 6063 Av Isla Verde; admission $5-15; ☽ 10pm-3am) A swinging club inside the El San Juan Hotel that frequently get breathless reviews from celeb spotters and all-night dance fanatics. The two-level interior is small, and the music is a mix of dance, reggaeton and salsa. The atmosphere's electric and the people-watching possibilities in the lobby beforehand strangely voyeuristic. Dress up, bring your credit card and get ready to jive to what is touted as the best sound system in the Caribbean.

El Chico Lounge (Map p101; ☎ 787-791-1000; El San Juan Hotel & Casino, 6063 Av Isla Verde; ☽ 10pm-2am) If you want to dance but discos aren't your style, then try El Chico. Professional dancers move among the crowd getting everyone in motion. Live music adds to the fun. Dressy attire required.

Cocobongo (Map p101; ☎ 787-727-3422; 2940 Av Isla Verde; ☽ 11pm-late) A Mexican-flavored restaurant/club with fine margaritas, this is a good place to catch live salsa and it rocks till late.

SANTURCE

Club Liquid (Map pp98-9; ☎ 787-647-3619; 1420 Av Ponce de León; ☽ 9pm-4am) The former Asylum Club has confusingly changed its name to Liquid (there's another Liquid bar in the Water & Beach Club Hotel). This one's darker, sweatier and more nocturnal. Night owls, of both straight and gay varieties, end their Sunday morning dance-a-thons here. Expect an

18-to-23 crowd here, except on gay nights when it's noticeably older.

Krash (Map pp98-9; ☎ 787-722-1131; 1257 Av Ponce de León; ⊗ 10pm-late) The former Eros club may have changed its name but it's still predominantly gay. Theme nights are the staple here and DJs shake the house nightly with the latest club sounds from LA, New York and beyond. Hot dancing is de rigueur and the toilets sport some strangely erotic Hellenic murals. There's a $10 cover charge after midnight.

Kouros (Map pp98-9; ☎ 787-977-0771; 1515 Av Ponce de León; ⊗ 10pm-late Sat & Sun) Open only on the weekends, Kouros is probably the most glamorous disco in town, and it caters to a well-heeled gay male and female crowd (although certainly anyone is welcome). If you want to put on something slinky and get hot and sweaty under a strobe light, check out Kouros.

Cups (Map pp86-7 ☎ 787-268-3570; 1708 San Mateo; ⊗ 10pm-late) Lesbian-friendly bars are hard to come by in San Juan, but this one in Santurce is a laid-back women's scene popular with couples and cruisers.

Classical Music, Opera & Ballet

Luis A Ferré Center for the Performing Arts (Bellas Artes; Map pp98-9; ☎ 787-724-4747; 22 Av Ponce de León; tickets $15-45) Built in 1981 in Santurce, this center has more than 1800 seats in the festival hall, about 700 in the drama hall and 200 in the experimental theater. The three concert halls fill when the Puerto Rican Symphony Orchestra holds one of its weekly winter performances. International stars also perform here, and it stages productions by the Ópera de Puerto Rico and Ballet de San Juan.

Theater

Something of a city emblem, the **Teatro Tapia** (Map pp90-1; ☎ 787-722-0407; Plaza de Colón; tickets $15-30) on the south side of Plaza Colón is an intimate neoclassical theater designed in the Italian style with three-tiered boxes and an elegantly decorated lobby. Dating from 1832 and named after the so-called 'Father of Puerto Rican literature,' Alejandro Tapia y Rivera, the building has long acted as a nexus for the island's rich cultural life and has hosted big names from the world of opera, stage and ballet from around the world. The theater was restored extensively in 1949 and then again in 1976, 1997 and 2007. Experts today rate it as the oldest free-standing drama stage in the US and its territories.

The Tapia's contemporary performances are usually in Spanish and frequently feature new works from Spain or Latin America. The acting is professional and performances attract Puerto Rico's literati and social elite.

Cinemas

Movie theaters can be found in most of San Juan's major shopping centers. You can also look in the yellow pages of the phone directory under *Teatros y Cines* (Theaters & Cinemas) for the one nearest you; be sure to ask someone you trust whether the movie house is in a safe area before you go wandering around its locale after dark. The average cost of a cinema ticket is adult/child/senior $6/2.50/4.

Reading Cinemas (Map pp86-7; ☎ 787-767-1363, 767-3505; Plaza Las Américas) In the Hato Rey district, this is the city's largest multiplex.

Teatro Metro (Map pp98-9; ☎ 787-722-0465; Parada 18, 1313 Av Ponce de León) This classic, restored cinema is in Santurce, edging towards Miramar.

UA Cinema 150 (Map p101; ☎ 787-791-0707; Laguna Gardens Shopping Center, 10 Av Laguna) This awaits viewers in Isla Verde.

Fine Arts Cinema (Map pp98-9; ☎ 787-721-4288; 654 Av Ponce de León) The island's only true art-house cinema was once a sanctuary for adult-only movies. These days it shows a good selection of independent films from around the world.

Movie buffs should refer to p108 for information on the city's up-and-coming annual cinema festival.

Casinos

Although it may not be Vegas, San Juan has certainly developed a reputation for being Las Vegas-on-sea, a mantle it stole from Havana when Castro threw the mob and their gambling syndicates out of Cuba in 1959. As a result a lot of travelers and islanders come down here purely for the action. All of San Juan's casinos are associated with resort hotels, and the gaming houses have now expanded to offer Caribbean Stud Poker, Let It Ride, Pai Gow Poker and the Big Six Wheel, as well as the standard blackjack, roulette, craps, baccarat and minibaccarat. Most of the city's casinos are open between noon and 4pm, and 8pm and 4am. Casual-smart dress is the norm.

Resorts featuring casinos include the InterContinental (p112), the El San Juan (p112) and the Ritz-Carlton (p113) in Isla Verde, the San Juan Marriott (p111) in Condado and the **Sheraton Hotel** (Map pp90-1 ☎ 787-721-5100; 100 Brumbaugh) in Old San Juan.

Sports
Estadio Sixto Escobar (p97) is a popular place for track-and-field competitions.

Home of the Montreal Expos until 2004, **Hiram Bithorn Stadium** (Map pp86-7; ☎ 787-725-2110; Plaza Las Américas, Av Roosevelt) is a small ballpark built on Astroturf. It's named after the first Puerto Rican to play in the majors.

The **Roberto Clemente Coliseum** (Map pp86-7; ☎ 787-754-7422; Roosevelt Ave) is the place to catch top boxing bouts and basketball games.

For a decent gym try **San Juan Fitness Club** (Map pp90-1 ☎ 787-877-0887; 259 Fortaleza; ☺ 5am-10pm Mon-Thu, 5am-8pm Fri, 8am-6pm Sat), which has an impressive array of equipment and charges $10 a drop-in ($20 for four visits).

SHOPPING
Arts & Crafts
The best arts and crafts shopping is in Old San Juan. San Francisco and Fortaleza are the two main arteries in and out of the old city, and both are packed cheek-by-jowl with shops. Running perpendicular at the west end of the town, Calle del Cristo is home to many of the old city's chicest establishments.

Shops worth looking out for are **Bóveda** (Map pp90-1 ☎ 787-725-0263; 200 Calle del Cristo; ☺ 10am-8pm Mon-Sat) and **Butterfly People** (Map pp90-1 ☎ 787-723-2432; 257 Cruz; ☺ 10am-6pm Mon-Sat), but your best bet is to wander at will and check out what's on offer. Popular Puerto Rican souvenirs include *santos* crafts, domino sets, cigars, rum and coffee.

Markets
Artisans Fair (Map pp86-7; Parques Muñoz Rivera & Sixto Escobar, Puerta de Tierra) Head here for more traditional shopping. The market is generally open on weekends, but call the PRTC (p88) ahead of time to inquire about changing hours of operation.

Mercado de Río Piedras (Map p102; Paseo de Diego) Of course, there's also the market for produce, meats and bargain clothing (p101).

Shopping Malls
Plaza Las Américas (Map pp86-7; ☺ 9am-9pm Mon-Sat, 11am-5pm Sun) Took the wrong turning at Miami airport? Well, no actually. The Caribbean's largest shopping mall is the 200-store Plaza Las Américas situated rather ostentatiously in Hato Rey. It's as indigenously Puerto Rican as Starbucks, but it sells almost everything you're ever likely to need.

Plaza Carolina (Map pp86-7; off Hwy 26; ☺ 9am-9pm Mon-Sat, 11am-5pm Sun) This is a similar operation,

---

DETOUR: LA PLACITA DE SANTURCE

Revitalized after a recent injection of municipal funds, the once dilapidated Santurce marketplace (Map pp98–9) is rocking just like old times. The show starts not long after dawn when bleary-eyed market traders stock up their permanent stalls with homegrown treats from around the island. There's chayote from Barranquitas, pumpkin from Coamo, pineapple from Lajas, and mango from Mayagüez – all glowing colorful, tasty and fresh in the morning sun.

Materializing mid-morning, inquisitive shoppers arrive en masse to finger and bag the best produce, before sitting down for a hearty lunch in one of the square's many family-run cafés. **Don Tello** (☎ 787-724-5752; 180 Dos Hermanos; mains $6-13; ☺ 11am-4pm Mon, 11am-10pm Tue-Sat) is a perennial favorite, although the vintage **El Popular** (787-722-4653; 205 Capitol; mains $5-7; ☺ lunch & dinner) lives up to its populist name with huge portions of delicious *comida criolla*.

At 5pm, with the market winding down for the evening, the square undergoes a heady transformation, particularly on Fridays. Still dressed in their smart work attire, groups of exhausted office clerks roll in to drink, chat, de-stress and unwind. As the myriad bars fill up, ties are loosened, a salsa band lets rip from a makeshift stage, and a bright and infectious energy infiltrates the humid yet congenial surroundings. It doesn't take long for the dancing to start. A shimmy here, a holler there, and suddenly the whole square is alive with inebriated marketing reps kicking off their high heels and slick-haired business analysts salsa-ing like repressed Ricky Martins into the morning light. Come 6am and there's little left, save for a handful of all-night revelers nursing premature hangovers and the familiar clatter of early morning traders setting out their wares for another day of business.

which lies to the east of the city, offering US standards such as JC Penney and Sears among its collection of 150 shops. It is off Hwy 26 (Expreso Baldorioty de Castro) in Carolina.

GETTING THERE & AWAY
Air
International flights arrive at and depart from Aeropuerto Internacional de Luis Muñoz Marin (LMM), which is about 8 miles east of the old city center. See p286 for information on airport services and for a list of international carriers that fly to San Juan.

Several airlines provide services between San Juan and the other parts of the commonwealth, though Puerto Rico's domestic air network is limited. Private aircraft, charter services and the bulk of the commuter flights serving the islands of Culebra and Vieques arrive at and depart from San Juan's original Aeropuerto de Isla Grande, on the Bahía de San Juan in the city's Miramar district. See p290 for details.

Cruise Ship
More than a dozen cruise lines include San Juan on their Caribbean itineraries, and as the second-largest port for cruise ships in the western hemisphere, the city is visited by more than a million cruise-ship passengers a year. All ships dock at the piers along Calle La Marina near the Customs House, just a short walk from the cobblestone streets of Old San Juan. See p289 for details.

Público
There is no islandwide bus system; públicos form the backbone of public transportation in Puerto Rico and can provide an inexpensive link between San Juan and other points on the island, including Ponce and Mayagüez. For more details see p290.

In San Juan the major público centers include the LMM airport, two large público stations in Río Piedras (Centro de Públicos Oeste and Centro de Publicos Este) and – to a lesser extent – the Plaza de Colón in Old San Juan. These are the places you should go first if you want to attempt to understand the intricacies of the fun – but sometimes difficult to fathom – público system. For detailed information see p290 and p141.

GETTING AROUND
To/From the Airport
The bus is the cheapest option. Look for the 'Parada' sign outside the arrivals concourse at LMM airport. The B40 bus will get you from the airport to Isla Verde or Río Piedras. From Isla Verde you can take bus A5 to Old San Juan and Condado. From Río Piedras you can take bus A9 to Santurce and Old San Juan.

There are also airport shuttle vans or limousine kiosks on the arrivals concourse. Chances are you can join some other travelers headed your way. Once the van fills, you'll pay around $7 to Isla Verde, $9 to Condado and $12 to Old San Juan.

Getting to LMM airport from hotels in the San Juan area is easy. Staff at virtually all of the midrange and top-end hotels will arrange for a taxi or airport shuttle van to pick you up in front of your lodging at your request. Depending on how many people share the cost of the ride, you can expect to pay between $4 and $20. If you go it alone, there are fixed prices to/from the airport and the following destinations: Isla Verde ($10), Condado ($14) and Puerta de Tierra/Old San Juan ($19).

Bicycle
San Juan is in the dark ages when it comes to provisions for cyclists. The only operator in the central tourist areas is Hot Dog Cycling (p105) in Isla Verde, which offers daily and weekly rates and allows you to take its bikes around the island. You can also rent bikes out in Piñones (p125). Rather surprisingly, cyclists can navigate a pleasant and safe cross-city route by following the shoreline from Old San Juan through Condado and Isla Verde as far as Piñones (the last part is on a designated bike lane). There is an additional bike path in Parque Lineal in Hato Rey (Map pp86–7). Elsewhere, getting in and out of the city by bike is difficult and – given the audacity of the drivers – not always advisable.

Bus
The **Autoridad Metropolitana de Autobuses** (AMA; Metropolitan Bus Authority & Metrobus; ☎ 787-767-7979) has a main bus terminal (Map pp90–1) in Old San Juan near the cruise ship piers. These are the routes taken most often by travelers (bus numbers are followed by associated route descriptions):

B40 LMM Airport, Isla Verde, Piñones and Río Piedras.

M1 & M9 Old San Juan, Río Piedras via various routes.

B21 Old San Juan, Condado, Stop 18 (Santurce), Plaza Las Américas.

A5 Old San Juan, Stop 18, Isla Verde.

C10 Hato Rey, Stop 18, Condado, Isla Grande.

In Old San Juan there is a handy free trolley bus that plies a route around the old quarter (see Mapp90–1). The trolley starts and finishes just outside the main bus terminal (see above), but you can get on and off at any one of two dozen designated stops.

Car

If you can avoid driving in the city, by all means, do so. Traffic, parking and the maze of thoroughfares make having, let alone driving, a rental car in the city a challenge.

Old San Juan has the city's two safest and most accessible parking facilities: Covadonga parking lot on Recinto Sur, just as you enter town; and Dona Fela, next door, which is slightly cheaper.

For access to El Morro or the nightlife of San Sabastián, check out the underground lot (beneath Plaza del Quinto Centenario off Calle Norzagaray) at the upper end of town. Parking costs $2.50 for the first hour, and 75c for additional hours.

For car rental, both **Avis** (800-874-3556) and **Hertz** (800-654-3131) have offices at LMM International Airport.

Ferry

A commuter ferry service called the **Acua Expreso** (☎ 787-788-1155; per trip $0.50) connects the east and west sides of Bahía de San Juan, Old San Juan and Cataño. In Old San Juan, the ferry dock is at Pier 2, near the Sheraton Old San Juan Hotel & Casino. The ferry runs every 30 minutes from 6am to 9pm.

Metro

The brand-new Tren Urbano, which opened in 2005, connects Bayamón with downtown San Juan as far as Sagrado Corazón on the south side of Santurce. Efficient trains run every five minutes in either direction between 5:30am and 11:30pm. Bicycles are permitted with a special permit. The 16 super-modern stations are safe, spacious and decked out with acres of eye-catching art and polished chrome. The line, which is a mix of sky-train and underground, charges $1.50 one-way

or $3 return for any journey, regardless of length. For more information contact **Tren Urbano** (☎ 866-900-1284).

Taxi

Cab drivers are supposed to turn on the meter for trips around town, but that rarely happens. Insist on it, or establish a price from the start. Meters – when or if they do go on – charge $1.75 initially and $1.90 per mile or part thereof. You'll also pay $1 per piece of luggage. There's a $5 reservation charge; add a $1 surcharge after 10pm.

Taxis line up at the south end of Fortaleza in Old San Juan; in other places they can be scarce. Don't make yourself a mugging target by standing on a deserted street waiting for one to pass by – call from the nearest hotel. Try **Metro Taxi Cabs** (☎ 787-725-2870) or **Rochdale Radio Taxi** (☎ 787-721-1900); they usually come when you call.

AROUND SAN JUAN

PIÑONES

Of the many arresting cultural contrasts visible in Puerto Rico, none is as striking as the abrupt transition from modern San Juan to pleasantly ramshackle Piñones, gateway to the east coast. The two worlds are linked by Punta Cangrejos, a small bridge on Rte 187 that spans Boca de Cangrejos (Crabmouth Point); once you cross it, 'resort-land' quickly becomes a distant memory.

Do as the visiting *sanjuaneros* do on weekends and saunter along the sandy curves that are backed by spiky pine groves, nosh on seafood snacks and *coco frío* (ice-cold coconut milk) sold at roadside stands, and soak up the strong Afro-Caribbean culture that permeates Loíza Aldea and Carolina, two neighboring towns that maintain strong indigenous identities in the face of urbanization.

Both a state forest – Bosque Estatal de Piñones – and a neighborhood of its parent municipality, Loíza Aldea, further to the east, Piñones presents an alternative to the high-rise condos and casino hotels of Isla Verde to the west, and the massive pharmaceutical plants of Carolina to the south. During vacations and on weekends, this entire stretch is filled with *sanjuaneros* and locals enjoying lots of African-influenced music, food and drinks.

Friquitines, also known as *buréns* in Piñones, are food kiosks of all shapes and sizes (and states of hygiene) that line the coastal road. Proprietors roast plantains, whole fish, codfish fritters and skewered pieces of seasoned pork over wood fires (it's a good idea to avoid oysters, seviche and other raw or lightly cooked dishes). Reefs just offshore create good surfing conditions and protect bathers from the full force of ocean swells, and on the days the ocean's just too rough, there's the recently completed Paseo de Piñones, a first-rate nature trail and bike path along the beach and through the forest reserve.

History

In the 16th century most of this fertile low-lying coastal region was farmed and inhabited by local people. Once the Spanish arrived and took over in 1719, huge tracts of land were turned into massive sugarcane plantations and captured natives were forced to provide the necessary labor, although they resisted mightily. Unable to keep many of their farmhands from melting into the nearby mountains, plantation owners began shipping in African workers, and sometimes stole them from other Caribbean islands. Most of the 30,000 residents living in the municipality today are freed descendants of these Yoruba slaves. The region is justifiably proud of its Afro-Caribbean heritage: Loíza Aldea is named after Luisa, a powerful Taíno *cacique* (chief) who ruled the area before the Spanish conquest.

Orientation & Information

Whatever is happening in laid-back and rural Piñones is happening on Rte 187, which parallels the ocean. Entering from the west side, coming from San Juan, there's a little bridge to cross and then immediately a sign on the left saying '*Bienvenidos a Boca de Cangrejos*' (Welcome to Crabmouth Point). The sign leads up a small incline and onto a cliff overlooking the water. Several popular *friquitines* and restaurants are located there; it's a popular drinking place and offers fabulous views, especially at sunset. The road circles and brings you back down onto Rte 187. Parking is available on the cliff top. About a mile down the road is another concentration of popular beach shacks, set just a little off the road overlooking the ocean. There are few accommodations and no real sense of the town

beyond what is immediately visible along Rte 187; eventually Rte 187 hits Rte 951, which returns to Hwy 3.

The nearest information center is located relatively close by in the LMM International Airport terminal bordered by Rte 187.

Dangers & Annoyances

Avoid walking along deserted strips of beach after nightfall, and be aware that some drug activity takes place on the beaches toward the west side of town. Don't venture onto the beach in that area at night. Watch your speed while driving; transit cops love to patrol scenic Rte 187.

Beaches

Piñones' wild beaches contrast sharply with the well-raked expanses of Isla Verde not two miles to the west – and this is part of their attraction. You can find a choice spot almost any place where Rte 187 parallels the coast. The most picturesque and deserted beaches start around Km 9. For swimming, avoid the corals at the western end of the strand of beaches. Unfortunately, this is where most of the food stands are, and it's where the bus from San Juan ends its route. Nonetheless the walk east is a pleasant ramble along a dedicated hiking/biking path.

Activities

To see a patch of the rarely viewed coastal wilderness, you can join up with a **kayak** flotilla on a three-hour guided ecotour of the Laguna de Piñones and Laguna la Torrecilla. The lagoon features fish, birds and the occasional manatee. Copladet Nature & Adventure Tours (p104) in San Juan can hook you up for $80. Boat hire is also available from Centro Cultural Ecoturístico de Piñones (see p126).

If the **surfing** is good at Piñones, you will see rows of cars with board racks parked by a good break. Or you can check ahead with one of the San Juan surf shops before you go (p104).

For **bicycling**, head across to the 5-mile-long Paseo de Piñones bike trail, running from the east end of Isla Verde along the shores of Playa Piñones and into the Bosque Estatal de Piñones. You can rent bikes from Domiro Sousa Brugal at El Pulpo Loco (p126), a beachfront restaurant on the bike trail, for $10/20 per hour/day. Alternatively head for COPI (p126) across the road.

Eating & Drinking

Although the ocean vistas, open-air seating and shade from the tall pine trees make the food kiosks a terrific place to kick back with a cold soft drink or beer, hygiene is not always a top concern for vendors in Piñones. If your stomach hasn't acclimatized yet, hit one of the more established restaurants listed below.

Piñones has a well-established nightlife, especially on weekends. There's no specific gay and/or lesbian bar in town, but gay couples won't attract any unwelcome attention at local spots.

There are countless bars, restaurants and beach shacks here and names come and go. To list them all would be nigh on impossible and detract somewhat from the joy of wandering between them and ending up where your senses carry you.

To get started you might want to try **Reef Bar & Grill** (☎ 787-791-1374; mains $15-20, beers $3; ☽ noon-10pm Wed-Thu, noon-2am Fri-Sun) with its seafood and African-flavored sides, or Dominican-run **La Terraza** (mains $15; ☽ lunch & dinner) which has live music on Saturday night. **Puerta del Mar** (mains $13-18; ☽ lunch & dinner) is also fun and serves classic *mofongo*, fritters, deep-fried fish and burgers, while **El Pulpo Loco** (☎ 787-791-8382; Rte 187 Km 4.5; mains $6-18; ☽ lunch & dinner) is a *criollo* place that also rents out bikes.

Just in front of El Pulpo Loco, **Soleil Beach Club** (☎ 787-253-1033; www.soleilbeachclub.com; Rte 187 Km 4.6; mains $8-24; ☽ 7pm-1am Wed-Fri, 10pm-1am Sat, 2-5pm Sun), the town's hottest night spot, showcases live jazz, '70s and '80s music, salsa, blues, and weekly *bomba y plena*.

Getting There & Away

The B40 bus picks passengers up near the Cockfight Arena on Isla Verde (connect with A5 for the rest of San Juan) and runs all the way to the settlement at the west end of the beach at Piñones. Walk a mile to the east for some decent swimming beaches. You can also cycle to Piñones from San Juan. A dedicated bike lane begins just west of Isla Verde.

LOÍZA ALDEA

Take Hwy 187 east from San Juan to catch some fresh air and rural scenery (and escape the commerce and traffic jams on Hwy 3). The road eventually breaks out of the Piñones forest. When you cross a bridge spanning the island's largest river, the Río Grande de Loíza, the road brings you to the center of Loíza Aldea, commonly called Loíza. This town is a largely rural municipality in the coastal lowlands east of LMM airport, and it includes Piñones as well as three other districts.

Loíza dates from 1719 and has a rich Taíno heritage. Sadly, there's little infrastructure to support tourism, and none of the settlements here are scenic. Most of the 30,000 residents are poor. There are only two reasons for a traveler to visit – a church and a fiesta. You will find some kiosks set up along the roads in Loíza that sell the usual snacks, but there's nowhere to sleep at night. Stay in nearby Piñones, San Juan or at any number of places around Luquillo, El Yunque or Fajardo.

GETTING AWAY FROM IT ALL

You don't have to run to the hills to get away from it all. In fact, some of San Juan's greatest escapes can be found only a mile or two from the city center.

The **Corporación Piñones Se Integra** (COPI; ☎ 787-253-9707; www.copipr.com) is a community based nonprofit organization that is involved in improving the facilities in Puerto Rico's poorer barrios, particularly Loíza. Concurrently, they are working hard to keep the island's traditional Afro-Caribbean culture alive. Headquartered in the **Centro Cultural Ecoturístico de Piñones** (Rte 187, Boca de Cangrejos, Loíza), situated to the right of Rte 187 immediately after you cross the bridge at Boca de Cangrejos, the organization promotes some of Puerto Rico's best *bomba y plena* performances at its on-site **Café El Búho** at 9pm on the second and last Friday of each month. You can also arrange traditional dancing and percussion lessons here (phone or check website for details) as well as enjoy regular expositions of local art.

Sitting on land that was recently saved from the developer's bulldozers via direct community action, COPI have also pledged to protect the region's priceless but precarious ecology. To discover it for yourself, you can hire both bicycles and kayaks at the cultural center to utilize on the adjacent Piñones bike path and lagoon.

Information

The center of the town is called the Plaza de Recreo, known as La Plaza, and is just east of the bridge over the Río Grande de Loíza. Here you will find the **Loíza Tourism Office** (☎ 787-886-6071; ⏰ 8am-noon & 1-4pm Mon-Fri).

Sights

At the northern end of the plaza, **La Iglesia del Espíritu Santo y San Patricio** (Church of the Holy Ghost and St Patrick) appears every bit as proud and colonial as the cathedral in Old San Juan, and stands out from the humble collection of surrounding modern buildings.

The church dates from 1646 and took its name from the patron saint of Ireland to honor Puerto Rico's famous Irish mercenaries, who designed many of the fortifications of Old San Juan.

Festivals & Events

Puerto Rico's African soul is unveiled for nine days every July and August in the **Fiesta de Santiago**, a cultural extravaganza of drums, masks and hybrid religious iconology relating to the Catholic Saint James the Moor Slayer.

Shopping

Handmade *vejigante* masks carved by local artisans are available in many places in Loíza (and are generally of higher quality for less money than what you'll find in San Juan). Wander the streets around the town center and you'll see plenty of colorful creations quite literally staring out at you.

The most famous shop in town is **Estudio de Arte Samuel Lind** (☎ 787-876-1494; Rte 187 Km 6.6). The studio, which is open to visitors when someone is at home, is 2 miles south of town on Rte 187. Samuel doesn't sell masks but his paintings, sculptures and serigraph prints cost between $15 and $350. To drive there, head toward Río Grande until you see a sign for the studio. Turn left and stop at the third house on the left. Públicos from San Juan to Rio Grande will stop at the studio on request. About 20 other mask makers work in the area. The tourist office will supply details.

Getting There & Away

You can catch a público to Loíza's plaza from Río Piedras in San Juan for about $2, which is not a bad way to go during the Fiesta de Santiago, when traffic into Loíza on Hwy 187 and Hwy 188 can be more frightening than a *vejigante* mask. Públicos return to Río Piedras from a terminal in Loíza (three blocks away from the plaza), but usually only during daylight hours.

CATAÑO & BAYAMÓN

Together, Bayamón and Cataño have a denser concentration of strip malls than any other area in Puerto Rico, which may be one reason why tourists don't seem to be flocking across the bay. Other reasons could be the heavy industrialization, traffic that could make you pull your hair out, and air that's often fouled with noxious chemicals. Nonetheless, there are a few things worth seeing in Bayamón and Cataño, although nothing warrants staying overnight.

To get here, you can take the Acua Expreso ferry from Old San Juan and enjoy a quick harbor tour along the way (p124). The new Tren Urbano now links Santurce, Hato Rey and Río Piedras to Bayamón; from Old San Juan/Condado you can catch bus B21 to Sagrado Corazon station and the start of the train route.

If you head about a mile north of town to where Hwy 165 meets Hwy 870, you can follow the latter to a secluded picnic site amid the dramatic setting of Isla de Cabras.

Sights

BACARDÍ RUM FACTORY

Called the 'Cathedral of Rum' because of its six-story pink distillation tower, the **Bacardí Rum Factory** (Map pp86-7; ☎ 787-788-8400; Hwy 888 Km 2.6; admission free; ⏰ 8:30am-4:30pm Mon-Sat) covers 127 acres and stands out like a petroleum refinery across from Old San Juan, near the entrance to the bay. The world's largest and most famous rum-producing family started their business in Cuba more than a century ago, but they began moving their operation to this site in 1936. Today the distiller produces some 100,000 gallons of rum per day and ships 21 million cases per year worldwide.

In exchange for some freebies you'll be escorted on a tram tour that lasts about 30 minutes. To get to the Bacardí factory, take a público (about $3 per person) from the ferry terminal in Cataño along the waterfront on Calle Palo Seco (Hwy 888). At Km 2.6 north of town, look for the Cathedral of Rum and other Bacardí factory buildings to your left, rising above the landscape. Free tours of the plant leave every 30 minutes on the half-hour.

THE BACARDÍ STORY

While the free guided tour of the famous Bacardí factory in Cataño is big on bonhomie and generous with the gratis drinks, there is a noticeable tendency to gloss over various elements of the company's 150 year history – and with good reason. Today the Bacardí brand retains its headquarters in the Bahamas and runs the largest rum factory in the world in Puerto Rico. But, with brutal irony, its roots were sown more auspiciously several hundred miles to the west, in Cuba, a country with whom the company's powerful bosses have been at loggerheads for the last 50 years.

Founded in 1862 in the city of Santiago de Cuba, the world's largest rum dynasty was the brainchild of Don Facundo Bacardí, an immigrant from Catalonia, Spain, who had arrived on the island in 1830 at the age of 16. Recognizing the unusual quality of the sugar cane in Cuba's eastern valleys, Facundo began experimenting with rum distillation using molasses until he was able to produce a refined, clear spirit that was filtered through charcoal and aged in oak barrels.

The new drink quickly caught on and, in time, Facundo passed his burgeoning rum business down to his sons Emilio and José. Emilio went on to become a well-known Cuban patriot during the Second Independence War against the Spanish and, in the 1890s, was exiled briefly for his revolutionary activities. He returned to Cuba a hero in 1898 and was promptly named as Santiago's first mayor. It was during this tempestuous period that Bacardí concocted its two famous rum cocktails, the Daiquiri (named after a Cuban beach) and the Cuba Libre, both mixed with their signature clear rum.

After the repeal of the US prohibition laws in 1932, Bacardí began expanding its operation outside Cuba, opening up a bottling plant in Mexico and establishing the Cataño distillery in Puerto Rico, a move that enabled them to combine cheap labor costs with direct entry into the American market. But, post WWII, with the whiff of revolution in the air, far more ominous changes loomed. Although the family initially supported Castro and his rugged band of Cuban patriots in the late 1950s (a banner on Bacardí's Havana HQ had greeted the rebels with a cordial *'Gracias Fidel!'*), they quickly changed tack when the new Cuban leader began nationalizing businesses island-wide in 1960. Abandoning a 100-year tradition, the company was promptly relocated overseas, lock, stock and rum-filled barrel.

In the years since, the Bacardí clan has remained a vociferous voice in the powerful anti-Castro movement in the US and gained rum-slinging notoriety for their sponsorship of dubious far-right groups and other clandestine political operations. In the early 60s, the family attempted to sponsor a plot to bomb Cuban oil refineries and thus spark a countrywide insurrection, until their cover was blown by a front page story in the *New York Times*. A couple of years later, Bacardí boss and one-time Fidel pal, José Pepin Bosch, is said to have bankrolled a CIA plot to assassinate the Castro brothers and Che Guevara using mafia hit-men.

Yet, despite controversy, Bacardí has remained the world's most popular rum selling more than 240 million bottles annually in 170 countries. In Puerto Rico, the Cataño factory reigns as the so-called cathedral of rum churning out over 70% of the company's annual global production.

ISLA DE CABRAS & FUERTE DEL CAÑUELO

Located at the end of Hwy 870, north of the Bacardí Rum Factory and the settlement of Palo Seco, **Isla de Cabras** (Goat Island; Map pp86-7; admission $2) is perhaps the greatest seaside refuge in metro San Juan for travelers craving privacy and nature. There isn't much here except some shade trees, park benches, rocky seashore, waves and litter. You can fish, but the offshore currents are too dangerous for swimming. The ruins at the north end of the island mark a late-19th-century leper colony.

On the island's south end stand the remains of Fuerte del Cañuelo (Cañuelo Fort). The fort, which is nothing but ruins today, dates from 1610 and once shared the responsibility of protecting Bahía de San Juan with El Morro, which is across the channel marking the entrance to the bay.

PARQUE CENTRAL DE BAYAMÓN

In the old tradition of urban oases like New York's Central Park, this pristine park (Map pp86–7) stands across from the new city hall (the industrial-looking bridgelike structure spanning Hwy 2) in the center of Bayamón. It is remarkable for its landscaping and the preserved country house located on the grounds. The train running around the park's perimeter is one of the last vestiges of the days when sugarcane railways laced the northern lowlands of the island.

MUSEO DE OLLER

Located in the former city hall on the plaza of Bayamón's historic district, this art and history **museum** (Map pp86-7; ☎ 787-785-6010; admission free; ⏰ 8:30am-4pm Mon-Fri) pays tribute to native son Francisco Oller (1833–1917), considered the first Latin American impressionist. Most of Oller's great works are displayed elsewhere, but the restored neoclassical museum building is worth a peek if you are in the area. The collection includes some Oller portraits, Taíno artifacts, and sculptures.

LUIS A FERRÉ PARQUE DE CIENCIAS

This 42-acre **science park** (Map pp86-7; ☎ 787-740-6868; Hwy 167; adult/child & senior $5/3; ⏰ 9am-4pm Wed-Fri, 10am-6pm Sat & Sun) is located in Bayamón on Hwy 167, south of the exit from the Hwy 22 toll road. Children seem to get a kick out of this science museum, despite the fact that the focal point of the park is education. It features pavilions that include a new planetarium, electrical energy museum, physics museum, rocket plaza, aerospace museum, transportation museum and zoo. There's also an artificial lake that kids can paddle-boat through just for the thrill of it – no educational lesson attached. Parking costs $1.

CAPARRA

This is the site of Juan Ponce de León's first settlement on the island, established in 1508. The site was rediscovered in 1936, and only the foundations of a few buildings remain. There is a small **museum** (Map pp86-7; ☎ 787-781-4795; Hwy 2 Km 6.6; admission free; ⏰ 8:30am-4:15pm Tue-Sat) featuring Taíno artifacts that is open irregularly. Located on a highly commercial section of Hwy 2 east of Bayamón in Guaynabo, the site is only worth a visit to ponder why the great conquistador ever imagined this spot on the fringe of a mammoth swamp could possibly be suitable as a location for a colony.

East Coast

The east coast is Puerto Rico shrink-wrapped; a tantalizing taste of almost everything the island has to offer squeezed into an area not much larger than Manhattan. Here in the foothills of the Sierra de Luquillo the sprawling suburbs of San Juan blend caustically with the junglelike quiescence of El Yunque National Forest, the commonwealth's giant green lungs and biggest outdoor attraction. At sea level, beach hedonists bask on the icing-sugar sand of Playa Luquillo while higher up among the forest's crinkled peaks heavy clouds gather like giant purple sponges ready to unleash their abundant rain into El Yunque's many waterfalls and rivers.

For golfers and the spring-break crowd, the east provides a different kind of nirvana. There are more mega-resorts here than in any other part of the island outside San Juan, a haul that includes the glitzy Conquistador – once used as a setting for the James Bond movie *Goldfinger* – and the colossal Palmas del Mar, a resort more reminiscent of a planned modern town than an authentic Caribbean getaway.

Scruffy Fajardo is the island's uncrowned water-sports capital, an interesting hodgepodge of the beautiful and the unsightly, where adventurous spirits gather to kayak, dive, snorkel and fish. Rich yachters park their sailboats at Puerto Real, the largest marina in the Caribbean, while a few miles north traditional fishing sloops nestle in a secluded little bay at Las Croabas.

Cutting through the region like a thin, green ribbon is the so-called northeastern ecological corridor, a slender tract of land that has been saved from the developers' axe thanks to persistent lobbying by local environmental groups. The jewel in its crown is Las Cabezas de San Juan Reserva Natural 'El Faro,' a tiny nodule of coastline that hosts seven different ecosystems and one of Puerto Rico's stunning bioluminescent bays.

HIGHLIGHTS

- Getting high on the challenging Tradewinds trail in **El Yunque National Forest** (p132)

- Escaping from the coastal chaos in the cool, green world of the **Casa Cubuy Ecolodge** (p136)

- Supping a fruit smoothie and chomping on a fried *surullito* on action-packed **Playa Luquillo** (p138)

- Admiring the sea views, iguanas and seven different ecosystems in **Las Cabezas de San Juan Reserva Natural 'El Faro'** (p142)

- Enjoying lunch among the fishermen in a plastic-knife-and-fork restaurant on **Playa Húcares** (p149)

- POPULATION: 450,000

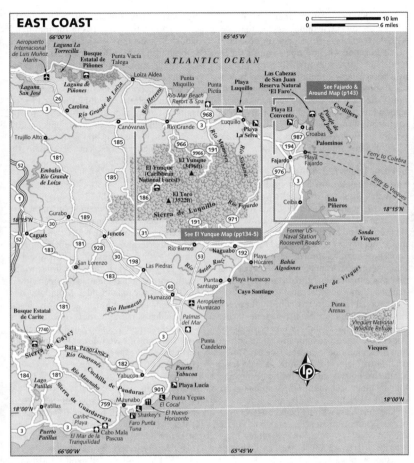

History

Much of this region was once covered with lighter variations of the dense foliage now found only in El Yunque, but native Taíno did manage to successfully farm the fertile land around the low-lying coasts. All that changed when the Spanish arrived en masse around 1700. The tremendous wealth of natural resources in El Yunque – lots of fresh water and timber, for example – attracted settlers, and existing farmlands were quickly turned into massive sugar plantations by colonizers. A small gold rush added to the need for a strong labor force, and after most of the indigenous population was either wiped out by disease or forced deep into the mountains, the Spanish brought in West African slaves

in considerable numbers. Descendants of those Yoruba people make up the bulk of the 30,000 residents who live in the municipalities around El Yunque today. The next wave of colonization came when the US took control of the island in 1898, eventually setting up the commonwealth status that continues to this day. Most of the highways and existing infrastructure on this part of the island were built by the US military, which maintained a base near Fajardo until 2003.

Climate

The east coast tends to follow the same weather patterns as San Juan. The exception to this rule is El Yunque, with weather catering to the unique needs of its ecosystem. Sudden surges of light rain can occur anytime during the year in this dense rainforest, but that goes with the territory – throw on some protective gear and get on with your day. During the island's hurricane season – late June through mid-November – El Yunque gets very wet indeed. Some trails might be closed down due to mud slides, and streams swell enormously. It's a good idea to check in at the visitors center for the latest weather update before heading out for a trek. Winter nights in the Luquillo Sierra can be damp and a little chilly.

Getting There & Around

Most of the east coast is traversable via Hwy 3, which – while far from pretty – gets the job done with relative efficiency. Once you leave San Juan, be it on Rte 187 (the scenic route via Piñones and behind Loíza Aldea) or on the main drag of Hwy 3, be prepared for bursts of concentrated development (fast-food restaurants, several strip malls and the occasional pharmaceutical plant) and distant views of El Yunque. Públicos serve most towns.

There are public vans running between Fajardo and San Juan, but to penetrate further into the countryside, a car or bike is necessary. It is easy to organize a tour with car and driver into the El Yunque rainforest (see p135). The driving trip from San Juan to Fajardo takes about two hours (without traffic). From San Juan to Yabucoa it's about three hours (again, without traffic).

The northeast with its high concentration of cars is not the most pleasant part of Puerto Rico in which to cycle. But stay off the main arteries of Hwys 3 and 66 and two-wheeled transport is possible.

EL YUNQUE

Covering some 28,000 acres of land in the Sierra de Luquillo, this verdant tropical rainforest – recently rebranded El Yunque National Forest – is a shadow of what it was before axe-wielding Spanish conquerors arrived in the 16th and 17th centuries. But, in common with other protected reserves on the island, the ecological degradation has been largely reversed over the past 50 years, and today, under the auspices of the US Forest Service, El Yunque is once again sprouting a healthy abundance of dense tree cover.

Compared to other Puerto Rican forest reserves, El Yunque is well staffed and crisscrossed by an excellent network of signposted trails. But adventurers beware. In contrast to national parks in the mainland US, there's no true wilderness experience to be had here. Unlike North Americans, Puerto Ricans have never truly incorporated wilderness hiking in the national psyche. As a result, most of El Yunque's hikes are short, paved and relatively mild compared to the trails of Yellowstone and Yosemite. Crowds populate El Yunque's popular spots in peak season, but if you stray off the standard tourist routes, there are still plenty of places to slip under the radar (p150).

Orientation

Once you've entered the El Yunque National Forest (see p137 for directions), all of the forest's visitors centers, major attractions and trailheads appear as Hwy 191 twists, turns and climbs steeply on its way south toward the summit. Although maps can make it seem like Hwy 191 descends through the forest to the south side, note that the road has been closed for decades due to landslides. Mountain-bike enthusiasts get their workout on this closed road, which is the *only route* open to bikers within the forest. It's also possible to follow Hwy 186 along the west side of El Yunque, but if you want to experience the forest's heart, Hwy 191 is the road to take.

Information

First port of call for aspiring rainforest explorers should be the well-blended **El Portal Visitors Center** (☎ 787-888-1880; www.southernregion.fs.fed .us/caribbean; Hwy 191 Km 4.3; adult/under 4yr/4-12yr & senior $3/free/1.50; ☺ 9am-5pm, closed Christmas Day). Built in 1996, El Portal is an intelligently landscaped visitors center that offers reams of information about both El Yunque and tropical rainforests in general. The facility has interactive exhibits, a 12-minute film in both English and Spanish, a walkway through the forest canopy and a gift shop. Vending machines serve up drinks and snacks, but there's no on-site restaurant. You can also pick up free basic maps and information on the forest. If you don't feel like paying the admission tariff or want to avoid crowds on weekends, head to one of the other visitors centers further up the mountain, where you can pick up brochures and basic maps for no charge.

Located after El Portal, the **Catalina Work Center** (☎ 787-888-1880; Hwy 191 Km 4.3; ☺ 8am-4:30pm Mon-Fri), connected to the National Forest

Office, is where you can get a camping permit – good for the day it is issued. Rangers hand out maps designating approved camping locations along with the permits.

It's worth enduring the switchbacks and steep road to get to the **Palo Colorado Visitors Center** (☎ 787-888-1880; Hwy 191 Km 11.9; ☺ 9:30am-4pm), which issues camping permits on weekends. Most of the short and spectacular hiking trails leave from this spot. The picnic area – which includes a series of sheltered concrete platforms hidden in the jungle, overlooking a ravine of rushing water – is hard to match anywhere on the island. The staff here offers first-aid service, and there's also a gift shop with maps and the like.

The Sierra Palm Visitors Center is a free visitors center on your way up the mountain. It is not always staffed, but its rest rooms are generally open for tour vans, and there's a food concession, Yuquiyú Delights (p137).

Sights

In addition to short and long hiking trails in El Yunque (see right), there are a few places directly accessible by road within the forest.

La Coca Falls is the first spectacular natural feature you see as Hwy 191 climbs south toward the forest peaks. There is an 85ft cascade as the stream tumbles from a precipice to the right of the highway onto boulder formations. The gate is open every day from 7am to 6pm.

Less than a half mile further up the mountain, you see the 65ft, Moorish-looking stone **Yokahú Tower**, which was built as a lookout in 1962. This is the first good place for vistas of the islands to the east, but there are better vantage points higher up on the mountain. The tower often gets crowded with tour groups. Pass it by unless you have a lot of time and the view to yourself.

The **Baño Grande**, a former swimming hole built during the Depression, lies across Hwy 191 from the Palo Colorado Visitors Center (above). A little further along the road, **Baño de Oro** is another former swimming hole that is now a popular spot for photo opportunities. The water hole takes its name from the Río Baño de Oro, which feeds the pool. The name means 'bath of gold' in English, and Spaniards gave the river this name because they mined for gold here in the 16th century. The Baño de Oro Natural Area surrounding the pool is the catchment area for the river and pool. In addition to the short Baño de Oro trail to

the pool there are two overgrown trails in the Natural Area, which the National Park Service plans to open in the future.

If you really want to paddle in some water, take the 30-minute walk from Palo Colorado down the mountain to the swimming hole at the base of **La Mina Falls**. Here you'll find a water cascade, quite stunning in its natural beauty. Come early if you want tranquility, because it's popular with cavorting families.

Activities
HIKING

With more than 23 miles of well-maintained trails, and plenty of rugged terrain, El Yunque has a plethora of easy day hikes. Come prepared and remember there are no water or trash or restroom facilities.

La Coca Trail

This popular 1.8-mile hike will take you a little over an hour each way. The trailhead is just up the road past the falls of the same name – just before the Yokahú Tower – and there is a small parking lot here. It's a fairly benign, low-altitude trail following streams through tabonuco forest. La Coca made its mark on El Yunque history when a US college professor disappeared here for 12 days in 1997, claiming after his rescue that he got off the trail and was lost. The Forest Service, which had enlisted a search party of 60 volunteers and aircraft, was hardly amused. If you follow La Coca to its end, you can go left (east) along Carrillo Trail to the eastern part of the forest, or right (west) to La Mina Falls on La Mina Trail (below).

Big Tree Trail

This short 0.86-mile trail of moderate difficulty gets its name from the size of the vegetation along the way. The walk takes about a half-hour each way, and it has interpretive signs along its route through tabonuco forest before ending at La Mina Falls. All these attractions make this probably the most popular trail in the park. The trailhead is at Km 10.4 on Hwy 191.

La Mina Trail

The forest's newest trail was opened in 1992 as an extension of the Big Tree trail, although it can be done in isolation from its starting point at the Palo Colorado Visitors Center. The trail heads downhill through Palo Colorado forest to La Mina Falls and an old mine tunnel.

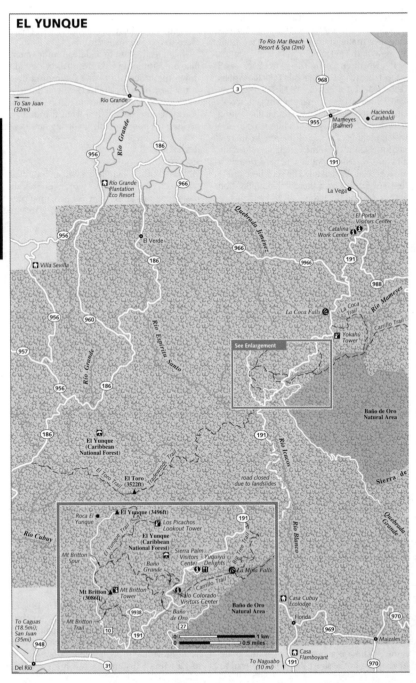

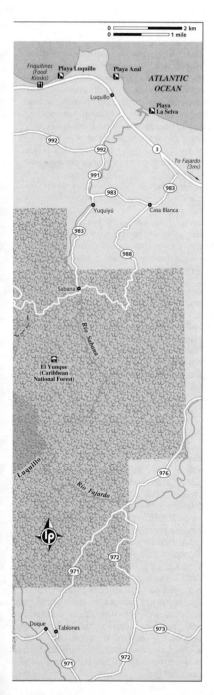

Mostly paved, it's an easy 0.7-mile walk down, but a bit of a hike back up. The La Mina trail connects with the Carrillo trail at La Mina Falls and with La Coca soon after.

Mt Britton Trail

If you are short on time and want to feel as if you have really 'summited,' take the 0.8-mile, 45-minute climb up through the midlevel types of vegetation into the cloud forest that surrounds this peak, which is named after a famous botanist who worked here. This is a continuous climb on paved surfaces to the Mt Britton Tower, built in the 1930s. The trailhead is at the side of Hwy 9938, which veers off Hwy 191 south of Palo Colorado. The more adventurous and fit can connect to El Yunque Trail (below) via the 0.86-mile Mt Britton Spur.

El Yunque Trail

This is the big enchilada for most visitors and takes you to the top of El Yunque (3496ft, 1049m) in 1½ hours or longer. Starting on Rte 191 Km 12.2 opposite the Palo Colorado Visitors Center, the 2.4-mile trail is mostly paved or maintained gravel as you ascend through cloud forest to the observation deck, which is surrounded by microwave communication towers that transmit to the islands of Culebra and Vieques. If you want a rock scramble from here, take Los Picachos Trail (0.17 miles) to another old observation tower and feel as if you have crested a tropical Everest. You can return via a different route by descending down the Mt Britton Spur/Mt Britton Trail and then down Rtes 9938 and 191 to your start point.

Tours

San Juan–based tour operators (see p284) are handy in that they can transport you to and from the park, highlight the main sights and provide you with a mine of interesting information. In addition to the standard options, the National Park Service offers guided one-hour hikes from the Palo Colorado Visitors Center through **Forest Adventure Tours** (☎ 787-888-1880; adult/child $5/3; ☼ tours every hr 10:30am-3:30pm), a body which aims to offer visitors a better understanding of conservation and forest management.

Other good ecosensitive operators include **Eco-Action Tours** (☎ 787-791-7509; www.ecoactiontours .com), which offers half-/full day tours from

EAST COAST

EAST COAST

EL YUNQUE'S FLORA & FAUNA

More than 240 species of tree and 1000 species of plant thrive in this misty, rain-soaked enclave, including 50 kinds of orchid. El Yunque is also the island's major water supply, with six substantial rivers tracing their sources here. The fauna is characterized by the presence of the critically endangered Puerto Rican parrot (el higuaca) and more than 60 other species of bird, nine species of rare freshwater shrimp, the coquí frog, anole tree lizards, and the 7ft-long Puerto Rican boa.

Four forest zones define El Yunque. The tabonuco forest grows below 2000ft and receives less than 100in of rain. This area is characterized by tall, straight trees such as the tabonuco and ausubo, and palms, epiphytes (including many orchids), flowers and aromatic shrubs of many kinds.

The palo colorado forest grows above 2000ft in the valleys and on gentle slopes. Here annual rainfall averages as much as 180in. This area is lush with ancient colorado trees (some more than 1000 years old). Vines and epiphytes hang from the trees.

Above 2500ft, look for sierra palms along the streams and on the steep valley slopes. The so-called mountain palm tree dominates here in the third zone, the Palma Sierra Forest, with mostly ferns and mosses growing beneath.

The highest forest zone, the so-called 'cloud forest,' grows above the Palma Sierra Forest and sees up to 200in of rain per year. Trees here are generally twisted from strong trade winds and are less than 12ft tall (hence the term 'dwarf forest' commonly applied to this ecosystem). Mosses and lichens hang from trees and cover the forest floor. Red-flowering bromeliads stand out like beacons in the fog.

$37/50, depending on size of group, for hikes to Mt Britton and La Mina Falls. Guides are knowledgeable, environmentally conscious and eager to talk about the rainforest ecosystem. They'll pick you up from your San Juan hotel.

You might also connect with one of the park's volunteer guides, who post themselves around the Palo Colorado Visitors Center. Many of these guides are members of local Boy Scout Explorer Post 919. **AdvenTours** (☎ 787-530-8311; www.adventourspr.com) is an eco-sensitive guiding company that offers birding tours, night hikes and biking excursions in the National Forest. Call for current prices.

Sleeping

It's free to camp in El Yunque National Forest, but don't forget your permit (see p132). Camping is prohibited along many of the popular trails surrounding Palo Colorado Visitors Center and El Yunque peak, but you can camp in the wilder parts of the forest, including at its highest peak, El Toro, where it feels as if you have slipped into a primeval forest. Camping is all off-trail, and you must pack everything in and out. There are no water, trash or restroom facilities on the trails.

Several beautiful inns, B&Bs and guesthouses have opened up along the edges of El Yunque – not actually in the forest, but along its fringe. The proximity to the rainforest means lots of loud animal activity: the sound of chirruping coquí will send you to sleep, and you'll wake to wild birds whistling. Most places are accessible along the north section of Hwy 191, coming from Río Grande (Luquillo beaches are only a few minutes away). Other accommodations are on the south side, also on Hwy 191. Due to mud slides, south side accommodations must be accessed from the Naguabo entrance to El Yunque. These are good choices if you want to be in close proximity to day trips in and around Fajardo.

ourpick Casa Cubuy Ecolodge (☎ 787-874-6221; www.casacubuy.com; Hwy 191 Km 22 from Naguabo; r $90-115; P X R) If listening to a frog symphony, conversing nightly around the dinner table, and relaxing on a shady balcony within hammock-swinging distance of a mystical tropical rainforest has you dashing for your jungle apparel, then this could be your place. Cocooned atop the winding Hwy 191 on El Yunque's wild and isolated southern slopes, Casa Cubuy Ecolodge offers a welcome antidote to the modern Puerto Rico of crowded beaches and spirit-crushing traffic. Ten cozy rooms rise just inches from the ethereal green forest, and a covered communal patio replete with games, books and an honesty bar encourages multilingual guest interaction. To top it all, the lodge even guards its own private trail to a nearby waterfall and natural swimming pool. Sublime.

Río Grande Plantation Eco Resort (☎ 787-887-2779; www.riograndeplantation.com; Hwy 956 Km 4.2, Río Grande; r $125-175, villas $150-300; P ⊠ ⊑) The Río Grande is rustic; indeed nature is so close here that small living parts of it sometimes find their way into your room in the form of the odd gecko or two. But with immense grounds, a rushing river and tons of birds flying in all directions, the sight of this parcel of greenery so close to San Juan's urban sprawl is rather refreshing. Lots of weddings and corporate retreats are booked here in the summer, but off-season it can be a bit on the quiet side (phone ahead to let them know you're coming). Two-story villas are equipped with rocking chair, TV and huge Jacuzzi tub. It's not luxury bracket, but it's definitely eco.

Villa Sevilla (☎ 787-887-5889; www.villasevilla.net; Rte 956 Km 7.8, Río Grande; r $145-250; P ⊑) This recent addition to the El Yunque accommodations stable is also arguably its finest. Villa Sevilla is a private estate with three different sets of digs that all share the same gorgeous swimming pool and foliage-framed Atlantic views. There's the three-bedroom Bella Vista chalet, the two-bedroom La Casita and the one-bedroom Pablo's Place. All apartments have kitchen, satellite TV, washer/dryer and linen. They're ideal for couples and families on longer stays. The service here is top-notch and the rainforest surroundings magnificent.

Casa Flamboyant (☎ 787-874-6074; Hwy 191 from Naguabo; r $200-250; P ⊠ ⊑) Some hotels try to create their own 'faux' paradise, others are located where paradise already exists. Tucked way up high in the mountains and offering panoramic views of El Yunque, the Casa Flamboyant is of the latter variety. With its three gorgeous rooms with private bathrooms, and a private villa set off to one side (accessed across a stone bridge), this is as elegant as Puerto Rico's rainforest gets. Guests love to watch storm clouds march past en route to glowering El Yunque while lounging in the heated pool.

Eating

Yuquiyú Delights (Hwy 191 Km 11.6) This small food concession with sheltered tables situated next to the Sierra Palm picnic area is the only real 'restaurant' in the forest. It does decent burgers ($6), *comida criolla* (traditional Puerto Rican cuisine) and smoothies and should replenish your legs ready for a few more miles of hiking. A few smaller kiosks sell snacks and soft drinks around Km 7 on Hwy 191.

Getting There & Away

There's no public transportation to El Yunque. The only way to get here is by private car, taxi (expensive), or in a pre-arranged tour (p135). You can see the rainforest from San Juan even though it lies 25 miles to the southeast. Driving from San Juan, there will be signs directing you from Hwy 3 to Hwy 191, but the sign for Hwy 191 is not always visible (heavy winds sometimes knock it down). If you see it, turn right as directed. Otherwise, watch for a large sign announcing 'El Yunque Portal' on the right-hand side of the road. It's

---

DETOUR: BACKCOUNTRY ADVENTURE

The lofty Tradewinds–El Toro trail is the closest El Yunque gets to a true backcountry adventure. Although the 7.8-mile jaunt up to El Toro (3522ft) and back might not sound particularly daunting, wet conditions, thick mud and poorly maintained paths render it an all-day excursion for most hikers (some parties even camp out overnight). El Toro is El Yunque's highest point and the trail up from Hwy 191 traverses dense jungle broken by intermittent views of both coasts. During the ascent you'll pass through all four forest life systems, ending up in a haunting 'dwarf forest' above 3000ft characterized by its ghostly epiphytes and ubiquitous mist.

The trailhead for the Tradewinds trail is situated at Km 13.3 on Hwy 191, behind a locked gate where the road ends. The unpaved path climbs 3.9 miles to the summit of El Toro, from where you can either retrace your steps or continue west on the similarly vague El Toro trail to Km 10.8 on Hwy 186 (2.1 miles from El Toro and 6 miles from Hwy 191). From here you'll need to turn around and do the hike again in reverse, or arrange for a car to pick you up and take you back to the start.

Aspiring hikers should pack good walking shoes, water, food and rainwear. You'll also need to obtain a permit from the Catalina Work Center (p132; adjacent to the El Portal Visitors Center) prior to setting out.

at an intersection that also features a big sign for the Westin Río Mar Resort. Turn right at that intersection and go through the village of Palmer (Mameyes in Spanish), keeping your eyes peeled for more signage directing you to Hwy 191 and the El Yunque National Forest – there's a sharp left shortly after turning off the main highway. Just after the road starts to rise abruptly into the mountains, you enter the El Yunque National Forest.

Take note that some highway maps suggest that you can traverse the forest on Hwy 191 (or access El Yunque from the south via this route), but south of the Palo Colorado Visitors Center, Hwy 191 has been closed by landslides for years. Road maps also suggest that El Yunque can be approached via a network of roads along the western border of the national forest. Don't try it: these roads are rugged, untraveled, unmaintained tracks that dead-end in serious jungle. El Yunque is not immune to thievery, so if you park in a remote area to take a stroll, be sure to lock up and don't leave anything of value in plain sight in the car.

LUQUILLO & AROUND
pop 20,000

In many ways Luquillo is a typical Puerto Rican town; a physically beautiful coastal strip of magnificent beaches backed by a dull, uninspiring mishmash of condo towers, strip malls and unsightly urban sprawl. But here, in the island's congested northeastern corner, beauty easily outweighs the beast. Playa Luquillo, the mile-long crescent of surf and sand to the west of the town, is regularly touted as being the commonwealth's finest balneario (public beach) and the proverbial home of Puerto Rican soul food. Meanwhile, winking a velvety shade of purple in the background, the crenellated ridges of El Yunque proffer a ghostly invitation.

Central Luquillo is a baffling place that has a dearth of easy-to-find accommodation and little in the way of history. Aside from the underrated Playa Azul and a couple of strung-out restaurants, there's little worth exploring here. Instead, most travelers head a mile west to Puerto Rico's so-called 'Riviera', the insanely popular Luquillo Beach that is as famous for its ramshackle strip of permanent food kiosks as it is for icing-sugar sand and sheltered bay.

Luquillo traces its history to an early Spanish settlement in 1797 and its name to a valorous Taíno *cacique* (chief), Loquillo, who made a brave standoff against the early colonizers here in 1513. These days the 20,000-strong town is bypassed by the arterial Hwy 3 that carries traffic to Fajardo. Here you'll find little of lasting architectural note save for a couple of craning condo towers that do their best to block out views of El Yunque. Thanks to Luquillo's popularity with vacationing *sanjuaneros* (people from San Juan), público bus links with the capital are fairly regular during the week. If you're going to the beach, make sure you disembark next to the kiosks, a mile or so before Luquillo Pueblo.

Orientation & Information

Hwy 3 will take you to Rte 193 (aka Calle Fernandez Garcia), which is the main artery of Luquillo. It passes right by the Plaza de Recreo, the town's central plaza. Playa Azul is the beach directly in front of the condominium development of the same name. Most of the shops and stores of interest to visitors are alongside Playa Azul, or on Fernandez Garcia. O the parallel street 14 de Julio you'll find the Luquillo Community Health Center.

Beaches

Luquillo is synonymous with its balneario, the fabulous **Playa Luquillo** (admission free, parking $2; 8:30am-5:30pm). Set on a calm bay facing northwest and protected from the easterly trade winds, the public part of this beach makes a mile-long arc to a point of sand shaded by evocative coconut palms. The beach itself is a plane of broad, gently sloping yellow powder that continues its gradual slope below the water. Although crowds converge here at weekends and during holidays, Luquillo has always been more about atmosphere than solitude. With its famous strip of 50-plus food kiosks congregated at its western end, it's also a great place to sample the local culinary culture, including scrumptious *surullitos* (fried cornmeal and cheese sticks). There is a bathhouse, a refreshment stand, a security patrol and well-kept bathrooms.

You do not have to park in the balneario lot if you want to visit the beach. Playa Luquillo extends at least another mile to the west. If you pull off Hwy 3 by the long row of food kiosks, you can drive around to the ocean side of the stalls and park under the

---

TOP FIVE WATER ACTIVITIES

- Kayaking in the bioluminescent waters of Laguna Grande (p142)
- Boating from Puerto del Rey marina (p145)
- Diving in the Cayos Palominos and Icacos (p145)
- Surfing off the secluded El Cocal (p149)
- Fishing out of Fajardo (p145)

---

palms, just a few steps from the beach and with more cold beer and *pastelillos* (fried dumplings) than you could consume in a year.

Luquillo also has a section known as **Sea Without Barriers** (☎ 787-889-4329), the island's only disabled-accessible beach. Sea Without Barriers has a ramp and other facilities to help anyone with limited mobility get into the water safely.

If the balneario feels too busy (and it does get cheek-to-jowl in high season), head for **Playa Azul**, east around the headland and in the town itself. While the beach is more exposed to the trade winds, seas and dangerous rip tides (people have drowned), Playa Azul is just as broad, white and gently sloping as Luquillo. Snorkeling enthusiasts particularly enjoy these waters, but swim with great caution.

A friendly contingent of surfers hang out at the east end of this beach – known as 'La Pared' (the Wall) – waiting for an offshore breeze to glass off a 3ft break. Scrambling over a stone jetty at the east end of Playa Azul will take you to a strand of beach and bays that stretch over 5 miles to the **Playa Seven Seas** balneario in Las Croabas (p143). The western section of this undeveloped beach is known as **La Selva**; the eastern end is called **El Convento** and features a beach house that is a retreat for government officials.

Activities

La Selva Surf Shop (☎ 787-899-6205; 250 Calle Fernández García) has been around for more than 25 years. Well-stocked and friendly, it rents out surfboards and body boards and offers the latest on surf conditions at La Pared (literally two blocks away), La Selva (further east) and around the Humacao area to the south. While not exactly hard-core, Luquillo's waves are less crowded and less daunting than the west coast's.

For a guided kayak tour along the coast, check out a host of different day and night options from mobile operations, including **Las Tortugas Adventures** (☎ 787-889-7734), whose tours focus on the importance of environmental conservation, and **Eco-Excursion Aquatica** (☎ 787-888-2887), whose trips have a similar vent as those of Las Tortugas. Prices start at about $50.

The **Berwind Country Club** (☎ 787-876-3056; Hwy 187 Km 4.7, Río Grande; greens fee $70) is open to the public Monday to Friday. The greens fee includes a golf cart.

Río Mar Beach Resort & Spa (p140) is frequented for its two excellent courses: the Greg Norman River Course and the Tom and George Fazio Ocean Course. Nonguests pay $150 for morning tee times and $90 after 2pm.

Hacienda Carabaldi (☎ 787-889-5820; Hwy 992 Km 5.1; adult/child per hr from $30/25), a 600-acre eco-adventure ranch southwest of town, does trail rides on Paso Fino horses along the Río Mameyes and into the foothills of the rainforest, with time out for swimming and a picnic. Beach rides and simple jaunts around the ranch are also offered, as well as two-hour mountain-biking tours along rainforest trails. Aluminum bikes, with helmet and gloves, are provided for $40 per person.

Sleeping

For decades Puerto Ricans and adventure travelers have camped with impunity at La Selva and El Convento (opposite). During holidays and on high-season weekends, you'll have plenty of company. Think twice, though, if it looks like you'll be out there alone. Groups of young men have been known to roam the area looking for vulnerable targets. Muggings do occur.

Balneario Luquillo (☎ 787-889-5871, 787-622-5200; Hwy 3, Playa Luquillo; campsites with power hookup $19; **P**) There are more than 30 campsites and a bathhouse at this beachside spot. Insanely popular in the summer, but best avoided in the quiet winter months (when it's often closed).

Hotel Yunquemar (☎ 787-889-5555; www.yunque mar.com; No 6 Calle 1, Fortuna Playa, Luquillo; r $95-110; **P ⊠ ⊠**) The name Yunquemar sums it up. Lying in the shadow of El Yunque and within pebble-pitching distance of the *mar* (sea), you've got the best of both worlds here. OK, so there's still the traffic bewilderment of Luquillo to negotiate, but when you're staying in a down-to-earth, family-run guesthouse with its own swimming pool and home-cooking restaurant, the view appears so much sweeter.

Luquillo Sunrise Beach Inn (☎ 787-889-1713; www .luquillosunrise.com; A2 Costa Azul; d $95-135; ✻ ⌨) Filling a gap in the midrange market, the newly opened Sunrise Beach Inn is caressed by cooling Atlantic sea breezes in each of its spiffy 14 ocean-facing rooms. There's a communal patio and all upper-floor rooms have large balconies overlooking the beach. Other facilities include a conference room, breakfast service, cable TV and wi-fi internet. Luquillo plaza is two blocks away and the famous balneario and food kiosks a 30-minute stroll along the beach.

Río Mar Beach Resort & Spa (☎ 787-888-6000; www.westinriomar.com; 6000 Río Mar Blvd; r/ste $315/675; Ⓟ ✻ ⌨ ⌨ ᴥ) Another sprawling east-coast resort where the reception staff dress like flight attendants and the guests get around in golf carts. The Río Mar inhabits an entire hill just west of Luquillo. Spread over a mammoth 500 acres on former plantation land, there are two golf courses here along with a 600-unit high-rise hotel facility with the obligatory casino. It's better landscaped than some of the island's mega-resorts with dotted palms and imaginative art that pays a nod to indigenous island culture. If you enjoy resort living in the style of Cancun and Acapulco this could be your nirvana.

Eating

Luquillo's famous line of *friquitines* (also known as *quioscos,* or food stalls) along the western edge of Hwy 3 serve all sorts of tasty fried treats and outstanding *comida criolla* dishes (snacks $1 to $2, meals $3 to $9). Some of these kiosks are very run-down, while others look well kept and clean. Walk the line and follow your senses – or the locals.

La Exquisita Bakery (☎ 787-633-5554; 1 Calle Jesús Piñero; dishes $1-6; ✆ 6am-9pm Mon-Sat, 8am-8pm Sun) Well perhaps not 'Champs Élysées' exquisite, but, as far as Luquillo goes, this place could satisfy a few sweet tooths. Slap-bang in the town's sleepy main square, this is where locals gather for cakes, pastry, coffee and sandwiches.

Erik's Gyros & Deli (☎ 787-889-0615; 352 Fernández García; sandwiches & combo meals $6-10; ✆ 7am-4pm Mon-Sat) It doesn't look much and opening times can be sporadic, but locals swear by this place a few blocks south of the main plaza in downtown Luquillo. If you're missing gyro sandwiches or have an incurable penchant for feta cheese, this is the place.

Lolita's (☎ 787-889-5770; Hwy 3 Km 4.8; mains $6-11; ✆ noon-10pm Tue-Sun) Lolita's is 3 miles east of town on the south side of Hwy 3. The Mexican meals are so popular that the owners have moved into a building twice the original size. A soft taco costs $2.50, and many dinners run under $10. Imported Mexican mariachis provide the music.

Sandy's Seafood (☎ 787-889-5765; 276 Fernández García; mains $8-15; ✆ 11am-10pm) Obscured on a quiet street, Sandy's is the most popular restaurant in town and, by word-of-mouth, manages to attract the odd tourist-resort escapee. Perhaps best described as a fish-and-chip joint for lobster eaters, it's certainly not posh – sauce bottles adorn the tables – though you can get the full gamut of seafood here, from a traditional red snapper to jalapeño peppers stuffed with shrimp or lobster.

Shimas (☎ 787-888-6000; 6000 Río Mar Blvd; dishes $12-28; ✆ 1-10pm) If you have a sushi craving that must be met while in Luquillo, head to Shimas at the Westin Río Mar resort. It serves authentic Japanese food, as well as some Thai and Chinese dishes. There are 12 restaurants and lounges in the Río Mar. Other good eating choices are Ajili Mójili, serving traditional Puerto Rican food, and Cactus Jack's, which has won awards for its innovative Tex-Mex cuisine.

Bamboo Lounge (☎ 787-889-5820; Hwy 992 Km 5.1; dishes $13-24; ✆ 10am-10pm) Aside from offering first-rate horse rides and mountain biking (see Activities, p139), Caraballo also has a great restaurant, with panoramic views of the ocean and the rainforest. There's great Puerto Rican fare, a kid's menu, and a bar and patio area that stays open until 2am.

Entertainment

Aside from the makeshift barbecues and myriad people-watching possibilities, you only have a couple of options here (outside of the swankier bars in the Río Mar).Then again, the beach itself is often a full-on party, especially at weekends.

El Flamboyán Café (☎ 787-889-2928; Hwy 193 Km 1.2; ☺ 8am-midnight Thu-Tue) Rub some chalk onto your pool cue and twist the top off your Medalla beer (preferably by hand); yes, the Flamboyán is one of those rustic open-sided seaside bars with heavy stone tables and perennially popular pool tables that serves simple food and $2 bottles of beer. The local gang shows up on weekend evenings to witness the sporadic African drumming, live salsa and reggaeton.

Brass Cactus (☎ 787-889-5735; Hwy 193 Km 1.3) Not at all prickly, the Brass Cactus serves big plates of American pub fare with the odd traditional dish thrown in (dishes $8 to $22). Children will find lots to eat (burgers, fries, chicken fingers) and the down-home decor (think license plates hanging from the walls) will give them plenty to look at. Around 11pm on weekends the Cactus gets more of a club vibe, with patrons coming in to drink rather than eat. Usually there's live rock music, at least during the high season.

Getting There & Away

Públicos run regularly during the week from the Río Piedras terminal in San Juan ($4) to and from the Luquillo plaza.

FAJARDO & AROUND
pop 40,700

For the uninitiated observer, Fajardo is no oil painting. A spread-out municipality of just over 40,000 inhabitants, it sprawls like an untidy suburb between the El Yunque foothills and the sea. Part downbeat ferry port, part luxury boat launch, part swanky resort, and part busy commuter town, there's little rhyme or reason to this hard-to-fathom conurbation spread over seven wards, although there are plenty of amenities and ample hotels hidden amid the characteristic low hills and small hidden bays.

But delve beneath the outer turbidity and Fajardo has its raison d'être. A mecca for wealthy yacht owners and tourists heading to the gargantuan Conquistador (a mega-resort that once featured in the 1964 James Bond movie *Goldfinger*), Fajardo reigns as one of Puerto Rico's biggest water-activity centers and is the primary disembarkation point for the Spanish Virgin Islands of Vieques and Culebra.

You can do everything from diving in the waters of the coral-rich cordillera islands to exploring one of Puerto Rico's three bioluminescent bays here. On dry land there's the

---

PÚBLICOS

To step into a Puerto Rican público (intertown public bus) is to immerse yourself into an entirely different world, a parallel universe where the modus operandi is carried out in harsh, guttural Spanish and the best way to turn up the air-conditioning is to wind down the window.

The colorful cast of characters is evident as soon as you take a seat by squeezing Houdini-like into a hot and often crowded interior. Beside you the joker, spluttering jibes in barely comprehensible Spanish; behind you the sage, lecturing a myriad audience on boxing and baseball; while, up front, a luggage-laden Dominican family is engaged in tough negotiations with the driver over the price of an off-route airport drop-off.

But beginners beware. Públicos are not for the claustrophobic, or anyone in an urgent hurry. In the true tradition of open-ended, spontaneous travel, these slow-paced 15-seater minibuses have no printed timetable and no pre-arranged departure times. Buses leave only when they're full or when the driver deems he has sufficient passengers to make the trip worth his while. At weekends, they barely run at all, unless you're willing to lure the driver out of his Sunday morning reverie with a tidy sum.

But the joy of público travel is not in their rocketlike speed or unflinching reliability, but rather in their earthy authenticity. Two hours inside one of these veritable street-theaters-on-wheels and you'll learn twice as much about Puerto Rico as you would in a coastal mega-resort – and for a fraction of the cost.

The best place to catch a público in San Juan is at the suburban terminal in Río Piedras (p123), where clearly marked buses fan out across the island. First-timers should allow themselves plenty of time to get to know the nuances of the none-too-simple system. Prices for the one-hour journey to Luquillo hover at around $4 (compared to $80 for an equivalent taxi ride).

affectionate fishing 'village' of Las Croabas with its creaky fishing sloops, and the commonwealth's oldest colonial lighthouse. There's even a rather attractive and ecologically important nature reserve – Las Cabezas de San Juan – juxtaposed, in true Puerto Rican fashion, against the ubiquitous out-of-town shopping infestations.

Founded in 1760, downtown Fajardo, which lies between Rte 194 and Hwy 3, has little to show for 250 years of history. Yachters head a few miles south to Puerto del Rey, the largest marina in the Caribbean, while the most interesting sights for travelers – including the bio-bay, the nature reserve and the well-maintained Seven Seas Beach – punctuate the strung-out neighborhood of Las Croabas to the north.

Orientation

The city is quite spread out and navigation will require a bike, a car or a (very) sturdy pair of legs. Hwy 3 (sometimes bumper to bumper with traffic) divides the city and connects you to other roads leading to popular attractions.

Jumping off onto Rte 195 from Hwy 3 will bring you to the ferry docks; follow signs that say 'Embarcadero' until arriving at Rte 987. There the roads split; continuing straight on Rte 195 goes to the docks, while turning left onto Rte 987 passes Villa Marina and eventually brings you to the beach, the nature reserve and Las Croabas.

Most restaurants and sleeping accommodations are either near the docks or spread out along Rte 987.

Information

Fajardo Mayor's Office (☎ 787-863-1400; www .fajardopr.org; cnr Muñoz Rivera & Dr López; ☺ 8amnoon & 1-4:30pm Mon-Fri) There's no real tourism office in town, but the mayor's office does what it can. Call with any questions.

Hospital San Pablo del Este (☎ 787-863-0505; Rte 194 off Ave Conquistador; ☺ 24hr) The largest hospital along the east coast and your best option for treatment for any medical issues that may arise.

Pizz@Net (☎ 787-860-4230; per 30/60min $3/5; ☺ 11am-11pm) At the marina in Villa Marina, this is a great place to nosh on a pizza and surf the net.

Wash-n-Post (☎ 787-863-1995; Villa Marina shopping center; ☺ 8am-8pm Mon-Sat, 10am-5pm Sun) A one-stop FedEx, Western Union and UPS service that also has fluff and fold.

Sights

Culture vultures should look elsewhere: Fajardo has few interesting historical artifacts and little indigenous culture. The area's best activities can be enjoyed on the beach, in or under the water, or at the small but illuminating Las Cabezas de San Juan nature reserve.

LAS CABEZAS DE SAN JUAN

A 316-acre nodule of land on Puerto Rico's extreme northeast tip, the **Las Cabezas de San Juan Reserva Natural 'El Faro'** (☎ 787-722-5882, 787-860-2560; www.fideicomiso.org; Hwy 987 at Las Croabas; adult/under 11yr & senior $7/4; ☺ 9am-4pm Wed-Sun, Spanish tours 9:30am, 10am, 10:30am & 2pm, English tours 2pm) protects an historic lighthouse, a bioluminescent bay, rare flora and fauna, lush rainforest, various trails and boardwalks, and an important scientific research center. Despite its diminutive size, the reserve shelters seven – yes *seven* – different ecological systems, including beaches, lagoons, dry forest, coral reefs and mangroves. Animal species that forage here include big iguanas, fiddler crabs, myriad insects and all kinds of birds. Such condensed biodiversity is typical of Puerto Rico's compact island status and 'Las Cabezas' is highlighted as an integral part of the commonwealth's vital – but dangerously threatened – northeast ecological corridor.

Adding historical value to a potent natural brew is the splendidly restored 19th-century **lighthouse** (El Faro de Las Cabezas de San Juan; Puerto Rico's oldest, dating from 1882) that overlooks the peninsula's steep, craggy cliffs where the stormy Atlantic meets the Sonda de Vieques (Vieques Sound). The lighthouse has an information center and observation deck, open the same hours as the reserve, which offers spectacular views of El Yunque.

There are about 2 miles of trails and boardwalks that lead through the park, but you can't follow them on your own: you must take a guided tour. This lasts more than two hours, including the short tram ride through the dry forest section. Reservations are required.

You can get a glimpse of some of the reserve by simply walking east down the narrow beach from the Playa Seven Seas. Better yet, take a kayak tour (see p145) at sunset, and head into **Laguna Grande** after dark for

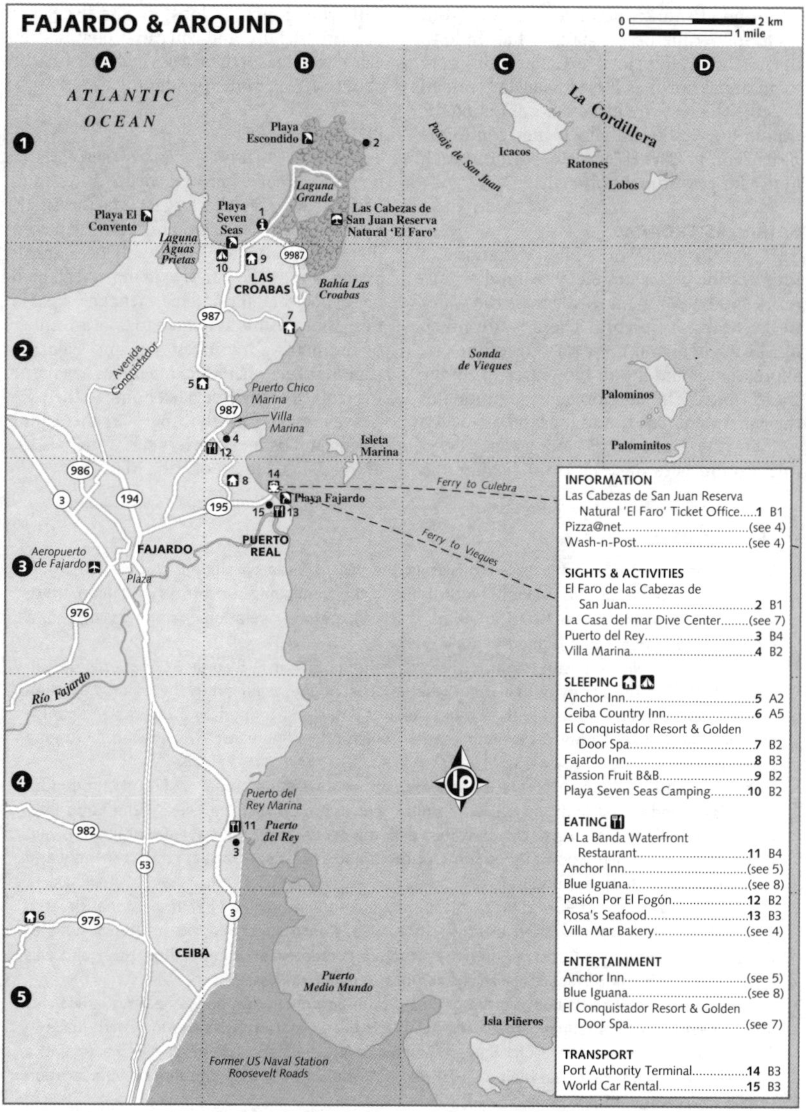
FAJARDO & AROUND
0 2 km
0 1 mile
ATLANTIC OCEAN
Playa Escondido
Laguna Grande
Playa El Convento
Playa Seven Seas
Laguna Aguas Prietas
Las Cabezas de San Juan Reserva Natural 'El Faro'
LAS CROABAS
Bahía Las Croabas
Icacos
La Cordillera
Pasaje de San Juan
Ratones
Lobos
Avenida Conquistador
Puerto Chico Marina
Villa Marina
Sonda de Vieques
Palominos
Palominitos
Isleta Marina
Playa Fajardo
Ferry to Culebra
Ferry to Vieques
FAJARDO
PUERTO REAL
Aeropuerto de Fajardo
Plaza
Río Fajardo
Puerto del Rey Marina
Puerto del Rey
CEIBA
Puerto Medio Mundo
Isla Piñeros
Former US Naval Station Roosevelt Roads
INFORMATION
Las Cabezas de San Juan Reserva Natural 'El Faro' Ticket Office.....1 B1
Pizza@net.....(see 4)
Wash-n-Post.....(see 4)
SIGHTS & ACTIVITIES
El Faro de las Cabezas de San Juan.....2 B1
La Casa del mar Dive Center.....(see 7)
Puerto del Rey.....3 B4
Villa Marina.....4 B2
SLEEPING
Anchor Inn.....5 A2
Ceiba Country Inn.....6 A5
El Conquistador Resort & Golden Door Spa.....7 B2
Fajardo Inn.....8 B3
Passion Fruit B&B.....9 B2
Playa Seven Seas Camping.....10 B2
EATING
A La Banda Waterfront Restaurant.....11 B4
Anchor Inn.....(see 5)
Blue Iguana.....(see 8)
Pasión Por El Fogón.....12 B2
Rosa's Seafood.....13 B3
Villa Mar Bakery.....(see 4)
ENTERTAINMENT
Anchor Inn.....(see 5)
Blue Iguana.....(see 8)
El Conquistador Resort & Golden Door Spa.....(see 7)
TRANSPORT
Port Authority Terminal.....14 B3
World Car Rental.....15 B3

the green-glowing, underwater 'fireworks' of bioluminescent micro-organisms. Make sure you go in a kayak or sailboat; engine pollution is slowly killing the very micro-organisms that create the bioluminescence. Check that you're not doing anything to harm the environment before making deals with local boat owners.

PLAYA SEVEN SEAS

On the southwestern shore of the peninsula of Las Cabezas, **Playa Seven Seas** (www.parquesnacionalespr.com; admission free, parking $3) is a sheltered, coconut-shaded horseshoe public beach. While not be quite as pretty as Playa Luquillo, fear not – it is attractive. The beach gets packed on weekends and during summer.

For good snorkeling or to get away from it all, follow the beach about a half mile to the northeast along the Las Cabezas property to an area known as **Playa Escondida** (Hidden Beach). The reefs are just offshore. Taking the trail to the west eventually brings you to the nearly empty **Playa El Convento**, with its beach house for government officials.

BAHÍA LAS CROABAS

You find this spot where Hwy 987 ends at a little seaside park rimmed by seafood restaurants and bars looking east across the water to the peaks of Culebra. There is not much of a beach here, but there's a view of the offshore islands and the air blows fresh with the trade winds. The anchorage accommodates the fishermen's co-op and the last half-dozen *nativos*, the 'out-island' sloops that everyone around here once used for fishing and gathering conch or lobster. The fishermen here are friendly, and you can probably strike a deal with one of them for a boat ride (usually about $100 per boat per day).

PUERTO DEL REY

This **marina** (☎ 787-860-1000; Hwy 3 Km 51.4) stands behind a breakwater in a cove 2 miles south of Fajardo. It is the largest marina in the Caribbean (1100 slips). You will find a complete marina village here with restaurants, stores, laundry facilities, banking and all manner of boat-hauling and maintenance capabilities. Many yachts stop here to take advantage of the marina's courtesy car and Fajardo's supermarkets when stocking up for a winter in the tropics or the ride back home to the USA. Travelers will find that many of the sailing, diving and fishing charters run from here. It's about 5 miles south of Villa Marina.

LIGHTHOUSES

In common with other small, seafaring islands, the Puerto Rican coastline is dotted with lighthouses. From the imposing hulk of El Morro fort to the formidable surf breaks of Rincón, these sturdy, storm-lashed sentinels (16 in all, of which 11 are still operational) stand as important historical monuments to a rugged bygone era.

Puerto Rico's oldest existing lighthouse, dating from 1882, is El Faro de Las Cabezas de San Juan, situated in the eponymous natural reserve on a craggy headland in the island's extreme northeastern corner. Adorned with rich neoclassical detail and topped by a distinctive Spanish colonial tower, it today houses a nature center which offers fine views over toward El Yunque rainforest.

You'll need to cross over to the island's extreme southwestern corner to find the commonwealth's second-oldest lighthouse, Los Morrillos, perched atop rust red cliffs in the Cabo Rojo National Wildlife Refuge. Recently renovated and still active, this rather austere gray-and-white late-colonial-era construction guards some of the island's most spectacular coastal scenery and is open periodically to the public.

Languishing as one of Puerto Rico's most endangered lighthouses, El Faro de Mona, situated on bleak Mona Island, has been inactive since 1976. Constructed in 1900 on the designs of famous French engineer Gustave Eiffel, the structure is redolent of a mini Eiffel Tower and was once crucial in guiding ships through the tempestuous Mona Passage.

An erstwhile west-coast beacon, the original Punta Borinquen lighthouse near Aguadilla was all but destroyed by a tsunami that swept through the area after a devastating earthquake in 1918, and today only a few crumbling walls remain. Nearby stands its modern replacement, a whitewashed cylindrical tower built in 1920 that is now used both as a lighthouse and a vacation retreat for coastguard personnel.

In operation since 1846, San Juan's El Morro fort houses Puerto Rico's oldest light station. After suffering severe damage during a US navy bombardment during the 1898 Spanish-American War, the original lighthouse was rebuilt with unique Spanish-Moorish features, a style that blends in surprisingly well with the rest of the fort.

Constructed in the early 1880s to demonstrate Spanish hegemony over the island of Culebra, the historic Culebrita lighthouse was deactivated in 1959 and subsequently decimated by a double whammy of terrifying hurricanes (Hugo in 1989 and Marilyn in 1995). In 2003 the Culebra Foundation was formed to save it from extinction.

Activities

Fajardo is decidedly amphibian – life is as exciting in the water as it is on land. This coastal region is blessed with many tiny islands (not to mention Culebra and Vieques) that provide fabulous opportunities for swimming, snorkeling, diving, fishing or just relaxing on a quiet beach.

BOATING

Almost all sailing trips advertised for travelers on the island sail out of one of the marinas in Fajardo. The operators listed here have been around for a while and know the area well, but there are many more good choices if these are all booked; *Que Pasa* (the island's tourism magazine) updates listings of new charter operators throughout the year. Many will pick you up in San Juan. Advance reservations are recommended for all charter tours.

Erin Go Bragh Charters (☎ 787-860-4401; www.egbc .net; Puerto del Rey Marina) offers ecofriendly sunset trips, dinner trips, daily trips (with BBQ and other lunches provided) and overnight charters to Vieques and Culebra. Captain Bill and his wife Ingrid visit various islands in the cordillera where you can swim, fish and snorkel.

East Island Excursions (☎ 787-860-3434; www .eastwindcats.com; Puerto del Rey Marina) has glass-bottomed catamarans that are in high demand, so book early. All kinds of day trips to La Cordillera islands are offered, and it even does quick runs over to St Thomas. One of the catamarans has a water slide that launches you right into the ocean. Day trips start at $69 per person (10am to 3:30pm).

Salty Dreams (☎ 787-717-6378; www.saltydreams.com; Villa Marina) offers day trips with lunch to Icacos, Lobos, Palominos and Palominitos cays in its 46ft catamaran *Salty Dogs* from $59 per day.

Traveler (☎ 787-863-2821; www.travelerpr.com; Villa Marina) offers similar daily tours with all-you-can-eat salad bars and snorkeling equipment provided for reasonable prices.

KAYAKING

This is absolutely the most entrancing way to see Fajardo's bioluminescent attractions – and the most environmentally sound as well. Swimming was banned in the bay in 2007.

Although technically located in Río Grande, **Eco Xcursion Aquatica** (☎ 787-888-2887; trips $45-65) is a mobile operation with guided flotilla trips to La Cordillera cays for snorkeling, and a sunset trip around Las Cabezas and into the bioluminescent Laguna Grande, where microorganisms glow in the dark water.

Yokahú Kayaks (☎ 787-604-7375, 863-5374) provides equipment, and the guides are very professional. Children under seven aren't allowed on the night trips, which leave at 7pm and generally last two hours. Their nonpolluting kayaks are one of the most environmentally friendly ways of seeing the laguna.

Eco-Action Tours (787-791-7509; www.ecoactiontours .com) offers kayak tours (one- to three-person kayaks) as well as excursions in a nonpolluting electric boat (minimum four people). Prices start at $25 per person.

FISHING

Capt Osva Alcaide (☎ 787-547-4851; www.deepseafish ingpr.com) offers half- and full-day deep-sea fishing charters out of Fajardo, and snorkeling to Icacos and Palomino Island. Expect to pay at least $400.

DIVING

There's no shortage of dive operators in Fajardo.

Operating since 1963, the **Caribbean School of Aquatics** (☎ 787-728-6606; www.saildiveparty .com; Villa Marina; ⏰ 7am-10pm) has National Association of Underwater Instructors (NAUI) and Professional Association of Dive Instructors (PADI) scuba classes, and Captain Greg Korwek will take you on all-day boat trips to the best spots around La Cordillera and elsewhere; two-tank dives start from $119 per person.

Set inside the grounds of El Conquistador resort, the PADI-certified **La Casa del Mar Dive Center** (☎ 787-860-3483; www.lacasadelmar.net; 1000 Ave Conquistador; ⏰ 8am-6pm) is great for all levels. The 'Bubblemakers for Kids' appeals to the younger crowd (8 to 15 years; $49); more experienced divers can take the trips to local reefs (one/two tanks $69/99). A two-tank dive over in Culebra is $125.

Sea Ventures Pro Dive Center (☎ 800-739-3483, 787-863-3483; www.divepuertorico.com; Puerto del Rey; ⏰ 8:30am-6pm) has three outlets in Fajardo, Palmas del Mar and Guánica. They're staffed by very experienced professionals offering one-week PADI certification courses. For those who just want the basics or already know how to dive, there are multiple trips to Palominos and Icacos Cays daily (one/two tanks $65/99), and on Sunday there are trips to Vieques and Culebra.

EAST COAST

Sleeping

Officials don't hassle people who pitch tents on Playa El Convento, which is reached by the path heading west from Playa Seven Seas. The area is popular so you'll usually find at least one or two tents up at all times; avoid pitching here if there are no other campers. Muggings do occur.

Playa Seven Seas Camping (☎ 787-863-8180, 622-5200; Hwy 987; campsites per tent $10) One of Puerto Rico's safest beaches, Playa Seven Seas near Las Croabas fills up fast. Make sure you reserve in advance if you plan to come during the summer or holidays. Showers and bathrooms are available and there's a restaurant on the beach; portable toilets are not allowed.

Anchor Inn (☎ 787-863-7200; frenchman@libertypr .net; Hwy 987 Km 2.7; r from $70;) The Anchor is a rather odd red, black and white construction situated in a similarly odd slice of spase land between Fajardo and Las Croabas. This place can be as dead as a dodo off-season, but arrive with low expectations and the cheap prices, no-frills rooms and reasonable on-site restaurant might be enough to make you stay.

Ceiba Country Inn (☎ 787-885-0471; www.geocities .com/countryinn00735; Hwy 997 Km 2.1; s/d $85/95;) A classic mountain retreat, this place has nine units overlooking the Caribbean and the offshore islands. On a clear day St Thomas can be seen on the horizon. Picture a landscaped hillside villa with decks, BBQ grill, continental breakfast and lounge. From San Juan, take Hwy 3 past Fajardo until the road becomes Rte 53. Take exit 5 (Ceiba North) and then make a right onto Rd 975 and go 1 mile. Turn right onto Hwy 977. Half a mile down the road is a sign for Ceiba Country Inn.

Passion Fruit B&B (☎ 800-670-3196; www.pas sionfruitbb.com; Hwy 987 Km 0.1; r $100-130;) A tropically themed guesthouse with a personal touch, the Passion Fruit is quite likely to inspire plenty of summer passion with its poolside breakfast spread and colorful 3rd-floor honeymoon suites. Discreet, private and bang for your buck.

ourpick Fajardo Inn (☎ 787-860-6000; www .fajardoinn.com; 52 Parcelas Beltrán, Hwy 195; r $100-300;) Perched on a hill overlooking the scruffy Fajardo corridor (and distant sea views), the Spanish hacienda-style Fajardo Inn is hard to miss. Recently extended to include a new pool, crazy golf, kid's playground, tennis court and a gym so huge it would look impressive in New York's Upper East Side,

this peach-hued Puerto Rican parador (country inn) exudes comfort, charm and a refreshing blend of unhurried ambience. Rooms are large and uncluttered, with cable TV, massive beds, wood furnishings and a daily dose of complimentary Puerto Rican coffee. A miniresort without the wristband.

El Conquistador Resort & Golden Door Spa (☎ 787-863-1000; www.elconresort.com; 1000 Ave Conquistador; r $300-700;) Lush, tropical paradise, or a spin-off of the allegorical 1960s sci-fi series *The Prisoner*? The gargantuan El Conquistador attracts and repels visitors in equal measure. A 900-unit mega-resort that encompasses a steep coastal escarpment a few clicks northeast of Fajardo, this mini-town boasts its own cove, cable car, mock Andalusian village, and – just in case you were harboring any James Bond allusions – private fantasy island. If your idea of a good vacation revolves around golf, tennis, spa pampering, water sports, fine dining and around-the-clock gambling, this could be your bag. If you're more intent on cross-fertilizing with the 'real' Puerto Rico, try the nice little guesthouse down the road.

Eating

Villa Mar Bakery (☎ 787-860-5590; Villa Marina; snacks $2-7) A kind of neighborhood bakery in the small row of shops adjacent to the Villa Marina; you can top up on coffee, pastries and sandwiches here. It's next to the Pizza@net (p142).

Blue Iguana (☎ 787-860-6000; dishes $7-21; 4-10pm Mon-Thu, to 1am Fri-Sun) The Fajardo Inn (left) has two restaurants, but this one is by far the best, with great Mexican fare, sharp service and unbelievably cheap prices (for sizable portions). In the earlier hours it's a good option for families; later on the pool table and ample bar attracts a drinking crowd. On weekends it's very popular after 10pm.

Anchor Inn (☎ 787-863-7200; Hwy 987 Km 2.7; dishes $8-24) This inn seems to focus more on its food than its accommodations. It has a big dining room specializing in lobster dishes that usually cost about $22. You can also go light here with a chef's salad for about $9.

A La Banda Waterfront Restaurant (☎ 787-860-9162; Puerto del Rey Marina, Hwy 3 Km 51.4; dishes $12-25) Live lobsters are easily transferred from the aquarium to your plate here – with a side trip to the kitchen, of course. If you prefer not to see your food swimming before you eat it, go for the Italian dishes or hearty steaks.

ourpick **Rosa's Seafood** (☎ 809-863-0213; 536 Tablazo; dishes $14-25; ☺ 11am-10pm Thu-Tue) Frustrated ferry passengers mix with loyal locals at this much vaunted seafood salon situated within anchor-dropping distance of Fajardo docks. You'll walk through a gauntlet of rusting cars and snarling canines to get here, but enter the bright-yellow building at road's end and the smell of fresh fish and the sound of sizzling onions will soon leave you forgetting about your ferry delays. Lobster, red snapper, and fish and chips are the more delectable in-house specialties, though Rosa's can also knock up a good steak – all for a tidy sum, of course.

Pasión por el Fogón (☎ 787-863-3502; Rte 987 Km 2.3; dishes $16-32) Lobster medallions, filet mignon and chicken stuffed with sweet banana and bacon – sound tasty? The governor of New York, Mariah Carey and Carlos Delgado obviously thought so, as they've all eaten here at one time or another. Listed as one of Puerto Rico's leading Mesónes Gastronómicos, Pasión por el Fogón is situated opposite the Villa Marina and – in keeping with its name – has a real passion for cooking.

Entertainment

Anchor Inn (☎ 787-863-7200; Hwy 987 Km 2.7) This place showcases music on weekend nights when salsa, merengue and Latin rock groups perform here.

The casino, bars and restaurants at the El Conquistador Resort & Golden Door Spa are actually open to the public; you're perfectly welcome to try your luck at the tables or take in a floor show from the bar no matter where you lay your head later that night.

Blue Iguana (opposite) gets busy on weekend nights during high season.

The stores and bars at Villa Marina sometimes put out tables for dominoes and become a popular hangout for locals on weekends. Friday night has live music.

Shopping

The malls are on Hwy 3 just north of town if you need a supermarket, Blockbuster Video, Payless Shoes or Wal-Mart fix.

Getting There & Away

AIR

The small, busy **Aeropuerto de Fajardo** (☎ 787-860-3110; 24hr parking $8.50) lies west of town near the intersection of Hwy 3 and Hwy 976.

All aircraft are Islander twins or tri-motor Trilanders. Typical one-way fares are $25 to Vieques (15 minutes), $30 to Culebra (15 minutes) and $80 to St Croix (30 minutes).

Isla Nena Air Service (☎ 787-761-6362) flies on demand to Vieques and Culebra.

Vieques Air Link (☎ 888-901-9247; www.viequesair link.com) offers daily on-demand flights to from Fajardo to Vieques, Culebra and St Croix.

Air Flamenco (☎ 787-801-8256; www.airflamenco.net) flights go to Culebra and San Juan.

CAR

There's a spacious outdoor parking lot on the right-hand side of the road as you approach the ferry docks. The lot is surrounded by secure fencing and has 24-hour surveillance. It's $5 a day.

Directly across from the public parking lot, the small **World Car Rental** (☎ 787-863-9696; Rte 195 at the docks; per day $35; ☺ 7:30-6pm) offers compact cars at daily and weekly rates.

FERRY

The ferries to Vieques and Culebra leave from the **Port Authority terminal** (☎ 787-863-3360, reservations 787-801-0250) for the islands. The terminal is about 1.5 miles east of town in the run-down Playa de Fajardo/Puerto Real neighborhood (follow the signs to either). For the ferry schedule for Culebra, see p165; for Vieques, see p180.

There's an irregular ferry that runs between Puerto Rico and the US Virgin Islands leaving Fajardo twice a month on Sundays at 1pm. Phone **Transportation Services Virgin Islands** (☎ 340-776-6282) for further details. The ferry takes approximately two hours and costs $125 per person. Reservations are required.

PÚBLICO

The **main público stop** (☎ 787-860-1820; www.fajar dopr.org; ☺ 4am-6pm Mon-Sat) is off the plaza in the old commercial center of town; but you will also find públicos at the ferry terminal (to meet incoming ferries) and near the seafood restaurants in Las Croabas. Many of the públicos at the ferry terminal will take you to and from the Río Piedras section of San Juan ($6, 1½ hours). You can also get to Las Croabas ($2, 20 minutes); a trip south to Humacao to catch another público on to Ponce and the south coast is around $5 and takes 30 minutes. Other options include

Luquillo ($1, 15 minutes) and Palmer (near El Yunque; $2, 20 minutes). If you are coming from San Juan and going to the ferry dock, make sure to tell the driver to go all the way to the port.

TAXI
You can always find taxis at the ferry terminal to take you to Luis Muñoz Marín (LMM) airport in San Juan ($80).

NAGUABO & AROUND
pop 24,800

There are two parts to modern Naguabo; the so-called downtown – which you'll curse for its nutty traffic and impossible-to-understand one-way system – and the unkempt Playa Húcares, where you might want to linger for views, a snooze, and lunch in one of its down-to-earth seafood restaurants.

Sights
Playa Húcares doesn't actually have a beach – the waterfront is a rock seawall overlooking a bay. It does, however, have a dramatic view of Vieques, 10 miles out to sea, and Cayo Santiago, closer to the coastline. It's worth visiting to get a look at the brightly painted fishing sloops and the two Victorian mansions that stand like sentinels over the sleepy little boardwalk, officially named Malecón Arturo Corsino. One of the mansions, the Castillo Villa del Mar, is on the National Registry of Historic Places (despite the dilapidation and the graffiti) and was once home to a restaurant and art gallery where local painters showed their work. These days it's a run-down old eyesore, but the mansion next to it has been somewhat restored, giving rise to hopes that both structures will eventually be returned to their former state of grace.

On weekends people flock to the line of open-air seafood restaurants just across the street for freshly caught *chillo* (snapper) and *sierra* (kingfish). If you follow Hwy 3 a half mile further south, you'll see about 2 miles of thin, tree-lined, vacant beach. Beyond this, the road carries you into the tiny village of **Playa Humacao**. Dilapidated Playa Humacao has one bright spot. There is a pristine balneario and *centro vacacional* (vacation center) at the neighborhood west of the village. **Punta Santiago** has become a bit of a weekend and holiday hotspot, and its bright *friquitines* offer lots of succulent treats like *arroz con jueyes*

(rice with crab chunks) and shark nuggets. During the busy season it's fun and upbeat and nowhere near as crowded as Luquillo.

Activities
Captain Frank López (☎ 787-850-7881, 787-316-0441) offers fishing or snorkeling trips and sea excursions to Cayo Santiago. Prices are negotiable: start your bidding at about $30. Look for *La Paseadora* boat at Playa Naguabo. At the Palmas del Mar Resort (below) you can also organize diving and snorkeling trips through the **Palmas Dive Center** (☎ 787-863-3483; Marina de Palmas), which will take you to Cayo Santiago and the deeper sites offshore (there are 35 within a 5-mile radius). Prices start at $60/89 for a half-day snorkel/dive.

Golfers can make reservations at either of the two **golf courses** (☎ 787-285-2256) at the Palmas del Mar resort. The greens fee for the 6800yd Reese Jones course is $125, or $80 after 2pm for nonguests; the old course (called 'the Palms') has similar prices.

The resort also has 20 **tennis courts** (☎ 787-852-6000), but you will need to make a reservation. Court fees are $25 an hour during the day, or $33 at night.

The **Palmas del Mar Equestrian Center** (☎ 787-852-6000; ☺ Tue-Sun) boards about 40 horses, including hunters and jumpers. One-hour-plus trail rides cost about $40.

Sleeping
There are several pretty guesthouses tucked into the south side of El Yunque that can be reached from Naguabo (see Sleeping, p136). Accommodations in Naguabo are very limited, with the exception of the Palmas del Mar Resort, which lies a few miles to the south. Yabucoa has more to offer.

Centro Vacacional Punta Santiago (☎ 787-852-1660; Hwy 3 Km 72.4, Playa Humacao; campsites with/without hookups $20/10, r/villas $66/110) This spot has a balneario and 36 cottages and 63 villas in a coconut grove on a pristine beach. Each unit can accommodate up to six people.

There are also more than 40 campsites around Playa Naguabo and Playa Humacao. Make reservations for the campsites through the central San Juan office of the **Recreational Development Company** (☎ 787-853-1660).

Palmas del Mar Resort (☎ 787-852-6000, 800-725-6273; www.palmasdelmar.com; 170 Candelero Dr; r $250-430) At first it's rather hard to work out exactly what Palmas del Mar *is*. A gargantuan resort?

An ultra-exclusive gated community? Or a manufactured minitown strangely redolent of Jim Carey's 'prison' in *The Truman Show*? Covering 2700 acres, this massive complex is significantly larger than most of Puerto Rico's state forests and is a world unto itself. At its opulent core lies a huge cluster of privately owned villas (ranging in price from $365,000 to $5 million) and time-share units built around a marina, 6.5 miles of beach and a golf course. Of more interest to itinerant travelers are the casino and token hotel: the Four Points by Sheraton, which has 107 amply furnished rooms and access to any of the resort's 19 restaurants. The only thing missing is *anything* inherently Puerto Rican.

Eating

While there's very little foodwise in Naguabo proper save the usual burger joints, the more easygoing strip of Playa Húcares is a cheapskate's heaven, and perfect for a bit of do-it-yourself research. Comb the kiosks and holes-in-the-wall at the north end for great *empanadillas* (dough stuffed with meat or fish), *mojito criollo* (rum, mint and lemon) sauce on fresh fish and tasty *surullitos*.

our pick **Restaurant Vinny** (☎ 787-874-7664; ☻ 8am-10pm) If you've no time to barter, head for Restaurant Vinny, a plastic-fork and -chair place that does a bang-up lunch for $4 (and the best *empanadillas* on the island).

Getting There & Away

Coming from San Juan, the easiest way to get to this part of the east coast is to follow Hwy 3 past Fajardo. Exits will soon follow for Naguabo and surrounding towns. Note that the Punta Santiago exit brings you off the highway and into a busy intersection with lots of fast-food restaurants, gas stations and shopping malls. If you are planning on going up into the south side of El Yunque or the Ruta Panorámica, gas up here first. Punta Santiago is 10 more minutes down the road by car; follow the signs.

The públicos vans in Playa Naguabo park near the promenade. They go to Naguabo ($1) or Humacao ($2), from where you can move on to the greener pastures of Fajardo, Ponce or San Juan.

The Palmas del Mar Resort will arrange for a minivan to haul you to and from LMM airport in San Juan – about a 40-minute trip in normal traffic. During peak season, the scheduled trip is $25 per person (four person minimum). For reservations call ☎ 787-285-4323.

The entrance to Palmas is a well-marked road off Hwy 3, a couple of miles south of Humacao. Driving from San Juan, take Hwy 52 south to Caguas and Hwy 30 to Humacao – all expressway, toll-road driving.

YABUCOA & AROUND
pop 39,200

Surrounded by hills on three sides and ocean on the other, Yabucoa sits on a tract of well-watered fertile land that once played host to Puerto Rico's all-encompassing sugar industry. Unless you have a penchant for poking around the ruins of old sugar mills, the town holds little for modern-day travelers. Out on the periphery, it's a different story. Yabucoa is the start point for two dramatic drives: the famed Ruta Panorámica and the less heralded, but no less spectacular, Hwy 901 that tracks the coast between Playa Lucia and the Punta Tuna lighthouse. On this road you'll find accommodations, restaurants and two of the island's most isolated surfing spots.

If you are traveling south to Yabucoa from the Humacao area, take the Hwy 53 toll road to avoid the traffic on Hwy 3. This lightly traveled section of road bisects miles of sugarcane fields and estuary where three mountain rivers meet.

Sights & Activities

The balneario at **Playa Lucía** (parking $2), near the intersection of Hwy 901 and Hwy 9911 in Yabucoa, has great shade under its coconut trees and several little beach bar-restaurants just off its premises. **El Cocal** is one of the few good surfing spots in the area (ask for directions at the balneario). Further southwest toward Maunabo is Sharkey's, another decent surf break where you're likely to have the waves to yourself.

Off Hwy 901 along the coast, you can ponder the ruins of **Hacienda de Santa Lucía**, an old sugar plantation a mile north of Playa Lucía. Don't expect a haunted mansion; there's only one wall left. **Central Roig** is the still active, old-time sugar hacienda and mill on the same road.

Lovers and solitary types like the view from the base of the **Faro Punta Tuna**, the lighthouse just southeast of Maunabo. From

---

GO FURTHER INTO THE COUNTRYSIDE

If you have an aversion to large crowds or can't face getting swallowed up by another ranger-led tour group from Texas, give El Yunque's northern highlights a body-swerve and head instead to the region's alternative entrance road just west of the town of Naguabo. Since mud slides closed the central section of Hwy 191 in the 1970s, this southern portion of the rainforest has remained relatively isolated and unexplored.

The best trail starts at the Casa Cubuy Ecolodge (p136) some 15 miles up the precipitous and winding Hwy 191. To tackle it, it's best to spend a night or two at the lodge itself, where you can park your car, procure directions, and enquire about the possibility of a guided hike with local expert **Robin Phillips** (☎ 787-874-2138; per person $22, minimum 5 people). If you choose to go it alone, start your excursion by hiking up Hwy 191 for 0.5 miles beyond Casa Cubuy until you reach road's end by a cluster of picnic pavilions. Turn right past the 'Do Not Enter' sign and follow a narrow trail alongside a half buried pipeline. After a mile or so you'll be forced to scramble across a landslide and pick up the trail again on the other side, just behind a copse of bamboo. Keep going alongside the pipeline until you reach a dam and aluminum bridge. Cross the bridge and proceed along the trail to a waterfall, where you'll encounter a steel ladder. Carefully ascend the ladder before climbing through a dry streambed and scrambling up to a small pool/swimming hole at the top.

This challenging out-and-back hike is approximately 12 miles round-trip and takes a good five to six hours. Go prepared for mud, rain and plenty of uphill scrambling. It is strongly advised that you enquire about current hiking conditions at the Casa Cubuy Ecolodge before setting out.

Hwy 901, take Hwy 760 toward the ocean. A path leads down to the extremely secluded **Playa Larga**.

Sleeping

Playa de Emajaguas Guest House (☎ 787-861-6023; Hwy 901 Km 2.5; dm/d $50/160) Ah…the view. Here in the island's southeastern corner, where the Cuchilla de Panduras Mountains meet the sea, you'll find Puerto Rico almost as Columbus must have found it. The no-frills Emajaguas Guest House nestles in verdant mountain foothills above a stunning deserted beach near El Cocal and Sharkey's surf breaks. The place is akin to a simple African 'rest-house,' light on luxuries and close to nature, but you come here for the surroundings and the sense of isolation (not always easy to find in Puerto Rico), not the complementary soap bars. The once grand house shelters seven scruffy but efficient apartments, with private baths and kitchenettes. Grab a hammock and turn off, tune in and drop out.

Caribe Playa (☎ 787-839-6339, 787-839-1817; www.caribeplaya.com; Hwy 3 Km 112; r $79-104; 🐾) You will spot this place where Hwy 3 runs along the seashore between Maunabo and Patillas. Tucked right on the shore under a slanting plantation of coconuts, this inn has 29 units, many with beachfront balconies; most rooms have a kitchen sink and fridge, but no stove.

There's a restaurant on the premises and a natural pool carved into the rocky coast. A licensed therapist can do beachside massages for $50 an hour.

Parador Costa del Mar (☎ 787-266-6276; Hwy 901 Km 5.6; r $84-102; 🐾 🐾) Well clear of the urban infestations of Yabucoa, the Costa del Mar is the younger sibling of the Palmas de Lucía (it's owned by the same family) and fits the same price and comfort bracket. Its position on a grassy bluff overlooking the ocean at the start of spectacular Hwy 901 gives it extra kudos, as do the vividly colored flowers, luminous pool and brilliant yellow paintwork. But there's substance under the superficiality. You can also bank on five-star cleanliness, zippy service and gym, sauna and a 100yd trek to the beach.

Parador Palmas de Lucía (☎ 787-893-4423; www.palmasdelucia.com; cnr Hwy 901 & Hwy 9911; r $90-109; 🅿 🐾 🖥 🐾) Just when you thought mall-infested Yabucoa was uninhabitable, you hit the end of the road at Playa Lucía and stumble upon what is surely one of Puerto Rico's best paradores. Backing up onto the beach, but with its own secluded pool and restaurant, the Palmas de Lucía is a light, airy place with huge, clean rooms decked out with rather plush furnishings. To add spice to an already strong brew, there's also a small but well-kept gymnasium which offers a good alternative to jogging around Yabucoa's traffic-clogged roads. Good service is par for the course at this family-friendly hotel, and it makes an excellent launch pad for a lengthy road trip across the Ruta Panorámica.

Eating

El Mar de la Tranquilidad (☎ 787-839-4870; Hwy 3 Km 118.9; dishes $7-22) Once the road returns to sea level (heading west), look for this establishment on the seaward side of Hwy 3. Beer on the outdoor terrace is a rare pleasure, and you can get *salmorejo de jueyes* (land crab in tomato sauce), lobster and some decent cocktails.

El Nuevo Horizonte (☎ 787-893-5492; Hwy 901 Km 9.8; dishes $7-23) Just a mile or two west of Parador Costa del Mar, the view rarely gets better than it does from this place. This restaurant is perched high on the mountainside overlooking the Caribbean. You can smell the *asopao de langosta* (lobster stew) cooking 200yd before you get here. A cauldron of the stew will set you back about $18 and serves at least two people.

Getting There & Away

Públicos link Yabucoa with the nearby urban centers of Humacao ($3) and Maunabo ($2), with connections onto Fajardo and San Juan. A new tunnel on Hwy 3 connects Yabucoa and Maunabo, although the oceanside Hwy 901 is a far more scenic route (especially if you're on a bike).

EAST COAST

Culebra & Vieques

Islands often have a reputation for being insular, eccentric and slightly rebellious, and Culebra and Vieques are no different. Separated from mainland Puerto Rico by a 7-mile stretch of choppy ocean, the first hints of seditious nonconformity appear as you dock at the ramshackle ferry ports of Dewey or Isabel II to be met by a colorful cast of American expats and maverick locals. Closer geographically to the US Virgin Islands than they are to the rest of the commonwealth (they are often referred to, colloquially, as the Spanish Virgin Islands), these two bejeweled Caribbean havens are noticeably slower and more easygoing than their main island counterpart. Covered in a blanket of dry subtropical forest and blessed with a handful of rare endemic plant and animal species, they also exhibit distinct physical characteristics. Disembark for a few days and you'll uncover more surreptitious surprises: wild horses in Vieques, rare turtles in Culebra – and quite a few rare people too, many of whom were instrumental in the fight to reclaim their prized islands from the US Navy in 1975 (Culebra) and 2003 (Vieques) after more than 50 years of military occupation.

Ironically, things couldn't have turned out better. Thanks largely to their military history; the Spanish Virgins – in keeping with their name – remain tranquil and refreshingly undeveloped. With former navy land recently given over to two new US Fish & Wildlife Refuges, the main draw card for contemporary visitors is the unsullied beaches – Vieques and Culebra protect some of the best arcs of sand in the Caribbean – and the unblemished countryside that glimmers invitingly with nary a resort, golf course or casino to break the natural vista.

HIGHLIGHTS

- Staking out leatherback turtles on a starlit volunteer turtle-watching program on **Playa Brava** (p158), Culebra

- Swapping four wheels for two and going on a picturesque spin to **Green Beach** (p173) on bike-friendly Vieques

- Finding dilapidated US tanks and a refreshing lack of tourists on paradisiacal **Playa Flamenco** (p159)

- Eating, drinking, playing or just plain chilling on the colorful 'strip' in laid-back **Esperanza** (p170)

- Foraging into the newly formed **Vieques National Wildlife Refuge** (p169) to discover unblemished beaches, thriving wildlife and excellent snorkeling

Culebra
Playa Flamenco ★   ★ Playa Brava

Vieques   ★ Vieques National Wildlife Refuge
★ Green Beach   ★   ★ Bahía Mosquito
Esperanza

- Seeing stars on a serene but distinctly surreal evening boat tour of bioluminescent **Bahía Mosquito** (p171)

- POPULATION: 12,000

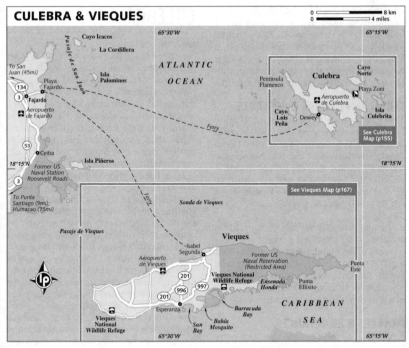

CULEBRA & VIEQUES

HISTORY

Some 500 years ago the islands east of Puerto Rico, including Culebra and Vieques, were disputed territory between the Taíno and the Caribs. Groups from both tribes came and went from the islands according to the season – probably to hunt the turtles nesting here. Vieques had more fertile, flatter land for farming and therefore was the more popular island. The first real settlement came to Culebra during the early 16th century, when Taíno and Carib refugees from Borinquen gathered here and on Vieques to make peace with each other, pool their resources and mount a fierce (but ultimately unsuccessful) campaign to drive the Spaniards from the big island. When Spain conceded Puerto Rico and her territories to the US following the Spanish-American War in 1898, both Culebra and Vieques became municipalities of the Republic of Puerto Rico. Therefore, residents are recognized as US citizens (half of them are expat Americans, in any case).

For most of the 20th century, the US Navy and Marine Corps used the islands for target practice and for rehearsing 20th-century military actions carried out on other shores, such as Iwo Jima, the Philippines, Haiti and Kuwait. The navy left Culebra several decades ago to concentrate its activities on Vieques, where it set up a military camp and proceeded to hold practice bombings in nearby waters with alarming regularity. After an errant bomb killed a civilian in 1999, *viequenses* reached their breaking point. A long struggle ensued, but the navy was eventually ejected. Of course, the tracts of pristine land that opened up with the military's departure caught the attention of many developers, including the Puerto Rican government itself, which wants a beefed-up tourism infrastructure on both Culebra and Vieques. Locals are trying hard to bring in new jobs through sustainable tourism that won't destroy the wild land and beaches that make the Spanish Virgin Islands truly special. So far so good – but the battle rages on.

CLIMATE

The famous Caribbean trade winds gently buffet these two islands, but it is still hot, hot, hot just about every day of the year. Average temperatures are around 85°F with relatively low humidity. Add the glare from surrounding water and white sand and it feels like 110°F in the shade. Rainy season, which doesn't do much to cool things off, is May through November. Hurricane season is August/September through November, with October generally being the wettest month.

TERRITORIAL PARKS & RESERVES

The Puerto Rico Department of Natural Resources protects more than 1500 acres of land along the Península Flamenco and from Monte Resaca east to the sea. Named the Culebra National Wildlife Refuge (p156), it includes the coastline as well as more than 20 offshore cays. The **US Fish & Wildlife Service** (☎ 787-742-0115; www.fws.gov) administers all of these lands.

Vieques National Wildlife Refuge (p169) protects 18,000 acres on the eastern and western ends of the island. Formed between 2001 and 2003, it is the largest natural reserve in Puerto Rico and offers visitors a chance to mountain bike, hike, snorkel and swim on newly opened beaches and pristine land.

DANGERS & ANNOYANCES

Culebra is virtually crime-free, but petty thievery is sadly somewhat common on Vieques, especially around the Sun Bay public beach. Lock hotel rooms and don't bring valuables to the beach. Be careful with cell phones, as thieves have been known to grab them right out of people's hands. Don't leave anything in sight in the car and lock the doors, always.

GETTING THERE & AROUND

There's frequent air service from San Juan, Fajardo and St Thomas in the Virgin Islands to both Vieques (see p180) and Culebra (see p165). Cheaper and more environmentally friendly are the government-run ferries that run from Fajardo to Vieques (see p180) and Culebra (p165) regularly. If you're lucky you might find a private operator to connect you by boat to St Thomas.

Many travel agencies will tell you that cars are a must on Culebra and Vieques, which is probably why there are far too many of them plying the islands' small towns and quiet lanes. However, with a little extra effort and some lung-expanding leg work, both islands can be negotiated via a mixture of públicos, taxis, bicycles and your own two feet.

CULEBRA

pop 2000

An elusive lizard (not seen since 1974) hides in a unique mountain 'boulder' forest, a couple of abandoned US tanks lie rusting on a paradisiacal beach, a sign on a shop door in the 'capital' Dewey reads 'Open some days, closed others.' Welcome to Culebra – the island that time forgot; mainland Puerto Rico's weird, wonderful and distinctly wacky smaller cousin that lies glistening like a bejeweled Eden to the east.

Long feted for its diamond dust beaches and world-class diving reefs, sleepy Culebra is probably more famous for what it *hasn't* got than for what it actually possesses. There are no big hotels here, no golf courses, no casinos, no fast-food chains, no rush-hour traffic, no postmodern stress and *no problemas, amigo*. Situated 17 miles to the east of mainland Puerto Rico, but inhabiting an entirely different planet culturally speaking, the island's peculiar brand of off-beat charm can sometimes take a bit of getting used to. Don't expect open-armed cordiality here. Culebran friendliness is of the more backwards-coming-forwards variety. Home to rat-race dropouts, earnest idealists, solitude seekers, myriad eccentrics, and anyone else who can't quite get their heads around the manic intricacies of modern life, the island is the ultimate 'riddle wrapped up in a mystery inside an enigma.' Among the traveling fraternity, it has long inspired a religiouslike devotion in some, and head-scratching bafflement in others. There's but one binding thread – the place is jaw-droppingly beautiful.

HISTORY

First hunting grounds for Taíno and Carib tribes, then a pirate stronghold during the days of the Spanish Empire, much of Culebra's 7000 acres has remained essentially the same ever since two-legged creatures took to walking its shores. The US Navy grabbed control of most of the island early in the 20th century and didn't cede its lands back to the locals until 1975. Some modern structures went up on the newly accessible land rather rapidly, but resident expats and native-born *culebrenses* were very quickly able to find a common language and they have continued to work together quite fiercely to hold over-development and commercialization at bay.

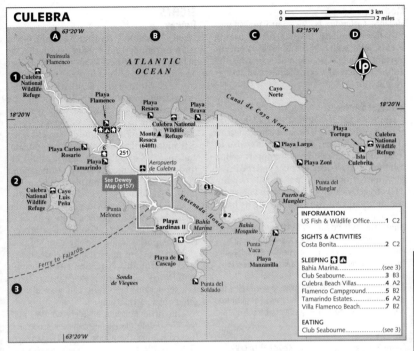

CULEBRA

INFORMATION
US Fish & Wildlife Office........1 C2

SIGHTS & ACTIVITIES
Costa Bonita.........................2 C2

SLEEPING
Bahía Marina.....................(see 3)
Club Seabourne....................3 B3
Culebra Beach Villas.............4 A2
Flamenco Campground............5 B2
Tamarindo Estates.................6 A2
Villa Flamenco Beach............7 B2

EATING
Club Seabourne..................(see 3)

CULEBRA & VIEQUES

ORIENTATION

There's very little you need to know to navigate the island. The cheery little ferry dock fronts a strip of shops and the Kokomo Hotel. Cab drivers and public vans also congregate here.

Heading left away from the dock will bring you to Calle Pedro Márquez, usually referred to as the 'main road,' which leads into Dewey, the island's principal settlement. There are only a few roads leading in and out of Dewey.

It is easier to walk than drive in town due to one-way streets and some parking congestion. The main road eventually leads out to the single landing strip airport on Rte 251; if you continue past the airport you get to Playa Flamenco. If you take Rte 250 east you'll come to turn-offs for Playas Resaca and Brava, eventually winding up at Playa Zoni. Another road, Calle Fulladoza, heads south to Punta del Soldado.

Culebrita and Cayo Norte are two of the more popular cays off Culebra and are easily visited; there are about 18 others surrounding the island.

INFORMATION

Few establishments have meaningful street addresses on Culebra; descriptive addresses are generally used here. Basic island maps are handed out by hotels and car-rental agencies. All of the services listed here are in Dewey.

Emergency

Culebrenses will tell you that if you have an emergency on the island, you will get a much faster, more professional response by calling the island detachment of the Puerto Rican police than by contacting the municipal police. There's a police station in Calle Pero Márquez.
Municipal police (☎ 787-742-0106)
Puerto Rican police (☎ 787-742-3501)

Internet

Excétera (Map p157; ☎ 787-742-0844; 162 Calle Escudero; per 15min/hr $5/15; ☻ 9am-5pm Mon-Fri, to 1pm Sat) Heftily priced internet. You can also buy stationary, newspapers and magazines such as *National Geographic*.

Laundry

Tommy's (Map p157; ☎ 787-742-0722; Calle Romero) Same-day laundry service.

Media

Culebra Calendar is the island newspaper and has complete listings of upcoming events, jobs, tide tables and articles on important Culebra issues. You can find the online version at www.theculebracalendar online.com.

Medical Services

Despite its small population, Culebra has good health services. Some basic toiletries are carried in local shops, but it's wise to bring things like condoms, tampons, saline solution, contact-lens supplies and medicine for tummy troubles – not that you are more likely to get sick on Culebra than anywhere else, but you will want something at hand if you do.

Clinic (Map p157; ☎ 787-742-3511) In town on the road to Punta Melones; has drugs and resident doctors. The island also keeps a plane on emergency standby at the airport overnight for medical transport to the main island.

Walgreens (☎ 787-860-1060) With no pharmacy on the island, *culebrenses* call Walgreens in Fajardo. The pharmacy ships drugs to the island on Vieques Air Link flights.

Money

Banco Popular (Map p157; ☎ 787-742-3572; Calle Pedro Márquez; ◷ 8:30am-2:30pm Mon & Wed-Fri) There's an ATM here.

Post

Post office (Map p157; ☎ 787-742-3862; Calle Pedro Márquez; ◷ 8:30am-4:30pm Mon-Fri, to noon Sat) Right in the center of town.

Tourist Information

There are some good websites available. Try www.islaculebra.com or www.culebra-island .com for a general overview.

Tourist office (Map p157; ☎ 787-742-3116; Calle Pedro Márquez; ◷ 8:30am-3:30pm Mon-Fri) Good island-wide information can be found at this booth outside the Alcaldía (Town Hall) on the main street 200m from the ferry terminal.

DANGERS & ANNOYANCES

Culebra breeds swarms of mosquitoes, especially during the rainy season (August to November). Some of the daytime species have been known to carry dengue.

Wear your seatbelt and obey local parking laws! Officers on Culebra love issuing traffic tickets.

SIGHTS
Dewey

Dewey, Culebra's diminutive main town, is an intriguing hodgepodge of ramshackle buildings and off-beat locals that lies nestled on a thin knob of land between two glistening bays. More gritty rural backwater than drop-dead gorgeous Caribbean idyll, the settlement's exotic charm is as idiosyncratic as it is hard to capture. Asthmatic trucks crawl along narrow muddy streets, grey cats muse in the sweltering afternoon sun, and snatches of pulsating *bomba* drums intrude like rhythmic invitations from behind the colorful pink and purple facades of the myriad guesthouses. Named after an illustrious US admiral, Dewey is generally referred to as 'Da Town' by locals, a large number of whom are US expats. You can buy groceries here, post a letter, shoot a game of pool and buy a decent meal, if the chef decides to wake up from his afternoon siesta. Beyond that, Dewey is a sleepy backwater that serves as a serviceable launching pad for Culebra's other rustic attractions.

The little **Museum of Ildefenso** (Map p157; ☎ 787-742-0240; Rte 250; ◷ 8am-noon & 1-3pm) is tucked behind the office of the Department of Natural Resources, and has some historical pictures of the island and lots of Taíno artifacts. Beware: the hours – like everything in Culebra – are rather sporadic.

Culebra National Wildlife Refuge

More than 1500 acres of Culebra's 7000 acres constitute a national wildlife refuge (Map p155), which US President Theodore Roosevelt signed into law almost 100 years ago, and which is protected by the Departamento de Recursos Naturales y Ambientales (DRNA; Department of Natural Resources & Environment). Most of this land lies along the Península Flamenco, and from Monte Resaca east to the sea, and includes all of the coastline as well as more than 20 offshore cays, with the exception of Cayo Norte. The **US Fish & Wildlife Service** (Map p155; ☎ 787-742-0115; www.fws.gov; ◷ 7am-4pm Mon-Fri) administers these lands. Monte Resaca, Isla Culebrita and Cayo Luis Peña are open to the public from sunrise to sunset daily, and all have some fairly challenging hikes. Stop by the office on the east side of Ensenada Honda for maps, literature and permission to visit other sections of the refuge.

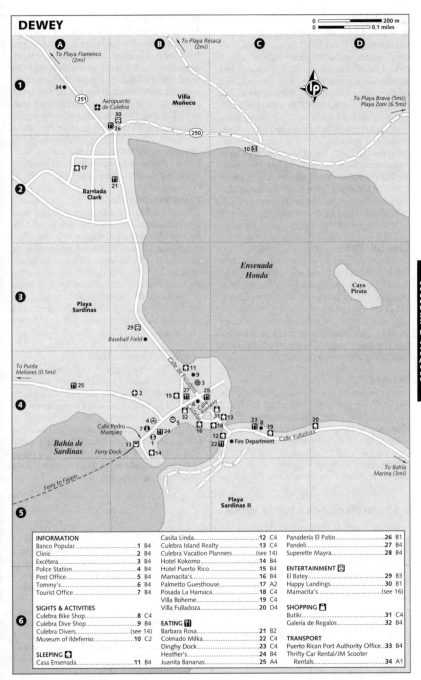

DEWEY

To Playa Flamenco (2mi)

To Playa Resaca (2mi)

To Playa Brava (5mi); Playa Zoni (6.5mi)

Villa Muñeco

Aeropuerto de Culebra

Barriada Clark

Ensenada Honda

Cayo Pirata

Playa Sardinas

To Punta Melones (0.5mi)

Baseball Field

Calle de Escudero

Calle Pedro Marquez

Calle Estrella Romero

Calle Fulladoza

Fire Department

Bahía de Sardinas

Ferry Dock

Ferry to Fajardo

To Bahía Marina (3mi)

Playa Sardinas II

CULEBRA & VIEQUES

INFORMATION	Casita Linda......................**12** C4	Panadería El Patio......................**26** B1
Banco Popular.....................**1** B4	Culebra Island Realty...............**13** C4	Pandeli.....................................**27** B4
Clinic..................................**2** B4	Culebra Vacation Planners.....(see 14)	Superette Mayra........................**28** B4
Excétera..............................**3** B4	Hotel Kokomo........................**14** B4	
Police Station.......................**4** B4	Hotel Puerto Rico...................**15** B4	**ENTERTAINMENT**
Post Office...........................**5** B4	Mamacita's..............................**16** B4	El Batey....................................**29** B3
Tommy's...............................**6** B4	Palmetto Guesthouse..............**17** A2	Happy Landings........................**30** B1
Tourist Office........................**7** B4	Posada La Hamaca..................**18** C4	Mamacita's............................(see 16)
	Villa Boheme..........................**19** C4	
SIGHTS & ACTIVITIES	Villa Fulladoza.......................**20** D4	**SHOPPING**
Culebra Bike Shop..................**8** C4		Butiki..**31** C4
Culebra Dive Shop..................**9** B4	**EATING**	Galería de Regalos....................**32** B4
Culebra Divers.....................(see 14)	Barbara Rosa..........................**21** B2	
Museum of Ildefenso..............**10** C2	Colmado Milka.......................**22** C4	**TRANSPORT**
	Dinghy Dock..........................**23** C4	Puerto Rican Port Authority Office..**33** B4
SLEEPING	Heather's................................**24** B4	Thrifty Car Rental/JM Scooter
Casa Ensenada......................**11** B4	Juanita Bananas......................**25** A4	Rentals..................................**34** A1

Isla Culebrita

If you need a reason to rent a kayak or hire a water taxi, Isla Culebrita (Map p155) is it. This small island, just a mile east of Playa Zoni, is part of the wildlife refuge. With its abandoned lighthouse, six beaches, tide pools, reefs and nesting areas for seabirds, Isla Culebrita has changed little in the past 500 years. The north beaches, such as the long crescent of Playa Tortuga, are popular nesting grounds for sea turtle, and you may see these animals swimming near the reefs just offshore. Bring a lot of water, sunscreen, a shirt and a hat if you head for Isla Culebrita, because there is little shade here. See Kayaking (p161) and Boating (p161) for details on renting and hiring boats to reach this island. The Isla is also home to a ruined lighthouse earmarked for extensive repairs.

Cayo Luis Peña

Less visited than Isla Culebrita, Luis Peña (Map p155) is the island of peaks, rocks, forests and coves you'll pass just a few minutes before the ferry lands you at Culebra's dock. This island is another part of the wildlife refuge, and it has a collection of small sheltered beaches. Luis Peña is a short kayak or water-taxi trip from town; it has good beaches and snorkeling all around the island.

Beaches

Culebra's beaches offer wild natural beauty, but little in the way of tourist facilities. The only beach that has amenities is Playa Flamenco, and even these are limited. Be sure to bring lots of water/snacks when venturing out and don't take risks swimming if you're on your own. The following beaches are listed clockwise around the island from Dewey.

PUNTA MELONES

The nearest beach to town. Take the road past the clinic about a half-mile north until you reach a development on the hill to your right. Ahead on your left, you'll see the rocky Melones point with a navigation light; to the right of the point is a stony beach. If you head down to this beach, you will find great snorkeling at both ends. The point's name comes from the prevalence of a species of melon cactus in this part of the island. It's a good idea to bring shoes you can wear in the water; cacti line the sea floor. There's also not a lot of shade on the beach, so strong sunscreen is imperative.

PLAYA TAMARINDO

A little bit beyond Melones, this is a very good snorkeling beach. You can swim here from Melones by heading north along the peninsula; it's also accessible by foot or car by turning off the Dewey–Flamenco Beach road at the bottom of the hill just before the lagoon. This is an often-overlooked beach; it's not as flashy and fabulous-looking as others are, but offers a good combination of sun and shade, gentle currents and lots of underwater life for good snorkeling.

PLAYA CARLOS ROSARIO

If you follow a path west from the parking lot at Playa Flamenco, a 12- to 15-minute hike over the hill will bring you to Playa Carlos Rosario, an antidote to the crowds at Playa Flamenco and one of the best snorkeling areas in Puerto Rico. But don't get confused: Playa Carlos Rosario is not the first beach you'll reach along this path. This first nameless beach is one of the few places in Puerto Rico where you'll see nude or topless bathers taking in the sun in privacy.

VOLUNTEERING FOR A TURTLE WATCH

Two of Culebra's most isolated beaches – Resaca and Brava – are nesting sites for the endangered leatherback sea turtle, the largest living sea turtle in the world. The nesting season runs April through early June and each year small groups of volunteers are recruited by the US Fish & Wildlife Refuge to oversee the delicate egg-laying process. Volunteers meet at sunset before traveling out to the beaches where they are required to count eggs, measure turtles, and document the event for environmental records. At the same time, participants are able to witness one of nature's most transfixing and timeless events in stunning close-up.

Volunteer postings are understandably limited so, if you are keen to take part, it is wise to plan ahead. Start by contacting either nonprofit organization **CORALations** (☎ 787-556-6234; www .coralations.org) or the **US Fish & Wildlife Service** (Map p155; ☎ 787-742-0115; www.fws.gov; ☺ 7am-4pm Mon-Fri) for more details. CORALations also undertakes important coral-reef restoration work on the island.

BEAUTY & THE BEAST

In *The Beach*, a widely-acclaimed novel by British writer Alex Garland, a group of idealistic back-packers go off in search of a paradisiacal beach that is, as yet, undiscovered by modern tourism. Take away the food kiosks and the sprinkling of summer sunbathers, and Flamenco on the rustic island of Culebra could quite easily fit the bill. Long touted by newspaper articles and travel spreads as 'the finest beach in the Caribbean' (and one of the top 10 in the world), this mile-long scimitar of sand is undeniably beautiful, though the history of the area is a little less beguiling.

Up until the early 1970s, Flamenco was part of a live firing range used by the US Navy for target practice. First requisitioned by the military in 1902 to counter a rising German threat in the Caribbean, Culebra's beaches were used to stage mock amphibious landings and myriad ground maneuvers. In 1936, with WWII in the offing, the Flamenco peninsula yielded to its first live arms fire and the beach was regularly shelled.

Burgeoning decade by decade, the military operations reached their peak during the late 1960s at the height of the Vietnam War, with the navy simulating gun attacks and submarine warfare. When the US government hinted at expanding the Culebra base in the early 1970s, public sentiment quickly turned bellicose. In what would become a dress rehearsal for the Navy-Vieques protests (see p168) 30 years later, a small committed group of Puerto Rican protesters – including Independence party leader Reubén Berríos – initiated a campaign of civil disobedience which culminated in squatters accessing the beach and having to be forcibly removed by police. Despite arrests and imprisonments, the tactics worked. In 1975 the US Navy pulled out of Culebra and the beach was returned to its natural state.

Well almost…. Over 30 years later you can still find graphic evidence of the war games that once wreaked havoc on Flamenco. At the beach's western end, contrasting rather sharply with the diamond-dust sand and translucent water, two rusty, seaweed-covered tanks sit like ghostly reminders of past military misdemeanors. Beauty and the beast – it's a photo opportunity too good to miss.

To reach Carlos Rosario, head north from this first beach, cross the narrow peninsula, and head down to the sandy basin and shade trees. A barrier reef almost encloses this beach, and you can snorkel on either side of it by swimming through the bottle channel – look for the white plastic bottle marker – at the right side of the beach. But be *very* careful: water taxis and local powerboats cruise this channel and the reef, and in 1998 a long-time Culebra resident and diver was struck and killed by a boat.

For really spectacular snorkeling, work your way along the cliffs on the point south of the beach, or head about a quarter mile north to a place called the **Wall**, which has 40ft drop-offs and rich colors. By the way, a lot of local gringos call Carlos Rosario 'Impact Beach' because of all the shelling it took back in the navy days, and you may see ordnance in the water. It could be live – don't mess with it!

PLAYA FLAMENCO

Stretching for a mile around a sheltered, horseshoe-shaped bay, Playa Flamenco is not just Culebra's best beach; it is also generally regarded as the finest in Puerto Rico, and quite possibly the whole Caribbean. In fact, certain discerning travel writers have suggested that it is among the top 10 in the world. While individual musings may sound trite, there is no denying that this gentle arc of white sand and crystal surf is something special. Backed by low scrub rather than craning palms, and equipped with basic amenities, Flamenco is the only public beach on the island. It is also the only place where you are allowed to camp. Facilities include two rudimentary guesthouses, a collection of kiosks (selling both snack food and beach gear), toilets, outdoor showers, lifeguards, picnic tables and a parking lot. There are currently no fully blown restaurants or stores in the area, so visitors should stock up with provisions before they arrive.

In contrast to the main island's gargantuan resorts, Flamenco is refreshingly rustic and crowd-free. In the winter months you'll feel like Robinson Crusoe contemplating the clarity of the water here, while on a busy day in summer with perhaps 200 people spread across nearly a mile of beach, it will still seem half-deserted. A nearby lagoon attracts fla-mingos in the winter – hence the name – while reefs at each end made for great snorkeling.

PLAYA RESACA

A *resaca* is an undertow and a metaphor for a hangover, an allusion to the state of the water perhaps, or the way you will feel after climbing up and down 650ft Monte Resaca to reach it. The **US Fish & Wildlife Service** (☎ 787-742-0115) maintains the trail here, and you should call them for permission as well as directions to the trailhead. Monte Resaca, the island's high-est point, is characterized by an ecologically unique boulder-strewn forest on its upper slopes that harbors rare types of flora and fauna (mainly lizards). It's a deceptively tough (and sometimes prickly) climb. Bring lots of water and sunscreen and don't try swimming from the beach.

PLAYA BRAVA

The beauty of Brava lies in the fact that there is no road here; you *have* to hike – make that bushwhack – along a little-used trail that is often overgrown with sea grape and low scrub. The rewards are immense when you finally clear the last mangrove and are con-fronted with an isolated but stunning swathe of sand that glimmers with a fierce but utterly enchanting beauty.

To get here, travel around to the east-ern side of Ensenada Honda. Pass the Km 4 marker and turn left a little way past the cemetery. Follow this road until the pave-ment ends and you come up against a gate. This is the entrance to a cattle farm, but it is also a public right-of-way, so park your car or bike and head due north on the trail beyond the gate. The second half of the trail

leads through a grove of trees that is often rife with butterflies.

PLAYA ZONI

Head to the extreme eastern end of the island and you'll eventually run out of road at Playa Zoni. It's a straightforward 20-minute drive – or 45 minutes on a bike – but the road can be treacherous after heavy rains. It's paved but sometimes large chunks wash away. There's a small parking spot next to the sign alerting you to the fact that endangered turtles cross the beach. Zoni is long and straight, with beautiful Caribbean islands popping up in the distance, but again, it's an isolated place, so don't swim alone.

Some locals think this is a better beach than Flamenco; it doesn't have quite the same soft sand and gentle curves, but it certainly is stunning in its own right and is usually less crowded. Be careful entering waters for a few days after a storm. Sometimes the heavier currents will have pulled sand away from the shoreline that usually covers rocks; it will eventually wash back in, but until then there's the distinct possibility that you can bark your shins on some very sharp projectiles.

PUNTA DEL SOLDADO

This site on the extreme southwestern tip of the island has a rocky beach and terrific snorkeling. To get here, follow the road south across the drawbridge for about 2 miles, pass-ing Club Seabourne and finally scaling a steep hill. Here the pavement stops, so pull over to the side of the road and park. Walk down the dirt road to the beach at the end (about 10 minutes). You will see the reef about 50yd off-shore to the southeast. Locals bring their chil-dren to snorkel in the shallow waters here.

THE COSTA BONITA DEBACLE

Gaze across Ensenada Honda on a peaceful sunlit evening and you'll see an incongruous-looking minivillage chiseled onto a bluff on the opposite side of the bay. This is the inaptly named **Costa Bonita** (Pretty Coast), a sprawling cluster of buildings that was constructed in the early 2000s on the promise of being Culebra's first ecoresort. But local suspicion quickly turned to fury when it transpired that Costa Bonita had obtained its building permits in an underhand manner and was about as 'green' as an overloaded Hummer. Following complaints by residents, and a long list of environmental misdemeanors – including raw sewage, pollution from motorboats and illegal landfill – documented by local protection agency CORALations, the resort filed for bankruptcy in 2006 just a few years after it opened. It now sits disused, like a wantonly discarded Christmas present, a shocking testament to the naivety, ignorance and downright greed that unplanned tourist development can sometimes wreak.

ACTIVITIES
Diving & Snorkeling
Despite reef damage caused during the US Navy testing era, Culebra retains some of Puerto Rico's most amazing dive spots, including sunken ships, coral reefs, drop-offs and caves. Highlights include the *Wit Power* tug boat (which sank in 1984), the Geniqui Caves, the El Mono boulders, and the fish-filled water-world of Cayo Ratón. Good snorkeling can be accessed many beaches, in particular Playas Carlos Rosario, Tamarindo and Melones.

The island's two main dive operators are **Culebra Divers** (Map p157; ☎ 787-742-0803; www.culebradivers.com), across from the ferry dock, and **Culebra Dive Shop** (Map p157; ☎ 787-742-0566; Calle de Escudero), in Dewey. Both offer similar services and prices, and are generally open during normal business hours. You can rent snorkel gear for about $10 to $12 or arrange a day trip for adult/child $50/35. The same vendors also offer dive instruction and trips. One-/two-tank dives cost around $65/90.

Kayaking
Ocean Safaris (☎ 787-379-1973) kayak trips have been featured in a number of magazine articles on Culebra – and for good reason. For just $45, you can get instruction and a half-day guided tour to places such as Isla Culebrita or Cayo Luis Peña. It also rents out kayaks for $25/40 for a half-/full day. **Culebra Water Toys** (☎ 787-742-1122) can help out with both kayaking and windsurfing – the latter is a popular activity in Ensenada Honda.

Boating
Culebra's only glass-bottomed boat, the **Tanama Glass Bottom Boat** (☎ 787-501-0011; trips $25-40) offers some really fantastic two-hour harbor cruises in and around the various reefs, snorkeling trips with equipment included, and trips out to Culebrita. The boat can generally be found at the Dinghy Dock (p164).

Culebra Boats (☎ 787-360-9807) rents fast inflatable dinghies with motors ($50 per hour) to get around Ensenada Honda. Alternatively you can join Captain Luis and his crew for a ride on the water taxi out to Culebrita ($45). Longer day excursions with kayaking and a lobster lunch go for $79 per person. Pick-up and drop-off is from the dock at Club Seaborne (p163).

Fishing
The real fish hawk on the island is **Chris Goldmark** (☎ 787-742-0412; per half-day $220). He can take you out to the flats for some superb bonefishing, or offshore for the big stuff.

Cycling
With its hills, dirt trails and back-to-nature ruggedness, Culebra is an excellent place to bike – not just for exercise but also as a handy means of transportation. **Culebra Bike Shop** (Map p157; ☎ 787-742-2209; Calle Fulladoza) is sometimes open, sometimes not. If no one answers your hollering, try yer man, Steve, on the phone. Still no luck, look him up in the Dinghy Dock next door. If you do manage to pin him down, Steve rents decent mountain bikes like Diamondbacks for approximately $25 a day, with discounts for longer rents. **Dick & Cathy** (☎ 787-742-0062) will also rent you wheels. Call them, tell them where you are, and they'll swiftly deliver it to you in their old-fashioned VW van – just like that!

Surfing
The island's not known for great waves, but you can sometimes catch some action at Carlos Rosario, Zoni and Punta Soldado. Culebra Dive Shop (left) has boogie boards for rent.

Hiking
Rejoice! The island is your oyster. The 2.5-mile hike from Dewey to Playa Flamenco is along a paved road with some inclines, but the destination is idyllic. You can veer off to Playa Tamarindo from a junction just before the lagoon. Playa Carlos Rosario is reached via a trail that starts at the west end of Playa Flamenco. The hike to Playa Brava begins at the end of a back road that cuts north from Rte 250 just past the graveyard. The trail rises to a ridge and then drops to the beach via thick bushes. The toughest hike on the island is the rough trail to Playa Resaca that traverses the eponymous mountain. Outside Dewey, Culebra's roads are light on traffic and excellent for an early morning jog.

SLEEPING
Aside from guesthouses, inns and hotels, Culebra has an excellent selection of rental properties of all shapes and sizes dotted around the island. **Culebra Vacation Planners** (Map p157; ☎ 787-742-3112, 866-285-3272;

www.culebravacationplanners.com) can fix you up with some stunners. Situated opposite the ferry dock, next door to the Hotel Kokomo (which it owns), the friendly and knowledgeable staff here can quickly find a one-, two-, three- or more bedroom house or apartment for you to stay in. Some are very remote and private, while others are within walking distance of all Dewey's 'hot spots.' Disabled and special-needs travelers can also be catered for. Rates depend on where you stay. There are basic rooms for under $100 and mansions with views of the British Virgin Islands for up to $500 per night.

Culebra Island Realty (Map p157; ☎ 787-742-0052; www.culebraislandrealty.com; Calle de Escudero) is another decent option that has numerous attractive secluded properties in the east of the island over toward Playa Zoni and Punta del Manglar.

Dewey

Hotel Puerto Rico (Map p157; ☎ 787-742-3372; r with fan/air-con $40/50; ✷) Right in the center of town, but bottom of the quality pile, this hotel gives new meaning to the term 'long in the tooth.' If your sloe consideration is price, then think about resting your bags in the rugged accommodation here.

Hotel Kokomo (Map p157; ☎ 787-742-0683; r $45-85; ✷) If you're anxious to dump your bags in the first visible crash pad in order to get out exploring, then Hotel Kokomo, the bright yellow building right on the ferry dock, is just the ticket. New management has given this old place a second lease on life, and rooms, while still basic, are clean and cheery enough. The cheapest have shared bathrooms.

Villa Fulladoza (Map p157; ☎ 787-742-3576; Calle Fulladoza; apt $70-85) Besides running a book exchange, Villa Fulladoza offers seven bright apartments in invigorating colors with clean kitchenettes and fans. The shared patio is shaded by several swaying mango trees and there's a boat dock if you are lucky enough to enjoy your own private water transportation.

Mamacita's (Map p157; ☎ 787-742-0090; www.mamacitaspr.com; 64 Calle Castelar; r $85-110; ✷) Screaming lurid pink, pastel purple, green, blue and perhaps a little yellow, Mamacita's is the raffish Caribbean crash pit you've been dreaming about. And although the water's invariably cold, and the reception staff will have probably gone home by the time your boat arrives, there's something strangely contagious about this old Culebra stalwart.

Rooms are simple but attractive, the vibe in the adjacent bar fun and casual (once you've got your head around the local eccentricities – of which there are many) and the on-site restaurant a living legend.

Posada La Hamaca (Map p157; ☎ 787-742-3516; www.posada.com; r $92-146) Wedged right next to Mamacita's, La Hamaca has a tough act to follow and lies somewhat in its neighbor's shadow. It's a shame because it's not a bad option. Rooms are basic but comfortable and overlook the canal, while locationwise you're right in the heart of Dewey with plenty of eating options within walking distance. The front desk is a good font of local information.

Palmetto Guesthouse (Map p157; ☎ 787-742-0257; www.palmettoculebra.com; r $95-115; ✷) Set up in Barriada Clark, this new business is a superfriendly and accommodating escape run by two ex-Peace Corps volunteers from New England. Five guestrooms have the run of two kitchens, a deck, a handy book exchange and a sporty magazine pile. Situated not far from the airport, it is possible to walk to most of Dewey's restaurants from here, as well as idyllic Flamenco Beach.

Casita Linda (Map p157; ☎ 787-742-0360; casitalindabeach@cs.com; r for up to 4 people $100) Right on the canal, this house harbors three apartments – two on the ground floor and one on the upper floor – and is much nicer inside than out. It's also right in the thick of what passes for 'action' in downtown Dewey. Rooms are air-conditioned and decked out in local handicrafts. The two two-bed apartments have kitchenettes and living spaces and can accommodate a maximum of six people. Alternatively, the ground floor one-bed apartment can accommodate a maximum of four. Phone ahead for reservations, as it is sometimes hard to track the owners down.

Casa Ensenada (Map p157; ☎ 787-742-3559; r $100-150; ✷) This pleasant B&B just north of town on the waterfront at Ensenada Honda is handily placed for almost everything. The inn has three units (two of which can accommodate four people) with kitchen, separate entrance, and air-conditioning. There are a lot of unexpected extras here such as free use of kayaks, free boat dock, beach towels, grill, hammocks and more. Throw away your Blackberry and tune into Culebra time, amigos!

Villa Boheme (Map p157; ☎ 787-742-3508; www.villaboheme.com; Calle Fulladoza; r $107-152; ✷) The breezy communal patio, lovely bay views, kayak rentals and proximity to town (not to mention the Dinghy Dock restaurant next door) are the highlights of Villa Boheme. Rooms are plain but clean and usually have bunk beds. Some are equipped with kitchenette for guests who don't care to make use of the shared cooking facilities.

South of Dewey

Bahía Marina (Map p155; ☎ 787-742-3112; www.bahia marina.net; Punta Soldado Rd, Km 2.4; r $150-300; ❄ 🔊) One of the island's newest accommodations is also one of its most luxurious – in fact, it's Buckingham Palace by Culebra standards. Billed as a condo resort, this is not your average high-rise environmentally unsound concrete block. Abutting a 100-acre nature preserve, it has 16 well-integrated apartments with modern kitchenettes, water pressure (a recent invention in this part of the world), cable TV, swimming pool, restaurant/grill and live music at weekends. It's also the venue for the annual Culebran jazz festival.

Club Seabourne (Map p155; ☎ 787-742-3169; www .clubseabourne.com; r/villas $165/549; ❄ 🔊) A deftly designed small resort that blends seamlessly into the southern portion of the island, Club Seabourne is Culebra luxury-style, with an outdoor bar, a secluded swimming pool and a restaurant decked out with tablecloths and wine glasses (see p164). The welcoming lobby has a library, video lounge and relaxing chairs, while the individual villas have sea views and are deliciously tranquil. Just remember that this is Culebra, so don't always expect Niagara Falls water pressure or room service waiting on your every beck and call. Seabourne is situated 1.4 miles south of Dewey on the road to Punta del Soldado.

Playa Flamenco Area

Flamenco Campground (Map p155; 787-742-0700; camp-sites $20; Ⓟ) The only place you can legally camp in Culebra is just feet from the paradisiacal Playa Flamenco. Report to the office at the entrance and you will be assigned a spot. Six people maximum per tent. There are outdoor showers with water available between 4pm and 7pm; bathrooms are open 24/7. The campground's pretty safe and reservations aren't usually necessary.

Villa Flamenco Beach (Map p155; ☎ 787-742-0023; studios $100-125, apt $130) Gentle waves lulling you to sleep, a night sky replete with twinkling stars, and one of the best beaches on the planet

just outside your window; this place would be a winner even if it was just a roof and four walls. To make your stay more comfortable, the management has added self-catering kitchen facilities, air-con units and inviting hammocks. Paradisiacal. It's right next to the Culebra Beach Villas.

Culebra Beach Villas (Map p155; ☎ 787-742-0319; www.culebrabeachrental.com; r $125-295) The only visible building on the beach is this three-story Caribbean villa with wraparound balconies. It acts as the main building to a small complex which rents out self-catering apartments with kitchen and cable TV for between two and eight people. The setting is stunning, though you'll have to stock up on provisions in Dewey, 2.5 miles away.

Tamarindo Estates (Map p155; ☎ 787-742-3343; www .tamarindoestates.com; r $175-210; 🔊) The Tamarindo is Culebran to the core; rustic, isolated and set facing one of the Caribbean's most serendipitous views overlooking Cayo Luís Peña and a national wildlife refuge. Being Culebra, the accommodations – which comprise 12 self-contained cottages spread over 60 acres – are not New York luxury. Then again, you probably didn't come here to watch Hollywood movies on flat-screen TV. Nestled near the water's edge there's a pool and restaurant, both of which may or may not be in operation, but remote Playa Tamarindo just down the road is guaranteed to be open 24/7 365 days a year. The main gripe here is the price, which is a tad high for such rustic accommodations.

EATING

Most restaurants close down in the mid-afternoon (around 2pm or 3pm), ostensibly to prepare for dinner (but probably for a siesta). Things stutter into action again sometime around 6pm. Many places only take cash.

Dewey

Panadería El Patio (Map p157; ☎ 787-742-0374; dishes $3-8) Positioned strategically at the end of the airport runway, El Patio offers fresh, warm *pan criollo* (a bit like French bread), coffee and sandwiches.

Pandeli (Map p157; ☎ 787-742-0296; dishes $4-10; 🕙 5:30am-5pm) Ideal if you're twiddling your thumbs waiting for the 6:30am ferry to Fajardo (the Pandeli opens at an eye-popping 5:30am), this deli/café sells pastries, pancakes, salads, sandwiches and coffee. Come 8am and it's inundated with school kids and stray travelers using the internet. A good place to take breakfast and lunch and catch up on the local gossip.

Barbara Rosa (Map p157; ☎ 787-742-3271; dishes $6-11) *You* are the waiter at this diminutive restaurant/bistro. You're also in Barbara's house – her front verandah to be more exact, so tread carefully. When you've decided what you want, take the menu into the front room and holler through the kitchen hatch at the busy Barbara as she scurries around the kitchen. Hey presto, 15 minutes later out comes fish and chips, a juicy burger or a plate of homemade crab cakes. It's rather quaint, once you get your head round the system. Barbara's is situated on the road north out of Dewey toward the airport.

Heather's (Map p157; ☎ 787-742-3175; pizza $8-20) In the center of town, across from the town hall, Heather's is a popular hangout at night and a great pizza parlor. It gets popular in the high season so expect a wait.

ourpick Mamacita's (Map p157; ☎ 787-742-0090; mains $11-20) The nexus of pretty much everything on Culebra, Mamacita's (also see Sleeping, above) offers some of the best-presented food outside of San Juan along with zero pretension and laid-back, quirky service. Fish and meat plates are tasty, seasoned and creative, and the menu – which always includes at least one vegetarian option – changes daily, as displayed on a handwritten blackboard. Of all the places on the island, this is where expats, locals and visitors mingle best. Fun is in the air at weekends when the *bomba* drums get warmed up.

Juanita Bananas (Map p157; ☎ 787-742-3855; Harbor Villas; dishes $12-24; ⏰ 5:30-10pm Fri-Mon; **V**) Opened in 2004, this revolutionary restaurant gives new meaning to the words 'fresh' and 'sustainable.' Sporting its very own greenhouse and garden, almost all of the fruit, vegetables and herbs listed on the menu will have traveled only a few hundred yards before hitting your plate. The seafood is also local and fished using sustainable methods. Specialties include tasty soups, fruity desserts and the famous *sofrito* sauce (garlic, onions and pepper browned in olive oil and capped with *achiote* – annato seeds). The restaurant is situated on a small rise about half a mile from Dewey. Reservations are necessary.

Dinghy Dock (Map p157; ☎ 787-742-0581; Calle Fulladoza; mains $13-28) If you can brave the gauntlet of cigarette-smoking expats that requisition the steps nightly, you'll find the DD to be something of a culinary revelation. Unusually for Puerto Rico, there's an all-you-can-eat salad bar to quell your early hunger pangs, and you can chomp on your lettuce and cucumber while watching the kitchen staff throw morsels of food to the giant tarpon that swim right up to the deck. Fish is the obvious specialty here – fresh catches such as swordfish and snapper done in creole sauces. The busy bar is a frenzy of expats nursing Medalla beers and acts as the unofficial island grapevine. If you haven't heard it here first, it's not worth hearing.

Just past Mamacita's is a bridge on your right. Cross it and keep right. **Colmado Milka** (Map p157; ☎ 787-742-2253; ⏰ 7am-6pm Mon-Sat, to noon Sun), the island's second-largest supermarket (that's not saying much), is there.

At **Superette Mayra** (Map p157; ☎ 787-742-3888; ⏰ 9:30am-1:30pm & 3:30pm-6:30pm Mon-Sat) you'll find all of the basic food supplies along with other nonedible essentials such as washing powder, diapers and toilet rolls.

South of Dewey

Club Seabourne (Map p155; ☎ 787-742-3169; mains $19-27) Aside from being an upscale inn (see p163), Club Seaborne is also the king of Culebran *cordon bleu*. With 36 covers arranged around a mosquito-free screened-in porch, you can sup on wine (the place has its own wine cellar), chomp on cerviches and feast on steak filets while enjoying calming views of glistening Ensenada Honda framed by palms. The adjacent poolside bar and gazebo hosts a popular happy hour and can conjure up a formidable mojito.

ENTERTAINMENT

If you ask a local about the nightlife in Culebra, they'll probably suggest you stand outside and look at the stars. But scratch around in Dewey and you could end up joining a drum circle, brandishing a karaoke mike, or putting the world to rights over several cold Medallas with a reformed shopaholic from Chicago.

El Batey (Map p157; ☎ 787-742-3828) Not a large place, but seemingly big enough to accommodate the majority of Culebra's population at weekends, when locals swing by to shake a leg to reggaeton with a bit of salsa and meringue mixed in. During the week the place is esteemed for its cheap burgers, cold beers and pool tables. It's situated on the road north out of Dewey toward the airport.

Happy Landings (Map p157; ☎ 787-742-0135) Planted at the end of the airstrip, Happy Landings is a drinks-only dive these days (it used to serve food). Though hardly a font of pulsating nightlife, it may be worth sticking your head around the door to see if anything spontaneous is happening.

Mamacita's (Map p157; ☎ 787-742-0090) Mamacita's has a lively happy hour and after-dinner scene. On weekends, locals, expats and yacht crews favor this place, with its open-air deck and selection of reggae, calypso and buffet. Mamacita's really smokes when *bomba y plena* drummers show up to rock the patio every Saturday night with *bomba* rhythms, as well as salsa and merengue. Everybody dances! See also the review in Eating (opposite).

Dinghy Dock (Map p157; ☎ 787-742-0581; mains $13-28) The 'dock' has karaoke on Thursdays – aarghhhh!

SHOPPING

Galería de Regalos (Map p157; ☎ 787-742-2294; cnr Calles Pedro Márquez & Castelar; 🕑 10am-5pm) A colorful gift-and-clothes shop that sells priceless República de Culebra T-shirts and plenty of other unique knickknacks.

Butiki (Map p157; ☎ 787-935-2542; cnr Calles de Escudero & Romero) A local art shop run by an American expat that sells paintings, jewelry, masks, T-shirts and plenty more. Almost everything is island-made.

GETTING THERE & AWAY
Air

Culebra gets excellent air service from San Juan and Fajardo on the commuter carriers that also serve Vieques: **Isla Nena Air Service** (☎ 787-812-5144; www.islanena.8m.com), **Vieques Air Link** (☎ 787-741-8331; www.vieques-island.com/val) and **Air Flamenco** (☎ 787-724-1818; www.airflamenco.net). There are at least five flights a day to/from San Juan's Isla Grande and Luis Muñoz Marín (LMM) airports (from $95), and more flights a day to/from Fajardo (from $50). Isla Nena Air Service flies once a day between Culebra and Vieques ($35 one way).

Boat Charter

Captain Luis of **Culebra Boats** (☎ 787-360-9807) will often charter a boat for one to four people to St Thomas in the US Virgin Islands. Phone to enquire about availability and prices.

Ferry

Puerto Rican Port Authority ferries travel between Fajardo and Culebra thrice daily. The high-speed passenger ferry takes about an hour and a half. Round-trip passenger fares are $4.50. Boats leave Fajardo daily at 9am, 3pm and 7pm, and Culebra at 6:30am, 1pm and 5pm. The cargo ferry (small/large car $15/19) takes two hours.

To confirm the schedule and to make reservations (required for vehicles), call the **Puerto Rican Port Authority** Culebra office (Map p157; ☎ 787-742-3161; ferry dock, Dewey; 🕑 8-11am & 1-3pm Mon-Fri); Fajardo office ☎ 787-863-0705, car reservations 800-981-2005; 🕑 8-11am & 1-3pm Mon-Fri). Note that neither of these offices is great at answering their phones. So it goes.

GETTING AROUND

Most of the island's natural attractions are not near the town, and chances are that your guesthouse or other rental isn't either. So you will need to organize a ride, by either rental car or taxi.

Biking, kayaking and water taxis are good options for reaching far-flung attractions around the island. See p174 for details.

To/From the Airport

If you have not arranged an airport pick-up/drop-off with your guesthouse proprietor, you'll need one of the three island cabs (see below); $5 to $7 will get you just about anywhere on the island.

Car & Scooter

It's not always necessary to hire a car on Culebra (there are too many cars on the island as it is). The Dewey area is all walkable, Flamenco Beach is a not unpleasant 30-minute hike, and everywhere else can be easily reached by público bus, taxi or, if you're energetic, bicycle. See p175 for bike hire. If you really can't be parted from your four wheels contact **Thrifty Car Rental/JM Scooter Rentals** (☎ 787-742-0521).

Taxi

There is taxi service on the island, but the taxis are basically público vans designed to get large parties of people back and forth between the ferry dock and Playa Flamenco (where they will be partying or camping) for a couple of dollars per person. The públicos are not radio-dispatched, so getting a timely pickup has been a problem for many people heading to or from dinner at a restaurant.

Willy (☎ 787-742-3537, 787-396-0076) generally meets every ferry and also arrives at your door when booked. If he's busy and you're stuck for a ride, try **Romero** (☎ 787-378-0250) or **Kiko's Transportation** (☎ 787-742-2678).

VIEQUES

pop 10,000

With a name stamped in infamy, Vieques was where Puerto Rico's most prickly political saga was played out in the public eye. For over five decades the US Navy used more than two-thirds of this lusciously endowed Spanish Virgin Island for military target practice. The war games ended in 1999 after a misplaced 500lb bomb caused the death of a Puerto Rican civilian and set in motion a protest campaign that led to the navy's long-awaited withdrawal.

Measuring 21 miles long by 5 miles wide, Vieques is substantially bigger than Culebra and distinctly different in ambience. Though still a million metaphorical miles from the bright lights of the Puerto Rican mainland, the larger population here has meant more luxurious accommodations, hipper restaurants and – unfortunately – more petty thievery (particularly on the beaches).

Since the official military withdrawal in 2003, Vieques has regularly been touted as the Caribbean's next 'big thing,' with a pristine coastline ripe for the developer's bulldozer. Fortunately, environmental authorities swept in quickly after the handover and promptly declared all of the former military land (which consists of 70% of the island's total area) a US Fish & Wildlife Refuge. The measure has meant that the bulk of the island remains virgin territory to be explored and enjoyed by all.

Development elsewhere has been slow and low-key. Although many guesthouses and restaurants have expanded their business since 2003, much of this growth has centered on ecoventures and small but luxurious boutique hotels. The only real 'resort' was closed at the time of writing, and the island has yet to succumb to golf, gambling or Las Vegas–style glitz. It's a situation that seems unlikely to change in the short term. Vieques' residents – many of whom are US expats – are fiercely protective

of their Caribbean nirvana and, fresh from seeing off the US military in 2003, they are boldly accustomed to putting up a fight.

The name 'Vieques' is a 17th-century Spanish colonial corruption of the Taíno name *bieque* (small island). The Spaniards also called Vieques and Culebra *las islas inútiles* (the useless islands) because they lacked gold and silver. But over the centuries, residents and visitors who share affection for this place have come to call Vieques 'Isla Nena,' a term of endearment meaning 'Little Girl Island.'

These days Vieques is synonymous with its gorgeous beaches, semiwild horses and unforgettable bioluminescent bay.

HISTORY

When Columbus 'discovered' Puerto Rico on his second voyage in 1493, Taíno people were living peacefully (save for the occasional skirmish with Carib neighbors) on Vieques. With the expansion of Puerto Rico under Ponce de León, more Taíno fled to the island; Caribs joined them and the two groups mounted a fierce resistance to Spanish occupation. It failed. Spanish soldiers eventually overran the island, killing or enslaving the natives who remained.

Even so, Spanish control over the island remained tentative at best. In succeeding years, both the British and French tried to claim the island as their own. In reality, Vieques remained something of a free port, thriving as a smuggling center.

Sugarcane plantations covered much of Vieques when the island fell to the Americans in 1898 as spoils from the Spanish-American War, but during the first half of the 20th century the cane plantations failed. Vieques lost more than half its population and settled into near dormancy; the remaining locals survived as they always had, by subsistence farming, fishing and smuggling.

Shortly after WWII broke out, the US Navy showed up on Vieques and grabbed about 70% of the island's 33,000 acres to build military bases (see p168). They held onto it until May 2003 when, after four years of peaceful protests, the land was ceded to the US Fish & Wildlife Refuge. In the years since, Puerto Rican, US and international developers have been salivating at the prospect of building mega-hotels and more. But for the time being, ecotourism, construction, cattle raising, fishing and some light manufacturing (such as the

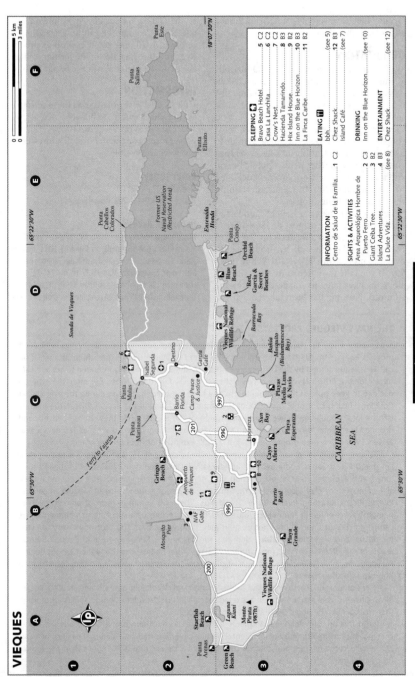

VIEQUES

CULEBRA & VIEQUES

INFORMATION
Centro de Salud de la Familia......**1** C2

SIGHTS & ACTIVITIES
Area Arqueológica Hombre de
  Puerto Ferro..................................**2** C3
Giant Ceiba Tree...........................**3** B2
Island Adventures..........................**4** B3
La Dulce Vida.............................(see 8)

SLEEPING
Bravo Beach Hotel........................**5** C2
Casa La Lanchita..........................**6** C2
Crow's Nest..................................**7** B3
Hacienda Tamarindo....................**8** B3
Hix Island House...........................**9** B2
Inn on the Blue Horizon..............**10** B3
La Finca Caribe...........................**11** B2

EATING
bbh...(see 5)
Chez Shack.................................**12** B3
Island Café.................................(see 7)

DRINKING
Inn on the Blue Horizon............(see 10)

ENTERTAINMENT
Chez Shack................................(see 12)

General Electric assembly plant) bring money and jobs to the island.

ORIENTATION

With slightly more than 10,000 people, Vieques is considerably more populated than its sleepy sister island, Culebra. Consequently, it has two towns to Culebra's one. The main settlement, Isabel Segunda (Isabella II), is on the north side where the ferry docks. Most people run through Isabel Segunda en route to Esperanza, on the Caribbean side. Esperanza is indisputably prettier, with a public beach, and a *malecón* (waterfront promenade) lined with numerous attractive and entertaining restaurants and guesthouses.

Hwy 200 originates in Isabel Segunda and heads west past the airport as far as Green Beach on the island's western tip. To get to Esperanza, take either of two routes south over the mountains: Hwys 201/996 or Hwy 997. If you take the latter route, you will pass along the navy fence as you descend from the summits. Nothing has been taken down yet,

so the Garcia Gate is clearly visible on your left. Head through the gate and east along an unpaved road and you'll end up at pristine Red and Blue Beaches in the former military zone (now a national wildlife refuge).

INFORMATION

Unless otherwise noted, all of these addresses are in Isabel Segunda. While some actual street addresses exist on Vieques, citizens and businesses rarely use them. Physical addresses are given when possible.

Emergency

Fire (☎ 787-741-2111)
Police (☎ 787-741-2020) Isabel Segunda only.

Internet Access

Blackbeard Sports (Map p170; ☎ 787-741-1892; 101 Muñoz Rivera, Isabel Segunda; per 15min $3) Has a small but efficient business center located in its Isabel Segunda store.
Museo de Esperanza (Map p172; ☎ 787-741-8850; Calle Flamboyán 138, Esperanza; per 30min $3; ☒ 11am-4pm) The museum has half a dozen computer terminals plus wi-fi.

THE NAVY-VIEQUES PROTESTS

In a country where the national status is more often a topic of apathy than anarchy, the 1999–2003 protests against the US Navy presence on the island of Vieques were something of a wake-up call. First requisitioned by the US military in 1941, Vieques was originally intended to act as a safe haven for the British Navy during WWII, should the UK fall to the Nazis. But after 1945 the US decided to keep hold of the territory to use as a base for weapons testing during the ever chillier Cold War. Taking control of over 70% of the island's total land in the east and west, the military left the local population to live in a small strip down the middle while they shelled beaches and dropped live bombs on off-shore atolls. On average the military bombed Vieques 180 days a year and in 1998 alone they dropped a total of 23,000 explosive devices on the island.

With the public ire raised, things came to a head on April 19, 1999, after Viequense civilian guard David Sanes Rodríguez was accidentally killed when two 225kg bombs missed their target and exploded near an observation post he was manning. The incident triggered a massive campaign of civil disobedience that reached far beyond the shores of Vieques, recruiting Puerto Ricans and non–Puerto Ricans worldwide. The most common form of protest involved demonstrators entering the military base illegally and setting up makeshift encampments. The campaign gained international notoriety in May 2000 when over 700 protesters were arrested for trespassing, including notable celebrities such as Robert Kennedy Jnr and Reubén Berríos, leader of the PIP (Puerto Rican Independence Party). Other names who threw their weight behind the cause were Jesse Jackson, Ricky Martin, boxer Felix Trinidad and Archbishop of San Juan Roberto González Nieves.

As in Culebra 25 years earlier, the pressure and publicity finally paid off and in 2001 Puerto Rican Governor Sila María Calderón brokered a deal with US President George W Bush promising that the US military would leave Vieques by May 2003.

Unfortunately, the clean-up campaign still continues. Furthermore, after decades of heavy shelling, various health and environmental bodies have reported that Vieques' eastern beaches are heavily contaminated and that its citizens have a cancer rate 27% higher than the Puerto Rican average.

Laundry

Familia Rios (Map p170; ☎ 787-438-1846; Calle Benitez Castaño 1) A few yards up the street from the ferry dock, across the street from the Chinese restaurant, this Laundromat can do same-day service for a fee or you can use self-serve washers. Change and detergent are available.

Media

Vieques Times (☎ 787-741-8508) Published monthly in both English and Spanish, this is no longer the only paper in town, but it is still one of the best.

Medical Services

Centro de Salud de la Familia (Map p167; ☎ 787-741-0392; Rte 997 Km 0.4; ☑ clinic 7am-3:30pm Mon-Fri, emergency 24hr) Just south of Isabel Segunda on Hwy 997.
Farmacia Antonio (Map p170; ☎ 787-741-8397; Calle Benítez Guzman; ☑ 7:30am-7pm Mon-Fri, 8am-6pm Sat, 11am-3pm Sun) For basic supplies and over-the-counter remedies, Antonio's is a good bet.

Money

It's a good idea to carry cash on the island (but watch out for petty thieves) as the ATMs have been known to run dry.
Banco Popular (Map p170; ☎ 787-741-2071; Calle Muñoz Rivera; ☑ 8am-3pm Mon-Fri) Has one of two ATMs in Isabel Segunda.

Post

Post office (Map p170; ☎ 787-741-3891; Calle Muñoz Rivera 97; ☑ 8:30am-4:30pm Mon-Fri, 8am-noon Sat) Across from the Banco Popular, this is the island's only post office. It will take poste-restante letters.

Tourist Information

Good websites include www.enchanted-isle .com or www.vieques-island.com for useful directories of island businesses, services and accommodations.
Puerto Rico Tourism Company (PRTC; Map p170; ☎ 787-741-0800; www.gotopuertorico.com; Calle Carlos Lebrun 449; ☑ 8am-5pm) Friendly and helpful staff is on hand every day to give out information, brochures and the classic Vieques map, www.theviequesmap.com.

SIGHTS
Vieques National Wildlife Refuge

This 18,000-acre **refuge** (Map p167; ☎ 787-741-2138; www.fws.gov/southeast/vieques) occupies the land formerly administered by the US military. The 3100-acre western segment – used mainly as a storage area during the military occupation – was instituted in 2001. The 14,700-acre eastern segment, which includes a former live firing range (still off-limits), was inaugurated two years later in 2003.

The refuge protects vast tracts of largely pristine land containing four different ecological habitats: beaches, coastal lagoons, mangrove wetlands and forested uplands. It also includes an important marine environment of sea grasses and coral reefs. Many colorful species survive in these areas, including the endangered brown pelican and the Antillean manatee. Vieques' dwarfish thicket-strewn forest, which includes some indigenous cacti, provides one of the best examples of dry subtropical forest in the Caribbean.

Existing as a military site until May 2003, much of the refuge's land is still officially off-limits to visitors. A potentially dangerous no-go zone is Punta Este in the far east of the island, where live ordinance is still being removed. Other restricted areas in the east include most of the north coast east of Isabel II along with the south coast east of Orchid Beach (although there are few obstacles to prevent you getting in). The most easily accessible area is the narrow ribbon of land that abuts the dirt road leading from the Garcia Gate to Orchid Beach.

Most of the western part of the refuge is open for business, and includes a lonely swathe of colorful wildflowers, locked up military bunkers and the looming hulk of Mt Pirata, the island's highest point at 987ft.

Perhaps the finest **Giant Ceiba Tree** (Map p167) in Puerto Rico is situated on the right-hand side of the road as you head toward Green Beach, adjacent to the Mosquito Pier. Rumored to be 400 years old, the tree resembles a gnarly African baobab, which is probably the reason why it was venerated so much by uprooted Afro-Caribbean slaves. The Ceiba is Puerto Rico's national tree.

Isabel Segunda

A calm yet hardworking coastal town dotted over low hills on Vieques' north coast, nontouristy Isabel Segunda is the island's administrative center and grittily authentic capital. Sometimes busy, sometimes quiet – depending on ferry activity – the town is more urban than anything on Culebra (though that's not saying much). Lines of cars disgorge daily at the dock, the odd down-and-outer languishes on a bench in the otherwise empty central square, and a handful of new snazzy restaurants pull in a burgeoning stream of affluent American visitors.

CULEBRA & VIEQUES

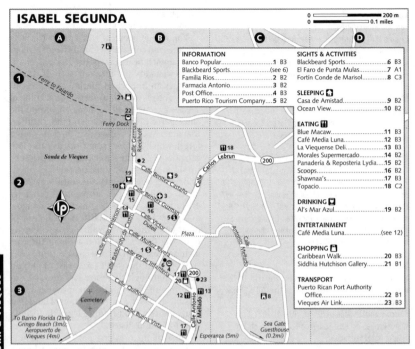

ISABEL SEGUNDA

Though less beguiling than its southern rival Esperanza, Isabel II is no ugly duckling. Named for the enigmatic Spanish queen who reigned between 1833 and 1868, the town is the island's oldest settlement, founded in 1843, and showcases a handful of historical sights, including an 1896 lighthouse and the last Spanish fort to be built in the Americas.

During the US naval occupation Isabel was a downbeat place with only basic amenities but, in more recent years, better services and a handful of boutique hotels in the hills to the east have established a more swanky reputation. But with only 5000 residents and more wild horses than wine waiters, it's a long way from sparkling modernity.

EL FARO DE PUNTA MULAS

One of Puerto Rico's 16 historic lighthouses, this pastel-shaded historic monument stands on the hilly point just north of the Isabel Segunda ferry dock. Built in 1896, it was restored in 1992 and contains a small **museum** (☎ 787-741-0060; admission free), which is open irregularly. Come for the vista and sunset, not the exhibition – a rather paltry collection of photos and artifacts depicting local maritime history, island history and natural history of the coast.

FORTÍN CONDE DE MIRASOL

This small **fort** (☎ 787-741-1717; 471 Calle Magnolia; adult $2; ☼ 10am-4pm Wed-Sun), on the hill above Isabel Segunda, is the last Spanish fort constructed in the Americas (1840s). Although never completed, the fort has ramparts and a fully restored central building that houses a history and art museum. It currently serves as a museum that showcases the island's 4000-year-old Indian and colonial history.

Esperanza

Esperanza is the quintessential Caribbean beach town; a shabby-chic cluster of wooden shacks and colorful open-fronted restaurants that has lifted many a dampened mainland spirit. If you've been fighting your way through the chaotic traffic and soulless suburbia of San Juan, this could be your nirvana; an exotic but laid-back mélange of infectious Latin music and friendly street-side sales-folk peddling rum, reggae and bioluminescent kayaking trips.

Set on Vieques' calm southern shores, Esperanza's waters are deep, clear and well sheltered to the north, east and south by two tall, lush islands. The white concrete railings of the modern *malecón* rise quaintly above the town's narrow beach and, if you arrive at sunset, you will see twinkling lights and hear ebullient music pouring from the cafés and restaurants that line the Calle Flamboyán 'Strip' facing the Caribbean.

Twenty-five years ago, Esperanza was a desolate former sugar port with a population of about 1500. Its residents survived by fishing, cattle raising and subsistence farming. But then a couple of expatriate Americans in search of the *Key Largo*, Bogart-and-Bacall life discovered the town and started a bar and guesthouse called 'Bananas' (p176). Gradually, word spread among independent travelers, and a cult following took root. Protected (rather ironically) by the presence of the US military on Vieques, Esperanza, despite a recent growth in popularity, has managed to retain much of its rustic pioneering spirit and remains an evocative but fun place to visit.

MUSEO DE ESPERANZA

This tiny **museum** (☎ 787-741-8850; www.vcht.com; 138 Calle Flamboyán; ☺ 11am-4pm Tue-Sun), on the Strip in Esperanza, is operated by the Vieques Conservation and Historical Trust (founded in 1984 to save the island's bioluminescent bays). The museum contains exhibits on the ecological efforts of the trust, the island's natural history and its early Indian inhabitants. Donations are welcome. Behind the gift shop, the museum runs what is supposedly the smallest aquarium on earth, a series of tanks in which baby sea creatures are displayed for a few weeks before being returned to the ocean. There's also a rotating exhibit on the island's flora and fauna, and an internet facility (see p168).

AREA ARQUEOLÓGICA HOMBRE DE PUERTO FERRO

You will find this site marked by a sign on Hwy 997, east of Esperanza. About a quarter mile east of the entrance to Sun Bay (Sombé), take the dirt road on your left (it heads inland). Drive for about two minutes until you find the burial site of the Indian known as the 'Hombre de Puerto Ferro' (Map p167), which is surrounded by a fence. Big boulders identify

a grave where a 4000-year-old skeleton (now on exhibit at the Fortín) was exhumed. Little is known about the skeleton, but archaeologists speculate that it is most likely the body of one of Los Arcaicos (the Archaics), Puerto Rico's earliest known inhabitants; this racial group made a sustained migration as well as seasonal pilgrimages to the Caribbean from bases in Florida.

Until the discovery of the Hombre de Puerto Ferro, many archaeologists imagined that the Arcaicos had reached Puerto Rico sometime shortly after the birth of Christ; the presence of the remains on Vieques could push that date back nearly two millennia if controversy surrounding the skeleton is resolved. Visitors are welcome to stop by the excavation site, but besides the original boulders, there's not much to see.

BAHÍA MOSQUITO

Locals claim that this bay (Map p167), a designated wildlife preserve about 2 miles east of Esperanza, has the highest concentration of phosphorescent dynoflagellates not only in Puerto Rico, but in the world (see p67). Indeed, it's also known as Bioluminescent Bay – and it's magnificent.

A trip through the lagoon is nothing short of psychedelic, with hundreds of fish whipping up bright-green sparkles below the surface as your kayak or electric boat passes by (don't ever accept a ride in a motorized boat – the engine pollution kills the organisms that create phosphorescence). But the best part is when you stop to swim: it's like bathing in the stars.

You can just drive east on the rough Sun Bay road (you'd better have a 4WD because the road's a mess) and jump in for a swim at any point that's glowing. However, an organized trip will give you far more opportunity to really take in the spread of phosphorescence.

There's another inlet to the east, Barracuda Bay, that's also filled with dynoflagellates, but most tour operators don't venture out that far.

Reservations are recommended for tours and kayak rentals in high season. For more information, see Boating (p174) and Kayaking (p174).

Beaches

Vieques' beaches are as legendary as Culebra's – and there are more of them. Environmentally

CULEBRA & VIEQUES

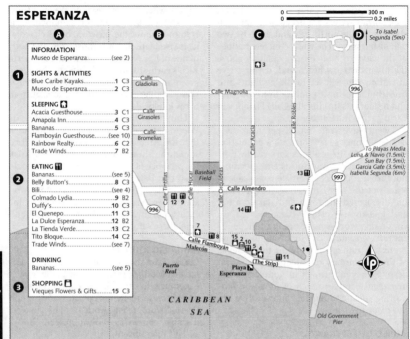

ESPERANZA

0 ——————— 300 m
0 ——————— 0.2 miles

To Isabel
Segunda (5mi)

INFORMATION
Museo de Esperanza..............(see 2)

SIGHTS & ACTIVITIES
Blue Caribe Kayaks..................**1** C3
Museo de Esperanza.............**2** C3

SLEEPING
Acacia Guesthouse.................**3** C1
Amapola Inn............................**4** C3
Bananas..................................**5** C3
Flamboyán Guesthouse........(see 10)
Rainbow Realty.......................**6** C2
Trade Winds...........................**7** B2

EATING
Bananas..................................(see 5)
Belly Button's.........................**8** C3
Bili...(see 4)
Colmado Lydia.......................**9** B2
Duffy's...................................**10** C3
El Quenepo...........................**11** C3
La Dulce Esperanza.............**12** B2
La Tienda Verde...................**13** C2
Tito Bloque...........................**14** C2
Trade Winds...........................(see 7)

DRINKING
Bananas..................................(see 5)

SHOPPING
Vieques Flowers & Gifts........**15** C3

Calle Gladiolas
Calle Girasoles
Calle Bromelias
Calle Magnolia
Calle Robles
Calle Acacia
Calle Horar
Calle Orquídeas
Calle Tintillas
Calle Almendro
Calle Flamboyán
Malecón

Baseball Field

To Playas Media
Luna & Navio (1.5mi);
Sun Bay (1.5mi);
Garcia Gate (3.5mi);
Isabella Segunda (6mi)

996
997

Puerto Real
Playa Esperanza
(The Strip)

CARIBBEAN SEA

Old Government Pier

speaking, the US occupation was a blessing in disguise, in that it has left many of the island's more remote beaches in an underdeveloped and pristine state. Now protected in a national wildlife refuge, areas such as Blue, Red and Green Beaches are clean, untrammeled and paradisiacal. Others, encased in the former weapons-testing zones, remain closed off and are, effectively, virgin territory. It's a good idea to check with the **US Fish & Wildlife Service** (☎ 787-741-2138; www.fws.gov) before heading off to explore so you don't wander into any contaminated areas.

Unfortunately many of Vieques' beaches are prone to petty theft. No matter how remote your beach, don't leave your valuables unguarded while you swim or snorkel, especially on the beach in downtown Esperanza. They'll be gone in a heartbeat.

PLAYA ESPERANZA
The advantage of slender Playa Esperanza (Map p172) is that it is within shouting distance of the *malecón* and most of Esperanza's bars, restaurants and guesthouses. The downside is that it is often dirty with litter, seaweed

and – even worse – shards of glass. Tread carefully. A popular option for those in the know is to journey across to the nearby islet of **Cayo Afuera** (Map p167), an uninhabited pinprick of land that is part of the Mosquito Bay Reserve. Situated a few hundred meters across the bay, many intrepid locals elect to swim (not advisable unless you are a strong swimmer and are aware of the local weather conditions), while others kayak or take a boat. There is great snorkeling here, both under the ruined pier and on the ocean side of the islet where a sunken sailboat languishes beneath the surface. Antler coral, nurse sharks and manatees have also been spotted in the vicinity.

SUN BAY
This long half-moon-shaped bay (Map p167; also known as Sombé), less than a half mile east of Esperanza, is the island's *balneario* (public beach), with all the facilities you have come to expect in Puerto Rico. Measuring a mile in length, Sun Bay is rarely busy. Indeed, such is its size that even with 100 people congregated in its midst it will still appear almost deserted. The beach is also not always staffed,

so you can often drive in without paying the usual $2. If the gate is locked, take the easy walk east along Playa Esperanza, and then walk across the narrow sand spit to Sombé.

PLAYAS MEDIA LUNA & NAVIO

If it really is isolation you're after, continue east on the dirt road past Sombé, and you'll enter a forest. Go left at the fork in the road. In a couple of hundred yards, you'll stumble upon Playa Media Luna (Map p167), a very protected, shady beach that is excellent for kids. Beyond this on the same road is Playa Navio (Map p167), where bigger waves are the domain of bodysurfers. Both of these beaches served as sets in the 1961 film version of the famous William Golding novel *The Lord of the Flies*. If Vieques has a specific beach that attracts gays and lesbians, Navio is the one.

If you climb the rocks at the west end of Playa Navio, you'll find a path along the shore that you can follow to find petrified clams and corals dating from 50 million years ago.

ORCHID, RED, GARCIA, SECRET & BLUE BEACHES

All these south-shore beaches (Map p167), which used to be on navy land, can be reached by entering the Garcia Gate on Hwy 997.

At the Garcia Gate, turn south on the dirt road to calm and clear **Red Beach** (Playa Caracas), which has a few gazebos with picnic tables to shade bathers from the sun. **Garcia Beach** is lesser known and has less shade, meaning that fewer people decamp here. **Secret Beach** is also in the vicinity. This deliciously deserted stretch of sand has absolutely no facilities – just jaw-dropping beauty. If you find it, don't tell anyone.

Blue Beach (Bahia de la Chiva), at the east end of the former Camp Garcia road, is long and open, and occasionally has rough surf. If you happen upon this beach during Semana Santa (the Holy Week preceding Easter), you'll see hordes of faithful Catholics camping on the beach, where they pray and party in honor of the death and resurrection of Jesus Christ. There's good snorkeling here at an island just off the coast. **Orchid Beach**, further eastward, is as far as you can go at present. Called Playa La Plata by locals, this gorgeously secluded beach has sand like icing sugar and a calm sea that seems to shimmer

---

TOP HIDDEN BEACHES

- Playa Brava (p160)
- Secret Beach (left)
- Playa Zoni (p160)
- Orchid Beach (left)
- Green Beach (p173)

---

in a thousand different shades of turquoise, cobalt and blue.

GRINGO BEACH

Gringo Beach (Map p167) is the site of the now defunct Martineau Bay resort, earmarked by 'W' hotels as a new venture in 2008–09. You will find a great reef for snorkeling just 10yd offshore, but seas can be lumpy here from December to March, when trade winds can blow from the northeast.

LAGUNA KIANI

Also at the western edge of the wildlife refuge, not far from Green Beach, is Laguna Kiani (Map p167), a large mangrove swamp. There is a wooden boardwalk around the lagoon with information panels on it about flora and fauna. It's an excellent area for hiking and wildlife observation. The dirt roads leading to Laguna Kiani or the surrounding beaches are excellent for biking, jogging or hiking. It is also an ideal area to view Mt Pirata, the highest elevation on the island and the original moist subtropical forest on Vieques.

STARFISH BEACH

On the other side of Laguna Kiani is the most wonderful beach (Map p167) on Vieques for children, with gentle surf, crystal-clear waters and immense starfish to catch the eye lying all along the shore. It's a really good place for families to relax, and perfect for teaching youngsters the look-don't-touch approach to fragile ecosystems.

GREEN BEACH/PUNTA ARENAS

Punta Arenas (Map p167) is the best beach for a quiet picnic, some family-friendly snorkeling, and up-close views of the big island and El Yunque across the water. To get here, pass through the former Nava Ammunitions Facility (NAF) Gate and head west for about 20 minutes through pastoral landscapes and herds of wild horses. At the western tip of the island, the road turns to dirt and you can park in the clearings.

The strand here is not very broad and is punctuated with coral outcroppings, but there are plenty of shade trees. Snorkeling reefs extend for miles, and you can expect to have this place pretty much to yourself, except on summer weekends, when a lot of yachts out of Fajardo come here on day trips. Since this beach is generally sheltered from the trade winds, you definitely want bug repellent.

PLAYA GRANDE
Mostly deserted, Playa Grande (Map p167) has a long, narrow strip of sand and water that drops off very quickly (not good for children or weak swimmers). If you head west on Rte 996 past Esperanza to Rte 201, you'll eventually come to a dead end. Park in the dirt (make sure to lock your car and hide valuables) and hit the sand.

ACTIVITIES
Diving
The island's biggest and best dive shop is **Blackbeard Sports** (Map p170; ☎ 787-741-1892; 101 Muñoz Rivera, Isabel Segunda). Based out of Isabel Segunda, these guys offer two-tank scuba dives from $100 and Professional Association of Dive Instructors (PADI) certified basic open-water courses from $350. You can also rent your own snorkel/scuba gear for $15/50 a day.

Snorkeling
Golden Heron Ecotours (☎ 787-615-1625; www.golden -heron.com) offers excellent snorkeling trips to almost virgin reefs that are reachable only by motorboat. The company only uses the boats of local fishermen and has a strong environmental ethos (helping people protect rather than exploit their local landscapes). Boats for up to six people can be chartered for $600. The trip with a qualified guide lasts all day. Children are welcome.

Boating
Vieques Sailing (☎ 787-508-7245) with Captain Bill and his boat *Willo* offer a variety of sailing trips. Pick from a two-hour sunset cruise ($30), a half-day sailing and snorkeling trip ($45), or an all-day sailing excursion including snorkeling, beach time and lunch ($95).

Run by one of the conservation groups trying to keep the bioluminescent bay in tip-top shape, **Island Adventures** (Map p167; ☎ 787-741-0720; www.biobay.com; Rte 996 Km 4.5) offers 90-minute tours ($30) in an electric boat just about every night, except when there's a full moon (take the trip to learn why!). Guides are bilingual and humorous although the groups are often a little on the large side. There's a Mexican restaurant next door to their offices where you dine either before or after your excursion.

Kayaking
Abe's Snorkeling & Bio-bay Tours (☎ 787-741-2134; www.abessnorkeling.com), based in Esperanza, offers guided kayaking and snorkeling trips to Cayo Afuera, a few hundred meters offshore (adult/child $35/17.50). This is a great trip for beginners and families. Its ecofriendly bio-bay tour (adult/child $30/15) is equally child-friendly with kayaks that can accommodate families of three or even four.

Blue Caribe Kayaks (Map p172; ☎ 787-741-2522; http://enchanted-isle.com/bluecaribe; Calle Flamboyán, Esperanza; trips $23-30) rents out kayaks to individuals ($10/25 for one/four hours) and offers trips through the bioluminescent bay ($30), with a swim stop included. Blue Caribe also does kayak/snorkeling trips in the day around Cayo Afuera. If nobody's in the office ask around for 'Pooch' – check the pier first.

Fishing
Fishing is sublime in Vieques. Imagine Florida Keys with about one-tenth of the fisherfolk and enough bonefish, tarpon and permit to stock a mini ocean. Fishing boats can also allow you access to isolated stretches of coastline in the former naval zone.

For operators, it's a toss up between **Caribbean Fly-fishing Company** (☎ 787-741-1337; www.caribbeanflyfishingco.com) and **Wildfly Charters** (787-435-4833; www.wildflycharters.com). They've both received favorable *New York Times* reviews and charge similar rates ($300 per half-day).

Horseback Riding
Penny Miller (☎ 787-741-4661) runs highly recommended guided trail rides through the mountains or by the ocean, whatever you prefer. Tours cost $65 for two hours. She is connected to the Sea Gate Guesthouse (opposite).

VIEQUES BY BIKE

A hidden blessing of the erstwhile US occupation is that Vieques remains refreshingly undeveloped and ideal for cycling. Free from the main island's legendary traffic jams and unforgiving drivers, this 135-sq-mile slither of land has subsequently become a little-heralded biker's paradise with a couple of decent cycle outlets ready to kit you out with the essentials.

As well as renting out bikes, helmets and child-seats, Blackbeard Sports (below) in Isabel II organizes guided rides around the island. It also promotes a free women's riding group that meets at the store every Saturday morning. If you're up for going it alone, Blackbeard Sports can furnish you with maps, routes and insider tips. A few wider suggestions are listed below.

■ The main road from Isabel II to Esperanza is Hwy 997, but head west on Hwy 200 and then south on Hwy 201 and you'll find a quieter, more pleasant alternative route. Halfway along, you can detour up Hwy 995, another lovely country road.

■ The ultimate Vieques loop involves heading west out of Isabel II on Hwy 200 all the way to Green Beach (the last section is unpaved). After some shore snorkeling and an idyllic picnic lunch, swing south through the old military bunkers to Playa Grande before linking up with Hwy 996 to Esperanza. The most direct route back to Isabel II on Hwy 997.

■ For the best off-road adventure, head south from Isabel II on Hwy 997 as far as the old Camp Garcia gate. Turn left along a dirt road and you'll encounter a plethora of pristine beaches spread out like golden jewels along the track. Pack a picnic, swimming gear and plenty of water.

Cycling

Some of the best bicycling is along Hwys 995, 996 and 201, which wind through the countryside north and west of Esperanza and are light on traffic.

Blackbeard Sports (Map p170; ☎ 787-741-1892; 101 Muñoz Rivera, Isabel Segunda) rents out North American standard bikes from its store in Isabel Segunda for $25 per day including helmet. It also rents child seats. These guys can fix you up with some fantastic tours (see boxed text, above).

La Dulce Vida (Map p167; ☎ 787-617-2453; www .bikevieques.com) are based on the south side of the island and offer similar prices and deals.

SLEEPING

Vieques is a rural island. You can expect to hear chickens, dogs, cats, cattle and horses making their barnyard noises day and night. Travelers will find guesthouses in both of Vieques' main towns, as well as elsewhere.

Just like Culebra, Vieques is an openminded and tolerant community, and you can safely assume that all tourist accommodations here are gay-friendly. Quite a few of the guesthouses and restaurants on the island are owned or staffed by lesbian or gay expats.

If you're looking for a rental agent, try gayfriendly **Rainbow Realty** (Map p172; ☎ 787-741-4312; www.enchanted-isle.com/rainbow; 278 Calle Flamboyan) in Esperanza. **Crow's Nest Realty** (☎ 787-741-0033; www.enchanted-isle.com/crowsnestrealty) can also help you out. These agents represent a variety of vacation properties ranging from apartments to villas. Expect to pay $675 to $2800 per week.

If you wish to camp, just east of Esperanza you can pitch your tent at **Sun Bay** (Sombé balneario; ☎ 787-741-8198; campsites $10). You'll need to make reservations, even though there are plans to add 50 new campsites. If you don't require facilities or security, you can camp with impunity on any of the more remote island beaches.

Isabel Segunda

There are a few accommodations in the heart of town, easily reached on foot from the ferry. Lots of new offerings have popped up just above the lighthouse on North Shore Rd, an area called Bravos de Boston. They're not far as the crow flies, but a long uphill trek on foot.

Sea Gate Guesthouse (off Map p170; ☎ 787-741-4661; r $50-110; P) Situated on a hill high above the town, the Sea Gate is a bit of a hike from the ferry dock, most of it uphill. But once you get here, it's a different world. Horses roam freely in the surrounding grounds (and can be rented for horseback riding, see opposite), lush vegetation fills the garden, and views of surrounding countryside are panoramic. The crux comes with the animals. This place is dog-friendly – yes, they'll accommodate your pet and give him/her a 'doggie bag' on arrival. If sharing a house with myriad canines ain't your cup of tea, you might want to try something a little closer to town.

Casa de Amistad (Map p170; ☎ 787-741-3758; www.casadeamistad.com; 27 Calle Benitez Castaño; r $70-90; ❄ ⚑) A fun and comfortable place to crash slap-bang in the middle of town, Casa de Amistad has seven rooms for rent with air-con and private bathrooms (two of the bathrooms, though private, are separated from bedrooms). Communal areas include an honor bar, sitting room/library, kitchen, landscaped yard and swimming pool, and rooftop deck.

Ocean View (Map p170; ☎ 787-741-3696; 751 Calle Plinio Peterson; r $75-100; ❄ ⚑) Vieques' old dockside stalwart is centrally-located, convenient and…well, that's about it. Don't expect a plethora of home comforts in this faded and rather bleak town-center hotel. Situated just 200yd from the ferry dock, you shouldn't have any problem wheeling your suitcase here, but once inside its echoing corridors you might begin to wish you'd nabbed that haggling taxi to take you elsewhere. For the unfussy, the Ocean View does, at least, have friendly staff, a swimming pool and – surprise, surprise – a lovely ocean view.

Casa La Lanchita (Map p167; ☎ 800-774-4717; www.viequeslalanchita.com; North Shore Rd 374, Bravos de Boston; r $95-140; ℗ ❄ ⌨ ⚑) In the same neighborhood as the Bravo Beach, but a little lower down the quality bracket, La Lanchita nonetheless turns out eight spiffy suites with private bathroom and kitchenette on the ocean's edge. The building's another whitewashed three-story colonial beauty that resembles an old plantation house rising up over the Atlantic. Bonus features include beach gear, view balconies and a placid pool with kid's section. There's a four-night minimum.

our pick Bravo Beach Hotel (Map p167; ☎ 787-741-1128; www.bravobeachhotel.com; North Shore Rd 1, Bravos de Boston; r $190-300, villa $550; ℗ ❄ ⌨ ⚑) Up above the lighthouse, in the burgeoning Bravos de Boston neighborhood, Vieques is fast creating its very own Beverley Hills. The trend is epitomized in the Bravo Beach Hotel, a former sugar merchant's hacienda whose gorgeous 'Viejo San Juan' style exterior looks like it's been lifted straight off the front cover of *Travel & Leisure* magazine. Nine fantastical guest rooms are set in lush tropical grounds

with ample verandahs and two mesmerizing swimming pools. There are shaded gazebos here, along with floating cushions, Italian linens, placid Atlantic views…you'll spend days checking out the details. Honeymoons were invented for this.

Esperanza

Bananas (Map p172; ☎ 787-741-8700; www.bananasguesthouse.com; Calle Flamboyán; r $65-80; ❄) This is where it all started. Bananas is Esperanza's original budget guesthouse-restaurant and it's a classic, in the mold of a backpacker's hostel in Thailand or a beach bar in Jamaica. Seasoned travelers will know the deal here: great prices; a lively downstairs bar; a funky and relaxed atmosphere; and basic but adequate rooms that receive the odd nightly visitor from the insect kingdom. Light sleepers should beware of noise from Esperanza's vibrant party strip outside.

Trade Winds (Map p172; ☎ 787-741-8666; Calle Flamboyán; r $70; ❄) Another vintage Vieques abode (vintage meaning since 1984). Situated on the far west end of the *malecón*, this popular guesthouse and inn has 10 rooms, most with air-con, including three terrace rooms that have a harbor view and catch the breeze. The biggest feature is probably the fabulous open-air deck where meals are served – it offers splendiferous views of the ocean.

Amapola Inn (Map p172; ☎ 787-741-1382; amapolainn.com; 144 Calle Flamboyán; r $75-125) The Amapola Inn has five rustic but secluded rooms in a separate building behind its popular Bili restaurant on the Esperanza strip. They're clean, cool and relatively quiet without being too far removed from the central action.

Acacia Guesthouse (Map p172; ☎ 787-741-1059; www.acaciaguesthouse.com; 236 Calle Acacia; r $95-140) Clean and airy are two words that spring to mind when you glimpse inside the four welllaid-out apartments encased in this threestory whitewashed building situated on a rise above Esperanza's beachside strip. From the 2nd- and 3rd-floor decks and rooftop patio you have spectacular views over hills and sea, and virginal St Croix is visible on clear days. The units have full kitchens, comfortable furnishings and friendly owners who live just across the street. There's also a free washing machine, and complementary air-con courtesy of the breezy trade winds that spread their freshness across the private terrace.

Flamboyán Guesthouse (Map p172; 140 Calle Flamboyán; r $135; ❄) These four à la mode rooms above Duffy's bar (p179) on the Strip in lively Esperanza are brand new and appear chic with their glass hand basins and luxuriant linens. Three of the rooms have small balconies that overlook Vieques' most happening beach boulevard with its soul-searching tourists and local dive operators bringing the boats in after a day on the waves. Duffy's and some frenetic bar action is just down the staircase. Bring earplugs or go to bed late.

Elsewhere on the Island

La Finca Caribe (Map p167; ☎ 787-741-0495; www .lafinca.com; Hwy 995; r from $85; ❄) Finca Caribe is Vieques personified. Sitting high up on a mountain ridge seemingly a million miles from anywhere (but only actually 3 miles from either coast), it's the kind of rustic haven stressed-out city slickers probably dream about. Despite its back-to-nature facilities – outdoor communal showers, shared kitchen and hippyish decor – it has a religious following and has inspired gushing reviews from numerous top newspapers and magazines. The secret lies in the nuances. Picture the swaying hammocks, the unhurried games of croquet, the tangible proximity of nature…

Crow's Nest (Map p167; ☎ 787-741-0033; www.crows nestvieques.com; r $124-190; P ❄ 🖳 ❄) Perched – figuratively speaking – in the Barrio Florida in the hills above Isabel Segunda, the Crow's Nest enjoys a rural airy setting with its pink bougainvillea contrasting with its rippling turquoise swimming pool. More funky than luxurious, the rooms here have lounging area and kitchenette just in case you need to escape the simmering action at the adjacent Island Café (p179). Inspiring a small inn feel, the staff are courteous and helpful, and local activity organizers regularly drop by to pick up budding recruits. Children under 12 are not admitted.

Hacienda Tamarindo (Map p167; ☎ 787-741-8525; www.enchanted-isle.com/tamarindo; r $170-275; P ❄) Lying along Hwy 996 about three-quarters of a mile west of Esperanza, on a hill looking across fields to the Caribbean, this is one of the largest guesthouses (15 rooms) on the south side of the island. Rooms or suites are tricked out in 'Caribbean deluxe' style, which means lots of elegant doors opening to wrought-iron balconies filled with bougainvillea. Quite lovely, all of it.

our pick Inn on the Blue Horizon (Map p167; ☎ 787-741-3318; www.innonthebluehorizon.com; r $200-400; P ❄ 🖳 ❄) Small is beautiful. The Inn on the Blue Horizon was surely invented with such a motto in mind. With only nine rooms harbored in separate bungalows wedged onto a stunning ocean-side bluff a few clicks west of Esperanza, the sense of elegance here – both natural and contrived – is truly breathtaking. The luxury continues inside the restaurant and cozy communal lounge, which overlook an Italianate infinity pool fit for a Roman emperor. Not surprisingly, the establishment has featured in *Architectural Digest* magazine where it received kudos from well-traveled literary critic Paul Theroux.

our pick Hix Island House (Map p167; ☎ 787-741-2302; www.hixislandhouse.com; r $235-295; Hwy 995; P ❄) And now for something completely different… Ecohip, new age–minimalist, environmental-austere; to describe the Hix house in a single sentence is nigh-on impossible, suffice to say that the place inspires robust opinions across the spectrum and is guaranteed to be like nowhere else you have ever visited. Designed by cutting-edge Canadian architect John Hix, this unique guesthouse consists of three industrial concrete blocks that arise out of the surrounding trees like huge granite boulders (or incongruous eyesores, if you're of a more cynical persuasion). Hosting 12 rooms, the ethos here is minimalist, ecological and close to nature – the idea is that the rooms open up to give you the feeling that you are actually living in the forest. Further green credentials are earned through solar panels, recycled water and natural air-conditioning (trade winds). It's a brave and surprisingly attractive experiment.

EATING

After busy weekends, many restaurants on Vieques close to regroup on Monday. Many of the newer, high-end and American-run restaurants want reservations, especially on weekends in high season.

Isabel Segunda

Panadería & Repostería Lydia (Map p170; ☎ 787-741-8679; cnr Calles Benitez Guzman & Plinio Peterson; snacks $1-5; ❄ 4am-noon) With a 4am opening call, this veritable hole-in-the-wall bakery-cum-coffee bar is ideal for insomniacs, late-night party animals and ferry workers on the graveyard shift. On a quiet weekend morning in sleepy Isabel, it's one of the only places likely to be open. Stop by for caffeine, pastries, sandwiches and sweet bread, and fight with the locals for one of the two plastic tables that furnish the sidewalk.

Scoops (Map p170; ☎ 787-741-5555; Calle Benitez Guzman; snacks $2-8) Junk food hasn't arrived on Vieques yet but, if you need something fast and palatable, you can grab a cheap pizza here and watch the local teenagers as they gamble away their pocket money on the arcade machines. An adjacent room holds more tasty treats with Häagen-Dazs ice cream and fresh fruit juices. They're ridiculously expensive, but what the hell?

La Viequense Deli (Map p170; ☎ 787-741-8213; Calle Antonio Mellado; dishes $5-12; ⏰ 6am-6pm Mon-Sat, to 2pm Sun) If it's breakfast you're after, this is the place to come for your 6am pancakes or hangover-curing coffee. If you miss the 11am cut-off you can feast instead on decent baked goods, tortillas and sandwiches. Service is no-nonsense and fast, the decor clean and modern, and the clientele local with a smattering of in-the-know tourists.

Shawnaa's (Map p170; ☎ 787-741-1434; Calle Antonio G Mellado; dishes $6-10; ⏰ lunch Mon-Fri) Bring a big appetite to Shawnaa's buffet. It's full of superb *comida criolla* dishes that you can take out onto the patio or consume in the shaded interior.

bbh (Map p167; dishes $12-28; closed Sun-Tue) With its high-end magazine cover setting in the Bravo Beach Hotel (p176), you would expect this restaurant to be trendy and chic. And naturally, it is. This place is foodie heaven, with European cheeses, New Zealand lamb and plenty of infused local ingredients. Tapas are the specialty, but there's also a wine room and the poolside Palms bar where you can enjoy an alcoholic appetizer.

Topacio (Map p170; ☎ 787-741-1179; Calle Carlos Lebrun; mains $17-24; ⏰ lunch & dinner) The newly opened Topacio has already cemented a firm reputation among those with a penchant for delicious seafood served Caribbean-style. Sheltered on an outside patio underneath colorful lights, you can sample the generous paella, fish in a creole sauce, seafood *mofongo* (mashed plantains) and lobster cooked in garlic. Unpretentious, efficient and brimming with fresh and locally caught ingredients, this place offers great Puerto Rican authenticity without sacrificing on the quality.

Café Media Luna (Map p170; ☎ 787-741-2594; 351 Calle Antonio G Mellado; mains $18-30; ⏰ dinner)

Romance is not dead in Vieques' original 'posh' restaurant where candlelit tables and a tiny street-side balcony add panache to any meal. And there's more. Isabel II's music scene more or less begins and ends in this attractive colonial building where smooth live jazz accompanies lamb chops, seared tuna and rather authentic pizza. OK, so the price is a little steep, but with a comprehensive wine list and free entertainment provided by the pizza-tossing chefs in the open-sided kitchen, you might just be inspired to dust off your credit card.

Blue Macaw (Map p170; ☎ 787-741-1147; Calle Antonio G Mellado; dishes $24-32; ⏰ dinner) No birds here, but plenty of fancy metal curves and elaborate downlighting. One of a trio of plush new eating houses that could quite easily have been plucked straight out of San Juan's SoFo neighborhood, the Blue Macaw was fire-damaged in 2005. Relaunched in 2007 in polished chrome, it's reignited itself (the restaurant, not the fire that is) with all its old vigor, displaying a menu that's as delicious as the decor is plush. Try the scampi, the lamb tenderloin or the tempura trout and leave room for a lavish dessert.

If you're looking to stock up on provisions, try **Morales Supermercado** (Map p170; 15 Calle Baldorioty de Castro, Isabel Segunda) There is a second store a mile west of Isabel Segunda on the road to the airport (Hwy 200).

Esperanza

La Dulce Esperanza (Map p172; ☎ 787-741-0085; Calle Almendro; dishes $1-12) On the west end of this back street, this pleasant eatery serves Danish for a dollar, thick creamy coffee for half that, fat sandwiches at lunch and pizza for dinner.

Trade Winds (Map p172; dishes $4-19; Calle Flamboyán; ⏰ breakfast, lunch & dinner) Unpretentious dining at its finest. Sit back in a wide chair on the breezy verandah and enjoy scrumptious scrambled eggs or island-spiced fish and meat dishes later in the day. They're all good.

Belly Button's (Map p172; Calle Flamboyán; dishes $5-11; ⏰ 7am-2pm Wed-Sun) Make a beeline for breakfast at Belly Button's and bring a good appetite. Your belly will be more than happy after you've heroically demolished the three Frisbee-sized pancakes that appear rather magically on your plate here. Consisting of a small collection of alfresco tables located outside a kitchen trailer on the *malecón*, this expat-run breakfast phenomenon conjures up enough food to keep you going until 6pm.

Grab a copy of the *San Juan Star,* help yourself to a mug of gourmet coffee and make plans for a day of breathtaking action – or indolence.

Bananas (Map p172; Calle Flamboyán; dishes $7-17) Bananas does everything in a sandwich: beef, red snapper, jerk chicken, you name it… The burgers are as thick as your forearm and the fries constitute a minimountain. You could easily while away a whole afternoon here eavesdropping on Navy-Vieques protest veterans and rat-race dodging expats. It's the people-watching potential that makes the place – as well as those juicy burgers, of course.

Tito Bloque (Map p172; Calle Acacia; dishes $7-18; ☻ dinner) Head to this spot, at the foot of Calle Acacia next to the mangroves, when you want something different from Esperanza. This raised outdoor patio draws a local crowd and is known for its good, cheap grilled lobster.

Bili (Map p172; ☎ 787-741-1382; 144 Calle Flamboyán; dishes $8-17; Ⓥ) Bili is the recently rebranded restaurant at the Amapola Inn. Offering the island's finest selection of vegetarian food, it's also a haven for noncarnivores who've grown tired of eating omelets. The yucca salads are good as is the seafood and you can shoot the breeze alfresco as the *malecón* crowds steam past.

Duffy's (Map p172; ☎ 787-741-7000; Calle Flamboyán; dishes $9-18) Esperanza's newest bar is a sleeker and slightly more refined version of Banana's next door. It fills a gap in the market with fresh salads and creative seafood, but still nurtures an undone Caribbean flavor. Opening out onto Esperanza's main strip, the laid-back street atmosphere infiltrates the shady interior where expats and locals mingle over beer and scallops.

El Quenepo (Map p172; ☎ 787-741-1215; Calle Flamboyán; dishes $11-20) The new kid on Esperanza's seaside block, El Quenepo has a lovely interior and an equally delectable menu. The food's catch-of-the-day fresh and the decor is – by normal Viequesian standards – remarkably chic. A new trend?

For groceries, **La Tienda Verde** (Green Store; Map p172; Calle Robles) and the **Colmado Lydia** (Map p172; Calle Almendro), near the baseball field in the center of town, are your best bets in Esperanza.

Elsewhere on the Island

Chez Shack (Map p167; ☎ 787-741-2175; Hwy 995 Km 1.8; dishes $12-20) What have '60s psychedelic band the Mamas and Papas and Vieques' most bohemian restaurant got in common? They both owe at least a part of their success to expat impresario and restaurateur Hugh Duffy. In the 1960s, Duffy owned a restaurant called 'Love Shack' on the nearby island of St Thomas, where he hosted folk-music nights with a quartet of spaced-out hippies called the New Journeymen. It was an important first break. But while the Journeymen changed their name to the Mamas and Papas and headed off to LA for some *California Dreamin'*, Duffy transplanted himself 13 miles to the west where he opened up Chez Shack, a quirky Caribbean hangout that quickly began to rival the luminous bio-bay as *the* place to go on Vieques. Two decades later both Duffy (now into his 80s) and the shack are still rustling up fine dinners that have become almost as celebrated as his erstwhile protégées. Monday is the big night, with live reggae and an outdoor grill featuring chicken, fish or steak.

Island Café (Map p167; mains $16-22) Cocooned in the Crow's Nest (p177) in the lofty barrio of Florida, the Island Café features a variety of Caribbean mains served on a 2nd-story terrace with great views of the main island. Try the fiery West Indies pork and plantain stew with coconut.

Inn on the Blue Horizon (Map p167; mains $16-28) A mile west of Esperanza on Hwy 996, the inn (p177) offers casual, elegant gazebo dining with a view like the name implies. Fresh trout goes for $18. Reservations are a must.

DRINKING

Al's Mar Azul (Map p170; ☎ 787-741-3400; Calle Plinio Peterson) shelters the ghosts of Charles Bukowski and Ernest Hemingway and is the nexus of local gossip. Locals come to play pool, and expats come to drink…and drink. Visitors teeter somewhere in between.

Bananas has an active pub scene with a popular dart board. At the Inn on the Blue Horizon, you'll find a friendly gringo crowd, especially on Friday night.

ENTERTAINMENT

Café Media Luna has salsa, jazz and Latin rock on weekends, and draws a mixed crowd of gringos and locals, straights and gays.

On Monday, Chez Shack boogies to live reggae.

SHOPPING

Vieques Flowers & Gifts (Map p172; ☎ 787-741-4197; Calle Flamboyán; ☻ 9am-6pm) On the Strip in Esperanza, this shop has everything from local crafts, pottery, clothes and – of course – fresh flowers.

Caribbean Walk (Map p170; ☎ 787-741-7770; Calle Antonio G Mellado; ☺ 10am-6pm) Tiny, but full of local art, this creative shop in Isabel Segunda harbors intricate jewelry and plenty of other dexterously sculpted crafts.

Siddhia Hutchinson Gallery (Map p170; 787-741-8780; 15 Calle 3; ☺ 10am-4pm Mon-Sat) At this gallery of a local artist and designer, Siddhia Hutchison, you can pick up first-class paintings of colorful tropical scenes. Siddhia also organizes periodic painting workshops.

GETTING THERE & AWAY
Air
Públicos greet just about every flight that comes in and will take you anywhere you want to go on the island.

The island has lots of air services from San Juan – both LMM International and Isla Grande airports – and Fajardo. There are a good 10 flights a day to/from San Juan's Isla Grande and LMM airports, and approximately half a dozen between Fajardo and the island. **Isla Nena Air Service** (☎ 787-863-4447) also links Vieques with Culebra. Round-trip prices start at $165 (25 minutes) from LMM, $90 from Isla Grande and $45 (10 minutes) from Fajardo. Phone any of the following companies for more up-to-date information.

Vieques Air Link (Map p170; for San Juan-Vieques flights ☎ 888-901-9247, 787-741-8331, for Fajardo-Vieques flights 787-741-3266; www.vieques-island.com/val) is the major carrier with an office in Isabel Segunda.

Isla Nena Air Service flies daily to Culebra, Fajardo and San Juan for roughly the same prices as Vieques Air Link.

Air Sunshine (☎ 800-327-8900, 787-741-7900; www.airsunshine.com) flies directly to St Thomas, St Croix, Tortola and Virgin Gorda in the US Virgin Islands. It also carries people between San Juan and Vieques, charging the same rates as the other carriers.

M&N Aviation (☎ 787-791-7008, 787-741-3911/2; www.mnaviation.com) flies to Fajardo, San Juan Isla Grande and San Juan International.

Cape Air (☎ 800-352-0714; www.flycapeair.com) flies four times a day from San Juan LMM International.

Ferry
The Puerto Rican Port Authority's high-speed passenger ferries run between Fajardo and Vieques four times a day (three at weekends). Boats leave Fajardo at 9:30am, 1pm, 4:30pm and 8pm and Vieques at 6:30am, 11am, 3pm and 5pm. Passage takes one hour 15 minutes, weather permitting. The round trip costs a giveaway $4. The thrice-daily cargo ferry from Fajardo to Vieques (weekdays only) takes two hours and costs $15 for a small car or $19 for a large one.

Call to confirm the schedule and to make reservations (particularly for trips on Friday, Saturday, Sunday and Monday). In Fajardo

---

DETOUR: MONTE PIRATA

During the navy occupation, the hilly western quarter of Vieques was riddled with scores of cavernous military-style bunkers that were used to store ammunition. The overgrown bunkers remain, but today most of the land that was off-limits pre-2003 is open for public access. One little-visited highlight is Monte Pirata (Pirate's Mountain); at 987ft, it's the island's highest point. The trail to the summit follows an old paved road that veers south off Hwy 200 a couple of miles before you hit Green Beach. While it's still officially closed to cars, there's nothing to stop hikers and bikers tackling the steep 3-mile grunt to the top.

The scenic rewards are breathtaking in more ways than one. Never cleared for sugar cane, Monte Pirata is covered in Vieques' oldest forest and is a haven for copious species of bird. With a sharp eye and a good pair of binoculars, count on seeing *carpinteros,* Puerto Rican woodpeckers, Adelaide warblers, and a handful of red-tailed hawks.

Pirata's summit hosts a radar facility run by the Department of Homeland Security, but the 360° views are stupendous and include glimpses of Culebra, St Thomas and the purplish hump of El Yunque glowering on the main island to the northwest.

Check on trail access before you tackle this trek. Restricted land on Vieques is an ambiguous topic and there is often conflicting information on where you can and can't go. For the most reliable information enquire at the Vieques National Wildlife Refuge (p169) or the Vieques Conservation and Historical Trust situated in the museum (p171) in Esperanza.

CULEBRA & VIEQUES

call the **Puerto Rican Port Authority** (☎ 787-863-0705, 800-981-2005; ☻ 8-11am & 1-3pm Mon-Fri) for vehicle reservations (required), or call the **Vieques office** (Map p170; ☎ 787-741-4761; ☻ 8-11am & 1-3pm Mon-Fri) at the ferry dock in Isabel Segunda. Note that neither of these offices is good at answering its phones.

GETTING AROUND
Bicycle
Vieques is excellent for cycling, and partaking in a little two-wheeled transport will help ease the proliferation of cars that goes hand in hand with tourist growth. The road across the island from Isabel II to Esperanza is less than 6 miles in length and can be tackled by any moderately fit cyclist. See p175 for bike rental.

Car
Unless you rent a scooter, almost all vehicles rented are Suzuki Samurai jeeps for about $45 to $65 a day.

Although Vieques is a big island, you may not need a car for your whole stay as most of the main facilities are located within close proximity to each other in the center of the island. Reliable operators include **Island Car Rentals** (☎ 787-741-1666) and **Maritza's Car Rental** (☎ 787-741-0078).

Public Transport
If you have not arranged for a rental car at the airport or an airport pick-up/drop-off with your guesthouse proprietor, you'll need one of the island cabs (below); $10 to $15 will get you just about anywhere on the island. Públicos usually greet both the ferries and the airplanes, and will take you where you need to go, but you can't be in a hurry to get there. Regulated fees are $3 for anywhere in the old civilian area and $5 for the beaches in the US Fish & Wildlife Refuge. Públicos run fairly regularly between Isabel Segunda and Esperanza.

Taxi
For a ride, try one of the following cabs. They can usually be found hanging out around the ferry terminal and airport at arrival times.
Angel (☎ 787-741-1370)
Coki Ayala Ayala (☎ 787-375-5195)
Eric (☎ 787-741-0448)
Fast Eddie (☎ 787-741-0082)

CULEBRA & VIEQUES

Ponce
& the South Coast

Ponce's fiercely proud history as the southern capital comes with lofty declarations; whether it's a place that 'does not repeat history, but improves it' (Rafael Pon Flores) or a 'land of Camelot: ideal, legendary, dreamlike, and real' (Antonio Gautier). All nice enough, but a common T-shirt captures the *ponceño* civic hubris best: it shows the entire island paved over with a crowded parking lot, except for Ponce, represented by a cluster of historic facades. The slogan reads simply: '*Ponce es Ponce.*'

Ponce owes its inimitable old-world charm to the island's topography: the craggy peaks of the Central Mountains long buffered it from the modernization that paved over San Juan. Today, a stream of traffic follows the sweeping curves of the San Juan–Ponce Autopista across the center of the island, reaching the south coast in only two hours. The completion of this highway has encouraged some unsavory hallmarks of the north: traffic and sprawl.

East and west of Ponce, along Hwys 2 and 3, the region is also rich in history and is rapidly changing. Crumbling chimneys of dead sugar mills dot the horizon of the coastal plains, neighboring their graying industrial replacements – chemical and pharmaceutical factories. History is still palpable among the colonial structures and seaside boardwalks of Arroyo, Yauco, and Guanica, but none are entirely free from the vestiges of the 21st century – American fast-food chains, coughing towers and honking motorists.

The rocky coast on the south can't compare with the postcard-perfect beaches on the Atlantic, but beyond a typical day at the beach, travelers can kayak the maze-like mangrove-lined routes of the Bahía de Jobos estuary or hike the arid hills of the Bosque Estatal de Guánica. Opportunities for game fishing and diving on the southern shores draw crowds southwest to the hard-partying La Parguera, which boasts the surreal glow of the Bahía de Fosforescente.

HIGHLIGHTS

- Standing in awe before *Flaming June* at the coolly air-conditioned **Museo de Arte de Ponce** (p188)

- Betting on little mechanical horses at a roadside stand outside of **Arroyo** (p195).

- Dancing to blasting reggaeton on Ponce's riotous **Calle Luna** (p192)

- Bombing down rocky trails out to the coast on a mountain bike at the **Bosque Estatal de Guánica** (p201)

- Staggering down the crooked streets of **La Parguera** (p205) after snorkeling off its keys.

Museo de Arte
de Ponce;
La Parguera   Calle Luna
★ ★Bosque ★   Arroyo ★
Estatal
de Guánica

- POPULATION: 195,000

History

The rolling foothills and broad coastal planes of the south coast were home to a number of indigenous tribes and were first colonized by Spaniards, who raised cattle and horses for the colonial expeditions in Mexico and South America in the 16th century. In 1630 they built a little hamlet on a good port between the mountains and the coast which would eventually become Ponce. Coamo, the third-oldest settlement on the island, is the oldest in the south.

For more than a century, goods and materials flowed through the welcoming harbors, which afforded ships shelter from the easterly trade winds and safe escape from hurricane winds. Ostensibly the port of Ponce was only open to Spanish vessels trading directly with Spain, but the watchful eyes of the island governor lay a universe away, over the mountains in San Juan, and with no one to enforce the law, free trade flourished, bringing with it goods, currencies, and people from across the New World and Africa.

During the 16th and 17th centuries freebooting traders grew rich on such commerce. When slave revolts erupted in the neighboring French-held island of Saint-Domingue in the 1790s and South America between 1810 and 1822, many wealthy refugees fled to the south coast, buying land and introducing efficient agricultural methods for coffee and sugarcane. Soon they imported former slaves from British colonies around the Caribbean to meet the ever-increasing harvesting demands of American traders, hungry for sugar, coffee and rum. Production and profits from agriculture skyrocketed throughout the 19th century, when agricultural barons built cities with elegant town squares, neoclassical architecture and imported French fountains.

The Spanish-American War put a quick end to the freebooting days, bringing instead an American military occupation, uniformly enforced trade laws and an economic freefall. This was aided by hurricanes which devastated the coffee industry, falling sugar prices, and the US government's decision to develop San Juan, not Ponce, as a strategic port. When the Great Depression hit in the 1930s, the region fell into an economic hibernation.

These days the south coast limps along littered with contradictions between the past and the future: a jumble of cranes mark Ponce's continual, if poorly planned, urbanization.

The breathtaking sunsets over the Caribbean are marred by huffing factory smoke stacks, and the smooth highways that cut through the ramshackle towns are littered with roadkill and choked by traffic, only affording occasional glimpses of the land's lush natural beauty. These paradoxes make Ponce and the surrounding south coast the place where the 18th and 21st centuries have collided, and an area of constant surprise.

Climate

Much drier and breezier than San Juan and other parts of Puerto Rico, much of the region is in a 'rain shadow,' meaning it gets significantly less rain than the north coast because it's downwind of a mountain range. The dry, sunny air is quite pleasant in winter, but also blisteringly hot, averaging in the 80s. In summer, especially around the Bosque Estatal de Guánica, the sun beats down mercilessly and temperatures soar even higher. Regardless of the season, sun block and water are essentials.

Getting There & Around

The south coast is reached by car from San Juan in only two hours via the Autopista Luis A Ferré (A-52), though there are coastal roads that circumnavigate the island and connect the region. The only airport with reliable commercial flights is in Ponce. For travel within the region, a car is necessary unless you have enough time to travel by the makeshift, irregularly departing público system. Terminals are in the center of all significant cities and towns, usually near the center of town. Some towns in the far corners of the south coast are serviced by public transportation with great infrequency.

PONCE

Ponce native son and author Abelardo Díaz Alfaro famously called Ponce a *baluarte irreducible de puertorriqueñidad* – a bastion of the irreducible essence of Puerto Rico – and strolling around the quaint square and narrow streets of the city's historic center certainly evokes the stately spirit of Puerto Rico's past. Unfortunately, the neighborhoods that surround the square bear witness to a woeful characteristic of Puerto Rico's present: irreducible snarls of congested traffic. Even though the honking and ceaseless construction are signs of the city's continual

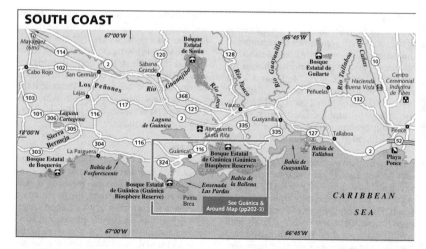

SOUTH COAST

growth, the communities surrounding San Juan have grown much faster, unseating Ponce's status as Puerto Rico's second-most populated metropolis.

To understand the essence of Ponce itself, start at the city center, lined with shops, banks and surprisingly affordable hotels. The city has a more easygoing spirit than other major cities on the island, with businesses that open late and close early, couples who stroll circles around the city's fountains, and breezy evenings 2 miles south at the shore line. There, at a developed facility called Paseo Tablado La Guancha, clusters of attractive restaurants and cafés draw families for open-air dinners on the weekend. After the kids go to bed, the drinks flow and the area jumps with a booming mix of reggaeton and salsa.

History

Unlike many destinations in the north, where history buffs have to navigate tourist attractions and do some digging, Ponce's celebrated past is a marquee feature. Present in preserved Spanish colonial buildings, statuary and more than a dozen museums, history is most readily visible at the city's historic Plaza Las Delicias. Those interested in the island's precolonial indigenous roots are only a short drive from Puerto Rico's largest and most educational archeological site, the Centro Ceremonial Indígena de Tibes.

The earliest western settlement saw a number of clashes between Spanish Conquistador Ponce de León (from whom the town gets both

its name and one of its many nicknames, 'City of Lions'), and the Taíno tribes, but the region was claimed for the Spanish Crown in 1511. The city was established around 1630, when the Spaniards built the first incarnation of the current cathedral and named it for the patron saint of Mexico, the Virgen de Guadalupe.

As the first port of call in the region – far from Spanish authorities in San Juan – Ponce grew fat off the rewards of smugglers who trafficked the Caribbean in the late 1600s. By the mid-1700s Ponce's bourgeois society wanted at least a patina of respectability; Spanish merchants and wealthy refugees from nearby Saint-Domingue (where slave revolts radically changed the order of things) poured resources into legitimate enterprises like tobacco, coffee and rum. Sugar, too, became an important business, and entire plains (the same denuded ones you see today) were shorn of greenery and replaced with silky, highly profitable sugarcane stalks. The added wealth and polyglot mixture of Spanish, Taíno, French and black West Indian peoples helped establish Ponce as the island's earliest artistic, musical and literary center.

The parlors of the bourgeoisie echoed with postured *danza* while satirical, boisterous strains of *bomba y plana* were shared by laborers.

That golden age ended in 1898 when Spain rejected America's demand to peacefully observe Cuban independence to start the Spanish-American War. Compared to modern definitions, it wasn't much of a scuffle, lasting a scant five months, but the Americans'

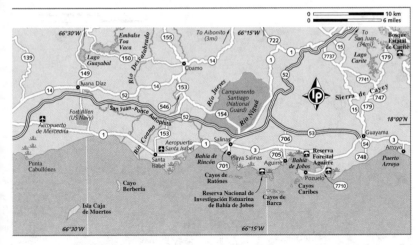

strategic Operation Bootstrap had a lasting impact on Ponce by only funding ports on the north coast. Shortly thereafter, a hurricane devastated the region's coffee and sugar crop and the region slid into near ruin. The sugar industry never fully recovered, and civil unrest a few years later resulted in the Ponce Massacre (see p187), which politically alienated Ponce from the rest of the island. In the decades since, Ponce has gradually reestablished itself as a historic center for tourists – helped dramatically by a highway connecting it to San Juan – and entered the modern age with an economy based on textiles, plastics, oil and rum.

Orientation

Cruising to Ponce from San Juan is easy on the smoothly paved A-52, a partially toll-controlled highway called the Autopista Luis A Ferré. You'll know when you get there after you come out of the mountains and drive through the towering letters by the roadside reading 'P-O-N-C-E.' The city center is about 2 miles from the south shore and 2 miles from the foothills of the Central Mountains to the north.

Once you're at the city center, park the car so you can avoid the frustrating traffic that seems to seize the streets at random. Most of the city's sights are a short walk from the city center and the grid of streets is easily navigable by foot. Should you ever get lost in Ponce, look to the skies for a sign from God: the town's two infallible landmarks are the towering steeples of the Catedral Nuestra Señora de Guadalupe, which sits regally at the center of the lovely Plaza Las Delicias, and an enormous concrete and glass cross, El Vigía, which overlooks the town to the north.

You don't have to drive through the center of town to get from one side of Ponce to the other – two bypass roads circle the city to the south. The inner road is Av Emelio Fagot/Av Las Américas (Hwy 163). The faster route is the outer road, Hwy 2, called the 'Ponce By Pass.' Here you will find the city's biggest mall and loads of American chain stores. To reach the port area, take the newly paved route just east of the square, Rte 12. It becomes a divided highway south of the Ponce By Pass. Follow the signs to La Guancha.

Information
BOOKSTORES

Amazingly, when American chain bookstore Borders packed up shingle and left the mall a few years ago it left Puerto Rico's historical center without a single polite bookstore. If you are hard up for something to read in English, you'll have to drive back to San Juan or Mayagüez.

Candy & Magazine Store (72 Reina Isabel; ☺ 7am-6pm Mon-Fri, 8am-6pm Sat, 8am-1pm Sun) This small shop has some dusty magazines (with an amusingly random assortment of English language titles including *Mountain Biker*) and one computer with a printer and limited internet access (about $3 per 30 minutes). It ain't much, but it's easily found downtown.

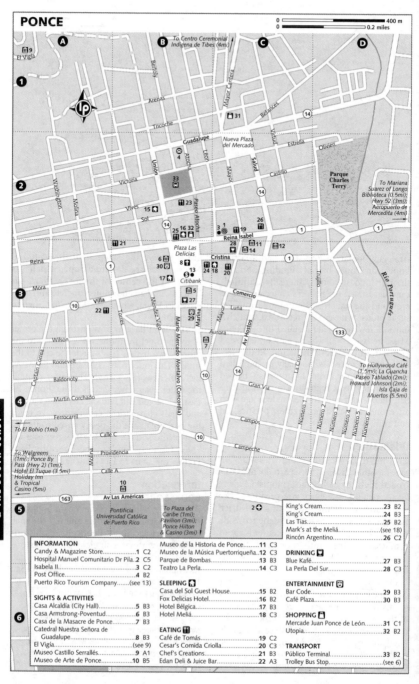

PONCE

INFORMATION	
Candy & Magazine Store	**1** C2
Hospital Manuel Comunitario Dr Pila	**2** C5
Isabela II	**3** C2
Post Office	**4** B2
Puerto Rico Tourism Company	(see 13)

SIGHTS & ACTIVITIES	
Casa Alcaldía (City Hall)	**5** B3
Casa Armstrong-Poventud	**6** B3
Casa de la Masacre de Ponce	**7** B3
Catedral Nuestra Señora de Guadalupe	**8** B3
El Vigía	(see 9)
Museo Castillo Serrallés	**9** A1
Museo de Arte de Ponce	**10** B5
Museo de la Historia de Ponce	**11** C3
Museo de la Música Puertorriqueña	**12** C3
Parque de Bombas	**13** B3
Teatro La Perla	**14** C3

SLEEPING	
Casa del Sol Guest House	**15** B2
Fox Delicias Hotel	**16** B2
Hotel Bélgica	**17** B3
Hotel Meliá	**18** C3

EATING	
Café de Tomás	**19** C2
Cesar's Comida Criolla	**20** C3
Chef's Creations	**21** B3
Edan Deli & Juice Bar	**22** A3
King's Cream	**23** B2
King's Cream	**24** B3
Las Tias	**25** B2
Mark's at the Meliá	(see 18)
Rincón Argentino	**26** C2

DRINKING	
Blue Kafé	**27** B3
La Perla Del Sur	**28** C3

ENTERTAINMENT	
Bar Code	**29** B3
Café Plaza	**30** B3

SHOPPING	
Mercade Juan Ponce de León	**31** C1
Utopia	**32** B3

TRANSPORT	
Público Terminal	**33** B2
Trolley Bus Stop	(see 6)

THE PONCE MASSACRE

In the turbulent 1930s, Puerto Rico's troubled economy created revolutionary fervor across the island, but it was in Ponce, with its reputation for culture and sophistication attracting a lot of students, that a march for independence went terribly wrong.

Originally the marchers had a parade permit for the demonstration, which was staged in the plaza on Palm Sunday, March 21, 1937, but at the last minute the governor of Puerto Rico withdrew his permission.

Angered, the nationalists defied the prohibition and marched. Slightly fewer than 100 young men and women faced off with 150 armed police near Plaza Las Delicias. When the nationalists started singing 'La Borinqueña' – the national anthem – a shot was fired and then the entire plaza erupted in gunfire. Seventeen marchers and two police officers died. Not one civilian carried a gun, and most of the 17 died from shots in the back. While the US government chose not to investigate, the American Civil Liberties Union did, and confirmed that the catastrophe warranted its popular name, 'Masacre de Ponce' (Ponce Massacre). Now a small museum called, appropriately, the **Casa de la Masacre de Ponce** (☎ 787-844-9722; cnr Marina & Aurora; admission $1; ⊗ 9am-4pm Wed-Sun), in the building that held the offices of the Nationalist Party in 1937, keeps the memory alive.

INTERNET

Many hotels have internet service for guests and the Plaza Las Delicias has wireless connectivity, a terrific convenience for travelers with a laptop.

Mariana Suarez of Longo Biblioteca (☎ 787-284-4141; Villa; ⊗ 9am-9pm Mon-Sun). A short walk from the plaza, this bright new facility is part of Archivo Municipal de Ponce and contains an impressive $114 million digital computing and education center. Puerto Rico Telephone footed the bill and did it right, with 50 new computers, laptop stations and wireless access.

MEDICAL SERVICES

Emergency (☎ 911)

Hospital Manuel Comunitario Dr Pila (☎ 787-848-5600; Av Las Américas, east of Av Hostos) 24-hour emergency room. Recommended.

Walgreens (☎ 787-812-5978; Rte 2 Km 225; ⊗ 24hrs) The only pharmacy that can accommodate a late night need for aloe.

MONEY

Banks line the perimeter of Plaza Las Delicias, so finding a cash machine is no problem. Most of the banks are open from 9am to 4pm weekdays, plus Saturday mornings, though they may close a little earlier in summer.

POST

Post office (☎ 787-842-2997; 93 Atocha; ⊗ 7:30am-4:30pm Mon-Fri, 8:30am-noon Sat) Three blocks north of Plaza Las Delicias, this is the most central of the city's four post offices.

TOURIST INFORMATION

Puerto Rico Tourism Company (PRTC; ☎ 787-284-3338; www.letsgotoponce.com; Parque de Bombas, Plaza Las Delicias; ⊗ 9am-5:30pm) You can't miss the big red-and-black structure in the middle of the park, where friendly, English-speaking members of the tourist office are ready with brochures, answers and suggestions.

Sights

PLAZA LAS DELICIAS

The soul of Ponce is its idyllic Spanish colonial plaza, within which stand two of the city's landmark buildings, Parque de Bombas and Catedral Nuestra Señora de Guadalupe. At any hour of the day a brief stroll around its border will get you well acquainted with Ponce – the smell of *panderias* (bakeries) follows churchgoers across the square each morning, children squeal around the majestic Fuente de Leones (Fountain of Lions) under the heat of midday, and lovers stroll under its lights at night. Even as the kiosks selling lottery tickets and trinkets, the commercial banks and the fast-food joints encroach at the edges (a Burger King and a Church's mar the plaza's west side), reminders of the city's prideful history dominate the plaza's attractions, including marble statuary of local *danza* icon Juan Morel Campos and poet/politician Luis Muñoz Marín, Puerto Rico's first governor. The Fuente de Leones is the square's most captivating and vibrant attraction, a monument rescued from the 1939 World's Fair in New York.

Parque de Bombas

Ponceños will claim that the eye-popping Parque De Bombas (☎ 787-284-3338; admission free; ⏰ 9:30am-5pm) is Puerto Rico's most frequently photographed building – not too hard to believe as you stroll around the black-and-red-striped Arabian-style edifice and make countless, unwitting cameos in family photo albums. Originally constructed in 1882 as an agricultural exhibition hall, the space later housed the city's volunteer firefighters, who are commemorated in a small, tidy exhibit on the open 2nd floor. Since 1990, the landmark has had a perfect function as a tourist information center – even the most hapless touristo can't miss it – where a pleasant, bilingual staff will sell you tickets for a trolley and point you in the right direction for local attractions and amenities.

Catedral Nuestra Señora de Guadalupe

The twin bell towers of this **cathedral** (Our Lady of Guadalupe Cathedral; ☎ 787-842-0134; admission free; ⏰ 6am-1pm Mon-Fri, 6am-noon & 3-8pm Sat & Sun) cast an impression of piety over the plaza, even as young punks gather to show off skate tricks on its steps. The structure was built in 1931, in the place where colonists erected their first chapel in the 1660s, which (along with subsequent structures) succumbed to earthquakes and fires. Its stained glass windows and lovely interior are picturesque, but be mindful of the fact that this is a fully functioning church, with a number of daily services.

Casa Alcaldía

Facing Plaza Las Delicias on the south side of the plaza, Ponce's current **city hall** (☎ 787-284-4141; admission free; ⏰ 8am-4:30pm Mon-Fri) started life in the 1840s as a general assembly house but soon became a jail. The last public hanging on the island happened in its courtyard, where you can see galleries that were formerly cells. The building has been Ponce's civic center for most of the 20th century; its balcony has seen speeches by four US presidents – Teddy Roosevelt, Herbert Hoover, Franklin Roosevelt and George HW Bush. The waggish head of Carnaval, El Rey Momo, also makes his pronouncements from here.

Casa Armstrong-Poventud

Like most publicly funded renovations in Ponce, the **Casa Armstrong-Poventud** (☎ 787-844-2540) has progressed slowly; its caryatid columns have been behind a veil of scaffolding for the better part of a decade. Even though the conversion into a museum and cultural center were promised for late 2008, it's best not to hold your breath. Still, the 1900 structure is beautiful and it promises to be another jewel in Ponce's encrusted crown of cultural landmarks when it is completed.

MUSEO DE ARTE DE PONCE (MAP)

With an expertly presented collection, this commanding **art museum** (☎ 787-848-0505; www.museoarteponce.org; 2325 Av Las Américas; adult/child/senior & student $5/1/2; ⏰ 10am-5pm) is the vibrant heart of the city's artistic community, easily among the best fine-arts centers in the Caribbean and itself worth the trip from San Juan. Set across from Universidad Católica, about 10 blocks to the south of Plaza Las Delicias, the museum's expertly curated collection – some 850 paintings, 800 sculptures and 500 prints – represents five centuries of Western art that was donated in large part by former governor Luis Ferré. While typical museum etiquette applies, the intimate spaces are loaded with works presented in a fully bilingual manner, and visitors can get up close and personal to take in every brush stroke. The building's blanched edifice, winged central stair and hexagonal galleries are the masterwork of architect Edward Durell Stone, who created Washington DC's Kennedy Center. The exceptional pre-Raphaelite and Italian baroque collections are offset by impressive installations and special exhibits (which usually cost a nominal extra fee). Lord Leighton's erotic *Flaming June* is the museum's sensual showpiece.

MUSEO DE LA MÚSICA PUERTORRIQUEÑA

After the MAP, this spacious pink villa designed by Juan Bertoli Calderoni, father of Puerto Rico's neoclassical style, offers Ponce's best museum experience, and is a must for those interested in the sound of the island. A guided tour of the **museum** (☎ 787-848-7016; www.icp.gobierno.pr; cnr Reina Isabel & Salud; admission $1; ⏰ 8:30am-4:30pm Wed-Sun) showcases the development of Puerto Rico's music, allowing hands-on demonstrations of the island's indigenous instruments. The collection of Taíno, African and Spanish instruments – especially the handcrafted four-string guitar-like *cuatros* and three-sting *trios* – and careful explanation of Puerto Rican musical traditions are highlights. The museum also hosts a three-week seminar on drum building in July, and holds traditional concerts in its courtyard and parlor.

MUSEO DE LA HISTORIA DE PONCE

This **history museum** (☎ 787-844-7071; 51-53 Reina Isabel; adult/child $3/1 🕑 9am-5pm Wed-Mon) is extensive for a city of less than 200,000, more evidence of Ponce's reverence for history. Located in the 1911 Casa Salazar, on the same block as Teatro La Perla, the museum has 10 galleries displaying centuries of the city's history in ecology, economy, education, architecture, medicine, politics and daily life. A refreshingly Ponce-centric perspective on the development of Puerto Rican culture, the building itself is an architectural treasure that blends typical *ponceño criollo* detailing with Moorish and neoclassical elements.

TEATRO LA PERLA

After closing its doors for structural renovations in 2005, the stately, 1000-seat **Teatro La Perla** (Pearl Theater; ☎ 787-843-4322; cnr Mayor & Cristina; 🕑 lobby 8am-4pm Mon-Fri) recently reopened its doors to theatrical and musical performances. The columned entrance, designed by Calderoni, the father of Puerto Rico's neoclassical style and designer of the Museo de la Música Puertorriqueña, was completed in the 1860s. It took 20 years to rebuild after the disastrous 1918 earthquake, but has since played a crucial role in the city's performing arts world, only underscored by the construction of the Instituto de Musica Juan More Campos, a music conservatory, across the street.

EL VIGÍA

It doesn't really compare to the hilltop monument at Corcovado in Rio de Janeiro, but the 100ft reinforced-concrete **Cruceta El Vigía** (El Vigía Cross; ☎ 787-259-3816; 17 El Vigía; admission $1; 🕑 9am-5:30pm Tue-Sun) looking over Ponce is one of the city's more reliable points of orientation. The site was first used for a similar purpose in the 19th century, when the Spanish Crown posted lookouts here to watch for smuggling along the coast. Today, the site is on shared grounds with the Museo Castillo Serrallés and a scrubby Japanese garden, but it still offers an expansive view. The $3 elevator ride to the top is optional; the view is probably better in the open air at the base, without the hazy obstruction of grubby Plexiglas windows.

Museo Castillo Serrallés

To cap the trip to El Vigía in style, try a tour of **Museo Castillo Serrallés** (Serrallés Castle Museum; ☎ 787-259-1770; 17 El Vigía; adult/child & senior $6/3; 🕑 9:30am-5.30pm Tue-Sun), on the same property as the mammoth cross. Docents lead bilingual walking tours dedicated to the Serrallés, the first family of Puerto Rican rum, and their Moorish-style castle. When the somewhat exhausting hour-plus tour ends there aren't freebie sips of the king-making product, but you can order snacks and drinks at the café and relax on the terrace under the red-tiled roof, enjoying a view of the city below and the quiet burble of the garden's fountains. A combo ticket with Cruceta El Vigía costs $9.50.

PONTIFICIA UNIVERSIDAD CATÓLICA DE PUERTO RICO

This **Catholic university** (☎ 787-841-2000) sits behind an arch on the south side of Av Las Américas, across from the art museum. It serves about 10,000 students with programs in all major undergraduate disciplines and a law school. While this is a commuter campus (like almost all universities on the island), its students shape Ponce's nightlife. While the draw for travelers to visit here is somewhat limited, when school's in session the grounds offer a bustling scene in pleasant contrast to quiet afternoons spent in the city's museums.

LA GUANCHA PASEO TABLADO

One of Ponce's most successful urban beatification projects of the last couple decades was this **boardwalk**, commonly known as 'La Guancha,' which lies about 3 miles south of the city center near the relatively lonely Ponce Hilton. Built in the mid-1990s, it's a haven for picnicking families and strolling couples to watch yachts slide in and out of the harbor. Its chief points of interest include a concert pavilion, a handful of open-air bars and food kiosks, a couple of fine-dining restaurants, a well-kept public beach and a humble observation tower. Monday and Tuesday are slow, but on the weekends the place picks up with a breezy, festive atmosphere. A newly built expressway makes reaching La Guancha much easier than it's been in the past.

ISLA CAJA DE MUERTOS

The name of **Isla Caja de Muertos** – which translates to Coffin Island – seems cribbed from the script of a swashbuckling adventure flick, but the big lizards here run a lazy show, trotting across dusty, cacti-lined trails and over the mangrove marsh. The morbid moniker itself even has a tame origin; it's thought to have come from an 18th-century French author's observation that the island's silhouette looked like a body in a casket.

But the opportunity for a refreshing, day-long escape from the congestion of Ponce is key, starting with some of the best snorkeling around and plenty of tranquil, if somewhat rocky stretches of beach. Day hikers can wander past a bounty of endangered plants and reptiles that thrive in the climate and a regal 19th-century lighthouse, occasionally used as a station for biologists. If you need more swashbuckling action, try a low-impact tour (below) to scuba at the 40ft wall that's just offshore. No longer serviced by a municipal ferry, the only way to make the 3-mile trip aside from haranguing with fisherfolk at La Guancha is through **Island Ventures** (☎ 787-834-8546; $30 round-trip; reservations necessary). Leave a message if there's no answer.

Activities
SWIMMING

The modest **beach** to the east of La Guancha was the result of a big civic project and, outside of it, Ponce doesn't have much by way of beaches. There's almost never a sizable surf and it can't compare to beaches on the Atlantic, but it's a stone's throw from La Guancha's cafés and restaurants and perfect for a few hours of lounging. It's also likely to get jammed on the weekends.

BOATING & SNORKELING

In not so distant memory, a government boat carried swarms of people to the now-quiet **beaches** on Isla Caja de Muertos, but since the ferry was repurposed for the Fajardo–Vieques–Culebra run, the wilds have reclaimed the place. Today Island Ventures sends boats over to Caja de Muertos with chair, umbrella, lunch and refreshments for a $17 ticket, and you can rent snorkeling gear for a nominal extra charge. It also can accommodate two-tank dives for about $60 to the Wall of the island's shore, which is magnificent with the right conditions.

Festivals & Events

Ponce may not have the biggest hillside cross or the biggest carnival, but in the lead-up to Lent, Ponce's **Carnaval** is a time of seriously huge partying. Events kick off on the Wednesday before Ash Wednesday with a masked ball, followed by a series of float parades and ending with the coronation of the Carnaval queen and the child queen. For most of Sunday afternoon a huge parade fills the streets with floats, *vejigantes* and music. Monday evening entails a formal *danza* competition, Tuesday brings an end to the whole shebang with yet another last parade around the square, and the party ends with the ceremonial burial of a sardine (the traditional significance of which has been washed away by booze) and the onset of Lent. By that time, there's a lot to give up for the Catholic holiday. Each parade and all of the critical activities take place in Plaza Las Delicias in front of Casa Alcaldía. If you're planning to visit Ponce during Carnaval, make your hotel and transportation reservations at least three months in advance.

In the **Fiesta Nacional de la Danza** (☎ 878-284-4141), held in mid-May, chamber orchestras perform under the lights in Plaza Las Delicias and well-groomed couples offer postured examples of the form that is regarded as 'Puerto Rico's classical music.' It's in the right place; Ponce was home to high society and composers who made *danza* a distinctive art form at the turn of the 19th century.

Drummers and *pleneros* (*plena* singers) arrive from all over the island to join in **Fiesta de Bomba y Plena**, the singing, dancing and drumming style that evolved in Ponce from citizens of African descent who came en masse to work the cane fields. Held in November.

Ponce adopted Mexico's patron saint – the Virgen de Guadalupe – as a result of the constant cultural exchange between the island and Mexico during the colonial era. In the **Fiesta Patronal de la Virgen de Guadalupe** in early December, fireworks are lit, booze is swigged and songs are sung during this week-long festival. The climax is at midnight on December 12, when Mexican mariachis called the Cantata Las Mañanitas arrive to lead a procession of citizens through the streets.

Sleeping

If you're planning on spending any quality time in Ponce, its best to make your bed at one of the hotels surrounding the Plaza Las Delicias, instead of the chain resort complexes outside of the city center. Names like Hilton and Holiday Inn might comfort the most cautious gringo, but the local flavor is nil and prices soar for accommodations that are only modestly more comfortable.

BUDGET

Hotel Bélgica (☎ 787-844-3255; 122 Villa; r $50-75; P 🕸) A traveler favorite for years, the Bélgica is just off the southwest corner of Plaza Las Delicias, a 20-room hotel with European-style high ceilings and wrought-iron balconies. Rooms near the front allow you to stare out over the plaza from a private balcony, but be prepared for noise on weekend nights.

Casa Del Sol Guest House (☎ 787-812-2995; www .casadelsolpr.com; 97 Union; r $60-75; 🕸 🖳 🐾) Situated just north of the Plaza, this nine-room guesthouse is the city's best deal, offering pleasant rooms and a welcoming staff within steps of the plaza. Shared balconies look over the busy street, and there's free wi-fi, a basic continental breakfast and a private terrace out the back with a small hot tub. Given the number of amenities, it's a steal; there's even a complementary drink from the bar downstairs included. If you are traveling with a large party and looking for a vacation rental in Ponce, it also may be able to accommodate you.

MIDRANGE

Hotel El Tuque (☎ 787-290-0000; www.eltuque.com; Rte 2 Km 220, 3330 Ponce By Pass; r $85-105; P 🕸 🖳 🐾) Recently taken over and renovated by a franchise, this adjoins a water park (open in summer only), drawing families in the summer and when thunderous events are on at the neighboring speedway. Don't expect attentive service, especially in the slow winters, but the outdoor hammocks and small pool are soothing when unaccompanied by the roar of car engines and squealing tots.

Fox Delicias Hotel (☎ 787-290-5050; www.foxdeli ciashotel.com; 6963 Reina Isabel; r $85-250; P 🕸 🖳 🐾) The Fox family refitted an old building on the corner of the plaza into a modern hotel. Opened in 2005, its plaza-facing rooms are a favorite among sophisticated *sanjuaneros*. The place has two different personalities depending on the calendar: its cocktail lounges swell in the high season and during festivals, but off-season amenities are limited and the place is pretty sleepy.

Howard Johnson (☎ 787-841-1000; Hwy 1 Km 123.5; r $95-110; P 🕸 🖳 🐾) Of the four modern chain hotels on the periphery of town, this

is the best deal. With tidy, tiled bathrooms and the typical chain hotel comforts (smooth jazz in the lobby, cheesy art work), it doesn't have a crumb of local personality, but it's a pristinely clean option and very near the airport. The amenities include an on-site restaurant, laundry, gym, wi-fi, and a patio with a shimmering pool.

Hotel Meliá (☎ 787-842-0260, 800-44-UTELL; www .hotelmeliapr.com; 2 Cristina; r $95-125; P 🕸 🖳 🐾) Just east of the plaza, this place might remind you of favorite three-star hotels in Spain and Portugal. Everything is clean and functional, the building is monumental and the staff is friendly and helpful; the rooftop sun deck, continental breakfast and a beautifully renovated pool are attractive bonuses. The 80 rooms are spread over four floors and bit by bit they are being updated. The beds are big and bathrooms fully modernized. The hotel has been in the family for generations – check out the pictures on the wall for a look at Ponce in its prime – and the manager/co-owner will happily tell you its history.

Holiday Inn & Tropical Casino (☎ 787-844-1200; www.sixcontinentshotels.com; 3315 Ponce By Pass; r $110-160; P 🕸 🖳) Perched atop a hill west of town on Hwy 2, the attractions include a small casino, modern rooms and a bilingual staff. The poolside bar offers a sweeping view of the Caribbean and surrounding mountains.

TOP END

Ponce Hilton & Casino (☎ 787-259-7676; www.hilton .com; 1150 Av Caribe; r $210-280; P 🕸 🖳 🐾) This 153-room Hilton stands within a gated area south of town, near La Guancha boardwalk on the Caribbean. As the most deluxe place in town, it has well-manicured grounds, on-site golf, a nightclub, restaurants and a casino. Sun-pink golfers and wealthy Americans are wont to gripe about their last round and the quality of the buffet, but the live music and ocean views give a touch of local flavor.

Eating

It's been a long time coming, but restaurateurs in Ponce are beginning to cater to the city's rising profile as a tourist destination with more exciting and adventuresome fine-dining offerings. La Guancha is a good bet for open-air cafés and restaurants take on a festive atmosphere at sunset. For something cheap and on-the-go, there are carts around Plaza Las Delicias where a hot dog with the works ($1.50) comes saddled with mustard, ketchup, onions, peppers, processed cheese, meaty chili and crispy shoestring potato chips. Perhaps by way of suggestion, many of them also sell gum and antacids.

BUDGET

King's Cream (9223 Marina; cones $1-3; ⊙ noon-9pm) On a pleasantly warm evening, lines stretch down the sidewalk at this excellent local institution, located across from Parque de Bombas. Within the smooth blended tropical licks are big chunks of pineapple, coconut, almond and passion-fruit, which come piled high for just over $1. If the line is too long, seek out the other location a few blocks north of the plaza on Calle Vives, between Calles Union and Marina.

Edan Deli & Juice Bar (☎ 787-259-7074; cnr Villa & Torres; mains $2-7, ⊙ lunch; **V**) This bright lunch counter sits in the back of an organic grocery store, offering veggie and vegan salads and sandwiches and fresh organic juices. It's only open for lunch, but the store keeps longer hours (8am to 6pm) and has the city's best supply of natural foods.

Cesar's Comida Criolla (cnr Mayor & Cristina; dishes $2-14; ⊙ lunch) The ultimate hole-in-the-wall for *comida criolla* (traditional Puerto Rican cuisine), this humble joint might be rough around the edges, but the savory piles of pork, chicken and seafood (most served with rice and beans) are the city's best home cookin'. If you can't choose from the daily offerings scrawled on the chalkboard, ask Cesar and his wife Freda; they might even walk you back to the kitchen to glimpse in the steaming vats of bliss.

Café de Tomás (☎ 787-840-1965; cnr Reina Isabel & Mayor; mains $4-20; ⊙ lunch & dinner) A lunch line hovers at this down-home eatery to see what's coming out of the kitchen, usually a reliable assortment of *comida criolla*, many of which cost less than $7. Within the heavy French doors of the adjoining Tompy's there's similarly tasty food with sit-down service, tablecloths and slightly higher prices.

Chef's Creations (☎ 787-848-8384; 100 Calle Reina; mains $6-$12; ⊙ lunch) On the 1st level of a former residence, this place exudes casual elegance. The menu changes every day and leans toward international fusions of local fare, like the delicious Paella Con Tostones.

MIDRANGE & TOP END

A flock of fine-dining options are opening downtown, but if you're up for a drive to the port area, *ponceños* will point you to a couple of traditionally popular seafood places with white tablecloths, water goblets, an armory of silverware and waiters in vests.

El Bohío (☎ 787-844-7825; Av Las Américas; mains $6-20; ⊙ lunch & dinner) Delectable, inventive *comida criolla* dishes that taste like nothing you've tried before. El Bohío is a little hard to find, but worth asking around for.

Rincón Argentino (☎ 787-284-1762; cnr Salud & Isabel; mains $10-22; ⊙ dinner) With tinkling piano, soft lights and heavy palm fronds, this is one of the more romantic options in town, as long as mosquitoes aren't feasting on diners who choose to sit on the patio. The mains veer toward slabs of garlicky red meat in a grilled Argentine preparation, but chicken, seafood and pasta creations round out the menu. It also boasts a lengthy wine list.

Mark's at the Meliá (☎ 787-842-0260; www.marksatthemelia.net; Hotel Meliá, 2 Cristina; mains $14-26; ⊙ dinner) Long regarded as Ponce's final word in fine dining, the cozily lit (though somewhat stuffy) restaurant within the Meliá Hotel has been lauded in every foodie magazine on the island for *comida criolla* treated to 'French' technique. Though more inventive newcomers threaten Chef Mark French's place at the top of Ponce's food chain, this is the place for upscale *mofongo* (mashed plantains), or try the salmon dinner ($25).

ourpick Las Tías (☎ 787-844-3344; www.lastiaspr.com; cnr Union & Reina; mains $15-30) This bilevel restaurant and lounge has an ideal corner spot and big balconies, making for exciting people-watching. The elegant French colonial atmosphere – wicker chairs and lazily turning fans – is backed up by a haute spin on regional dishes. The food alone makes it the best fine dining in the city center, even if the unhurried service and the atmosphere still need a little polish. The key lime cheesecake is killer.

Drinking & Entertainment

Ponce is a little slow during the week, but the weekends bring college crowds to a row of clubs on Calle Luna, one block south of the plaza, to slam drinks and grind to reggaeton. The scene at La Guancha is also festive, but a bit more reserved. Both the Ponce Hilton and the Holiday Inn have modest casinos, but there's more stylish action at the Hilton, which claims to be one of the biggest on the island.

PUBS

ourpick **La Perla Del Sur** (cnr Christina & Mayor) This chipper little bar opposite the Teatro La Perla attracts a crowd of amiable older gents who leisurely push pool balls around the table and practice their English swear words when nothing drops. The drinks are about as cheap as they come (a Medalla will set you back $1.50), making cheerful exchanges of rounds common. There's no phone and the hours are random, but it's usually open from about noon to dinner time.

Blue Kafé (☎ 787-248-3774; cnr Luna & Concordia; 5pm-late) You'd never know by strolling past, but hidden within this monocolored lounge is an expansive, open-air courtyard where young *ponceños* chat and toast the balmy weather, offering a reprieve from some of the more wild options on the block.

Hollywood Café (☎ 787-843-6703; Rte 1 Km 125.5; 6pm-late Wed-Mon) In the neighborhood near the Howard Johnson, this is off the beaten path, but a mid-20s crowd sprawls into the parking lot from Thursday to Sunday, getting rowdy with Latin rock, competitive pool and cheap swill.

DANCE CLUBS

Bar Code (☎ 787-432-3313; cnr Luna & Marina; 6pm-late Wed-Sun) Like its adjoining neighbor Ksy Ksy, this dance club is sweaty and riotous on the weekends, bringing in Ponce's young and restless who tend to drink like fish, dance like dogs (the local term for a distinctive step) and party like every animal in between. Beware the Wasikoki, a five rum concoction that's served out of jugs. Expect a thorough security check at the door.

Café Plaza (☎ 787-432-3313; 3 Union; 5pm-late) After graduating from the Calle Luna party scene, a slightly classier crowd comes here to thin their blood on juice drinks and beer. The tables on the sidewalk fill quickly, especially when they host live music or DJs. When it gets late, the crowd migrates into the narrow quarters to dance.

Pavilion (Ponce Hilton & Casino, 1150 Av Caribe) The disco at the Hilton is one of Ponce's weekend hot spots, catering to a mostly English-speaking crowd and Ponce's young and wealthy.

Shopping

Paseo Atocha, just north of the plaza, is closed to traffic, serving as a busy pedestrian marketplace with food stands and cheap goods. Here and along the cross streets merchants create a street-bazaar feel with racks of clothing, leather goods and suspiciously affordable designer wear. The city's enormous mall, Plaza del Caribe, has typical American-chain clothiers and is located south of downtown at the intersection of Rte 2 and the Ponce By Pass.

CHARLIE APONTE & LA UNIVERSIDAD DE LA SALSA

If you'd never heard salsa before, it'd be best to start with El Gran Combo de Puerto Rico, the island's authorities on the sound. Founded by Rafael Ithier in 1962, they've existed in one form or another ever since, playing thousands of gigs across Latin America and abroad. Charlie Aponte, one of the group's vocalists, joined the so-called *La Universidad de la Salsa* (The University of Salsa) in 1973 and has toured with them since then. When asked about the continued vibrancy of Puerto Rico's legendary musical ambassadors, Aponte replies with a wry smile, 'It's in the sound. The feel of the music, and that sound, are eternal, and that is the secret to our long life.'

Aponte's seen the world with the group, performing as one of the group's three vocalists, himself being introduced to the traditional songs as a child. 'Many Puerto Ricans, many Cubans, many Dominicans, grew up with that sound in their homes, singing along,' he says. 'That's how I got started. But after hearing that rhythm your entire life, it's not just a kind of music or a kind of dance, it becomes a kind of life. The beat is the soul of the music and maybe the soul of Puerto Rico. When you hear it you feel it instantly, and it hits you and gets in your body and there's nothing like it.'

Seeing El Gran Combo on its home turf is not uncommon, though the group continues to maintain a relentless schedule of international touring. Still, Aponte says, 'there's nothing like playing at home, here, in the place where it was born.'

Charlie Aponte was interviewed by Nate Cavalieri

Utopia (☎ 787-845-8742; 78 Reina Isabel; ☾ 10am-6pm) Selling colorful *vejigantes* (masks), *santos* (small carved figurines representing saints) souvenirs and Puerto Rican trinkets, Utopia is the nicest souvenir shop on the square. The bonus? The little bar up front will sell six-packs of beer to go, the only such place on the plaza.

Nueva Plaza Del Mercado (Between Paseo Atocha and Victoria; ☾ 6am-6pm Mon-Sat) Winding through crowds of shoppers on Paseo Atocha will lead you to the city's most exciting indoor market, four blocks north of the Plaza. The selection of produce – freshly hacked off the vine – is marvelous, and can be complimented by less healthful options like cheapie sweets and fried snacks, as well as lottery tickets. Just up the block, the slightly more crowded Mercade Juan Ponce de León has stalls hocking pan-religious voodoo charms and salsa tunes on vintage vinyl platters, reconditioned boots and hand-rolled cigars.

Getting There & Away

Four miles east of the town center off Hwy 1 on Hwy 5506, the Aeropuerto de Mercedita (Mercedita Airport) looks dressed for a party, but still waiting for the guests to arrive. **Cape Air** (☎ 787-848-2020; www.capeair.com) has five flights a day to San Juan (one-way/return $87/105) and **jetBlue** (☎ 800-538-2583; www.jetblue.com) also services the city from a number of American cities.

There's a nice, new público terminal three blocks north of the plaza, near Plaza del Mercado, with services connecting to all major towns on the island. There are plenty of long-haul vans headed to Río Piedras in San Juan (about $20) and Mayagüez (about $10) and an inexpensive café on-site.

Getting Around

TO/FROM THE AIRPORT

Taxis in Ponce are not exactly filling the streets and tend to gravitate to the Plaza Las Delicias. Expect to pay $15 for the 4-mile taxi trip to or from the airport (right).

CAR

Ponce has rental-car agencies (mostly located at the airport), including the following:

Avis (☎ 787-842-6184)
Dollar (☎ 787-843-6940)
Hertz (☎ 787-842-7377)

TAXI

A handful of cab companies operate in the city, and flagging one down at the Plaza Las Delicias is much quicker than calling for one. They charge $1 to drop the flag and about $1.30 per mile, but meters are used infrequently, so ask about the destination price before you get an unpleasant surprise. **Coop Taxi del Sur** (☎ 787-848-8248) and **Ponce Taxi** (☎ 787-642-3370) are reliable.

TROLLEY

The city tourist office operates trolley and fake train trips for visitors ($2), which are informative and entertaining. If you're going to be in Ponce for a day or two, this makes an excellent way to get your bearings. Supposedly both trolley and train follow the same route, but the two-hour trolley ride makes stops allowing passengers to get out and snap photos, while the train makes no stops, completing its circuit in about an hour. Of the two options, the trolley is recommended. There are supposed to be regular trips between 8am and 7:30pm daily, but if demand is low the drivers will change the schedule or routes on a whim. They all leave and return to the stop in front of the Casa Armstrong-Poventud, on the west side of Plaza Las Delicias. Trolleys are supposed to appear about every 15 minutes.

CENTRO CEREMONIAL INDÍGENA DE TIBES

Tropical storm Eloíse hit Ponce in 1975, causing the Río Portugués to overflow its banks. When the floodwater retreated from local farmland, it exposed the ruins of **Tibes** (Tibes Indian Ceremonial Center; ☎ 787-840-2255; Hwy 503 Km 2.2; adult/senior & child $2/1; ☾ 9am-4pm Tue-Sun, closed major holidays), an ancient ceremonial center. The municipal government quickly expropriated more than 30 acres, and a team of archaeologists, historians, engineers and geologists moved in. To date they have excavated slightly more than 5 acres of the property.

While Tibes lacks the dramatic scale of a place like Uxmal in Mexico, the evidence of both Igneris and other pre-Taíno cultures makes it among the most important archaeological sites in the Caribbean. The site is in the foothills just north of town and is a recommended way to spend an afternoon while visiting the Ponce area.

Current excavations have uncovered seven *bateyes* (ball courts), two ceremonial plazas, burial grounds, around 200 skeletons, pottery, tools and charms. As you tour the manicured pastoral setting – with its *bateyes* and plaza rimmed by bordering stones (some with petroglyphs) – guides explain that the first settlers on this spot were Igneris, who probably migrated from the Orinoco Valley in Venezuela and arrived at Tibes about AD 300. They were farmers and sought out fertile river valleys like Tibes to grow their staple crop of cassava.

As part of their cassava culture, the Igneris became fine potters, making vessels for serving and storing food. Many of these bell-shaped vessels have been found buried with food, charms and seashells in more than 100 Igneri graves, where individuals were buried in the fetal position in the belief that they were bound back to the 'Earthmother' for rebirth. Many of the Igneri graves have been discovered near or under the *bateyes* and walkways constructed by the pre-Taíno, who probably came to the site around the first millennium.

In a well-developed museum on the property you can see many of the axes, dishes, *cemíes* (deities), spoons and adzes that they used. You will also see some reconstructed pre-Taíno *bohíos* (huts) amid this natural botanical garden with its fruit trees, including the popular *guanábana* (soursop). There's a cafeteria open seasonally at Tibes if you get hungry.

All visits include a tour, which takes about an hour and includes a movie and a visit to the small museum, where you can see Indian ceremonial objects, pottery and jewelry. Sometimes the tour gets sold out, so you should make reservations in advance.

Tibes lies about 2 miles north of Ponce at Km 2.2 on Hwy 503. If you're driving this route, the best way to not get lost is to follow the brown signs leading to Tibes: pick these out on Hwy 14 (Calle Fagot) on the northeast side of Ponce. It's also easy to get there on a público from Ponce (opposite), which costs about $6, but getting back can be tricky.

ARROYO

On the southeast corner of the island, Arroyo is a drowsy beach town with a curious history, a place which seems to have dozed off shortly after the rein of 'king sugar' and never quite woke up. It's the first town on the south coast of interest to travelers heading clockwise along the island from San Juan, and typical of many of the seaside bergs in the area, with economies that hobble along though a trickle of tourism and small commercial fishing industries. The dusty main drag, Calle Morse, passes 19th-century structures and salt-beaten wooden homes with sagging tin roofs and shuttered windows, eventually ending at the still, blue Caribbean.

Like the regional hub of Ponce, Arroyo was a rough-and-tumble smugglers' port during the colonial days, when New England sea captains and Caribbean traders built many of the slouching wooden houses that still stand. Arroyo's early notoriety came when American Samuel Morse, inventor of the telegraph, installed communication lines here in 1848. This event put Arroyo on the map and made Morse a local hero; they named the main street after him and sing about him in the town's anthem.

Entering the village from Hwy 3 to Calle Morse, you'll notice that the upside of Arroyo's isolation is a lack of modern commercial development – there's not a Burger King in sight. Still, little effort and money is spent on preserving its inherent historical charm. The nearby Tren del Sur, which was the last working railway on the island, sits just up the road in a rusting heap, with whispers of a (unlikely) renovation floating about town.

Orientation & Information

Hwy 3, the old southern coastal road, skirts the edge of town but Hwy 753 brings you to the center and becomes the main street, which has a number of eateries, a pharmacy and a string of cheap watering holes. If you visit during peak season in the summer, you might get lucky and find someone at the **Arroyo Tourist Office** (☎ 787-839-3500; 87 Morse) but don't count on it; the hours are erratic.

Sights & Activities

The long, narrow strand adjoining the Centro Vacacional Punta Guilarte has a public **balneario** and is the only decent beach around, even though the waters have suffered from pollution. It's about 3 miles east of Arroyo on a property with grills and tables. Parking costs $2.

The **Antigua Casa de Aduana** (Old Customs House; ☎ 787-839-8096; 67 Morse; 9am-4pm Wed-Sun) is housed in an elaborately carved former customs house and filled with Morse memorabilia. Be sure to call ahead, as hours are varied and seasonal, and the building is often closed for 'renovations.'

Sleeping & Eating

Centro Vacacional Punta Guilarte (☎ 787-839-3565; Hwy 3 Km 126; campsites/cabins/villas $10/65/109; **P** **ⅹ** **ⅹ**) About 2 miles east of Arroyo, this well-maintained government facility has rustic cabins and slightly more refined (read: hot water and air-con) villas, 40 basic campsites and a pool. The cabins sleep six. The place bustles during the summer months, when you should reserve a room well in advance through the San Juan office of the Compañía de Parques Nacionales (☎ 787-622-5200). In the winter, you might have it mostly to yourself.

La Familia (53 Morse; sandwiches $1.25-$5; ⏲ lunch & dinner) This popular cafeteria and bakery is next to a ramshackle old-time general store that is loaded with unlikely finds.

Getting There & Away

Most públicos bound for Guayama will take you the few extra miles into Arroyo for a nominal charge, leaving you at the terminal near the town hall on Calle Morse. It might take a while to get a público back to Guayama ($3), but from there you can find a connecting ride to Río Piedras in San Juan or back to Ponce.

GUAYAMA

A few miles up the hill from the coast is Guayama, the bigger, less attractive older sister to little Arroyo. The two cities have been linked since the colonial days when the shadowy brokering of Arroyo's ports – illegally bringing in goods from across the Americas and sending out sugarcane and rum – fattened the wallets of Guayama's society families. In the century since, these sister towns have grown apart, with the sprawling asphalt parking lots of big box stores and commercial development offering evidence of how Guayama has left ragged little Arroyo behind.

Today, Guayama's 45,000 residents pay the rent with jobs at pharmaceutical and light industrial factories that lie west of town, and the place once called the 'City of Witches' (a result of Santería worship brought here by African laborers) suffers from the typical contemporary spells of hasty development and heavy traffic. The jewel of the city is the fountain at the center of the plaza, which was imported from France in 1918.

During the first weekend of March the upscale **Feria Dulce Sueño** (The Fair of Sweet Dreams; ☎ 787-834-1988) bring thousands of equestrian zealots to town for a Paso Fino horse race.

Sights

MUSEO CASA CAUTIÑO

On the north side of the plaza, this **museum** (☎ 787-864-9083; cnr Palmer & Vicente Pales; adult/child $1/0.50; ⏲ 9am-4pm Tue-Sun) was built as a *criollo*-style town house in 1887 to house the wealthy Cautiño family, who profited from a typical trio of cane, cattle and tobacco. Almost 100 years later, the government claimed the property for back taxes (a common event on the island, which has saved many heirlooms). Now the house has been restored to its dignified Victorian state, with Oriental carpets and period furnishings.

CENTRO DE BELLAS ARTES

A symbol of Guayama's rising status, this former courthouse was made into a **fine arts center** (☎ 787-864-7765; Rte 3 Km 138; admission free) that lies just west of town. The collection focuses on emerging and established Puerto Rican artists, though the walls are occasionally hung with student works.

RESERVA NATURAL MARIPOSARIO LAS LIMAS

Hiding in the hills about 5 miles north of Guayama, this family-operated **butterfly sanctuary** (☎ 787-864-6037; admission $3; ⏲ 10am-3pm Thu-Sun) covers nearly 200 acres of semi-tropical land carefully watched over by a Puerto Rican couple. The 90-minute tour reveals an enormous variety of flora, fauna and wildlife and a chance to savor the fresh mountain air. Reservations are recommended. To find the sanctuary, go north on Rte 15 to Rte 179. Turn onto Rte 747 and make a right at the sign at Km 0.7.

Sleeping & Eating

It'd be a bit harsh to call the hotel options in Guayana the choice between a rock and a hard place; it might be more accurately summed up as the choice between a largish stone and a slightly smaller one. Neither is close to the city's charming center or within a short walk of…well, anything. If it's late and you're tired, consider pulling in here, but better sleeping options abound to the east. For eats, inexpensive fare comes from the cafeterias by the central plaza, but the best food is a few miles down the road, in the fishing community of Pozuelo.

Hotel Brandemar (☎ 787-864-5124; end of Rte 748; r $54-75; P ⓧ ⓢ) Following a twisting road through a residential neighborhood just outside of town, you'll come to the Brandemar, a serviceable family-run hotel which is Guanica's best by a nose. It's a small compound of buildings including a hotel with inexpensive, no-frills rooms situated around a pool, buttressed by a building with well-stocked bar and restaurant with fresh fish plates.

El Molina (☎ 787-866-1515; Hwy 54 Km 2.1; r from $97; P ⓧ ⓢ) Set on 9 acres of a former sugar plantation, this 20-room inn is dominated by a crumbly old sugar mill, and is a solid bet for travelers looking for a place to rest their heads and little more. Its adjoining sports bar/restaurant turns to thumping nightclub on the weekends, which can be exciting or unruly, depending on whether you want to party or sleep. The relatively big price tag reflects a sellers' market.

Supreme Bakery (☎ 787-864-8175; cnr Derkes & Hostos; mains $3-15; ☽ 6am-7pm) The lines get long at lunch and it can be hard to get a seat, but the fat pork sammys and other *comida criolla* dishes are worth it. The baked goods are also out of sight. In the summer and on weekends they offer take out until 9:30pm.

ourpick La Casa de Los Pasteliollos (☎ 787-864-5171; Rte 7710 Km 4; mains $3-30; ☽ 10:30am-6pm Mon-Wed, 10:30am-10pm Thu, 10:30-11pm Fri) After seeing the sorry excuse for what passes for *pasteliollos*

elsewhere – dry as dirt and trapped under a merciless heat lamp– you might not recognize the namesake of this seaside patio restaurant. The ambitious variations of the fried staple (shark? octopus? pizza?) are made to order, arriving as greasy, seafood-stuffed slices of heaven. More ample, healthful options are also lovingly made, based around fresh catches. Add in the view of crashing waves and dreamy hammocks tied between palms, and this is the best lunch spot on the south coast.

Getting There & Away
To find a público, look for the parking structure two blocks southeast of the plaza. Local services to neighboring towns including Patillas and Salinas cost $3 and longer hauls to San Juan or Ponce are about $8. Check the decals on the windshields of the públicos to discern their destinations. Coming by car, you can't miss the town – it's at the junction of Hwy 3 and the Hwy 53 toll road.

BAHÍA DE JOBOS
If you're traveling west from Guayama and Arroyo, the only way to get a feel for the region is by skipping the smoothly paved Hwy 53 and navigating the two-lane Hwy 3. The feel in this area is not the typical fodder for postcards – a lot of one-stoplight towns, roadkill, and crumbling smokestacks from failed sugar mills but the slow route's highlight is the sprawling Reserva Nacional de Investigación Estuarina de Bahía de Jobos, which has hiking trails, camping and a labyrinth of mangrove canals for kayaking. The marshy reserve

---

DETOUR: POZUELO FISHING EXCURSION

The Puerto Rican government has put in a number of smooth, swift highways and tollways over the last few decades, making navigating the island in your sweet little rental car a speedy affair. However, a much more savory taste of the south coast can be discovered by taking the trusty old two-lanes of Hwys 2 and 3, which traverse the heart of a handful of local fishing communities' joints for *comedia creolla* home cooking. The best of these might be Pozuelo, a little collection of buildings on the end of a peninsula just east of Arroyo, about 40 minutes from Ponce. Turning off Hwy 3 onto Rte 7710 will bring you past a handful of places where the catches are fresh, but the classiest lunch is at **La Casa de Los Pasteliollos** (above). For dinner, wander over to **Villa Pesquera Punta Pozuelo** (☎ 787-864-5522; Rte 7710 Km 6; ☽ 10:30am-6pm). Surrounded by dry-docked boats at the end of the dusty road, this restaurant serves cheap food and beers all evening and is a magnet for local fishermen, who tend to crack a few colds one early in the afternoon. They'll rent boats and kayaks, but if you want to get into deeper water, you can hire a boat through the restaurant, or negotiate a half-day fishing charter for around $40 from one of the locals. It's the best way to truly dig into the fishing culture of the south coast, and probably the cheapest option for chartering a boat on the island.

borders the nearly abandoned sugar town of Aguirre, which makes a compelling detour.

Sights & Activities

RESERVA NACIONAL DE INVESTIGACIÓN ESTUARINA DE BAHÍA DE JOBOS

Bursting with wildlife, the rarely traveled National Estuarine Research Reserve at Bahía de Jobos is an enormous protected mangrove bay, one of the largest and least visited patches of pristine coastal wilderness in Puerto Rico. The Bahía de Jobos covers almost 3000 acres of brackish water, including associated coastal wetlands and 15 offshore mangrove keys known as Los Cayos Caribes. West of the research reserve, the Reserva Forestal Aguirre adds even more undeveloped coastal land to this wilderness.

Get your bearings and check out the educational displays at the reserve's **lab and visitors center** (☎ 787-864-0105; Hwy 705 Km 2.3; ☑ 7:30am-noon & 1-4pm Mon-Fri, 9am-noon & 1-3pm Sat & Sun). In addition to a veritable ark of brown pelicans, great blue herons, black-crowned night herons, snowy egrets, ospreys, peregrine falcons and American oyster catchers, this is probably the best place to see manatees (sea cows) in Puerto Rico. Well over 100 feed here (best seen early in the morning) and play free, untroubled by the comings and goings of humans. There are also dolphins and hawksbill sea turtles in the area.

You can go on a superb hike along the **Jagueyes Forest Interpretive Trail**, which twists around mangroves, wetlands and saltflats for about 30 minutes, with bilingual signs posted along the way. The path can be reached from the visitors center by driving west on Rte 3, then turning left at Km 154.6.

AGUIRRE

Crumbling monuments to the sugar industry are evident everywhere on the southeast part of the island, but there's no more heartbreaking reminder of departed 'King Sugar' than sleepy little Aguirre, which borders the Bahía de Jobos and is so far off the beaten path that it doesn't appear on many tourist maps. The moldering sugar town was booming in the early-20th-century, complete with a mill, company stores, hospital, theater, hotel, bowling alley, social club, golf course, marina, executive homes and narrow-gauge railroad. This was the planned private community of the Central Aguirre sugar company, and at its height (around 1960) it processed 12,500 tons of sugarcane per day. Declining prices for sugar, foreign competition and escalating production costs drove the company under in 1990 and Aguirre became a virtual ghost town. The rusting train tracks remain, as does a weedy **golf course** (☎ 787-853-4052; Rte 705 Km 1.6; tee $12; ☑ 7am-6pm Tue-Sun).

Sleeping & Eating

Aside from fending off mosquitoes and camping in the Bahía de Jobos reserve, there are no places to stay in Aguirre. The nearest options are Coamo, Guayama and Playa Salinas.

Getting There & Away

The only way to visit Reserva Nacional de Investigación Estuarina de Bahía de Jobos and Aguirre is by car. Take Hwy 705 south from Hwy 3. Watch for the barely visible sign pointing to 'Historic Aguirre.'

PLAYA SALINAS

Salinas proper, the town at the center of the south coast agricultural economy, lies about a mile north of the coast and a mile south of the highway. Even though it's the birthplace of baseball legends Roberto and Sandy Alomar and a pair of Miss Universe queens, the town itself isn't so easy on the eyes; like many other small cities in the region, it's never replaced the sugar-based economy. There is a tourist office on the central plaza, but it's open seasonally, and even then infrequently.

The coastal barrio of Playa Salinas is quite a different story. The name is a bit of a misnomer since there's no actual sand here, but the geographical features of its protected harbor make it an important port for the northern Caribbean. With deep water and a dense barrier of coastal mangroves, it's an ideal 'hurricane hole,' perfect for cruising sailors looking to hide from the tempest. Even when the seas are still, the port attracts scores of yachters, and though many of them are captained by retired Americans and Europeans, locals will be wont to gab about frequent celebrity sightings. Notables of late have included JLo and Marc Anthony.

Following Rte 701 along the coast you'll pass a cluster of candlelit surf-and-turf joints then arrive at the Marina de Salinas, a complex that includes the Posada El Náutico hotel. Travelers looking for a berth aboard a cruising sailboat headed to the Dominican Republic, the Bahamas, the US, Cuba or Jamaica will do well to check the bar within the Marina de Salinas, especially in late March and early April. If you can't get a ride, it's still a good place to watch the boats roll in and out of the harbor.

Sights & Activities

Even if you don't stay at the Posada El Náutico, most activities in the water are available through the front desk of the **Marina de Salinas** (☎ 787-824-3185; 8-G Playa Ward), where you can rent kayaks ($15/40 per hr/day), water bikes ($15/60 per hr/day) and bicycles (per half-day $10). They'll also help you arrange day trips, deep-sea fishing expeditions and jaunts to the local cays.

With a blasting stereo and boisterous families, trips on the **La Paseadora** (☎ 787-824-2649; dock near El Balcón del Capitan; tours $3, trips to local cays $5) leave weekend mornings in good weather. They offer snorkeling tours and round-trips to a nearby island with a beach.

East of town on Hwy 3 is the office of the **Departamento De Recursos Naturales** (☎ 787-824-3185; 8-G Playa Ward), which can provide information and a place to pay fees for the many surrounding natural areas.

The only place to get in the water without some kind of floating vessel is at Polita's Beach (Ctra 701).

Sleeping & Eating

Marina de Salinas & Posada El Náutico (☎ 787-824-3185; 8-G Playa Ward; r $84-125; P ⊠ ⊠ ⊒) This is the best coastal hotel east of Ponce, part of the all-in-one marina complex that has cheerful, clean rooms decorated with some tropical flair, a pool, playground, café and slightly more upscale restaurant overlooking the harbor. Find it easily by heading south on Rte 701, past the line of seafood restaurants. The snack bar near the pool is where the cruising fraternity, mostly American, comes for cheap breakfasts in the morning and cheap beers through the afternoon.

La Playa Minimarket (Calle A & Hwy 701; snacks up to $5; ⏰ noon-late) Run by brothers Evan and Irving, this little place is a well-situated (though not too well-stocked) bar and grill/minimarket, though the latter is only evident from a stock of dusty cans, mosquito repellent and dish soap. The food here is certainly a family affair: homemade sandwiches *criolla* and blood sausage come steaming from the tiny small

kitchen, and the food is available to go. The beer is cheap and the locals feisty; they dance to a TV in the corner playing videos of old salsa bands. This is the ideal place to get away from the other tourists.

Ladi's Place (☎ 787-824-2035; Calle A 86, off Hwy 701; mains $10-30; ⏰ lunch & dinner) Like its west-facing neighbors up and down the road, the sunset views are a nightly show from the breezy patio. Ladi's claims to have created 'Mojo Isleño,' a zesty garlicky sauce that dresses most local fish dishes. A crooner plays the keyboard in the corner and the song list calibrated to please gringo sailors, who sway along to 'Margaritaville' at least once an evening.

Getting There & Away

You cannot miss where the públicos gather in the lot near the town plaza. You can get to Guayama for about $2 or Ponce for $5. To get to Playa Salinas and the marina, you have to walk about 1.5 miles or negotiate with your público driver.

From the east, Hwy 3 becomes Hwy 1 as it passes through Salinas. From Ponce, drivers should take Hwy 1 east or the Hwy 52 toll road to Hwy 1 south.

COAMO

Ponce de León's obsessive search for the Fountain of Youth – which, according to some historians, was sought in hopes of curing sexual impotence – led not only to the discovery of North America, but perhaps also to the founding of this city, still famous for its thermal springs. There's no word if they helped solve León's problem; the miraculous waters are known by natives as a geothermic, not supernatural, phenomena. Regardless, León's lagging libido might be responsible for making Coamo the third-oldest colonial settlement on the island (after San Juan and San Germán), a place that also staged a decisive battle of the Spanish-American War years later.

Bathing conquistadors and battlefields aside, Coamo today is a major chicken-processing center with more than 30,000 residents. The main draw for travelers continues to be the *baños* (baths) south of town. Over the years they've hosted former US President Franklin Roosevelt and millions of visitors.

Coamo's more recent claim to fame is a footrace, the hilly 20km San Blás de

Illescas Marathon (actually more like a half-marathon), which happens every February.

Sights & Activities

If you're a connoisseur of natural springs, the **Los Baños de Coamo** (Coamo's Baths; admission free; ☺ 8am-6pm) are worth a detour, though the environs are basic and swimsuits are required – bathing au naturel isn't tolerated by local families.

Taking a dip early in the morning, during a rain shower or at dinnertime might give you the place to yourself. The upper pool has thermal water at about 110°F and the lower one is cooler, and they are a good place to take in the scene as trade winds blow across the fields and down the Río Coamo on its way to the sea. This isn't a plush spa; both pools are simple structures of poured concrete but more swish thermal experiences can be had at the neighboring hotel.

To get here, take Hwy 153 from Hwy 1 or Hwy 52. Head north for about 3 miles and look for the sign that points off to the left (west) to the Parador Baños Coamo, which is Rte 546. You'll pass a number of recent condo developments and the **Coamo Springs Golf Coure** (☎ 787-825-1370; Rte 546 Km 1; rounds weekday/weekend $38/$60), but continue down the hill a half mile to the dirt parking lot. The parador is right by the river, which flows near the right side of the fence. You'll see some ruins and two pools built high on the side of the riverbank.

There's very little public transportation to the *baños*. A público from Ponce will drop you at the intersection of Hwys 546 and 153, about 1 mile away ($3). For more money they may go to the baths, but you'll need to arrange it in advance.

If you're interested in poking around town after a dip, check out **San Blás Catholic Church** on the plaza, which has paintings by the island masters Campeche and Oller, including a painting of one of Oller's girlfriends being tortured in Purgatory. As in Guayama, Coamo has also converted an old mansion on the plaza into a **museum**; it opens upon a request through the town hall.

Sleeping & Eating

Parador Baños de Coamo (☎ 787-825-22186; www .banosdecoamo.com; end of Hwy 546; r $85-95; P ✖ ⚑) Situated around an enormous Samanea saman (rain tree), this is the most recent incarnation of hotels that have stood on this site for 150 years. The ruins of its predecessors give it a historic colonial feel, as little lizards scurry around the grounds and guests enjoy the open-air bar and thermal pools. There's an award-winning restaurant on-site and the rooms are modern, if a little worn. Nonguests can use the hotel's swimming and thermal pools between 10am and 5:30pm for $5/3 per adult/child.

YAUCO

Yauco's well-scrubbed public squares, friendly tourist office and pleasant shopping district stand in gleaming contrast to the ragged little bergs that dot the southwest highway. Hidden up in the hills, the city was founded in 1758 by merchants tired of pillaging pirates. Now the so-called 'City of Coffee' is a perfect stop for supplies before heading into the Guánica forest and a charming afternoon side trip in its own right, famous for bold coffee, yucca plantations and well-preserved art deco, colonial and creole architecture.

To get there, exit Hwy 2 at Km 359 and go right on Calle 25 de Julio, which runs alongside **Parque Arturo Lluberas**. You'll be in town when you reach the Yauco Garden, a large, futuristic sculpture tree that might have developed from plans drawn by Dr. Seuss. East of the plaza, in the basement of the brightly painted Alejandro Franceschi Art Museum is the **tourist office** (☎ 787-267-0350; cnr 25 de Julio & Batences; ☺ 8am-3pm Mon-Fri, 9am-2pm Sat & Sun), with information about local indigenous and precolonial ruins and **trolley tours**, which run regularly in the summer and by appointment in the off-season.

Sights

In sharp contrast to the modern Parque Arturo Lluberas is the city's more traditional **Plaza de Recreo**, just a few blocks up the hill upon which the massive **Iglesia Católica Nuestra Señora del Rosario** casts a long shadow over domino players and strolling lovers. The plaza hosts a small wireless café where you can sample local coffee, and sits just off a bustling stretch of shops on Calle Comercio, which has a number of jewelers who will make gold pendants with your name on them.

The **Centro de Arte Alejandro Franceschi** (☎ 787-267-0350; cnr 25 de Julio & Batence; ☺ 8am-3pm Mon-Fri, 9am-2pm Sat & Sun) is the city's immaculate little art museum, a 1907 building chock-full of Victorian oil paintings and gilded frescos.

Sleeping & Eating

For something inexpensive, stroll down Calle Comercio, which has good cafeterias and cafés. The same strip also has a franchise of the delightful Ponce institution, **King's Cream** (☎ 787-267-0505; 27 Comercio; ☯ 9am-8pm).

Hotel & Restaurante El Cafetal (☎ 787-856-0345; Rte 368 Km 10; s/d $57/87 P ☒ ⬚ ⬚) This is the only place to stay in Yauco: a multilevel maze of stairs and hallways running through this clean, inexpensive hotel, which has balconies overlooking the mountains and a retired limestone quarry. It also hosts Yauco's best restaurant, with a menu that gravitates toward fish dishes for about $15. The elaborate, slightly bizarre facility was designed by its owner and includes an attractive pool with waterfalls. There's also an adjoining motel with hourly rates – technically for travelers who get in late – but the mirrored ceiling, hidden entrance and covered parking might give you a different impression of its purpose.

GUÁNICA & AROUND

A plush resort east of town draws a top-flight of international travelers, but Guánica doesn't much notice the happenings of the relatively rich and famous: it exudes the feel of a simple fishing village where folks unwind after a long week of tending the lines by hitting their favorite open-air bar on the *malecón*. In many ways similar to Arroyo, Guánica has been largely passed over by the bland commercial and housing developments. After a long day in the sun at the Bosque Estatal de Guánica, this is an excellent spot to recharge with a few cold ones and a meal of the freshest seafood – some of it caught only hours earlier by the guy at the end of the bar.

Orientation

The small fishing town of Guánica is situated around the well-protected Bahía de Guánica, just a few miles south of Hwy 2 on Rte 116. The village itself is unlikely to grace a picture postcard – it's just a scrubby town square and a row of bars and restaurants facing a large factory across the bay. However, just east of town the Bosque Estatal de Guánica is stunning, sitting in hills that ramble down into the ocean. The park is reached by turning south off Rte 116 at Rte 334. The winding Rte 333 leads out of town, past a swish hotel and beaches to the south of the reserve.

Sights

BOSQUE ESTATAL DE GUÁNICA

The immense 10,000-acre expanse of the Guánica Biosphere Reserve is one of the island's great natural treasures and a blank slate for the outdoor enthusiast. Trails of various lengths and difficulty make loops from the visitors center, lending themselves to casual hikes, mountain biking, bird-watching and broad views of the Caribbean.

This remote desert forest is among the best examples of subtropical dry forest vegetation in the world – a fact evident in the variety of extraordinary flora and fauna – present at every turn. Scientists estimate that only 1% of the earth's dry forest of this kind remains, and the vast acreage makes this a rare sanctuary, crossed by 30-odd miles of trails that lead from the arid, rocky highlands, which are covered with scrubby brush, to over 10 miles of remote, wholly untouched coast. Only a two-hour drive from the humid rainforests of El Yunque, this crumbling landscape and parched vegetation makes an unexpected, thrilling contrast.

There are no hotels in the forest but the nearby towns of Guánica, La Parguera and Ponce have many places to stay. Bring food and water for hikes; there are no kiosks or food stands anywhere inside the forest.

History

The protected forest got its start in 1919 with the government acquisition of about half the current property. Over the years the government has added to the acreage and efforts to buy adjacent land continue. During the 1930s the Civilian Conservation Corps (CCC) cut many of the roads and built essential buildings here, and in the years since it has continued to expand under the protection of the Puerto Rico forest service.

In 1981 the UN acknowledged the value of this dry forest by designating it a Unesco 'biosphere reserve.' This accolade, Unesco says, makes it one of 529 such preserves in 105 countries around the world, where scientists and local people work with government agencies to create model land management.

Climate

The dry forest owes its distinctive and quite unusual microclimate to the presence of the nearby Central Mountains. This mountain range creates, guides and exhausts tropical

GUÁNICA & AROUND

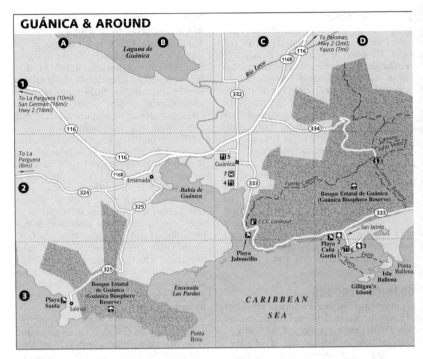

rainstorms as the easterly trade winds drive warm, moist air over the cool peaks. As a consequence, the cordillera gets totally inundated with rain while Guánica, located to the south, gets very little – usually about 35in a year, which mostly falls from June to September.

Meanwhile, December through April is so sunny, hot and dry that the deciduous trees shed all of their leaves. Temperatures fluctuate from 80° to 100°F, virtually tropical desert conditions. The flora and fauna that survive here must be hearty and attuned to the seasons.

Wildlife

Just over half the forest, in the highest elevation, consists of deciduous trees, while near the coast there's more than 1000 acres of semi-evergreen forest and scrub forest; at the waterline are the familiar mangroves. One of the most unusual plants here is the squat melon cactus with its brilliant pink flowers that attract hummingbirds. Another plant, with the unseemly name of the Spanish dildo cactus, grows into huge treelike shapes near the coast and attracts bullfinches and bats.

The forest's uneven rainfall and drainage patterns have created an unusual array of habitats for more than 700 varieties of plants (many in danger of extinction), which attract a large number of birds. Some studies claim that almost all of the bird species found in Puerto Rico turn up in Guánica – some say the area is better for bird-watching than El Yunque. Guánica is a preferred habitat for nine of the island's 14 endemic species, including the Puerto Rican woodpecker, the Puerto Rican emerald hummingbird and – the ultimate prize for bird-watchers – the exceedingly rare 'prehistoric' Puerto Rican nightjar, of which there are estimated to be as few as 1500. Long thought extinct, the nightjar has a recent unlikely enemy that troubles ecologists: a proposed windfarm in Guayanilla. Wind turbines are thought to be responsible for as much as 5% of nightjar deaths.

Scientists also come here to see the crested toad (*Bufo lemur*), which is critically endangered and has a current population estimated to be in the hundreds; the *Amelva wetmorei* lizard, with its iridescent tail; and the purple

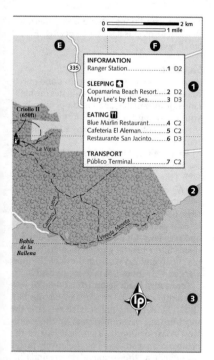

INFORMATION
Ranger Station.....................1 D2

SLEEPING
Copamarina Beach Resort.....2 D2
Mary Lee's by the Sea..........3 D3

EATING
Blue Marlin Restaurant..........4 C2
Cafeteria El Aleman.............5 C2
Restaurante San Jacinto........6 D3

TRANSPORT
Público Terminal..................7 C2

land crab. Green and leatherback turtles still lay their eggs here, but their hatchlings may be in a losing contest against the predation of mongooses, which have overrun the island since their introduction to control the rats in the cane fields.

Geography

The Bahía de Guánica divides the forest into two sections. The highest elevation here is 650ft, and many of the forest's hills rise abruptly from the coast to nearly equivalent heights. The terrain is undulating, with steep slopes in the east and moderate, rolling terrain in the west. Limestone underlies most of the forest and is overlaid by several yards of calcium carbonate. Erosion by both water and sun has created sinkholes, caves and a forest floor that often looks like brittle Swiss cheese.

Orientation & Information

To get to the eastern section of the reserve and the **ranger station** (☎ 787-821-5706; admission free; ☼ 9am-5pm), which has trail maps and brochures, follow Hwy 116 southeast toward

Guánica town from Hwy 2. Turn left (east) onto Hwy 334 and follow this road as it winds up a steep hill through an outlying barrio of Guánica. Eventually, the road crests the hills, ending at the ranger station, a picnic area and a scenic overlook of the forest and the Caribbean.

The southern extent of the eastern section of the forest – including Bahía de la Ballena (Whale Bay) and the ferry to Gilligan's Island – is also accessible by Hwy 333, to the south of Guánica. Parking is free.

Hiking

Guánica's lengthy system of hypnotic trails offers a million surprises, and although none of the foliage is particularly dense and getting lost isn't easy, be safe and bring water, sunscreen and bug repellent; the sun is unrelenting any time of year and there's little shade. Hikers should wear protective clothing against insects, thorns and the poisonous *chicharron* shrub with its reddish spiny leaves. Trails open and close seasonally to protect the wildlife and minimize human impact so it's hard to plan specifics about your hike until you get there. Parking is free.

The **Camino Ballena** 1-mile trail starts from the dusty parking lot of the ranger station, descending on a partially paved old road through some gnarled and wild scenery and eventually ending at a beautiful stretch of beach. As you leave the forest office, you'll pass a mahogany plantation and deciduous forest, passing chalky limestone scrub and cacti. A small side trail at the 1km marker will send you to the cool ravine where the 700-year old 'Centenario' Guayacán tree lives, before you continue on an easy downhill hike past agave and twisted gumbo limbo trees and eastward along Rte 333 toward Camino Cueva. After relaxing on the shore, the most challenging part of the hike is the return.

A 2-mile circular hike, the **Camino Julio Velez/Camino Los Granados** trail leaves from the ranger station and follows a broad, well-marked path through several areas inhabited by big birds, with a short detour to La Vígia, a fabulous lookout. It takes about one hour at a leisurely pace.

Ending at an observation tower built by conservationists, **Fuerte Caprón** doesn't go through the most eye-catching vegetation, but it's an easy, meandering 2.5-mile walk with changes in gradation to get your heart pumping. It takes about 60 minutes to get to the tower, then the trail continues for another 30 minutes before coming to a dead end.

Activities

Route 333 encounters several decent options for swimming before ending at the best one, Bahía de la Ballena. It twists and turns right along the coast, but keep your eyes peeled for unmarked dirt paths along the way where you can fight your way though mangroves to find sparsely populated waters.

Playa Caña Gorda (Stout Cane Beach; ☎ 787-821-6006; Hwy 333 Km 6.2; parking $2) is the balneario adjacent to the southern edge of the dry forest on Hwy 333 and where the locals come to grill fresh fish, play volleyball and lie around in the shade. The modern facilities are the most developed in the area, including a small shop with cold soda and sunblock.

Gilligan's Island and **Isla Ballena** (Whale Island) are small mangrove islands off the tip of the Caña Gorda peninsula and technically part of the dry forest reserve. Neither are too sandy, but both offer good sunbathing and passable snorkeling. The ambitious can reach these via kayak (rentals are available at Playa Caña Gorda and the Copamarina Resort) or you can catch a small **ferry** (adult/child $4/2; ☺ 9am-5pm Tue-Sun) in front of Restaurante San Jacinto every hour, barring bad weather. To get to the less-visited Ballena, you'll probably have to pony up an additional $2.

At the very end of Rte 333 is the most secluded beach, a long crescent of mixed rocky and sandy shore bordering **Bahía de la Ballena**. The road ends at the east end of the bay, and you can park anywhere along the road to picnic and sunbathe (you can also pick up the Vereda Meseta trail here).

There's also **Playa Santa**, west of Bahía de Guánica at the very end of Hwy 325. Here you can listen to a symphonic duet of jet-ski motors and reggaeton, courtesy of the Ancala Flotante, a half-built bar at the end of the road that keeps its jukebox cranked. **Pino's Boat & Water Fun** (☎ 787-821-6864) rents kayaks and paddle boats for about $15 an hour. You can also arrange boat tours and banana-boat thrill rides.

Part of the Copamarina resort, **Dive Copamarina** (☎ 787-821-0505, ext 729) has one- and two-tank wall dives about 30 minutes away for $75; it's $25 extra to rent equipment.

Weather conditions often prevent afternoon dives. It also rents snorkeling gear ($15) and small boats.

Sleeping

A community of vacation houses and guesthouses called San Jacinto dominates the highlands of the small Caña Gorda peninsula. If you're looking for a cheap option, drive up there and poke around, many of the houses rent out space.

Mary Lee's by the Sea (☎ 787-821-3600; www .maryleesbythesea.com; 25 San Jacinto; studios from $120, apt $250) This guesthouse run by US expat Mary Lee Alverez is one of the best on the island, set on a steep hillside overlooking the mangrove cays. Each well-designed apartment feels like its own villa, with decks, hammocks, barbecue and sea views. One even has a bathroom that opens into a private garden shower. You can rent boats and kayaks from the dock. Be forewarned – she does not take credit cards.

Copamarina Beach Resort (☎ 800-468-4553; www .copamarina.com; Hwy 333 Km 6.5; r $165-400, villas $859; P ☒ ☐ ☒) This full-service resort is the most upscale vacation retreat on the southwest coast of Puerto Rico, just east of the balneario on a shallow bay. Relatively pricey but worth it, the immaculate grounds include a pair of beautiful pools, tennis courts, and two upscale restaurants. There's even an on-site dive shop and a 24-hour service desk. Most of the plush, elegantly outfitted rooms open to ocean breezes and swaying palms, making it idyllic for honeymooners, who drag beach chairs into the shallow waters under the shade of the palm trees. The only drawback is the resort's isolation but, for those who enjoy peace and quiet, it can also be its greatest attribute.

Eating & Drinking

Cafeteria El Aleman (106 Ochoa; dishes $1-8; ☺ lunch & dinner) If you're of the mindset that you're not truly vacationing in the Caribbean until you're sipping a high-octane rum drink out of a coconut, this tiny roadside cafeteria is the answer to your prayers. Patrons park themselves on stools at the shoulder of the road, choose their coconut (and their poison – the house recommends Cutty Shark) and order thick, homemade sandwiches and sundry *comida criollas*.

Restaurante San Jacinto (☎ 787-821-4941; San Jacinto Km 0.5; dishes $2-20; ☺ lunch & dinner) At the

Gilligan's Island ferry landing, this beach bar and eatery has sandwiches, seafood and chicken, as well as outdoor tables and bench seating. It gets mobbed on weekends with day-trippers going or returning from the ferry. Order cheap to-go options outside for lunch, or head to the nautical interior for a more expensive dinner.

Blue Marlin Restaurant (☎ 787-821-5858; 59 Av Esperanza Idrach; mains $8-13; ☯ dinner) Rather than breaking the bank on the fancy place at the Copamarina, try this family-run restaurant on the *malecón*. Locals consider it the best, with a large outdoor deck and economic seaside drinking ($1.50 Medalla beers). If you ask for the freshest catch, your waiter will most likely bring you something that was in the water only a few hours earlier.

Getting There & Away

Público vans stop on the plaza in Guánica, a few blocks west of the shore. Getting to or from Ponce or Mayagüez costs about $7. During the summer and on sunny weekends you may be able to catch vans to the beach at Caña Gorda and Playa Santa or the ferry dock to Gilligan's Island, but don't count on it.

If you're driving to Guánica, follow Hwy 116 south from the Hwy 2 expressway.

LA PARGUERA

La Parguera is a lazy, lovable seaside town, a somewhat disorderly magnet for vacationing Puerto Ricans and US expats who seem to spend most of the morning in bed, most of the day on the water, and most of the weekend half in the bag. During the day, the streets clear out as fishermen and divers head out to navigate the maze of mangrove canals through to open water, to land snapper and shark or dive the 40-ft wall 5 miles off shore.

When the sun goes down on the weekends and during the long summer months between Easter and September, La Parguera parties hard despite its diminutive population. The bars' jukeboxes blast salsa and reggaeton, and the streets fill with students and travelers, who traverse the crooked, disorderly sidewalks with a wobble in their step.

At the busy waterfront, boats shuttle tourists to the amazing, glowing waters of the town's big draw – Bahía de Fosforescente – simultaneously diminishing its glow with the pollution from their motors.

The ramshackle mix of new and old buildings has a chaotic charm, from the occasional house on stilts over the water to less quaint vacation condo developments that have sprouted on upland fields beneath a tall, steep hill.

Orientation & Information

Even though many of the streets don't have signs, it doesn't take long to get acquainted with La Parguera; Rte 304, which brings you into town, takes a sharp bend at the water to become the main drag. It's lined with dive and surf shops, trinket galleries, bars and cafeterias.

The **El Muelle Shopping Center** (Ave los Pescadores, one block off Rte 304) has a book exchange, a well-stocked, brightly lit grocery store, and a contract post office.

Sights

BAHÍA DE FOSFORESCENTE

These glittering waters are La Parguera's biggest tourist draw, though it's actually not one bay but two: Bahía Monsio José and Bahía La Parguera. Both lie east of town and are nearly encircled by mangroves. You reach them via narrow canals through the mangrove forest and, if you come here at night, bioluminescent micro-organisms in the water put on a surreal light show (see p67).

But the light show at La Parguera, while the most famous, can no longer claim to be the best – you have to go to Vieques for that; see p171. Pollution from illegal building, boating and sewage has diluted the concentration of the little lights. Nevertheless, the $7 you pay **Cancel Boats** (☎ 787-899-5891) at the town docks, for a ride to the Bahía de Fosforescente aboard the *Fondo Cristal II* (Glass Bottom II) is the least expensive way to witness this phenomenon in Puerto Rico. If you want to be ecologically minded, however, eschew this bahía for a place where nonpolluting kayaks or electric boats are used – and tell motorized-boat operators why you're saying no.

ISLAS MATA LA GATA & CARACOLES

These two mangrove keys lie less than a half mile offshore. The sandy strands on the seaside are really the only places in La Parguera to spend a traditional day at the beach, and both are overused and the sand is not spectacular. You can come here in your own rental boat or kayak, but the boat operators at the town docks will also take you for a $7 round-trip.

ISLA DE MAGUEYES & ISLA DE MONOS

Magueyes Island lies about 200yd south of the boat docks and is used as a marine science station for the Universidad de Puerto Rico. The island was formerly a zoo, though now it's overrun by some frighteningly large iguanas, many of which were originally brought from Cuba. They occasionally make their way to the mainland. Monkeys held for research on Isla de Monos (Monkey Island), about a mile to the west, have also escaped and are breeding ashore – pests to local farmers, but amusement for children and local wags.

Activities

DIVING & SNORKELING

It's possible to travel offshore to Cayo Enrique or Cayo Laurel with **Paradise Scuba Center** (☎ 787-899-7611; paradisescubapuertorico@hotmail.com). A four-hour snorkeling excursion costs $35, and the fee includes drinks and snacks, homemade by the wife of owner Luis. For $50, you can take a sunset snorkeling trip that includes swimming after dark in the bioluminescent waters of Bahía de Fosforescente. Many scuba fanatics use this operator to dive places like the Wall and Trench Alley. A two-tank dive at the Wall is $80; a night dive runs at $50. Travelers can rent snorkeling gear for $12 per day.

More recently, **West Divers** (☎ 787-899-3223; Rte 304 next to police station) has beefed up their operation in the area. They offer three-hour snorkeling trips ($35) and two-tank trips to the Wall ($80). If you're in a party smaller than three call ahead to inquire about joining with another group.

WINDSURFING

La Parguera's sheltered waters and reliable breezes make it a prime destination during the peak of the windsurfing season. See Eddie 'Gordo' Rodríguez at **Ventolera** (☎ 787-808-0396), a water-sports shop in the Muelle plaza.

BOATING

Travelers have a number of vendors to choose from in this town. **Cancel Boats** (☎ 787-899-5891; boats per hr $15), at the town docks, has a lot of loyal customers renting its 15ft whaler-type boats with 10HP engines. Competitor Torres Boat Service nearby has similar prices.

Across the street from the El Muelle shopping center is **Aleli Kayak Rental** (☎ 787-899-6086; 1-/2-person kayaks per hr $10/15, half-day $30/40, full day $50/60), which is the most ecologically responsible way to see the magical waters. It also offers a chartered catamaran tour ($700 per day) and ecotours through the mangrove channels. For any rentals, call ahead, as opening hours are variable.

FISHING

You can fish the reefs for grouper, snapper and mackerel, or head into deeper water for blue marlin, tuna and dorado. **Parguera Fishing Charters** (☎ 787-382-4698) runs half- and full-day trips (from $175) on its 31ft Bertram out of a well-marked dock at the west end of town.

THE WALL

Although landlubbers can have plenty of fun in Parguera, divers know the real draw – the underwater treasure hidden 6 miles offshore.

The Wall (advanced dive, 50ft to 125ft) features a 'swim through' at the base of an immense reef that has a sheer 60ft drop. Plenty of good diving takes place above that mark, but the real treat is wiggling in and out of the 'swim through' hole and checking out the impressive reef structure at 80ft and below. Divers have reported seeing manatees, dolphins, manta rays and much, much more.

Here are some other diving highlights near La Parguera:

The Motor (novice, 55ft to 75ft) An unclaimed airplane motor adds mystery to a reef.

Barracuda City (novice, 60ft to 70ft) You'll get the hairy eyeball from big silver predators.

Super Bowl (intermediate, 55ft to 75ft) Swim-throughs and overhangs.

The Chimney (intermediate, 55ft to 75ft) A north-facing ledge honeycombed with holes.

Black Wall (intermediate, 60ft to 130ft) A smaller version of the big coral wall.

Two For You (advanced, 55ft to 120ft) This reef looks like an underwater flower shop.

Fallen Rock (advanced, 65ft to 120ft) A magnet for abundant coral and bright blue fish – you can even get a little 'nitrogen narcosis' intoxication if you go real deep.

Festivals & Events

La Parguera takes its name from the abundant pargo fish and in the middle of June hosts the **Fiesta de San Pedro** to honor the patron saint of fishermen. The party closes the main street where there's live music, food kiosks, childrens' activities and vendors who pour untold gallons of Medalla.

Sleeping

There are plenty of sleeping options within walking distance of La Parguera, so unless it is the peak of the summer season or during the annual San Pedro festival, it won't be hard to find a clean, comfortable place to sleep for well under $100. There are guesthouses and a pair of larger, slightly more polished hotels all within walking distance of the dock.

Glady's Guest House (☎ 787-899-4678; 42 Calle 2; r $60-74 🅿 😺) This great guesthouse option sits across the street from Lucerna's bakery. The tidy grounds are a few steps from the center of the action, but just far enough away to allow a good night's sleep.

our pick **La Parguera Guest House** (☎ 787-899-3993; www.pargueraguesthouse.com; Rte 304 Km 4; r $65 🅿 😺 🖵) This cheerfully painted guesthouse might be the best deal in town, right on the strip with 18 clean, small rooms all with a small refrigerator and cable. There are also two apartments; one sleeps six and goes for $120, another sleeps eight and can be had for around $150. During peak season prices go up a little.

Nautilus Hotel (☎ 787-899-4004; nautilus@caribe .net; 238 Rte 304; r Mon-Fri $65, Sat & Sun $80-90; 😺 😸) This hotel sits behind its own small parking lot and faces a mangrove lagoon, just east of the center of town. The Nautilus is a well-appointed modern place with 18 rooms, a pool and Jacuzzi.

Parador Villa del Mar Hotel (☎ 787-899-4265; www.pinacolada.net/villadelmar; 3 Av Albizu Campos; r $80-90; 😸) This place is outside of town at the top of a hill with a view of the Bahía de Fosforescente. There 25 rooms here feature the usual modern conveniences, and there's also a swimming pool.

Parador Villa Parguera (☎ 787-899-7777; www.villa parguera.net; Hwy 304 Km 3.6; r $107-187; 😺 🖵 😸) On the main street across from the church, this two-story hotel with 63 units is a long-time favorite of travelers, and the closest to luxury that you're going to find in town. There is a gourmet restaurant and nightclub on-site.

Eating

It's easy to follow your nose here; there are plenty of bars and food kiosks at the waterfront by the docks. All of the fancy paradores have at least one high-end restaurant on-site offering creative takes on *comida criolla* and traditional seafood dishes.

Doña Luisa (Rte 304, near La Parguera Guest House; empanadas $1-2; 😺 lunch until late) The best place for cheap empanadas in town, nothing costs over two bucks. In terms of atmosphere, this beat-up cafeteria doesn't have much polish, but it more than makes up for it in character. The empanadas with *pulpo* (octopus) are the best.

La Lucerna Bakery (☎ 787-899-9637; Hwy 304 Km 3; dishes $1.50-5; 😺 breakfast, lunch & dinner) This is Carlos José Ramos' gem, with a friendly staff, careful cooking and low prices. Pancakes cost under $2. The bakery's sandwiches, such as a *medianoche* (midnight) run less than $3.

El Manglar (☎ 787-899-4742; next to El Mulle Shopping Center; mains $6-18; 😺 9:30am-midnight) International with a Middle-Eastern flair, the menu has hummus and babaganoosh, salads, burgers, pizza and Puerto Rican food, all served in a relaxed atmosphere. It transforms from one of the city's best restaurants to one of its most festive nightspots, featuring a live combo of some sort, playing Latin rock or jazz, folk or occasionally traditional music on a breezy outdoor patio.

our pick **Aguazul Tamara Zoe** (☎ 787-899-8014; Rte 304 near Hotel Nautilus; mains $10-22; 😺 lunch & dinner Tue-Sat, lunch Sun) The focus on fresh local, organic ingredients and a menu of homemade raviolis, *churrasco* (grilled meat) and creole fish dishes with a haute presentation leaves Zoe with few peers. Finish with a plate of fresh local cheese and it's the best fine dining in La Parguera.

Entertainment

Nightlife in La Parguera is an outdoor affair: people drink, eat and stroll from one end of the waterfront road to the other.

Mar y Tierra (☎ 787-899-4627; Rte 304; 😺 4pm-midnight, later on weekends) This stands out among the cluster of places packed together between the main street and the docks. It is more of a pavilion with indoor and patio seating than a traditional bar, and it pumps out live Latin rock and salsa on the weekends. Right in the center of town, it's impossible to miss.

El Karacol (Rte 304, at the docks; 😺 4pm-midnight, later on weekends) This brightly lit bar/diner has the ambience of a fluorescent-lit fast-food chain, making a bizarre partner to the dark and noisy adjoining game room. The 'sangria coño' is their famous drink, which tastes like rum-spiked wine.

Parador Villa Parguera (☎ 787-899-7777; Hwy 304 Km 3.6; admission from $20) The Parador Villa Parguera (p207) draws an older crowd, including many couples. There's always dancing and a show on Saturday night, which usually features performances by well-known island singers and comedians.

Getting There & Away

Públicos come and go irregularly from a stop near the small waterfront park and boat piers in the center of the village. Service is basically local and travels to nearby towns such as Lajas ($1), where you can move on to bigger and better van stands in bigger and better municipalities.

The fastest way here is on Hwy 116, off Hwy 2, from Guánica or San Germán. Follow the signs for the last couple of miles on Hwy 304.

West Coast

'Go West, surfer dude,' was the unofficial mantra for a whole generation of '60s wave-riders who ran out of untrammeled Californian coastline to colonize. Intuitively, they switched south to a utopia not too far removed from the golden sands that they had left behind. Puerto Rico's west coast is a paradisiacal amalgam of crashing surf, sultry fishing villages and psychedelic sunsets. Its pièce de résistance is Rincón, a tropical surfin' safari that throws grizzled expats among wacky locals in a laid-back town that was once immortalized in a song by the Beach Boys.

Collectively rebranded and renamed, Puerto Rico's 'Wild West' now goes under the rather anodyne pseudonym of Porta del Sol (Gateway to the Sun), a tourist-company invention that does little justice to its diverse scenery and colorful heritage. San Juan – although only two hours' drive to the east – is a distant memory out here in a grandiose land of stormy shorelines and blinking lighthouses where resorts are low-key and deep-fried cod fritters from a Caribbean food shack are considered a cordon bleu meal.

Even the region's biggest city Mayagüez retains a proud and slightly bolshie sense of independence, stoked perhaps by the belief that Columbus allegedly hit these shores first. Adding authenticity to myth is San Germán, the island's second-oldest city with colonial relics to rival anything in Mexico, and Boquerón, one of the commonwealth's most down-to-earth fishing villages with an atmosphere that is more Montego Bay than South Beach.

The southwest also has nature, a compact triangle of land around the Cabo Rojo lighthouse that falls outside Puerto Rico's main road grid and defies conventional island ecology with its prickly cacti and eerie salt flats.

HIGHLIGHTS

- 'Taking the tube' and 'walking the nose' with a posse of multitalented, multinational surfers in **Rincón** (p228)
- Bargaining at myriad seafood stalls along Calle José de Diego in downbeat **Boquerón** (p213)
- Contemplating the well-preserved architectural artifacts of colonial **San Germán** (p217)
- Climbing an observation tower to spy abundant birdlife at the **Corozo Salt Flats** (p211)
- Experiencing the animated but subtle local vibe in lovingly restored Plaza Colón in **Mayagüez** (p221)
- Braving rough seas to visit the 'Galápagos of Puerto Rico' on **Isla Mona** (p234)

★ Rincón

★ Mayagüez

★ Isla Mona

San Germán ★

Boquerón ★

Corozo Salt Flats ★

- POPULATION: 400,000

lonelyplanet.com

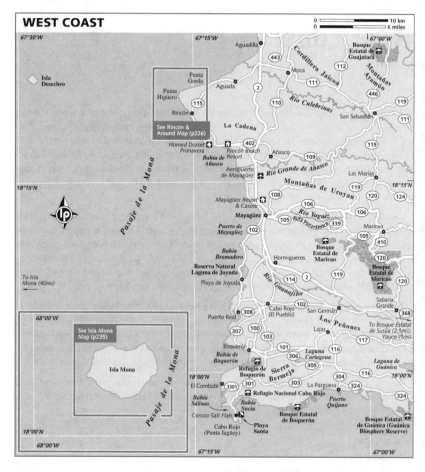

History

The consensus is that Columbus first arrived in Puerto Rico in November 1943 and docked somewhere off the west coast (though there is some dispute as to actually *where*). Fifteen years later he was followed by Juan Ponce de León who landed near Cabo Rojo before heading off north to found the settlement of Caparra. San Germán, the island's second-oldest city, was founded near Mayagüez in 1511 and moved to its present site in 1573. More recently, the west has spawned many great liberal thinkers including Dr Ramón Emeterio Betances, the inspiration behind the revolutionary Grito de Lares (p35) in 1868. The details of this abortive rebellion were fine-tuned in a series of safe houses on the outskirts of Mayagüez.

Climate

The west coast of Puerto Rico is pleasantly hot all year round. Late in the summer and early in the fall rains get heavy. Otherwise, it's sunny, breezy and around 80°F nearly every day.

Territorial Parks & Reserves

The 4775-acre Bosque Estatal de Boquerón is split into eight different segments spread around the Cabo Rojo area. The two of most interest to travelers are the Refugio de Boquerón (p214) with its mangrove wetlands and excellent bird-watching opportunities, and the Reserva Natural Laguna de Joyuda (p217) which plays host to numerous species of waterfowl. Close by, the Refugio

Nacional Cabo Rojo (p212) is another bird-watchers haven with trails, a visitor's center and guided hikes.

In the foothills of the Central Mountains further east the 3300-acre Bosque Estatal de Susúa (p219) exhibits an interesting blend of dry forest and tropical jungle.

Getting There & Around

The west is easily accessed by Hwy 2, the island's nominal ring road – although it's not as fast as the newer toll roads further east. Públicos serve most of the main towns, with Mayagüez acting as the regional hub. You can fly direct from the US into Aguadilla airport 30 minutes northeast of Rincón. Mayagüez also has its own airport (flights from San Juan and the US Virgin Islands only). The area around Cabo Rojo southwest of Hwy 2 is ideal for cycling.

CABO ROJO

Cabo Rojo (Red Cape) is the name of both a small administrative town, 8 miles west of San Germán, and the wider municipality that surrounds it. To add to the confusion, it is also the name used to describe the rugged coastline that constitutes Puerto Rico's extreme southwestern tip. Characterized by rust-red limestone cliffs that fall precipitously away into the ocean, the region is dominated by the Faro de Cabo Rojo (Red Cape Lighthouse), which sits atop a wild and windswept promontory surrounded by coastal mangroves, dry cacti and crystalline salt pans.

Busy Hwy 2 cuts inland west of Yauco, leaving this rather isolated corner of the island refreshingly untrammeled and unspoiled. There's an extensive patchwork of wildlife refuges here along with a quiet network of country roads that make for excellent cycling. Closer to the lighthouse you'll find trails, extensive salt pans and the bejeweled but little-known Playuela Beach. In-the-know locals will tell you in surreptitious whispers that this is one of the island's best stretches of sand.

The Cabo Rojo municipality incorporates the settlements of Boquerón, El Combate, Playa de Joyuda and Cabo Rojo (El Pueblo), which lies 10 miles north of the eponymous cape. There's little to see in the town today aside from a small museum dedicated to local heroes such as Dr Ramón Emeterio Betances,

the father of Puerto Rico's independence movement, and Roberto Confresí, a once notorious local pirate. The best selection of accommodations lie in Boquerón and the best restaurants in Joyuda.

Information

The Porta del Sol branch of the **Puerto Rico Tourism Company** (PRTC; ☎ 787-255-1560; www.gotopuertorico.com; La Campana Bldg, Muñoz Rivera; ⏰ 8am-4pm) is located in Cabo Rojo (El Pueblo).

Sights & Activities

MUSEO DE LOS PRÓCERES

If you've got a half hour to kill in the town of Cabo Rojo and have more than a passing interest in Puerto Rican history, this small **museum** (☎ 787-255-1560; Rte 312 Km 0.5; admission free; ⏰ 7am-4pm Tue-Fri, 8am-4:30pm Sat) can enlighten you on local painting, indigenous Taíno culture and the life and times of various 19th-century liberal luminaries such as native-born Ramón Emeterio Betances.

COROZO SALT FLATS, PUNTA JAGÜEY & PLAYA SANTA

For a serene drive through undeveloped coastal plain or a cycling adventure, approach Cabo Rojo from La Parguera (p205) via Hwy 304, Hwy 305 and Hwy 303. Then follow Hwy 301 south until it turns to dirt, where you'll traverse a spit of sand between Bahía Salinas (Salt Bay) and the aptly named Bahía Sucia (Dirty Bay).

Vast salt flats surround this narrow peninsula, especially to the east; humans have been gathering salt here since AD 700. When the first Spaniards arrived, they quickly took over the evaporation pools used by the Taíno to collect salt and expanded the business, making it a sustaining force in the local economy until efficient sugarcane farming arrived in the 18th century.

At the Corozo Salt Flats you'll see pools of evaporating brine and mounds of salt waiting to be shipped to market alongside the dirt road as you head south toward the headland of Punta Jagüey, where scrub forest sets in and the land rises to the steep limestone cliffs. Go to the end of the road and park on the left near the crescent beach known as Playa Santa. Although this is not a designated camping area, Puerto Ricans have been pitching tents on Playa Santa for years. Swimming is safe, but salty.

REFUGIO NACIONAL CABO ROJO

This **refuge** (☎ 787-851-7258, ext 35; Hwy 301 Km 5.1; admission free; ☺ 8am-4pm Mon-Fri) is about a mile north of the Hwy 3301 turnoff to El Combate. Its visitors center contains displays on local wildlife and wildlife management techniques. Outdoors you will find bird-watching trails among the ruins of an old farmstead in the Valle de Lajas (Lajas Valley). This area around the coastal plains and shores of Cabo Rojo is a major winter ground for migratory ducks, herons and songbirds, and more than 130 bird species have been sighted here. You can arrange guided hikes through the refuge at the Centro Interpretativos Las Salinas de Cabo Rojo (below).

CENTRO INTERPRETATIVOS LAS SALINAS DE CABO ROJO

A small **center** (☎ 787-851-2999; Hwy 301 Km 11; admission free; ☺ 8:30am-4:30pm Wed-Sat, 9:30am-5:30pm Sun) further south along Hwy 301 toward the lighthouse explains the geology and ecology of the salt pans. It is staffed by knowledgeable ecosensitive guides who can give thorough explanations of the local flora and fauna. Across the road is a three-story wooden lookout tower that offers a bird's-eye view of the salt pans, a major bird migratory corridor.

CYCLING

There are numerous cycling trails around the Cabo Rojo lighthouse and wildlife refuge. Ask at the Centro Interpretativos Las Salinas de Cabo Rojo (above) for details. The nearest bike rental is at the **Wheel Shop** (☎ 787-255-0095; www.wheelshoppr.com, in Spanish; Hwy 100 Km 5.9) in Cabo Rojo (El Pueblo). Expect to pay from $20 per day.

Sleeping & Eating

Punta Aguila Resort (☎ 787-254-4954; Hwy 301 Km 11.5; r $100-160; Ⓟ 🍴 🛖) Next door to Parador Bahía Salinas Beach Hotel and paling somewhat by comparison, this small resort rents out a variety of efficiency apartments in a multilevel condo-style building facing the Pasaje de la Mona. There is a free-form pool and seaside cabanas (for shade).

Parador Bahía Salinas Beach Hotel (☎ 787-254-1212; www.bahiasalinas.com; Hwy 301 Km 11.5; r $150-190; Ⓟ 🍴 🛖 🛖) As if the location wasn't enough – rust-red cliffs, salt flats and an adjacent wildlife refuge – this gorgeous parador goes one step further. Imagine drape-covered sun loungers,

TOP AUTHENTIC PUERTO RICAN EXPERIENCES

▪ Sampling Brazo Gitano at E Franco & Co in Mayagüez (p224)

▪ Hitting the Surfer's beach at Dogman's in Rincón (p229)

▪ Sunday Service at the Catedral de San Germán de Auxerre in San German (p219)

▪ Strolling along the 'Gourmet Golden Mile' in Playa Joyuda (p216)

▪ Soaking up the late night ambience of the beachside strip in Boquerón (p216)

canopy beds and marble statues of lions and maidens surrounding an infinity pool that frames some of the island's most spectacular sunsets. Added to this is the award-winning Aqua al Cuello Restaurant (below) and Bohemio Bar where you can recline next to the lapping ocean waves amid pretty palms and lush vegetation in perfect serenity. In contrast to bigger resorts, the low-rise, low-key Bahía Salinas is gentle with the environment and threads its luxury quite seamlessly into the surrounding landscape.

Aqua al Cuello Restaurant (☎ 787-254-1212; www.bahiasalinas.com; Parador Bahía Salinas Beach Hotel, Hwy 301 Km 11.5; meals $8-28; ☺ lunch & dinner) On a beautiful deck over the water this place cooks up equally beautiful food that has bagged it Puerto Rico's best Mesón Gastronómico award in recent years. The mahimahi in creole sauce is backed up by some surprising specials. Ever tried kangaroo?

Getting There & Away

There is no regular público service available to the Punta Jagüey area, which is the most remote corner of the island. Some days there is a morning público that runs between the town of Cabo Rojo (El Pueblo) and the point, but you can't count on it. A more reliable option is to come by rental car or bike (following the route from La Parguera via Hwy 304, Hwy 305 and Hwy 303; see p211).

EL COMBATE

Named after a 1759 colonial turf war waged for control of the lucrative salt flats to the south, El Combate (The Battle) retains its wayward and embattled image. Indeed, people from this gritty seaside settlement, wedged incongruously between Boquerón beach and the Cabo Rojo lighthouse, are still known locally as Los Mata con Hacha (Those Who Kill with Axes) for their historical penchant to wield sharp weaponry against rivals from the nearby town of Lajas.

Situated at the end of Hwy 3301, a short spur road that branches west from Hwy 301, El Combate today is an untidy sprawl of tawdry guesthouses, backyard trailer-camping sites, beach houses and restaurants. But while the down-at-heel bar scene might be a little on the rough side, the thin 3-mile-long strip of sand that affronts the Pasaje de la Mona is a perennially popular vacation spot for Puerto Rican families and high-school and college kids looking for some fun during the weekends.

Sleeping & Eating

Luichy Sea Food Restaurant & Guest House (☎ 787-254-7053; Hwy 3301 Km 2.9; r $80-100; ✷) Among more than half a dozen guesthouses at the south end of town, this place is a good bet for cleanliness. Rooms are very basic with private bathrooms.

Combate Beach Hotel & Restaurant (☎ 787-254-7053; Hwy 3301 Km 2.7; d/q $90/110; P ✷ ✹) A favorite oasis in El Combate, this hotel is right on the beach about a quarter of a mile from all the development in the town. The motel-style rooms are simple but clean with private bathrooms. There's a casual restaurant serving seafood and *comida criolla* (traditional Puerto Rican cuisine).

Villas Mojacasabe (☎ 787-254-4888; www.mojacasabe.com; Hwy 3301 Km 3.2; r/cabins $90/141; P ✷) Nothing fancy here; then again, it is El Combate. Built inside a sturdy fence on the north side of the village, these cabins come in concrete or wood and sleep up to six people. There are also double bedrooms in a larger block. Scattered around the complex is an amusement hall with a bar, a boardwalk and a launch ramp for boats. The crowds pile in to listen to live Latin rock, salsa and merengue on weekends, so don't expect too much tranquillity.

Annie's Place (☎ 787-254-0021; Hwy 3301 Km 2.9; mains $5-15) Annie's is a bar and restaurant with great *empanadillas* (dough stuffed with meat or fish), lobster soup, fish salad and homemade burgers. Right on the water, it's very popular in the early evening when

young kids on double dates drop by to play billiards and watch the sun set.

Getting There & Away

Públicos run frequently to and from the town of Cabo Rojo (El Pueblo) from April to the end of August ($2). In Cabo Rojo you can connect to Mayagüez ($4, 30 minutes) or Ponce ($7, two hours).

If you're arriving by car, El Combate is at the bitter end of Hwy 3301. Go west at the turnoff from Hwy 301.

BOQUERÓN

pop 8000

Easy-going Boquerón, where Puerto Rico meets the Caribbean with a cool Calypso twist, is a colorful west-coast fishing community with wooden-shack restaurants and open-air food stalls that pulsates at weekends to a jaunty but inherently Puerto Rican nightlife. Rightly famous for its sheltered balneario (public beach) and up-and-coming marina, Boquerón is surrounded by a verdant patchwork of refuges, nature reserves and state forests – a nuance that lends the settlement a refreshing small-town, semi-rural feel. Down here in the island's extreme southwestern corner, a tangible sense of isolation contrasts with the maelstrom elsewhere and many stressed-out *sanjuaneros* happily tackle the three-hour drive from the capital to bliss out on the region's palm-shaded beaches.

Historically, Boquerón's legacy is possibly even older than Caparra's. Certain scholars have claimed that this is where Columbus first set anchor when he 'discovered' the island of Puerto Rico in 1493. However, no town existed here until the 1700s and the new colony's administrative focus was ultimately centered further to the east.

Boquerón attracts travelers of all types, from cell-phone-wielding yacht owners to colorfully attired Rastafarians, and has lately become a favorite destination for wealthy islanders. But with few restaurants outside the standard mom-and-pop luncheonettes and zero resort hotels, the atmosphere remains informal and relaxed. There's a lot of fun to be had at the waterfront here, particularly at night when the two main roads are shut down to traffic and people can indulge in that favorite Caribbean pastime of *limin'* – hanging out, chilling, and moving from one bar to another with a drink in hand.

WEST COAST

Sights

REFUGIO DE BOQUERÓN

The western part of the Bosque Estatal de Boquerón carries the name Refugio de Boquerón. It is made up of more than 400 acres of mangrove wetlands, about 2 miles south of town between the coast and Hwy 301. This is an excellent area for bird-watching; more than 60 species are commonly sighted. A number of duck species migrate here in the winter, as well as osprey and mangrove canary. An excellent way to see this sanctuary is to rent a kayak (right) and paddle south across Bahía de Boquerón (Boquerón Bay). The **main office** (☎ 787-851-7260; Rte 101 Km 1.1, Boquerón; ☺ 7:30am-3:30pm) can provide more information and has a 700ft walkway leading into the mangroves. Or stop at Km 1.1 just off Rte 101 and start walking along the trail you see there. Insect repellent is a must-carry in dry season, as is water, and always watch where you put your feet: tiny crabs scuttle about.

BEACHES

Rated as one of the best public beaches in Puerto Rico (along with Luquillo), the **Balneario Boquerón** (parking $3) is a mile-long arc of sand backed by coconut palms and ample grassy lawns. Facilities include showers, changing rooms, toilets and picnic tables. The waters here are calm making it popular with Frisbee-throwing families who come down at weekends. To get there turn left (heading towards town) off Hwy 101 at the Boquerón Beach Hotel and proceed along a small spur road for a ¼-mile.

Playa Buyé is a smaller palm-fringed beach that's about 2½ miles north of town off Hwy 307.

Activities

DIVING & SNORKELING

Next to the *club náutico* (marina), west of the center of town, **Mona Aquatics** (☎ 787-851-2185; Calle José de Diego; www.monaaquatics.com) has a 40ft dive boat – *Orca Too* – that takes you on local dives ($125) or longer excursions to Isla Desecheo ($150). Prices include snack, weights, instruction and two dives. Mona Aquatics also rents out snorkeling gear and operates boats to Isla Mona (p234).

Nearby La Parguera has good diving and snorkeling opportunities as well (see p206).

KAYAKING

North of Shamar Bar-Restaurant & Hotel you'll find **Kaipo Kayak Rentals** (☎ 787-254-3413; Calle José de Diego), which rents out boats, kayaks and surf bikes (half surfboard, half bicycle) at hour and day rates.

Boquerón Kayak Rental (☎ 787-255-1849; Calle José de Diego) has pedal boats and surf bikes, as well as kayaks (all from $15 per hour). Boat rides are also available. Cash only.

GOLF

Near the intersection of Hwy 102 and Hwy 308 in Cabo Rojo (El Pueblo) is **Club Deportivo de Oeste** (☎ 787-851-8880; greens fee walk/cart from $10/30). It's a Jack Bender–designed 18-hole course with a panoramic view along its 3360yd. Greens fees vary depending on the time you play.

Sleeping

Shamar Bar-Restaurant & Hotel (☎ 787-851-0542; Calle José de Diego; r $60-85) If you've been backpacking around Thailand you'll know the deal – a glorified beach bar that sells cheap snacks and rents out slightly more expensive 'shacks.' Clean, bright and comfy – though not particularly quiet – the upstairs rooms are good crash pads if you want to be in the thick of Boquerón's small but vibrant commercial strip. For history buffs, the Shamar is the oldest commercial building in Boquerón and has been a working bar for more than 50 years.

Centro Vacacional Boquerón (☎ 787-851-1900, reservations 787-622-5200; apt s/d $68/109) Each of the 158 apartments (in two-story duplex units) holds six people and comes with bathroom, kitchen, bunk beds and ceiling fans. Activity rooms, a convenience store and a first-aid station are on the premises. The place gets booked a year in advance for summer and holidays; it's right on the beach.

Buyé Beach Resort (☎ 787-255-0358; Hwy 30 Km 4.8; cabins $75; 🏊 📶) Located on a popular beach north of town, this clean and simple operation has 16 cabins on the beach. Each cabin accommodates three to four people and includes a private bathroom and kitchen. There is a coin laundry here, too.

Adamari's Apartments (☎ 787-851-6860; Calle José de Diego; r $85; 🅿 🐾) Adamari's is the tall building right next to Parador Boquemar, with a laundrette out the front. While not state of the art, this place does have nine clean efficiency apartments (each with a kitchenette and many with ocean views).

Parador Boquemar (☎ 787-851-2158; Calle José de Diego; r $85-110; P X 🕭) There's a bit of a rabbit-hutch feel to the 60 generic rooms here, which are piled on top of each other over three crowded stories. That said, because this is Boquerón and because you're essentially 'downtown,' the Boquemar is rather popular. In common with standard Puerto Rican paradores, there's a pool, an above-average on-site restaurant and friendly down-to-earth service.

El Muelle Guest House (☎ 787-254-2801; Calle José de Diego; apt $85-125; P X) For a quiet night, El Muelle's the best bet. Rooms are spacious and have been nicely decorated. Check carefully for cleanliness before handing over any cash; it's a good idea to ask to see the room before agreeing to anything. Prices drop in the low season.

Boquerón Beach Hotel (☎ 787-851-7110; www.boqueronbeachhotel.com; r $88-149; P X 🕭) Plunked conveniently at the turnoff for the balneario (a quarter of a mile away and the primary reason why a lot of people visit the area), the Boquerón Beach Hotel offers good bang for your buck. Rooms in the front have been redecorated and are now passably pretty. You certainly won't fall in love with this place, but it's clean, brightly painted and efficiently run. Beware of the beach tag – it's actually on a busy road.

Cofresí Beach Hotel (☎ 787-254-3000; www.cofresibeach.com; 57 Calle Muñoz Rivera; apt $89-219; 🕭) OK, so it's not exactly a hotel, rather it's a three-story building with one-, two- and three-bedroom apartments for rent. Each unit is fully equipped, including a microwave and TV with VCR, and there's a limited maid service available by pre-arrangement. There's a view of the bay from the pool.

Wildflowers (☎ 787-851-1793; 13 Calle Muñoz Rivera; r $100-125; P X) An attractive Victorian-era house in the heart of Boquerón, Wildflowers feels like a homey B&B out of a small New England town. Doubling up as a gallery, both the cozy rooms and sleek communal areas display the work of deft local artists. There's no maid service or breakfast, but economically priced rooms can sleep up to four and there's shared use of a microwave and coffee machine with private refrigerators. Dark-wood floors and furnishings add a dash of 19th-century romance.

Eating

Shamar Bar-Restaurant & Hotel (☎ 787-851-0542; Calle José de Diego; lunch $2-7) Need a seat? Tough luck, the Shamar doesn't have any, unless you can locate one of its much-sought-after bar stools or are happy perching on the corner of the pool table while your partner cleans up. Right up against the water, this laid-back beach joint is where you come in your swimming gear to order anything and everything – as long as it's deep-fried. Try the empanadas or the tasty *surullitos* (fried cornmeal and cheese sticks) and come back in the evening when the action really kicks off (see p216).

Fish Net (☎ 787-859-6009; Calle José de Diego; mains $5-20) Boquerón is famous for its fish and this is as good a place as any to get it. In keeping with the image of the downbeat town center, there's nothing fancy about the decor here. But Boquerón has always been more about authenticity than architectural awards. Owner Roberto is the local Jamie Oliver and has been known to serve up a mean *pilones* (mashed plantain mixed with shrimps and salsa).

Pizzeria Lykken (☎ 787-851-6335; Calle José de Diego; pizza $8-15) Mimicking the main strip's vaguely Caribbean/bohemian air, the Lykken has myriad beads, jewelry and mobiles hanging from its wooden rafters. Its specialty is pizza, but you can get much more here, including potent cocktails.

Pika-Pika (☎ 787-851-2440; 224 Calle Estación; mains $12-24) A first-rate Mexican cantina located on Boquerón's back street, just a short block north of all the commerce on Calle José de Diego. Deep-dish burritos and tacos are savory and can be prepared vegetarian-style.

Galloway's Bar & Restaurant (☎ 787-254-3302; Calle José de Diego; dinner mains $12-24) 'Snowbirds Welcome' reads the sign out the front, but those four-seasoned spring-breakers from Minneapolis you've just spied sitting out on the waterfront deck aren't the only birds pecking at the food. Small black feathered creatures will make a beeline for any spare tasty morsels, so hold on to your seafood crab salad and freshly prepared octopus before it all ends up as birdfeed. Something of a local legend, Galloway's combines great seafood with a picturesque waterfront setting on Boquerón's rustic downtown strip. It's terrific for children, too.

Entertainment

The minute you hit the ground running in Boquerón you can tell from the shabby-chic bars and relaxed Caribbean ambience that this is a party town. Strangely, it is also one of the few towns on the island that puts a cap on serving alcohol – midnight on weekdays, 1am on weekends.

Shamar Bar-Restaurant & Hotel (☎ 787-851-0542; Calle José de Diego) Shirtless dudes down beers at the bar, reggaeton blasts out of the speakers set up in the street outside, and the pool table becomes a psychological battleground between well-known cue masters and wannabe hustlers; the Shamar is that kind of place – laid-back, cool and friendly on its own terms. People jams can occur at the bar during happy hour, but the street's a good refuge, as is the space out front which offers up a nightly show of awe-inspiring sunsets. Dress down, polish up on your Puerto Rican slang, and try not to look too geeky when you shimmy your hips to the live salsa.

Galloways Bar & Restaurant (☎ 787-254-3302; Calle José de Diego) All pretense of being a restaurant is dropped by 9pm on weekends, when a yuppie crowd shows up for live 1980s and '90s rock. There's live Spanish guitar music on Sundays.

Crash Boat Café (☎ 787-851-5003; Calle José de Diego; ☺ 9pm-3am) Wedged with its bows sticking out into the bay, the Crash Boat is – exactly as its name implies – shaped rather ingeniously like a crashed boat. The bar is in the bows and sports an authentic ship's wheel along with some deftly sculpted male torsos (minus heads). Behind is a stage where live music entertains a mixed bag of gay and straight revelers with techno, house and reggaeton music. Trendy without being trashy, this is quite the place for a raucous late-night beer or six.

Getting There & Away

The easiest way to get to Boquerón by público is via the town of Cabo Rojo (El Pueblo). From April to August, it's easy to find one for about $2. From El Pueblo, you can also catch a van to Mayagüez ($4, 40 minutes), Ponce ($7, two hours) or San Germán ($5, 20 minutes).

If you're driving from El Pueblo or Mayagüez, follow Hwy 100 south to Hwy 101 and turn right (west). Driving from San Germán, it's a straight shot west on Hwy 101 south of Lajas.

PUERTO REAL

Another coastal village that is part of the Cabo Rojo municipality, Puerto Real lies about 4 miles north of Boquerón (follow Hwy 307 north and then head west on Hwy 308) and is frequently referred to as 'the biggest fishing port on the west coast.' That's not saying much on an island where fishing brings in less than 1% of the GNP, but Puerto Real is starting to look a bit more prosperous with extra yachts at the docks these days.

Water-sports enthusiasts should not overlook this port. The local marina operator offers first-rate diving trips, and whale-watching, as well as boat safaris out to the marine sanctuary of Isla Mona, 50 miles offshore.

Captain Bill Casperson, who you will find at **Driftwood Charters** (☎ 787-323-8682), can take you on half-day snorkeling trips, two-tank dives from a 46ft dive boat and whale-watching trips; call for prices.

You can access Puerto Real via público from the station on the eastern fringe of Cabo Rojo (El Pueblo). The trip costs $2. These vans don't leave in a timely fashion, so don't depend on them if you are planning to make a fixed departure time for a diving or nautical excursion.

PLAYA DE JOYUDA

Acting as a kind of alternative Boquerón, Joyuda is famous for its cheap seafood restaurants and known island-wide as the Milla de Oro del Buen Comer (Gourmet Golden Mile). More than 35 family-owned eating establishments specializing in oysters, crab and shrimp have popped up in recent decades along a 3-mile stretch of Hwy 102. They abut a scrubby shoreline of sand and dirt that has suffered after years of coastal erosion. Problems with erosion in 2006 led to the island's temporary closure while local biologists replanted the coastal areas with *Mangle rojo* (red mangrove).

While Joyuda isn't a standard beach haven, there are plenty of accommodation options in this sprawling west-coast outpost, and with a couple of decent sailing/dive operators and a nearby nature reserve, there's enough outdoor adventures to work up an appetite for an evening of shellfish-restaurant-hopping. Just offshore, the tiny Isla de Ratones has a white sandy beach and is great for snorkeling.

Sights & Activities

The heart of the 300-acre **Reserva Natural Laguna de Joyuda** is a saltwater lagoon a mile long and a half-mile wide, with a depth that rarely exceeds 4ft. The sanctuary is of great importance to waterfowl and other migratory birds that come here to prey on more than 40 species of fish. Humans come here for the same reason.

The reserve is also home to another of Puerto Rico's famous bioluminescent bodies of water, which is like its famous cousins in La Parguera and Vieques but free of commercial tourism. After dark, micro-organisms give the dark water a green glow. Travelers with access to a kayak can launch a nighttime exploration of the lagoon; watch for the access road off Hwy 102 near Parador Perichi's.

For trips or tours around the area on a 33ft lobster boat, try **Tourmarine Adventures** (☎ 787-375-2625; www.tourmarinepr.com; Rte 102 Km 14.1). If you've got a big enough group (10 or more people), the owner will arrange trips to Isla Mona for approximately $150 per person. There are also snorkeling trips offered around the nearby cliffs ($40 without equipment), deep-sea fishing in the Pasaje de la Mona ($375 per half-day charter) and diving off Isla Desecheo ($75 per person). The owner also has a handful of apartments for rent.

Sleeping

Hotel Costa de Oro Inn (☎ 787-851-5010; Rte 102 Km 14.7; r $50-85; 🏊) A tiny pool and spotless rooms make this little guesthouse a great deal. There are no big luxuries on the property, but you'll be very comfortable.

Joyuda Plaza (☎ 787-851-8800; Hwy 102 Km 14.7; r $65-125; P 🍴 🏊) If you're a sucker for luxury then you shouldn't really be staying in Joyuda in the first place, though this 55-room hotel on the famous seafood strip does the job in terms of facilities and friendliness. There are TVs, private room phones, two swimming pools, corporate meeting facilities and some of the best fish restaurants in Puerto Rico a mere rod and line's length from the front door.

Parador Joyuda Beach (☎ 787-851-5650; Hwy 102 Km 11.7; r $70-125; P 🍴 🏊) Further up the road from Parador Perichi's and the Joyuda Plaza, this hotel is actually *on* a narrow strand of beach (as opposed to the other hotels that abut a road and a muddy shoreline). It's not exactly Boquerón, but the snorkeling right offshore is OK, as long as the wind stays southerly. The hotel has a restaurant, a swimming pool and 41 standard rooms with those ubiquitous flowery bedspreads. Arrive expecting a tropical-flavored motel and you shouldn't be disappointed.

Parador Perichi's (☎ 787-435-7197; Rte 102 Km 14.3; r $75-139; P 🍴 🏊) Close to Joyuda Plaza and across the road from the ocean (but no beach), Perichi's is high-end Joyuda style (which is a bit of an oxymoron). More popular with Puerto Ricans than Americans, it's definitely seen better days, although the 41 rooms have air-con, there's a large pool downstairs and the on-site restaurant carries a Mesón Gastronómico tag.

Eating

Joyuda is a great place for a bit of culinary exploration. Park your car or bike, stroll up and down the strip a few times and see where your nose leads you. For informal dining, locals swear by El Bohio, Raito and Vista Bahía. Others champion El Gato Negro. You might end up in all or none of these, sampling lobster, *mofongo* (mashed plantains), oysters or crab. Joyuda's restaurants aren't always fancy in terms of decor, but the food is legendary – and for good reason. If you're really short on time the following two places are tried and proven.

Island View (☎ 787-851-9264; Hwy 102 Km 13.7; dishes $7-21; 🕑 lunch & dinner Thu-Tue) Great views of the few small cays that dot the water off the coast and big steaming dishes of seafood specialties, such as rice and crab, have made Island View very popular.

Tino's (☎ 787-851-2976; Hwy 102 Km 13.6; dishes $10-25; 🕑 lunch & dinner Wed-Sun) If you want a really nice meal – with real silverware and paper plates that don't bend under their load – then Tino's is your best bet in Joyuda. It's not got the pretty views, but it does have the tourist office's stamp of approval as a Méson Gastronómico.

Getting There & Away

Joyuda isn't on a regular público route, but you can drive here easily enough from either Mayagüez or Cabo Rojo on Rte 102. Alternatively, take a taxi or hire a bike from The Wheel Shop in Cabo Rojo (p212).

SAN GERMÁN

pop 37,700

Puerto Rico's second-oldest city (after San Juan), San Germán is also one of its best preserved. Founded in 1511 near present-day Mayagüez on the orders of Juan Ponce

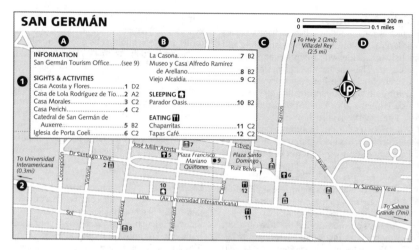

SAN GERMÁN

INFORMATION		
San Germán Tourism Office.......(see 9)		
SIGHTS & ACTIVITIES		
Casa Acosta y Flores....................1 D2		
Casa de Lola Rodríguez de Tío....2 A2		
Casa Morales.............................3 C2		
Casa Perichi.............................4 C2		
Catedral de San Germán de		
Auxerre.............................5 B2		
Iglesia de Porta Coeli...............6 C2		
La Casona..............................7 B2		
Museo y Casa Alfredo Ramírez		
de Arellano........................8 B2		
Viejo Alcaldía.........................9 C2		
SLEEPING		
Parador Oasis.........................10 B2		
EATING		
Chaparritas............................11 C2		
Tapas Café.............................12 C2		

To Hwy 2 (2mi);
Villa del Rey
(2.5 mi)

To Universidad
Interamericana
(0.3mi)

To Sabana
Grande (7mi)

de León, the original coastal settlement was moved twice in its early life to escape the unwelcome attention of plundering French corsairs. The current town, which lies about 10 miles inland from the Cabo Rojo coast, was established in 1573 and once administered a municipality that encompassed the whole western half of the island. Downsizing itself over the ensuing four centuries, contemporary San Germán (named for Germaine de Foix, the second wife of Spain's King Ferdinand) is far more unassuming than the colonial capital of yore, although the historical buildings – some of which date from the 17th century – retain a regal grandiosity.

Despite its rich architectural heritage and lofty listing on the National Register of Historic Places, San Germán is largely ignored by its modern inhabitants. Few tourists make it this far either. As a result, the classic four-square-block colonial center – laid out in an unusual irregular pattern – is a veritable ghost town after dark as busy locals head for out-of-town shopping malls and time-poor travelers whiz past on their way to Boquerón and the beaches. The city's one downtown hotel sports cobwebs, few of the numerous historic buildings are open for public viewing, and the uninspiring nightlife is confined to just one – admittedly good – tapas restaurant.

Fortuitously, San Germán's semi-abandonment lends it an air of authenticity. It is also one of the few settlements in Puerto Rico where the central city core hasn't been demeaned by thoughtless development.

Information

The government recently changed the name of Calle Luna to Av Universidad Interamericana; nobody uses it, however, so addresses in this book still refer to Calle Luna.

San Germán Tourism Office (☎ 787-892-3790; Viejo Alcaldía, Plaza Francisco Mariano Quiñones; ☎ 8am-4pm) This office also runs the San Germán trolley bus around the town's main sights, but schedules are erratic; phone ahead.

Sights
IGLESIA DE PORTA COELI

This small church might not look much, but it is actually one of the oldest surviving ecclesial buildings in the Americas. Originally constructed between 1606 and 1607 on the orders of Queen Isabella of Spain, it once served as the chapel for a Dominican monastery that stood on this site until the 1860s. The current structure dates from a 1692 renovation and despite its architectural simplicity it retains a dramatic position at the crown of a long, steep flight of steps overlooking Plaza Santo Domingo. The Porta Coeli ('Heaven's Gate' in Latin) has an interior with ausubo pillars and roof beams, and a ceiling made from palm wood, which is typical of construction in Puerto Rico during the 17th and 18th centuries. Inside, a small **museum** (☎ 787-892-5845; Plaza Santo Domingo; admission $1; ☒ 8:30am-4:30pm Wed-Sun) displays statues of the black Virgin of Montserrat, folksy carvings of Christ imported from the early days of San Juan, choral books dating back 300 years and other curios.

CATEDRAL DE SAN GERMÁN DE AUXERRE

San Germán's **cathedral** (☎ 787-892-1027; ⊗ 8-11:30am & 1-3pm Mon-Fri, 8-11am Sat, mass 7am & 7:30pm Mon-Sat, 7am, 8:30am, 10am & 7:30pm Sun) is named for the town's patron saint and is noticeably grander than the diminutive Porta Coeli. Facing Plaza Francisco Mariano Quiñones, it dates back to 1739, but major restorations and expansions over the years (especially in the 19th century) have created a mélange of architectural styles, including colonial, neo-classical and baroque elements. This is an active parish; if you visit for a Saturday or Sunday service, take note of the crystal chandelier that helps to light the main nave and the trompe l'oeil fresco.

CASA PERICHI

Situated on the main drag, this **house** (94 Luna) is a 1920s estate that's been on the National Register of Historic Places since 1986. Its eclectic architectural style featuring wraparound balconies and decorative wood trim has been called 'Puerto Rican ornamental artisan.' It's not currently open for public viewing.

CASA MORALES

Highlighting the eclecticism and historical diversity of San Germán's architecture this Victorian-era **house** (38 Ramos) was built soon after the American occupation in 1898. With its gables, porches and roof turrets, it is redolent of a Queen Anne–style structure from the plush neighborhood of a US mainland city. It also exemplifies how quickly American aesthetics infiltrated the island. It is a private home and not open to the public.

CASA ACOSTA Y FLORES

Built in a crisscross of styles, this **house** (70 Dr Santiago Veve), dating from 1917, exhibits elements of criollo, Victorian and art-nouveau architecture. Painted in cream and white with intricately decorated iron railing it resembles a beautifully crafted wedding cake. The house is a private residence, but can be admired from the outside.

VIEJO ALCALDÍA

The old city hall, which acts as a dividing line between the city's two central squares, is a classic example of a 19th-century colonial municipal building with its stately facade and cool inner courtyard. The building currently serves as a police station and the headquarters for San Germán's rather low-key tourist office (opposite).

LA CASONA

The beguiling yellow and blue Spanish-colonial building that dominates the north side of Plaza Francisco Mariano Quiñones is

---

DETOUR: BOSQUE ESTATAL DE SUSÚA

Although geographically Susúa lies closer to the south coast than the west, locals in San Germán have long considered it their backyard and have subsequently claimed unofficial 'ownership' rights. Juxtaposed between the dry coastal flats and the humid mountain foothills of the Cordillera Central, the forest's diminutive 3300 acres is certainly no Yellowstone; indeed, it's only marginally bigger than Puerto Rico's largest resort, the gargantuan Palmas del Mar on the east coast.

But what it lacks in acres it makes up for in peaceful solitude. Well off the main tourist trails and notoriously difficult to find, Susúa is invariably deserted year-round – save for the odd binocular-wielding ornithologist (the forest boasts 44 species of bird) and in-the-know mountain biker.

To get here, drive east out of Sabana Grande on Rte 368 to Km 2.1. Turn left and keep going until you arrive at the shack for the **Departamento de Recursos Naturales y Ambientales** (DRNA; Department of Natural Resources & Environment; ☎ 787-721-5495; admission free; ⊗ 7am-3:30pm Mon-Fri, 9am-5pm Sat & Sun). There's not much in the way of amenities at the entrance – just a few picnic tables, a toilet, a scattering of fire pits and some campsites (though you'd be wise to check on availability/hours before arrival; camping per tent $4).

The hiking trails that leave from the entrance are – surprise, surprise – poorly marked and can be quite hard to find. Speak to a ranger and they should be able to furnish you with a hand-drawn, worryingly simplistic map that will clarify things momentarily. For mountain bikers, there's a very challenging 6.3-mile trail that incorporates river crossings and a technical ravine reverently called La Pared (The Wall). The nearest bike rental is in the town of Cabo Rojo (see p212).

La Casona (cnr José Julián Acosta & De la Cruz), a mid-19th-century townhouse that was once the meeting place for an elite San Germán social group known as the Círculo de Recreo. In more recent times it has served as a cultural center and a shop. At the time of writing it was undergoing refurbishments.

CASA DE LOLA RODRÍGUEZ DE TIÓ

Built in 1843 in a neoclassical criollo style and said to be an excellent example of local 17th-century domestic architecture, this **house** (☎ 787-892-3500; 13 Dr Santiago Veve) is said to be the most continually occupied residence in the town. Its most famous resident was a 19th-century poet and patriot named Lola Rodríguez de Tió, who was exiled in the 1860s for her revolutionary activities. Lola's mother was a descendant of Ponce de León. The house is supposed to act as a museum, but is often closed. Phone ahead.

MUSEO Y CASA ALFREDO RAMÍREZ DE ARELLANO

Another eclectic house, built in 1903, this building is home to the local art and history **museum** (☎ 787-892-8870; 7 Esperanza; admission free; 🕓 10am-3pm Wed-Sun). Rooms are dedicated to different subjects, such as Taíno artifacts, religious curios like an old confessional booth, and colonial furniture.

UNIVERSIDAD INTERAMERICANA

Founded in 1912, this **university** (☎ 787-892-3090; Luna) is now the largest private facility of its kind in the Western hemisphere. The 267-acre campus just west of San Germán is probably the most attractive college setting in Puerto Rico and it draws about 6000 students from all corners of the globe. There are branch campuses in San Juan, Arecibo, Barranquitas, Bayamón, Fajardo, Guayama and Ponce, and tens of thousands of students work toward degrees in both its Spanish and English programs.

Festivals & Events

If you're here for the **Sugar Harvest Festival** (☎ 787-892-5574), held late in April, you'll be able to drink huge quantities of rum (which is distilled from sugarcane) while learning about the farming process.

Sleeping

Parador Oasis (☎ 787-892-1175, 800-942-8086; 72 Luna; r $75; P 🕸 🖥 🏊) If you wanted luxury, you've come to the right place – the catch is, you're 20 years too late. Hidden under the cobwebs of the lackluster modern-day Oasis is a once grand dame of Puerto Rican paradores. Down on its luck and seemingly bereft of guests, the place today has the air of Miss Havisham's house in Charles Dickens' *Great Expectations*, though the Italianate pool still glistens invitingly and the staff try hard to plug the gaps (of which there are many). Framed testimonies on the wall highlight favorable reviews from years past; the most recent dates from 1984. Get the drift?

Villa del Rey (☎ 787-642-2627; www.villadelrey .net; Rte 361 Km 0.8; s $85-110; P 🕸 🏊) Your only alternative to the antiquated Oasis is this family-run country inn just north of town. A sturdy midrange option, it has big rooms, suites with kitchenettes, and an unhurried west-coast ambience (you may have to holler to raise the receptionist). Certainly fit for the kids – though perhaps not for a king (*rey*).

Eating

Tapas Café (☎ 787-264-0610; 48 Dr Santiago Veve; tapas $4-11; 🕓 dinner Wed-Fri, lunch & dinner Sat & Sun) Central San Germán has a perplexing dearth of decent restaurants so if you're staying in town for more than one day you'll probably end up here at least twice. Thankfully both the food and atmosphere are great, and on a busy night with a little bit of imagination you can picture yourself in the Triana district of Seville. Flamenco and bullfighting paraphernalia adorn the walls, while the plates are decorated with delicious fare such as *albondigas* (meatballs), *queso manchego* (Manchego cheese), *tortilla española* (Spanish omelette) and *jamon serrano* (cured Spanish ham).

Chaparritas (☎ 787-892-1078; 171 Luna; mains $10-15; 🕓 Wed-Sun) Vegetarians might have a hard time finding something to eat here, because Chaparritas puts meat on everything and cooks with a lot of lard, but the food is undeniably hot and tasty when it comes to the table. It's the usual Mexican burritos, tacos and enchiladas, but presented with flair.

Getting There & Away

San Germán enjoys frequent público services to and from Ponce ($6, 90 minutes) or Mayagüez ($4, 45 minutes). It lies just south of the Hwy 2 expressway, so if you are driving here from the west coast, follow Hwy 102 from the town of Cabo Rojo (El Pueblo).

MAYAGÜEZ
pop 98,400

Ah…Mayagüez, the Sultan of the West, the commonwealth's underrated and slightly disheveled dock town that has always had to play third fiddle to San Juan and Ponce. But savvy travelers should take note. Mayagüez is undergoing a dramatic rebirth. Positive signs are everywhere. Examine the deftly renovated cathedral and adjoining central plaza (Plaza Colón). Mull over the rebranding of Puerto Rico's west coast as the 'Porta del Sol' with Mayagüez as its HQ. Consider the prospect of

Mayagüez hosting the 2010 Central American and Caribbean Games.

Founded in 1760 by émigrés from the Canary Islands, Mayagüez had an inauspicious early history considering its current size and importance. The emerging economy was based on fruit production and agriculture, and even today the city remains noted for the sweetness of its mangos. In the mid-19th century Mayagüez developed a contrarian nature and sheltered numerous revolutionary thinkers including Ramón Emeterio Betances, architect of the abortive Grito de Lares (p35). Disaster struck in 1918 when an earthquake measuring 7.6 on the Richter scale all but destroyed the central business district, but the city rose from the rubble.

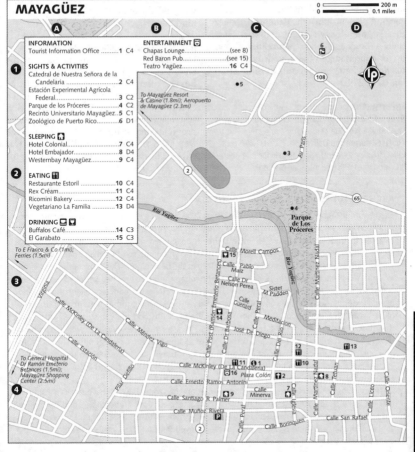

Mayagüez today boasts a vibrant university (specializing in sciences), numerous historic buildings, a couple of parks and one of the most salubrious central plazas on the island. Exciting local taste buds, the settlement has also been heralded for its contributions to Puerto Rican gastronomy and drinking. Two 19th-century bakeries concoct a locally famous delicacy known as *brazo gitano* (gypsy's arm; a jam sponge cake presented in the style of a Swiss roll). Additionally, there's a factory producing Medalla beer, a popular ice-cream store and a dive bar that invented an insanely sweet rum-and-wine cocktail known as Sangría de Fido.

Little visited by tourists who veer northwest to Rincón or south toward Cabo Rojo, Mayagüez has enough distractions to fill a long afternoon (including Puerto Rico's only zoo and planetarium), the delightful Yagüez theater and a lively student nightlife. Then there's the congenial *mayagüezians*, always up for a spontaneous fiesta, such as **Cinco Días con Nuestro Tierra**, an agricultural-industrial fair (see p279).

Information

General Hospital Dr Ramón Emeterio Betances (☎ 787-735-8001; Rte 2 Km 157)

Tourist Information Office (☎ 787-833-1650; cnr Calles McKinley & Peral; 8am-4pm) In the main square, it's well stocked with local maps and has helpful staff.

Sights

CATEDRAL DE NUESTRA SEÑORA DE LA CANDELARIA

Consecrated in 1760, Mayagüez' original Catholic church was replaced by the current model in 1836.

The cathedral suffered many blows over the subsequent 100 years, culminating in the 1918 earthquake which destroyed its ceiling, and a lightning bolt that toppled one of its bell towers. Ambitious renovation plans were drawn up by architect Luis Perocier in 1922, but due to lack of funds they were never truly realized.

The full refurbishment wasn't actually completed until 2004. The cathedral now sparkles afresh and survives as one of Puerto Rico's most evocative ecclesial monuments with gilded scenes from the life of Christ behind the altar.

RECINTO UNIVERSITARIO MAYAGÜEZ

Over 12,000 students are enrolled at this **university** (RUM; ☎ 787-832-4040; 259 Post) in a host of disciplines. Over the years, RUM has become the premier math and science campus of the University of Puerto Rico system and boasts internationally respected programs in agriculture and engineering, as well as in the physical and biological sciences. The campus lies just out of town off Calle Post (Hwy 2).

ARCHITECTURAL ICONS: TEATRO YAGÜEZ

The beautiful **Teatro Yagüez** (☎ 787-834-0523; cnr Calles McKinley & Dr Barbosa) would be an architectural icon in any European capital, let alone quiescent Mayagüez, a city that sometimes struggles to assert its understated cultural identity. Dubbed the 'Cathedral of Sonorous Art' by enamored locals, the building was the brainchild of Francisco Maymón, the son of Italian immigrants who was an early pioneer of silent movies in Puerto Rico at the beginning of the 20th century. Maymón inaugurated his first theater in 1909, an opulent neobaroque structure that was filled with Italian ceilings and tiles imported from Spain. Hosting opera, orchestral concerts, silent movies and plays, it rapidly became the font of polite society in the island's proud western city. But the glory wasn't to last. Although the Yagüez miraculously withstood the catastrophic earthquake that rocked Mayagüez in 1918, the theater faced disaster the following year when it burned down in a mysterious fire that claimed the lives of 150 people. After several bitter lawsuits with potential land-grabbers, Maymón finally won the right to rebuild the Yagüez on its original site in the early 1920s. The building that rose from the ashes was designed by the brilliant architect Sabás Honoré and was every bit as opulent as its predecessor.

Today, sparkling after a recent $4-million restoration, the Yagüez is a national historic monument that is widely feted by architectural buffs for its pilasters, cornices, French doors and decorative red-and-black dome. In Mayagüez' cultural life it continues to act as an important venue for concerts, drama, expositions and – yes – those beloved Puerto Rican beauty pageants.

ESTACIÓN EXPERIMENTAL AGRÍCOLA FEDERAL

Strolling is an attraction at both the **Estación Experimental Agrícola Federal** (☎ 787-831-3435; Av Paris; admission free; 🕑 7am-4pm Mon-Fri), the tropical agricultural research station of the US Department of Agriculture, and in the adjacent city park known as **Parque de los Próceres** (Patriots' Park; 🕑 dawn-dusk). These grounds lie just southeast of the RUM campus. At the agricultural station you will see plantations of yams, plantains, bananas, cassavas and other tropical 'cash crops' as researchers evaluate new hybrids and species introduced to the island (including a cinnamon tree from Sri Lanka). The gardens have one of the largest collections of tropical plants in the world known to have beneficial effects on human health. The Parque de los Próceres, on the south side of Hwy 65, has more verdant walkways.

ZOOLÓGICO DE PUERTO RICO

The only serious **zoo** (☎ 787-834-6330; Bario Miradero, Hwy 108 Interior; admission $6; 🕑 8:30am-4pm Wed-Sun) in Puerto Rico is just to the northeast of the university, off Hwy 108, in the same neighborhood as the agricultural research station and city park. Here you can see some 300 species of reptiles, birds, amphibians and mammals moving around in habitats somewhat similar to what they would have in the wild. Refurbished a couple of years ago, the zoo's still not exactly on the cutting edge, but it has done a lot to get away from steel cages.

Sleeping

Hotel Colonial (☎ 787-833-2150; www.hotelcolonial.com; 14 Calle Iglesia; s/d incl breakfast $39/59; P ❄ 💻) A former convent, the Colonial looks rather picturesque from the outside. Upstairs, however, the 29 rooms hold slightly dustier secrets. The thing to remember is that this place is cheap (possibly the cheapest on the island), local (Mayagüez isn't exactly a tourist town) and exhibits few luxury pretensions. Keep this in mind when you're suffering the basic breakfast, up-and-down water pressure and hard, plastic beds, and you should be just fine.

Hotel Embajador (☎ 787-833-3340; 111 Calle Ernesto Ramos Antonini; r $45-95; P ❄) Wake up in one of these rooms and you'll swear you've been transported back to 1972 – a tatty, sepia-toned version of 1972, that is. In dire need of a refurb, the Embajador, despite its shortcomings, is friendly and rather handily placed a few blocks west of the central Plaza Colón. It also boasts an interesting literary history. A number of years ago, when the famous Caribbean poet Derek Walcott visited RUM for a reading, the English faculty put him up at the Embajador and he allegedly composed some of *Omeros* here, the work that won him the Nobel Prize in 1992. If the poet in you is not quite up to emulating Walcott, try retiring to the new downstairs Chapas Lounge (p224), which has lent the establishment a new sophistication.

Westernbay Mayagüez (☎ 787-834-0303; www.westernbaymayaguez.com; 9 Calle Santiago R Palmer; r $75-85; P ❄ 💻 🏊) This six-story '70s high-rise one block from the main square was recently revamped and renamed, though it essentially remains a parador. There's nothing knockout about the rooms, but they're comfortable enough if you like small. Downstairs there is the standard pool and fountain (par for the course in Puerto Rico), and a reasonable Italian-themed restaurant. The hotel's probably designed more for the business traveler than the tourist, but you can't argue about the price.

Mayagüez Resort & Casino (☎ 787-831-7575; www.mayaguezresort.com; Rte 104 Km 0.3; r $160-325; P ❄ 💻 🏊) Just when you thought the resort frenzy had gone into hibernation, up springs another hotel-and-casino combo. Located off Hwy 2 north of town, this 140-unit property – with tennis courts, pool and casino – will be strangely familiar to travelers who have frequented the hotels of Isla Verde or the megaresorts that populate Fajardo and the east coast. Surprisingly, it is not on the water, but on 20 acres of tropical gardens – actually an adjunct to the nearby agricultural research station.

Eating

Rex Cream (Calle Méndez Vigo; dishes $1-3) Rex is a small Puerto Rican ice-cream chain that was founded in Mayagüez in the 1960s by Chinese immigrants who came to the island via Costa Rica. This signature store near the central plaza is still something of a local tradition and gets full, particularly on public holidays. Among the numerous weird and wonderful flavors you can sample are corn sherbet and tamarind.

Ricomini Bakery (☎ 787-832-0565; 101 Calle Méndez Vigo; dishes $2-8; ☽ 5am-1am) The Ricomini bakery and deli has been on this corner for well over a century and is still packing in the punters. Business deals are made here, relationships forged (and broken), and gossip boisterously exchanged. Ricomini's is always happy to serve the odd stray traveler and you can roll up for steaming coffee, scrambled eggs or a slice of the famous *brazo gitano*. The decor is open and clean and the atmosphere local.

Vegetariano La Familia (☎ 787-833-7571; José de Diego 151; mains $5-12; **V**) Bankers, teachers, students, office workers and itinerant travelers; they all line up here at another Mayagüez classic where the portions are huge, the tastes are rustic and the price is…well…peanuts. The lunch buffet on its own is a sight to behold – tofu dishes and salads stretching across a big table. Then there are the rice dishes, the pasta, the beans and the strangely tasty vegan lasagna. Even incurable carnivores have been known to lick their lips.

ourpick **E Franco & Co** (☎ 787-832-0070; www .brazogitano.com, in Spanish; 3 Manuel Pirallo; dishes $7-16) Most of Puerto Rico's culinary legends are less than 20 years old, but this salt-of-the-earth grocery-store-cum-café has been here for over a century and a half and is still drawing in punters from as far away as San Juan for a monthly stock up. Cocooned in the waterfront warehouse district, Franco's is an upmarket place with tables scattered around a glass-topped deli counter in the style of an old English tearoom. Order your lunch from a set menu and you'll receive a complimentary *brazo gitano* that goes down well with a cup of fine Puerto Rican coffee. Stocked with assorted condiments, fresh baked goods and opulent hampers, the store affords plenty of people-watching opportunities as shoppers from around the island arrive to pick up their favorite treats.

Restaurante Estoril (☎ 787-834-2288; cnr Calles Méndez Vigo & Iglesia; mains $12-20) Across the street from Ricomini Bakery, Estoril is known for its romantic setting and authentic Portuguese food. It's got murmuring fountains on the patio, festive plates on the walls and a stellar lunch buffet.

Entertainment

For entertainment and upscale atmosphere, head to the Mayagüez Resort & Casino (p223).

Otherwise, stay around town where a tight knot of student bars at the end of Calle Post has created a gregarious nighttime buzz.

Red Baron Pub (☎ 787-265-5770; 102 Calle Post; cover with live band $6; ☽ 9pm-2am) The dance club above El Garabato, Red Baron often has a DJ spinning reggaeton, rap, hip-hop and Spanish rock. Lots of students get tanked up downstairs and then come up to work the dance floor until the small hours. Cash only.

El Garabato (☎ 787-834-2524; 102 Calle Post; ☽ 1pm-2am) In the same building as Red Baron but on the 1st floor, El Garabato is more of a typical pub than a dance hall. Here students swing by for a quick one between classes or stop to play dominoes with the regulars. Happy-hour prices are laughably low – $2 for a mixed drink and $1 for a beer.

Buffalos Café (☎ 787-265-1395; 252 Calle Post; ☽ 11am-midnight) Another stop on the Calle Post crawl is this amiable place where you can munch on hot wings, sip on cold beer and dance salsa with people who know all the moves.

Chapas Lounge (☎ 787-834-0577; 111 Calle Ernesto Ramos Antonini; ☽ 11am-11pm Tue-Sat) On the ground floor of the faded 1970s Hotel Embajador (p223) is a rather plush restaurant and cocktail lounge that has developed into something of a hotspot in the city's nightlife. Come for a filet mignon and stick around for a few mojitos afterwards.

Getting There & Away

AIR

The Aeropuerto de Mayagüez is about 3 miles north of town, just off Hwy 2. **Cape Air** (☎ 800-352-0714) currently has several flights daily to and from San Juan ($98 one-way). There are also direct flights to the towns of St Thomas and St Croix ($335 one-way) in the US Virgin Islands.

CAR & MOTORCYCLE

Hwy 2, part of the island's nominal ring road, brings you to town from the north or south. While this is a four-lane road, it is plagued by traffic lights. Hwy 105 is the west end of the Ruta Panorámica, which leads from Mayagüez into the mountains and to Maricao.

FERRY

Mayagüez is Puerto Rico's gateway to the Dominican Republic, at least by sea. **Ferries**

Del Caribe (☎ 787-832-4800; www.ferriesdelcaribe.com, in Spanish), on the docks of Mayagüez north of the tuna canneries, offers the serious 'off-island' adventure across the Pasaje de la Mona. Its massive M/S *Caribbean Express* sails every other day across the Pasaje de la Mona for Santo Domingo in the Dominican Republic (a 12-hour trip). On board you will find a restaurant, cafeteria, bar, casino and disco, as well as conference rooms, private cabins, a sauna and a Jacuzzi. There is room for 250 cars along with 1125 passengers.

The ferry usually leaves Mayagüez at 8pm Monday, Wednesday and Friday, and Santo Domingo at 8pm Sunday, Tuesday and Thursday, arriving in the respective destinations at 8am the following morning.

One-way tickets start at $115 for a sleeping chair and $165 for a single cabin. Returns go from $165 for a chair to $250 for a cabin, though there are more deluxe options. If you buy a one-way ticket you must have an airplane ticket or some other proof of departure from the Dominican Republic. You pay extra for your car on a round-trip journey – up to $150. Reserve a day in advance, especially with a car, and show up two hours early.

PÚBLICO
The terminal is in Barrio Paris, about two blocks north of Plaza Colón. Públicos make the trip to west-coast beach towns such as Aguadilla and Rincón (each about an hour away), and the long trek to San Juan ($18 to $25, plan on four hours at least).

Getting Around
A few taxis usually show up at the airport when the flights arrive from San Juan; if none are there, or if you need to get to the airport, call **White Taxi** (☎ 787-832-1115). The one-way fare to town is about $8.

To rent a car you will find the following vendors at the airport or in Mayagüez Shopping Center, 2.5 miles south of the town on Hwy 2.
Avis (☎ 787-833-7070)
Budget (☎ 787-831-4570)
Hertz (☎ 787-832-3314)

RINCÓN
pop 14,300
You'll know you've arrived in Rincón when you pass the group of sun-grizzled gringos cruising west in their rusty 1972 Volkswagen Beetle with a pile of surfboards attached to the roof. Shoehorned far out in the island's most psychedelic corner, Rincón is Puerto Rico at its most unguarded, a place where the sunsets shimmer scarlet and the waiters are more likely to call you 'dude' than 'sir.' For numerous Californian dreamers this is where the short-lived summer of love ended up. Arriving for the Surfing World Championships in 1968, many never went home. Hence Rincón became a haven for draft-dodgers, alternative lifestylers, back-to-the-landers and people more interested in catching the perfect wave than bagging $100,000 a year in a Chicago garden suburb.

Rincón's waves are often close to perfect. Breaking anywhere from 2ft to 25ft, the names are chillingly evocative: Domes, Indicators, Spanish Wall and Dogman's. The crème de la crème is Tres Palmas, a white-tipped monster that is often dubbed the 'temple' of big wave surfing in the Caribbean.

Though Rincón is crawling with American expats (many of them residents), the tourist/local divide is more seamless and less exclusive than in the resorts out east. However, with a new, more affluent surfing generation demanding a higher quality of living than their 'turn off, tune in, drop out' parents, Rincón has increasingly embraced car culture and witnessed a noticeable expansion in the boutique hotel market. Indeed, these days the dudes with the boards are more likely to be lawyers than high school dropouts.

History
Rincón traces its history to the 16th century and a few low-key sugarcane plantations. And while many people believe it gets its name from the Spanish word *rincón* (corner) because of its shape, the municipality is actually named after one of the area's original planters, Don Gonzalo Rincón. For most of its history, the town survived on cane farming and cattle raising.

Things changed when the World Surfing Championships arrived in 1968. Glossy images of Rincón were plastered all over international magazines and TV – and the word was out. Every year since then has seen successive generations of wave riders make the pilgrimage. And while they pursued an endless summer, they began to invest in the community, building their own restaurants, guesthouses and bars.

RINCÓN & AROUND

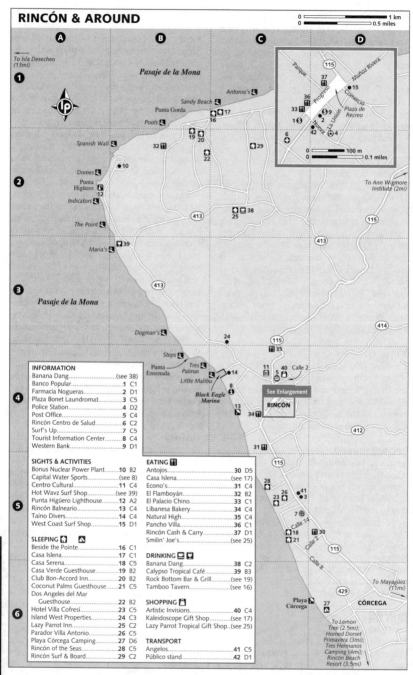

INFORMATION

Banana Dang............................(see 38)	
Banco Popular.............................**1** C1	
Farmacia Nogueras.....................**2** D1	
Plaza Bonet Laundromat..............**3** C5	
Police Station...............................**4** D2	
Post Office...................................**5** C4	
Rincón Centro de Salud...............**6** C2	
Surf's Up.....................................**7** C5	
Tourist Information Center...........**8** C4	
Western Bank..............................**9** D1	

SIGHTS & ACTIVITIES

Bonus Nuclear Power Plant......**10** B2	
Capital Water Sports.................(see 8)	
Centro Cultural.........................**11** C4	
Hot Wavz Surf Shop................(see 39)	
Punta Higüero Lighthouse.........**12** A2	
Rincón Balneario......................**13** C4	
Taíno Divers.............................**14** C4	
West Coast Surf Shop...............**15** D1	

SLEEPING

Beside the Pointe......................**16** C1	
Casa Islena...............................**17** C1	
Casa Serena..............................**18** C5	
Casa Verde Guesthouse.............**19** B2	
Club Bon-Accord Inn.................**20** B2	
Coconut Palms Guesthouse.......**21** C5	
Dos Angeles del Mar	
Guesthouse...........................**22** B2	
Hotel Villa Cofresí....................**23** C5	
Island West Properties..............**24** C5	
Lazy Parrot Inn.........................**25** C5	
Parador Villa Antonio................**26** C5	
Playa Córcega Camping.............**27** D6	
Rincón of the Seas....................**28** C5	
Rincón Surf & Board..................**29** C2	

EATING

Antojos....................................**30** D5	
Casa Islena............................(see 17)	
Econo's....................................**31** C4	
El Flamboyán...........................**32** B2	
El Palacio Chino.......................**33** C1	
Libanesa Bakery.......................**34** C4	
Natural High.............................**35** C4	
Pancho Villa.............................**36** C1	
Rincón Cash & Carry.................**37** D1	
Smilin' Joe's...........................(see 25)	

DRINKING

Banana Dang............................**38** C2	
Calypso Tropical Café................**39** B3	
Rock Bottom Bar & Grill..........(see 19)	
Tamboo Tavern......................(see 16)	

SHOPPING

Artistic Invisions......................**40** C4	
Kaleidoscope Gift Shop...........(see 17)	
Lazy Parrot Tropical Gift Shop..(see 25)	

TRANSPORT

Angelos....................................**41** C5	
Público stand............................**42** D1	

WEST COAST

As the baby-boomer generation of surfers got older, they continued to harbor romantic images of Rincón. But when they traveled with their own children, they demanded better accommodations, slicker restaurants and a broader variety of activities – and the town responded. Today, you can rent distinctive vacation homes or stay in luxurious hotels. While the old-style bunkhouses are all but gone, imaginative and moderately priced guesthouses remain a staple in Rincón.

Orientation

The actual municipal center is only about four square blocks, encircling the Catholic church and the Presbyterian church that face each other across the small Plaza de Recreo. While this urban core has many essential services, most of the inns, restaurants and beach attractions lie north or south of the town.

The best swimming beaches are south of the village, as are many of the larger hotels. A number of different snorkeling and surfing sites lie off Hwy 413 along the west side of the peninsula as it runs north to the lighthouse and the side road to the Bonus nuclear power plant. Moving further north, Hwy 413 climbs into steep hills.

There is a strong representation of guesthouses and a few bar-restaurants in this area, especially on a loop of road that circles down to the north-facing beach and rejoins Hwy 413 a mile further to the northwest. The larger, plusher accommodations generally lie to the south of town along Hwy 429.

Many of the accommodations, restaurants and pubs listed later do not have street addresses per se; in these cases we offer descriptive addresses.

MAPS

The Tourism Association of Rincón puts out a great, amusing map, complete with site descriptions, cartoon drawings and essential phone numbers (it's completely not to scale). You can get one from your innkeeper. Sometimes you can get a map for free; sometimes it's $1.

Information

EMERGENCY

Police station (☎ 787-823-2020) In the south corner of the village off Nueva.

INTERNET ACCESS

Banana Dang (☎ 787-823-0963; Hwy 413 Km 4.1; per 30mins $3; ☺ 7am-7pm Mon & Wed-Sat, 9am-7pm Sun) Wi-fi and terminals available here.

Surf's Up (Hwy 115 Km 12; per 30mins $3; ☺ 6am-8:30pm) Internet, wi-fi, coffee and bagels.

LAUNDRY

Plaza Bonet Laundromat (☎ 787-823-3504; Hwy 115 Km 12.3) South of town. No washing service (ie DIY only). Wash/dry $1/$1.50.

MEDICAL SERVICES

Farmacia Nogueras (☎ 787-823-1704; 11 Muñoz Rivera) Downtown next to the Plaza de Recreo.

Rincón Centro de Salud (☎ 787-823-5171/2795/3120; 28 Muñoz Rivera) In town next to Paco's Grocery, this health center is a block south of Plaza de Recreo.

MONEY

Banco Popular (☺ 9am-2:30pm Mon-Fri, 9am-noon Sat) Downtown near Plaza de Recreo. Has an ATM.

Western Bank (☺ 9am-2:30pm Mon-Fri, 9am-noon Sat) Also downtown near Plaza de Recreo, with an ATM.

POST

Post office (☎ 787-823-2625; ☺ 7:30am-4:30pm Mon-Fri, 8:30am-noon Sat) A mile north of the Plaza de Recreo on Hwy 115.

TOURIST INFORMATION

Tourism Association of Rincón (☎ 888-237-2073; www.rincon.org) For a complete list of the area's offerings, check out the virtual office here. There are links to accommodation websites.

Tourist Information Center (☎ 787-823-5024; Sunset Bldg, Cambija St; ☺ 8am-4:30pm Mon-Fri) In the new Sunset Building adjacent to Rincón public beach.

Sights

PUNTA HIGÜERO LIGHTHOUSE

Nicknamed El Faro, the lighthouse dates from 1892 and rises almost 100ft above the terrain. It was restored in 1922 after being severely damaged by a tsunami set off by the devastating 1918 earthquake. The 26,000-candlepower light has been automated since 1933 and still helps ships navigate the Pasaje de la Mona.

The lighthouse park is a popular attraction in Rincón. There are picnic tables, the odd food kiosk and a small **museum** (admission free; ☺ 10am-2pm) inside the lighthouse building that displays artifacts from shipwrecks and relays anecdotes from the area's maritime history. The principal reason to come here, however, is for the view. Five great surf breaks are nearby, and sometimes, during the winter, humpback whales come within 100yd of the coast.

BONUS NUCLEAR POWER PLANT

To purists, Rincón and nuclear energy probably go together like Nixon and Brezhnev. But paradise is full of surprises. That telltale green dome that pokes out from behind the palm trees behind the Punta Higüero lighthouse isn't a Maharishi yoga retreat or a temple to expired surfers. Rather, it's a building that once housed the first nuclear-powered electrical generating facility in the Caribbean. Back in the days when the Beach Boys led the Surfin' Safari, the Boiling Nuclear Superheater Plant (known half-sarcastically by the acronym of Bonus) was a test facility that produced a minuscule 16,000kW of electricity in order to introduce Latin America to the benefits of nuclear power and to train visiting engineers.

The plant never functioned properly, however, and in its short life from 1960 to 1968 it allegedly contaminated employees and suffered a reactor failure. Finally, the US government closed the plant and at the time claimed to have decontaminated it.

For 20 years Bonus became a rusting relic of the nuclear age and a favorite venue for graffiti writers, who had everything from anti-nuke to pro-marijuana biases. The locals even named a surf break after it: Domes, one of Rincón's most consistent breaks. In the mid-1990s cooperation between the town and the electrical company brought about the reopening of the building and total decontamination of the site.

Now, with the building 'clean,' dollars have been spent to paint and polish everything as a museum. At the time of research the Museo Technológico Dr Modesto Iriarte Beachamp was due to open in 2008.

CENTRO CULTURAL

Contrary to popular opinion, Rincón's history didn't begin in 1968 with the World Surfing Championships. Proof lies in this tiny **museum** (Hwy 413 Km 0.3; admission free; ⊙ 9am-2pm Thu & Sat), which harbors articles salvaged from shipwrecks and testimonies on the area's social history. Like a lot of the municipal museums on the island, the Centro Cultural is open irregularly and is dependent on the state of the current municipal budget and volunteerism. Enquire first at the Tourist Information Center (p227); staff there should be able to enlighten you as to current opening times and/or the possibility of a private viewing.

Activities

SURFING

Downtown on the Plaza de Recreo you will find the **West Coast Surf Shop** (☎ 787-823-3935; www.westcoastsurf.com; 2e Muñoz Rivera), a cool and funky place with some excellent graphics and big-screen TV images. Aside from selling all the appropriate gear, the owners have great local knowledge and can organize lessons for any standard or age at short notice. **Hot Wavz Surf Shop** (☎ 787-823-3942) is on the lighthouse road and can rent you a surfboard to fit conditions for $20 to $25; boogie boards cost about $15.

DIVING & SNORKELING

Rincón has two good dive shops thanks to the popularity of diving the pristine reefs around Rincón and Isla Desecheo.

Located inside the little marina on the north side of town, **Taíno Divers** (☎ 787-823-6429; www.tainodivers.com; Black Eagle Marina; 2-tank dive $109, snorkeling $75) is probably the best outfit on the west coast. Guides are responsible, professional and very environmentally aware. They do almost daily runs to Desecheo (8am to 2pm) and shorter trips to nearby reefs (8am to noon). Snorkel trips, one-tank dives, whale-watching and sunset cruises are also available, as well as chartered deep-sea fishing trips.

Snorkelers should head for either **Playa Shacks** or **Playa Steps** near Black Eagle Marina for the best of what the beaches have to offer.

SWIMMING

The surf is often too rough for swimming at many sites along the coast. Fortunately, there's a safe and newly renovated **Rincón balneario** about half a mile from the Plaza de Recreo. Here you'll find restrooms, showers, some temporary food shacks and a new mall which contains the tourist office, harbor restaurant and lookout tower.

There is also good, safe swimming on the adjacent strand in front of Parador Villa Antonio and Hotel Villa Cofresí.

SURFING BEACHES

As far as surfing folklore goes, Rincón wins the ultimate accolade: it's mentioned in a song by the Beach Boys. Released in 1962, *Surfin' Safari* name checks Rincón as the place where 'they're walking the nose,' surfer slang for moving forward on the board toward the front. But, to save you trying to translate all of that other unintelligible babble that cool dudes with surfboards shout from their car windows, here's a quick rundown on Rincón's hottest surfing beaches (running south to north):

Little Malibu Just north of the marina. OK in the winter, with easy 4ft breaks.

Tres Palmas The big kahuna, with breaks of up to 25ft. Requires *bon courage* and a long paddle out. Handle with care.

Steps Also known by its Spanish name, *Escalera,* this is the 'inside' break to Tres Palmas' 'outside' break. Good snorkeling spot when it's calm.

Dogman's A local favorite that is anything but predictable. Expect waves that are high and hollow.

Maria's A good right, but needs a decent swell. Three times a year the waves break big here, but otherwise it's average.

The Point In front of the lighthouse, this one is not for amateurs. Waves can break big here while Maria's is lying flat.

Indicators Good powerful rights. Watch out for rocks and a pipe and coral bottom.

Domes Named for the nearby former nuclear facility (opposite). Good rights with the occasional left. A strong undercurrent, but probably the most consistent spot in Rincón.

Spanish Wall A beautiful secluded spot only reachable by a rough path, this place gets up in the winter and can be particularly fabulous after a cold front.

Pools Offers a few shallow reef-break peaks that can occasionally barrel.

Sandy Beach Good beginner's beach with decent waves when the swell is right.

Antonio's Used heavily during the 1968 World Surfing Championships, this has a right wall with a shorter left. Two take-off points spread the crowd.

KAYAKING

You can rent kayaks from **Capital Water Sports** (☎ 787-823-2789; Sunset Village, Rincón Balneario) and at Taíno Divers (opposite) for approximately $25 an hour for use around the balneario.

FISHING & WHALE-WATCHING

Taíno Divers (opposite) does responsible whale-watching tours (about $35 per person). Boats are required to keep a minimum distance from the gentle giants, but less scrupulous operators don't always adhere to that rule. Taíno Divers can also take you on half-day deep-sea fishing excursions for $725 per chartered boat (eight people maximum). Whale-watching is also possible from the Punta Higüero lighthouse park in December.

Captain Pepi Alfonso is a licensed US Coast Guard who runs **Makaira Charters** (☎ 787-823-4391, 787-299-7374; www.makairafishing chaters.com; half/full day $525/800). He does deep-sea fishing charters for up to six people and can sometimes split charters if your party is smaller. Drinks are included, but bring your own food – no bananas (an old fishing superstition)!

Festivals & Events

The **Rincón Triathlon** (www.rinconpr.com/triathlon/home.htm) has been going since 1982, which is pretty much ancient history in the triathlon world. Held every June, it's a classic ironman contest that's starting to draw some quality international athletes – it makes for a serious fiesta for spectators.

Sleeping

Reservations are recommended, especially in high season (see p273).

Rincón is awash with rental properties of all shapes and sizes. To make your search easier you can enlist the services of **Island West Properties** (☎ 787-823-2323; www.rinconrealestateforsale.com) which maintains an office on Hwy 413 about a mile out of town toward the lighthouse. Villa rentals with one to eight bedrooms go from between $120 and $700 per night.

NORTH OF TOWN

Rincón Surf & Board (☎ 787-823-0610; dm $20, d $55-65, ste $85-95) In the Sandy Beach area north of town, this place advertises basic apartments 'over the jungle.' It's a favorite haunt of the

WEST COAST

RINCÓN SURFER, JOAQUIM CRUZ

What's so special about surfing in Rincón? It was the first place in Puerto Rico to sponsor surfing in a big way after the 1968 World Championships. It also embraces surfing culture in its entirety, with friendly people, plenty of places to stay, a decent local mayor, rural tranquillity and an excellent array of other sports.

What's your favorite spot to surf and why? Dogman's, because the waves there are really hollow. Often the waves elsewhere are just as high, but Dogman's invariably has the best tubes.

What kinds of dudes come here? All kinds – young, old, rich, poor, European and American.

What's the best time of year to surf? From the second week in October through April.

Where do surfers go after hours? To bars like the Calypso (p233), where you can hear good bands playing Latin, rock, salsa and reggae.

What was your hairiest moment in the water? Fifteen years ago I was out on my board at Domes surfing way too hard. I had made the Point to the rocks six or seven times and went for one last wave, but it was too much. I ended up on the rocks below the lighthouse, with my board attached to me by the lead trying to suck me back out to sea. I clung onto the rocks for dear life until someone threw a rope down from the lighthouse. There were plenty of cuts and bruises to count later.

When and where did you catch the perfect wave? Ten years ago I was surfing with my friend, Rasta, up at Crashboat Beach near Aguadilla. The swell was so awesome that the local dudes with boogie boards were actually fighting with each other for space in the water. I took a gorgeous wave and dropped down, turning as I went, hand on the wall. I think I took the tube three times before I ran out of water and hit the shore. There was this guy behind me watching and whooping. I'm not sure whether he was wishing he was up there with me or he was just sharing in the moment.

As told to Brendan Sainsbury

'surf trolls' who show up to ride the waves all winter, and the guesthouse offers 10% to 15% discounts if you stay a week or more. Facilities are basic and the service is pretty hands off.

Casa Verde Guesthouse (☎ 787-605-5351; www.find-paradise.com; Beach Rd off Hwy 413; apt $60-180; P ☒) This faded green house has horses in front and the popular Rock Bottom Bar & Grill (p233) next door. Casa Verde is a surfer-friendly guesthouse with supermodern accommodations. There are one-, two- and three-bedroom choices available – with the added plus of a late-night bar scene right next door. Well, it's a plus if you are willing to trade great lobster and live music for peace and quiet!

Beside the Pointe (☎ 787-823-8550; www.besidethepointe.com; r $75-125; P ☒) Right on Sandy Beach, this guesthouse has a very popular restaurant, Tamboo Tavern (p233), which attracts a fun crowd. Rooms are actually like small apartments, with cooking facilities and kitchenettes, but overall aren't quite as well cared for as the newer places. If you just want somewhere to rest your surfboard while you hit the beach bars, this could be the place. Expect plenty of background noise after hours.

Dos Angeles del Mar Guesthouse (☎ 787-431-6057; www.dosangelesdelmar.8k.com; Beach Rd off Hwy 413; r $99-149; P ☒) Right up the street from Casa Verde, this guesthouse has four immaculate rooms with ocean views and daily maid service. Everything's impeccably clean and rooms are attractively tricked out with wicker furniture.

our pick Lazy Parrot Inn (☎ 787-823-5654; www.lazyparrot.com; Hwy 413 Km 4.1; r $110-155; P ☒ ☐ ☎) Claiming the middle ground between high quality and high quirky, the Lazy Parrot captures the unique essence of Rincón without scrimping on the home comforts. A venerable inn crammed full with all kinds of parrots – including real ones, carved ones, inflated ones and stuffed ones – it occupies the high country above Rincón, offering peekaboo glimpses of the sparkling ocean. Rooms are comfortable, but not flash; the restaurant, Smilin' Joe's (p233), is a culinary corker; and the inviting pool and Jacuzzi – not to mention the leafy Bamboo bar – are positively sublime (especially at night). The staff is friendly and the clientele well-dressed gringos with surfing aspirations.

Club Bon-Accord Inn (☎ 787-823-2525; Hwy 413 Km 3.3; r $120-220; P ⛝ 🖥 🐾) Anchored on the so-called 'Fun Coast' overlooking Punta Gorda and Sandy Beach, the Bon-Accord is the new kid on the hotel block and, like all new-generation Rincón kids, it's measurably swisher and richer than its parents. That's not to say that this hyperhip 10-room boutique hotel is out of step with the traditional west-coast eccentricities. Despite a clientele of surfing doctors, lawyers and businessmen, the ambience here is intimate, laid-back and dude friendly. All that's missing is the rusted up old VW Beetle.

Casa Islena (☎ 787-823-1525; www.casa-islena.com; Hwy 413, Beach Rd; r incl breakfast $145-195; P ⛝ 🖥 🐾) Location, location, location. You could have built a shack at this gorgeous spot on moody and magnificent Sandy Beach and got away with it. But, Casa Islena is a minipalace, an elegant Mediterranean-style guesthouse that takes paradise and subtly blends in a bit of extra magic. The secrets lie in nine delicious sea-view rooms, a full poolside breakfast bar and free front seats to Rincón's dazzling surfing show. Roll in at 9am-ish and you'll spy the more chilled out guests practicing their early-morning yoga under the palm trees. For information on the restaurant, see p232.

Ann Wigmore Institute (☎ 787-868-6307; www.annwigmore.org; dm/r incl therapy & meals per fortnight $900/1900; P) You'll find this retreat and spa 4 miles northeast of central Rincón on Hwy 115 (on the way to Aguadilla). Clients are drawn here for wheat-grass therapy, 'internal cleansing' and lots of organic gardening.

SOUTH OF TOWN

Tres Hermanos Camping (☎ 787-826-1610; Hwy 115 Km 5; campsites $17) The nearest tent camping to Rincón is at this public beach off Hwy 115 just west of the town of Añasco and 5 miles south of Rincón. The shaded sites are steps from a lovely beach. There's showers and toilets, and RVs are accepted.

Playa Córcega Camping (☎ 787-823-6140; Hwy 115 Km 10.8; RV sites with/without power $25/15) This is for RVs only; there is no tent camping here. It's a few minutes south of the Rincón of the Seas resort. Rates vary depending on the season. Amenities include showers, toilets, and electricity.

Coconut Palms Guesthouse (☎ 787-823-0147; www.coconutpalmsinn.com; 2734 Calle 8, Comunidad Estela; r $75-150) Sandwiched in between Rincón's more upscale southern resorts lies this fun and un-

pretentious guesthouse in a residential neighborhood just off Hwy 115. The Coconut's best feature is its fern-draped and bird-filled courtyard along with its lovely setting right on a calm, nonsurfing stretch of beach. This is a great choice for those who want to relax with a good book or just laze around on the sand.

Lemon Tree (☎ 787-823-6452; www.lemontreepr.com; Hwy 429 Km 4.1; r $110-185) You can wrap yourself in a Japanese *yurkata* (robe) and enjoy a fresh morning coffee on your own private ocean-front deck at this luxury beachside property. Six self-contained suites with fully furnished kitchens are decorated in thematic tropical colors. There's the indulgent Banana suite with its Jacuzzi tub and terrazzo floors, or the three-bedroom Papaya suite with its flat-screen TV and sweeping beach views. An extra bonus is the on-site PADI-certified Lemon Tree Divers.

Hotel Villa Cofresí (☎ 787-823-2450; www.villacofresi.com; Hwy 115 Km 12.3; r $115-160; P ⛝ 🐾) If Rincón of the Seas is the 'plush new resort,' the down-to-earth Villa Cofresí is the older place down the road that puts fabulous customer service over fabulous art and wicker furniture over wood. Standard rooms have king-sized beds and some come with kitchenettes. There's also a pool, restaurant, bar and water-sports concession on the property.

Parador Villa Antonio (☎ 787-823-2645; www.villa-antonio.com; Hwy 115 Km 12.3; r $115-170; P ⛝ 🐾) Rincón's token parador is atypical of the genre: family-friendly, affordable and good with the basics. It's also got a loyal following among Puerto Rican families and seniors thanks to its playground, games room and lovely beachside setting. Suffice to say, many aspiring surfers or travelers on a budget gravitate to the quirkier, more Rincónesque places.

Casa Serena (☎ 787-823-2026; 2730 Calle 14, off Hwy 115 Km 11.4; apt $175) A good option, this informal beach house sits in a tropical garden on a quiet, wide, sandy beach. There are two apartments, each with two bedrooms, two bathrooms, a kitchen, a living/dining room, and a 15ft covered patio. You can swim and snorkel in the Caribbean right outside your garden gate, pick your own exotic fruit in season and watch the sun setting over the Pasaje de la Mona. Minimum stay: three nights.

Rincón of the Seas (☎ 787-823-6189; www.rinconoftheseas.com; Hwy 115 Km 12.2; r $235-495; P ⛝ 🖥 🐾) This is a resort with all the usual upscale touches, yet it somehow retains a more laid-back

Rincón feel than the bigger piles further east. Maybe it's the tasteful antiques that adorn the lavish lobby, or the gaggles of nouveau-riche surfers who congregate around the swimming pool. Parked right on a calm stretch of beach, the Rincón is a modern hotel with a swathe of beautifully landscaped grounds. Regular rooms go for under $200 in summer, but travelers with a penchant for art deco will have to fork out over $400 for the special ocean-view suite. There are tons of on-site amenities and staff more than willing to hook you up with snorkeling and diving adventures.

Rincón Beach Resort (☎ 787-589-9000; www.rincon beach.com; Hwy 115 Km 5.8; r/ste $240/459; **P** 🔀 🖳 🔊) Not quite as luxurious as the Dorset, this neighboring resort is also outside of Rincón proper. It's a boutique hotel that has some private villas, a gorgeous beach and lots of opulent amenities for guests. If you like all-inclusive places where you rarely have to leave the property unless it's to head into the water, then try this place – tennis, massages, golf and more right at your fingertips. The rates for suites drop in low season.

Horned Dorset Primavera (☎ 787-823-4030; www.horneddorset.com; Hwy 429 Km 0.3; r $650-4000; **P** 🔀 🖳 🔊) Undoubtedly the best small resort in Puerto Rico – and perhaps even the Caribbean (though you may have to re-mortgage your house to stay here). Forget the rather obscure name; this place claims to offer the 'epitome of privacy, elegance and service,' and it certainly delivers. There are 30 suites in private villas that are furnished with hand-carved antiques and come equipped with their own private plunge pools (just in case you get bored of the communal infinity pool). Dripping with exclusivity, the Horned Dorset doesn't accept children under 12, shuns TVs in the rooms and encourages people to dress up – especially for dinner (see above). It's a long way from Rincón's surf scene, but it's blissful.

Eating

A lot of Rincón's guesthouses and hotels also serve food, so the list of restaurants in this small municipality is impressive. Vegetarian options can be had at most places.

Libanesa Bakery (☎ 787-823-4440; 52 Muñoz Rivera; snacks $3-7) There's quite a smattering of bakeries in Rincón, but first prize for freshness and variety has to go to this Lebanese-run

place that guards the entrance to the small downtown core.

El Palacio Chino (☎ 787-823-3300; 18c Progresso; mains $4-8; 🕑 lunch & dinner) This local Chinese restaurant doesn't look much but commands a loyal local following. Sweet-and-sour chicken costs $5.

El Flamboyán (Hwy 413 Km 3.1 Interior; mains $6-11; 🕑 lunch & dinner) With its faded Che Guevara posters and vaguely bucolic setting overlooking the surf break at Pools, the Flamboyán is definitely old-school Rincón. This is where you come for *comida criolla* and inexpensive fish and chicken dishes and to converse with weather-beaten expats about the days before the dudes with money crashed in.

Natural High (☎ 787-823-1772; Hwy 115 Km 14.3; sandwiches $7-9; 🕑 11am-3pm Thu-Tue, 5-9pm Fri; **V**) Glowingly healthy and unadulterated enough to suit even the strictest vegans, Natural High is – much to the surprise of visiting carnivores – also rather tasty. Mixing good old-fashioned home cooking with an unusual blend of raw, organic ingredients, the dishes here are as delicious as they are different. Try the crunchy fresh salads or the fruit-infused smoothies and save the muesli-munching for another day.

Casa Islena (☎ 787-823-1525; www.casa-islena.com; Hwy 413, Beach Rd; tapas $7-10; 🕑 11am-3pm & 5-9pm) They could serve tripe here and it would still taste good, so evocative is the ocean-side setting. Fortuitously, so is the food. Casa Islena serves delicious tapas washed down with rum-laced sangria. Picture grilled swordfish in spicy coconut broth and skirt steak marinated in ginger, soy and garlic, enjoyed over a scarlet-streaked sunset. The restaurant also follows a good environmental code using filtered water (no plastic), biodegradable take-out containers and sustainably harvested seafood. For accommodation information, see p231.

Antojos (☎ 787-823-4377; Hwy 115 Km 11.2; dishes $8-14) In Spanish *antojos* means 'cravings' and you can satisfy a few at this local bar and restaurant situated on Hwy 115 south of the town. The specialty is fish served up with *comida criolla* side dishes, such as rice, beans and fried plantains. It's nothing fancy, but after a day of catching the waves it will replenish a hearty surfer's appetite.

Pancho Villa (☎ 787-823-8226; Plaza de Recreo; mains $10-12; 🕑 11am-3pm & 5-10pm Tue-Sun) If you have long grown bored of lukewarm enchiladas or unpalatable refried beans, this modest place in Rincón's main square could quite easily reignite your taste buds for all things Mexican. Though the decor's nothing fancy and the service only so-so, the Rancho Villa delivers the goods where it matters: the food's damn tasty. Try the house burrito or the crispy chimichanga washed down with a salt-laced margarita and beware the rose-toting mariachis on Friday nights.

Smilin' Joe's (☎ 787-823-5654; www.lazyparrot .com; Hwy 413 Km 4.1; mains $16-21; ☯ noon-9:30pm) Wonderfully creative food is par for the course at this happening restaurant situated in the Lazy Parrot Inn (p230). Try the sesame-ginger churrasco steak or the mango-glazed chicken breast and choose something full-bodied from the comprehensive wine list. Then there's the guesthouse itself, which provides a strangely romantic setting (considering all the parrot paraphernalia) with its cleverly lit swimming pool and strategically positioned Rum Shack bar, which lives by its rather Hemingway-esque motto 'Conserve water – drink rum.'

Horned Dorset Primavera (☎ 787-823-4030; www .horneddorset.com; Hwy 429 Km 0.3; mains $30-50; ☯ dinner) Weird. One of Puerto Rico's most formal restaurants in one of its most informal towns. Don't even think about dragging your flip-flops, shorts or surfboard here. The dress code requires smart casual and appreciates suits. Suffice to say, the place is exquisite, with stunning views and equally stunning French-influenced food that would have Gordon Ramsey looking over his shoulder. People propose marriage here or carve out high-powered business deals over skillfully seasoned duck, mahimahi, chateaubriand, porterhouse steaks and delicately prepared seafood dishes. For accommodation information, see opposite.

Self-caterers will find **Rincón Cash & Carry** (☯ 10am-6pm Mon-Sat, 10am-4pm Sun) in the center of town, right across from the Plaza de Recreo, and **Econo's** (☯ 10am-6pm Mon-Sat, 10am-4pm Sun) on Hwy 115, a half-mile south of the village.

DRINKING
Rock Bottom Bar & Grill (☎ 787-605-5351; Beach Rd off Hwy 413; ☯ noon-2am) Rock Bottom is a 'tree-house' style bar situated next to the Casa Verde Guesthouse (p230) in the Sandy Beach neighborhood. It has ladies nights, surf videos, tasty bar snacks (buffalo wings and mozzarella sticks) and a novel, less tacky version of

karaoke which it calls the 'Acoustic Jam.' Swap your surfboard for a guitar and become the next Brian Wilson.

our pick Calypso Tropical Café (☎ 787-823-4151; ☯ noon-midnight) Wall-to-wall suntans, svelte girls in bikini tops, bare-chested blokes nursing cold beers, and syncopated reggae music drifting out beneath the sun-dappled palm trees; the Calypso is everything you'd expect a beachside surfers' bar to be – and perhaps a little more. All that's missing is a prepsych-edelic-era Brian Wilson propping up the jukebox (then again, Brian never *could* surf). On the ocean side of the leafy road to the lighthouse, Calypso hosts the oldest pub scene in Rincón and regularly books live bands to cover rock, reggae and calypso classics. Not surprisingly, it's a microcosm of the region at large and *the* place to go to find out about surf gossip, weather and waves.

Tamboo Tavern (☎ 787-823-8550; www.besidethe pointe.com; Sandy Beach; ☯ noon-midnight) You don't have to be a surfer to hang out at Tamboo, but it helps. This is actually the patio bar of the Beside the Pointe guesthouse, but it doubles up as a great place for burgers, relaxation and a congenial après-surf scene. You may not always get live music here, but the sound system is pretty good and the twilight beach panorama something to behold. For information on the guesthouse, see p230.

Banana Dang (☎ 787-823-0963; Hwy 413 Km 4.1; ☯ 7am-7pm Mon & Wed-Sat, 9am-7pm Sun) Set up in 2007 by two committed coffee and banana addicts from LA, Banana Dang comes pretty close to delivering the best shots of caffeine on the island. Next door to the Lazy Parrot Inn in the hills above Rincón, it's well worth stopping off here to – in the words of the owners – think, drink and link (yes, there are computer terminals and wi-fi access). The banana smoothies are pretty memorable too.

Shopping
Artistic Invisions (☎ 787-431-2439; cnr Hwy 115 & Parada Muñoz; ☯ 11am-5pm Wed-Sat, 11am-4pm Sun) This gallery displays and sells the work of local artists, including paintings, mosaics and sea glass. You can even get your favorite piece reproduced on a mug or T-shirt.

Lazy Parrot Tropical Gift Shop (☎ 787-823-5654; www.lazyparrot.com; Lazy Parrot Inn, Hwy 413 Km 4.1; ☯ 9am-6pm) In the Lazy Parrot Inn (p230), this shop is a must-stop for parrot-heads. You will also see Lisl Voigt's handmade sea-glass jewelry here.

Getting There & Away

Rincón doesn't have an airport, but there are two in the area. If you are coming from San Juan, fly into Mayagüez. Aguadilla's Aeropuerto Rafael Hernández generally has a couple of flights a day from the New York area or Miami.

The público stand is just off Plaza de Recreo on Calle Nueva. Expect to pay about $4 if you are headed north to Aguadilla or $2 to go south to Mayagüez (you can access San Juan from either of these cities). Both trips take about 40 minutes.

In spite of what your map might suggest, the easiest way to approach the town is via the valley roads of Hwy 402 and Hwy 115, both of which intersect Hwy 2 south of the Rincón peninsula.

Getting Around

Now for the bummer: Rincón – despite its mantle as an 'alternative' beach haven – has little provision for nonmotorized transport. Perhaps all the references to '49 Chevy's and vintage 'woodies' in erstwhile Beach Boys' songs have been taken a bit too literally. A spaced out community with minimal public transport, Rincón has few sidewalks and almost no facilities for bicycles (the nearest bike rental is in Aguadilla; see p254). The only reliable way to get around the area is by rented car, taxi, irregular públicos or – if you're energetic and careful – walking. You will pay $18 or more for a taxi from either the Aguadilla or Mayagüez airports. Car rentals can also be found at both of these destinations (see p256 and p225) or you can try **Angelos** (☎ 787-823-3438; Hwy 115 Km 12), in the town itself.

ISLA MONA

There is no rarer wilderness adventure in the Caribbean than a trip to Isla Mona, Puerto Rico's 'Jurassic Park,' 50 miles to the west of the main island in the Pasaje de la Mona. And although few Puerto Ricans or travelers actually ever visit Mona, this nearly circular island of 14,000 acres looms large in many people's imagination.

A nature reserve since 1919 and uninhabited for more than 50 years, Mona is so full of history, dramatic geological formations and wildlife that it can overwhelm your senses and pique your curiosity in ways you cannot even imagine. Keep in mind, though, that concerns about safety on the island caused the Departamento de Recursos Naturales y Ambientales (DRNA; Department of Natural Resources & Environment) to close the island to visitors for months, so make sure Mona is open to visitors before you plan your trip.

You suddenly begin taking the 'long view' of our planet's history when you see the violet cliffs of the tabletop island rising like a *fata morgana* (mirage) above the deep blue waves, or a collection of giant iguanas scrambling onto a trail to sniff your scent. Puerto Rican traffic jams seem like only the tiniest wrinkles in time when a pod of humpback whales near Mona begin breaching in front of you, a nurse shark surprises you beneath some antler coral, or you scramble through one of the island's limestone caves toward a point of light until you come to a hole that opens in the side of a cliff 100ft above the sea.

Then there are fish-eating bats, wild goats and pigs, Taíno petroglyphs on cave walls and the stories – stories of enslaved Indians, sunken galleons holding treasures of gold, skeletons of 18th-century pirates uncovered on Playa Pájaros, buried buccaneer loot and a government-sponsored search for the same that ended abruptly when a member of the search party committed suicide.

All this serves as ample food for thought when you are sitting around your campfire in the starlit night – and a reminder that a trip to Mona cannot be undertaken on a whim. While the DRNA provides toilets and saltwater showers at Playa Sardinera, Mona is a backcountry camping experience and boat trips here can take more than five hours in rough seas.

The rangers and police detachment (in their small station at Playa Sardinera) can provide basic first aid and have radio contact with the main island, but beyond this you are on your own in a beautiful – but hostile – environment.

History

Scholars believe that Mona was first settled about 1000 years ago as pre-Columbian peoples migrated north through the Caribbean archipelago. Petroglyphs in some caves and the subtle ruins of *bateyes* (Taíno ball courts) are the chief remnants of the Indian presence. Another remnant is the island's name, a corruption of the original indigenous name 'Amona.' Most likely the Indians used Mona as a way station in their travels between

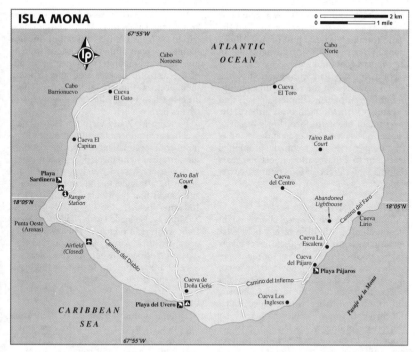

ISLA MONA

Puerto Rico and Hispaniola, and owing to the rich soil on the island, the Indians developed farms of cassava and sweet potatoes here to replenish the larders of voyagers.

Columbus stopped at Mona on September 24, 1494 (at the end of his second New World voyage) and remained several days to gather water and provisions for the long trip back to Spain. When the Spaniards returned in 1508, Mona had become a sanctuary for Taíno people escaping the slavery that the Spanish were impressing on the islanders of Hispaniola.

But, like Columbus, this small group of Spaniards had not come to conquer the island people, but simply to trade with them for water, cassava and sweet potatoes. This group of voyagers – led by Juan Ponce de León – was on its way to start a colony in Puerto Rico. In successive years Mona served as the breadbasket for the new Puerto Rican colony.

The Spanish government did eventually claim the island to guard the ship traffic through the Pasaje de la Mona, which was fast becoming the highway to and from the gold coast of the Americas. But after two decades of enslaving and decimating the population of Indians throughout the New World, the Crown found its resources of men and money stretched too thin and withdrew. Abandoned and defenseless, Mona fell into the hands of pirates by the late 1500s, when French corsairs used Mona as a staging ground and refuge in their attacks on the Spanish colony at San Germán.

During the next 300 years, Mona became the refuge of a host of privateers, including Sirs Walter Raleigh and Francis Drake, John Hawkins, William Kidd and the Puerto Rican buccaneer Roberto Cofresí. The 1832 execution of the freebooter Almeida, known as 'El Portugués,' brought an end to Mona's days as a pirates' den.

Throughout the next century, Mona went through cycles of activity and decline as various entrepreneurs tried to get rich mining the bat guano from Mona's caves. Rich in phosphate, the guano made exceptional agricultural fertilizer, but by 1924 the mines went dry and the citizens left (except for the family of Doña Geña Rodríguez, who lived in a cave – called Cueva de Doña Geña – on the south end of the island until 1943). It was about this time that a German submarine fired on the island (thinking it was a post for the Allies), probably scaring the living daylights out of the iguanas, goats and pigs.

Following Civilian Conservation Corps (CCC) activities on the island, the comings and goings of treasure hunters, WWII and a scam to turn Mona into an airbase, the government of Puerto Rico slowly began to take seriously its duty to protect the island as a nature preserve, and eventually prohibited development. Finally, after almost 500 years of human interference, Mona returned to her wild state.

Wildlife

Although its dry, semitropical climate might suggest an area with little variety in vegetation, Mona claims about 600 species of plants and 50 species of trees. Four of the plant species here are endemic, unknown to the rest of the world. Over the years many exotic species have been introduced to the island. Mahogany and coconut palms are two such species that still thrive. If you are exploring here, wear protective clothing. Mona has four types of venomous trees and bushes: indio, papayo, manzanillo and carrasco. Almost 3000 acres of the island consist of cactus thickets, while 11,000 acres are in scrub forest.

The biggest stars of the island's wildlife menagerie are the giant rock iguanas, *Cyclura stejnegeri* (similar to the iguanas at Anagada in the British Virgin Islands and Allan's Cays in the Bahamas). These guys can grow a body the size of a very large tomcat with a tail that makes them 5ft long. But it is their large heads and powerful jaws that are most fascinating, giving the iguanas the appearance of small-scale *Tyrannosaurus rexes*. Generally, these critters hunt and nest among the limestone ruts of the coastal plain, but you may see their tracks on the island's trails or beaches.

Do not offer food to these animals, and keep your distance. They have sharp teeth and claws, and they could charge if they feel cornered.

This advice also holds true for the feral pigs, goats and cattle whose ancestors got left behind by former settlers. There is a hunt here every winter to thin the herds, but there are still plenty around. Store your food out of their range or you may find your campsite invaded.

Humpback whales breed during the winter around the Pasaje de la Mona and during a trip to or from the island it is not uncommon to see pods of these gregarious animals breaching, spy-hopping with their heads out of the water to look around and slapping their pectoral flippers on the water. There are also schools of dolphins and pygmy sperm whales here.

Between May and October, Isla Mona's beaches are important nesting grounds for a number of species of marine turtle, including the chronically endangered Carey turtle.

If you are a bird-watcher, you will no doubt be attracted to the osprey, pelicans and hawks that hunt here, as well as about 100 other species.

Mona is also loaded with all kinds of bugs, so be aware and prepared. Fifty-two species of spider, three kinds of scorpion and four types of centipede are here for your pleasure. Several are venomous, including the black widow spider.

Orientation

Isla Mona is almost a perfect oval, measuring about 7 miles from east to west and 4 miles from north to south. Most of the island's coastline is made up of rough, rocky cliffs, especially along the north side. The south side, meanwhile, has a number of narrow beaches that fringe the highlands. The most approachable of these beaches is Playa Sardinera, where you will find toilets, showers and the concrete living quarters of the rangers and police detachment. The airfield, lying about a mile further east, has been closed since 1999.

The island's terrain consists of a broad rim of coastal plain that rises gently to a central mesa. Because the land is relatively flat and overgrown with vegetation, it is very difficult to find landmarks on the horizon. More than a few people have gotten lost here – including the pirate William Kidd. In 2001 a boy scout and his father were hiking on Mona and got lost; the boy died of dehydration and heat exhaustion.

Beware – if you venture to Mona, stick to main roads near Playa Sardinera. The basic photocopied map you get from the DRNA in San Juan is useless; the US Geological Survey (USGS), an agency of the US Department of the Interior, publishes a better map ($4). But even this map is of little help in the flat, featureless scrub terrain of the interior. Mona veterans strongly recommend first-time visitors go in company with a knowledgeable guide.

Sights & Activities

CAVES

Mona has 18 named caves that tunnel through the limestone in every part of the island. Many, like Cueva Lirio (Lily Cave), were mined for their guano, and some caves contain remains of railway tracks and machinery. Cueva de Doña Geña (Doña Geña Cave) was inhabited by a family for many years. A number of the most dramatic caves lie near the southeast cliffs, including Cueva La Escalera (Stairway Cave), Cueva del Pájaro (Bird Cave) and Cueva Los Ingleses (English Cave).

DIVING

This is one of the main reasons to come here. You will find spectacular 150ft visibility (or better) in the waters around the island. There are excellent barrier and fringe-reef dives filled with lagoons and ruts on the south side of the island, with eight different kinds of coral. Divers particularly enjoy the sharp drop-off along one reef that creates an overhanging wall; some fascinating creatures come to drift in its cool shadow. If you hang there too, you'll see spectacular things. **Scuba Dogs** (☎ 787-783-6377; www.scubadogs.net) is a San Juan–based diving outfit that organizes diving trips to the island.

Tours

Acampa Nature Adventure (☎ 787-706-0695; www .acampapr.com) Organizes four-day trips of the island with guided hikes; billed as 'roughing it with all the comforts.'

AdvenTour (☎ 787-889-0251; adventourspr.com) Respected eco-operator organizing adventure trips.

Adventures Tourmarine (☎ 787-375-2625; www .tourmarinepr.com; Rte 102 Km 14.1, Playa de Joyuda) The esteemed Captain Hernández is based in Joyuda in Cabo Rojo and is an old Mona hand; call for prices and availability.

Copladet (☎ 787-765-8595; www.copladet.com, in Spanish; 528 Calle Soller, San Juan) An acronym for the Corporación de Planificacion y Desarollo Turistico.

Sleeping

The only option for staying overnight on Mona is to camp. This is totally primitive camping to the point where you must bring your own water. The DRNA office in San Juan (p87) issues permits to camp on Mona (in designated areas on the south side of the island) for a maximum of three days. It's best to apply at least a week in advance. Campsites cost $2 per night per person. If you go with an outfitter, the outfitter will take care of the permits for you.

Visitors on a diving expedition will probably pitch camp at Playa Sardinera on the west end of the island. You can head up to the old grass airstrip at Punta Oeste (Arenas) to get away from the detachment of rangers and police who are here to protect the environment and watch for illegal immigrants crossing from the poorer Dominican Republic.

With time to trek, you can hike across the island on the Camino del Diablo (Devil's Rd) to rough it at the camping areas of Playa del Uvero, on the south of the island, or further on the Camino del Infierno (Hell's Rd) to Playa Pájaros on the southeast side.

Getting There & Away

The only way to get to Isla Mona is by boat. It is highly recommended you go with a professional and experienced guide as part of an organized trip. A number of people have actually died on the island after getting lost or becoming stranded (usually through dehydration).

All of the tour operators listed earlier run regular trips, although there are rarely set schedules. Prices vary depending on the length of trip and number of people. Phone ahead for a quote. Visiting Mona requires advanced planning. Don't expect to turn up on the west coast and leave the next day. If you are prone to seasickness, beware, the Pasaje de la Mona makes for a rough crossing.

North Coast

Head west out of San Juan on Hwy 2 and the suburban sprawl can seem never-ending. But it's not all drab satellite towns. Peer beyond the big box warehouses and glaring fast-food advertisements of Manatí and Barceloneta and more subtle secrets serendipitously reveal themselves. Here, the shadowy outline of a haystack-shaped hill. There, a glimpse of sun-flecked ocean sparkling like crumpled tin foil amid the ubiquitous concrete. And then, as if by magic, a side road beckons and you are drawn dreamily off the main drag and into an ethereal world of towering cliffs, hidden sinkholes and foaming Atlantic surf.

Wedged spectacularly between escarpment and sea, the north coast of Puerto Rico is known as karst country, a distinctly surreal landscape of bulbous *mogotes* (limestone hillocks) and limestone caves that resembles a giant papier-mâché experiment gone wrong. Nestled within this exotic haven of narrow valleys and dripping jungle lies a quartet of fecund state forests, all of which offer excellent DIY adventures for travelers with no fixed timetable.

Despite the challenges of the precipitous terrain, the north coast also showcases some of Puerto Rico's biggest outdoor attractions, many of which can be tackled in a day trip from San Juan. A 'grand tour' for weekend warriors includes the Río Camuy caves, the Observatorio de Arecibo (the largest radio telescope in the world) and the Parque Ceremonial Indígena Caguana – all must-sees on any itinerary and all consequently crawling with day-trippers. For an alternative escape, forge south into the mountain foothills around Río Abajo where placid lakes and out-of-the-way yoga retreats give new meaning to the word 'tranquil.'

HIGHLIGHTS

- Destressing with an early-morning yoga session at the **Casa Grande Mountain Retreat** (p247)

- Going underground with stalagmites and stalactites in the **Parque de las Cavernas del Río Camuy** (p245)

- Searching for alien life forms at the **Observatorio de Arecibo** (p245)

- Cycling with the wind in your hair along the surf-lashed beaches on the coast west of **Isabela** (p251)

- Finding a signposted trail (at last!) in the **Bosque Estatal de Guajataca** (p249)

Isabela ★   Parque de las
              Cavernas del
sque Estatal ★   Río Camuy
le Guajataca   ★ ★ Observatorio de Arecibo
                        ★ Casa Grande
                          Mountain Retreat

- POPULATION: 1 MILLION

History

The north coast contains one of the island's largest and oldest Native Indian ceremonial sites near Utuado, an archaeological find that provides dramatic proof that a well-organized Taíno culture thrived on the island before the arrival of the Spanish. Though Arecibo is the third-oldest city on the island, there is little of historical note remaining on the north coast outside of a couple of picturesque Spanish-colonial lighthouses. The 20th century saw a burgeoning of San Juan's suburbs westward into satellite towns such as Vega Alta and Manatí. At the same time a concerted effort has been made to protect karst country through tree-planting projects and the formation of half a dozen forest reserves in the 1940s.

Climate

Outside of the island's rainy months (late summer to early fall), the north coast is generally sunny, although big Atlantic storms can come barreling out of nowhere to whip the waves into a white-capped frenzy. Inland, the humidity increases, but on the shore the 80°F temperatures aren't at all oppressive.

Territorial Parks & Reserves

The north coast is dotted with small karst-country parks and reserves, although they're not nearly as well-equipped (or as well-trodden) as El Yunque. From east to west, there's the diminutive 1000-acre Bosque Estatal de Vega and the equally tiny Bosque Estatal de Cambalache. Around Arecibo the heavily populated San Juan suburbs give way to larger reserves such as the 5000-acre Bosque Estatal de Río Abajo, which has better-maintained trails and a wider range of facilities, although even this pales in comparison to the Parque de las Cavernas de Río Camuy, one of Puerto Rico's most oft-visited tourist attractions. Nestled in the northwest, the Bosque Estatal de Guajataca has caves, *mogotes* and plenty of signposted trails.

Getting There & Around

Aguadilla has an international airport that is widely used by vacationers heading for the west-coast beaches and scientists keen to study the stars at the Observatorio de Arecibo. Públicos run between the smaller coastal towns and from San Juan out to the main population centers along Hwy 2. Renting a car is probably the most popular option of getting around. The Isabela region is good for cycling.

DORADO
pop 13,200

For aspiring golfers, the legend of Dorado has always been more about putting greens than gold. This aptly named north coast town of just over 13,000 inhabitants boasts five championship-standard golf courses that draw Tiger Woods wannabes from as far apart as Miami and Melbourne. But, if you're the sort of person for who tee time is 'a drink with jam and bread' rather than an amble down the fairways, several stunning local beaches offer a welcome break from the clubhouse banter.

Founded in 1842, Dorado first rose to prominence as a resort town in the early 1900s when the Rockefeller family sailed in and started to construct their idyllic Caribbean Shangri-la on a golden stretch of beach. The venture went public in 1958 when Laurence Rockefeller, the well-known philanthropist and conservationist, opened up the region's first hotel, the Dorado Beach, a pioneering ecoresort where no building was taller than the surrounding palm trees. More resorts followed, including the grandiose Hyatt Regency Cerromar, with its exotic 1776ft swimming river, but by the early 2000s, with the Hyatt group struggling to maintain the hotels in tip-top shape, the town's fortunes started to slide.

Today, with both the Dorado Beach and Cerromar operations closed and awaiting takeovers (and makeovers), the town feels as if it's slipped into temporary hibernation. Elsewhere the building frenzy has shifted to newer holiday homes in plush gated communities meaning that Dorado, while retaining its ritzy image, has lost much of its erstwhile atmosphere.

Away from the resorts, Dorado has a timeless public beach in town and an even prettier free option a few miles to the west at Cerro Gordo (p243). Back in town, the original 19th-century settlement, with its teardrop-shaped lights rimming the main plaza, is a pleasant spot to while away a lazy afternoon.

Orientation

Rte 165 turns into Calle Méndez Vigo, the town's central road, and takes you past the shopping center. Then the road becomes Rte 693 (you'll see several nice restaurants on Vigo before it morphs into 693). Turn right at the gas station onto Rte 697 and you'll arrive at the town's closest public beach. If you

NORTH COAST

continue straight on Rte 693, you'll hit the two Hyatts and Playa de Cerro Gordo.

Sights & Activities

MUSEUMS

Dorado has a trio of small museums that could fill a short afternoon or a breather between golf rounds. The **Museo y Centro Cultural Casa del Rey** (☎ 787-796-5740; Calle Méndez Vigo) is an old Spanish garrison that displays antique furniture, the **Museo del Plata** (☎ 787-796-9031; Industria; 8am-4pm Mon-Sat) showcases local art, sculpture and paintings, and the **Museo de Arte e Historia de Dorado** (☎ 787-796-5740; cnr Calles Méndez Vigo & Juan Francisco; 8am-3:30pm Mon-Sat) gives you the rundown on local history and archaeology. Admissions are free.

BEACHES

Although nobody is advertising it, there is, in fact, a public beach in Dorado where you can swim. **Balneario Manuel Morales** (parking $2) is at the end of Rte 697. But it's a rather boring bit of sand surrounded by rocky outcrops and marred by litter. For a far better experience try Playa de Cerro Gordo several miles to the west (p243).

You can also get to nearby Toa Alta's beach, **Punta Salinas**, about 20 minutes east of Dorado on Rte 165. It's got food kiosks, lifeguards, restrooms and basketball courts.

SURFING

For those not staying at a resort, try **Kalichee Surf Shop** (☎ 787-796-3852; Rte 693 No 500; 9:30am-6:30pm Mon-Sat). Inside the Grande Shopping Center, Kalichee rents all sizes of surfboards for $25 to $45 a day and offers advice on where to find the best surfing. A credit card is needed to rent. They can also hook you up with the many local instructors who say they can get a beginner standing up by the end of a two-hour lesson.

GOLF

Look no further. Dorado has the best golf courses in the Caribbean, period. There are five 18-hole courses here and all remain open despite the recent closure of the adjoining Hyatts. The famed **East Course** (☎ 787-796-8961) at the former Hyatt Dorado is the green jewel – Jack Nicklaus has ranked its 540yd 4th hole as one of the best in the world. Its major-league

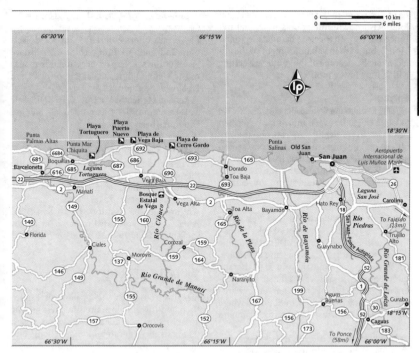

water hazards have helped it earn its rating as one of the planet's finest golf courses by *Golf Digest*. Next door lies the 6975yd **West Course** (☎ 787-796-8961), while across the road you'll find the **Pineapple** and **Sugarcane** (☎ 787-796-8915) courses at the Plantation Club. Dorado's fifth and newest course is the Chi Chi Rodríguez–designed **Dorado El Mar** (☎ 787-796-3070) at the Embassy Suites. Greens fees at these courses range from $100 to $150 for guests and $130 to $190 for nonguests depending on tee times.

Sleeping

Costa de Oro Guest House (☎ 787-278-7888; B28 on Calle H, off Rte 697; r $75-110; ⚌) Just a few hundred yards from the public beach in a residential section of town, this locally run establishment is the other side of Dorado: diminutive, no-frills and fairway-free. There are 14 plain but clean rooms, a minuscule pool the size of a resort Jacuzzi tub and friendly staff.

Embassy Suites Dorado del Mar Beach & Golf (☎ 787-796-6125; www.embassysuitesdorado.com; 201 Dorado del Mar Blvd; r $150-300; P ⊠ 🖳 ⚌) Dorado's newest resort has taken center stage since the

gargantuan golf hotels to the west have gone into hibernation. Situated close to town amid a phalanx of gated communities, it has its very own Chi Chi Rodríguez–designed course along with a business center, a gym, tennis courts and four specialty restaurants. The open-plan lobby is a fountain-filled state-of-the-art extravaganza where smooth-talking salespeople in Hawaiian shirts leap out from behind pillars and try to sell you timeshares. If you can survive this relatively innocuous form of initiation, you could be in for a ball.

Hyatt Regency Hacienda del Mar (☎ 787-796-3000; www.hyatt.com; Hwy 693 Km 12.8; r $200-1200; P ⊠ 🖳 ⚌) Something of a ghost town since the adjacent Hyatt Dorado Beach Resort and Cerromar closed a couple of years ago, this condo timeshare is so quiet it's almost spooky. Some visitors revel in their new-found isolation, while others find the strangely abandoned million-dollar resort…well…rather eerie. Since it's a timeshare, the Hacienda del Mar only has availability when one of the unit owners is away, so you need to call first and see what's vacant. Potentially, its facilities are top class, with golf, a secluded beach and the

NORTH COAST

Lazy River, one of the world's largest (1776ft long) leisure swimming pools/water features (once shared with the now-defunct Cerromar Hotel), but with the abandonment of the adjacent facilities, some of the rooms are getting a little long in the tooth.

Eating

ourpick **Restaurante Rancho Mar** (☎ 787-796-3347; Calle G; dishes $10-28) Every morning, fishermen head out to see what they can hook; every afternoon, the fruits of their labor are served at this restaurant, just across from the public beach, which has amassed quite a reputation for creating the freshest, most delectable seafood dishes in town. Menu changes daily, depending on the catch.

Villa Dorada d'Alberto Seafood Restaurant (☎ 787-278-1715; 99 Calle E; dishes $12-25) This is a lively seafood restaurant on Dorado's public beach strip that is always buzzing after dark. Fresh fish is the mainstay and it's generally good enough to attract the flush vacationers out of their resort nirvanas. Afterwards you can wander next door to El Portal where romantic guitar trios play Puerto Rican and Cuban classics.

El Ladrillo (☎ 787-796-2120; 334 Calle Méndez Vigo; dishes $15-35) El Ladrillo has been around for over 30 years and continues to lure guests out of the plush hotels for a night of intimacy and good food. Filled with old-world charm, the restaurant specializes in to-order steaks with plenty of back-up seafood; everything from octopus salad to lobster *asopao* (an island specialty, a delicious thick stew). It also functions as a mini art gallery, displaying a selection of local paintings.

Zen Garden (☎ 787-796-1173; Hwy 693 Km 12.8; dishes $18-33) Though they shut the Hyatt Cerromar a couple of years back, the Asian/sushi restaurant has remained open and outside of the golf clubs it's pretty much the only place to eat on this slumbering megaresort. If you don't mind braving the half-empty lobby, the food is still delectable and the staff will be more than happy to see you.

Entertainment

Your best bet for entertainment is to wander down to the public beach area where a clutch of lively seafood restaurants often host live music.

The Calypso Bar at the Embassy Suites also puts on live music at the weekends.

La Terraza (☎ 787-796-1242; Marginal Costa de Oro, Calle 1, off Rte 693) Yes, it serves a mean paella, but La Terraza offers entertainment for dessert on a 2nd-floor rooftop terrace with distant views of the sea. Expect occasional live salsa music – although it's usually pop rock from Hollywood soundtracks.

Restaurante Rancho Mar (☎ 787-796-3347; Calle G) This restaurant (left) stays open late and lets you nurse beers at the bar.

Getting There & Away

It is easy to get a público to and from Río Piedras in San Juan (40 minutes) or the ferry terminal in Cataño (about $3; 20 minutes).

Taxi de Dorado (☎ 787-796-3806) can get you around the locality or into San Juan. Alternatively, you can hire a car at **Dorado Car Rental** (☎ 787-796-2633; Hwy 693 No 26). Phone for rates.

MANATÍ & AROUND
pop 16,000

Despite its title as the 'Athens of Puerto Rico,' you won't find anything resembling an acropolis in Manatí. In fact, the closest you're likely to get to budding Hellenic culture in this thoroughly metropolitan town is the classical 18th-century Catedral Nuestra Señora de la Candelaria and the neo-Grecian Salon de los Poetas, a posthumous nod to poets past.

Modern Manatí, which was named for the endangered manatee (sea cow) that once prospered in these waters, is an industrial hub for workers in local pharmaceutical factories and a nearby pineapple canning plant. But, body-swerve the industrial eyesores and you'll quietly uncover some little-heralded beaches along with two inland forest reserves, Bosque Estatal de Cambalache and Bosque Estatal de Vega, set among the sinkholes and limestone *mogotes* of karst country.

TOP FIVE GREEN ESCAPES

- Bosque Estatal de Guajataca (p249)
- Laguna Tortuguero (opposite)
- Parque de las Cavernas del Río Camuy (p245)
- Bosque Estatal de Río Abajo (p246)
- Lagos Dos Bocas & Caonillas (p246)

Orientation

Manatí sprawls between the two east–west island thoroughfares of Hwy 2 and Expressway 22 (a toll road). The beaches and Laguna Tortuguero lie on a thin coastal strip to the north, while the Bosque Estatal de Vega lies just south of the main highways approximately 6 miles to the east. The Bosque Estatal de Cambalache is situated 5 miles west of Manatí, a mile or so north of Expressway 22.

Sights & Activities
BEACHES

Unlike most of Puerto Rico's public beaches, **Playa Mar Chiquita** is not alongside a main thoroughfare, and therein lies its charm. There's a hardly visible sign to the beach off Hwy 685, about 2 miles north of Manatí and just beyond the entrance to the town of Boquillas. If you miss the sign, go north on Hwy 648 (about a mile east of Boquillas). This road takes you over a steep hill to the beach, which lies at the bottom of an escarpment where the plateau of the coastal plain has been hollowed out into caves.

As you continue east on the seaside road (which has now become Hwy 686), you'll pass through a coastal forest. When the road creeps back to the edge of the coast, the long strand of **Playa Tortuguero** will be on the left. A couple of miles further east is a normal balneario (public beach), **Playa Puerto Nuevo** – a narrow crescent of sand sheltered by a broad headland to the east and surrounded by clusters of beach homes.

If this place seems too tame for you, head east from here upon Hwy 692, a road that comes to a halt in a mile or so at the spot where the Río Cibuco joins the sea. The beach along this road is exposed and punctuated with reefs and rocks. To the south lie cow pastures and savannas. This beach is known variously as **Playa de Vega Baja** and **La Costa Roja**. Strong riptides make it dangerous for swimming, but the surfing can be excellent and the peace you find sitting here under a coconut palm may be as good as it gets in Puerto Rico.

After a long detour inland (to clear the swampy mouth of the Río Cibuco), the network of coastal roads takes you to one more surprising beach as you head east. **Playa de Cerro Gordo** (parking $2) lies at the end of Hwy 690. This was once the north coast's best-kept secret, but word is definitely out; the government just pumped several million dollars into creating restrooms, showers, fire pits and other beach necessities to put Cerro Gordo on the tourist map – and the additions have improved what was already a first-rate area. Camping is possible here (p244).

BOSQUE ESTATAL DE VEGA

This is a small forest of approximately 1000 acres set among the *mogotes* south of the Hwy 22 expressway, just to the northwest of the town of Vega Alta. You enter off Hwy 676, where you'll see the **forest office** (☎ 787-724-3724; ☼ 9am-4pm). There are picnic shelters and a few modest hiking trails (signage isn't great), but the forest isn't very developed. Its principal function is to preserve some of the aquifer that lies beneath the sinkholes and to provide a green buffer against the outer suburbs of San Juan, which are pressing rather alarmingly on its borders. The hours here are seasonal; if you will require a ranger it's best to call ahead.

LAGUNA TORTUGUERO

This **lagoon** (☎ 787-844-2587; ☼ 8am-4pm Wed-Fri, 6am-6pm Sat & Sun) is the only natural lake in Puerto Rico, making its protection extra precious. It is also one of the most ecologically diverse spots on the island, listing 717 species of plant and 23 different types of fish. Hiking around this pretty spot yields ocean views, and you can also fish and kayak in the lake – though you'll have to bring your own equipment. Ask the rangers on duty about the trails, though they're pretty obvious. Some locals use them for jogging. One of the lake's stranger problems is its caiman infestation. In the 1990s there was an odd craze to buy striped South American caimans. Locals bought them in their droves, only to discover they don't make good pets. Hundreds were ditched in the lagoon, with unfortunate results for the ecosystem. Rangers run an extermination program and have succeeded in getting the population under control; in theory, caimans only hunt at night, but you want to watch what you're doing at all times. To get to Tortuguero from Hwy 22, take Exit 41, take a right on Hwy 2, then left on Rte 687 until you see a big sign for the lagoon on your left.

BOSQUE ESTATAL DE CAMBALACHE

Cambalache covers an area of just 1000 acres, making it smaller than a lot of Puerto Rican resort hotels. The entrance to this compact but little-visited forest reserve lies west of Barceloneta, in front of – wait for it – a Job Corps facility. Despite this rather inauspicious introduction, the forest is ecologically varied and characterized by distinctive karstic formations; countless *mogotes* pop straight up from the landscape to heights of 160ft. Its many caves provide homes for fruit bats, which often swarm like bees into the evening sky.

The forest has a picnic area, 8 miles of hiking trails, two designated trails for mountain bikes (though they're often washed out) and one that is wheelchair-accessible, and two camping areas (below). Note that a permit is required for cycling ($1). Call the Departamento de Recursos Naturales y Ambientales (DRNA; p87) in San Juan to obtain one. Basic on-the-ground information can be obtained at the **ranger station** (☎ 787-878-7279; Hwy 682 Km 6.6; ☒ 9am-4pm) to the right of the entrance gate. Since the forest only enjoys a couple of thousand visitors in any given year, the ranger should be very pleased to see you.

The forest is also home to a rather rundown looking **ornamental trees nursery** (☒ 7:30am-3pm Mon-Fri).

Sleeping & Eating

Bosque Estatal de Cambalache (campsites per person $4) To camp in karst country at this forest (p243), you need to make reservations. There are two campsites: La Boba holds four tents and La Rosa holds eight. A free permit is required; contact the DRNA in San Juan (p87).

Playa de Cerro Gordo (☎ 787-883-2730; campsites $13; ☒ beach 8am-6pm) There's camping available on this popular beach west of Dorado (p243). Lifeguards are present daily, and the food kiosks sell the usual fried finger foods that you can eat at pine picnic tables. If you're looking to camp in the summer months call ahead for a reservation and don't expect too much privacy. Parking costs $2.

Su Casa Steak House (☎ 787-884-0047; Hwy 670 Km 1; dishes $12-22) Breaking the fast-food monotony, this casual place (which is on the Mesón Gastronómico hot list) serves up some of the best steaks in the area. Also on the menu are seafood, *comida criolla* (traditional Puerto Rican cuisine) and plenty of other Puerto Rican delicacies served up with an international vent.

Getting There & Away

While you can get to and from Manatí by público (about 45 minutes from San Juan), you'll need wheels to avoid being stuck in the undesirable town with no way of getting around the sights. By car, Manatí can be reached from the east or west via Hwy 2, or by taking Hwy 149 south from Hwy 22.

ARECIBO & AROUND

pop 49,000

Approaching Arecibo today, it's hard to imagine that this sprawling modern municipality of nearly 50,000 people is Puerto Rico's third-oldest city, after San Juan and San Germán. Founded in 1556, the original town was named after an esteemed Taíno cacique (chief) and gained notoriety in 1702 when Spanish captain Antonio Correa thwarted a full-scale British invasion off the coast. But, while little of historical note remains in the present-day city, save a restored 19th-century cathedral and the emblematic Spanish-colonial Arecibo lighthouse, veer further inland and the view gets a lot more interesting.

Indeed, today the name Arecibo is more synonymous with the world's largest radio telescope than with its historic lighthouses and erstwhile Spanish military tacticians. The Observatorio de Arecibo lies several miles to the south in the heart of karst country, a tree-studded pastiche of haystack-shaped hills and plunging depressions that flicker like folds on a badly indentured map. Harboring a fascinating museum and a view worthy of a futuristic James Bond film set, the observatory is open to public viewing and reigns as one of the island's most rewarding must-sees. Back on the coast you can pass a short afternoon at the lighthouse and its surrounding historical park or saunter off in search of ancient Taíno petroglyphs in one of the north coast's many karstic caves.

The popular Hatillo Mask Festival, held on December 28, is one of Puerto Rico's most symbolic ceremonies whose innovative masks and costumes adorn the front of numerous books, postcards and tourist literature (see p279).

Orientation

Arecibo's city center is trapped between Hwy 2 and the Atlantic Ocean – it's a thin strip of restaurants and strip malls. The main attractions lie about 15 to 20 minutes outside of town in karst country, just off Hwy 129.

Sights & Activities
OBSERVATORIO DE ARECIBO

The Puerto Ricans reverently refer to it as 'El Radar.' To everyone else it is simply the largest radio telescope in the world. Resembling an extraterrestrial spaceship grounded in the middle of karst country, the **Arecibo Observatory** (☎ 787-878-2612; www.naic.edu; adult/child/senior $4/2/2; ☿ noon-4pm Wed-Fri, 9am-4pm Sat, Sun & most holidays) looks like something out of a James Bond movie – probably because it is (007 aficionados will recognize the saucer-shaped dish and craning antennae from the 1995 film *Goldeneye*).

The 20-acre dish, set in a sinkhole among clusters of haystack-shaped *mogotes,* is planet Earth's ear into outer space. The telescope, which is supported by 50-story cables weighing more than 600 tons, is involved in the SETI (Search for Extraterrestrial Intelligence) program and used by on-site scientists to prove the existence of pulsars and quasars, the so-called 'music of the stars.' Past work has included the observation of the planet Mercury, the first asteroid image and the discovery of the first extra-solar planets.

Top scientists from around the world perform ongoing research at Arecibo, but an informative visitors center with interpretative displays and an explanatory film provide the public with a fascinating glimpse of how the facility works. There's also a well-positioned viewing platform offering you the archetypal 007 vista.

To get to the observatory follow Hwys 635 and 625 off Hwy 129. It's only 9 miles south of the town of Arecibo as the crow flies, but the rollercoaster ride through karst country will make it seem more like 90.

PARQUE DE LAS CAVERNAS DEL RÍO CAMUY

For centuries now, the Río Camuy has been imposing its will on the soft karstic underground limestone to create this incredible system of caves, the world's third-largest. This **park** (☎ 787-898-3100; Hwy 129 Km 18.9; adult/child $12/6, parking $2; ☿ 8am-5pm Wed-Sun & holidays) spreads over an area about 10 miles long and has 17 entrances in the area between the towns of Hatillo, Camuy and Lares.

Over the years, the caves have been important shelters for indigenous people, home to millions of bats that help keep the island's insect population under control, and a source of fertilizer. But no modern explorers went to the trouble of making a thorough investigation of the caves until 1958. This was when Russell and Jeanne Gurnee and Bob and Dorothy Rebille accompanied José Limeres (a Puerto Rican doctor) into a Río Camuy sinkhole. The upshot of this trip was a suggestion that the government purchase 300 acres of land around the Río Camuy caves as a nature preserve. Later, the Speleological Society of Puerto Rico explored and mapped the caves, eventually proposing that the government develop the Cueva Clara de Empalme (at the site of the Cavernas del Río Camuy) for tourism, and in 1986 the attraction opened.

It is a good idea to call the park for local conditions (too much rain can cause closures or abbreviated tours), and arrive before 10:30am to avoid crowds or a long wait.

Your visit begins with a film about the caves at the visitors center. Then you take a trolleybus that follows a spiraling road down through the jungle into a 200ft-deep sinkhole to **Cueva Clara de Empalme** (Clear Cave Junction), where you take a 45-minute guided walk through the cave. Here you walk past enormous stalagmites and stalactites, and into rooms littered with boulders. At one point, the ceiling of the cavern reaches a height of 170ft; at another, you can see the Río Camuy rushing through a tunnel.

After leaving the cave from a side passage, you take another tram to the **Tres Pueblos sinkhole**, which measures 650ft across and drops 400ft. Forty-two petroglyphs that you can now inspect have been found in **Cueva Catedral** (Cathedral Cave).

The last tour leaves at 2pm if you want to see all three areas, or at 3:45pm if you want to see just one sinkhole.

For information on camping in this park, see p247.

PARQUE CEREMONIAL INDÍGENA CAGUANA

Like the archaeological site at Tibes near Ponce, this **Taíno ceremonial site** (☎ 787-894-7325; admission free; ☿ 9am-4pm), off Hwy 111, is not dramatic in the sense of having monumental ruins. The power of the place comes from its first-rate setting in a natural botanical garden of ceiba, ausubo and tabonuco trees shading the midslopes of the Central Mountains.

There are also 10 ceremonial *bateyes* (Taíno ball courts), which date back about 800 years to the time of the original Taíno inhabitants. Stone monoliths line many of the courts; some weigh up to a ton, but most are small. One court measures 60ft by 120ft. Quite a few have petroglyphs, such as the famous Mujer de Caguana, who squats in the pose of the traditional 'earth mother' fertility symbol.

The discovery of this site dates from the beginning of the 20th century, when it was originally excavated by the respected archaeologist J Alden Mason. He and subsequent archaeologists have concluded from the size and number of the ball courts that Caguana was not much of a village, but rather a central ceremonial site, perhaps one of the most important Taíno sites in the Caribbean.

Caguana is a place to walk and reflect, not to be stimulated by exhibits. Nevertheless, there is a small **museum** with artifacts and skeletons on the property, and a gift shop that sells inexpensive but attractive reproductions of Taíno charms, including the statues called *cemíes*.

LAGOS DOS BOCAS & CAONILLAS

These two lakes – each more than 2 miles long – fill a deeply cleft valley at a point where karst country gives way to the actual mountains of the Central Mountains, east of Hwy 10 and north of Utuado. The lakes are the principal reservoirs for the north-central part of the island, and for years they caused anxiety to communities downstream, who worried that the lakes could not absorb a torrential rainfall without overflowing or bursting a dam.

As it turned out, drought was the first plague to hit the lakes. At one point, the water dropped so low at Lago Caonillas that the bell tower of a 1930s-era chapel was exposed. The chapel had been built in the valley before the Aqueduct & Sewer Authority claimed the land and flooded it with a reservoir. Thousands of islanders flocked to the site, hoping for a miracle, as if the image of the bell tower rising above the water was the sign of the second coming of Jesus.

But the miracle was short-lived. When Hurricane Georges passed over Puerto Rico in 1998, more than 25in of rain fell on the Central Mountains, and a lot of that water found its way to Caonillas and Dos Bocas. The dams did not break, but the reservoirs overflowed, sending a wall of water down the Río Grande de Arecibo valley. The flood destroyed crops, houses, possessions and even the bridge over the river's mouth in Arecibo.

In calm weather, you can ride Dos Bocas' free launch, which serves as a taxi service to the residents in the area. The boat landing is on Hwy 123, on the west side of the lake. Boats leave almost every hour. You can disembark at restaurants around the lake or just sit back and enjoy the two-hour ride. You can similarly pick up the boat launch on the other side of the lake at the end of Hwy 612, about 3 miles beyond the Casa Grande Mountain Retreat (opposite). There's a restaurant here called **Vista al Lago** (☎ 787-814-6934), perched on a steep bluff where the boat stops. It serves decent *comida criolla* and hires out kayaks for $20 an hour. On the opposite shore nearby – easily reached by kayak – there are two more well-maintained restaurants, **Otoao** (☎ 787-312-7118) and **Rancho Marina** (☎ 787-894-8034) that do good seafood.

BOSQUE ESTATAL DE RÍO ABAJO

This 5000-acre forest has a **visitors center** (☎ 787-880-6557; ☉ 9am-5pm) just off Hwy 621, halfway between Utuado and Arecibo, and some of the most rugged terrain on the island. Situated in the heart of karst country, the forest's altitude jumps between 700ft and 1400ft above sea level. The steep sides of the *mogotes* are overrun with vines, and the forest is a jungle of tropical hardwoods, including Honduran mahogany and Asian teaks, and huge clumps of bamboo.

A century ago this land was logged almost bare. In the mid-1930s, the US government and the Civilian Conservation Corps (CCC) stepped in with their plan to reforest Puerto Rico. The remains of the lumber roads cut by the loggers and the CCC workers have now become trails. The two most popular and the best maintained are the **Visitors Center Trail** (a 500m-long stroll with three gazebos set up along the way) and **Las Perdices** (about 2km long). Others are often poorly maintained or affected by recent weather conditions. Enquire at the visitors center and you should be able to piece together a more substantial hike through karst country. If there are enough people around the amiable rangers will sometimes lead an ecohike. The Visitors Center Trail has water, interpretive displays and occasional wildlife lectures.

To reach Bosque Estatal de Río Abajo from San Juan, take Hwy 22 west toward Arecibo.

Turn south on Rte 10 toward Utuado. Turn west on Hwy 621 and continue to Km 4.4 and the park entrance.

The ranger station is near the entrance, where Hwy 621 snakes into the forest. At the end of this road, there is a picnic and recreation area and an aviary, where the DRNA is working to reintroduce the Puerto Rican parrot and other endangered species.

FARO Y PARQUE HISTÓRICO DE ARECIBO

This **theme park** (☎ 787-817-1936; Rte 655; adult/child $9/7; 🕑 9am-6pm Mon-Fri, 10am-7pm Sat & Sun) off Hwy 2 is a bit gimmicky and overpriced, though it does offer a tantalizing glimpse of the historic Arecibo lighthouse and provides enough diversions for kids to warrant a break on the long car journey east or west. Perched on a headland on the hill at Punta Morrillos, east of Arecibo, the **Faro de los Morrillos**, dating from 1897, is an excellent example of Spanish neoclassical architecture with its whitewashed facade and gracefully refined cylindrical shape. Inside, a tiny **museum** displays artifacts salvaged from shipwrecks. There are fantastic views of the Atlantic Ocean and karst country from the roof.

Elsewhere the park boasts a reconstructed Taíno village, two pirate ships, a pirate's cave, a mini-zoo and a substantial children's playground.

CUEVA DEL INDIO

Heading east from the Faro de los Morrillos, Hwy 681 takes you along a rugged coastline punctuated by coral outcroppings, dunes and lagoons. The countryside is largely rural, but clutches of beach houses have grown up along sections of the road. You will find the **Cueva del Indio** (Indian's Cave) near one such settlement, about 2 miles east of the lighthouse. Look out for an Esso gas station on the right. You can park here (ask permission) and follow the well-worn path across the road to the shore.

The surf crashes around the cave's entrance, which leads to a descending staircase and a substantial collection of Taíno petroglyphs on the walls. Bring a flashlight and good footwear.

BEACHES

There are two good beaches in the area of the Faro de los Morrillos. On the cove side,

south of the point and the commercial pier, just off Hwy 681, you will see the manicured facilities of a **town beach** with broad sand and totally protected water. This is a great place for families.

If you follow the road past the lighthouse (less than a quarter of a mile), you come to the **Balneario Morrillos** (parking $2). There is a big parking lot and all the usual facilities. The beach is about a half mile of low dunes and white sand, and it usually gets plenty of surf.

Sleeping & Eating

María Soto Campground (☎ 787-817-0984, 787-880-6557; adult/child under 10 $4/2) In Bosque Estatal de Río Abajo, this campground holds 40 people and is run by rangers. There are campfires, restrooms, gazebos and tables. Reservations are necessary.

Cavernas del Río Camuy Camping (☎ 787-898-3100; Hwy 129 Km 20; sites $5) You can camp at this site 1km from the famous caves. Facilities include showers, restrooms and electricity. Reserve a good 15 days in advance. It makes a handy base for exploring the surrounding attractions.

our pick **Casa Grande Mountain Retreat** (☎ 888-343-2272; www.hotelcasagrande.com; Hwy 612 Km 0.3; r $90-135; 🏊) Serenity has arrived. Materializing like a leafy apparition out of Puerto Rico's gorgeous karst country, the Casa Grande ought to be on the prescription list of all North American doctors as an antidote for stress and rat-race burnout. Nestled in its own steep-sided valley and run efficiently by an ex–New York lawyer, the Casa is an ecologically congruous hotel that stops you in your tracks, forcing you to slow down and take it easy. While there are no TVs or phones in any of the 20 jungle-esque rooms, there are daily yoga classes, a scrumptious on-site restaurant and every available excuse to sit around all day and do – absolutely nothing. Try it, you might just get hooked.

Parador El Buen Café (☎ 787-898-1000; Hwy 2 No 381 Km 84; r $95-160; 🅿 🏊) Little more than a journey-breaker on Hwy 2 between San Juan and the west coast, El Buen Café is nonetheless a clean and efficiently run parador that provides a welcome respite from the car chaos outside. The friendly staff, placid pool and adjacent cafeteria-style restaurant are the perfect antidote to any suppressed road rage. It's 5 miles west of Arecibo.

TJ Ranch (☎ 787-880-1217; Rte 146; cabins $100; Ⓟ Ⓡ) A charming stop on any karst country driving/cycling tour, TJ Ranch is a little known Eden that harbors three beautiful cabins surrounded by lush foliage next to Lago Dos Bocas. It's actually a working coffee plantation and the congenial hosts are known to be formidable cooks who will concoct all sorts of mini-feasts from the ultimate Puerto Rican cookbook.

Hotel Rosa del Mar (☎ 787-262-1515; Hwy 2 Km 86.6; r $119-149; Ⓡ) Right on the main drag of Hwy 2, this is another conveniently located and comfortable pit stop on the road west 6 miles out of Arecibo. It's also perfectly located for day trips to the Observatorio de Arecibo and the Río Camuy caves, as well as a drive through karst country. Redolent of a Holiday Inn Express (or some other midrange business hotel), this place has sharp and efficient service, business-like rooms and on-site convention facilities. But there's also a gym, a spa and interconnecting rooms for family-oriented travelers.

El Buen Café (☎ 787-898-1000; Hwy 2 No 381 Km 84; dishes $6-15; Ⓥ 5:30am-10pm) A lifesaver on Hwy 2, this no-nonsense cafeteria-style restaurant is open all hours (nearly) and serves cheap but tasty *comida criolla* with plenty of options. You can grab a 5:30am coffee and pastry here or a 9pm rice and beans; food and service are consistent throughout the day and the locals love it.

Lighthouse Bay Restaurant (☎ 787-878-5658; dishes $6-19; Ⓥ lunch & dinner) Near Arecibo's commercial pier on the way to the lighthouse, this is a good stop for lunch or dinner when you are in the area, or if you want to go to the beach or visit the lighthouse and Cueva del Indio. It's $18 for a large platter of *mariscos* (four types of shellfish) or you can go light with a burger for $7.

Entertainment

Lighthouse Bay Restaurant (☎ 787-878-5658) At this eatery you'll find a big crowd on the patio deck and bar every Friday and – sometimes – Saturday, when there is always live music including salsa, merengue and Latin rock.

Getting There & Away

Arecibo is accessible from San Juan or Aguadilla by the Hwy 22 expressway, or from Ponce by Hwy 10. Catch a público just east of the plaza to San Juan ($8, two hours) and to Aguadilla ($6, 1½ hours).

LAGO GUAJATACA

Beautiful and serene, Lago Guajataca has some of Puerto Rico's best fishing – on the north side of the lake are two clubs for anglers hoping to catch the tucunare fish that are stocked in this lake. Right in the middle of karst country, the easiest approach to the lake is along Hwy 2 to Rte 119, and then into the forest to the **DRNA** (☎ 787-896-7640; Rte 119 Km 22.1; Ⓥ 6am-6pm Tue-Sun). You'll need to get a permit here if you want to fish and you can pick up a loaner bamboo fishing pole

---

KARST COUNTRY DRIVING/CYCLING TOUR

Duration Three to four hours without breaks (two days by bike).
Distance 60 miles.
Season Anytime it's not raining.

Start in **Arecibo** (p244) and head south toward Lares, birthplace of the *independenista* movement. Take a scenic detour along the way to the **Observatorio de Arecibo** (p245) and the **Parque de las Cavernas del Río Camuy** (p245). Homing in on Lares, you'll want to stop in the main plaza for ice-cream from the renowned **Heladería de Lares** (p250). Head east next on Hwy 111 (up and down lots of ridges) to the **Parque Ceremonial Indígena Caguana** (p245). After a quiet walk, follow signs toward Utuado, but turn off when you see signs for **Lago Dos Bocas** (p246) and **Lago Caonillas** (p246). You'll find serene accommodations and early-morning yoga nearby at the **Casa Grande Mountain Retreat** (p247). Regular boats ply the lake and ramshackle restaurants sell all the regular Puerto Rican favorites. You can walk off the deep-fried cod fritters by pausing at **Bosque Estatal de Río Abajo** (p246) up Rte 621 where former lumber roads have been converted to trails. Stay on Hwy 10 as it approaches the edge of Arecibo city and hook up with Hwy 681. That will bring you down to the **Faro y Parque Histórico de Arecibo** (p247), where a picturesque lighthouse stands guard over the Caribbean.

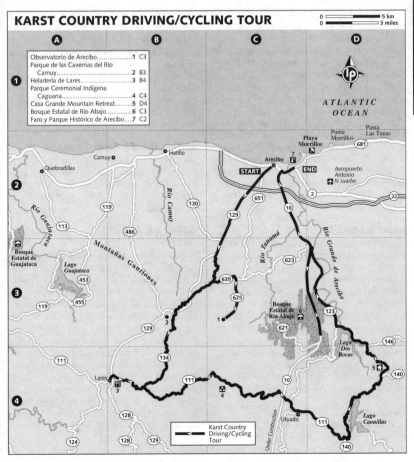

KARST COUNTRY DRIVING/CYCLING TOUR

Observatorio de Arecibo.................1 C3
Parque de las Cavernas del Río
  Camuy..............................2 B3
Heladería de Lares.....................3 B4
Parque Ceremonial Indígena
  Caguana............................4 C4
Casa Grande Mountain Retreat......5 D4
Bosque Estatal de Río Abajo..........6 C3
Faro y Parque Histórico de Arecibo....7 C2

(no bait) from the office. You are also free to use the bathrooms (with showers) and picnic tables. Kayaking is allowed in the lake, but it's best to bring your own kayak. The **Guajataka Kayak Club** (www.ninoscamping.com) meets at 8am on the first Saturday of every month; it's $5 to join in. Swimming in the lake is prohibited.

If you want to stay the night shoreside, try the rustic Hotel Lago Vista (p252). It's also good for a bite to eat, as is the Cafetín Vista al Lado (p252).

BOSQUE ESTATAL DE GUAJATACA
Despite its diminutive size (2300 acres) and proximity to the northwestern coastal towns, the Bosque Estatal de Guajataca contains

more trails (27 miles) than any other forest in Puerto Rico – including El Yunque. Set in dramatic karst country, the distinctive local terrain rises and falls between 500ft and 1000ft above sea level and is characterized by bulbous *mogotes* and rounded *sumideros* (funneled depressions). Covered by a moist subtropical forest and watered by 75 annual inches of rainfall, there are 45 species of bird to be found here along with 186 different types of tree. One of the highlights of the forest is the limestone **Cueva del Viento** (Cave of the Wind), which is rich with stalactites and stalagmites. There is also an observation tower and plantations of blue mahoe trees. The area is a favorite habitat of the endangered Puerto Rican boa.

Compared to other Puerto Rican forests and parks, the trails in Guajataca are relatively well marked, though it's wise to procure a map beforehand to see how the various paths link up. True to form, the **ranger station** (☎ 787-872-1045; Rte 446; ⏰ 8am-5pm) near the trailheads, 5 miles into the forest, is not always open, and when rangers do emerge they don't always have much in the way of printed information. The moral: come prepared. The best bet is to call the Aguadilla office of the DRNA (p253) before you arrive at the forest, find things closed and feel a little lost. Be warned that 'official' maps of the area are usually hand-drawn, photocopied and not to scale.

There are no eating facilities in Guajataca forest.

Sights & Activities

Most of the main hikes depart from, or near, the ranger station on Rte 446. The most popular is the 1.5-mile **Interpretative Trail** that passes the **observation tower** and several other points of interest (be sure to hike to the observation tower to get the best views of the surrounding countryside). It's a moderate walk that takes about two hours. **Trail Number One** breaks off from the Interpretative Trail and heads toward **Cueva del Viento**. There, wooden stairs will take you down into the depths of the dark cave (bring a flashlight). Let rangers know if you are going into the caves.

Sleeping

La Vereda (campsites per person $5) There are 10 campsites here, on Rte 446, about 5 miles

south of Hwy 2. Call the DRNA in San Juan (p87) for a permit and to make reservations, or try the Aguadilla office (p253).

Nino's Camping & Guesthouse (787-896-9016; Rte 119 Km 22.1; campsite/cabins $25/50; 🏊) Near Lago Guajataca, this is a nice lakeside option. The cute little cabins for four to 12 people have everything except sheets and utensils. There's a swimming pool and an activities room on-site.

Getting There & Away

There are no buses to Guajataca. If you're driving, take the Rte 446 south of Hwy 2 and follow it for 5 miles. Bike hire is available at Aquatica Dive & Surf (p254) near the Ramey Base.

ISABELA & AROUND
pop 12,300

Isabela is more famous for its surroundings than its urban attractions. Nicknamed the 'Garden of the Northeast' for its local cheeses and elegant Paso Fino horses, the coastline here is wild and rugged, with classic surfing beaches such as Jobos and Shacks emulating anything that Rincón has to offer. While there's plenty of accommodations and eating joints scattered along Rtes 466 and 4466, the 'scene' here is less cliquey and more isolated. The vistas are spectacular too. After a heavy dose of the ghastly urban sprawl on Hwy 2, the miles of sand dunes, inlets and untrammeled beaches that lie sandwiched between the lashing Atlantic and a 200ft coastal escarpment are a sight for sore eyes.

DETOUR: HELADERÍA DE LARES

For unbiased visitors, sleepy Lares is famous for two reasons. First, it was the site of the short-lived Grito de Lares (p35) independence call in 1868 and, second, it sells some of the best ice-cream on the island, if not in the Caribbean.

To the chagrin of modern-day *independistas*, the bulk of the people who visit the town these days come to consume large quantities of ice-cream rather than plot surreptitious rebellion; and what better place to do it? Their fixation is the understated **Heladería de Lares** (☎ 787-897-3290; Plaza de Recreo, Lecaroz; ⏰ 9am-4pm), an ice-cream store that occupies the ground floor of a three-story building in the town's pleasant main plaza. Though it may not have sparked any history-shaping insurrections since its inception four decades ago, the store's crafty concoction of over 1000 exotic ice-cream flavors, including avocado, *arroz con pollo* (chicken with rice) and – urghhhh – garlic, could certainly be seen as revolutionary.

Wacky, wonderful or just plain weird, the Lares Heladería today is celebrated across the island and is well worth a mile or two's diversion from a karst country driving tour for a fleeting sample. If you prefer your garlic in a curry rather than a cone, don't worry. There are plenty of delicious traditional flavors to choose from such as chocolate, almond and vanilla.

If you stay off the main roads, Isabela is great cycling country and there's a bike rental store close by (p254). Alternatively, you can explore the web of back roads that skirt the edge of karst country around the Bosque Estatal de Guajataca (p249) and nearby Lago Guajataca (p248). The former has a handful of well-signposted hikes (unusual in Puerto Rico), while the latter offers kayaking and fishing.

Orientation & Information

What locals refer to as Playa Jobos is actually one long coastline made up of different beaches – Jobos is the biggest one, at the intersection of Rtes 466 and 4466. That's also where you will find most of the hotels and restaurants. Bosque Estatal de Guajataca is 7 miles inland on Hwy 2. The nearest information center is at the Aguidilla airport on Ramey Base (p253).

Sights & Activities

BEACHES

The wonderfully dramatic crescent of **Playa Jobos** is protected by a large headland of dead coral to the east, and the surf breaks pretty consistently off this point. The site of the 1989 World Surfing Championships, Jobos is a good place to surf or watch professional athletes doing their wave thing. There is also fine swimming off the eastern beach, where the point protects you from the surf. The bar-restaurants on the south side of the cove offer a laid-back après-surf scene, especially on weekends.

Another beach, **Playa Shacks**, lies less than a mile west of Jobos, near Ramey Base on Rte 4466. There are good submarine caves here for snorkeling.

SURFING

While Isabela might lack the dude appeal of Rincón, the waves here are just as legendary. **Playa Jobos** has the best breaks on the island in some books, while other favorite spots include **Surfer's Beach** (preferred location for local contests, with diverse breaks from multiple directions and strong northwestern swells), **Table Top** (named for a flat, exposed reef that looks like a table with a round barrel coming up against cliffs) and **Gas Chambers** (known as Puerto Rico's best 'right tube,' these waves head right for a sharp and unforgiving cliff). Also check out **Secret Spot**, **Sal Si Puedes**, **Shore Island** and **Las Dunas**. See pp74–5.

To get the scoop on what's breaking and where, stop by the appropriately named **Hang Loose Surf Shop** (☎ 787-872-2490; Rte 4466 Km 1.2; ⏰ 11am-5pm Tue-Sat) near Playa Jobos. The shop has a complete selection of gear. Lots of overseas surfers come here to rent boards ($30 a day) for their surfin' safari around Puerto Rico. You can get lessons, too.

DIVING & SNORKELING

La Cueva Submarina Dive Shop (☎ 787-872-1390; www .lacuevasubmarina.com; Rte 466 Km 6.3) – named after the nearby underwater caves – is situated on Rte 466 at Playa Jobos and offers a complete list of dives and dive courses, including underwater cavern dives for skilled divers ($55), as well as guided snorkeling and scuba safaris for inexperienced divers.

CYCLING

Hit the ocean road on or around Rtes 466 and 4466 for some of the best bike rides on the north coast. Bike rental and route details are available from Aquatica Dive & Surf (p254) on Ramey Base.

HORSEBACK RIDING

A horseback ride along a nearly deserted beach is one of the joys of Isabela. You can take a ride along the fields, dunes and beaches with **Tropical Trail Rides** (☎ 787-872-9256; Rte 4466 Km 1.8; rides $35), which works out of stables at Playa Shacks.

Sleeping

It's not legal, but surfers and beach-lovers have been camping on Playa Jobos since the surfing championships were held here more than a decade ago.

Happy Belly's (☎ 787-398-9452; Rte 4466; r $40; P) A few rooms are available in this ugly green building that also houses a popular restaurant (p253), but ignore the facade and this is a good deal, especially if you're looking to rise early and hit the waves. It's perched above Playa Jobos.

Parador Vistamar (☎ 787-895-2065; www.paradorvis tamar.com; Hwy 2 Km 102; r $75-115; P ✕ ♿) A bog-standard Puerto Rican parador with 55 rooms located in two hilltop buildings overlooking the Atlantic, the Vistamar is a little close to traffic-heavy Hwy 2 for comfort. Bland rooms are fine if you're not fussy, or in dire need of a refurb if you are. Unhappy campers can console themselves with private decks, ocean views, a fun kiddie pool, tennis courts and a passable on-site restaurant. The Vistamar is situated 5 miles east of Isabela.

Hotel Lago Vista (☎ 787-896-5487; Hwy 119 Km 22; r $85-135; P ⛽ 🍽) Move a few miles inland and a halcyon world quickly emerges. Set on the shore of rural Lago Guajataca (p248), Lago Vista is a rustic country inn with a pool and sun deck. Simple but elegant rooms overlook the placid lake from balconies. It's peaceful and serene, and there's a restaurant serving *comida criolla*.

Hotel Restaurante Ocean Front (☎ 787-872-0444; www.oceanfrontpr.com; Rte 4466 Km 0.1; r $85-150; P 🍽) Imagine a classic Caribbean-style beach hotel situated on a wild and tempestuous stretch of sand popularly regarded by aficionados as being surfers' heaven. That's the Ocean Front; small, compact, suitably modern but not too flash. Rooms have balconies and good views of the incoming surf and there's a popular on-site restaurant-bar (opposite) that hosts occasional live music. Room rates are lowest Monday to Friday. The hotel is situated 5 miles west of Isabela on Playa Jobos.

Parador Villas del Mar Hau (☎ 787-872-2045; www.paradorvillasdelmarhau.com; Rte 466 Km 8.3; cabins $95-165; P 🍽 ⛽) Places like this barely exist anymore: a gorgeous clutch of brightly painted beach huts scattered like bucolic homesteads along a breathtaking beach where offshore coral islets create bathing lagoons. This rustic retreat has been continuously run by the Hau family for nearly 50 years and aside from the distant glimmer of encroaching condo towers, little has changed. The huts, nestled under wind-gnarled pine trees, have sea-facing decks and basic but comfortable fittings in keeping with the back-to-nature surroundings. Although popular during the summer, off-season this has to be one of the most tranquil places on the island. You can ride a horse, take a cycling tour, kayak, snorkel, hike the beach or sleep undisturbed under a palm tree. The villas are 4 miles west of Isabela.

Hotel El Guajataca (☎ 800-964-3065; www.hotel guajataca.com; Hwy 2 Km 103.8; r $107-139; P 🍽 ⛽) About 5 miles east of Isabela in Quebradillas, El Guajataca is a run-of-the-mill parador – ie slightly jaded rooms, keen-to-please staff and good family facilities – notable for its stupendous north-coast setting. Perched on a grassy cliff overlooking the Atlantic, this is Puerto Rico at its wildest and most romantic, although the inn doesn't come close

to emulating the setting. There's a pool, a tennis court and a so-so restaurant, along with easy access to a great surfing (but no swimming) beach.

Hacienda Jibarito (☎ 787-280-4040; Rte 445 Km 6.4; r $129-279; P 🍽 ⛽) Opened in 2006, this innovative new ecolodge bills itself as an 'agro-tourist complex,' that is, a hotel that doubles up as a hacienda (working ranch). But you don't have to be a full-blown cowboy to stay here. Although the facilities retain suitably rustic touches such as hammocks, rocking chairs and antique farming implements, this is not the complete back-to-nature experience you get in the outback. Comfortable rooms sport TVs, phones and bathtubs, and a laid-back poolside bar shakes up some refreshing piña coladas. But the hacienda's real forte lies in its beautifully landscaped grounds and positive environmental practices. The adjacent *granja* (farm) – which guests may visit – makes use of its own chicken, cows, shrimp farm and greenhouse to send produce directly to the on-site restaurant. The Hacienda is 8 miles south of Isabela heading along Hwy 112.

ourpick Villa Montaña (☎ 787-872-9554; www.villamontana.com; Rte 4466 Km 1.2; villas $250-350; P 🍽 💻 ⛽) At last, a large, posh resort that makes a successful effort of blending in with its natural environment. No golf courses, no casinos and no view-spoiling high-rises here; just 48 plantation-style villas in splendid isolation abutting tempestuous Playa Shacks. Even better, this place has a fine environmental record and there's an on-site organic kitchen garden that is raided daily to season the delicious restaurant food to prove it. Villas are one, two or three bedrooms and are brightly decorated in ebullient Caribbean patterns. Tucked away amid the tropical foliage, meanwhile, you'll find a tennis court, a gym, a spa and the Moroccan-themed Eclipse restaurant. Not surprisingly, accommodations get booked up fast.

Eating

Cafetín Vista al Lado (☎ 787-895-6877; Hwy 453 Km 4.2; dishes $5-10; ☾ lunch & dinner) If you are exploring karst country, stop on the east side of Lago Guajataca (p248) for some grilled chicken or pork. You can eat it at a picnic table with a view of the lake and dairy farms. There's also live music (opposite).

Happy Belly's (☎ 787-398-9452; Rte 4466; dishes $5-17; ☺ lunch & dinner) When the swell is good you could almost surf right up to the verandah here and place your lunch order with the dude waiter before paddling back out to catch a last wave. Perched above magnificent Playa Jobos, Happy Belly's confronts the sea head on, offering front-row seats for one of Puerto Rico's most visually dazzling surfing 'shows.' Food is of the simple burger and fish variety, but this place is more about setting than scrumptious cuisine. Order a cold Medalla beer and grab a wooden booth among the suntanned surf groupies and boogie boarders. There are also rooms available here (p251).

Hotel Restaurante Ocean Front (☎ 787-872-0444; www.oceanfrontpr.com; Rte 4466 Km 0.1; dishes $6-22; ☺ lunch & dinner) Tiny glowing lights and wavy green plants give this restaurant a relaxed, romantic atmosphere that perfectly complements the seafood dishes. The owner is famous for his secret salmon recipe. Live music nightly. Rooms available (opposite).

Cano's Trattoria Italiana (☎ 787-830-9154; Hwy 2 Km 108; dishes $7-22; ☺ lunch & dinner) A new location 8 miles east of Isabela has worked wonders for Cano's and added a nice touch of Tuscany to the otherwise cultureless Hwy 2. Cano's has deep-dish lasagna, calzones, homemade pastas and great pizza.

El Pescador (☎ 787-872-1343; Rte 466; dishes $8-26; ☺ lunch & dinner) This decent spot just west of Isabela does excellent seafood with a Caribbean twist. Beyond the fresh fish and loyal following of locals, there's evening karaoke mixed in with the occasional live salsa and meringue band.

Entertainment

Happy Belly's (☎ 787-398-9452; Rte 4466; ☺ until midnight) Lots of gringos pass by this popular eatery (above) on Thursday nights for some ear-splitting karaoke. If you can't handle amateur demolitions of old Bruce Springsteen numbers, try the live salsa and meringue on Wednesday, Friday and Saturday nights or the DJ on Sunday.

Mi Casita Tropical (☎ 787-872-5510; Rte 466; ☺ 1pm-midnight) Next to Happy Belly's, Mi Casita attracts a similar crowd and the two places often swap patrons all night.

Cafetín Vista al Lado (☎ 787-895-6877; Hwy 453 Km 4.2) In karst country, this restaurant (opposite) on Lago Guajataca has live music Saturday and Sunday until about 1am.

Getting There & Away

The easiest way to access the region, from San Juan or the west coast, is via the four-lane Hwy 22. But to really enjoy this area (and its lack of traffic), you need to get off the main highway and explore the back roads.

No públicos serve these back roads or beach areas such as Playa Jobos.

AGUADILLA
pop 15,700

Central Aguadilla occupies a small sliver of land wedged between Hwy 2 and the sea. Famous for its world-class surf beaches, colorful marine life and now defunct US air-force base, it is not an ugly place, but like many Puerto Rican towns the older sections have been largely abandoned in favor of generic out-of-town shopping malls (most of which infest Hwy 2).

The early colonizers of Aguadilla (founded in 1780) were Spanish loyalists fleeing from the Haitian invasion of Spanish Hispaniola in 1822. By the late 19th century the settlement had become an important port, but in 1918 its fortunes changed for the worse when it was ravaged by the destructive San Fermin earthquake and subsequent tsunami.

Attractions in town are thin on the ground, though a recent renovation has spruced up the central Plaza Colón. Surfers head north to the unblemished beauty of Crash Boat, Shacks and Jobos beaches, while committed golfers wheel their clubs to the windy Punta Borinquen course built for President Dwight Eisenhower. If neither activity appeals to you, give Aguadilla a body-swerve and head west to Rincón.

Orientation & Information

All of Aguadilla's accommodations are north of the city center, which is located on a tiny strip of land trapped between Hwy 2 and the coast. Rte 111 runs north–south through the city and then crosses Rte 107, which will take you to Ramey Base.

Departamento de Recursos Naturales y Ambientales (DRNA; Department of Natural Resources & Environment; ☎ 787-890-4050/2050)

Puerto Rico Tourism Company (PRTC; ☎ 787-890-3315) For more information about this region, check out this helpful office at the Aeropuerto Rafael Hernández, north of town on the old Ramey Base.

Sights & Activities

RAMEY BASE

Vieques, Culebra, Desecheo and Roosevelt Rds; sometimes it's hard to avoid bumping into erstwhile US military anachronisms when you're traveling through Puerto Rico. And, just when you thought you'd had your fill, here comes Ramey, near Aguadilla, a Cold War strategic command base created by the US Air Force in 1939 to serve as its Caribbean HQ. For 30 years the Americans poured money into Ramey and watched as the surrounding area burgeoned into a populous municipality of 64,000 people. And then in 1973 the base closed leaving behind a weirdly homogeneous stretch of track housing and the usual American fast-food restaurants.

Today, the former base hosts the international Aeropuerto Rafael Hernández, a university campus, a couple of hotels, a housing project and the only **ice-skating arena** (☎ 787-819-5555; admission $10-13; ⏰ 9:30am-11pm) in the Caribbean.

If you are traveling to the base from the south, take Hwy 107 north from Hwy 2. This route brings you through what is called Gate 1. The traffic can get a little nutty on this road, so you may want to approach from the east via Hwy 110 (the route to the airport), which brings you through Gate 5. Once you're in, have fun getting lost on the maze of roads that lead you around the airfield, administration buildings and the nearly endless plots of former base housing that have been sold off or rented to Puerto Rican families.

BEACHES

For some swimming, snorkeling and legendary surf breaks, the most popular place to go is **Playa Crash Boat**. It got its name because the air force used to keep rescue boats here to pick up crews from the Strategic Air Command's bombers that didn't make the runway. The beach lies off Hwy 107, halfway between town and the former air base. You will see a sign for Crash Boat that directs you west on the short Hwy 458.

If you are more adventurous and want to avoid the crowds, follow Hwy 107 past the Crash Boat turnoff and onto the base. Eventually, you will see the golf course on your left and a road that heads west through the golf course. Follow this road as it winds down to rough, lonely **Playa Wilderness** and the ruins of what must have been air-force

recreation clubs. Surfers like this desolate place, but also congregate up and down this coast (see p251).

GOLF

Punta Borinquen Golf (☎ 787-890-2987; greens fee Mon-Fri $18, Sat & Sun $20) Although Aguadilla is no Dorado when it comes to golf, it does boast this 6800yd 18-hole course on the former air-force base that was designed for President Dwight D Eisenhower – no less. The course offers a cafeteria, a pro shop, a practice range and lessons.

CYCLING

Aquatica Dive & Surf (☎ 787-890-6071; Rte 110 Km 10), just outside Gate 5 of Ramey Base, is one of Puerto Rico's best bike-rental establishments. The staff here can also help you with route planning. There are plenty of decent circuits in the Aguadilla/Isabela area that steer clear of the main roads and incorporate some magnificent rural scenery.

Sleeping & Eating

Hacienda El Pedregal (☎ 787-891-6068; www.elpedregal .com; Hwy 111 Km 0.1; r $70-90; P ⚑) Right next to the Cielo Mar Hotel but set back a bit (thus not enjoying the same stupendous views), El Pedregal is nonetheless a decent midrange option with lush grounds (palms, gazebos and birds) and a good selection of facilities (swimming pool, basketball court, activity room and on-site laundry). Situated north of Aguadilla in a quiet leafy neighborhood, the Hacienda has 27 well-appointed rooms and a renovated restaurant serving *comida criolla*.

Parador JB Hidden Village (☎ 787-868-8686; Hwy 416, Aguada; r & ste $70-125; P ⚑) Five miles south of Aguadilla on the way to Rincón you'll see this 33-room parador, which has marble floors, big beds, a restaurant and a pool. Some rooms have kitchenettes or you can chance your arm in the on-site Meson Las Colinas.

Cielo Mar Hotel (☎ 787-882-5959; www.cielomar .com; 84 Av Monemar, Hwy 111; r $80-105; P ⚑ ⚑ ⚑) In Aguadilla's strung-out hotel strip, the Cielo Mar takes first prize for location, situated high atop the area's famous surfing breaks with spectacular views over the town, an old sugar factory, Rincón, Isla Desecheo and those blood-red west-coast sunsets. Although the building itself with its bright orange chocolate-box architecture is hardly a stunner, the rooms are adequate and the

BIKE SHOP OWNER, JOSÉ RAFOLS SALLABERRY

Is there a cycling culture in Puerto Rico? There's no full-blown cycling culture, but non-competitive cycling is becoming ever more popular. Lance Armstrong made an important impression among Americans with his Tour de France wins and this effect has filtered through to Puerto Rico.

Where can you find it? Various cycling groups operate on different parts of the island. There's one in San Juan and another in the Cabo Rojo area. They generally meet on Sunday mornings for group rides.

What are the classic routes? Cabo Rojo on the southwest of the island offers some of the best on- and off-road routes. Rte 10 between Arecibo and Ponce also has some winding, precipitous terrain. Closer to home, there are some good 50km to 80km rides around the Isabela area in the northwest.

What aggravations do you face? Glass on the road, the occasional pothole and those famously unforgiving Puerto Rican motorists.

What safeguards are there for cyclists? More than you'd imagine – at least on paper. A few years ago a Puerto Rican senator got knocked off his bike and broke his leg. As a result, he suggested some important new safety legislation for bikers and his proposed bill was passed. Cyclists now have an official right to use the road and motorists must respect this. Drivers should only pass cyclists on the left, leaving at least 4ft of space, and they are not supposed to honk.

What's your favorite ride? Off-roading in the Cabo Rojo area. It mixes technical climbs with smooth stretches and has some pretty views.

Can you tour the island by bicycle? There's no reason why you shouldn't, as long as you take the normal precautions and stay off the main toll roads. An official 'Vuelta' ride takes place in late November in three stages between San Juan, Mayagüez and Guayama. There's also an organized ride that calls in at each of the island's nine historic lighthouses.

As told to Brendan Sainsbury

substantial swimming pool with its huge whale-shaped slide and obligatory fountain conjures up a family atmosphere. The best of the view can be enjoyed from the on-site Restaurant Terramar (p256).

Parador La Cima (☎ 787-890-2016; www.lacimahotel.com; Hwy 110 Km 9.2; r $85-140; P ✕ ▣ ▨) More motel than hotel, La Cima's a three-story concrete building in the no-man's-land just outside Gate 5 of Ramey Base. But what you sacrifice in location you make up for with a plethora of handy facilities. Count in an on-site gym, a swimming pool, a business center (with wi-fi access), two restaurants and a laundry room. You're also just round the corner from a rare Puerto Rican bike-rental store (opposite) giving you instant access to a whole host of other treats. The hotel also rents two-bedroom apartments from $175 per night.

Parador El Faro (☎ 787-882-8000; Hwy 107 Km 2.1; r $85-155; P ✕ ▨) On a rather nondescript highway between Aguadilla and Ramey Base, El Faro hides some sweet horticultural surprises. The main attraction is the lush tropical grounds – you walk through a vine-covered canopy to get from the swimming pool to

your room – plus the ultrafriendly front-desk service and decent on-site restaurant. The 50 rooms are the simple but clean accommodations you have come to expect from an unpretentious parador, but encased in such splendiferous natural surroundings they appear colored with a more luxurious tint.

our pick Cocina Creativa (☎ 787-890-1861; Hwy 110 Km 9.2; snacks $5-7; ☯ 9am-5pm Sun-Wed, 9am-6pm Thu-Sat; Ⓥ) Just when you'd given up hope of ever seeing an inventive, unique, nonfranchised eating establishment again, up pops Cocina Creativa, a fresh, cozy, homegrown resting place tucked rather incongruously behind a gas station on one of the northwest's ubiquitous big box strips. You can realign your zen here with a kind of organic-meets-European-meets-Jamaican menu. Try the yucca and fish-cakes, the jerk chicken with mango chutney or the amazing bruschettas.

Restaurant Garibaldi's (☎ 787-997-4730; Rte 107 Km 2.2; dishes $7-24) If you are really hungry, you might possibly finish one of these burritos by yourself – the Mexican dishes here are impossibly large, but very tasty. Enchiladas, tostadas, tacos and more, served daily.

ISLA DESECHEO

The alluring hump-shaped island that appears Robinson Crusoe–like across the horizon in spectacular Rincón sunsets is Isla Desecheo, a 1-sq-mile knob of prickly cacti and bushy scrub that is situated 13 miles off Puerto Rico's northwest coast. One of four outlying islands that make up the Puerto Rican archipelago (the others are Culebra, Vieques and Mona), Desecheo was first 'discovered' by Columbus in 1493 but remained unnamed until Spanish explorer Nuñez Alvarez de Aragón passed through in 1517. Buccaneers and pirates frequented these wild shores during the 16th and 17th centuries to hoard booty and hunt feral goats that had been introduced by the Spanish, but in the years since the only permanent inhabitants have been lizards, seabirds and the odd ugly rat. From WWII to the early 1950s, Desecheo was – surprise, surprise – used as a bombing range by the US military who left behind a dangerous cache of unexploded ordnance, a fact that has meant that the island is still officially off-limits to visitors (trespassers will be arrested).

But all is not lost. Thanks to its favorable position to the west of the geologically important Puerto Rican Trench, the waters around Desecheo are free from murky river run-off from the main island. As a result the sea here is unusually clear (visibility is generally 30m to 45m), making it one of the best spots for diving in the Caribbean. Desecheo was declared a US Fish and Wildlife Refuge in 1976 and a National Wildlife Refuge in 1983.

Restaurant Terramar (☎ 787-882-5959; www.cielo mar.com; 84 Av Monemar, Hwy 111; dishes $13-28; Ⓥ lunch & dinner) At the Cielo Mar Hotel (p254) north of Aguadilla, this restaurant takes prime spot on a pretty patio overlooking the sea. Dishes include a $28 lobster, *mofongos* (mashed plantains) and prawns.

Entertainment

The Cielo Mar Hotel (p254) features lightweight rock and salsa bands on weekends for dancing. For a more raucous scene, check out the many American-style bars near Ramey Base.

Getting There & Away

Scheduled airline services to Aguadilla's Aeropuerto Rafael Hernández change seasonally. Flights come in from New York and Newark (US) and the Dominican Republic about three times a week.

There is a público terminal in town right off the central plaza, if you really want to wait around for a ride to your next destination. Expect to pay $18 to San Juan (about 3 hours).

If you are driving between San Juan and the west coast (and want to avoid rush-hour traffic), consider taking the back road Hwy 443, which breaks off Hwy 2 just east of town, then rejoins it to the south.

Getting Around

If you have reached Aguadilla by público or plane, you can rent a car to explore the interesting backcountry of the surrounding area. Try **Budget** (☎ 787-890-1110) at the airport. Cycling is another feasible option; see p254.

Central Mountains

Exotic birds swoop majestically over mist-enveloped peaks, vivid red flamboyán trees punctuate lush valleys covered in a velvety green foliage, and a rustically clad *jíbaro* stops by the roadside to adjust his wide-brimmed straw sombrero. Welcome to Puerto Rico's central mountains, a verdant pastiche of small-scale coffee plantations and half-forgotten towns that still reverberates with the echoes of island's earliest inhabitants. Colored by rich Taíno legends and immortalized by poets in popular folklore, the island's traditions remain strong up here in a world so detached from the coast it's almost eerie. Throw away your maps, prize yourself away from the baccarat table, and get ready to find out why Puerto Rico really isn't that 'American' after all.

Crossing the magic line that separates the sierra from the shoreline is relatively easy. You can penetrate the island's mountainous backbone from either coast and lose yourself in a world of narrow roads and hidden viewpoints seemingly within minutes. The ultimate thrill is to tackle the crenellated peaks east to west via the Ruta Panorámica, a narrow, winding road laid down in the 1950s that dips like a primordial roller coaster from valley to ridge and back down to valley. Along the way you'll spy homey *colmados* (small grocery stores), isolated farms, and a way of life that has all but disappeared from the modern dog-eat-dog cities. For outsiders, this is Puerto Rico from another era, a deliciously tranquil rural haven that is often more redolent of Cuba or the Dominican Republic than of the Caribbean's US-sponsored economic powerhouse.

HIGHLIGHTS

- Lining up with the locals at the *lechoneras* in **Guavate** (p261)
- Whiffing the aroma of homegrown Puerto Rican coffee in **Hacienda San Pedro** (p269)
- Bushwhacking your way up an overgrown trail in the **Reserva Forestal Toro Negro** (p265)
- Jumping on and off the rural roller coaster that is the **Ruta Panorámica** (p269)
- Uncovering a lost world on the **Cañon de San Cristóbal** (p262) hike

- POPULATION: 350,000

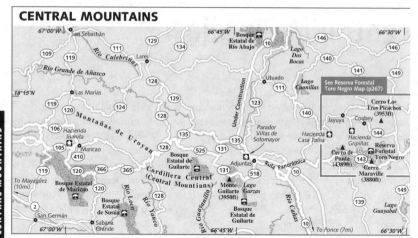

History

Thanks to their impregnable terrain, the central mountains have long acted as a haven for the rebellious and the repressed. Legend has it, native Taíno survived here until the mid-19th century and, even today, Indian traditions run strong in the festivals and artisan workshops scattered along the Ruta Panorámica. In more recent times, notoriety has struck these mountains twice. In 1950, an abortive uprising in Jayuya marked the death knell of the Puerto Rican independence movement as an effective political force. A further scandal erupted in 1978 when two young independence supporters were shot by policeman posing as revolutionaries on Cerro Maravilla in an incident that uncovered corruption, ballot-box fraud and an alleged FBI cover-up.

Climate

The climate in the mountains is wetter, cloudier and cooler than down on the coast. Cerro Maravilla in the Toro Negro forest records average high/lows a good 10°F to 15°F lower than in San Juan. Expect highs of 68°F and lows of 56°F in January. Rainfall is higher in the Cordillera Central. The Ruta Panorámica is often blanketed in mist on its loftier sections.

Getting There & Around

The Ruta Panorámica (p269), a chain of 40 mountain roads, travels 165 miles across the roof of Puerto Rico, from Yabucoa in the east to Mayagüez in the west. This chapter takes you along this route from east to west. It is generally well marked with distinctive brown road signs and highlighted on almost all commercial maps of the island. If you're driving, proceed carefully and never drive after dark.

The major towns in the central region such as Aibonito, Barranquitas and Adjuntas are easily accessed by público from either coast. Some of the more remote places, however, are a little more difficult to reach and, if you're without your own car, you may require lifts, taxis or plenty of forward planning. Bikes can be precarious on the Ruta Panorámica where drivers are famously erratic. Riders should stick to the wider link roads such as Rte 15 between Cayey and Guayama and listen to local advice.

BOSQUE ESTATAL DE CARITE

Less than an hour south of San Juan, the **Bosque Estatal de Carite** (Carite Forest Reserve; ☎ 787-747-4545; Rte 184 Km 27.5; ☼ 7am-3:30pm Mon-Fri) was created in 1935 to protect the watersheds of various local rivers from the forces of erosion. Measuring 6000 acres in area, the mountain reserve is easily accessed from the San Juan metro area, and it can get crowded on weekends and during the summer when *sanjuaneros* come here to enjoy the 72°F temperatures, green shade, and dozens of *lechonerías* (restaurants specializing in suckling pig) that line Hwy 184 as it approaches the northern forest entrance (see box, p261). The forest is one of the first points of interest you will hit if you are traversing the Ruta Panorámica east to west.

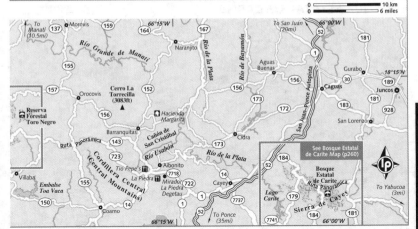

As with most Puerto Rican forest reserves, facilities are spartan and ranger stations are often unmanned.

If you are intending to stay in the reserve, bring water, insect repellent and food; no supplies are sold inside.

Orientation

The only way to enter the forest is by car. From the north, take Hwy 52 to the Cayey Este exit to Hwy 184. From the south, take the Ruta Panorámica from Yabucoa. You can also reach the forest from Patillas on the south coast via Hwy 184.

Sights & Activities

Carite, like many of Puerto Rico's forest reserves, is a great place for hiking, camping, fishing, toe-dipping (in pools and streams) and bird-watching, as long as you're up for a bit of DIY adventure. There are 49 species of bird here – including the endangered native *falcón de sierra* (mountain hawk) – and numerous species of tree. If you are passing through the forest on the Ruta Panorámica, you can stop for a picnic at the **Area Recreativa Charco Azul** (🕐 9am-6pm), a recreation/camping area near the southeastern entrance on Hwy 184, and take a short walk to the Charco Azul natural pool (see Charco Azul Trail, right). You can also stop off at **Area Recreativa Guavate** (🕐 9am-4.30pm Mon-Fri, 8am-5pm Sat & Sun) at the northern end for a spot of sunbathing and bird-watching (see Charles Rivera

Rodriguez Trail, p260) or some local food tasting at the nearby *lechonerías* (see box, p261). The third potential stopping place is the **Area Recreativa Real Patillas** (🕐 9am-6pm) on Hwy 184 to the south, at the start of the El Seis trail.

HIKING

Hurricanes have wreaked havoc on Carite's trails in the past and paths are constantly being cleared and restored. Of the trails below, Charco Azul, El Radar and Charles Rivera Rodríguez are the most reliable. It's best to phone ahead to check current conditions if you're a serious hiker.

At Las Casas de la Selva (p260), managers can provide information and guides for long hikes through Carite, including the six-hour trek through Hero Valley which is for experienced hikers only.

Charco Azul Trail

The most popular trail in the reserve and the most easily accessible is Charco Azul, which takes you to the swimming hole and camping/picnic area of the same name. It is an easy half-mile walk from Hwy 184, near the southeast corner of the forest. Beyond here a sketchy trail leads to the top of Cerro La Santa (2730 feet), Carite's highest point.

El Radar Trail

El Radar trailhead departs to the south, off Hwy 184 near the northwest corner of the

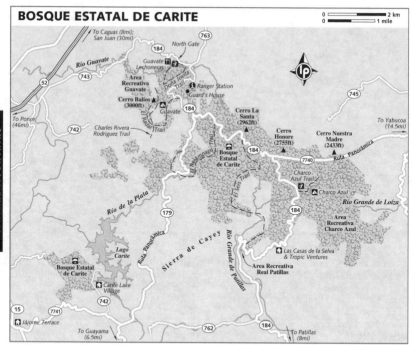

BOSQUE ESTATAL DE CARITE

forest, and makes a steep, one-mile climb to the peak of Cerro Balíos. There is a Doppler radar weather station here, plus vistas of the north and south coasts, as well as toward El Yunque.

Charles Rivera Rodriguez Trail

Starting at Guavate Recreation Area, this path goes up a steep and somewhat muddy trail. It takes about 35 minutes to ascend and offers some good bird-watching.

El Seis Trail

This steep three-mile jaunt starts at the Real Patillas recreation area on Hwy 184 a few miles south of Charco Azul. Unless you have a car to meet you at the other end, you'll have to do it as a six-mile out-and-back hike.

El Relámpago Trail

This path veers south off Hwy 184 a mile or so before the junction with Hwy 179. It follows the Río La Plata before winding round to cross Hwy 179 and veering north on the other side. It's about four miles one way and is fairly challenging.

Sleeping & Eating

The forest has two **camping areas** (campsites per person $4, children under 10 free). At the northwest corner of the reserve is Guavate, with room for six tents and 30 people. Charco Azul, the more attractive choice, is the pondside camping area at the southeast end of the reserve. It can accommodate 10 tents and 50 people. Both areas have toilet and bathing facilities. Reserve 15 days in advance with the Departamento de Recursos Naturales y Ambientales (DRNA; p87).

Las Casas de la Selva & Tropic Ventures (☎ 787-839-7381; Hwy 184 Km 16.1; campsites $10, cabin $50) This reserve is on the south slope of the Sierra de Cayey in the Río Grande de Patillas watershed. There was once a coffee plantation here, but 20 years ago it was turned into a sustainable-growth tree farm and a model for rainforest protection. The 1000-acre reserve has scientific relationships with local schools, colleges and Earth Watch expeditions. Students of a variety of ages come to work, learn about rainforest ecology and explore (see Volunteering, p285). Tourists can come here for a rustic vacation experience, sleeping in the heart of the forest. To find Las Casas de la Selva, follow Hwy 184 southeast toward Patillas through the Bosque Estatal de Carite to Km 16.1, where you will see a sign for the reserve. Note: the gate will be locked unless you make a reservation. If you want to stay here, there are tent sites, rent-a-tents ($35 for two people) and one rustic cabin with bathroom.

Carite Lake Village (☎ 787-763-4003; Rte 742 Km 2; r $75-90) Lots of peach-colored villas around the lake don't exactly make a village, but this place comes close. There are basketball courts, a boat ramp, a playground and an on-site restaurant. This is not exactly a place that's in tune with nature, but it's fun.

Jájome Terrace (☎ 787-738-4016; Rte 15 Km 4.6; r $107-124) Rich in both history and setting, the lush Jájome, which sits 2800ft up in the mountains of the Cordillera Central with satellite map views over towards Ponce, has been in business since the 1930s. In its early years, national icon Luis Muñoz Marín was a regular visitor. Almost wiped out by Hurricane George in 1998, the wooden Jájome was revamped in sturdy brick in 2002 and reopened with its 10 fully renovated rooms and popular open-terrace restaurant fresh with nouveau rustic charm. With no TVs or phones and no cell phone reception, the Jájome can sometimes feel like it's miles from anywhere, particularly from Mondays to Fridays when the restaurant is closed and there may be no other guests. Their loss could be your gain.

Getting There & Around
While a few públicos pass this way, they can be infrequent. Getting to the insanely popular restaurant strip of Guavate may be your best bet – the forest's northern gate (plus trails and camping access) is less than half a mile from here. The most popular way of seeing the mountains in their entirety is still a rental car.

AIBONITO & AROUND
pop 9200

Once the de facto capital of Puerto Rico, after the Spanish Governor Romualdo Palacios González established residence here in 1887, Aibonito has long been a retreat for the island's political leaders, its devout people, and the most wealthy. The town has a number of other claims to fame that include being the island's highest town (at about 2000ft), the site of the island's lowest recorded temperature (40°F in 1911) and the home of an

---

DETOUR: GUAVATE

Puerto Ricans invariably speak of Guavate in reverential tones. It's almost as if they know something you don't, an in-joke perhaps or a modus operandi that isn't written in the standard tourist textbook. During the week, this unkempt strip of scruffy, shack-like restaurants that abuts the Carite Forest is, well…just that. But come here at weekends and you'll witness a heady transformation – a country with its guard down, a nation with its mask off, a free-spirited populace united in its taste for good food, spontaneous dancing and plenty of boisterous revelry.

Considered the font of traditional Puerto Rican cooking, Guavate is the spiritual home of the island's ultimate culinary 'delicacy,' *lechon asado,* or whole roast pig, a locally reared hog turned on a spit about five meters from where you're sitting. But first impressions can be deceiving. Although the myriad *lechoneras* that pepper the roadside might look a little rough around the edges (cardboard plates, plastic forks, Formica tables), the assembled crowds tell another story. Everyone from millionaire businessmen to cigar-puffing *jíbaros* flock to this no-holds-barred food fest to sample the best in authentic Puerto Rican cuisine and culture. If it's the island's uninhibited 'soul' you're after, look no further.

The best action takes place on weekend afternoons between 2pm and 9pm, when old-fashioned troubadours entertain the crowds and live salsa, meringue and reggaeton music gets diners out of their chairs and onto any available floor space for libidinous dancing. With over a dozen restaurants and stalls all offering similar canteen-style food and service, your best bet is to follow the crowds and sample anything that gets put in front you. More daring creations include *arroz con grandules* (rice and pigeon peas), *pasteles* (mashed plantain and pork) and – brave, this one – *morcillas* (rice and pigs blood).

To get to Guavate from San Juan, follow expressway 52 to exit 31, halfway between Caguas and Cayey. Turn onto Hwy 184 and let your adventure begin.

impressive flower festival. For all these reasons, and because it's on the Ruta Panorámica, Aibonito is the most visited mountain town in Puerto Rico.

The town has a euphonious name that suggests a Spanish exclamation meaning 'Wow, how beautiful,' but the name is probably derived from a Taíno word that the first Spanish settlers heard when they arrived here in the 1630s. Today, travelers should associate Aibonito with beauty only in very specific ways. The town itself, which shelters a little less than half of the municipality's 25,000 residents, is something of a mixed bag. It sprawls across a high plateau in a slight rift between surrounding peaks. There are traffic jams every day on the narrow roads at the center of town, as rural families gravitate here for shopping, banking and – naturally – a visit to the drive-thru McDonald's. Thriving flower-growing, poultry-raising and poultry-processing industries have brought prosperity to the region, with little thought to urban planning and only belated attention to the area's natural gifts.

Yet there are two extraordinary natural treasures here. One, Mirador La Piedra Degetau, is a cluster of boulders on a peak bordering the Ruta Panorámica; there are great views from this place. Even more spectacular is the Cañón de San Cristóbal (St Christopher Canyon), which lies north of town in a deep volcanic rift cut into the rolling fields between Aibonito and the neighboring town of Barranquitas.

Aibonito-lovers claim that the weather in their town is perpetually spring-like. They are not exaggerating: the average temperature is 72°F. Gentle showers are common.

Most drivers approach Aibonito via the Ruta Panorámica. A less-traveled and more dramatic route (if you like hairpin turns) is to take Hwy 173 and Hwy 14 south from Cidra.

Sights

CAÑÓN DE SAN CRISTÓBAL

The canyon is so unexpected in both its location and appearance that it may take your breath away. The deep green chasm with its rocky crags and veil of falling water lies less than 5 miles north of Aibonito. The canyon is a fissure that cuts more than 500ft down through the Central Mountains. But you probably will not see it even as you approach its edge, because the rift is so deep and narrow

that the fields and hills of the surrounding high-mountain plateau disguise it.

The highest waterfall on the island is here, where the Río Usabón plummets at least 500ft down a sheer cliff into a gorge that is deeper, in many places, than it is wide. For fit mountaineering enthusiasts, the descent into the canyon is a first-class thrill whether you take steep trails or make it a technical descent. Not so long ago, San Cristóbal was a garbage dump, but the Conservation Trust of Puerto Rico saved the canyon by buying up most of it for preservation.

You can catch a glimpse of the canyon from a distance by looking east from the intersection of Hwy 725 and Hwy 162. But to get close, you have to take one of the side roads off Hwy 725 or Hwy 7725, and then cross private land to approach the rim of the canyon. Do not try this: you will be trespassing unless you actually get permission to cross private property, and you could easily put yourself at risk if you do not know the terrain. Cañón de San Cristóbal has sheer cliffs that are prone to erosion and landslides, and the trails into the canyon are so steep as to be an invitation for suicide when they get wet (and it rains a lot around here).

The best way to visit the canyon is to plan ahead, make reservations and join an organized trek with **San Cristóbal Hiking Tour** (☎ 787-857-2094; www.viajes.barranquitaspr.com) run by local historian and geographer Samuel Oliveras Ortiz. Trips run on weekends and holidays and vary from a three- to four-hour basic tour ($60) to a five- to six-hour adrenalin-junkie fest with rock climbing and rappelling ($85). Wear secure shoes and appropriate clothing that you can take off at the canyon floor, where temperatures can be more than 10°F warmer than up on the brink. Of course, you will need water and maybe some energy bars to get you back up the canyon wall.

MIRADOR LA PIEDRA DEGETAU

This nest of boulders lies on a hilltop alongside the Ruta Panorámica (Hwy 7718 here) at Km 0.7, just south of Aibonito. Once the 'thinking place' of Ponce-born writer Federico Degetau y González, who became the island's first resident commissioner in Washington DC, from 1900 to 1904, this must have been a truly sublime place in its day, with views of the mountains, the Atlantic and the Caribbean. On a clear evening, you can actually see cruise ships leaving San Juan more than 20 miles to

CENTRAL MOUNTAINS

the north and the lights of Ponce beginning to glow to the south.

Sadly, the natural beauty of the site has been marred by an architecturally horrific park and lookout tower that dwarf the actual rocks, which huddle like small pebbles to the side. Myriad picnic shelters, a playground and a paved parking lot further hinder the lyrical ruminations of potential poets. It's still an awe-inspiring view but one can't help feeling that the erstwhile Degetau must be turning in his grave.

LA CASILLA
This yellow 1880s lodge on the edge of town now serves as the **Centro Cultural Angel R Ortiz** (☎ 787-735-6093; Hwy 14 Km 51.8; admission free), a small museum maintained by the Puerto Rican Institute of Culture. The building was once part of a network of 27 such huts that housed so-called 'road keepers' (in this case, convicts). The lodge stands on the old 'pick and shovel' road built by slaves of Spanish landowners and later maintained by black convicts over the centuries. In the last years of Spanish colonization, decadent *criollo* landowners of Aibonito used to boast that the government had killed all of the town's people of African descent by forcing them to build the road. Phone ahead for reservations.

Festivals & Events
The **Festival de Flores** (Flower Festival) at Aibonito has grown into a major rite of summer during the last 30 years. Today it draws hundreds of commercial growers and amateur horticulturists and tens of thousands of flower lovers to see the town and the surrounding countryside ablaze with roses, carnations, lilies and begonias. Of course, along with the flowers there are food and craft stalls as well as the ubiquitous Puerto Rican beauty pageant. This event takes place at the end of June and often runs into the July 4 holiday (US Independence Day), so you had better plan to get here before the crowds or expect to spend your holiday in a traffic jam.

Sleeping & Eating
El Coquí Posada Familiar (☎ 787-735-3150; Rte 722 Km 7.3; r $80-90) Not the first place in the world you'd expect to find an American-style motel but, there it is, perched over one of those ubiquitous Puerto Rican fast-food joints in the improbable mountain town of Aibonito. The thing is, El Coquí is actually rather good, with amiable service, well-equipped rooms (fridges, microwaves and cable TV), huge beds, and facilities so clean you could safely perform brain surgery in the bathroom. Get a takeout from the adjacent mall and nestle down in bed with the Food channel on the tube. It's a good idea to call ahead to let them know you are coming. El Coquí can be hard to find and the reception is not always staffed.

La Piedra (☎ 787-735-1034; Hwy 7718 Km 0.7; dishes $10-25; 11am-7pm Wed & Thu, 11am-10pm Fri-Sun) Cough too loudly here and you could end up on the local radio. La Piedra, situated next to the Piedra Degetau Park is a long-time mountain institution that also accommodates the recording studios of Radio Cumbre. Yes, that guy on the next table behind the thick pane of reinforced glass isn't a waiter wearing ear muffs; he's a DJ reaching out over the airwaves on 1470AM. Broadcasting credentials aside, La Piedra serves up some rather decent food to accompany its regular diet of music and topical chat – chicken in a tamarind sauce and chicken broth and *mofongo* (mashed plantains) are popular local favorites. Thanks to its prime Ruta Panorámica location it also acts as a nexus point to chicane weary motorists, Federico Degetau pilgrims (and poets), and local walking groups setting off into the Cañon de San Cristóbal.

ourpick **Tio Pepe's** (☎ 787-735-9615; Hwy 723 Km 0.3; dishes $12-25) Good old Uncle Joe's (*Tio* means 'uncle' and *Pepe* is a standard Spanish nickname for José) is a traditional Aibonito favorite stuck a few miles to the west of the town on a wooded knoll surrounded by trees and flowers. There's a well-placed sundeck, function room and regular musical entertainment from passing troubadours and trios. The decor is easygoing but elegant and you'll be served up good old home-style mountain cooking. Pass the *mofongo*.

TOP FIVE MOUNTAIN HIDEAWAYS

Getting There & Away

Públicos will take you to Aibonito from Cayey or Caguas for about $3. These cities have connections to the Río Piedras district of San Juan for another $3.

BARRANQUITAS

One of the most quintessential of Puerto Rico's lofty mountain towns, Barranquitas is a diminutive but picturesque settlement that clings like a toy village to the muddy slopes of the rain-lashed Cordillera Central. Lying on the north side of the Cañón de San Cristóbal, about a 20-minute drive out of Aibonito on Hwy 162 (or an even shorter detour off of the Ruta Panorámica via Hwy 143), the town is known locally as the Cuna de Próceres (Cradle of Great People) for its historical propensity to produce poets, politicians and governors of national (and international) distinction. Most notable in this list is the legendary Muñoz clan (see box opposite), Puerto Rico's substitute 'royal' family whose evocative mausoleum has assured Barranquitas' place as a pilgrimage site for both local patriots and curious visitors for a long time to come.

This is not, however, a fairy-tale village of architectural heirlooms. Hurricanes and fires have ravaged Barranquitas several times (the name translates to 'Place of Little Mud Slides'), and the oldest structures, such as the church, date only from the early 20th century. Barranquitas' charm lies in its narrow streets, tightly packed with shops and houses, which fall away into deep valleys on three sides of the plaza. Indeed, the view from the mountain road descending into town, when the afternoon sun sets the church tower ablaze above the shadowy and thickly settled central neighborhoods, is truly memorable.

Orientation

Streets are poorly marked and the general populace only uses descriptive addresses, but navigating Barranquitas is pretty easy. Rte 162 becomes Calle Rivera, the main street, and then after passing the plaza it becomes Rte 156 headed east (incidentally, downhill is always east).

Sights & Activities

CASA MUSEO LUIS MUÑOZ RIVERA

This **house** (☎ 787-857-0230; cnr Calles Muñoz Rivera & Padre Berrios; admission $1; ☼ 8:30am-4:20pm Wed-Sun) honors the so-called grandfather of Puerto Rico's autonomy movement and the 20th-century architect of the Puerto Rican commonwealth. This is where Luis Muñoz Rivera was born in 1859, and it contains a collection of furniture, letters, photographs and other memorabilia.

MAUSOLEO FAMILIA MUÑOZ RIVERA

Just south of the plaza is a **family tomb** (7 Calle Padre Berrios; admission free; ☼ 8:30am-4:20pm Tue-Sun) that holds the remains of Muñoz Rivera, his famous son Luis Muñoz Marín and their wives. Photographic displays at the tomb evoke the funeral of Luis Muñoz Marín.

MUSEO DE ARTE Y ANTROPOLOGÍA

Just to the north of the mausoleum, you'll find this small **museum** (☎ 787-857-2065; admission free), which displays the painting and sculpture of local artists. It's open by appointment and for exhibitions.

PLAZA DE RECREO DE BARRANQUITAS

Barranquita's charming central plaza is overlooked by the **Parroquia de San Antonio de Padua**, a small church that was first constructed in 1804 but subsequently destroyed by two catastrophic hurricanes (the first of which wiped out the whole town). Rebuilt in 1933 in a quaint postcolonial style, the church was recently renovated and gleams amid the surrounding mountain greenery. The centerpiece of the plaza is a decorative wrought-iron gazebo/bandstand adorned with distinctive art nouveau flourishes and surrounded by four individual classical fountains. The 19th-century **alcaldía** (town hall) was undergoing renovation at the time of writing.

Sleeping & Eating

Hacienda Margarita (☎ 787-854-0414; Barrio Quebrada Grande, Sector Tres Caminos; r/ste $75/100; ☒ ☒) Destroyed in a 1998 hurricane, Hacienda Margarita has risen from the ruins with a modern two-story building housing 27 units, a pool, a restaurant and a bar (live local music Saturday nights). Rooms feature patios/balconies with views of the surrounding mountains. Some have rock walls and one has a Jacuzzi. Call the owners for directions, as you have to wind your way through a housing subdivision to find the hotel.

   Heladería Los Próceres (☎ 787-857-4909; 21 Calle Muños Rivera; ☼ 9am-9pm) Situated a block from the plaza, this is a classic Puerto Rican

---

THE MUÑOZ CLAN

While America spawned the legendary Roosevelt dynasty, Puerto Rico has produced its very own influential establishment family, the iconic Muñoz clan, two generations of charismatic politicians who changed the course of the island's postcolonial history and set the commonwealth on the road to dazzling modernity.

Born in the mountain town of Barranquitas in 1859, Luis Muñoz Rivera was the son of a former town mayor and the grandson of an enterprising Spanish sea captain. With politics planted firmly in his DNA, he formed the Autonomist Party in 1887, an organization that called for Puerto Rican autonomy within the confines of the Spanish colonial system. Three years later he upped the ante further by founding a newspaper, *La Democracia,* to act as a journalistic mouthpiece for his cause.

With the Spanish driven out by a US military government in 1898, Muñoz Rivera switched his focus to the United States. Initially an advocate of outright independence, he dropped his claims in the early 1900s to ensure the replacement of the one-sided Foraker Act by the 1917 Jones Act and a more equitable relationship with the United States. Although Muñoz Rivera died a year before its implementation, he was considered instrumental in drafting the new laws (that granted US citizenship to Puerto Rican nationals) and is still revered as one of Puerto Rico's most important homegrown personalities. His mausoleum in Barranquitas remains an important and oft-visited historical monument.

A chip off his father's block, Rivera's son, Luis Muñoz Marín, was a prodigious poet and journalist who studied law in the United States. Returning to Puerto Rico in 1916, the younger Muñoz joined the socialist party and became a leading advocate for Puerto Rican independence. But, just like his father before him, Luis retracted on his initial promises during a spell as President of the Puerto Rican Senate in the mid-1940s in order to enlist US economic backing for an ambitious industrialization campaign codenamed 'Operation Bootstrap.'

In 1949, Muñoz Marín became Puerto Rico's first democratically elected governor, a position he held for an unprecedented four terms (until 1965). During his time in office, he orchestrated Puerto Rico's economic 'miracle,' transforming the island from a poverty-stricken agrarian society into a thriving economic powerhouse based on tourism, manufacturing and pharmaceuticals. Often touted as the 'Father of modern Puerto Rico,' Muñoz commanded huge popularity at home for his efforts in tackling poverty while, at the same time, extracting greater freedoms from the United States. Other more nationalistic voices depict him as a turncoat who was coerced out of his independence ideals by a belligerent US military establishment.

Today, the Muñoz legacy is still evident all over Puerto Rico, from the mausoleum and museums of Barranquitas to the island's Aeropuerto Internacional de Luis Muñoz Murín (LMM international airport), named in honor of its most celebrated native son.

---

ice-cream joint. Milkshakes and 100% natural ice creams are concocted from strawberry, papaya, tamarind and *bizcocho* (sweet pastry). They also serve nachos, tostados and coffee.

Entertainment
You can check out the upcoming program in the small theater at the **Centro Cultural Luis Muñoz Rivera** (☎ 787-857-0520; Plaza de Recreo) in the main square. The activity heats up here during the Feria Nacional de Artesanías (Artisan's Festival) in mid-July.

Getting There & Away
Públicos to and from surrounding towns stop on Calle Padre Berrios, three blocks south of the plaza past the Mausoleo Familia Muñoz Rivera. You'll pay $1 to go to Aibonito, or $8 for the long (plan on four hours) roller-coaster ride to/from San Juan (Río Piedras terminal).

RESERVA FORESTAL TORO NEGRO
Covering 7000 acres and protecting some of Puerto Rico's highest peaks, the Toro Negro Reserve provides a quieter, less developed alternative to El Yunque. Bisected by some of the steepest and windiest sections of the Ruta Panorámica (Hwy 143 in this section), the area is often shrouded in mist and blanketed by a dense jungle foliage of primordial proportions. This is where

CENTRAL MOUNTAINS

you come to truly escape the tourist throngs that frequent the coast. But don't expect El Yunque–style signage here. Toro Negro's facilities – which comprise a campground, a few trails and a recreation area – are spartan and often poorly staffed. Rather than just turning up, it's far better to plan ahead and enquire about current conditions at the DRNA in San Juan (p87), as mudslides are common. Properly prepared and with a decent topo map, you should be able to carve out some memorable DIY adventures in the mountains. Alternatively you can get up close and personal with the wilderness via an organized trip (p268).

The highlight of Toro Negro – in more ways than one – is Cerro de Punta which, at 4389ft, is Puerto Rico's highest peak. You can drive most of the way to the top on the Ruta Panorámica or, alternatively, attempt to bushwhack your way up from Jayuya on an infuriatingly unkempt (and vague) trail. Other notable peaks include Monte Jayuya and Cerro Maravilla, scene of a notorious 1978 murder case when two pro-independence activists were shot by Puerto Rican police.

Orientation & Information

The Ruta Panorámica (Hwy 143) is your artery to and from the forest, and it is none too wide. Honk your horn when approaching blind curves.

All of the forest's public facilities lie at the east end of the reserve in the Area Recreativa Doña Juana, clustered in the vicinity of the ranger station at Km 32.4 on Hwy 143.

The **ranger station** (☎ 787-867-3040; Hwy 143 Km 32.5; ☺ 8am-noon summer, irregular hrs winter) has blurry photocopies of park literature, and some of this material is extremely misleading. The trail map lacks a compass rose and has been rotated so north it is not at the top of the page.

You're not likely to get anything better in San Juan from the DRNA, nor is it easy to get USGS maps on the island without ordering through a bookstore. You can get a USGS map from your favorite map supplier in the USA or mail-order one on the island. Otherwise, the map in this book is the best you will find.

Barranquitas is an hour away, so you'd better come prepared. Bring plenty of food, water and some insect repellent.

Activities
AREA RECREATIVA DOÑA JUANA

This is the area of about 3 sq miles at the eastern end of the park surrounding the ranger station. You will find picnic sites, toilets, showers, the camping area and a half-dozen short trails branching off Hwy 143. Come here in the winter and the place will probably look empty and abandoned. One trail leads to the **swimming pool**, open in summer only. Three others lead to the observation tower, less than a half-mile south of the highway.

CERRO DE PUNTA

In an island where the car rules, it's hardly surprising to find that there's a road to the top of the commonwealth's highest peak. Rising to 4389ft, the summit of **Cerro de Punta** lies in the Toro Negro Forest Reserve just off Hwy 143 (the Ruta Panorámica). Although there's a narrow unmarked cement road to the peak itself, it is actually better to stop in a parking lot on the northern side of Hwy 143 and walk the last 1.5 miles. Not surprisingly, the spur road can be treacherous in bad weather, plus going by foot will enable you to soak up the sights and sounds of the surrounding jungle. The summit is dominated by communication towers, though the view north is stupendous – cloud permitting. Cerro de Punta lies in the west of the reserve, almost 10 miles of tortured driving from the Area Recreativa Doña Juana.

Perplexingly, hiking Cerro de Punta is a difficult and little-attempted feat. Technically, a trail leaves from behind the Hacienda Gripiñas (p269), close to the town of Jayuya. The problem is a) finding it, b) following it (it is badly signposted and in a poor state of repair), and c) getting a local to admit it is open (routinely they'll tell you it's closed or – even better – deny all knowledge of it). If you're determined to give it a shot, ask around at the Hacienda Gripiñas and be persistent. The trail is a steep two- to three-hour alpine grunt.

HIKING

There are approximately 11 miles of trails around Doña Juana, but mostly they are short walks to the swimming pool. Longer hikes are listed below, but always consult with the ranger station. Two other popular trails are Vega Grande and La Currenta.

RESERVA FORESTAL TORO NEGRO

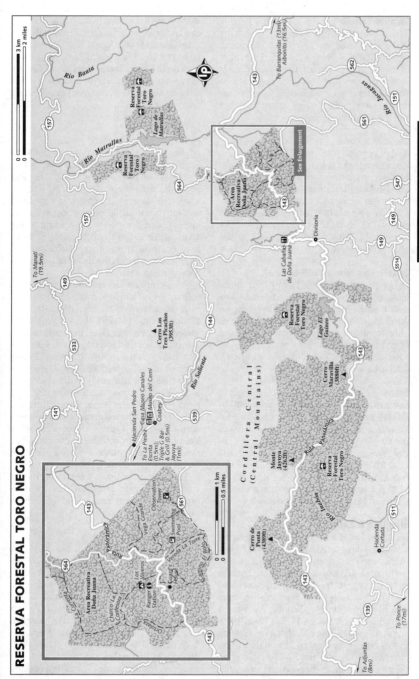

Camino El Bolo

Across from the visitor's center, through the parking lot, you'll spot a narrow trail heading uphill. That's El Bolo, a 2.5-mile jaunt that takes you up to a mountain ridge and great southern views, and then crosses Vereda La Torre to take you even higher. Come down on the same path; circling around can get you lost real fast.

Vereda La Torre

A very popular path that starts in the Area Recreativa Doña Juana, La Torre goes up to an observation tower with some great views. The 2-mile trail starts at the picnic tables and slowly gets more hilly and rough as you ascend. You'll see a tiny road feed into Vereda after about 20 minutes of walking – that's Camino El Bolo. Continue ahead to the observation tower.

Charco La Confesora/Ortolaza

Leaving directly from the Los Viveros camping area, Charco La Confesora is a half-mile trek to a little bridge. You can keep going on the muddy trail next to it, which is Ortoloza, until you reach a grove of orange trees and Hwy 143, which will bring you back to Los Viveros. If you don't want to walk on the road, double back on the same path.

Tours

Acampa Nature Adventure Tours (Map pp86–7; ☎ 787-706-0695; www.acampapr.com; 1221 Av Jesús T Piñero, San Juan) offer one day hiking/adventure tours to the Toro Negro rainforest. The excursion involves hiking/scrambling along the Quebrada Rosa River, rappelling off a 60ft cliff and zip-lining 200ft across the treetops. Prices start at $149 per person and include transportation from San Juan, equipment and lunch.

Sleeping & Eating

Los Viveros (Hwy 143 at Km 32.5; campsites per person $4) This is the designated camping area, and it is in the forest just north of the ranger station in the Area Recreativa Doña Juana. There is space for 14 tents (pretty close together), and part of the area is often reserved for larger groups such as the Boy Scouts. You need a permit from the DRNA in San Juan (p87). Apply 15 days in advance. If you're lingering in this area of the Central Mountains, bring charcoal and lighter fluid so you can cook your food over one of the open-air picnic grills

at the Area Recreativa Doña Juana near the east end of Reserva Forestal Toro Negro.

Las Cabañas de Doña Juana (☎ 787-897-3981; Hwy 143 Km 30.5) This place is actually a rib joint of sorts on the main Ruta Panorámica. It serves all types of grilled meats for under $10 in little open-air shacks by the roadside. Opening times are sporadic.

JAYUYA

Puerto Rico's unheralded mountain 'capital' lies a few kilometers north of the Ruta Panorámica in an isolated steep-sided valley overlooked by three of the island's highest peaks – Cerro de Punta, Cerro Tres Picachos, and Cerro Maravilla. Fiercely traditional and verdantly beautiful, the precipitous geography in this region has created a lost world where many of the island's old traditions live on. If you're on a 'mission impossible' to find Puerto Rico's last authentic *jíbaro*, this is a good place to start.

Steeped in Taíno legend, the original settlement of Jayuya had little contact with the rest of the island until 1911, when it was declared a municipality. In 1950, the fledgling town gained notoriety when local nationalist leader Blanca Canales led a revolt against US occupation known as the 'Jayuya Uprising.' Rebels stormed the police station, burned down the post office and audaciously declared a Puerto Rican Republic from the town square. The rebellion lasted just three days before US planes bombed the town, causing widespread destruction, but Jayuya's independent spirit lived on. Either by coincidence or conscious municipal planning Jayuya remains one of the island's most un-Americanized towns.

The town attempts to keep Taíno Indian culture alive with a festival that includes music, food, games and a Miss Taíno pageant (see p279).

Sights

Located in a small park in the barrio of Coabey, the **Casa Museo Canales** (☎ 787-828-4094; Rte 144 Km 9.3; ☒ noon-4pm Sat & Sun) is a reconstructed 19th-century coffee *finca* (rural smallholding) with quintessential *criollo* features that once belonged to Jayuya's first major, Rosario Canales. Rosario spawned two famous offspring. His son, Nemesio, is recognized as a great Puerto Rican poet, playwright and political activist, while his daughter, Blanca Canales Torresola, became a

---

TACKLING THE RUTA PANARÓMICA

If there was a mantle for the world's windiest road, Puerto Rico's Ruta Panarómica would surely be in the reckoning. Running the length of the island from Yabucoa in the east to Mayagüez in the west, this narrow but spectacular scenic highway has more twists and turns than a cagey Puerto Rican boxing champ, and is almost as dangerous.

Hit the mountain foothills somewhere east of Maricao and distances suddenly become mysteriously elongated as the island appears to double in size. Drives that would normally take 20 minutes on the coast quickly turn into two- to three-hour road trips with only a few brief glimpses of the faraway ocean reminding you that you haven't actually disappeared into the Amazonian jungle. But, first timers beware. Driving in these parts is no Sunday afternoon dawdle. Maneuvering deftly through dense rainforest and sleepy mountain villages, the Ruta's roadsides are populated by innumerable posses of stray dogs, escaped chickens, straw-hatted *jíbaros* and – more disturbingly – the burnt-out wrecks of several hundred abandoned cars. The latter sight should be enough to remind wannabe speed-freaks to steer carefully at all times (at no more than 25mph). Unfortunately, the locals aren't always so fastidious, often taking the precarious hills and tricky chicanes at 35mph or more. Drive defensively and be on your guard.

Motoring logistics aside, the Ruta's premier draw card is its bucolic authenticity and soothing sense of isolation. In marked contrast to the car chaos that plagues the coast, the central mountains exist in a different world. You can get lost here for days and never set eyes on a golf course or a fast-food joint. For an unhurried trip, reserve a minimum of three days and be prepared for plenty of stop-offs. See also Itineraries, p27.

---

notorious figure in the Puerto Rican nationalist movement when she led an independence revolt against the American-backed authorities in Jayuya in 1950. The house displays traditional antiques and has a pleasant aspect in the shadow of the surrounding mountains.

Across the park, the **Museo del Cemí** (☎ 787-828-1241; Rte 144 Km 9.2; ☉ 9am-4:30pm Mon-Fri) is housed in what is perhaps the oddest building on the island. Designed by Río Piedras architect, Efrén Badía Cabrera, the weird fish-like structure is supposed to represent a gigantic *Cemí* or native talisman. The exhibits inside are made up mostly of Taíno artifacts and photos of local petroglyphs.

La Piedra Escrita (Rte 144 Km 7.3) is supposedly one of the island's best preserved native petroglyphs carved on a large rock in the middle of the Río Saliente. Forming a natural bathing pool, it has become a popular stopping-off point for curious (and hot) travelers. There's a small car park and restaurant nearby (p270).

Hacienda San Pedro (☎ 787-615-3083; Rte 144 Km 8.4; ☉ 8am-6pm Mon-Sat, 10am-5pm Sun) is a small, working coffee farm with an attached museum and tasting room where you can get an intimate tour of the whole coffee-making process from green bean to dark-roast espresso. The gourmet blends served here are some of the best brews you'll taste anywhere.

Rustically packaged beans are sold on-site and there's a small museum.

Sleeping & Eating

Posada Jayuya (☎ 787-828-7250; 49 Guillermo Esteves; s/d incl breakfast $69/79; ✷ ⊠) This solid place in the town center is a good journeyman sleepover with 27 rooms that include TVs and refrigerators, and there's a pancake breakfast. The air-con unit might sound like the inside of a 1956 Buick, but at least it'll work, and the passable downstairs restaurant sometimes hosts live music.

Hacienda Casa Taína (☎ 787-828-2270; www.hacienda casataina.com; Hwy 528 Km 1.8; s/d $80/150; ✷ ⊠) Not two hours out of San Juan, but you could quite conceivably be in a different world. Isolated Casa Taína revitalizes Jayuya's independent spirit with it's unique architecture and priceless tranquility. No global conglomerate has colonized this small corner of the island yet – and hopefully never will. Instead, here amid the exotic statues, trickling fountains and mountain greenery you can find the sweet serendipity which other places so often lack, with nary a phone, TV or slot machine to bother you. The on-site restaurant's a classic.

our pick **Hacienda Gripiñas** (☎ 787-828-1717; www .haciendagripinas.com; Hwy 527 Km 2.5; s/d $90/155; ✷ ⊠) In-the-know back-road travelers face off against jaded big resort escapees at Hacienda

Gripiñas, another beautifully restored coffee hacienda dating from 1858 that is nestled picturesquely in the shadow of Cerro de Punta in the bucolic Jayuya valley. Among the strangely-shaped antiques and framed coffee posters lie more than a few nods to modern taste – a couple of swimming pools, for instance. But don't expect coastal-style luxury. This place is over 150 years old and remains true to its historical ethos. Bring a good book, throw away your alarm clock and fall asleep to a fine chorus of croaking frogs.

Triple G Bar & Grill (☎ 787-828-9999; Hwy 144 Km 7.3) A small thatched-roof restaurant in the parking lot at La Piedra Escrita (p269), this place serves up the best *comida criolla* in the valley.

ADJUNTAS
pop 20,000

Adjuntas goes by many exotic pseudonyms. Some call it the 'Switzerland of Puerto Rico'; others, the 'town of the sleeping giant' (due to the silhouettes of surrounding mountains); more still, the island's juicy 'citron capital.' But while it's certainly no Geneva in terms of fancy architecture and lavish rock-star appeal, this small mountainside town of 20,000 wedged into the Cordillera Central has quietly earned its environmental credentials. After the discovery of copper in the area in the 1960s, local community groups fought successfully to prevent their cool subtropical jungle haven from being turned into a huge open-cast mining pit. Instead, Adjuntas today has become something of an environmental steward whose livelihood remains rooted in bananas, coffee and citrus fruits.

Marking the spot where one of the island's major north–south arteries (Hwys 123 and 10) crests the Central Mountains, Adjuntas is a traffic bottleneck in the summer months. If you venture into town at this time, beware of the complicated one-way system and allow plenty of time for delays.

One of the main attractions in this area is the Bosque Estatal de Guilarte, with the seventh-highest peak on the island and a lake and cabins for rusticators.

Sights

You can visit the locally organized environmental group **Casa Pueblo** (☎ 787-829-4842; www.casapueblo.org; 30 Rodolfo Gonzáles; donation $2; ☺ 8am–4pm) in their pastel-pink Adjuntas HQ. Visits

include a talk on the body's development and environmental achievements, along with a tour of the library, photo exhibition, artisan's shop, butterfly garden and alternative energy schemes. Phone ahead to let them know you're coming.

Sleeping

Monte Río Hotel (☎ 787-829-3705; 18 Calle Cesar Gonzales; r $60-90; ☒) This no-frills town-center hotel stands about a mile from the Ruta Panorámica, one block south of the plaza of Adjuntas. There are 26 rooms with fresh air, mountain views and an Olympic pool. The restaurant and bar on the 1st floor are as good as they come in this town, with *comida criolla* dishes starting at less than $10.

Parador Villas de Sotomayor (☎ 787-829-1717; www.welcome.to/villas; Hwy 123/10 Km 36.3; r $65-$130; ☒) You're not exactly spoilt for choice in the Adjuntas area when it comes to finding accommodation, but the Sotomayor will satisfy most overnighters with its 26 solid but slightly run-down villas arranged around a central swimming pool, basketball courts, cooking grills, and horseback riding. While it is extremely popular with island families throughout the summer, don't be fooled by the Parador's accompanying literature which claims that it's the 'premier eco-tourism hotel in the Caribbean.' An overstatement, to say the least.

BOSQUE ESTATAL DE GUILARTE

This forest, west of Adjuntas, actually consists of a number of parcels of land totaling about 3600 acres. Most of it is rainforest dominated by sierra palms. Coming from the east, you first see Lago Garzas, a popular fishing site. West of the lake, the road rises toward the park's ranger station, near the intersection of Hwy 518 and Hwy 131. Here you will find a picnic area with shelters, cooking grills and toilets. There is also a trail that leads to the top of Monte Guilarte (3950ft) and five cabins you can rent for overnight stays.

The **DRNA** (☎ 787-829-5767, 787-724-3647; cabins $20) maintains the basic cabins, toilets and shower facilities (no camping is allowed in the Bosque). Each cabin sleeps up to six; cooking facilities are outdoors and there's no electricity. You must bring all of your own gear, including bedding. Make your reservations 15 days in advance with the DRNA at its offices in San Juan (p87). You can make an open reservation, which allows you flexibility with dates. Camping is not permitted in Guilarte.

MARICAO
pop 6200

With a population of fewer than 7000 citizens, Maricao is the smallest municipality on the main island of Puerto Rico, and a gem of a mountain retreat near the western end of the Ruta Panorámica. This is a town of little commerce, with rushing streams, gorges, bridges, terraced houses, switchback roads, and weather so cool and damp that some houses have stone fireplaces to take the nip out of the air. Outside the town, you will find dramatic vistas, coffee plantations and the largest state forest in Puerto Rico, the Bosque Estatal de Maricao.

With its peaks, dark forests and fog, Maricao is just the kind of place in which legends take root.

Admirers of Maricao claim that it was the strong coffee grown here that woke up the devil on the island. Another story claims that 2000 Taíno survived here into the 19th century, centuries after the last native Puerto Ricans were thought to have disappeared.

Yet another myth tells how the town takes its name from the demise of a local Taíno princess, María. According to legend, María was in love with a Spanish conquistador, and she told her beloved of Taíno plans to attack the local Spanish encampment. When the Taíno discovered her treachery, the princess was tortured to death. The Spanish honored her by naming the town after a fusion of María's name and the suffix 'cao' (from *sacrificio*) to signify her sacrifice for love. Less romantic scholars say the town's name comes from the Taíno name for a local tree.

Stopping here for a day or two is probably as close as a traveler can come to experiencing the charms of the legendary *jíbaro's* existence.

Maricao hosts a popular coffee harvest festival in mid-February, with crafts and traditional coffee-making demonstrations.

Orientation

In addition to approaching Maricao from the east or west on the Ruta Panorámica, you can get here by heading south on Hwy 119 from San Sebastián (then going east on the Ruta Panorámica to Maricao; about two hours' drive) or driving north from Sabana Grande

on Hwy 120 (about one hour's drive). Both routes involve a spectacular climb into the mountains on twisting roads.

Sights & Activities
BOSQUE ESTATAL DE MARICAO

This **forest** of more than 10,000 acres lies along the Ruta Panorámica south of Maricao, and the drive is spectacular, with sharp curves snaking over ridges as the mountainsides fall away into steep valleys. As you make this drive, you will see places to pull your car off the road at trailheads that lead into the woods or traverse down steep inclines.

Curiously, few of the trails are maintained or mapped by the DRNA. In fact, guides to Bosque Estatal de Maricao are difficult to come by, both at the department's office in San Juan and in Maricao. So if you are coming here to hike, get yourself a topo map of the area from a map supplier in the USA, or ask an island bookstore to order one from the USGS.

While the landscape is generally categorized as high-mountain rainforest, scientists note that the 845 species of plant here are less 'exuberant' than they are in a tropical rainforest such as El Yunque. Birds are the most studied fauna here, with 44 identified species. Tanagers, cuckoos and warblers are some of the remarkable types spotted in the forest.

LOS VIVEROS

Follow the signs south out of the center of Maricao to **Los Viveros** (Fish Hatcheries; ☎ 787-838-3710; Hwy 410; admission free; ☷ 8:30-11:30am & 1-3:30pm Thu-Sun). Or take the short trail off Hwy 120 if you want to see the buildings and streamside reservoirs where the commonwealth raises the tilapia and bass that stock the island's freshwater lakes. To say the least, this place is a quiet attraction. There is little to see here other than thousands of small fish, little to hear besides the sounds of the surrounding woods, birdsong and the rush of running water. But all this is totally in keeping with the ambience of Maricao. Call if you want a tour.

Sleeping & Eating
Parque Ecológico Monte de Estado en Maricao

(☎ 787-873-5632, reservations 787-622-5200; Hwy 120 Km 13.1; cabins $60; ☒) East of Maricao, this well-positioned campground has 24 remodeled cabins to rent in the state forest. Cabin sizes vary from three-person ($15) to six-person

($30) to 12-person ($55) and most have refrigerators, fireplaces and hot water. The area also has a swimming pool, basketball courts, restrooms, showers and an observation tower. Make reservations as far in advance as possible by calling the Compañía de Parques Nacionales (opposite) in San Juan.

our pick **Hacienda Juanita** (☎ 787-838-2550; www .haciendajuanita.com; Hwy 105 Km 23.5; s/d $100/130; ⚑) Ah…history and the natural world coexisting in perfect harmony. Add a pinch of exotic evening entertainment and stir in some aromatic Arábica coffee and you've got an almost perfect brew. If you really want a taste of authentic *jíbaro* lifestyle, come to the Hacienda Juanita, about 2 miles west of Maricao. Dating from 1834, this working coffee plantation with 21 units was also one of Puerto Rico's earliest paradores (established in 1976). There's a lovely pool here, a tennis court, short trails through foliage-rich grounds and a Mesón Gastronómico restaurant that hosts weekly music shows. The defining factor, however, is the setting which, like the hacienda itself, is rustic and unmolested by the passage of time.

Getting There & Away

Público vans leave the town's plaza on the Maricao–Mayagüez run and charge $4. As is usually the case, the vans leave when they are full or on the driver's whim.

Directory

CONTENTS

ACCOMMODATIONS

Puerto Rico's proximity to the United States has its upsides and its downsides. On the one hand the standard of accommodations is generally better than it is elsewhere in the Caribbean (although rarely as consistent as the US). On the other hand, prices are generally higher.

For package tourists there are plenty of high quality resorts, although few of them are all-inclusive (you must pay extra for food, drink and other activities). Prices for these establishments can vary depending on the season, ongoing offers and who you book through. Elsewhere there's a good system of paradores or midrange accommodations scattered across the island, often in historical buildings or old coffee haciendas. Vacation rentals are a more economical option for long-term guests or big groups. There are no youth hostels in Puerto Rico, and very few dorm-style accommodations, even near local universities. Motels in the traditional American sense are also thin on the ground. All this means that, aside from camping, there's a huge dearth of budget options.

Lodging rates in Puerto Rico vary, sometimes by more than 30%, from season to season and even from day to day, as hotels adjust rates according to the perceived demand. In general, rates are highest from December 15 through the end of May. They are also high from mid-June to August, when many island families take their vacations. Rates are lowest from September 1 to December 14. Because prices change so frequently, the rates listed in this book are often given as ranges. The prices given in this book do not include room taxes, which are 15% at hotels with casinos, and 9% elsewhere.

Camping
PUBLIC CAMPGROUNDS

These are on public lands such as national forests and commonwealth *reservas forestales* (forest reserves). To camp in one of the reserves, contact the **Departamento de Recursos Naturales y Ambientales** (DRNA; Department of Natural Resources; Map p87; ☎ 787-999-2200; www.drna.gobierno .pr in Spanish; Rte 8838 Km 6.3, Sector El Cinco, Río Piedras) at least 15 days in advance for reservations and a permit. Commonwealth-run forest-reserve campgrounds are likely to have showers and RV hookups available; national forest campgrounds tend to be less developed.

If you want to camp on the beach but don't want to risk running afoul of the law, call the

---

BOOK YOUR STAY ONLINE

For more accommodation reviews and recommendations by Lonely Planet authors, check out lonelyplanet.com/hotels. You'll find the true, insider lowdown on the best places to stay. Reviews are thorough and independent. Best of all, you can book online.

Compañía de Parques Nacionales (CPN; National Park Company; ☎ 787-622-5200, ext 355 or 369; www.parques nacionalespr.com in Spanish; Apartado Postal No 3207, San Juan, 00904), which allows camping at six public beaches: Cerro Gordo, La Monserrate, Seven Seas, Punta Guilarte (near Arroyo), Vieques and Culebra.

The grounds are big and grassy, and get packed during holidays. They've got picnic tables, showers and toilets. Not all CPN sites have 24-hour guards.

Never camp alone at a site without a guard, and be extra careful at Cerro Gordo and La Monserrate. You don't need a reservation to camp at these places, but in high season if you don't call ahead you'll likely be out of luck if you just pull up. To make a reservation, you must pay with Visa, MasterCard or Discover Card.

Summer is high camping season on the island; during the other seasons, camping areas at the balnearios and *reservas forestales* are often closed (although sometimes you can just set up camp for free and no one will bother you).

Getting in touch with the DRNA or CPN isn't always easy; your best bet is to call early and often – someone will eventually pick up the phone.

There is no fee or reservation necessary to camp in El Yunque, but you must get a permit at the Catalina Work Center (p132) in the forest.

PRIVATE CAMPGROUNDS

These are on private property and are usually close to or in a town. Most are designed with RVs in mind; few accept tents. Facilities can include hot showers, coin-operated laundry, a swimming pool, full RV hookups, a games area, a playground and a convenience store.

Guesthouses

Places calling themselves 'guesthouses' can differ vastly from one to another. While some guesthouses may have as few as two rooms for travelers, others may boast 25. While one guesthouse may look like a roadside motel, another may be a beach house with a pool, bar and restaurant.

The cheapest establishments, with rooms around $75, may have clean but unexciting rooms with a shared bathroom. Pricier places have rooms with private bathrooms, balconies, sun decks and public dining rooms with extensive menus and table service (at extra cost). They may be in a modern structure, quaint country home or urban beach house. Rooms at most guesthouses fall in the $75 to $180 price range, but some cost more than $200.

Hotels

Puerto Rico has plenty of top end resort hotels and a growing number of boutique options. Major chains represented include Marriott, Hilton and Sheraton. There are also a couple of unique world-class hotels, namely the Horned Dorset Primavera (near Rincón; p232) and El Convento in Viejo San Juan (p109). Ecohotels are another growing area, particularly around El Yunque and on the island of Vieques. Ocean Park has some rather deluxe beachside B&Bs and in recent years Rincón and Boquerón have gone more upmarket.

There are only a few accommodations on the island with rooms for less than $75, and almost all of these are found in small towns or unsavory neighborhoods of the cities. Rooms are usually small, and beds may be soft or saggy, but the sheets should be clean. A minimal level of cleanliness is generally maintained, but expect scuffed walls, old furniture and strange noises from your shower.

PRACTICALITIES

Electricity Puerto Rico has the 110V AC system used in America.

Newspapers & magazines *San Juan Star* (www.thesanjuanstar.com) is a bilingual daily newspaper. *Puerto Rico Breeze* is a biweekly newspaper on gay nightlife in San Juan. *Que Pasa!* is a bimonthly magazine put out by the Puerto Rico Tourism Company (PRTC).

TV American TV is broadcast across the island. Radio is mostly in Spanish; the English-language radio station is WOSO San Juan, at 1030AM.

Video systems Puerto Rico uses VHS for videos.

Weights & measures Puerto Rico follows the American imperial system with two exceptions: all distances you see on road signs are in kilometers and gas is pumped in liters. See the Quick Reference page (inside front cover) for a metric conversion chart.

Resorts are ubiquitous in Condado and Isla Verde. Further east, you'll find the mega-resorts, self-contained fantasy worlds of 500 to 2500 acres with championship golf courses, restaurants, spas, tennis courts and a complete array of water sports: the El Conquistador Resort & Golden Door Spa (near Fajardo; p146); the Río Mar Beach Resort & Country Club (near Luquillo; p140) and the Palmas del Mar Resort (near Humacao; p148) are the three fanciest piles.

Because of changing marketing strategies and seasons, the prices in this guide can be only an approximate guideline at best, though you'll be lucky to find a quality hotel for under $150.

Be prepared to add the 9% room tax, and probably a 10% service charge as well, to quoted rates. Children are often allowed to stay free with their parents, but rules for this vary. If traveling with a family, call and inquire.

Remember advertised hotel prices are not set in stone. If you simply ask about any specials that might apply, you can often save quite a bit of money. Nowadays booking online can also net you a special deal.

Paradores & Inns

Years ago, the Puerto Rico Tourism Company (PRTC) adopted the Spanish idea of creating a network of government-endorsed country inns for islanders and travelers looking for retreats in alluring natural settings.

Today, the PRTC endorses about 20 paradores (inns) scattered across the island and they are a mixed bag. How you view them depends on your expectations. If you're used to upmarket resorts you might find paradores a bit old-fashioned and pokey. If you're keen to get away from it all, you'll probably enjoy the experience.

The good thing about paradores is that they are invariably located in attractive areas (often in historic coffee haciendas) and are frequented primarily by Puerto Ricans. As a result, you'll be able to get out and discover the 'real' Puerto Rico here, as opposed to being cocooned in some manufactured, Americanized resort.

The trade-off comes in the form of iffy water pressure, basic furnishings and sometimes overdue renovations. On the upside, service is usually friendly and there's nearly always a swimming pool. If you've

traveled in Spain, you'll find Puerto Rican paradores are rarely comparable to their more luxurious Iberian equivalents.

Prices for rooms in both the endorsed and nominal paradores are comparable to the cost of rooms in guesthouses, ie between $75 and $150.

For reservations, a complete list and pictures of the government-endorsed paradores, contact **Paradores Puertorriqueños** (☎ 800-866-7827; www.gotopuertorico.com). You can also check with **Puerto Rico Small Inns** (☎ 787-725-2901; http://prhtasm allhotels.com).

Motels

Unfortunately there's no real network of cheap motels in Puerto Rico á la the United States. Such motels that do exist are strictly of the 'rooms-by-the-hour' variety. Not for the average tourist.

Vacation Centers

The Commonwealth of Puerto Rico maintains clusters of rental cottages around the island in Arroyo, Boquerón, Añasco, Humacao and Maricao. These *centros vacacionales* are popular with island families on weekends, holidays and summer vacations. Most of the accommodations are two-bedroom condos in attractive new duplex structures. These units are available to 'bona fide family groups' only, so don't show up with three college-age couples.

There is a minimum stay of two nights and a maximum stay of seven. Short-term rates run about $85 a night for a unit that sleeps six, but you may get a special weekly rate from September 1 to May 31 (when island kids are in school).

Bring your own sheets, or be prepared to rent them for $15 to $20 per set. Kitchen gear is not included in the price.

Reserve up to 120 days in advance through the Oficina de Reservaciones at the Compañía de Parques Nacionales (p273).

ACTIVITIES

Puerto Rico offers innumerable outdoor activities for travelers with ants in their pants. Some will surprise (ice-skating), some may disappoint (hiking – at least for the hardcore backcountry adventurers) while others will exceed even the highest expectations (surfing into the sunset in Rincón). The

Outdoors chapter (p71) will fill you in on the details. Meanwhile, here's a brief run-down on what to expect.

- Some of the best surf breaks in the Caribbean
- Excellent diving spots and crystal clear water
- Two of the brightest bioluminescent bays on the planet
- Safe snorkeling, often accessible directly from the shore
- Well-equipped public beaches
- Playa Flamenco, regularly touted as one of best beaches in the Caribbean
- The only tropical rainforest hikes in the US national park system
- Excellent bird-watching possibilities
- Deep-sea fishing
- Golf courses to rival anything in the US and Europe
- The largest marina in the Caribbean

BUSINESS HOURS

Businesses are open 8am to 5pm, but there are certainly no hard-and-fast rules. Shops are usually open 9am or 10am to 5pm or 6pm (often until 9pm in shopping malls and on Friday evening), except on Sunday, when hours are 11am to 5pm (often later in malls).

Post offices are open 8am to 4pm or 5:30pm weekdays, and some are open 8am to 1pm Saturday.

Banks are usually open 8am to 5pm on weekdays (in some areas such as Ponce, they close at 2:30pm), and 9:45am to noon on Saturday.

CHILDREN
Practicalities

There are a few places in Puerto Rico that don't take children under age 16, but generally that kind of attitude goes against the family-loving grain.

Children often get discounted rates at larger hotels, and providing an extra cot is rarely a problem.

In smaller facilities like guesthouses, children are welcomed but cots and cribs are less likely to be at hand.

Two of Puerto Rico's megaresorts offer full-day, camp-style programs for children aged three to 15. These are: El Conquistador Resort & Golden Door Spa (near Fajardo

on the east coast; p146) and the Palmas del Mar Resort (near Humacao on the east coast; p148).

Unless you know someone reliable on the island or you are staying at a big hotel, you'll have difficulty finding a baby-sitter. There are no reliable agencies that provide this service, but many hotels have day-care programs, activity programs for older kids, and trusted staff happy to make some extra money baby-sitting at night.

Motorists should note that Puerto Rican law requires children younger than four to be restrained in an approved child's seat while traveling in an automobile.

Specify this if you're booking a taxi. Alternatively, bring your own seat. Many car rentals also rent child seats. Enquire when you're booking.

If you see a diaper-changing station more than twice during your visit to Puerto Rico, consider yourself lucky. Puerto Rican parents get creative and change diapers on whatever flat surface is at hand.

Diapers and formula are available in the many drug stores in the populated areas, but travel with supplies in the Central Mountains and in more remote areas like Culebra and Vieques.

Breast-feeding in public is not frowned upon, but generally women should do it as discreetly as possible.

Sights & Activities

Big hits with kids are the Museo del Niño (p93) and the Casa de Ramón Power y Giralt (p92).

The Río Camuy caves (p245) and Observatorio de Arecibo (p245) are popular, and the Luis A Ferré Parque de Ciencias (p129) is a perennial favorite.

Blackbeard Sports (p175) on Vieques rents bicycles with rear child-seats (and helmets) and can organize guided trips for all the family.

For information on enjoying travel with young ones, read Lonely Planet's *Travel with Children*.

CLIMATE CHARTS

Temperatures in Puerto Rico are very consistent. At their coolest, daily temperatures seldom go below 73°F, and at their hottest rarely rise above 86°F. For a complete breakdown of the seasonal variations, see p20.

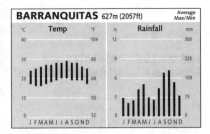

BARRANQUITAS 627m (2057ft) — Average Max/Min
Temp / Rainfall

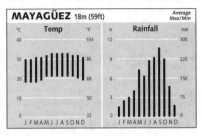

MAYAGÜEZ 18m (59ft) — Average Max/Min
Temp / Rainfall

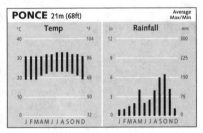

PONCE 21m (68ft) — Average Max/Min
Temp / Rainfall

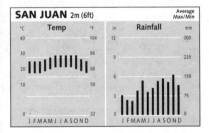

SAN JUAN 2m (6ft) — Average Max/Min
Temp / Rainfall

CUSTOMS

US Customs allows each person over the age of 21 to bring 1L of liquor and 200 cigarettes duty free into Puerto Rico or the USA. US citizens are allowed to import, duty free, $400 worth of gifts from abroad, while non-US citizens are allowed to bring in $100 worth. US law permits you to bring in or take out as much as $10,000 in US or foreign currency, traveler's checks or letters of credit without

formality. Larger amounts of any or all of the earlier – there are no limits – must be declared to customs.

DANGERS & ANNOYANCES
Personal Security & Theft

There are more than a few desperate people on the island, although most violent crimes are related to drugs and gang turf wars. Muggings occur on many public beaches after dark, so avoid them at night; leaving personal articles out on the beaches anywhere is inviting theft. Unfortunately, this includes the isolated beaches on Vieques.

However, even though street crime is a serious issue in urban areas, visitors need not be obsessed with security. A few commonsense reminders should help keep you secure.

Always lock cars and put valuables out of sight, whether you're leaving the car for a few minutes or longer, and whether you are in a town or in the remote backcountry. Rent a car with a lockable trunk. If your car is bumped from behind in a remote area, it's best to keep going to a well-lit area or service station. Never allow yourself to get into a conflict with another driver on Puerto Rican roads: road rage is common here, and more than a few antagonized drivers have been known to retaliate with gunfire.

Be aware of your surroundings and who may be watching you. Avoid walking on dimly lit streets at night, particularly when alone. Walk purposefully. Avoid unnecessary displays of money or jewelry. Divide money and credit cards to avoid losing everything and also aim to use ATMs in well-trafficked areas.

In hotels, don't ever leave valuables lying around your room. Use safety-deposit boxes or at least place valuables in a locked bag. Don't open your door to strangers – check the peephole or call the front desk if unexpected guests try to enter.

Carjacking does occur in Puerto Rican cities though it is rare that a tourist is targeted. To minimize the risk, avoid driving alone late at night in rough neighborhoods; take a taxi instead.

Recreational Hazards

In wilderness areas the consequences of an accident can be very serious, so don't ever head into the forest without leaving someone – either the ranger on duty, someone back at your hotel or your friends who chose to stay at the beach – your planned itinerary. Minor cuts and scrapes can get infected easily in this climate, so it's a good idea to hike with disinfectant.

WILDLIFE
Wild horses roam parts of Vieques, and although they look gentle and placid while grazing on the tropical underbrush, they can kick, bite and trample. Even small animals are capable of inflicting serious injury or even fatal wounds on unsuspecting tourists. Some also carry rabies. Keep your distance from all wild animals, and that goes double for any mongooses you see in El Yunque. The monkeys and iguanas on some of the cays off the south coast can be downright fierce.

PESTS
Mosquitoes are ubiquitous – and they do not restrict their activities to the hours around sunset. In fact, one type of daylight mosquito carries dengue fever (p296), although the risk of contracting it is extremely low.

Hookworm – which can be contacted by simply walking barefoot through infected sand or dirt – once plagued the island. And while public health initiatives have reduced the prevalence of the disease, the possibility of catching it still exists. Frequent bathing and the use of footwear is the very best prevention.

DISCOUNT CARDS
Senior Cards
Though the age when discounts begin varies with the attraction, travelers 55 years and older can expect to receive cut rates and benefits. Be sure to inquire about such rates at hotels, museums and restaurants. All you need to get the senior discount offered at many local attractions is a valid ID showing you are 55 or older.

Visitors to national parks – including the forts in Old San Juan – and to campgrounds can cut their costs greatly by using the Golden Age Passport, a card that allows US citizens aged 62 and over (and those traveling in the same car) free admission nationwide and a 50% reduction on camping fees. You can apply in person for the card at any national park or regional office of the US Forest Service or National Park Service.

Student & Youth Cards
If you're a student, an international student ID card or school or university ID card can get

you discounts for theater/museum tickets and public transportation. There are no hostels, so discounts don't apply here.

EMBASSIES & CONSULATES
Embassies & Consulates in Puerto Rico
Most nations' principal diplomatic representation is in Washington DC. To find out the telephone number of your embassy or consulate in DC, call ☎ 202-555-1212.

In addition, some nations with 'interests' in Puerto Rico maintain consulates and honorary consulates on the island. The foreign consulates in Puerto Rico are in San Juan or the surrounding suburbs:

Austria (☎ 787-766-0799; Plaza Las Américas, Río Piedras)

Canada (☎ 787-790-2210; 107 Calle Cereipo Alturas, Guaynabo)

Netherlands (☎ 787-759-9400; Mercantil Plaza, Hato Rey)

UK (☎ 787-727-1065; 1509 Calle Lopez Landron, Santurce)

FESTIVALS & EVENTS
Every Puerto Rican town honors its patron saint annually. These *fiestas patronales* occur throughout the year and generally begin on a Friday 10 days before the saint's day. The fiestas usually take place in the town's central plaza and have the carnival atmosphere typical of such celebrations throughout Latin America. The fiestas climax with a parade on the Sunday nearest the saint's day in which parishioners of various churches carry large wooden effigies of the saint through the streets. Frequently, the music, dance and rituals associated with the parade blend African and some Taíno traditions with Roman Catholic protocol. For a complete and up-to-date list of these *fiesta patronales,* contact the PRTC (p284).

The **Festival Casals** (www.festcasalspr.gobierno.pr), the premier musical event in Puerto Rico and probably all of the Caribbean, is held annually in San Juan. Founded by the great cellist Pablo Casals, who retired to Puerto Rico, the festival is now more than 40 years old and draws world-class conductors and musicians for two weeks of concerts celebrating orchestral music. Concert tickets can cost $20 to $40, but students, seniors and disabled persons can get a 50% discount. Dates vary.

Following is a list of other island events that have cultural as well as entertainment value. The telephone numbers listed will connect travelers with event organizers or local tourist offices.

January

Festival San Sebastián (☎ 787-724-0910) Sponsored by the Instituto de Cultura Puertorriqueña, this three-day shindig of parades, food, dancing and music is one of the island's hippest street carnivals and draws in crowds from around the Caribbean and beyond.

February

Coffee Harvest Festival, Maricao (☎ 787-838-2290) Held midmonth, this is like a *fiesta patronal,* but with demonstrations of traditional coffeemaking and local crafting. The rugged mountain setting of the town is sublime, and the fresh air fills with the scents of roasting beans.

Carnaval, Ponce (☎ 787-841-8044) During the six days preceding the beginning of Lent, Catholics and folks who love to party come to Ponce to celebrate and give themselves up to food, alcohol and romance before Lent begins. During Lent, they deny themselves the pleasures of the body until after Easter. While this event is not up to the standards of Rio de Janeiro's Carnaval or New Orleans' Mardi Gras, it is a hopping good time in the tradition of put-on-a-mask (or just pretend), wear funny clothes (cross-dressing is always cool) and party 'til you drop. This is one of the great places to see parades of *vejigantes,* the traditional horned maskers.

March

Cinco Días con Nuestro Tierra, Mayagüez (☎ 787-265-3855) Held in the second week of March, this is one of the island's agricultural-industrial fairs, featuring local produce.

April

José de Diego Day Celebrates the birthday of patriot José de Diego (born April 16, 1867). It's a national holiday, celebrated with particular enthusiasm in Aguadilla, where he was born.

May

Fiesta Nacional de la Danza, Ponce (☎ 787-224-1844) This event, held in mid-May, features a week of music and dance concerts that celebrate the stately music of string quartets and the 19th-century ballroom dance that was the hallmark of island sophistication in the days when elegance and manners were more important.

June

Fiesta de San Juan Bautista, San Juan (☎ 787-735-3871, 787-721-2400) Here you have the *ne plus ultra,* the *fiesta patronal* of the island capital. On June 24 you will find the narrow streets of Old San Juan filled with a crush of party animals. At midnight, legions of people walk backward into the sea (or sometimes fountains) three times to demonstrate their loyalty to the saint of Christian baptism and gain his blessing for the coming year.

Festival de Flores, Aibonito At the end of June you can see acres of roses, carnations, lilies, begonias etc come to life in the fresh air of this attractive mountain town.

July

Fiesta de Santiago, Loíza Aldea (☎ 787-876-3570) Loíza is the place to come if you want to see one way that Puerto Ricans of African descent keep their ties to Africa alive. This is a fiesta worthy of Bahía in Brazil: parades, fabulous drum ensembles, masks and costumes revive saints, such as Santiago, who, according to the traditions of Santería, are incarnations of West African gods. Held at the end of the month.

November

Jayuya Indian Festival, Jayuya (☎ 787-828-0900) Although all pure-blooded Taíno have been gone for about 400 years, this festival, held midmonth, does a decent job of reviving the games, costumes, food and music of the original islanders. As with almost all Puerto Rican fiestas, there is a beauty pageant, this time with young women in Indian dress.

December

Hatillo Mask Festival, Hatillo (☎ 787-898-3835) Held on December 28, this is the island's third major festival of maskers. This one features masked devils prowling the streets as incarnations of the agents of King Herod, who sent his soldiers into the streets of Judea to find and kill the Christ Child. Kids think it is great fun to run and hide from the maskers.

FOOD

For detailed descriptions of island eating patterns, see Food & Drink (p56). Prices run the gamut in Puerto Rico and in certain sections of town compete with those you'd see in Tokyo, New York and London. The least expensive meals are found in fast-food restaurants, *friquitines* (roadside kiosks) and the bodegas that serve snacks.

GAY & LESBIAN TRAVELERS

Puerto Rico is probably the most gay-friendly island in the Caribbean. San Juan has a well-developed gay scene, especially in the Condado district, for Puerto Ricans and visitors. Other cities, such as Mayagüez and Ponce, have gay clubs and gay-friendly accommodations as well. Vieques and Culebra have become popular destinations for an international mix of gay and lesbian expatriates

DIRECTORY

and travelers. In the cities and in major resort areas, it is easier for gay men and women to live their lives with a certain amount of openness. As you travel into the middle of the island, it is more difficult to be out, as people are not used to seeing same-sex couples holding hands or displaying affection publicly. It might be wiser to keep your canoodling to a minimum when mixing with the crowds.

On the island, pick up a copy of the **Puerto Rico Breeze** (☎ 787-724-3411), a bilingual tabloid of events and listings for accommodations, restaurants, clubs etc, for gay men and lesbians.

Also, check with the staff at the gay venue **Atlantic Beach Hotel** (☎ 787-721-6900), in Condado, for information on current events in the lesbian and gay community.

Another good resource is the **Gay Yellow Pages** (☎ 212-674-0120; PO Box 533, Village Station, NY 10014-0533), which has a national edition and regional editions. Also check out these definitive gay sources: www.go-breeze.com and www.planetout.com.

HOLIDAYS

US public holidays are celebrated along with local holidays in Puerto Rico. Banks, schools and government offices (including post offices) are closed, and transportation, museums and other services are on a Sunday schedule. Holidays falling on a weekend are usually observed the following Monday. Nearly all museums in Puerto Rico close on Mondays. Some also remain closed on Tuesdays.

New Year's Day January 1
Three Kings Day (Feast of the Epiphany) January 6
Eugenio María de Hostos' Birthday January 10 – honors the island educator, writer and patriot
Martin Luther King Jr Day Third Monday in January
Presidents' Day Third Monday in February
Emancipation Day March 22 – island slaves were freed on this date in 1873
Palm Sunday Sunday before Easter
Good Friday Friday before Easter
Easter A Sunday in late March/April
José de Diego Day April 18
Memorial Day Last Monday in May
Independence Day/Fourth of July July 4
Luis Muñoz Rivera's Birthday July 18 – honors the island patriot and political leader
Constitution Day July 25
José Celso Barbosa's Birthday July 27
Labor Day First Monday in September
Columbus Day Second Monday in October

Veterans' Day November 11
Thanksgiving Fourth Thursday in November
Christmas Day December 25

INSURANCE

No matter how you're traveling, make sure you purchase travel insurance. This should cover you not only for medical expenses and luggage theft or loss, but also for cancellations or delays in your travel arrangements. You should be covered for the worst possible case, such as an accident that requires hospital treatment and a flight home. Coverage depends on your insurance and type of ticket, so ask both your insurer and your ticket-issuing agency to explain the finer points. **STA Travel** (☎ 800-777-0112) offers travel insurance options at reasonable prices.

Travel insurance also covers lost tickets. Make sure you have a separate record of all your ticket details – or better still, a photocopy of the tickets. Also make a copy of your policy in case the original is lost.

INTERNET ACCESS

Finding a good internet café outside of San Juan can be incredibly frustrating. If you can't find anything open (cybercafés tend to open and shut within weeks), most public libraries have computers with internet access. Free wi-fi access is increasingly available in the better hotels, although whether it is working is another matter. Popular resort towns such as Rincón, Ponce and Fajardo tend to have more options.

LEGAL MATTERS

If you are stopped by the police for any reason, bear in mind that there is no system of paying fines on the spot. Attempting to pay the fine to the officer is frowned upon at best and may compound your troubles by resulting in a charge of bribery. For traffic violations, the police officer will explain your options to you.

If you are arrested for more serious offenses, you are allowed to remain silent. There is no legal reason to speak to a police officer if you don't wish, but never walk away from an officer until given permission. All persons who are arrested are legally allowed (and given) the right to make one phone call. If you don't have a lawyer or family member to help you, call your embassy. The police will give you the number upon request.

Puerto Rico follows US laws in all criminal and most legislative matters. In the event that you are arrested, you have the same rights as you would have on US soil.

Drinking Laws

The drinking age is 18 on the island – three years younger than in the US! Legally you need identification with your photograph on it to prove your age. In Puerto Rico, minors are not permitted in bars and pubs, even to order nonalcoholic beverages. Ostensibly, this prohibition means that most dance clubs are also off-limits to minors, but door guards seem to make liberal exceptions for pretty young women.

Old San Juan has enacted a stiff law to stop the drinking in the streets. If you get caught, you will be fined $500. The establishment that served you the drink will be charged $1000. Furthermore, you could incur stiff fines, jail time and penalties if caught driving under the influence of alcohol. During fiestas, holidays and special events, roadblocks are sometimes set up to deter drunk drivers. The legal blood alcohol limit for drivers is 0.08%.

Nevertheless, alcohol is much more a part of the social scene on the island than it is in many parts of the US and Europe. Puerto Rico has few 'blue laws' prohibiting the times and places where alcohol can be consumed. This means that drinking (even underage drinking) is rampant during fiestas – as it is every Thursday to Sunday in San Juan and beach resort towns when islanders are in party mode. Drinking on the beach is legal.

MAPS

Navigating Puerto Rico can be a challenge because of missing road signs and changes in street names. Furthermore, none of the major maps totally agree. Rand McNally publishes a foldout road map that includes detailed city maps of Aguadilla, Arecibo, Caguas, Mayagüez, Ponce and San Juan, as well as the islands of Culebra and Vieques. The map is available at bookstores and newsstands around the island for about $3.

A similar map produced by **Metro Data** (www .metropr.com), the mapmakers of Puerto Rico, is the most up-to-date product. If you want something even more detailed – right down to housing plots – pick up Metro Data's *Guía Urbana* for San Juan and Ponce ($15), stocked in most San Juan bookstores.

The US Geological Survey (USGS), an agency of the US Department of the Interior, publishes very detailed topographic maps of Puerto Rico, at various scales up to 1:250,000. Maps at 1:62,500, or approximately 1in = 1 mile, are ideal for backcountry hiking and backpacking. Some bookstores and outdoor equipment specialists on the island carry a selection of topographic maps.

MONEY

Puerto Rico uses US currency. The US *dolar* or *peso* (dollar) is divided into 100 cents (¢). Coins come in denominations of 1¢, called the *centavo* or *chavito* (penny); 5¢, called the *villon* or *ficha* (nickel); 10¢ (dime); 25¢, called the *peseta* (quarter); and the seldom-seen 50¢ (half-dollar) coin. Quarters are the most commonly used coins in vending machines and parking meters, so it's handy to have a stash of them. Notes, commonly called bills, come in $1, $2, $5, $10, $20, $50 and $100 denominations – $2 bills are rare but perfectly legal. There is also a $1 coin that the government has tried unsuccessfully to bring into mass circulation; you may get them as change from ticket and stamp machines. Be aware that they look similar to quarters.

ATMs

Called ATHs in Puerto Rico for *a todos horas* (at all hours), ATMs are a convenient way of obtaining cash from a bank account back home. Even many small-town banks in the middle of nowhere have ATMs. They are common in most shopping areas and are often available 24 hours a day.

There are various ATM networks, and most banks in Puerto Rico are affiliated with several. Exchange, Accel, Plus and Cirrus are the predominant networks. For a nominal service charge, you can withdraw cash from an ATM using a credit card or a charge card. Some American banks take advantage of Puerto Rico's commonwealth status to charge a hefty $7 dollar fee on each 'international' withdrawal you make.

Remember that ATMs in remote locations and on Vieques and Culebra run out of money sometimes on weekends.

Credit Cards

Major credit cards are accepted at hotels, restaurants, gas stations, shops and car rental agencies throughout Puerto Rico. In fact, you'll find it hard to perform certain trans-actions, such as renting a car or purchasing tickets to performances, without one.

Even if you loathe credit cards and prefer to rely on traveler's checks and ATMs, it's a good idea to carry one for emergencies. If you're planning to rely primarily upon credit cards, it would be wise to have a Visa or MasterCard in your deck, since other cards aren't as widely accepted.

If you should lose your credit cards or they are stolen, contact the company imme-diately. Contact your bank if you lose your ATM card.

Following are toll-free numbers for the main credit-card companies:

American Express (☎ 800-528-4800)
Diners Club (☎ 800-234-6377)
Discover (☎ 800-347-2683)
MasterCard (☎ 800-826-2181)
Visa (☎ 800-336-8472)

Moneychangers

Most banks on the island will exchange cash or traveler's checks in major foreign curren-cies, though banks in outlying areas don't do so very often, and it may take them some time. It is probably less of a hassle to exchange foreign currency in San Juan.

Banco Popular (☎ 787-791-0326; 🕙 8am-4pm) has a currency-exchange office in Terminal C at the Luis Muñoz Marín (LMM) airport. You can also exchange currency at just about any Banco Popular office in the capital San Juan (p87).

Though carrying cash is more risky, it's still a good idea to travel with some for the convenience. Make sure you carry small bills though, as outside of banks, few places can break $50s or $100s – even $20s are some-times too much. Cash is useful to help pay all those tips, and some smaller, more re-mote places may not accept credit cards or traveler's checks.

Carry copies of your traveler's check num-bers and credit card numbers separately.

Tipping

On the island, tipping is in order in restau-rants and better hotels. Taxi drivers, hair-dressers and baggage carriers expect tips, and waiters and bartenders rely on tips for their livelihoods. Tip 15% unless the service is terrible (in which case a complaint to the manager is warranted), or about 20% if the service is great. Never tip in fast-food, take-out or buffet-style restaurants where you serve yourself. Baggage carriers in airports and hotels get $2 for the first bag and $1 for each additional bag. In hotels with daily housekeeping staff, leave a few dollars in the room when you check out – ask at the desk regarding the appropriate amount per day. In budget hotels, tips are not expected, but are always appreciated.

Taxes

There is no national sales tax (such as VAT) in the US or Puerto Rico, but almost everything you pay for on the island is taxed. You also won't see a sales tax or a restaurant tax, but there is a 9% accommodation tax in most guesthouses and motels, and if you stay in a hotel with a casino, expect the amount to jump to 15%. Unless otherwise stated, the prices given in this book don't include local taxes. There's also a 5% tax on jewelry sold on the island.

POST

You'll find a **US post office** (☎ 800-275-8777; www .usps.gov) in almost every Puerto Rican town, providing familiar postal services such as parcel shipping and international express mail. Private shippers such as **United Parcel Service** (UPS; ☎ 800-742-5877) and **Federal Express** (FedEx; ☎ 800-463-3339) ship much of Puerto Rico's load of parcels and important time-sensitive documents to both domestic and foreign destinations.

If you have the correct postage, you can drop your mail into any blue mailbox. However, to send a package that's 16oz or heavier, you must take it to a post office. If you need to buy stamps or weigh your mail, go to the nearest post office. Larger towns have branch post offices and post-office cent-ers in some supermarkets and drugstores. Addresses for main local post offices are given in this book.

You can have mail sent to you, addressed as 'c/o General Delivery,' at any post office that has its own zip (postal) code. Mail is usually held for 10 days before it's returned to the sender; you might request that your correspondents write 'hold for arrival' on letters. Alternatively, have mail sent to the local representative of American Express or Thomas Cook, which provide mail service for their customers.

SHOPPING

Shoppers will find a lot of tempting, pretty things in the shops of Old San Juan, Condado and Ponce, but few bargains. Puerto Rico is not a duty-free port. The only economic advantage to shopping in Puerto Rico is that there is no sales tax.

Travelers looking for souvenirs are usually drawn to the island's folk arts. *Santos* are probably the most popular purchase, but these carved religious figures can cost well over $100. *Mundillo,* the intricately woven island-made lace, is also a popular purchase, as are woven hammocks like the ones Columbus admired when he first stopped at Borinquen. You can also pick up *vejigantes,* masks typical of those worn in the fiestas at Ponce and Loíza. Island-made macramé and ceramic items are also widely available in the shops catering to tourists.

Since Puerto Rico is the leading producer of rum in the world, you would be right to expect that many travelers find this beverage the one thing they must buy on the island. You will not only find a dizzying variety of rum in Puerto Rico (see p57), but you'll also discover that it is significantly cheaper here than in the US. Most bottles cost between $6 and $15, depending on size and quality. And there is no limit to how much you can take out of Puerto Rico when you leave, but bear in mind the limits imposed by the country you are next entering.

The second-most popular consumable among island travelers is the rich, mountain-grown coffee. Both Adjuntas and Rioja are popular premium products with fancy labels and packaging, but islanders say that Puerto Rican coffee is of such high quality that you cannot go wrong buying the local supermarket brands.

Bargaining is not appreciated or widely practiced in Puerto Rico. There's nothing wrong with asking if there's a discount available at a guesthouse or hotel – especially when there are empty rooms – but full-on haggling over prices in stores is likely to get you nothing but an expression of contempt from the shopkeeper.

SOLO TRAVELERS

There's no stigma attracted to traveling alone in Puerto Rico – in fact it's a great way to make friends – but you do need to take precautions simply because you're missing the safety of numbers. Watch out for someone who accidentally bumps you and then apologizes profusely, engaging you in conversation. When you turn around, your bags may be gone. Likewise, pickpockets will work in tandem to rid you of your wallet. If you are going solo, travel light and keep track of your belongings. Avoid traveling at night, and don't hitch – ever.

TELEPHONE

All phone numbers within Puerto Rico consist of a three-digit area code (787) followed by a seven-digit local number. If you are calling locally, just dial the seven-digit number. To call the island from the US, dial ☎ 1 + 787 + the seven-digit number. Call the island from any other overseas destination the same way, after dialing the appropriate code for an international line in your country.

For directory assistance on the island, dial ☎ 411. For US directory assistance outside Puerto Rico, dial ☎ 1 + the three-digit area code of the place you want to call + 555-1212. For example, to obtain directory assistance for a toll-free number, dial ☎ 1-800-555-1212 or 1-888-555-1212. If you need Puerto Rican directory assistance while you're outside the country, dial ☎ 1-787-555-1212.

The 800, 866 and 888 area codes are designated for toll-free numbers within Puerto Rico, the US and sometimes Canada as well. These calls are free (unless you are dialing locally, in which case the toll-free number is not available).

To make a direct international call from Puerto Rico, dial ☎ 011 + the country code + the area code + phone number. You may need to wait as long as 45 seconds for the ringing to start. International rates vary depending on the time of day and the destination. Call the operator (☎ 0) for rates. The first minute is always more expensive than extra minutes. To make a reverse-charge (collect) call, call the operator (☎ 0) and let them know you wish to make a collect call.

Hotels hike up the price of local calls by almost 200%, and long-distance rates are raised between 100% and 200%. Many hotels (especially the more expensive ones) add a service charge of between 50¢ and $1 for each local call made from a room phone, and they also add hefty surcharges for long-distance calls. Public pay phones, which can be found

DIRECTORY

in most lobbies, are always cheaper. You can pump in quarters, use a phone debit card or make collect calls at pay phones. Phonecards are available and sold at kiosks, in bodegas and around town. Cell phones are popular and operate just about everywhere. Puerto Rico is on the US system, so all the US networks are present.

TIME
Puerto Rico is on Atlantic Standard Time. Clocks in this time zone read an hour later than the Eastern Standard Time zone, which encompasses such US cities as New York, Boston, Washington DC and Miami. During Daylight Saving Time in those cities – from 1am on the first Sunday in April until 2am on the last Sunday of October – the time is the same in Puerto Rico. There is no Daylight Saving Time observed on the island.

When making appointments, most Puerto Ricans generally follow the American style of using a 12-hour clock and adding am or pm to connote morning or afternoon. Occasionally you'll hear the 24-hour clock used, mostly when people are speaking Spanish.

TOURIST INFORMATION
Local Tourist Offices
The **Puerto Rico Tourism Company** (PRTC; www .gotopuertorico.com) is the commonwealth's official tourist bureau and a very good source for thorough brochures on island accommodations, sports, shopping, dining and festivals. The PRTC also sponsors a variety of folk and fine-arts shows around the island. From abroad, you can call any of the PRTC offices worldwide and request a tourist information packet. On the island, call the offices or stop by for up-to-date information and calendars of current events. PRTC has offices in Aguadilla (p253), Boquerón (p213), Ponce (p187), San Juan (p87) and Vieques (p169).

Tourist Offices Abroad
All of the following countries have Puerto Rico Tourism Company offices:
Argentina (☎ 1-314-4525; 882 Calle Santa Fe, piso 9, 1059 Buenos Aires)
Canada (☎ 416-368-2680; 41-43 Colbourne St, Suite 301, Toronto, ON M5E 1E3)
France (☎ 01 44 77 88 00; Express Conseil, 5 bis Rue du Louvre, 75001 Paris)
Germany (☎ 49-69-350047; Eifelstrasse 14-A, 60529 Frankfurt)

Mexico (☎ 525-553-2730; Vicente Saúrez 64-A, Colonia Condesa, 06140 Mexico City, DF)
Spain (☎ 3491-431-2128; Calle Serrano No 1-20 Izquierda, 28001 Madrid)
USA Los Angeles (☎ 213-874-5991, 800-874-1230; 3575 W Cahuenga Blvd, Suite 405, Los Angeles, CA 90068); Florida (☎ 305-445-9112; 901 Ponce de León Blvd, Suite 101, Coral Gables, FL 33134); New York City (☎ 212-599-6262; 666 Fifth Ave, New York, NY 10103)
Venezuela (☎ 58-2-761-7929; Centro Profesional del Este, piso 6, Suite 265, Calle Villaflor, Caracas 1050)

TOURS
While nothing can compete with the adventure of planning and executing a wilderness trip on your own, these tour operators can take a lot of the worry out of the adventure and give you a chance to interact with fellow adventure travelers:
Acampa (Map pp86-7; ☎ 787-706-0695; www.campapr .com; 1211 Av Jesús T Piñero, San Juan) If you want to go to Isla Mona, Reserva Forestal Toro Negro, El Yunque, Río Camuy or any other adventure spot on the island, Acampa has all the latest gadgets to give you a spectacular trip.
Aquatica Dive & Bike Adventures (☎ 787-890-6071; www.aquatica.cjb.net) Bicycle tours in Aguadilla, Cabo Rojo and Quebradillas, with the option of taking a swim en route.
Aventuras Puerto Rico (☎ 787-380-8481; www .aventuraspuertorico.com) Kayaking, custom tours, horseback rides and snorkeling around Ponce, Arecibo, Camuy and Isabela.
Aventuras Tierra Adentro (Map p102; ☎ 787-766-0470; www.aventuraspr.com; 268-A Av Jesús T Piñero, San Juan) Camping, caving, rock-climbing, river-touring, with a specialty in canyon adventures.
Copladet Nature & Adventure Tours (☎ 787-765-8595; www.copladet.com) Birding, caving, hiking, horseback riding, kayaking; trips to Isla Caja de Muertos.
Eco Xcursion Aquatica (☎ 787- 888-2887; ecoxcursion @libertypr.net) Nature-conscious educational tours and outdoor activities including kayaking, biking, hiking around Fajardo, Luquillo, Ceiba and more.
Encanto Ecotours (☎ 787-272-0005) Mangroves, manatees, turtle nesting; trips to Culebra, Vieques and Isla Mona – this tour group does just about everything on every part of the island.

TRAVELERS WITH DISABILITIES
Travel to and around Puerto Rico is becoming easier for people with disabilities. Public buildings (including hotels, restaurants, theaters and museums) are now required by law to be wheelchair-accessible and to have appropriate rest-room facilities. Public transportation services (buses, trains and taxis) must

be made accessible to all, including those in wheelchairs, and telephone companies are required to provide relay operators for the hearing impaired.

Many banks now provide ATM instructions in Braille. Curb ramps are common, and some of the busier roadway intersections have audible crossing signals. Playa Luquillo has a beach especially for the mobility-impaired (p138), and ferries to the Spanish Virgin Islands (p147) are disabled-accessible.

Larger private and chain hotels have suites for disabled guests. Major car-rental agencies offer hand-controlled models at no extra charge. All major airlines and intercity buses allow guide dogs to accompany passengers.

A good website to find access information is www.access-able.com. A number of organizations and tour providers specialize in the needs of disabled travelers:

Mobility International USA (☎ 541-343-1284; www .miusa.org; PO Box 10767, Eugene, OR 97440) Advises disabled travelers on mobility issues. It primarily runs an educational exchange program.

Wheelchair Getaways Rent-A-Car (☎ 787-726-4023, 800-868-8028) Provides livery service as well as tours of Puerto Rico.

VISAS

You only need a visa to enter Puerto Rico if you need a visa to enter the US, since the commonwealth follows the United States' immigration laws. As a commonwealth, Puerto Rico subscribes to all the laws that apply to traveling and border crossing in the United States. US citizens can enter the commonwealth with proper proof of citizenship, such as a driver's license with photo ID, a passport or a birth certificate. Visitors from other countries must have a valid, scannable passport. Countries participating in the Visa Waiver Program – the EU, Australia, New Zealand and much of Latin America – don't need visas to get into Puerto Rico. The **US State Department** (www.state.gov) has current information about visas, immigration etc. See p286 for passport information.

VOLUNTEERING

As a relatively rich country in close geographic and economic proximity to the United States, Puerto Rico offers limited opportunities for volunteering. Your best bet to find work on a worthwhile ecological project is on the island of Culebra where the US Fish and Wildlife Refuge

run a volunteer turtle watch (p158) on Playa Brava during nesting season. You can also access this project through CORALations, a non-profit organization that is involved in coral reef protection in and around the island.

The US-based **Earthwatch Institute** (☎ 1-978-461-0081) runs one-to-two-week research missions to the Bosque Estatal de Carite (p258), where participants learn forest management skills and aid in the rejuvenation of the tropical rainforest. Volunteers stay in tents in the Casas de la Selva complex inside the park and spend their time planting seedlings, studying trees and monitoring local frog populations. Some of the trips are family friendly.

WOMEN TRAVELERS

Puerto Rico's status as a US commonwealth means that women enjoy a position in society not dissimilar to the United States or any other western-style democracy. The fact that the island has elected many influential women to high political office, including the late San Juan mayor Felisa Rincón de Gautier and ex-Puerto Rico governor Sila María Calderón, has proved that powerful females are no cultural pushovers and have garnered new-found respect among formerly misogynistic males.

Puerto Rican women crisscross the island all the time by themselves, so you won't be the only solo woman on the ferry or public bus, but as a foreigner you will attract a bit more attention. Most of it will be simple curiosity, but a few may assume you'd much rather be with a man if you could, so hey – they'll be friendly and give you the option. If you don't want the company, most men will respect a firm but polite 'no thank you.'

Bookstores, found in the Yellow Pages under *Librerías,* are good places to find out about gatherings, readings and meetings. University campuses are also good sites to network, and their social centers often have bulletin boards where you can find or place travel and short-term housing notices.

One international organization with an affiliate office in Puerto Rico is **Profamilia** (Planned Parenthood; ☎ 787-765-7373; 117 Padre Las Casas, El Vedado, San Juan). The staff here can refer you to clinics and offer advice on medical issues. Another good source of information on health and safety issues for women is the government office **Comisión Para Los Asuntos de Mujer** (Commission for Women's Affairs; ☎ 787-722-2977; 151 Calle San Francisco, Old San Juan).

Transportation

TRANSPORTATION

GETTING THERE & AWAY

ENTERING THE COUNTRY

Even if you are continuing immediately to another city, the first airport that you land in is where you must carry out immigration and customs formalities. The customs process can be quick and painless or it can involve a more prolonged exchange between you and officials.

A certain number of passengers are set aside to be searched randomly on just about every flight. You may be tapped, and it may be for no reason other than that your number came up.

Customs officials are mostly focused on excluding those who are likely to work illegally or overstay their welcome in Puerto Rico, so visitors will be asked about their

---

THINGS CHANGE...

The information in this chapter is particularly vulnerable to change. Check directly with the airline or a travel agent to make sure you understand how a fare (and ticket you may buy) works and be aware of the security requirements for international travel. Shop carefully. The details given in this chapter should be regarded as pointers and are not a substitute for your own careful, up-to-date research.

---

plans and perhaps about whether they have sufficient funds for their stay.

It's a good idea to be able to list an itinerary that will account for the period for which you ask to be admitted, and to be able to show you have $300 to $400 for every week of your intended stay. These days, a couple of major credit cards will go a long way toward establishing 'sufficient funds.'

Remember that the list of items that can't be brought on to airplanes now includes many implements used by divers, campers and hikers. Check the **US State Department** (www.state .gov) for an updated list, and make sure you check those bags.

Flights, tours and rail tickets can be booked online at www.lonelyplanet.com /travel_services.

Passports

Unless you are an American or Canadian citizen, you need a scannable passport to enter Puerto Rico. No passport is automatically denied, but in the high-scrutiny world of airports, you can expect to garner some extra attention or questioning from officials if you have stamps showing recent travel to countries known for drug trafficking.

If you are asked to step aside, the best thing to do is stay calm and answer the questions as best you can.

Carry a photocopy of your passport separately from your passport. Copy the pages with your photo and personal details, passport number and US visa. In the event of loss, call your local consulate or embassy. You can find your consulate's telephone number by dialing information on the island (☎ 411). To reach your embassy, call directory assistance for Washington DC (☎ 202-555-1212). See also Visas (p285).

AIR

Airfares to Caribbean destinations such as Puerto Rico vary tremendously depending on the season you travel, the day of the week you fly, the length of your stay and the flexibility the ticket allows for flight changes and refunds. Still, nothing determines fares more than demand, and when things are slow,

---

CLIMATE CHANGE & TRAVEL

Climate change is a serious threat to the ecosystems that humans rely upon, and air travel is the fastest-growing contributor to the problem. Lonely Planet regards travel, overall, as a global benefit, but believes we all have a responsibility to limit our personal impact on global warming.

Flying & Climate Change

Pretty much every form of motor travel generates CO_2 (the main cause of human-induced climate change) but planes are far and away the worst offenders, not just because of the sheer distances they allow us to travel, but because they release greenhouse gases high into the atmosphere. The statistics are frightening: two people taking a return flight between Europe and the US will contribute as much to climate change as an average household's gas and electricity consumption over a whole year.

Carbon Offset Schemes

Climatecare.org and other websites use 'carbon calculators' that allow jetsetters to offset the greenhouse gases they are responsible for with contributions to energy-saving projects and other climate-friendly initiatives in the developing world – including projects in India, Honduras, Kazakhstan and Uganda.

Lonely Planet, together with Rough Guides and other concerned partners in the travel industry, supports the carbon offset scheme run by climatecare.org. Lonely Planet offsets all of its staff and author travel.

For more information check out our website: lonelyplanet.com.

---

regardless of the season, airlines will lower their fares to fill empty seats.

Airports & Airlines

San Juan's recently modernized Aeropuerto Internacional de Luis Muñoz Marín – commonly shortened to LMM – lies just 2 miles beyond the eastern border of the city in the beachfront suburb of Isla Verde. Chances are that you will be arriving and departing from the airport in San Juan, but Aguadilla's Aeropuerto Rafael Hernández, at the former Ramey Base on the island's northwest tip, has some scheduled international flights from the US (mainly New York). Ponce and Mayagüez each have a small airport for domestic flights. San Juan's original airport at Isla Grande, on the Bahía de San Juan in the Miramar district, services private aircraft and the bulk of the commuter flights to the Puerto Rican islands of Culebra and Vieques; see p290.

Puerto Rico is the most accessible island in the Caribbean. San Juan is served by a number of North American carriers that fly between Puerto Rico and a score of mainland US cities; Miami has the most frequent flights. British Airways has services from London, Iberia flies from Madrid and Lufthansa's subsidiary Condor provides travelers with a link from Frankfurt.

Tickets

The easiest and cheapest way to book tickets is through the website of any major carrier. Many offer discounted fares online that aren't available over the phone or through a travel agency. For North Americans, the 'no-frills' carriers that don't offer any meal service or other amenities but get you to your destination expeditiously are usually the best deals. Most of these tickets are non-refundable but can be held and used again if something keeps you from flying on the appointed day. Other websites known to offer discounted fares:

www.bestfares.com/home.asp
www.cheaptickets.com
www.expedia.com
www.travelocity.com

If you have any particular needs – traveling with children, taking a guide dog, kosher or vegan meal requests – it's always better to book directly with the company over the phone or through a travel agent.

At holiday times travelers to Puerto Rico will probably find it difficult to get the flights and fares they want unless they plan – and purchase their tickets – well in advance. Holiday times include Christmas, New Year's Eve, Easter, Memorial Day, Labor Day and Thanksgiving.

Asia

Most Asian countries offer fairly competitive airfare deals, with Bangkok, Singapore and Hong Kong the best places to shop around for discount tickets. Hong Kong's travel market can be unpredictable, but some excellent bargains are available if you are lucky. **STA Travel** (www.statravel.com) is a good and reliable place to start.

Australia

Two well-known agents for cheap fares are **STA Travel** (☎ 1300 360 960; www.statravel.com.au), which has offices in major cities and on many university campuses, and **Flight Centre** (☎ 13 16 00; www.flightcentre.com.au), which has dozens of offices throughout Australia.

Qantas flies to Los Angeles from Sydney, Melbourne (via Sydney or Auckland) and Cairns. United flies to San Francisco from Sydney and Auckland (via Sydney), and also flies to Los Angeles. Connector flights are available to San Juan.

Canada

Canadian discount air-ticket sellers are also known as consolidators, and their airfares tend to be about 10% higher than those sold in the USA.

Travel CUTS (☎ 800-667-2887; www.travelcuts.com) is Canada's national student travel agency and has offices in all major cities.

Caribbean & Latin America

Many flights to San Juan from Central and South America are routed through Miami, Houston or New York. A few countries' international flag carriers, such as Lacsa and Mexicana, fly directly to San Juan from Latin American cities.

Puerto Rico's link to Antigua, Barbados, Haiti, Jamaica and Trinidad is American Airlines and BWIA. ALM Antillean Airlines also has flights to/from Puerto Rico connecting to Aruba, Bonaire, Colombia, Panama, Venezuela and St Maarten.

Cape Air, Air St Thomas, Vieques Air Link, Air Sunshine and others also fly this route.

Continental Europe

Though London is the travel-discount capital of Europe, there are several other cities where you will find a range of good deals. Generally, there is not much variation in airfare prices from the main European cities. The major airlines and travel agents usually have a number of deals on offer, so shop around.

STA Travel (www.statravel.com) has offices throughout the region. **Nouvelles Frontières** (www.nouvelles-frontieres.com) also has offices throughout the world.

France has a network of student travel agencies that can supply discount tickets to travelers of all ages. **OTU Voyages** (☎ 0820 817 817; www.otu.fr) and **Voyageurs du Monde** (☎ 01 42 86 16 40; www.vdm.com) have branches throughout the country and offer some of the best services and deals.

Recommended agencies in Germany include **STA Travel** (☎ 01805 456 422; www.statravel.de), which has branches in major cities across the country.

In Spain, recommended agencies include **Barcelo Viajes** (☎ 902 116 226; www.barcelo-viajes.es), with offices in major cities.

Lufthansa's subsidiary line Condor flies from Frankfurt to San Juan. Iberia has direct flights from Madrid to San Juan and connecting flights through the Dominican Republic.

New Zealand

STA Travel (☎ 0800 874 773; www.statravel.co.nz) is a good source of information, and **Flight Centre** (☎ 0800 243 544; www.flightcentre.co.nz) also has a lot of options. New Zealanders might also want to look at www.roundtheworldflights.com, which has lists of carriers from all over the place who fly to Puerto Rico via Wellington.

UK

Discount air travel is big business in London. Advertisements for travel agencies appear in the travel pages of the weekend broadsheet newspapers and in *Time Out*.

For students or travelers under 26 years, a popular travel agency in the UK is **STA Travel** (☎ 0870 160 0599; www.statravel.co.uk), which has branches across the country. STA sells tickets to all travelers, but caters especially to young people and students.

British Airways offers daily connecting flights to San Juan through Miami. Several other airlines feed Miami and Fort Lauderdale from the UK, including American Airlines, Delta Air Lines and Virgin Atlantic. American Airlines offers a connecting service to San Juan.

For information about flights from Aberdeen, Scotland, directly to San Juan, check out **Kasbah Travel** (www.kasbah.com).

The **Globetrotters Club** (www.globetrotters.co.uk; BCM Roving, London WC1N 3XX) publishes a newsletter called *Globe* that covers obscure destinations, and can help you find traveling companions. Check the free magazines widely available in London – start by looking outside the main railway stations.

USA

The most popular routes to Puerto Rico from the US are via New York and Miami, but direct flights from about a dozen other cities in the continental US also serve the island. Some carriers now offer continued service through San Juan to Ponce and Aguadilla, or they fly directly into Aguadilla's airport. Almost all major carriers fly to Puerto Rico; Jet Blue is currently the most popular and economical option.

STA Travel (☎ 800-781-4040; www.statravel.com) has offices in all major cities.

In addition to the scores of online ticket vendors, a few 'old-school' discount ticket agencies sell reduced-rate tickets to the Caribbean by telephone and by placing small advertisements in newspapers like the *New York Times*. Sometimes these vendors can come up with fares well below internet fares. Try **Pan Express Travel** (☎ 212-719-9292; www.panexpresstravel.com; 25 W 39th St, New York, NY 10018).

SEA
Cruise Ship

San Juan is the second-largest port for cruise ships in the Western Hemisphere (after Miami). More than 24 vessels call San Juan their home port or departure port, and every year new cruise ships either originate sailings in San Juan or make San Juan a port of call. More than one million cruise-ship passengers pass through San Juan per year. Their ships dock at the piers along Calle La Marina near the Customs House and the Sheraton Old San Juan Hotel & Casino, just a short walk from the cobblestone streets of Old San Juan.

Per diem prices vary according to the standard of the ship, but you will be lucky to pay less than $1700 for a seven-day cruise out of San Juan. However, this price will probably include your airfare and transfers to the ship, as well as all your meals and entertainment.

The **Cruise Line International Association** (CLIA; ☎ 212-921-0066; www.cruising.org; 500 Fifth Ave, No 1407, New York, NY 10110) provides information on cruising and individual lines. Or you can contact the cruise lines directly:

Carnival Cruise Lines (☎ 800-327-9501)
Celebrity Cruise Lines (☎ 800-437-3111)
Club Med Cruises (☎ 212-997-2100)
First European Cruises (☎ 888-893-8767)
Holland American Line (☎ 800-628-4855)
Mediterranean Shipping Cruises (☎ 800-628-4855)
Norwegian Cruise Line (☎ 800-327-7030)
Princess Cruises (☎ 800-421-0522)
Radisson Seven Seas (☎ 800-285-1835)
Royal Caribbean Cruise Line (☎ 800-327-6700)

Ferry

TO/FROM THE DOMINICAN REPUBLIC

For a true seafaring adventure, consider the ocean-going ferry between Mayagüez, on Puerto Rico's west coast, and Santo Domingo, in the Dominican Republic. Currently the massive rainbow-colored ship sails three or four days a week in each direction. See p224.

TO/FROM THE US VIRGIN ISLANDS

Transportation Services Virgin Islands (☎ 340-776-6282) runs an irregular ferry service between Puerto Rico and the US Virgin Islands, with ferries leaving Fajardo twice a month; see p147.

Yacht

Crewing aboard a yacht destined for the West Indies from North America or Europe is a popular way of getting to Puerto Rico.

Marinas are located at most major resorts and at principal ports around the Puerto Rican coast.

Upon reaching the island, however, you *must* clear immigration and customs unless you are coming directly from a US port or the US Virgin Islands. There are now numerous online clearinghouses for those seeking yacht-crew positions (both experienced and inexperienced mariners).

These services usually charge a registration fee between $25 and $40. Two operations known for their professionalism are the **Yacht Crew Register** (☎ 604-990-9901; www.yachtcrewregister.com) and **Yacht Crew Inc** (☎ 954-788-3832; www.yacht-crew.com).

TRANSPORTATION

GETTING AROUND

AIR

Because Puerto Rico is such a small island, its domestic air transportation system is understandably basic. Suffice to say there are daily flights between San Juan, Ponce, Aguadilla and Mayagüez. The bulk of Puerto Rico's domestic air traffic links San Juan to the offshore islands of Culebra and Vieques.

Domestic Airports & Airlines

From its Isla Verde location on the eastern edge of San Juan, LMM (p123) handles a fair amount of the island's scheduled domestic air traffic.

Isla Grande (SJG) airport in San Juan's Miramar district, on the Bahía de San Juan, is the center for private aviation as well as Puerto Rico's air-taxi operations. To get to Culebra and Vieques from this convenient downtown airport, you can fly on **Vieques Air Link** (San Juan–Vieques flights ☎ 787-741-8331, San Juan–Culebra flights ☎ 787-722-3736; www.vieques-island.com/val). Fares to Vieques are $50/95 one way/round-trip; fares to Culebra are about $55/95. **Air Flamenco** (☎ 787-724-1818; www.airflamenco.net) also flies these routes at similar fares. Other airports include the following:

Culebra Airport (CPX; ☎ 787-742-0022; Culebra)

Eugenio María de Hostos Airport (MAZ; ☎ 787-833-0148; Mayagüez)

Fajardo Airport (FAJ; ☎ 787-860-3110; Fajardo)

Mercedita Airport (PSE; ☎ 787- 842-6292; Ponce)

Rafael Hernandez Airport (BQN; ☎ 787-891-2286; Aguadilla)

Vieques Airport (VQS; ☎ 787-741-0515; Vieques)

BICYCLE

While bicycling hasn't traditionally been a popular means of getting around the island, things are changing. Most resorts have at least one bicycle-rental outlet, and independent bicycle supply shops can be found in a few select places. For serious long-distance bicycling, you'll need to bring your own bike or buy one in Puerto Rico. Some of the best routes are highlighted in the Itineraries chapter (p28). For further cycling tips see the Outdoors chapter (p79).

The hazards of cycling in Puerto Rico include nightmare traffic, dangerous drivers and a general lack of awareness about cyclist's needs. Puerto Rico is a country where the car is king and most natives simply aren't used to seeing touring bikes on the road. Bear this is mind before venturing out on two wheels and stick to quiet back roads and the smaller towns. Never cycle after dark. For further advice (and empathy) contact the Puerto Rican Cycling Federation (p79).

BOAT
Charter Yacht

All of the island's major resorts have marinas where you can charter yachts or powerboats, either with a crew or a 'bareboat.' Crewed boats come with a skipper and crew, and you don't need any prior sailing experience. With bareboat charters, you rent the boat and be your own skipper.

Charter companies include the following:

Caribbean School of Aquatics (☎ 787-728-6606; Condado)

Castillo Watersports (☎ 787-791-6195; Isla Verde)

Driftwood Charters (☎ 787-255-0690; Puerto Real)

Erin Go Bragh (☎ 787-860-4401; Fajardo)

Traveler (☎ 787-863-2821; Fajardo)

Ferry

The **Puerto Rican Port Authority** (☎ 787-863-0705, car reservations ☎ 800-981-2005) has large, high-speed ferries that run from Fajardo to Culebra and Vieques. While timetables can be changeable and getting on is a bit of a scrum, the boats are generally quick and reliable. See p165 and p180 for schedule and fare details. For reservations, contact the Puerto Rican Port Authority or call the island offices on **Vieques** (☎ 787-741-4761) and **Culebra** (☎ 787-742-3161); reservation office hours are 8am to 11am and 1pm to 3pm weekdays. If you have reservations, plan to pick up your tickets at the ferry terminal a half-hour before the scheduled sailing. If you haven't, the ticket office opens an hour before departure.

Note: reservations go quickly for boats bound for the islands on Friday evening to Saturday morning, and returning to Fajardo on Sunday afternoon to Monday morning, so plan ahead.

BUS

See p292 for information on traveling by bus within San Juan. For intertown travel by público, see p293.

CAR & MOTORCYCLE

Despite the occasional hazards of operating a car in Puerto Rico, driving is currently the most convenient way to get around the countryside, see small towns, cross sprawling suburbs and explore wide, open spaces. This is particularly relevant to roads such as the Ruta Panorámica where public transport is scant and cycling deemed too dangerous.

On the other side of the coin, it's easy to list the circumstances in which you *won't* want a car. In San Juan, for example, the hassles of traffic, parking and navigating the maze of thoroughfares make using a car in the city a challenge, to say the least. Elsewhere, a liberal scattering of wrecked abandoned vehicles that litter numerous roadsides across the country provide ample testimony to the evils of driving in Puerto Rico. While islanders certainly share a North American love of motor cars, their driving skills inhabit a whole different ballpark (think Mexico City or Guatemala rather than LA).

Puerto Rico's best roads are its Expressway toll roads; these include numbers 22 (San Juan–Arecibo), 66 (San Juan–Canóvanas), 52 (San Juan–Ponce) and 53 (Fajardo–Yabucoa). You must pay a fee on these roads at a booth at one of various entry-exit checkpoints. Prices for 2-axle vehicles range from 50c to $1.50. It is wise to have the right money available.

The next best roads are the main highways such as Hwys 2 and 3 (which effectively ring the island), Hwy 10 (Arecibo–Ponce) and Hwy 30 (Caguas–Humacao). These roads have two to three lanes in either direction but are infested with traffic lights and are often jammed packed with cars – especially during rush hour. With their ubiquitous shopping malls and unsightly concrete satellite towns, they're hardly the best advert for the island's scenic attractions.

Lesser roads are far more charming, but considerably narrower (often only 1½ lanes wide). Crisscrossing the island's precipitous inland terrain, they are also invariably slow and winding. Bank on an average speed of 25mph in the mountains.

In Puerto Rico – rather bizarrely – speed limits are posted in mph and road distances in kilometers.

Driver's License

Any valid driver's license can be used to rent and operate a car or scooter in Puerto Rico. If you stay longer than 90 days, residency laws say you have to get a Puerto Rican license.

Fuel & Spare Parts

Esso, Shell, Texaco and other major oil companies maintain gas stations across the island. In rural areas, stations usually close on Sunday. Almost everywhere on the island, gas stations generally stay open until about 7pm. At the time of research, the price was about 90¢ a liter for economy gas, which is remarkably inexpensive by international standards. You can use credit cards for fuel purchases in all but rural areas. Don't let your tank go dry, though, because the next station could be a long way up the road.

Garages aren't as readily available, so you should always take a spare tire and a jack with you, and carry some water in case the engine overheats.

Rental

All of the major international car-rental companies operate, along with dozens of smaller, local firms. The trusted names such as Avis and Hertz are usually the safest bet. Most companies require that you have a major credit card, that you be at least 25 years old and that you have a valid driver's license (your home license will do). Some companies (Budget, for example), may rent to drivers between the ages of 21 and 24 for an additional charge. Larger companies will accept debit cards, but expect them to put at least a $500 hold on your funds until the car is safely returned.

Car-rental agencies are listed in the local Yellow Pages and in the Puerto Rico Tourism Company's (PRTC) publication, *Qué Pasa*. You will find plenty of rental companies at the LMM airport, in major cities and in resort towns ringing the island's coast. Agencies in San Juan include the following:

AAA (☎ 787-791-1465)
Alamo (☎ 787-753-2265, 800-327-9633)
Avis (☎ 800-874-3556)
Budget (☎ 787-791-0600, 800-468-5822)
Charlie Car Rental (☎ 787-728-2418)
Dollar Rent-A-Car (☎ 787-591-5500)
Hertz (☎ 787-791-0840, 800-654-3131)
L&M (☎ 787-725-8307, 800-666-0807)
National (☎ 787-791-1805, 800-568-3019)
Target (☎ 787-728-1447, 800-934-6457)
Thrifty (☎ 787-253-2525, 800-367-2277)
Wheelchair Getaways Rent-A-Car (☎ 787-883-0131, 800-868-8028)

TRANSPORTATION

Insurance

Liability insurance is required in Puerto Rico, as in most US states. Insurance against damage to the car, called Collision Damage Waiver (CDW) or Loss Damage Waiver (LDW), is usually optional, but will often require you to pay for the first $100 or $500. Some credit-card companies cover car rentals, so extra coverage may not be needed. Always take some insurance – accidents happen far too easily. Note also that most rental agencies don't cover accidents that happen on Culebra or Vieques. You aren't supposed to take cars there because there's no way to get a tow-truck to you in an emergency. Nobody at the ferry will stop you from bringing a rental to the island, but any accidents, nicks or dings will be paid for with your money.

Road Conditions & Hazards

Puerto Rico has the best roads in the Caribbean – and the worst traffic jams!

What you need to watch out for are island animals – dogs, chickens, horses, pigs – that wander across the roads, particularly in the mountains, and on Culebra and Vieques.

Road Rules

You must be at least 16 years old to drive a car in Puerto Rico. Going more than 10 miles an hour over the speed limit will eventually result in a speeding ticket. In rural areas, where speed limits aren't always posted, use common sense and watch for school zones, where 15mph (strictly enforced during school hours) is the norm. Most highway signs employ international symbols, but one common source of confusion is that distances on island roads are measured in kilometers, while speed limits are posted in miles per hour.

Driving rules here are basically the same as they are in the US. Traffic proceeds along the right side of the road and moves counterclockwise around traffic circles; seat belts and motorcycle helmets must be worn; and children younger than four must travel in child safety seats.

Carjacking, though rare, is not unheard of in Puerto Rico so stopping for anyone who waves you down or approaches your vehicle carries significant risk. Letting a stranger into your car is – sadly – like playing Russian roulette. Many island drivers notoriously ignore stoplights and stop signs late at night – supposedly for fear of making themselves targets for carjackers.

HITCHING

Hitching is not recommended in Puerto Rico.

LOCAL TRANSPORTATION
Bus

Puerto Rico does not presently have an islandwide bus service. San Juan, however, is a different matter and buses are cheap, abundant and well-run. The system is administered via the **Autoridad Metropolitana de Autobuses** (AMA; Metropolitan Bus Authority; ☎ 787-767-7979; www.dtop.gov.pr/ama/default.htm, in Spanish) and **Metrobus** (☎ 787-763-4141). AMA buses charge 50¢ to any destination on their routes; Metrobuses usually charge 75¢. See p123 for specifics on routes and schedules. Visitors can identify bus stops by an obelisk marker that reads 'Parada' or 'Parada

---

LOW-IMPACT TRANSPORTATION

■ Puerto Rico is a small island and in-country flying is largely superfluous – unless you're the president or in a major hurry. Rather than catching a plane to the outlying islands of Culebra and Vieques, get the scenic 1- to 1½-hour ferry from Fajardo instead.

■ San Juan has a great public transportation system that is both far-reaching and cheap, making car hire in the capital largely unnecessary.

■ Hire a bike where feasible and discover Puerto Rico's quieter corners on two wheels.

■ Resist renting a car on the tiny island of Culebra (there are far too many of them already). Instead, use públicos, a bicycle and your own two feet.

■ Aim to take at least one journey on a público and find out what these colorful street-theaters-on-wheels are all about.

■ Experience the space age modernity of San Juan's new Tren Urbano.

de Guaguas' (Bus Stop). Bus system maps are everywhere.

See opposite for information on públicos.

Metro

The Tren Urbano is the brand new public transportation system that shuttles people around San Juan. The only one of its kind in the Caribbean, it runs 12 miles from Sagrado Corazon in Santurce to Bayamón, stopping at 16 stations along the way. Ultramodern and efficient, the Tren opened in 2005 after years of delays.

Although it still avoids the areas of main tourist interest, plans are afoot to extend it in the future. Tickets are a standard $1.50 one-way. See also p124

Públicos

Públicos are essentially intertown minibuses that run prescribed routes during daylight hours. Some públicos make relatively long hauls between places such as San Juan and Ponce or Mayagüez, but most make much shorter trips, providing a link between communities. Públicos usually make their pickups and drop-offs at a van stand on or near a town's central plaza, so you will pay extra if you want the driver to take you to a destination that is off the route. The catch is that travel takes a long time, as the driver stops frequently to let people on and off.

For schedules and fares, inquire at the público stands in town plazas or at San Juan's LMM airport. You can also look under *Líneas de Carros* in the Yellow Pages telephone directory. **Choferes Unidos de Ponce** (☎ 787-764-0540) makes the San Juan-Ponce run; **Líneas Sultanas** (☎ 787-765-9377) will get you from San Juan to Mayagüez.

As públicos stop almost everywhere they are also useful for getting around the smaller spread-out municipalities such as Fajardo and Mayagüez. Once again, you'll need to be patient. For more information on públicos see p141.

Taxi

Taxis are available in most of the midsized to large cities on the island, and in theory they all use meters. Getting the driver to turn it on can be quite a challenge, however, so either establish what you are willing to pay up front or threaten to get out if the driver won't hit the button. San Juan is the exception to this haggling hassle: its 'tourist taxis' have fixed rates for all their trips. See p124.

TRANSPORTATION

Health Dr David Goldberg

Prevention is the key to staying healthy while traveling. Travelers who receive the recommended vaccines and follow common-sense precautions usually come away with nothing more than a little diarrhea.

BEFORE YOU GO

Bring medications in their original containers, clearly labeled. A signed, dated letter from your physician describing all medical conditions and medications, including generic names, is also a good idea. If carrying syringes or needles, be sure to have a physician's letter documenting their medical necessity.

INSURANCE

If your health insurance does not cover you for medical expenses abroad, consider supplemental insurance. US travelers can find a list of medical evacuation and travel insurance companies on the **US State Department website** (www.travel.state.gov). Find out in advance if your insurance plan will make payments directly to providers or reimburse you later for overseas health expenditures.

RECOMMENDED VACCINATIONS

Since most vaccines don't produce immunity until at least two weeks after they're given, visit a physician four to eight weeks before departure. Ask your doctor for an International Certificate of Vaccination (otherwise known as the yellow booklet), which will list all the vaccinations you've received. This is mandatory for countries that require proof of yellow fever vaccination upon entry, but it's a good idea to carry it wherever you travel.

No vaccines are required for Puerto Rico, but a number are recommended; see p297.

INTERNET RESOURCES

There is a wealth of travel health advice on the internet:

Lonely Planet (www.lonelyplanet.com) A great place to start.

MD Travel Health (www.mdtravelhealth.com) Another website of general interest which provides complete travel health recommendations for every country, updated daily, at no cost.

World Health Organization (www.who.int/ith) Available online at no cost as well as in book form – *International Travel and Health* – which is revised annually.

It's usually a good idea to consult your government's travel health website before departure, if one is available:

United States www.cdc.gov/travel
Canada www.hc-sc.gc.ca
United Kingdom www.dh.gov.uk

FURTHER READING

If you're traveling with children, you might want to read Lonely Planet's *Travel with Children* before you leave. The *ABC of Healthy Travel,* by E Walker et al, is another valuable resource.

IN TRANSIT

DEEP VEIN THROMBOSIS

Blood clots may form in the legs (deep vein thrombosis; DVT) during plane flights, chiefly because of prolonged immobility. The longer the flight, the greater the risk. Though most blood clots are reabsorbed uneventfully, some may break off and travel through the blood vessels to the lungs, where they could cause life-threatening complications.

MEDICAL CHECKLIST

- Antibiotics
- Antidiarrheal drugs (eg loperamide)
- Acetaminophen (Tylenol) or aspirin
- Anti-inflammatory drugs (eg ibuprofen)
- Antihistamines (for hay fever and allergic reactions)
- Antibacterial ointment (eg Bactroban) for cuts and abrasions
- Steroid cream or cortisone (for poison ivy and other allergic rashes)
- Bandages, gauze, gauze rolls
- Adhesive or paper tape
- Scissors, safety pins, tweezers
- Thermometer
- Pocket knife
- Insect repellent for the skin
- Permethrin-containing insect spray for clothing, tents, and bed nets
- Sun block
- Oral rehydration salts
- Iodine tablets (for water purification)
- Syringes and sterile needles

The chief symptom of deep vein thrombosis is swelling or pain of the foot, ankle or calf, usually but not always on just one side. When a blood clot travels to the lungs, it may cause chest pain and make breathing difficult. Travelers with any of these symptoms should seek immediate medical attention.

To prevent the development of deep vein thrombosis on long flights you should walk about the cabin, perform isometric compressions of the leg muscles (ie contract the leg muscles while sitting), drink plenty of fluids and avoid alcohol.

JET LAG & MOTION SICKNESS

Jet lag is common when crossing more than five time zones, and can result in insomnia, fatigue, malaise or nausea. To avoid jet lag try drinking plenty of fluids (nonalcoholic) and eating light meals. Upon arrival, get exposure to natural sunlight and readjust your schedule (for meals, sleep etc) as soon as possible.

Antihistamines such as dimenhydrinate (Dramamine) and meclizine (Antivert, Bonine) are usually the first choice for treating motion sickness. Their main side effect is drowsiness. An herbal alternative is ginger, which works like a charm for some people.

IN PUERTO RICO

From a medical standpoint, Puerto Rico is generally safe and its close relationship with the US means standards are generally higher than elsewhere in the Caribbean. The most common travel-related diseases, such as dysentery and hepatitis, are acquired by consumption of contaminated food and water. Mosquito-borne illnesses are not a significant concern in most of the islands, except during outbreaks of dengue fever.

AVAILABILITY & COST OF HEALTH CARE

For emergencies in Puerto Rico, call ☎ 911. Excellent medical facilities are available in Puerto Rico. A number of hospitals have emergency rooms, including:

Ashford Presbyterian Memorial Community Hospital (Map pp98-9; ☎ 787-721-2160; 1451 Av Ashford, Condado, San Juan)

General Hospital Dr Ramón Emeterio Betances (off Map p221; ☎ 787-735-8001; Rte 2 Km 157, Mayagüez)

Hospital Manuel Comunitario Dr Pila (Map p186; ☎ 787-848-5600; Av Las Américas east of Av Hostos, Ponce)

Hospital Damas (☎ 787-840-8686; 2213 Ponce By Pass, Ponce)

Hospital Dr Dominguez (☎ 787-852-0505; 300 Font Martello, Humacao)

University of Puerto Rico School of Medicine (Map p102; ☎ 787-758-7910; UPR School of Medicine, A-878 Main Building, Medical Sciences Campus, San Juan) For more complicated medical problems, make an appointment here. The Faculty Practice Plan at the university offers a broad array of specialists and sophisticated diagnostic facilities.

Many doctors and hospitals expect payment in cash, regardless of whether you have travel health insurance. If you develop a life-threatening medical problem, you'll probably want to be evacuated to a country with state-of-the-art medical care. This could cost tens of thousands of dollars, so be sure you have insurance to cover this before you depart.

HEALTH

Pharmacies *(farmacias)* in Puerto Rico are generally well-stocked with medications up to North American standards. All pharmacists are fully trained and professionally licensed.

INFECTIOUS DISEASES
Dengue Fever

Dengue fever is a viral infection found throughout the Caribbean. In Puerto Rico, the incidence usually peaks between September and November. Major outbreaks occurred in 1994 and 1998. Dengue is transmitted by Aedes mosquitoes, which tend to bite during the daytime and are usually found close to human habitations, often indoors. They breed primarily in artificial water containers such as jars, barrels, cans, cisterns, metal drums, plastic containers and discarded tires. As a result, dengue is especially common in densely populated, urban environments.

Dengue usually causes flulike symptoms, including fever, muscle aches, joint pains, headaches, nausea and vomiting, often followed by a rash. The body aches may be quite uncomfortable, but most cases resolve uneventfully in a few days. Severe cases usually occur in children under age 15 who are experiencing their second dengue infection.

There is no treatment for dengue fever except to take analgesics such as acetaminophen/paracetamol (Tylenol) and drink plenty of fluids. Severe cases may require hospitalization for intravenous fluids and supportive care. There is no vaccine. The cornerstone of prevention is insect protection measures – see Mosquito Bites (p299).

Hepatitis A

Hepatitis A is the second most common travel-related infection (after travelers' diarrhea). It occurs throughout the Caribbean, particularly in the northern islands. Hepatitis A is a viral infection of the liver that is usually acquired by ingestion, though it may also be acquired by direct contact with infected persons. It occurs throughout the world, but the incidence is higher in developing nations. Symptoms may include fever, malaise, jaundice, nausea, vomiting and abdominal pain. Most cases resolve without complications, though hepatitis A occasionally causes liver damage. There is no treatment.

The vaccine for hepatitis A is extremely safe and highly effective. If you get a booster six to twelve months later, it lasts for at least 10 years. It's a good idea to get it before you go to Puerto Rico or any other developing area. Because the safety of the hepatitis A vaccine has not been established for pregnant women or children under the age of two, they should instead be given a gammaglobulin injection.

Hepatitis B

Like hepatitis A, hepatitis B is a liver infection that occurs worldwide but is more common in developing nations. Unlike hepatitis A, the disease is usually acquired by sexual contact or by exposure to infected blood, generally through blood transfusions or contaminated needles. The vaccine is recommended only for long-term travelers (on the road more than six months) who expect to live in rural areas or have close physical contact with the local population. Additionally, the vaccine is recommended for anyone who anticipates sexual contact with the local inhabitants or a possible need for medical, dental or other treatments while abroad, especially if a need for transfusions or injections is expected.

The hepatitis B vaccine is safe and highly effective. However, a total of three injections are necessary to establish full immunity. Several countries added the hepatitis B vaccine to the list of routine childhood immunizations in the 1980s, so many young adults are already protected.

Malaria

In the Caribbean, malaria occurs only in Haiti and certain parts of the Dominican Republic. Malaria pills aren't necessary for Puerto Rico.

Rabies

Rabies is a viral infection of the brain and spinal cord that is almost always fatal. The rabies virus is carried in the saliva of infected animals and is typically transmitted through an animal bite, though contamination of any break in the skin with infected saliva may result in rabies. Rabies occurs in several of the Caribbean islands, including Puerto Rico.

Rabies vaccine is safe, but a full series requires three injections and is quite expensive. Those at high risk for rabies, such as animal handlers and spelunkers (cave explorers), should certainly get the vaccine. In addition, those at lower risk for animal bites should

RECOMMENDED VACCINATIONS

Vaccine	Recommended for	Dosage	Side Effects
hepatitis A	all travelers	one dose before trip; booster six to 12 months later	soreness at injection site; headaches; body aches
typhoid	extended stays in rural areas	four capsules by mouth, one taken every other day	abdominal pain; nausea; rash
hepatitis B	long-term travelers in close contact with the local population	three doses over six-month period	soreness at injection site; low-grade fever
rabies	travelers who may have contact with animals and may not have access to medical care	three doses over three- to four-week period	soreness at injection site; headaches; body aches. Expensive.
tetanus-diptheria	all travelers who haven't had booster within 10 years	one dose lasts 10 years	soreness at injection site
measles	travelers born after 1956 who've had only one measles vaccination	one dose	fever; rash; joint pains; allergic reactions
chickenpox	travelers who've never had chickenpox	two doses, one month apart	fever; mild case of chickenpox

consider asking for the vaccine if they might be traveling to remote areas and might not have access to appropriate medical care if needed. The treatment for a possibly rabid bite consists of a rabies vaccine with rabies immunoglobulin. It's effective, but must be given promptly. Most travelers don't need a rabies vaccine.

All animal bites and scratches must be promptly and thoroughly cleansed with large amounts of soap and water, and local health authorities need to be contacted to determine whether or not further treatment is necessary (see Animal Bites, p299).

Other Infections

An outbreak of **viral meningitis** caused by echovirus 30 occurred between June and September 2004, resulting in more than 400 cases, chiefly in children. The outbreak began in the southern coastal town of Arroyo, then spread to the eastern coastal town of Cieba and the mountain town of Aibonito. Echoviruses are spread by direct contact with the respiratory secretions or feces of an infected person. To protect yourself from viral meningitis, you should pay careful attention at all times to hand-washing and personal hygiene, especially after using the toilet, before eating, and after changing diapers (nappies). The chief symptoms of meningitis are fever, severe headache, stiff neck, sensitivity to bright light, drowsiness or confusion, and nausea and vomiting. Anyone who develops these symptoms should immediately seek medical attention. Viral meningitis, unlike bacterial meningitis, does not in general lead to serious complications.

An outbreak of **acute hemorrhagic conjunctivitis** (pink-eye), a viral infection characterized by the sudden onset of painful, swollen, red eyes with bleeding and tearing, occurred between August and October 2003. Almost half a million people were involved, chiefly school-aged children and those living in crowded urban areas. A previous outbreak was reported in 1997. In most cases, the illness resolves uneventfully, but may cause significant discomfort and temporary incapacity. You can protect yourself from acute hemorrhagic conjunctivitis by frequent hand-washing and by not sharing towels or bedding.

Schistosomiasis is a parasitic infection acquired by swimming, wading, bathing or washing in fresh water that contains infected snails. Early symptoms may include fever, loss of appetite, weight loss, abdominal pain, weakness, headaches, joint and muscle pains, diarrhea, nausea and cough, but most infections are asymptomatic at first. Long-term complications may include kidney failure, malabsorption, enlargement of the liver and spleen, engorgement of the esophageal blood vessels, and accumulation of fluid in the abdominal cavity.

To protect yourself from schistosomiasis, you should avoid swimming, wading or rafting in bodies of fresh water, such as lakes,

HEALTH

ponds, streams or rivers. Unless known to be safe, water for bathing or showering should be heated to 150° F for at least five minutes or held in a storage tank for at least three days. Toweling yourself dry after unavoidable or accidental exposure to contaminated water may reduce the likelihood of schistosomiasis, but does not reliably prevent the disease and is no substitute for the precautions above. Swimming in the ocean or a chlorinated swimming pool carries no risk of schistosomiasis.

Typhoid fever is caused by ingestion of food or water contaminated by a species of *Salmonella* known as *Salmonella typhi*. It's reported in most of the Caribbean islands, but is uncommon. Typhoid vaccine is recommended only for those planning an extended stay in rural areas or expecting to consume potentially contaminated food. The vaccine is usually given by mouth, but is also available as an injection. Neither vaccine is approved for use in children under age two. If you get typhoid fever, the drug of choice is usually a quinolone antibiotic such as ciprofloxacin (Cipro) or levofloxacin (Levaquin), which many travelers carry for treatment of travelers' diarrhea.

Fascioliasis is a parasitic infection that is typically acquired by eating contaminated watercress that has been grown in sheep-raising areas. Early symptoms may include fever, nausea, vomiting and painful enlargement of the liver.

HIV/AIDS has been reported from all Caribbean countries. Be sure to use condoms for all sexual encounters.

TRAVELERS' DIARRHEA

To prevent diarrhea, avoid tap water unless it has been boiled, filtered or chemically disinfected (iodine tablets); only eat fresh fruits or vegetables if cooked or peeled; be wary of dairy products that might contain unpasteurized milk; and be highly selective when eating food from street vendors.

If you develop diarrhea, be sure to drink plenty of fluids, preferably an oral rehydration solution containing lots of salt and sugar. A few loose stools don't require treatment but, if you start having more than four or five stools a day, you should start taking an antibiotic (usually a quinolone drug) and an antidiarrheal agent (such as loperamide). If diarrhea is bloody or persists for more than 72 hours or is accompanied by fever, shaking chills or severe abdominal pain you should seek medical attention.

FOLK REMEDIES

Problem	Treatment
Jet lag	Melatonin
Motion sickness	Ginger
Mosquito bite	Eucalyptus oil
Prevention	Soybean oil

ENVIRONMENTAL HAZARDS
Water

The tap water in Puerto Rico is generally safe to drink. If you have a sensitive stomach or prefer filtered water, most shops stock bottled varieties.

If you're camping or out in the 'wilds,' another option is to disinfect water with iodine pills. Instructions are usually enclosed and should be carefully followed. Alternatively, you can add 2% tincture of iodine to 1L of water (5 drops to clear water, 10 drops to cloudy water) and let stand for 30 minutes. If the water is cold, longer times may be required.

The taste of iodinated water may be improved by adding vitamin C (ascorbic acid). Iodinated water should not be consumed for more than a few weeks. Pregnant women, those with a history of thyroid disease and those allergic to iodine should not drink iodinated water.

A number of water filters are on the market. Those with smaller pores (reverse osmosis filters) provide the broadest protection, but they are relatively large and are readily plugged by debris. Those with somewhat larger pores (microstrainer filters) are ineffective against viruses, although they remove other organisms. Manufacturers' instructions must be carefully followed.

Sun

To protect yourself from excessive sun exposure, you should stay out of the midday sun, wear sunglasses and a wide-brimmed sun hat, and apply sunscreen with SPF 15 or higher, with both UVA and UVB protection. Sunscreen should be generously applied to all exposed parts of the body approximately 30 minutes before sun exposure and should be reapplied after swimming or vigorous activity.

Travelers should also drink plenty of fluids and avoid strenuous exercise when the temperature is high.

HEALTH

Animal Bites

Do not attempt to pet, handle or feed any animal, with the exception of domestic animals known to be free of any infectious disease. Most animal injuries are directly related to a person's attempt to touch or feed the animal.

Any bite or scratch by a mammal, including bats, should be promptly and thoroughly cleansed with large amounts of soap and water, followed by application of an antiseptic such as iodine or alcohol. The local health authorities should be contacted immediately for possible postexposure rabies treatment, whether or not you've been immunized against rabies. It may also be advisable to start an antibiotic, since wounds caused by animal bites and scratches frequently become infected. One of the newer quinolones, such as levofloxacin (Levaquin), which many travelers carry in case of diarrhea, would be an appropriate choice.

Snakes are a hazard in some of the Caribbean islands. In the event of a venomous snake bite, place the victim at rest, keep the bitten area immobilized, and move the victim immediately to the nearest medical facility. Avoid tourniquets, which are no longer recommended. Spiny sea urchins and coelenterates (coral and jellyfish) are a hazard in some areas.

MOSQUITO BITES

Mosquito-borne illnesses are usually not a concern in Puerto Rico. However, outbreaks of dengue fever have occurred in the recent past, so you should be aware of the means of preventing mosquito bites, if necessary. If dengue or other mosquito-borne illnesses are being reported, you should keep yourself covered (wear long sleeves, long pants, hats and shoes rather than sandals) and apply a good insect repellent to exposed skin and clothing. A bug spray containing DEET does the best job of warding off insects, but try to use it sparingly as it also is known to kill some of the natural organisms that live in the island's bays and inlets. Do not apply DEET to eyes, mouth, cuts, wounds or irritated skin. Products containing lower concentrations of DEET are as effective, but for shorter periods of time. In general, adults and children over 12 should use preparations containing 25% to 35% DEET, which usually lasts about six hours. Children between two and 12 years of age should use preparations containing no more than 10% DEET, applied sparingly, which will usually last about three hours. Neurologic toxicity has been reported from DEET, especially in children, but appears to be extremely uncommon and generally related to overuse. DEET-containing compounds should not be used on children under age two.

Insect repellents containing certain botanical products, including eucalyptus oil and soybean oil, are effective but last only 1½ to two hours. Products based on citronella are not effective.

For additional protection, you can apply permethrin to clothing, shoes, tents and bed nets. Permethrin treatments are safe and remain effective for at least two weeks, even when items are laundered. Permethrin should not be applied directly to skin.

CHILDREN & PREGNANT WOMEN

In general, it's safe for children and pregnant women to go to Puerto Rico. However, because some of the vaccines listed on p294 are not approved for use in children or during pregnancy, these travelers should be particularly careful not to drink tap water or consume any questionable food or beverages. Also, when traveling with children, make sure they're up-to-date on all routine immunizations. It's sometimes appropriate to give children some of their vaccines a little early before visiting a developing nation. You should discuss this with your pediatrician.

HEALTH

Language

CONTENTS

Many seasoned Spanish speakers find themselves a little off balance when they first hear Spanish in Puerto Rico. In fact, two very different forms of Spanish are spoken on the island. Every Puerto Rican learns to speak Standard Modern Spanish in school, and this is the language you'll hear from hotel and restaurant staff if you address them in Spanish.

However, the Spanish you hear on the streets is Antillian Spanish or, as it's also known, Boricua (the language of Borinquen). For a number of reasons, the rhythm and sound of spoken Boricua takes an ear trained in Castillian, Mexican or South American dialects a little time to get used to.

Most of the original Spanish colonists of Puerto Rico came from Andalucía, Extremadura and the Canary Islands and brought with them the regional tendencies to relax or devoice consonants. This style persists to the extreme on the island's streets. When you hear two well-acquainted Puerto Ricans of any social class speaking together, you will notice their strong tendency to totally drop the pronunciation of final consonants like s and d, and sometimes articles like *el* or *la*. A standard Spanish sentence such as *vamos a la ciudad* (let's go to the city) becomes 'vamo a ciudá' in Boricua, and *muchas gracias* (thanks very much) becomes 'mucha gracia.'

The sounds of consonants are changed or even dropped in the middle and ends of words. A classic example is the tendency to drop the d in past participles, so that the standard Spanish *asopado* (stewed or stew) becomes 'asopao,' the accepted name and spelling for a traditional Puerto Rican stew. When an r appears next to another consonant in the middle (and sometimes at the end) of a word, it is often pronounced as an 'l,' thus *farmacia* (pharmacy) becomes 'falmacia' and *comprar* (buy) becomes 'compral.'

Some Puerto Ricans – especially those from the interior – reverse this, replacing an r next to another consonant in the middle or at the end of the word with a spoken 'l.' A word like *dulce* (a sweet or candy) becomes 'durce' and *hotel* changes to 'hoter.'

Several other linguistic variants characterize Boricua: *seseo* is the pronunciation of the soft c sound as an 's' rather than the 'th' of Castilian Spanish – *placer* (pleasure) is pronounced 'pla-thair' in Madrid, but 'plasair' in San Juan. *Yeísmo* is the tendency to pronounce the trilled ll of a Spanish word like *amarillo* (yellow) as an English 'y' or even a 'j,' so the word in Boricua sounds like 'amariyo' or even 'amarijo.' When Puerto Ricans come across a word like *carro* (car), they change the trilled rr to an 'h' – 'cahro.' The letter v is always pronounced like a 'b,' as in most Spanish-speaking countries. Hence, *Venga!* (Come!) sounds like 'benga.'

Travelers hoping to submerge themselves in the island's rich culture need to have some command of basic Spanish vocabulary, as well as some sense of the distinctions between Puerto Rican and other kinds of Spanish. However, even if you speak Spanish well, you can expect Puerto Ricans, proud of their hard-earned English skills, to address you in English. One of the great rewards for many travelers to Puerto Rico is remaining long enough at a destination to hear the locals address them in Spanish.

For a more detailed guide to the language, get a copy of Lonely Planet's compact *Latin American Spanish Phrasebook*.

PRONUNCIATION

Pronunciation of Spanish is not difficult. Many Spanish sounds are similar to their English counterparts, and the relationship between pronunciation and spelling is clear and consistent. Unless otherwise indicated, the English examples used below take standard American pronunciation.

Vowels & Diphthongs

a	as in 'father'
e	as in 'met'
i	as the 'i' in 'police'
o	as in British English 'hot'
u	as the 'u' in 'rude'
ai	as in 'aisle'
au	as the 'ow' in 'how'
ei	as in 'vein'
ia	as the 'ya' in 'yard'
ie	as the 'ye' in 'yes'
oi	as in 'coin'
ua	as the 'wa' in 'wash'
ue	as the 'we' in 'well'

Consonants

Spanish consonants are generally the same as in English, with the exception of those listed below.

The consonants **ch**, **ll** and **ñ** are generally considered distinct letters, but in dictionaries **ch** and **ll** are now often listed alphabetically under **c** and **l** respectively. The letter **ñ** still has a separate entry after **n** in alphabetical listings.

b	similar to English 'b,' but softer; referred to as 'b larga'
c	as in 'celery' before **e** and **i**; elsewhere as the 'k' in 'king'
ch	as in 'choose'
d	as in 'dog'; between vowels and after **l** or **n**, it's closer to the 'th' in 'this'
g	as the 'ch' in the Scottish *loch* before **e** and **i** ('kh' in our pronunciation guides); elsewhere, as in 'go'
h	invariably silent
j	as the 'ch' in the Scottish *loch* ('kh' in our pronunciation guides)
ll	as the 'y' in 'yellow'
ñ	as the 'ni' in 'onion'
r	as in 'run,' but strongly rolled
rr	very strongly rolled
v	similar to English 'b,' but softer; referred to as 'b corta'
x	usually pronounced as **j** above; as in 'taxi' in other instances
z	as the 's' in 'sun'

Word Stress

In general, words ending in vowels or the letters **n** or **s** are stressed on the second-last syllable, while those with other endings have stress on the last syllable. Thus *vaca* (cow) and *caballos* (horses) are both stressed on the next-to-last syllable, while *ciudad* (city) and *infeliz* (unhappy) are stressed on the last syllable.

Written accents generally indicate words that don't follow the rules above, eg *sótano* (basement), *América* and *porción* (portion).

GENDER & PLURALS

In Spanish, nouns are either masculine or feminine, and there are rules to help determine gender (there are of course some exceptions). Feminine nouns generally end with -**a** or with the groups -**ción**, -**sión** or -**dad**. Other endings typically signify a masculine noun. Endings for adjectives also change to agree with the gender of the noun they modify (masculine/feminine singular -**o**/-**a**). Where both masculine and feminine forms are included in this language guide, they are separated by a slash, with the masculine form first, eg *perdido/a* (lost).

If a noun or adjective ends in a vowel, the plural is formed by adding **s** to the end. If it ends in a consonant, the plural is formed by adding **es** to the end.

ACCOMMODATIONS

I'm looking for ...

Estoy buscando ...	e·stoy boos·*kan*·do ...	

Where is ...?

¿Dónde hay ...?	*don*·de ai ...	
a hotel	*un hotel*	oon o·*tel*
a boarding house	*una pensión*	*oo*·na pen·*syon*
a youth hostel	*un albergue juvenil*	oon al·*ber*·ge khoo·ve·*neel*

Are there any rooms available?

¿Hay habitaciones libres?	ay a·bee·ta·*syon*·es *lee*·bres

I'd like a ...	*Quisiera una*	kee·*sye*·ra *oo*·na
room.	*habitación ...*	a·bee·ta·*syon* ...
double	*doble*	*do*·ble
single	*individual*	een·dee·bee·*dwal*
twin	*con dos camas*	kon dos *ka*·mas

MAKING A RESERVATION

(for phone or written requests)

To ...	A ...
From ...	De ...
Date	Fecha

I'd like to book ...	Quisiera reservar ...
	(see the list under
	'Accommodations' for bed
	and room options)
in the name of ...	en nombre de ...
for the nights of ...	para las noches del ...
credit card ...	tarjeta de crédito ...
number	número
expiry date	fecha de vencimiento

Please confirm ...	Puede confirmar ...
availability	la disponibilidad
price	el precio

How much is it	¿Cuánto cuesta	kwan·to kwes·ta
per ...?	por ...?	por ...
night	noche	no·che
person	persona	per·so·na
week	semana	se·ma·na

private/shared	baño privado/	ba·nyo pree·va·do/
bathroom	compartido	kom·par·tee·do
full board	pensión	pen·syon
	completa	kom·ple·ta
too expensive	demasiado caro	de·ma·sya·do ka·ro
cheaper	más económico	mas e·ko·no·mee·ko
discount	descuento	des·kwen·to

Does it include breakfast?
  ¿Incluye el desayuno? een·kloo·ye el de·sa·yoo·no
May I see the room?
  ¿Puedo ver la pwe·do ver la
  habitación? a·bee·ta·syon
I don't like it.
  No me gusta. no me goos·ta
It's fine. I'll take it.
  OK. La alquilo. o·kay la al·kee·lo
I'm leaving now.
  Me voy ahora. me voy a·o·ra

CONVERSATION & ESSENTIALS

Hello.	Hola.	o·la
Good morning.	Buenos días.	bwe·nos dee·as
Good afternoon.	Buenas tardes.	bwe·nas tar·des
Good evening/	Buenas noches.	bwe·nas no·ches
night.		

Bye/See you soon.	Hasta luego.	as·ta lwe·go
Yes.	Sí.	see
No.	No.	no
Please.	Por favor.	por fa·vor
Thank you.	Gracias.	gra·syas
Many thanks.	Muchas gracias.	moo·chas gra·syas
You're welcome.	De nada.	de na·da
Pardon me.	Perdón.	per·don
Excuse me.	Permiso.	per·mee·so
(used when asking permission)		
Forgive me.	Disculpe.	dees·kool·pe
(used when apologizing)		

How are things?
  ¿Qué tal? ke tal
What's your name?
  ¿Cómo se llama? (pol) ko·mo se ya·ma
  ¿Cómo te llamas? (inf) ko·mo te ya·mas
My name is ...
  Me llamo ... me ya·mo ...
It's a pleasure to meet you.
  Mucho gusto. moo·cho goos·to
The pleasure is mine.
  El gusto es mío. el goos·to es mee·o
Where are you from?
  ¿De dónde es? (pol) de don·de es
  ¿De dónde eres? (inf) de don·de er·es
I'm from ...
  Soy de ... soy de ...
Where are you staying?
  ¿Dónde está alojado/a? (pol) don·de es·ta a·lo·kha·do/a
  ¿Dónde estás alojado/a? (inf) don·de es·tas a·lo·kha·do/a
May I take a photo?
  ¿Puedo sacar una foto? pwe·do sa·kar oo·na fo·to

DIRECTIONS

How do I get to ...?
  ¿Cómo puedo llegar a ...? ko·mo pwe·do ye·gar a ...
Is it far?
  ¿Está lejos? es·ta le·khos

SIGNS

Entrada	Entrance
Salida	Exit
Información	Information
Abierto	Open
Cerrado	Closed
Prohibido	Prohibited
Comisaria	Police Station
Servicios/Baños	Toilets
Hombres/Varones	Men
Mujeres/Damas	Women

Go straight ahead.
  Siga derecho.   *see*·ga de·*re*·cho
Turn left.
  Voltée a la izquierda.   vol·*te*·e a la ees·*kyer*·da
Turn right.
  Voltée a la derecha.   vol·*te*·e a la de·*re*·cha
Can you show me (on the map)?
  ¿Me lo podría indicar   me lo po·*dree*·a een·dee·*kar*
   (en el mapa)?   (en el *ma*·pa)

north	*norte*	*nor*·te
south	*sur*	soor
east	*este*	*es*·te
west	*oeste*	o·*es*·te
here	*aquí*	a·*kee*
there	*allí*	a·*yee*
avenue	*avenida*	a·ve·*nee*·da
block	*cuadra*	*kwa*·dra
street	*calle*	*ka*·ye

EMERGENCIES

Help!	*¡Socorro!*	so·*ko*·ro
Fire!	*¡Incendio!*	een·*sen*·dyo
I've been robbed.	*Me robaron.*	me ro·*ba*·ron
Go away!	*¡Déjeme!*	*de*·khe·me
Get lost!	*¡Váyase!*	*va*·ya·se
Call ...!	*¡Llame a ...!*	*ya*·me a
an ambulance	*una ambulancia*	oo·na am·boo·*lan*·sya
a doctor	*un médico*	oon *me*·dee·ko
the police	*la policía*	la po·lee·*see*·a

It's an emergency.
  Es una emergencia.   es *oo*·na e·mer·*khen*·sya
Could you help me, please?
  ¿Me puede ayudar,   me *pwe*·de a·yoo·*dar*
   por favor?   por fa·*vor*
I'm lost.
  Estoy perdido/a. (m/f)   es·*toy* per·*dee*·do/a
Where are the toilets?
  ¿Dónde están los baños?   *don*·de es·*tan* los *ba*·nyos

HEALTH

I'm sick.
  Estoy enfermo/a.   es·*toy* en·*fer*·mo/a
I need a doctor.
  Necesito un médico.   ne·se·*see*·to oon *me*·dee·ko
Where's the hospital?
  ¿Dónde está el hospital?   *don*·de es·*ta* el os·pee·*tal*

I'm pregnant.
  Estoy embarazada.   es·*toy* em·ba·ra·*sa*·da
I've been vaccinated.
  Estoy vacunado/a.   es·*toy* va·koo·*na*·do/a

I'm allergic to ...	*Soy alérgico/a a ...*	soy a·*ler*·khee·ko/a a ...
antibiotics	*los antibióticos*	los an·tee·*byo*·tee·kos
nuts	*las fruta secas*	las *froo*·tas *se*·kas
penicillin	*la penicilina*	la pe·nee·see·*lee*·na
I'm ...	*Soy ...*	soy ...
asthmatic	*asmático/a*	as·*ma*·tee·ko/a
diabetic	*diabético/a*	dee·ya·*be*·tee·ko/a
epileptic	*epiléptico/a*	e·pee·*lep*·tee·ko/a
I have ...	*Tengo ...*	*ten*·go ...
a cough	*tos*	tos
diarrhea	*diarrea*	dya·*re*·a
a headache	*un dolor de cabeza*	oon do·*lor* de ka·*be*·sa
nausea	*náusea*	*now*·se·a

LANGUAGE DIFFICULTIES

Do you speak (English)?
  ¿Habla/Hablas (inglés)?   *a*·bla/a·blas (een·*gles*) (pol/inf)
Does anyone here speak English?
  ¿Hay alguien que hable   ai al·*gyen* ke *a*·ble
   inglés?   een·*gles*
I (don't) understand.
  (No) Entiendo.   (no) en·*tyen*·do
How do you say ...?
  ¿Cómo se dice ...?   *ko*·mo se *dee*·se ...
What does ... mean?
  ¿Qué quiere decir ...?   ke *kye*·re de·*seer* ...

Could you please ...?	*¿Puede ..., por favor?*	*pwe*·de ... por fa·vor
repeat that	*repetirlo*	re·pe·*teer*·lo
speak more slowly	*hablar más despacio*	a·*blar* mas des·*pa*·syo
write it down	*escribirlo*	es·kree·*beer*·lo

NUMBERS

0	*cero*	*ce*·ro
1	*uno/a*	*oo*·no/a
2	*dos*	dos
3	*tres*	tres
4	*cuatro*	*kwa*·tro
5	*cinco*	*seen*·ko
6	*seis*	seys
7	*siete*	*sye*·te

LANGUAGE

8	ocho	o·cho
9	nueve	nwe·ve
10	diez	dyes
11	once	on·se
12	doce	do·se
13	trece	tre·se
14	catorce	ka·tor·se
15	quince	keen·se
16	dieciséis	dye·see·seys
17	diecisiete	dye·see·sye·te
18	dieciocho	dye·see·o·cho
19	diecinueve	dye·see·nwe·ve
20	veinte	vayn·te
21	veintiuno	vayn·tee·oo·no
30	treinta	trayn·ta
31	treinta y uno	trayn·tai oo·no
40	cuarenta	kwa·ren·ta
50	cincuenta	seen·kwen·ta
60	sesenta	se·sen·ta
70	setenta	se·ten·ta
80	ochenta	o·chen·ta
90	noventa	no·ven·ta
100	cien	syen
101	ciento uno	syen·to oo·no
200	doscientos	do·syen·tos
1000	mil	meel

SHOPPING & SERVICES

I'd like to buy ...
Quisiera comprar ...   kee·sye·ra kom·prar ...

I'm just looking.
Sólo estoy mirando.   so·lo es·toy mee·ran·do

May I look at it?
¿Puedo mirarlo?   pwe·do mee·rar·lo

How much is it?
¿Cuánto cuesta?   kwan·to kwes·ta

That's too expensive for me.
Es demasiado caro   es de·ma·sya·do ka·ro
para mí.   pa·ra mee

Could you lower the price?
¿Podría bajar un poco   po·dree·a ba·khar oon po·ko
el precio?   el pre·syo

I don't like it.
No me gusta.   no me goos·ta

I'll take it.
Lo llevo.   lo ye·vo

Do you accept ...?	¿Aceptan ...?	a·sep·tan ...
credit cards	tarjetas de crédito	tar·khe·tas de kre·dee·to
traveler's checks	cheques de viajero	che·kes de vya·khe·ro

less	menos	me·nos
more	más	mas
large	grande	gran·de
small	pequeño	pe·ke·nyo

I'm looking for (the) ...   Estoy buscando ...   es·toy boos·kan·do

ATM	el cajero automático	el ka·khe·ro ow·to·ma·tee·ko
bank	el banco	el ban·ko
bookstore	la librería	la lee·bre·ree·a
embassy	la embajada	la em·ba·kha·da
exchange office	la casa de cambio	la ka·sa de kam·byo
general store	la tienda	la tyen·da
laundry	la lavandería	la la·van·de·ree·a
market	el mercado	el mer·ka·do
pharmacy	la farmacia/ la droguería	la far·ma·sya/ la dro·ge·ree·a
post office	los correos	los ko·re·os
supermarket	el supermercado	el soo·per·mer·ka·do
tourist office	la oficina de turismo	la o·fee·see·na de too·rees·mo

What time does it open/close?
¿A qué hora abre/cierra?   a ke o·ra a·bre/sye·ra

I want to change some money/traveler's cheques.
Quiero cambiar dinero/   kye·ro kam·byar dee·ne·ro/
cheques de viajero.   che·kes de vya·khe·ro

What's the exchange rate?
¿Cuál es el tipo de   kwal es el tee·po de
cambio?   kam·byo

I want to call ...
Quiero llamar a ...   kye·ro ya·mar a ...

airmail	correo aéreo	ko·re·o a·e·re·o
letter	carta	kar·ta
registered mail	certificado	ser·tee·fee·ka·do
stamps	estampillas	es·tam·pee·yas

TIME & DATES

What time is it?	¿Qué hora es?	ke o·ra es
It's (one) o'clock.	Es la (una).	es la (oo·na)
It's (seven) o'clock.	Son las (siete).	son las (sye·te)
midnight	medianoche	me·dya·no·che
noon	mediodía	me·dyo·dee·a
half past two	dos y media	dos ee me·dya

now	ahora	a·o·ra
today	hoy	oy
tonight	esta noche	es·ta no·che
tomorrow	mañana	ma·nya·na
yesterday	ayer	a·yer

LANGUAGE

Monday	lunes	loo·nes
Tuesday	martes	mar·tes
Wednesday	miércoles	myer·ko·les
Thursday	jueves	khwe·ves
Friday	viernes	vyer·nes
Saturday	sábado	sa·ba·do
Sunday	domingo	do·meen·go

January	enero	e·ne·ro
February	febrero	fe·bre·ro
March	marzo	mar·so
April	abril	a·breel
May	mayo	ma·yo
June	junio	khoo·nyo
July	julio	khoo·lyo
August	agosto	a·gos·to
September	septiembre	sep·tyem·bre
October	octubre	ok·too·bre
November	noviembre	no·vyem·bre
December	diciembre	dee·syem·bre

TRANSPORTATION
Public Transportation

What time does	¿A qué hora ...	a ke o·ra ...
... leave/arrive?	sale/llega?	sa·le/ye·ga
the bus	el autobus	el ow·to·boos
the plane	el avión	el a·vyon
the ship	el barco	el bar·ko

airport	el aeropuerto	el a·e·ro·pwer·to
bus station	la estación de autobuses	la es·ta·syon de ow·to·boo·ses
bus stop	la parada de autobuses	la pa·ra·da de ow·to·boo·ses
luggage check room	guardería/ equipaje	gwar·de·ree·a/ e·kee·pa·khe
ticket office	la boletería	la bo·le·te·ree·a

I'd like a ticket to ...
   Quiero un boleto a ...   kye·ro oon bo·le·to a ...
What's the fare to ...?
   ¿Cuánto cuesta hasta ...?   kwan·to kwes·ta a·sta ...

student's (fare)	de estudiante	de es·too·dyan·te
1st class	primera clase	pree·me·ra kla·se
2nd class	segunda clase	se·goon·da kla·se
one-way	ida	ee·da
return	ida y vuelta	ee·da ee vwel·ta
taxi	taxi	tak·see

Private Transportation

pickup (truck)	camioneta	ka·myo·ne·ta
truck	camión	ka·myon
hitchhike	hacer dedo	a·ser de·do

ROAD SIGNS	
Acceso	Entrance
Aparcamiento	Parking
Ceda el Paso	Give Way
Despacio	Slow
Dirección Única	One-Way
Mantenga Su Derecha	Keep to the Right
No Adelantar/ No Rebase	No Passing
Peaje	Toll
Peligro	Danger
Prohibido Aparcar/ No Estacionar	No Parking
Prohibido el Paso	No Entry
Pare	Stop
Salida de Autopista	Exit Freeway

I'd like to	Quisiera	kee·sye·ra
hire a/an ...	alquilar ...	al·kee·lar ...
bicycle	una bicicleta	oo·na bee·see·kle·ta
car	un auto/ un coche	oon ow·to/ oon ko·che
4WD	un todo terreno	oon to·do te·re·no
motorbike	una moto	oo·na mo·to

Is this the road to ...?
   ¿Se va a ... por esta carretera?   se va a ... por es·ta ka·re·te·ra
Where's a gas/petrol station?
   ¿Dónde hay una gasolinera?   don·de ai oo·na ga·so·lee·ne·ra
Please fill it up.
   Lleno, por favor.   ye·no por fa·vor
I'd like (20) liters.
   Quiero (veinte) litros.   kye·ro (vayn·te) lee·tros

diesel	diesel	dee·sel
leaded (regular)	gasolina con plomo	ga·so·lee·na kon plo·mo
gas/petrol	gasolina	ga·so·lee·na
unleaded	gasolina sin plomo	ga·so·lee·na seen plo·mo

(How long) Can I park here?
   ¿(Por cuánto tiempo) Puedo aparcar aquí?   (por kwan·to tyem·po) pwe·do a·par·kar a·kee
Where do I pay?
   ¿Dónde se paga?   don·de se pa·ga
I need a mechanic.
   Necesito un mecánico.   ne·se·see·to oon me·ka·nee·ko
The car has broken down in ...
   El carro se ha averiado en ...   el ka·ro se a a·ve·rya·do en ...

The motorbike won't start.

No arranca la moto.   no a·*ran*·ka la *mo*·to

I have a flat tyre.

Tengo un pinchazo.   *ten*·go oon peen·*cha*·so

I've run out of gas/petrol.

Me quedé sin gasolina.   me ke·*de* seen ga·so·*lee*·na

I've had an accident.

Tuve un accidente.   *too*·ve oon ak·see·*den*·te

TRAVEL WITH CHILDREN

I need ...

Necesito ...   ne·se·*see*·to ...

Do you have ...?

¿Hay ...?   ai ...

   a car baby seat

   un asiento de seguridad para bebés

   oon a·*syen*·to de se·goo·ree·*da* pa·ra be·*bes*

   a child-minding service

   un servicio de cuidado de niños

   oon ser·*vee*·syo de kwee·*da*·do de *nee*·nyos

   a children's menu

   una carta infantil

   oo·na *kar*·ta een·fan·*teel*

   a creche

   una guardería

   oo·na gwar·de·*ree*·a

(disposable) diapers/nappies

pañales (de usar y tirar)

pa·*nya*·les de oo·*sar* ee tee·*rar*

an (English-speaking) babysitter

una niñera (de habla inglesa)

oo·na nee·*nye*·ra (de *a*·bla een·*gle*·sa)

infant formula (milk)

leche en polvo para bebés

le·che en *pol*·vo *pa*·ra be·*bes*

a highchair

una trona

oo·na *tro*·na

a potty

una pelela

oo·na pe·*le*·la

a stroller

un cochecito

oon ko·che·*see*·to

Do you mind if I breast-feed here?

¿Le molesta que dé   le mo·*les*·ta ke de
de pecho aquí?   de *pe*·cho a·*kee*

Are children allowed?

¿Se admiten niños?   se ad·*mee*·ten *nee*·nyos

Glossary

See p61 for a list of common food terms.

aldea – village, hamlet
Arcaicos – Archaics; first known inhabitants of Puerto Rico

bahía – bay
balneario – public beach
barrio – neighborhood or city district
bateyes – Taíno ball courts
boca – mouth, entrance
boleros – ballads/love songs
bomba – musical form and dance inspired by African rhythms and characterized by call-and-response dialogues between musicians and interpreted by dancers; often considered as a unit with *plena*, as in *bomba y plena*; see also *plena*
Boricua – Puerto Rican; a person of Puerto Rican descent
Borinquen – traditional Taíno name for the island of Puerto Rico
bosque estatal – state forest
botánica – shop specializing in herbs, icons and associated charms used in the practice of Santería

cacique – Taíno chief (male or female)
callejón – narrow side street; alleyway
capilla – chapel
caretas – traditional masks worn at island festivals; see also *máscaras, vejigantes*
Caribs – original colonizers of the Caribbean, for whom the region was named
casa – house
caserios – government-sponsored, low-income housing projects
cayos – cays; refers to islets
cemíes – small figurines carved from stone, shell, wood or gold, representing deities worshipped by the Taínos
centros vacacionales – literally 'vacation centers'; form of rental accommodation popular with island families, with facilities ranging from basic wooden cabins on the beach to two-bedroom condos
cerro – hill or mountain
Changó – Yoruba god of fire and war believed to control thunder and lightning; one of several principal deities worshipped in Santería; see also *orishas*
comida criolla – traditional Puerto Rican cuisine
Compañía de Parques Nacionales – CPN; National Park Company
coquí – a species of tiny tree frog found only in Puerto Rico; the island's mascot
cordillera – a system of mountain ranges

criollo – island-born person of Spanish parentage; in colonial times considered inferior by peninsular Spaniards; see also *mestizo*
culebrenses – residents of Culebra
curandero – healer

danza – form of piano music and stylized figure-dance with origins in Spain, fused with elements of island folk music
Departamento de Recursos Naturales y Ambientales – DRNA; Department of Natural Resources & Environment

espiritismo – spiritualism
Estado Libre Asociado – associated free state; the term describes Puerto Rico's relationship with the USA

fiestas patronales – the annual celebrations staged in Puerto Rican cities and towns to honor each community's patron saint
fortaleza – fortress
friquitines – roadside kiosks
fuerte – fort

galería – gallery
garitas – turreted sentry towers constructed at intervals along the top of Old San Juan's fortifications
gringo – term used on the island to describe Americans

hacienda – agricultural estate, plantation

iglesia – church
Igneris – Indian group of the Arawakan linguistic group; early settlers of Puerto Rico
independentistas – advocates for Puerto Rican independence

jíbaro – rural mountain resident, often cast as archetypal Puerto Rican

laguna – lake or lagoon
lechonera – restaurant specializing in roast suckling pig
LMM – abbreviation for San Juan's Aeropuerto Internacional de Luis Muñoz Marín

malecón – pier, waterfront promenade
máscaras – masks; see also *caretas, vejigantes*
mercado – market
Mesónes Gastronómicos – a Puerto Rico Tourism Company–sponsored program involving a collection of restaurants in the island that feature Puerto Rican cuisine

mestizo – person of mixed ancestry (usually Indian and Spanish); see also *criollo*
mogotes – conical peaks
monasterio – monastery
mundillo – traditional form of intricately woven lace, made only in Puerto Rico and Spain
municipios – town and city government units composed of mayors and assemblies

Nuyoricans – Puerto Rican exiles in the US

orishas – Yoruba deities worshipped in Santería, often associated with Catholic saints; see also *Changó*

palacio – palace
parador – country inn
parque – park
pasaje – passage
pava – typical straw hat of the *jíbaro*
playa – beach
plazuela – small plaza
plena – form of traditional Puerto Rican dance and song that unfolds to distinctly African rhythms beat out with maracas, tambourines and other traditional percussion instruments; often associated with *bomba*
pleneros – *plena* singers
ponceños – residents of Ponce
PRTC – Puerto Rico Tourism Company
públicos – shared taxis, usually minivans equipped with bench seats, which pick up passengers along a prescribed route and provide low-cost local transport islandwide
puerta – gate/door
puerto – port
punta – tip, end

reserva forestal – forest reserve
ron – rum

sanjuaneros – residents of San Juan
Santería – Afro-Caribbean religion representing the syncretism of Catholic and African beliefs, based on the worship of Catholic saints and their associated *Yoruba* deities, or *orishas*
santero – an artist who carves *santos*; one of many names for practitioners of the rites of *Santería*
santos – small carved figurines representing saints, enshrined and worshipped by practitioners of *Santería*
sonda – sound
supermercado – supermarket
sur – south

Taínos – indigenous Puerto Ricans
tapones – traffic jams
tienda – store
turismo – tourism
turista – tourist

universidad – university
urgente – urgent

valle – valley
vegetales – vegetables
vejigantes – traditional masks; see also *caretas, máscaras*
ventana – window
vereda – path or trail
vino – wine

Yoruba – West Africans brought to Puerto Rico as slaves

zoologico – zoo

The Authors

BRENDAN SAINSBURY
Coordinating Author, San Juan,
East Coast, Culebra & Vieques, North Coast,
Central Mountains

Brendan is a Brit from the London area now based in Vancouver, Canada. His interest in the Spanish-speaking Caribbean Islands was first ignited after a memorable visit to Cuba in 1997. Suitably seduced, he returned in the mid-2000s to pen the Lonely Planet guides to Cuba and Havana. The short hop east to the 'Enchanted Island' of Puerto Rico was a natural progression. For this book Brendan wrote destination chapters, most of the front chapters and Directory and Transport.

NATE CAVALIERI
Ponce & the South Coast

The miles covered by Nate Cavalieri during the research of this book passed at a leisurely pace – he explored the south coast entirely on bicycle, recovering from the blisteringly hot afternoon rides with icy Medallas. When not traveling, he lives in Sacramento, California, where he is a writer and musician. Nate also wrote the Music chapter.

Behind the Scenes

THIS BOOK

This 4th edition of *Puerto Rico* was researched and written by Brendan Sainsbury and Nate Cavalieri. The previous edition was written by Ginger Adams Otis, with contributions by Mario A Murrillo (History) and Dr David Goldberg (Health). Randall Peffer was the author of the first two editions of Puerto Rico. This guidebook was commissioned in Lonely Planet's Oakland office, and produced by the following:

Commissioning Editors Erin Corrigan, Jennye Garibaldi, Evan Jones

Coordinating Editors David Carroll, Averil Robertson

Coordinating Cartographer Andy Rojas

Coordinating Layout Designer Pablo Gastar

Managing Editor Brigitte Ellemor

Managing Cartographer Alison Lyall

Managing Layout Designer Adam McCrow

Assisting Editors Carly Hall, Charlotte Orr, Diana Saad, Gabrielle Stefanos

Assisting Cartographer Peter Shields

Cover Designer Pepi Bluck

Assisting Layout Designer Indra Kilfoyle

Project Managers Rachel Imeson, Craig Kilburn

Language Content Coordinator Quentin Frayne

Thanks to Jennifer Garrett, Lisa Knights, Adriana Mammarella, Suyin Ng, Malcolm O'Brien, Celia Wood

THANKS
BRENDAN SAINSBURY

Thanks to Erin for writing the script, Jennye for reining it in, Nate for his erudite support, Maria Antonia for the gorgeous apartment, Shannon for the two-wheeled tour of Vieques, Liz for her iron nerves on the Ruta Panorámica, Emilio for his enthusiastic *recorrido* of El Yunque and Kieran for – well – just being Kieran.

NATE CAVALIERI

Without the saintly kindness, technical aptitude and good humor of Berto, of Berto's Bicycle Shop, the research for this book might never have been completed. His garage in Jauca materialized from the heat waves rising off the asphalt in my hour of most desperate mechanical and spiritual need. Warm thanks as well for the support of Brendan, Florence, and my folks.

OUR READERS

Many thanks to the travelers who used the last edition and wrote to us with helpful hints, useful advice and interesting anecdotes:

Mary Jo Allen, Peggy Ball, Sashti Balu, David Bekhor, Edo & Simone Berger-Bleumink, Judy Clark, Barry Conchie, Dan Coplan, Marti Copleman, Hope Curry, Helene Eichholz, Natalie Enck, Steve Frank,

---

THE LONELY PLANET STORY

Fresh from an epic journey across Europe, Asia and Australia in 1972, Tony and Maureen Wheeler sat at their kitchen table stapling together notes. The first Lonely Planet guidebook, *Across Asia on the Cheap,* was born.

Travelers snapped up the guides. Inspired by their success, the Wheelers began publishing books to Southeast Asia, India and beyond. Demand was prodigious, and the Wheelers expanded the business rapidly to keep up. Over the years, Lonely Planet extended its coverage to every country and into the virtual world via lonelyplanet.com and the Thorn Tree message board.

As Lonely Planet became a globally loved brand, Tony and Maureen received several offers for the company. But it wasn't until 2007 that they found a partner whom they trusted to remain true to the company's principles of traveling widely, treading lightly and giving sustainably. In October of that year, BBC Worldwide acquired a 75% share in the company, pledging to uphold Lonely Planet's commitment to independent travel, trustworthy advice and editorial independence.

Today, Lonely Planet has offices in Melbourne, London and Oakland, with over 500 staff members and 300 authors. Tony and Maureen are still actively involved with Lonely Planet. They're traveling more often than ever, and they're devoting their spare time to charitable projects. And the company is still driven by the philosophy of *Across Asia on the Cheap*: 'All you've got to do is decide to go and the hardest part is over. So go!'

Jerry Gabay, Krishna Gagné, Laurie Gardner, Andrew Gorlin, Cherry Greiner, Chris Hardin, Ellen Harris, Elliot Hen-Tov, Roland Jestremski, Irene Jorgensen, Camilla Lamer, Murray Lantner, Fei Lauw, Pedro H Lopez, Liz Mccartney, Steph Mcdougal, Greg Meier, Bastiaan Meyers, Jon Newhard, J Nino, Isabelle Noirot, Ali Oren, Jessica Raymond, Linda Reynolds, Nancy Ross, Janina Rusiecki, Stephen Rutenberg, Genevieve Schaer, Susanne Schindler, Catherine Smith, Thomas Spear, Doris Taylor, Jeff Tecosky-Feldman, Ben Walker, Rose Wong and Aned Yarelis

ACKNOWLEDGMENTS
Many thanks to the following for the use of their content:

Globe on title page ©Mountain High Maps 1993 Digital Wisdom, Inc.

Internal photographs: p6 (#4) Bill Bachmann/Alamy; p14 (#5) Mark Bacon/Alamy; p10 (#1) Danita Delimont/Alamy; p13 (#2) Robert Fried/Alamy; p6 (#2) Kim Karpeles/Alamy; p14 Ray Pfortner/Photolibrary; p11 (#5) Kevin Schafer/Alamy; p16 Kennan Ward/Corbis. All other photographs by Lonely Planet Images, and p8 (#3) Jerry Alexander; p5 Donald C & Priscilla Alexander Eastman; p8 (#2), p9 (#5), p11 (#4) John Elk III; p10 (#3) Greg Johnston; p9 (#1) Alfredo Maiquez; p7 (#1) Aaron McCoy; p9 (#4), p15 (#4) John Neubauer; p6 (#5), p12, p15 (#1) Steve Simonsen.

SEND US YOUR FEEDBACK

We love to hear from travelers – your comments keep us on our toes and help make our books better. Our well-traveled team reads every word on what you loved or loathed about this book. Although we cannot reply individually to postal submissions, we always guarantee that your feedback goes straight to the appropriate authors, in time for the next edition. Each person who sends us information is thanked in the next edition – and the most useful submissions are rewarded with a free book.

To send us your updates – and find out about Lonely Planet events, newsletters and travel news – visit our award-winning website: **www.lonelyplanet.com/contact**.

Note: we may edit, reproduce and incorporate your comments in Lonely Planet products such as guidebooks, websites and digital products, so let us know if you don't want your comments reproduced or your name acknowledged. For a copy of our privacy policy visit www.lonelyplanet.com/privacy.

BEHIND THE SCENES

Index

GreenDex

This new GreenDex is designed to allow you to sift through Puerto Rico's myriad hotels, restaurants and points of interest and carefully select the greenest and most environmentally friendly options. Places have been chosen on the basis of their sustainability credentials regarding three key factors: the environment, the culture and the economy. In weighing up various companies for inclusion we have attempted to answer the following questions. Do they make positive contributions to the environment? Do they respect local traditions and encourage cultural interaction? And, do they offer financial benefits to the host community? The list is by no means exhaustive and we would appreciate traveler feedback to aid in the formulation of future GreenDexes. You can communicate your thoughts via the talk2us network. For further information see www.lonely planet.com/responsibletravel.

Top scale (left to right): 12pm | 1pm | 2pm | 3pm | 4pm | 5pm | 6pm | 7pm | 8pm | 9pm | 10pm | 11pm | 12am

Bottom scale (left to right): 12pm | 1pm | 2pm | 3pm | 4pm | 5pm | 6pm | 7pm | 8pm | 9pm | 10pm | 11pm | 12am

Mon / Sun

International Date Line

Svalbard *(Norway)*
Zemlya Frantsa-Iosifa *(Russia)*
Severnaya Zemlya *(Russia)*
Novaya Zemlya *(Russia)*
KARA SEA
LAPTEV SEA
Novosibirskie Ostrovo *(Russia)*
EAST SIBERIAN SEA
BARENTS SEA

Sweden 1pm
Norway
2pm
Finland
Estonia
Latvia
Lithuania
Belarus
Denmark
Germany
Poland
France Austria
Ukraine
Italy
Romania
Bulgaria
Greece
Turkey
Tunisia MEDITERRANEAN SEA
Syria
Iraq
Iran
3.30pm
Afghanistan 4.30pm
Tibet (China)
5.45 pm
China
North Korea
South Korea
Japan
SEA OF OKHOTSK
BERING SEA
NORTH PACIFIC OCEAN

3pm
4pm
5pm
Russia
6pm
Kazakhstan
Uzbekistan
Kyrgyzstan
Mongolia
7pm
9pm
11pm
12am
10pm
3am
2am

Algeria
Libya
Egypt
Saudi Arabia
2pm
Turkmenistan
Nepal 5.45 pm
India
5.30 pm
8pm
EAST CHINA SEA
Taiwan
Niger
Chad
Sudan
Eritrea Yemen
Oman
4pm
UAE
Myanmar
6.30 pm
Laos
Thailand
Vietnam
Philippines
Northern Mariana Is *(US)*
9pm
Marshall Is *(US)*
12am

1pm
Nigeria
Central African Republic
Ethiopia
3pm
Somalia
ARABIAN SEA
BAY OF BENGAL
5.30pm
Sri Lanka
Federated States of Micronesia 11am
Palau
Kiribati

Congo
Gabon 1pm
Congo (Zaire)
Kenya
Tanzania
Maldives
Malaysia
Indonesia
Nauru EQUATOR

Angola
Malawi
Zambia Zimbabwe
Madagascar
Mauritius
Reunion *(Fr)*
Seychelles 4pm
6.30 pm
Cocos (Keeling) Is *(Aust)*
East Timor
Papua New Guinea
Solomon Is
SOUTH PACIFIC OCEAN
Namibia
Botswana
Mozambique
INDIAN OCEAN
Vanuatu
Fiji

South Africa
9.30 pm
Australia
New Caledonia *(Fr)*
10.30 pm
Lord Howe Is *(Aust)*
11.30 pm
Norfolk Is *(Aust)*

Prince Edward Is *(S. Africa)*
French Southern & Antarctic Territories *(Fr)*
TASMAN SEA
New Zealand

Heard & McDonald Is *(Aust)*
SOUTHERN OCEAN

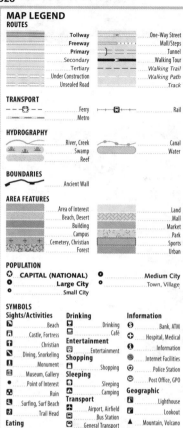

LONELY PLANET OFFICES

Australia

Head Office
Locked Bag 1, Footscray, Victoria 3011
☎ 03 8379 8000, fax 03 8379 8111
talk2us@lonelyplanet.com.au

USA

150 Linden St, Oakland, CA 94607
☎ 510 250 6400, toll free 800 275 8555
fax 510 893 8572
info@lonelyplanet.com

UK

2nd fl, 186 City Rd,
London EC1V 2NT
☎ 020 7106 2100, fax 020 7106 2101
go@lonelyplanet.co.uk

Published by Lonely Planet Publications Pty Ltd

ABN 36 005 607 983

© Lonely Planet Publications Pty Ltd 2008

© photographers as indicated 2008

Cover photograph: Yellow-and-black carnival mask, Ponce, Macduff Everton/Corbis. Many of the images in this guide are available for licensing from Lonely Planet Images: www.lonelyplanetimages.com.

Printed by Hang Tai Printing Company.
Printed in China.